Raise Happy Children... Teach Them Joy!

By
Mary Ann Budnik

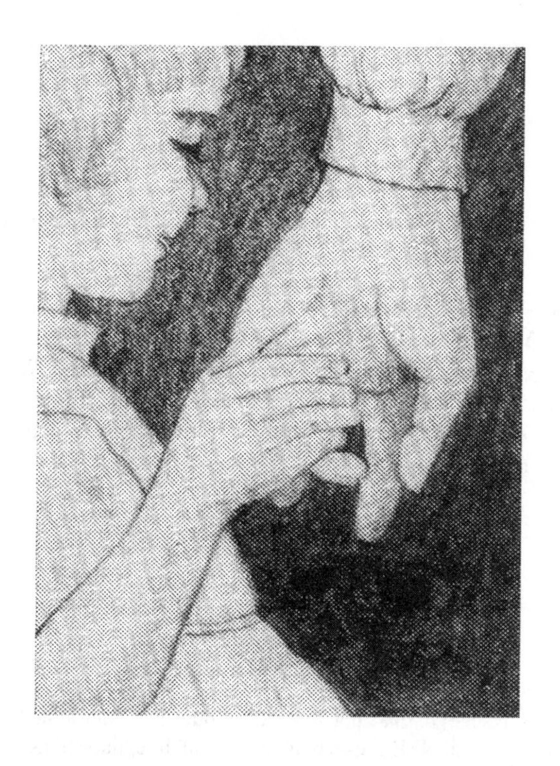

R. B. Media, Inc.
Springfield, IL

IMPRIMATUR: Most Reverend Gerald Scarpone, O.F.M.
Bishop of Comayagua, Honduras
February 14, 2004
The Imprimatur is a declaration that a book or pamplet is considered to be free from doctrinal or moral error.

Central American Edition: May 1, 2004
First USA Edition: May 1, 2004

Illustrations by Christine Mack
Inside front cover and Chapter 2 illustrations Giedre Vaitys
Published by R.B. Media, Inc.

For additional copies of ***Raise Happy Children...Teach Them Joy!,*** or for copies of Mary Ann Budnik's other books, ***Raise Happy Children Through A Happier Marriage!, Raise Happy Children...Raise Them Saints!, Raise Happy Children...Teach Them Virtue!, You Can Become A Saint!, You Can Become A Saint! Workbook, Looking For Peace? Try Confession!*** and her "***Why Suffer?*** booklet contact:

R.B. Media, Inc.
154 Doral
Springfield, IL 62704
Phone: (217) 546-5261 Fax: (217) 546-0558
Website: www.rbmediainc.com
E-mail: MABudnik@worldnet.att.net

Library of Congress catalog card number: 2002094921
R.B. Media, Inc.: ISBN 0-9700021-6-5

Dedication

When I think of joy and happiness, two Jesuit friends, Fr. Hal Cohen, S.J., and Fr. John Hardon, S.J., pop instantly to mind. They not only supported my writing apostolate but brought me many blessings and graces through their friendship, their example of passionate love of God as well as their virtuous lives. Both died within weeks of each other leaving a void in my life and in the world. But since we are all members of the Mystical Body of Christ, they are simply a prayer away. To them and to St. Josemaría Escrivá I dedicate this final book in the ***Raise Happy Children*** series.

Fr. Harold Cohen, S.J., brought the love and joy of Christ to everyone he met with his infectious smile, his thoughtfulness and ready laughter that bubbled over with joy. He hungered to bring souls closer to God through personal contact and his TV series, *A Closer Walk*.

Likewise, Fr. John Hardon, S.J., radiated a quieter but no less authentic happiness and joy to everyone he encountered as he traveled the world proclaiming the Gospel of Christ, working tirelessly for the Holy See and the salvation of souls...a 20th century Athanasius.

Last, but most important, is St. Josemaría Escrivá who taught me how to achieve joy so that I could share this information with you. Without his example, formation, and writings the ***Raise Happy Children Series*** would not have been possible for me to write.

These three priests were heroic examples to me of people striving for sanctity, struggling to live virtuous lives and exhibiting the fruit of virtue which is joy and happiness, the topic of the ***Raise Happy Children*** series of books.

Acknowledgements

This book would not be possible if not for the help of:

- My husband, Bob, who sacrificed himself in countless ways so that this book could now be in your hands.
- Reverend Jack Kubeck and Reverend Michael Giesler, of the Prelature of the Holy Cross and Opus Dei who acted as my chief editors, theologians and coaches.
- Christine Mack who provided several illustrations for this book.
- Giedre Vaitys who provided the inside page illustration of the little girl and the weightlifter. Giedre's illustrations were originally used in ***Family Future Digest.***
- My copy editors, Nancy Hanlon and Carol Kelly. Their input and editing skills added the polish.
- Dr. David Isaacs of the University of Navarre in Pamplona, Spain, for permitting me to quote extensively his course material on families.
- Mr. James Stenson for allowing me to quote his material and books at length.
- Mary Jo Paulson for permitting me to use her lecture material.
- Annie Lang for her contribution on Teen Fashion.
- My daughters, Mary Kate Stangel, Marianne Budnik, and Mary Terese Wills who permitted me to use them as examples, sometimes not too flattering, to make a point.
- Dick and Lou Prince who audiotaped Dr. Isaacs' course, "Parents and Their Adolescent Children," for us at the Univesity of Navarre in Spain.
- Other resource material that I was permitted to use freely.
- Tom & Mary Magnor for allowing me to use their beautiful family for my cover and chapter pictures: (L-R) Patrick, Bridget, Tom, Kathryn, Eileen, John Paul being held by Elizabeth and Anne Marie in front of Elizabeth.
- Zachary Kitson who permitted me to use his picture for Chapter 6.
- Scepter Publishers, Inc. for allowing me to freely quote their publications.
- My readers who suggested this book, then sent audio tapes, videos, books and prayers. The latter kept me writing!

In writing this book I found inclusive language awkward. For this reason I use the traditional meaning of he/him as including men and women, boys and girls.

Table Of Contents

INTRODUCTION

"Virtue consists in the firm resolve to obey the Lord." St. Fulbert of Chartres

Last week I met a charming woman from Ohio by the name of Judy. As she had heard that I had written a book on teaching children virtues, she began questioning me on the topic. Another woman, who overheard our conversation, piped in to ask, *Which virtue do you think, Mary Ann, is the most basic?* When I replied *obedience because without self-discipline it is impossible to practice any of the other virtues,* quiet spoken Judy took the floor. Sadly she disclosed, *My parents had no rules. I could do whatever I wanted. There were no limits. It made me feel that my parents did not love me...or even care for me.* There was dead silence in the group. Each of us could see that Judy is still hurting from the effects of her parents' permissiveness. Finally, Judy herself broke the silence by stating firmly, *My children have rules and limits. I want them to know that they are cared for and deeply loved!*

"Take care of these children of yours because they are my children also!"[1]

Our Lady to St. Bridget

In ***Raise Happy Children...Teach Them Joy!***, the fourth and final book of the ***Raise Happy Children Series***, we are continuing our discussion on how to teach children the various virtues that will make them happy, holy, responsible children, teens, and adults. By virtue of one's baptism *we commit ourselves to a certain behavior. If we accept the true faith in Christ, we thereby obligate ourselves to a certain mode of life*, Monsignor James Turro reminds us.[2] That mode of living, which consists in striving to live daily in a more virtuous manner, includes not only us but our children, teens, and young adults. Please realize that people who decide to live lives of virtue change the world! St. Olaf, the patron saint of Norway, wasn't always a saint. In fact, he was a vicious Viking chief who raided Western European countries. His underlings were permitted to pillage, murder, and commit other atrocities. Finally, converted to the Catholic faith, he settled down in Norway, devoted himself to reparation for his misdeeds and developed a life of virtue thereby becoming a saintly leader.

St. Stephen of Hungary's father, Duke Gesa, headed the dreaded Magyars, the most vicious of the invading barbarian hordes. The Magyars thought nothing of killing all the inhabitants of the towns they captured. They spread their terror from Bavaria up through Flanders and France. As Church historian, H. Daniel-Rops recounts: *During most of the eleventh century every inhabitant of Western Europe could foresee the possibility of his being killed or sold into slavery by the terrible successors of the Huns...[T]he Hungarian peril lasted until the year 1000 when the conversion of their king, Stephen, transformed these nomads into a sedentary*

1 Ferdinand Holböck, ***Married Saints and Blessed Through the Centuries*** (San Francisco: Ignatius Press, 2001) p. 250.

2 *Magnificat,* Oct. 2002, p. 171.

agricultural nation, saving both Europe and themselves.[3] Duke Gesa *saw that the one hope of his nation's survival was its conversion to Christianity.*[4] His wife, a Slav princess, St. Adelaide, helped to bring about his conversion and that of the Magyars. At the same time, she raised their son, St. Stephen, to be a holy, wise monarch who based his kingdom on Christian "federalism." In order for the barbarian Magyars to exchange their violent, nomadic lives for farming, the Magyars had to first exchange their vices for virtues. If the barbarians could learn virtues, certainly your teens can learn them as well!

Let's take a closer look at the Dark Ages, a time devoid of the pursuit of virtue. *Tied to the goods of this world by the dreadful bond of fear, men gave no thought to the doctrine of renunciation and love of one's neighbor...The truly Christian spirit was absent from the services of the Church which people too often attended without understanding much of the liturgy, and from almsgiving, which was practiced without charity in the heart....Let us repeat, there were exceptions which is proper to recognize; but on the whole the above description applied to nearly all men, including the ruling class...Nor, of course, did the morals reflect the Gospel. Violence, which had been endemic since the barbarian invasions, attained its zenith...*[It was] *the law of the fist...Jealousy, envy, the unbridled wish to enlarge one's estate at the neighbors' expense were rampant; perfidy joined hands with violence, and political assassination was as common throughout Western Europe in the tenth century as in Italy during the fifteenth. Brigandage, destructiveness, and looting were so commonplace that such risks were provided for in commercial contracts.* (Sounds like our insurance policies!)

Daniel-Rops continues: *Would you care to take a look at one of those "Christians" of the year 1000, one of those terrible*

---

[3] H. Daniel-Rops, ***The Church In The Dark Ages*** (NY: E. P. Dutton & Co. Inc., 1960) p. 531.
[4] *Ibid*, p. 555.

fellows who were at that time masters of the world? Here is one. His name is Fulk Nerra (987-1040) and he was related to the counts of Anjou. He is credited with the idea of replacing the old wooden palace forts with the enormous stone buildings...He was filled with unbridled passion, a temper directed to extremeness. Whenever he had the slightest difference with a neighbor he rushed upon his lands, ravaging, pillaging, raping, and killing; nothing could stop him, least of all the commandments of God! He cared nothing for the respect due to the priest of the Lord: we find him attacking the convent of St. Martin of Tours, plundering the house of a canon, setting fire to the monastery of St. Florentine...This appalling man had countless crimes upon his conscience, but when seized with a fit of remorse he abandoned himself to well nigh incredible penances. Thus the very tomb of St. Martin, whose monks he had ill treated, saw him prostrate, with bare feet and in penitent's dress; and four times during his life he went to Jerusalem as a devout pilgrim, treading half naked the sorrowful road of the Passion while two of his servants flogged him till blood came, crying: "Lord, receive thy perjured Fulk!" He was typical of his age.[5]

As you can see, during the Dark Ages, men lived a distorted form of Christianity. A form we want our teens and young adults to avoid. But our culture is beginning to look a lot like the Dark Ages because parents not only are not living virtue themselves but they are not teaching virtues to their teens.

> *"Virtues demand discretion and all excess is vice."* St. Bede

Let's consider a bit of philosophy to understand the importance of learning virtues better. But don't panic. I promise that this section will not be deep.

First of all, there are many common facts about man (man used in a universal sense) but we are only interested in the

[5] *Ibid.*, pp. 541-542.

common facts that impact man's happiness since happiness is the topic of this series of books. These common facts profoundly impact one's ability to be happy. They include: man's free decision about his actions; his capacity for love and self-sacrifice; his concern about right and wrong; his sense of guilt and responsibility; his (hopefully) deliberate efforts of self-reform and self-improvement; his insistent need for and sense of personal dignity; his restless search for happiness; his need to love and be loved; his constant questioning about his origin and destiny, and his inability to fulfill himself from within himself. Furthermore, each individual has the power to rise above instinct, passion and coercion. Likewise, man is free to act or not, and to make choices so as to decide his own course of action or inaction because of the self-determining power of his will. For this reason an ancient proverb insists that *character determines destiny.* Because of free-will, each person is personally responsible for his actions.[6] We can't claim, *The devil made me do it!* We personally have to take responsibility for everything we do.

Fr. Cormac Burke in his essay, ***Man and Values***, explains that *Man is ever seeking a lasting, meaningful happiness, which is not found in a life of pleasure seeking or self-enjoyment. He wants more. Man finds deeper satisfaction in certain kinds of achievements and good works...At his core man is a responsible acting person who is shaping himself. He is a work in progress. He is inescapably intelligent and free, and therefore responsible for himself—and for others. He must make free choices to respond to his conscience, which calls him to take charge of his life, act responsibly to see the good, and respond to the needs around him. Through the exercise of his higher powers of intellect and will, man is able to recognize ("conscience") good and evil, and to freely choose to do one, avoid the other. He is aware of thereby becoming a certain kind of person. If he is thoughtful and uses his mind honestly and chooses wisely, he is "acting*

[6] John Young, ***Reasoning Things Out,*** Chapter 5 "Free Will."

according to right reason" as Aristotle said. He is able to acquire virtue and thereby become what he was intended to be—a fully responsible, committed, socialized and moral person. Growth in virtue requires that he exercise self-mastery and self-possession: that he subdue himself, direct his passions, control his bodily appetites, and order his emotions (editorial emphasis).[7]

Since man is a composite of soul (conscience, mind, intellect, reason, understanding and will) and body, his happiness/fulfillment depends on giving himself to God and to others within a framework of true good. Fr. Marcial Maciel, founder of the Legionaries of Christ and Regnum Christi, points out: *By nature man is homo religious. When this dimension of man is ignored, his personal and family life, and society itself, gets thrown out of balance.*[8] Happiness and a balanced life can only be achieved through the acquisition of specific virtues which lead us to become more Christ-like. It was for this purpose we were created. If our children do not fulfill the purpose for which they were created they will never achieve happiness no matter how hard they pursue it. To achieve happiness on one's own terms is impossible. Just look at the rich and famous who commit suicide. One example is Nobel Prize winner Ernest Hemingway. He told a friend a month before he shot himself to death: *[I]f I can't exist on my own terms, then existence is impossible. Do you understand? That is how I've lived, and that is how I must live—or not live."*[9]

Hemingway did not realize that he could not fulfill himself on his own terms. His fulfillment/happiness calls for a free response to objective values that lie outside and above him. To be happy, man must be open and be prepared to respond and to rise to them.[10] When man does not respond, not only is he unhappy but it causes psychological problems.

[7] Class 6, "Christian Anthropology," p. CA-7.

[8] Jesús Colina, ***Christ Is My Life*** (Manchester, New Hampshire: Sophia Institute Press, 2003) p. 248.

[9] Cormac Burke, ***Man And Values.***

[10] Christian Anthropology, p. 36.

Dr. Frank J. Moncher, director of clinical training at the Institute for the Psychological Sciences in Arlington, Virginia, discussed the psychotherapy of virtue in a Zenit interview. He feels that patients who would benefit from this specialty would be those struggling with parenting issues, marital problems, addictions and other life adjustment problems. But Dr. Moncher also believes others would likewise benefit because *problems occur in someone's life when he is prevented from acting toward that which he knows is truly good—as opposed to something that merely feels good in the short term. People may be prevented by needs, wants, feelings or passions that compel them toward different goals than what they know to be good.* He elaborates even more: *Clinically, many of the clients we see are suffering psychologically from a restriction in their ability to choose freely; in fact, that is maybe the best way to understand counseling and psychotherapy from a Catholic perspective, that is, the goal from this perspective is to free people to freely choose God, lives of holiness,...to choose virtue* (editorial emphasis).

Individuals, who are hindered in their ability to know, freely choose, or act upon their choices because of psychological problems, are compromised in their ability to demonstrate virtue. Because of this connection between the two—psychological problems interfering with virtue—people can benefit from performing the opposite, that is, through exercising virtue in the face of emotional struggles.[11]

Fr. Cormac Burke insists that *the presence and operation of human freedom means that there is no such thing as automatic fulfillment for anyone. A man's life, according to his choices, can take different ways that lead to different results and destinations. His experiences and responses can be enriching, or impoverishing; they can open his horizons and widen his understanding of values, of others, of the world; or close his ambition and range of interests in on himself, so directing his life down the dead-end of personal insufficiency.*

[11] Zenit, May 9, 2002.

Man can grow towards happiness and fulfillment, or shrink towards misery and frustration.[12] Read these words to your teens. Let them know that by aiming low he/she reduces the possibility of achieving happiness.

To develop as a person, one must be open to values, discern values, respond to values, and assimilate values. That is why ***Raise Happy Children...Raise Them Saints!*** preceded the books on teaching children virtues. First we need to teach our children and teens to love God. From their love of God comes the desire, the longing, and the willingness to do the will of God who becomes their Beloved. The rules, summed up in the moral law and the Ten Commandments, lead to the Beatitudes which point out how to specifically love God by living virtuous lives. This leads to goodness which in turn leads to happiness and joy. It's similar to learning an instrument. We can try to play the violin without instruction but we will never play it correctly or beautifully. Our bow will slide up and down the neck of the violin rather than gripping the strings. Without knowing the correct finger positions, the instrument will squeak rather than be melodious. Instead of a beautiful musical piece, the experience will be like nails scratching a chalk board...dreadful.

Fr. Edward Leen, CSSP, insists: *God wishes His creatures not only to exhaust all the possibilities of natural happiness but, rising beyond all that, to experience a happiness that of its nature is divine.*[13] He further explains: *Happiness is the result of a full life. The infinite happiness of God springs from His infinitely perfect life. Man, vivified by the re-creative breath of God, is enabled to exercise vital activities like those of God and thus participate in God's happiness. That beatitude was not, of course, to be enjoyed straightaway in full measure. A period of growth and imperfection, measured by the time of earth's pilgrimage, was to be followed by an*

---

[12] Christian Anthropology, p. 65.

[13] Edward, Leen, CSSP, ***Why The Cross?*** (NJ: Scepter, 1938) p. 103.

eternity of maturity and perfection. But happiness was to be man's lot in both periods of his existence—a happiness strictly proportioned to the perfection with which he should live God's life in each: God, incompletely and dimly seen in this world, would be contemplated face to face in the world to come...The soul tastes divine happiness by entering into intimate and vital union with God dwelling within it. The privilege of entering into God's life and consequent happiness, though granted in its perfect form in heaven is not denied to earth, though in a form less perfect (editiorial emphasis).[14]

We taste this happiness when we utilize the theological virtues of faith, hope and charity which are infused in baptism, then given a booster shot in confirmation.

John Paul II repeatedly admonishes teens to seek true happiness by striving for holiness. In Slovakia, September 14, 2003, he told young Slovaks: *You are the hope of the Pope! Do not be afraid to become true friends of Jesus. Learn from Him how to love this world properly and you will build with His help the civilization of love.*

At World Youth Day (WYD) in Canada, he told young people: *Too many lives begin and end without joy, without hope. That is one of the principal reasons for the World Youth Day...I pray that the World Youth Day will offer all Canadians an opportunity to remember the values that are essential to good living and to human happiness...The "spirit of the world" offers many false illusions and paradises of happiness. There is perhaps no darkness deeper than the darkness that enters young people's souls when false prophets extinguish in them the light of faith and hope and love. The greatest deception, and the deepest source of unhappiness, is the illusion of finding life by excluding God, of finding freedom by excluding moral truths and personal responsibility* (editorial emphasis).

At difficult moments in the Church's life, the pursuit of

[14] *Ibid.*

holiness becomes even more urgent. And holiness is not a question of age; it is a matter of living in the Holy Spirit, just as [Bl.] Kateri Tekawitha and so many other young people have done...

The enthusiasm and joy that you are showing are a sure sign of your love for the Lord, and of your desire to serve Him in the Church and in your brothers and sisters.[15]

[Jesus] calls us to be His: He wants us all to be saints. Dear young people, may it be your holy ambition to be holy, as He is holy.

You will ask me: but is it possible today to be saints? If we had to rely only on human strength the undertaking would be truly impossible. You are well aware, in fact, of your successes and your failures; you are aware of the heavy burdens weighing on man, the many dangers which threaten him and the consequences caused by his sins. At times we may be ripped by discouragement and even come to think that it is impossible to change anything either in the world or in ourselves.

Although the journey is difficult we can do everything in the One who is our Redeemer...Young people of every continent, do not be afraid to be the saints of the new millennium! Be contemplative, love prayer; be coherent with your faith and generous in the service of your brothers and sisters, be active members of the Church and builders of peace. To succeed in this demanding project of life, continue to listen to His Word, draw strength from the Sacraments, especially the Eucharist and Penance. The Lord wants you to be intrepid apostles of His Gospel and builders of a new humanity.[16]

Eight months after World Youth Day in Canada, John Paul II again reminded the youth of the world where to find the happiness they seek: *No one apart from Christ can give you*

---

[15] Zenit, July 23 and July 28, 2002.

[16] Zenit, July 29, 2002.

true happiness. By following the example of Mary, you should know how to give Him your unconditional "yes". There is no place in your lives for selfishness or laziness...Humanity is in urgent need of the witness of free and courageous young people who dare to go against the tide and proclaim with vigor and enthusiasm their personal faith in God, Lord and Savior.[17]

Two months later the Pope explained that *if every baptized person is called to be a missionary, children and adolescents must also respond to this challenge in their own environment.* He then recommended that youth pray the missionary Rosary. The missionary Rosary consists of five decades, each of which is a different color representing a different continent: *White for old Europe, so that it will be able to recover the evangelizing strength it has generated in so many Churches; Yellow for Asia, full of life and youth; Green for Africa, subjected to the trial of suffering; Red for America, seedbed of new missionary energies; Blue for Oceania, which awaits a more capillary diffusion of the Gospel.*[18]

To the youth of Bulgaria John Paul II stressed: *True, Jesus is a demanding Friend who sets high goals and asks us to go out of ourselves in order to come to meet Him:* ***"Whoever loses his life for My sake and the Gospel's will save it"*** **(Mk.** 8:35). *This statement can seem difficult, and in some cases can even be frightening. But I ask you: is it better to resign yourself to a life without ideals, to a society marked by inequality, oppression, and selfishness, or rather to seek with a generous heart what is true, good, and just, working to build a world which shows forth the beauty of God, even at the price of having to face the many difficulties which this brings...There are no short cuts to happiness and light! Only Jesus can supply answers which are neither illusion nor delusion! Therefore, accept with humble courage what God sets before you. In His great power and tenderness, He calls you to be saints. It would be foolish to vaunt such a call, but*

[17] Zenit, March 19, 2003.

[18] Zenit, May 16, 2003.

it would be reckless to refuse it. It would be condemning yourself to failure in life.[19]

Just as the Holy Father is exacting with young people, you must also be exacting with your teens and young adults. They have the generosity and enthusiasm to respond positively to great challenges.

"Work as if you were to live a hundred years. Pray as if you were to die tomorrow."
Benjamin Franklin

The participation of the will and intellect are needed to acquire each virtue. As your teen develops virtues, these virtues give the teen's intellect and will firmness, promptitude, and pleasure thereby strengthening his intellect and will. As Dr. David Isaacs writes: *This means that if man develops virtues, his intellect will perceive what is really good for him and his will, as with his affective appetites, will follow his intellect in seeking true perfection.* Therefore, the more virtues acquired the more perfect a person becomes. The more perfect a person becomes, the happier he is.

What is meant by firmness and promptitude? "Firmness" means that a person can act without doubting. Moreover, he sees improvement and security in various aspects of his life. *"Promptitude" means that it is easier to do good things because they have been incorporated as a basic part of life; they have become part of man's way of thinking and doing things. In this way the intellect and the will are left free to apply themselves to other things in greater depth so as to achieve greater efficiency. Without having to devote a great deal of thought and struggle, the person acts, reacts, and decides positively. And lastly, the person comes to know, in part, what true happiness is. Virtue allows him to do things with satisfaction, with pleasure,* according to Dr. David

---

[19] Zenit, May 26, 2002.

Isaacs.[20]

"No one is suddenly made perfect."
St. Bede

Will teaching teens and young adults virtue be easy? No. Will it bring perpetual peace to the family? No. **Only when all members practice virtue will there be true peace.** The challenge of teaching virtue can bring conflict as well as turmoil in the beginning when dealing with rebellious teens or reluctant young adults. Calling on the virtue of fortitude, we must forge ahead despite the anger or resentment of our teens and young adults by being demanding (in a kind, patient manner) that they persist in struggling to develop the various virtues. It will mean for you confronting problems rather than ignoring them to keep a false sense of peace. It means establishing standards, then sticking with them even if your children or young adults angrily protest, seem to resent you, or separate themselves from you emotionally. It means explaining clearly what each virtue is, why it is important to cultivate it, then how to go about acquiring it.

Dr. Isaacs emphasizes that *[n]othing of what we have said is easy in everyday life, and if the parents do not give a good example it will be even more difficult. The demanding atmosphere in the family means that the parents are struggling themselves to improve in different aspects related to the human virtues.* Isaacs then cautions parents that children may *perceive their parents' achievements as something totally unattainable for themselves, and become downhearted. For this reason the parents should explain the effort that that improvement has required, without pride, showing that the merit is not so much in what one has achieved but rather in the effort that it has required...Parents who haven't extensively developed some virtue should not be downhearted either...Parents who are demanding with themselves, although they do not achieve much, will still be a*

[20] David Isaacs, University of Navarre Course "Teaching Younger Children Virtue," Washington, D.C., 1986.

good example to their children.[21]

To be demanding does not mean sternness, bad temper or rigidity. Rather it means firmness, determination, constancy followed through with good temper and joy despite the suffering it entails. *We want children to be able to choose between beneficial alternatives,* insists Isaacs. *As educators we are not interested in the possibility of choosing between good and bad. We prefer to put what is bad over to one side so that the child can choose between what is good and what is better. An important reason for being demanding...is to keep children away from what can unnecessarily hurt them, without, obviously, excessive protection, calculating the risk so that the child learns when to say yes and when to say no. The virtue of fortitude comes into play here in its two aspects: resisting and undertaking enterprises. The second motive for demanding, therefore, is that the child should learn to resist possible harm.*[22]

When our children are small we worry that they may be hit by a car, or they may burn themselves or fall from a high perch. But as our children grow into teens, "harm" takes on even more urgency when mixed with drugs, alcohol, gangs, Satanism, and sex. Teach your teens the reason for seeking the good, even when the good is difficult.

Then teach your teens to discern between fact and opinion. Try training them by using newspaper articles. Have the teen read the article then quiz him. What are the facts, what are opinions? Use the same technique with the TV news. Next teach your child to analyze situations by using his reason.

Help your teen to understand the consequences of his actions and decisions, the cause and the effect. Also teach him to distinguish between what is important and what is secondary.

Lead your teen to realize his capabilities and weakness,

---

[21] *Ibid.*   [22] *Ibid.*

especially the areas in which he needs to improve. Rather than giving lectures, help your child to discover his weak points on his own with subtle help. If he protests that he does not need your help, read to your teens and young adults these words of Sister Elvira Petrozzi, the founder of the Community of the Cenacle: *If we don't accept the help of others, who see and suffer from our defects every day, we run the risk of accumulating a lot of anger, sadness, and superficiality inside of us.*[23]

Dr. Isaacs adds, let the teen fail in some of his endeavors *so that he should come to recognize his shortcomings, as well as how to ask for help when necessary. If he learns the value of asking for help, it will be the child who goes to his parents asking for their counsel.*[24] If we prevent our teen from failing in the normal course of his activities, he will become so proud that he will be unwilling to take any advice as he grows older. More about this later in the virtue of humility.

In relation to the will, the child needs to learn to recognize what he really wants and what is secondary. He must recognize his capacity for making an effort, for struggling to improve, for taking the initiative, for making decisions, etc. If he does not recognize these, he will continually make mistakes, blindly following what looks superficially attractive or skipping from one thing to another without rhyme or reason, notes Isaacs.

In the case of the adolescent, he should know if he tends to be emotive or non-emotive, active or non-active, and other aspects of his character so as to be able to judge in which areas he should try to improve. We can begin to help him in this from his early childhood...by telling him, for example, "Haven't you noticed that you always get angry when you're hungry?" [25]

---

[23] Rev. Raymon Peyret, "Our First Vocation is Love," *Resurrection Magazine,* Year 2, Dec. 2001.

[24] University of Navarre Course "Teaching Younger ..." *Op. Cit.*

[25] *Ibid.*

Famous authors Drs. Henry Cloud and John Townsend insist that *the most important thing parents can give children is a sense of responsibility—knowing what they are responsible for and knowing what they aren't responsible for, knowing how to say no and knowing how to accept no. Responsibility is a gift of enormous value.*

They continue: *We've all been around middle-aged people who have...tantrums or sulk when others set limits on them, or they simply fold and comply with others just to keep the peace. Remember that these adult people started off as little people. They learned long, long ago to either fear or hate boundaries. The relearning process for adults is laborious.*[26] While Drs. Cloud and Townsend were using literary license to stress the importance of responsibility, we all know that the most important thing we can give our children is a vibrant Catholic faith and understanding of correct moral conduct. Responsibility ranks after faith and morals in importance. George Washington in his "Farewell Address" made this point very clear. He told his listeners: *Let us with caution indulge the supposition that morality can be maintained without religion. Whatever may be conceded to the influence of refined education on mind...reason and experience both forbid us to expect that national morality can prevail in exclusion of religious principle.*[27] St. Josemaría reiterates: *What a sorry state someone is in when he has marvelous human virtues but a total lack of supernatural outlook, because he will apply those virtues quite easily to his own selfish ends. Meditate upon this.*[28] He continues: *...There are many Christians who follow Christ and are astonished by His divinity, but forget Him as Man. And they fail in the practice of supernatural virtues, despite all the*

[26] Drs. Henry Cloud and John Townsend, ***Boundaries*** (Grand Rapids: Zondervan, 1992) pp. 169-170.

[27] "Pro-Christian Activist Blasts Federal Tyranny," in the *American Free Press*, July 7, 2003, p. 13.

[28] St. Josemaría Escrivá, ***Furrow*** (NY: Scepter, 1987) #427.

external paraphernalia of piety, because they do nothing to acquire human virtues.[29]

"*Our chief peril is not attack; it is decay.*"
G. K. Chesterton

In ***Raise Happy Children...Teach Them Virtues!*** we discussed **the twelve foundation virtues of obedience, sincerity, order, fortitude, perseverance, patience, industriousness, generosity, freedom, responsibility, justice, and charity.** Without these foundation virtues it will be difficult, if not impossible, to develop the **additional twenty virtues discussed in this book: temperance, moderation, modesty, chastity, sociability, friendship, respect for others, simplicity, patriotism, prudence, flexibility, understanding, loyalty, audacity, hospitality, tact, courtesy, humility, optimism and cheerfulness.** It would be like trying to build your dream house in the air rather than on a concrete foundation. It just won't work! That does not mean that the virtues need to be lived perfectly by our preteens and teens before we can teach them the next virtues. It takes a lifetime of struggle to truly develop each of the virtues. We can never say, *I've acquired the virtue of humility,* or *patience* or *charity.* There will always be aspects of each virtue that we can live better. Do you recall how Benjamin Franklin found that the harder he tried to acquire virtue the more aware he became of his lack of virtue?

Venerable Cardinal John Henry Newman had a keen understanding of this. He writes: *In books, everything is made beautiful in its way. Pictures are drawn of complete virtue; little is said about failures, and little or nothing of the drudgery of ordinary, everyday obedience, which is neither poetical nor interesting. True faith teaches us to do numberless disagreeable things for Christ's sake, to bear petty annoyances, which we find written down in no book. In most*

[29] *Ibid.,* #652.

books Christian conduct is made grand, elevated, and splendid; so that any one, who only knows of true religion from books and not from actual endeavors to be religious, is sure to be offended at religion when he actually comes upon it, from the roughness and humbleness of his duties, and his necessary deficiencies in doing them. It is beautiful in a picture to wash the disciples' feet; but the sands of the real desert have no luster in them to compensate for the servile nature of the occupation.[30]

St. Francis de Sales adds: *Selfishness, complacency, false liberty of spirit, these are things, which one cannot well uproot from the human heart; one cannot do more than prevent them from bearing their fruit, which is sin, for one can never altogether stop their uprising, their first impetus, their shoots, as it were, their first impact and stirring; but one can moderate their number and frequency by the practice of opposite virtues and chiefly by the love of God. So we must be patient and amend and curb our bad habits little by little, get the better of our aversions, and master our inclinations and moods as they come up; for in short this life is continual warfare and there is no one who can say: I am not being attacked. Rest is reserved for heaven where the palm of victory awaits us. On earth we must fight our battle between fear on the one hand and hope on the other, in the knowledge that hope is always the stronger because He who comes to our help is almighty. So never give up working constantly towards your amendment and perfection....Because of the love you owe yourself you should be on your guard to eradicate your wrong inclinations. Never be dismayed to find that you are worthless and thoroughly ill-tempered. Alas! Deal gently and lovingly with your heart, raising it up when it falls, and longing ardently for its perfection. Above all, do what you can to strengthen the superior part of your spirit, not stopping short at feelings and consolations but passing on to resolutions, definite purposes, and projects* (editorial emphasis).[31]

[30] From ***Parochial and Plain Sermons*** (San Francisco: Ignatius, 1997).

[31] Elizabeth Stopp, ***St. Francis de Sales*** (NY:Harper & Brothers, 1960).

St. Peter Damian especially addresses young people. He counsels them: *Beware, lest any vice should increase with the growth of your body, lest the knots of any perversity should harden within you; rather, be vessels of honor and not of reproach, ready for any good work in the house of the Lord. If you desire to shine with the uprightness of manhood, and to abound in virtue...take up at once the weapons of continence, and fight with all your strength against the violent temptations of the flesh. At this, the very beginning of your apprenticeship, assure yourselves of certain victory with God on your side; bodily wage implacable war on the hostile spirits...Tread your pride underfoot, crush envy, curb your tongue with a strict silence, let meditation on the Scriptures quench the desires of your palate; your tongue must not utter detraction, nor give countenance to it by listening to it...It is not, however, detraction to reveal a brother's fault to him whose duty it is to correct it...*[32]

Don't become discouraged if you have worked to instill the virtues in your teens but your teens seem fairly virtueless at home. This is not uncommon. In fact, many children and teens may act up at home but are virtuous outside the home. Parents can become truly concerned about the lack of virtue in their children until they receive positive feedback from teachers, parents of their friends, coaches and relatives. Then parents begin to think, *Are we talking about the same child?* It is important to remember that you are instilling the foundation of each virtue in your children. It is not going to be, most likely, the edifying, heroic virtue we see in saints or in older people who have struggled for years with their defects. Our teens are just beginning along the inclined path of virtue. They will stumble, get side-tracked, and even slip back now and then, just as we do as adults. This is to be expected but certainly **not** accepted.

---

[32] Patricia McNulty, ***Selected Writings on the Spiritual Life*** (London:Faber & Faber, 1959).

"Motivation is the mother of all virtues."
St. Hildegard of Bingen

The Midtown Education Foundation, a not-for-profit corporation, tutors inner city children to help them excel in their studies while at the same time teaching their students virtues. Each student receives an "All Star Goal Sheet" that *tracks goals for daily life. Students in the Walgreen's One-on-One Program...set up to five goals each week, most of them related to academics and character.* Study the sample of The All Star Team Sheet below.

The goals are small, precise, and achievable. *For one student, a weekly goal might be not to hit a sibling. Later that might evolve to actually smiling at the sibling. Still later, the goal might expand to do something nice for the sibling without their even knowing.* Another student's goal might be *to make his bed regularly, to write down homework assignments, to exercise.* As Program Director John Zimmer adds, *All Star Sheets help our students to develop good habits through small steps. The key to acquiring a virtue is to acquire a habit.*[33] Why not adopt something similar for your children? As you work with your children/teens on a specific virtue, why not have several goals related to the virtue you are trying to train them in? Include several other goals from prior virtues that need more work. For example, if obedience is still a problem, pick an achievable goal for obedience. Or order may be a problem. Do not pick a vague goal such as *I'm going to be orderly every day this week.* Instead, plan a specific, achievable goal such as, *each day at 4 p.m. I will do my homework* or *when I go to bed I will put my shoes in the closet* or *I will make my lunch for tomorrow right after dinner.* Slowly you will see progress.

Bishop Thomas V. Daily, who heads the Diocese of Brooklyn, was interviewed on NBC's *News Forum* in regard to the problems within schools and families. He responded: *While we all talk about teaching values in the schools, we seldom talk about instilling virtue in our children: Virtues are the muscles of the soul—just the basic virtues of prudence, justice, fortitude, temperance, and self-discipline. The more we practice those virtues the stronger we become in the spirit and in the soul, even as exercising the muscles of the body builds up the body...[W]e all want a solid education for our kids. So let's work to build a conscience in our kids that strengthens the person and at the same time benefits the commonweal* (editorial emphasis).

Certainly there are many great dedicated teachers in New York's parochial and public schools; but we must work more

[33] MEF, "Small Goals Lead To Virtue," Spring, 2003. www.midtown-metro.org

to develop virtues in the kids, virtues such as respect and self-control, for example and patience, obedience, and perseverance.[34]

King St. Louis of France was so concerned about the upbringing of his son that he wrote a book for him entitled ***Instructions To His Son.***[35] Likewise, my concern for you and your children, as well as for my daughters and my grandchildren, has prompted me to devote six years of my life to the ***Raise Happy Children Series***. During this time I have made friends with several of the postal clerks at the local post office. One of the women, the mother of four, asks me periodically, *Are children becoming more virtuous because of your books?* Dr. David Isaacs insists that we will not see the fruits of our labors until our children have children. So be patient and persevering. The efforts you are making to teach your children virtue are taking root, even if you cannot see it. Let me give you an example of how this works. Ever since I can remember, I have had the annoying habit of sitting on the edge of my chair. It's very uncomfortable but no matter if I'm working at my computer, sitting in church, doing a TV interview or having lunch with friends, I always perch on the edge of the seat. I simply cannot break this habit. Lately I've been trying to figure out why in the world I persist in sitting like this. Then, last week I went to a music store to buy some beginner violin books as a gift for a friend. When I opened one, there was a young girl perched on the edge of her chair in position to play her violin. Suddenly I knew why I perch on the edge of chairs. As a child I was trained by my strict, Hungarian violin teacher (a descendent of the Magyars) to sit in that position to play correctly. The habit that I learned in third grade has persisted with me into middle age. Although it is simply a habit, not a virtue, the virtues you teach your children will likewise surface in their lives if you are as

[34] Henry King, "Work To Develop Virtues..." *The Wanderer* (MN), Jan. 12, 1995, p. 1.

[35] H. Daniel-Rops, ***Cathedral And Crusade*** (NY: E.P. Dutton & Co., Inc., 1961) p. 44.

consistent in teaching the virtues as my violin teacher was in teaching me correct form.

"Raise this child very carefully, for God has chosen her for Himself."

An inner locution to Bl. Alda Bellanti[36]

Once your teens and young adults have the firm foundation of all the virtues discussed in books three and four in the ***Raise Happy Children Series*** they will also have the beginnings of joy in their lives. My friend, Sarah, saw first hand how this works.

Sarah, was on "Grandma" duty for several weeks when her daughter, Kit, had her fifth baby in St. Louis. Kit's four children are ages nine, seven and four-year-old twins. Over a quiet lunch Sarah shared her three-week experience with me: *I wanted to test your method for teaching children virtues to see if it really works. It does work, as long as the parent is consistent for at least three weeks. There was a profound change in my grandchildren from the time I arrived to the time I left. While my daughter, Kit, prides herself on being a parent who disciplines her children, when I arrived I felt that the children were in control of the home rather than the parents. Kit loves her children so much that she is afraid to say "no" to them. She doesn't realize that "no" is a loving word. She may begin by saying "no" but when the kids pester, she always gives in to them. If her husband corrects a child she comes to the child's defense. The children, as young as they are, have learned to play one parent against the other.*

My plan was to try to establish the foundation virtues during the time I was with my grandchildren. Quite frankly I found it exhausting to be consistent, to be on one's toes constantly in supervising the children but by the time I went home, the tone in Kit's home had changed. My consistency was well worth the effort. The children were happier. There was more order as well as cooperation. It was amazing to see the changes but it did not begin on a positive note.

[36] ***Married Saints and Blessed Through the Centuries***, *Op. Cit.*, p. 227.

As I walked into my daughter's home, her nine-year-old son, Brian, was sprawled out on the sofa with the TV blaring. He was concentrating so deeply on the gameboy in his hands that he never noticed my arrival. I was hurt. As I walked back and forth bringing in my suitcases, he never looked up to greet me or to offer to help. After a half hour of this I finally walked up to him saying, "Brian, aren't you even going to say 'hello'?" Looking sheepish, Brian looked up at me, greeted me, then went right back to his gameboy. Next his brother, Liam, bounded in from a soccer game eager to tell his mother the highlights of his game. Again I had to stop him to ask if he was going to say "hello". He gave me a brief "hello" but continued on with his tale. His twin sisters were more gracious. They said "hello" but then went outside to play with friends. I certainly didn't feel very welcomed into their home.

Later that evening Kit complained to me that Brian was becoming sullen and moody, not the upbeat, vivacious little boy he used to be. I gave her an article I was reading from Zenit that cited studies that showed that children who played gameboy more than thirty minutes a day developed personality problems relating to people. I tried to tactfully suggest that the gameboy combined with liberal TV privileges could very well be the cause of Brian's sullenness. Kit looked the article over then told me Brian never played his gameboy more than thirty minutes. Unfortunately I found that Kit was not keeping track of the time. Brian told me he could play it anytime he wanted to...and he did.

Kit knows how I feel about the TV being on so that was turned off during the day while I was there.

Surveying the situation, I decided my best bet was to start with the four-year-old twins, Grace and Rosemarie. At bedtime I offered to read the girls some stories. First we read some stories about St. Therese and other saints, then some secular stories. The little girls were filled with questions about angels, God, and saints. We must have talked religion for about an hour but I kept referring everything back to doing the will of God. The next day, when the girls misbehaved I would ask them, "Are you doing God's will or your will?" It was surprising to hear the four-year-olds honestly tell me, "I was doing my will." Their brothers, listening to our conversation, easily picked up the points I was trying to make.

Kit had taught her children to do specific chores which the children do each day. I worked along with them discussing how since they had offered their day to God in their morning prayers their work had to be done well. The children listened then tried to do their work better. Each time they became "bored" I found another project or task for them to do. The little girls learned to wash the floor moldings in each room while I taught the boys to paint the front stairs and decorative ceiling pieces. All of them learned to fold laundry. As I taught the children the new tasks they would ask me questions of faith such as, "Did you ever have a miracle happen?" or "Did your angel ever help you?" This gave me an opportunity to combine faith with the virtues I was trying to instill.

It was fun to see how excited the children were with their new accomplishments. It was a way for them to show their love for their parents while at the same time it expanded their ability to do new tasks. Next they helped me landscape the front yard. As the weeks passed, the children were visibly more cheerful, helpful, and happy. We had a lot of fun together.

The day before Kit came home from the hospital with the baby, she hired a woman to come in for the day so I could have a day off. When I returned from my day away I wished I had never left! The sitter was even more permissive than Kit. The kids were watching TV as they munched on candy at dinnertime. From the color of their mouths they had been eating candy most of the day and they were wired! When I told Grace to put the candy away, she thrust out her chin defiantly telling me, "I don't have to listen to you anymore." The house was torn-up and dirty. Quite frankly I wanted to have a good cry, pack up and go home. I was outnumbered and the kids knew it. Just then the phone rang. It was my brother. When I told him my situation he laughed, then said, "Sarah, your job's not to teach the children virtues. Just keep them from killing each other!" While I laughed with him, I love my grandchildren too much to have such a small goal for them. There had to be a way to regroup. With the help of prayer and my guardian angel, I was able to restore order, then get the kids to help cleanup. After the evening family rosary, Brian surprised me by asking me to tell them some stories about the saints. The rest of the children then began to ask me questions about God, heaven and how to become a saint. It struck me that they had had a whole day to do whatever they wanted to do...eat candy and junk, watch TV and videos, tear-up the house, skip chores, be naughty but subconsciously they knew that had not made them happy. While Brian would roll his eyes when I talked about God or virtues the first week I was there, now he was actually questioning me about them. That I found interesting. Even children realize they are happier when they live virtuous, faith-filled lives.

Several months later Sarah and I stopped to see Kit and her family in St. Louis. When I parked the car, the children ran from the house and the neighbor's to greet Sarah. The grandchildren swarmed around her, talking to her, hugging her, kissing her. I was touched to see little Rosemarie constantly kissing her. Sarah actually couldn't move because of the press of the children. They all wanted to talk to her, to be with her. Grace and Rosemarie asked if they could help carry anything in. Even the boys cheerfully took packages into the house for their grandmother. Sarah's experiment was a success but more important, the fruit of it, joy, was visible in those children. It was touching to see that Sarah's grandchildren loved her because she showed that she loved them and cared about them by setting limits, helping them to expand their potential while exposing them to ways to love God more deeply. If you are consistent in teaching each virtue to your children you will have a similar success story.

> *"What is youth? It is a time given by providence to every person and given to him as a responsibility. During that time he searches...for the answers to basic questions; he searches not only for the meaning of life but also for a concrete way to go about living his life."*
> John Paul II

Teens have a great capacity for heroically giving themselves to a cause. Be sure that you are teaching them to give themselves to God rather than to a gang, or a cult! Fr. Marcial Maciel recalls the violent persecutions against Catholics in Mexico in the 1920s. The martyrdom of his friend, José Sánchez del Río, for the faith, laid the groundwork in his soul for the founding of the Legionaries of Christ. Fr. Maciel recalls: *José, who was fourteen, asked me to go into the mountains with him and fight with the Cristeros (Christians), but I was very young (about seven). He took off to the mountains. A few days later he was caught by government troops...They asked him to renounce his faith in Christ, under pain of death. José refused to apostatize...So they skinned the soles of his feet and forced him to walk through the town towards the cemetery. He cried and moaned in pain. But he would not give in. Every so often they stopped and said to him, "If you shout 'Death to Christ the King,' we will spare your life. Say 'Death to Christ the King.'" But he would answer, "Long live Christ the King." Once they got to the cemetery, before shooting him, they asked him for the last time if he would give up his faith. He didn't, and they killed him right there. Like many other Mexican martyrs, he died shouting, "Long live Christ the King!"...I believe that God made use of all this to shape my soul and prepare it for the mission of founding the Legion of Christ*[37] when Maciel was

---

[37] ***Christ Is My Life,*** *Op. Cit.,* pp. 8-9.

a sixteen-year-old seminarian.

It is also during the critical teen years that vocations develop whether it is a vocation to the priesthood, religious life, celibate lay life or to marriage. St. Peter of Chavanon (1003-1080) received the call to the priesthood during his schooling.[38] Bl. Joan Soderini (1301-1367) joined the Third Order Servites of Mary in Florence, Italy at the age of twelve. St. Bernard, in his late teens, sought out his wise uncle, Gaudry, to discuss his possible vocation. When it was agreed that he did have a vocation to the cloister, Bernard, at the age of twenty-two, left the world to give his life to God but he didn't go alone. He brought with him a total of 30 knights, among them his uncle Gaudry, five of his six brothers, other family members, and friends. But before he left home he told his youngest brother Nivard, who at fifteen was too young to join the cloister: *See how rich you'll be [as heir to all the family lands].* Nivard responded, *What, you take heaven and leave me the earth? I won't agree to any such arrangement.* He later joined his brothers in the monastery.[39]

Two cardinals found not only their conversion during their teens but also their vocations to the priesthood. Kenyan Cardinal Maurice Michael Otunga, recently deceased, was the product of a pagan family. On his own he embraced the Catholic faith at the age of twelve then was ordained at 27. Influenced by his pagan family roots, in his work he gave great importance and support to families.[40] Cardinal Francis Arinze, the Prefect of the Congregation for Divine Worship and the Sacraments, converted to Catholicism at the age of nine. He is a member of the Ibo tribe of Nigeria. It was only after he was in the seminary that his mother converted. His father converted after Cardinal Arinze was ordained a priest in 1958. Recently deceased Cardinal Francis Xavier Nguyên Văn Thuân of Vietnam discerned his vocation when thirteen-years-old. Coming from a devout family whose

---

[38] *Magnificat,* Sept. 2003, Vol. 5, No. 7.

[39] ***Cathedral And Crusade,*** *Op. Cit.,* p. 81.

[40] Zenit, Sept. 7, 2003.

relatives were martyrs for the faith, his father simply asked if he had *sufficiently considered such a serious decision. Had he prayed long and hard enough? Had he asked God to show him His will in this matter?*[41] When assured that Thuân was serious, his parents helped him to enroll in the minor seminary. Fr. Marcial Machiel recalls how he found his vocation as a young teen: *[My mother] told me that when I was an adolescent and she couldn't make out what would become of me, she entrusted me to the Blessed Virgin. The very day she told Mary to take care of me—she was by then almost at wits end with my adolescent mischief—I came to her that night to tell her I wanted to go and become a priest.*[42]

If a teen is not striving for virtue, any vocation will be difficult if not impossible to faithfully live. Drs. Cloud and Townsend believe that *the teens...are a crucible for kids. We find out what kind of character has actually been built into our children during this difficult passage.*[43] Or, stated in a more negative way, we discover the lack of character which we have permitted to develop in our teens by allowing vices to set deep roots into their souls as children.

Let's look at some other famous teens. The Apostle St. John was in his teens when Christ called him off his father's fishing boat to follow him. Our Lady was in her early teens when God the Father sent St. Gabriel to ask for her consent to be the Mother of God. Going back even further in salvation history, did you realize that the Prophet Jeremiah was about 14 when God called him? In fact, Jeremiah reminds the Lord: ***Lord Yahweh; look, I do not know how to speak: I am a child!*** (***Jeremiah*** 1:5) His difficult task was to foretell the coming destruction of Jerusalem while at the same time calling the king and people to repentance. For his efforts he was stoned to death.

In ***The Confession of Patrick,*** St. Patrick exposes his

---

[41] André Nguyên Vãn Châu, ***The Miracle of Hope, Political Prisoner, Prophet of Peace*** (Boston: Pauline Books & Media, 2003) pp. 29-30.
[42] ***Christ Is My Life,*** *Op. Cit.*, p. 11.
[43] ***Boundaries***, *Op. Cit.*, p. 175.

initial lack of faith and virtue. He discloses: *My father was a certain man named Calpornius, a deacon, son of the late Potitus, a presbyter, who was in the town of Bannaventa Berniae. He had a small estate nearby. There I was captured and made a slave. I was not even sixteen-years-old. I was ignorant of the true Lord, so I was led to Ireland in captivity with many thousands of others, who deserved this fate, because we cut ourselves off from God, because we did not keep His commandments, because we were disobedient to our priests who admonished us about our salvation.*[44] Although raised in a family of clerics, St. Patrick had not been taught the faith or virtues by his parents. God had to intervene to save his soul by permitting him to be enslaved in order to turn him around. We certainly don't want God to have to intervene in such a difficult manner with our children, do we? Reading further in his ***Confession*** and ***Letter*** he publicly accuses himself of the vices of pride, ambition and self-righteousness. Author Greg Tobin points out that *[a]lthough he ultimately won his battles against his moral defects, it took tremendous sustained effort to do so. This is the manifestation of his courage.*[45]

St. Bernard of Menthon (996-1081) was a teenager who lived with his parents in Val d'Aosta on Annecy Lake in Italy. His father, although a nobleman, had the apostolate of safely leading travelers and pilgrims through the passes in the Alps during winter. Bernard, impressed by his father's care for travelers, decided to found an order to establish hospices where travelers could find help, a warm meal, and spend the night safely as they journeyed through the Alps. Special dogs were kept at the hospices to find lost travelers or those buried in avalanches. These dogs came to be known as St. Bernards.[46]

Around the year 1000 AD, St. Romuald, a young prince of Ravenna, Italy, exchanged his palace for a monastery to

---

[44] Greg Tobin, ***The Wisdom of St. Patrick*** (NY: Ballantine Books, 1999) p. 197.
[45] *Ibid.*, p. 180.
[46] ***Cathedral and Crusade,*** *Op. Cit.*, p. 257.

make reparation for a murder committed by his royal father. Over time he founded the Camaldolese congregation.[47] Then there is Bl. Margaret of Louvain (1207-1225), a young maid of eighteen, who worked in her uncle's inn. Her uncle gave free lodging to the poor and pilgrims. Eventually her uncle and aunt decided to sell the inn so they could become religious. Thieves, hearing of the inn's sale, went there to steal the money. Margaret, having been away on an errand, walked in on the robbery that resulted in the brutal murder of her uncle and aunt. One of the murderers offered to spare her life if she kept quiet about his part in the murder and married him. When she refused, she was likewise murdered.[48]

On a more cheerful note, there is the beautiful story of St. Clare, the eighteen-year-old daughter of the powerful Italian Sciffi family. Frequently Clare accompanied her mother to hear St. Francis of Assisi preach. She found his spiritual fire and words captivating. She had made his acquaintance when he came to her palace to beg alms. Later she learned that her wealthy cousin, Rufino, had given up all his wealth to joined Francis' new order of Brothers Minor. Although Lady Clare had many suitors because of her beauty, sweetness, and wealth, she rejected them all. Then two weeks before the Easter of 1212 her father, Lord Faverone, told her that a handsome, wealthy knight had asked for her hand in marriage and her father had consented. Clare was told she would meet the young man at Easter when he came to discuss the arrangements for their marriage. Clare was heartbroken. Marriage was not in her plans. The night of Palm Sunday, Clare and her cousin, Pacifica, secretly left the Sciffi castle to go to St. Mary of the Angels. There they were greeted by cousin Rufino, St. Francis and the rest of the brothers who were waiting for them. Standing before the altar, St. Francis cut Clare's golden tresses off after accepting her vows to serve God and the poor. Pacifica made her vows that evening too.

[47] ***The Church In The Dark Ages***, *Op. Cit.*, p. 582.
[48] *Magnificat*, Sept. 2003.

Following the ceremony, the two teens were then taken to a convent to stay until St. Francis could find them a convent of their own. When Lord Faverone discovered where Clare and Pacifica were, he stormed into the chapel where Clare was praying. Although her father tried to remove her by force she clung tightly to the altar railing. Not able to budge her, her father went home in a fury. But the turmoil wasn't over for the Sciffi family. Shortly afterwards, Clare's fifteen-year-old sister, Agnes, disappeared. Her father knew exactly where to find her. This time he successfully tore Agnes away from Clare. As Agnes sobbed, *Oh, sister, sister! Save me, save me!* Clare dropped to her knees to storm heaven for help. Suddenly petite Agnes became so heavy that the men carrying her away had to drop her leaving her to roll away into the bushes. Terrified by this event, as they ran they yelled out to Lord Faverone, *It's a sign from God. Surely He wishes her to remain in the convent!* And she did.[49]

Not all saints had virtue as teens. St. Vincent Strambi (1745-1824) had to struggle long and hard to acquire virtue. Using his slingshot, he once shattered a pitcher of water a neighbor lady was carrying on her shoulder. Not only did she lose her pitcher, she was drenched with water!

The successful struggle for virtue is not limited to the far distant past. Let's look at more recent teen saints and blesseds. Two young catechists, Daudi Okelo, 16-18 years of age and Jildo Irwa, 12-14 years old, were speared and knifed to death because they refused to stop teaching the Gospel in Uganda in 1918.[50] Both of these young boys were products of pagan homes. They converted to the Catholic faith without the support of their families. When a young catechist was killed, Daudi offered to take his place while Jildo volunteered to go as his assistant. When Fr. Gambaretto warned the boys that they also could be

---

[49] Helen Walker Homan, ***Francis and Clare, Saints of Assisi*** (NY: Farrar, Straus & Cudahy, 1956).

[50] Zenit, Sept. 12, 2002.

killed Daudi replied. *I am not afraid to die. Jesus, too, died for us!* Although Daudi was naturally shy he overcame his shyness to work with the children in his village and neighboring villages. At dawn he would beat his drum calling the children to morning prayers and catechism instruction. To help the children retain his lessons he taught them in a singsong manner. At sunset he would again call the children to come for evening prayers and the rosary. Jildo was also the product of a pagan family but his parents eventually converted to Catholicism. While Daudi was shy, Jildo was outgoing, and lively. He would entertain the children with games to attract them to Daudi's lessons. After witnessing Daudi's death, Jildo was told he could go free if he gave up teaching the Catholic faith. In tears over his friend's death, he told his attackers, *We have done nothing wrong. For the same reason you killed Daudi you must also kill me, because together we came here and together we have been teaching God's word.* At that he was grabbed then killed by a spear.[51]

Bl. Pier Giorgio Frassati, one of the special patrons of World Youth Day, was born in 1901 in Turin, Italy. He died from polio which he caught while caring for the sick. He was 24 years old, and only months away from receiving his degree in mining engineering.

Frassati came from what we would term a wealthy, influential, dysfunctional family. He had just one younger sister, Luciana. His mother was a famous painter and his father was an agnostic politician who held positions as an Italian Ambassador and senator besides owning the liberal newspaper *La Stampa.*

Despite the lack of faith of his parents, Pier developed a deep devotion to Our Lady and her rosary as well as to the Blessed Eucharist. While his father thought he spent many of his nights carousing, Pier was actually taking part in nocturnal adoration. At the age of 17 he joined the

[51] Zenit, Oct. 18, 2002.

St. Vincent de Paul Society to help the poor, the sick, orphans, and the demobilized servicemen of World War I. He gave up family summer vacations to stay in Turin to work with these people. He bestowed his bus fare on the poor so they could purchase food then ran home to be on time for dinner. When a friend asked him how he could go into the slum housing Pier replied, *[r]emember always that it is to Jesus that you go: I see a special light that we do not have, around the sick, the poor, and the unfortunate.* A German reporter caught him giving his coat to a poor person outside the Italian Embassy, then overheard his father chastising him for doing so. Pier simply replied: *But you see, Papa, it was cold.* He would say, *Jesus comes to me every morning in Holy Communion and I repay Him in my very small way by visiting the poor.* John Paul II nicknamed him "the man of eight beatitudes" for his charitable work covered all the beatitudes.

In fact, Frassati decided to become a mining engineer so that he could help the miners. Around this same time, attracted by the writings of St. Catherine of Siena, he became a Dominican tertiary.

At Turin's Royal Polytechnic Institute, Pier promoted Marian devotion, chastity, and of course, Eucharistic Adoration. Saying *charity is not enough, we need social reform,* he joined Catholic Action, the Catholic Student Federation, and the People's Party which promoted the principles of Pope Leo XIII's encyclical, ***Rerum Novarum***. This was in opposition to the political views of his father. Author Michael Persica notes, *though not prone to violence, Pier Giorgio did not shy away from standing up for his beliefs, both political and religious, even under the threat of turbulent confrontation. In one such confrontation with Roman police, he seized his group's fallen banner and raised it high above his head to rally the other youths, using the staff to protect himself from the officers' violent blows. "To live without Faith," he wrote, "without a heritage to defend, without* *battling constantly for truth, is not to live, but to 'get along'; we must never just 'get along.'* " [52] He strongly opposed the communists and the Fascists.

Pier was not all work. He loved Italian culture and was an accomplished mountain climber. He enjoyed the theatre, opera, art galleries, and playing pool. In fact, he used his skill in pool to wager bets with his friends, who he called "The Shady Characters". If he won, they would have to attend adoration with him. They always agreed to the wager and naturally, he always won the bet. If they teased him about his deep faith he would respond: *True happiness, dear friends, does not consist in the pleasure of the world or in earthly things, but in peace of conscience which we only have if we are pure in heart and mind.* He was never known to use profanity or drink to excess although he was called the "holy Terror" because of his love of practical jokes. On hiking or mountain climbing expeditions with his friends he would begin the rosary or other prayers as they hiked or climbed. He counseled them: *Learn to be stronger in spirit than in your muscles. If you are, you will be real apostles of faith in God.*[53]

When Frassati fell in love with Laura Hidalgo, also a member of Catholic Action but of a lower class than he, he realized that his parents would not permit their marriage. Rather than disobey them he decided to turn his love into a Christian friendship. Writing to a friend he explained: *So, my program is this: to transform that special feeling that I had for her,* [into]... *the restful bonds of Christian friendship, respect for her virtues, imitation of her outstanding gifts. Perhaps you will tell me that it is mad to hope this. But I believe, if you pray a little for me, in a short time I can achieve that state of prayer.*[54]

Only twenty-four, he wrote to his sister on the topic of cheerfulness vs. suffering saying: *You ask me whether I am*

[52] Zenit, July 14, 2001.

[53] Michael Persica, "The Man of the Beatitudes," *The Mir Response*, April/May 1995 p. 5. [54] *Ibid.*

cheerful. How could I not be, so long as my trust in God gives me strength? We should always be cheerful. Sadness should be banished from all Christian souls. For suffering is a far different thing from sadness, which is the worst disease of all. It is almost always caused by lack of faith. But the purpose for which we have been created shows us the path along which we should tread, perhaps strewn with many thorns, but not a sad path. Even in the midst of intense suffering it is one of joy.[55]

When Pier Giorgio contracted poliomyelitis his parents' attention was focused on his dying grandmother. As he was dying his mother scolded him for not helping her. *Not even in those desperate final days could he ever forget his closest friends, the poor. It was Friday, the day he visited them. While lying on his deathbed he wanted the usual material assistance to be brought to them. He asked his sister to take a small packet from his jacket and with a semi-paralyzed hand he wrote the following note to Grimaldi: "Here are the injections for Converso. The pawn ticket is Sappa's. I had forgotten it; renew it on my behalf."*[56] He died July 4, 1925. The day of his funeral the streets of Turin were lined with the people he had helped. His parents were stunned by the crowds. His niece, Wanda Gawronska, speaking about her uncle in Canada on All Saints Day, 1999, pointed out: *God gave Pier Giorgio all the external attributes that could have led him to make the wrong choices: a wealthy family, very good looks, manhood, health, being the only heir of a powerful family. But Pier Giorgio listened to the invitation of Christ:* ***"Come and follow me."*** *He anticipated by at least 50 years the Church's understanding and new direction on the role of the laity.*[57]

Conversions and virtuous teens are not limited to the past but are living with us today. On June 28, 2002 the statutes of the Neocatechumenal Way were recognized by the Pontifical Council for the Laity. This organization has spread to 105 nations. It was founded by a most unlikely young

---

[55] *Ibid.* [56] Zenit, July 14, 2001. [57] *Ibid.*

man, Kiko Argüello of Madrid, in 1964. Kiko, from a middle class Madrid family, was a self-described atheist. He studied fine arts, even winning the National Award for Painting. Yet he wasn't happy. He recalls, *I had died interiorly and I knew that sooner or later my end would undoubtedly be suicide. To live each day was a suffering. Every day the same thing: why get up? Who am I? Why are we living? Why earn money? Why get married? Nothing had meaning for me. I would ask the people around me: "Excuse me, but do you know why you are living?" They could not answer me. A great chasm opened within me. I would escape from myself. That chasm was a profound call from God, who was calling me from my deepest interior.*[58]

At the height of Kiko's despair he cried out to God for help and God responded in a manner that startled him. Kiko gave up his painting to live among the poor where he began a community to teach catechesis based on the Gospel and the Eucharist. With the help of his co-founder, Carmen Hernandez, and priest friends, their experiment was tried successfully in several parishes. Kiko explains: *The Neocatechumenal Way does not intend to create a movement in itself, but tries to help parishes to open a way of Christian initiation [leading] to baptism, in order to discover what it means to be Christian. It is an instrument at the service of bishops within parishes, to bring back to the faith the many people who have abandoned it. The renewal that has taken place in parishes thanks to the neocatechumenate has, in fact, caused an amazing missionary impulse, which has made many catechists and whole families offer themselves to be sent to those places on earth in need of evangelization. Another important fruit in the local Church is the flowering of numerous vocations, both to the religious as well as the priestly life. It has made possible the resurgence of 40 missionary diocesan seminaries, which can go to the assistance of so many dioceses in difficulty, at this time of lack of vocations.*[59] Kiko, now middle aged, is still actively

[58] Zenit, June 28, 2002.

[59] Zenit, June 28, 2002.

pursuing souls.

Your job is to inspire your teens and young adults to "go for the gold" of God's eternity by deepening their faith as they live lives of virtue. Despite the culture we are living in, many parents around the world are doing precisely that. My sixteen-year-old niece recently discovered that she has an outstanding operatic voice. Months ago I overheard her choral director telling her parents that if this young woman wanted to pursue a career in music there was no limit to how far she could climb. Since then I've watched as this high school junior began private voice lessons. When I asked if she was thinking of attending Julliard after high school, she laughed as she told me, *My voice teacher talks about me attending Julliard and then singing at the Met, but singing is a pleasant hobby. I don't think that I will make it a career.* What she did not tell me is that she is seriously considering giving her life to God through a specific vocation that may conflict with an operatic career. She is placing God's will before her own personal desires.

My nephew, her older brother, is a freshman in college. He selected his second choice college so that he would be closer to home. This would enable him to come home twice a month to help his grandfather care for his tree farm. This young man was concerned that his grandfather, 89, would not be able to care for the property himself. His spirit of service is rooted in personal virtue. These teens are able to practice self-sacrifice because their parents have taught them not only a deep Catholic faith, but virtues as well.

Another young man I know is a sophomore in college. While I've always thought he had a priestly vocation, last Spring he fell in love with a lovely girl from a great family. Then last summer he worked at Midtown in Chicago to help inner city children. Upon returning home he asked his parents if he could speak with them about his future. He explained that working at Midtown he began to see that God may be calling him to a special vocation that would exclude marriage. When his father explained that it would be difficult to give up an earthly love, the young man agreed but said, *I always thought I would marry but if God wills this vocation for me, I am willing to give up my plans to marry in order to do His will.* Again, these parents gave their son a deep faith in God, a wonderful foundation in the virtues as well as the willingness to live a life of self-sacrifice.

We have been discussing teens that have a strong faith base. But virtues are prized by all people, not only Christians, because of the natural law written by God in the heart of everyone. So let's consider human virtues from a Native American prospective. Pulitzer Prize nominee Allan W. Echert writes an interesting, balanced, historical series on the development of the United States. In his ***A Sorrow In Our Heart, The Life of Tecumseh,*** (please read this footnote)[60] The author explains how the Indians taught their children self-control and why tantrums, crying and whining were not permitted. He explains that children learned as babies not to cry. In addition they were trained not to express vocally their anger, frustration or pain. Outbursts by children not only disgraced their parents but *could often have grave consequences; a noisy child could easily ruin a hunt by frightening off game and, in times of hostilities, a wailing baby or whining toddler could direct an enemy to their location and result in disaster.* Self-control was taught through affection, anticipating the needs of infants before they began crying then as the children grew older through rewards of praise. ...*No Shawnee infant or toddler was ever struck as a method to curtail its crying or other outburst.*[61]

The Indians based their teaching of virtues on their strong faith in the Great Spirit, Moneto. Like Christians they

---

[60] This book of 1,068 pages is fascinating but pp. 196-197, the last line of 268 and the three top lines of 269 are not appropriate for young readers. The mating ritual is described in too much detail.

[61] Allan W. Echert, ***A Sorrow In Our Heart, The Life of Tecumseh*** (NY: Bantam Books, 1993) p. 55.

believed that after death, depending on how one lived his life, each person would either go to a place of peace and happiness or eternal torment. Listen in as a war chief explains to a seventeen-year-old captive from West Virginia their beliefs. This white teen had asked to join the tribe. He eventually became the famous Indian warrior, Blue Jacket: *No one is forced to believe in these matters... Morality is a fixed law...From our earliest childhood it is instilled in our minds that deceitfulness among ourselves is a crime. We live according to our standards and principles and not for what others might think of us. Absolute honesty toward others of our tribe is the basis of character and the standards and rules of conduct are followed scrupulously. The foundation of all Shawnee intercourse is this: "Do not kill or injure your neighbor, for it is not him you injure, you injure yourself; but do good to him, therefore add to his days of happiness as you add to you own. Do not wrong your neighbor, nor hate him, for it is not him that you wrong—you wrong yourself; but love him, for Moneto loves him also as he loves you.*[62]

Although women followed the same law as the braves, gossip was considered a great crime; *meaning deliberate and malicious lying meant to cause harm, shame, humiliation or pain.*[63]

Rather than threats or punishments to make children obey, the Shawnees appealed to the child's personal pride and family pride to carry out directives and instructions. The reward for right behavior was praise, not only from the parents but also from the other villagers who all took part in the formation of the children. When children did something wrong a parent would only have to say, *Oh, how sad I am that my child has done this bad thing. I truly hope he will never do it again,* to change the child's conduct.[64]

Order was lived by again appealing to the child/teen's pride. The child was allowed to carry out the task when and how he chose to do it but by doing the task promptly,

---

[62] *Ibid.* p. 63. [63] *Ibid.* [64] *Ibid.*, p. 65.

the teen was guaranteed praise.

In the particularly severe winter of 1780 when the Mississippi as well as all the other major rivers froze solid, Tecumseh was given the responsibility of feeding his family of nine, plus the widows and elderly of his village since the braves would be away defending their land. Tecumseh was only twelve-years-old! He was capable of this task because he had become a skilled hunter at the age of six. Each day he went out to hunt with his bow and arrows for their food. His skill was such that *[h]e brought in to the village hundreds of rabbits, scores of turkeys, large numbers of grouse and squirrels, raccoons and opossums, and even, on three separate occasions, bear. Most often, however, he hunted deer and buffalo...In one day he killed seventeen deer and five buffalo.*[65]

Saving his tribe from starvation, he was accorded warrior status, again at age twelve. As such he had a voice in the Indian Councils. He could also lead war and hunting parties. Tecumseh, at the age of fifteen, took advantage of his right to address the Councils speaking out against the torture of prisoners. After one prisoner was tortured to death, Tecumseh stepped in to stop the victim's body from being further defiled saying: *You will say that I am young and inexperienced in such matters...but I cannot keep from speaking. What I have seen here has made me sick and ashamed for you and for myself. What bravery, what courage, what strength is there in the torturing of a man unable to defend himself?...Now I see that in the very act of committing it, we lower ourselves to something beneath animals, to something evil and hideous and revolting...I will gladly kill any foe in battle, but I will not be part of killing any man helpless in our grasp. I will not accept as friend...any man who will do this...Never again will I take part in the torture like this of any living creature, man or animal. Never! Nor, as I have said, will I consider as friend any man who will allow himself to take part in so degrading a measure.*[66] Due to his courage in speaking out against

[65] *Ibid.*, p. 245.

[66] *Ibid.*, pp. 312-313.

the evil of torture the Shawnee nation, for the most part, vowed to no longer torture prisoners. Teenagers, if formed well in the virtues, can have a great impact on the world.

Now It's Time To Get To Work!

Photocopy the prayer written by St. Thomas Aquinas on page 49. Give a copy to each of your teens but also keep one for yourself. Pray it daily together or encourage your teens to pray it daily on their own. It's a beautiful summation of what each of us should strive to become.

Virtue is also its own reward. Isaiah tells us:

Canticle of Isaiah

He who practices virtue and speaks honestly,
Who spurns what is gained by oppression,
Brushing his hands
Free of contact with a bribe,
Stopping his ears lest he hear of bloodshed,
Closing his eyes lest he look on evil.
He shall dwell on the heights,
His stronghold shall be the rocky fortress,
his food and drink
in steady supply.

If you and your children live a life of virtue you will not only experience happiness on earth then later in eternity with God, but you will know true joy, the joy that the saints write about. That does not mean that you will not experience the cross, tribulation or chaos in your life, but even in the midst of suffering or chaos you will experience true peace and joy. The struggle to acquire all the virtues is well worth the effort. Try it and see!

Mary Ann Budnik
May 1, 2004,
Feast of St. Joseph the Worker

Prayer For Help In Developing Virtue
by
St. Thomas Aquinas

O God, all-powerful and all-knowing, without beginning and without end, you who are the source, the sustainer, and the rewarder of all virtues, grant that I may abide on the firm ground of **faith,** be sheltered by an impregnable shield of **hope**, and be adorned in the bridal garment of **charity**. Grant that I may through **justice** be subject to you, through **prudence** avoid the beguilements of the devil, through **temperance** exercise restraint, and through **fortitude** endure adversity with **patience**. Grant that whatever good things I have, I may share generously with those who have not and that whatever good things I do not have, I may request humbly from those who do. Grant that I may judge rightly the evil of the wrongs I have done and bear calmly the punishments I have brought upon myself, and that I may never envy my neighbor's possessions and ever give thanks for your good things. Grant that I may always observe **modesty** in the way I dress, the way I walk, and the gestures I use, restrain my tongue from frivolous talk, prevent my feet from leading me astray, keep my eyes from wandering glances, shelter my ears from rumors, lower my gaze in **humility**, lift my mind to thoughts of heaven, contemn (despise) all that will pass away, and love you only. Grant that I may subdue my flesh and cleanse my conscience, honor the saints and praise you worthily, advance in goodness, and end a life of good works with a holy death. **Plant deep in me, Lord, all the virtues**, that I might be **devout** in divine matters, **discerning** in human affairs, and burdensome to no one in fulfilling my own bodily needs. Grant to me, Lord, fervent contrition, pure confession, and complete reparation. Order me inwardly through a good life, that I might do what is right and what will be meritorious for me and a good example for others. Grant that I may never crave to do things impulsively, nor disdain to do what is burdensome, lest I begin things before I should or abandon them before finishing. Amen

CHAPTER I

THE TEEN YEARS: AGES 13 TO 15

"What is youth? It is a time given by providence to every person and given to him as a responsibility." John Paul II

Once your child hits thirteen, the "golden years" end. No longer children but not yet adults, adolescents are young men and women saddled with rapid physical, emotional, and psychological changes. Suddenly the sweet, intelligent, docile child becomes a spacey, lazy, defensive, self-conscious, vain, moody, frustrated, short-fused, uncommunicative, mouthy teen. This unfortunately is normal due to original sin. Just as the "terrible twos" are normal, likewise the "terrible teens" are normal. Along with the physical and emotional changes, the teen years shape the adult character. The degree of virtue or lack of virtue your teen achieves during adolescence determines the type of adult he will become. If he doesn't struggle to control his temper as a teen, he is not going to be able to control it as an adult. If he doesn't control his urge to pound his little brother in anger now, he will most likely physically abuse his wife as an adult. If your teen does not push himself to work now, he will not be industrious as an adult. The same can be said of all the other defects of character.

Although seemingly "mature" it is important for parents to pay particular attention to the spiritual, physical and psychological development of their teens. This transition from childhood to adulthood, John Paul II points out, is marked by the child's need to *discover and, at the same time, organize, choose, foresee and make their most personal decisions. [It] is a time of discovering oneself and one's own inner world, the time of generous plans, the time when the feeling of love awakens, with the biological impulses of sexuality, the time of the desire to be together, the time of a particularly intense joy connected with the exhilarating discovery of life. But often it is also the age of deeper questioning, of anguished or even frustrated searching, of a certain mistrust of others and dangerous introspection, and sometimes the age of the first experiences of setbacks and disappointments.*[1]

In St. Louis, the Holy Father developed this idea even further: *During the time he searches, like the young man in the Gospel, for answers to basic questions; he searches not only for the meaning of life but also for a concrete way to go about living his life. This is the most fundamental characteristic of youth...*

It is for this reason that our availability to our teenage children is critical. Fathers need to spend more time with their teens, rather than less time. Moms should be home when the teens return from school. Parental availability gives the teen someone to confide in, to open up to, to question on the topics that puzzle or frighten him.

---

[1] John Paul II, ***Apost. Exhort. Catechesi Tradendae***, October 16, 1979, no. 38.

Fr. Marcial Maciel also stresses the importance of parents being physically available to their teens. He explains how *adolescents are extremely malleable, for good and for evil, and there are many other alternatives available that can easily lead them astray...Many parents understand this, and then the results are very good. Others give in to the pressures and easily leave their children adrift, directionless, at the mercy of circumstances, without a guide to motivate them, guide them, and point them towards the good. Worse still, in some cases there are parents who facilitate their drifting away from Christ.*[1A]

After decades of experience working with youth Fr. Marcial Maciel admits: *Working with adolescents is exhausting but exhilarating. It's exhausting because adolescents are charged with surplus energy and an educator has to be with them always in everything they are up to. You can't follow them from a distance, because they are not yet fully mature and they need an adult to guide them. That's why it is very demanding work, even physically...But it is exhilarating because their souls are still receptive and, with the utmost respect for their freedom, you can instill in them many human and Christian values...[T]hey are open to the great ideals of life: they have huge reserves of generosity, and they will respond eagerly to what you ask of them--as long as you give them a motivating ideal...[T]his ideal is friendship with Christ.*[1B]

Brace yourself for the big "R" (rebellion). But take heart. Many of the greatest saints were rebellious teens who worried their parents. Two who come to mind are St. Augustine and St. Teresa of Avila. Then there is St. Josemaría who rebelled against his father's wishes that he become a lawyer. Josemaría wanted to become an architect. This difference of opinion not only caused tension between the father and son but also a bit of estrangement. Cardinal Francis Xavier Thuân when he turned fifteen

[1A] ***Christ In My Life,*** *Op. Cit.*, pp. 172-173.
[1B] *Ibid.*

likewise began to challenge his elders, particularly his father. Prior to this time *he had never before dreamed of talking back to his parents, but now Thuân suddenly found himself ready to challenge his father's critical remarks and sometimes had to control himself in order to avoid explosive confrontations.*[1C]

The teen years usher in a time of rebellion against parents, discipline, school, and sometimes against the Catholic faith if the teen has received a superficial spiritual formation or been given poor example by their parents or siblings. Adolescence, the age of idealism, should actually bring teens closer to God. If given the proper spiritual and doctrinal formation, faith fueled by this idealism will move teens to give their lives to God in whatever vocational choice they make. Consider the parable of the "Rich Young Man." John Paul II writes: *his decision to go away from Christ was influenced only by exterior riches: by what the young man possessed, not by what he was. What he was—a young man, with all the interior treasure of youth—had led him to Jesus. It has also impelled him to ask questions which clearly encompassed the whole of life: What must I to do? What must I do to inherit eternal life? What must I do so that my life may have full value and full meaning?*[2] These are the questions we have to answer for our children by giving them a deeper, more intensive spiritual formation through classes on Catholic morality and Church doctrine, by sending them on retreats, to World Youth Day, getting them involved in Catholic youth groups and taking them on pilgrimages. If we do not give our youth the answers to these questions which the Pope outlined above, they will seek them elsewhere in satanic cults, fundamentalism, gangs, the drug culture, and in promiscuity. If your teen challenges the faith, get him the answers. He is searching and looking to you to provide the answers to his doubts. Fr. Robert Sirico, founder of the Acton Institute, left the Church as a teen when the nun who taught his theology class and the priest

[1C] ***The Miracle of Hope***, *Op. Cit.*, p. 61
[2] John Paul II, Letter ***Parati semper***, March 31, 1985, no. 3.

he questioned in confession refused to answer his doubts about the faith. They thought he was a smart aleck. He was sincerely searching for the truth. Don't make the same mistake as these people did with your teen. If you do not know the answers, take your teen to someone who *can* answer their questions.

John Paul II told the youth gathered at World Youth Day in Rome: *Do not be afraid to be the saints of the third millennium!* Bishop Rylko elaborates on the Holy Father's challenge to youth: *The Pope says: I am a friend of young people, but a demanding friend. A true friend does not agree with everything, applaud everything his friend wants or says. At times young people say they want things which, in the end, they themselves do not accept. The Pope is not afraid to ask them to be saints, to be faithful to purity before marriage, to accept the call to a life of consecration. Sometimes youth leaders may take young people's expectations, things that seem to please them, as basic criteria for education. However, these desires fail to express the deepest longing for the truth. It is important to accept young people, but they must be accepted in love and truth, calling "good" what is good, and "evil" what is evil.*[3]

Teens need a catechesis that will help them *grasp a genuinely Christian understanding of life. This catechesis must shed the light of the Christian message on those realities which have greater impact on the adolescent, such as the meaning of bodily existence, of love and the family, the standards to be followed in life, in work and leisure, in justice and peace, and so on.*[4]

Do not depend on the Catholic high school or youth ministry to give this catechesis to your teens. As the primary educator of your children this catechesis must first come from you. The others only supplement what you give your children. John Paul II insists: *The parents' ministry of*

[3] Zenit, August 16, 2000.

[4] The Sacred Congregation for the Clergy, ***General Catechetical Directory***, April 11, 1971, no. 84.

evangelization and catechesis are to play a part in their children's lives also during adolescence and youth, when the children often challenge or even reject the Christian faith received in earlier years.[5] Besides, at the Bishops' Meeting in Washington, D.C., November, 2003, it was reported that none of the books being used for catecheses in high schools is in conformity with the ***Catechism of the Catholic Church***. The books must be completely rewritten.[5A]

If you shirk this duty, it is a sin of omission. Why not join with other families with teens to give religion classes, to practice the works of mercy? Make the sacrifice to see that your teen attends these classes. To put soccer or other activities before God is spiritually dangerous. It teaches the teen that God is not our main priority in life. *When it is a question of the healthy education of youth,* wrote Pope Leo XIII, *no limit should ever be placed upon the effort and concern brought to bear, no matter how great these may be.*[6]

Teens who have a living faith are better able to control their rebellious impulses by using the spiritual means of frequent confession, reception of the Holy Eucharist, the daily rosary and prayer. Cardinal Thuân used these means to try to control his rebellion. He read the lives of the saints, attended daily Mass, prayed and got lots of exercise swimming, mountain climbing and hiking.

The Rebellious Years

In some teens rebellion is delayed until college and even beyond but each child goes through it in some manner in varying degrees. It is a time of suffering and loneliness for the child. *Adolescence is the lonely time of life, whether it be the moment when the ego begins to assert itself in the face of parental authority, or the time when the ego is disgusted with*

[5] John Paul II, Letter ***Parati semper***, March 31, 1985, no. 13.

[5A] Catechism suggestions for teens can be found in Appendix A, p. 423 in ***Raise Happy Children...Raise Them Saints!*** and "Additional Helps" at the end of Chapter 4.

[6] Leo XIII, Enc. Letter ***Sapientia christianae***, Janurary 10, 1890.

itself because it threw off all authority and became its own god, notes Archbishop Fulton J. Sheen. *This void comes from a void inside.*[7]

In teens, idealism incongruently meshes with materialism. While a teen expresses rage against the injustices he sees in the world, on weekends he stalks the Mall looking for "in" clothing rather than giving his money to alleviate the injustices.

Teens likewise find themselves pulled in different directions. Gone are the carefree days of childhood:

1. The adolescent is on the one hand an imitator and on the other, a rebel...
2. The adolescent is torn between looking his worst and looking his best...
3. Another tension is that which develops between cockiness and timidity...
4. Silence and loquaciousness are other tensions...lonely at home...on the telephone the adolescent can talk for hours.
5. The greatest tension of all is between two kinds of steadiness...The boy has a prepossession for possession; the girl has a prepossession to be possessed. But the boy soon wants a new model and peculiarly enough that affects the girl.[8]

Teens VS. Authority

When your happy, obedient child grows moody, sullen, terribly self-conscious, at times defiant and prone to worry, realize that the "terrible teens" have arrived. The limits you set and your authority will be tested for the next four to six years by your teen.

Dr. Rudolf Allers writes: *The formation of the definite self is the central phenomenon and the real problem of*

[7] Archbishop Fulton J. Sheen, ***Children and Parents*** (NY: Simon and Schuster, 1970) p. 55.

[8] *Ibid.*, pp. 57-58.

adolescence...The dawning consciousness of self, and connected therewith the still vague but nevertheless very impressive awareness of being a person, makes the adolescent feel that he ought to rely on himself, that he ought to be independent in his decisions, that he ought to become fully responsible for his actions. From this arises the longing for independence, the tendency for self-assertion, the unwillingness to listen to advice and the repugnance to blind obedience.[8A] Your teen may no longer take your values or beliefs for granted. He has to be convinced that they are legitimate values. *Young people are attracted, in a marked way, by all kinds of revolutionary and destructive ideas. Dissatisfaction with the existing state of things always leads to the adoption of disruptive views, but these are not always succeeded by constructive ideas...Traditional views are upheld by authority, and authority is the only reason why the child believes...The child is not yet capable of understanding and of justifying these ideas rationally...Authority, however, is one of the things that adolescents most resent. It is, strange enough, at the same time one of the things for which they long for most,* adds Dr. Allers (editorial emphasis).[8B] That is why many young people join the military, particularly the most difficult branches such as the Marines. They want to be subjected to strong discipline. Others may join a street gang or satanic cult that has a strong authority figure. It also gives the teen a sense "of belonging," of being accepted.

To manage this age group you must persistently practice the virtue of fortitude. If you do not, you will either become a permissive parent with your teens "raising" you rather than vice versa or you will become a dictator. Likewise, restrain yourself from treating your teen as an equal. Dr. Allers asserts that *[i]n placing himself on exactly the same level with the adolescent...the... [parent] renounces every possibility of creating a real understanding of authority;*

[8A] Rudolf Allers, M.D., Ph.D., ***Forming Character In Adolescents*** (Fort Collins, CO:Roman Catholic Books,1940) p. 20, p. 31.

[8B] *Ibid.*, p. 62, pp. 63-64.

and without such an understanding the further development of the adolescent especially in his attitude towards work and towards social life, will probably go amiss.[8C]

It takes courage to say "no" when you anticipate your teen throwing a major tantrum. When tempted to give in to keep peace, remember that to be permissive is to teach your teen vices. An example of a permissive parent is Martha Washington. George Washington married a young widow, Martha Custis, who had two children—Jack who was four-years-old and Patsy who was almost two at the time of their marriage. When Jack caused a serious uproar in the household, Washington gave him a whack much to Martha's horror. Washington believed that Jack resented his unlimited freedom and was acting up to force his mother to set limits. Martha was unwilling to accept Washington's observation. She also refused to allow Washington to discipline her children telling him: *You may not punish him—I forbid it—you may not...Speak to him, but gently. Explain to him, but don't frighten him. You must not put a finger on him—ever...I refuse to let you touch him.* To which Washington responded: *A child cannot grow up without discipline...And I wish I had the right to refuse to let you ruin him.*[8D] As a concession Martha told Washington that she had sent the boy to bed without dinner but when Washington went to say good-night to his stepson he found a tray of food there. Martha lacked the fortitude to follow through on her method of discipline. The little boy apologized for his misbehavior so Washington cleverly used the opportunity to try another manner of discipline. He asked the little boy, who was hungry: *If you would please me, punish yourself. Don't touch a bite of that food—have absolutely nothing till breakfast. Is that possible?* The boy nodded.[8E] As a young adult, Jack told his mother that she would have *ruined him if it wasn't for Washington's struggle*

[8C] *Ibid.*, p. 73.

[8D] Mary Higgins Clark, ***Mount Vernon Love Story*** (New York: Pocket Books, 1968) p. 145.

[8E] *Ibid.*, p. 149.

to make him a man despite her interference.[8F] Don't ruin your teens by being permissive.

On the other hand, to be a dictator breeds contempt for you and authority in general. We find such an example in the teen years of Maria von Trapp of *Sound of Music* fame. Maria had a very tragic childhood. She did not know her mother, who died from pneumonia when Maria was two. Her distraught father took Maria to be raised by an elderly cousin, who was in her sixties, then he left the country. She saw her father only on rare visits. Her foster mother not only raised her but taught her the Catholic faith. Upon the death of her father, her foster sister's husband was appointed her guardian. He accused and punished Maria for things she never did. He forbade her to participate in activities with her friends. He refused to hear of her going on to college to become a teacher. Timid as a child, she accepted his harsh treatment of her but as a teen, she rebelled. Maria relates, *all the things he had insinuated—that I was skipping school, playing hooky, hanging around with the other girls, asking him for money for copy books but instead spending it on cookies and candies—were put into action...I eagerly accepted an invitation to come upstairs in somebody's house [visit a friend], and I arrived home at any time—even after dark, stoically expecting my spanking—but having lived!...I suddenly felt a bottomless contempt for the man who had punished me all these years for no reason at all. Having lied to me by insinuating all these things which I had never done, I made up my mind that for this most cruel punishment I would never, as long as I lived, say one true word to him, so help me God.*[8G] Needless to say, at this same time, she lost her Catholic faith. Learn to trust your teens. Even if your teen fools you every now and then, if he sees that you trust him he will try to live up to your trust, counseled St. Josemaría.

[8F] *Ibid.*, p. 240.
[8G] Maria von Trapp, ***Maria, My Own Story*** (Carol Stream, IL: Creation House, 1972) pp. 24-25.

Since the rebellion against authority is universal in some manner during the teens, let's consider this topic. We began this discussion in ***Raise Happy Children...Teach Them Virtues*** under the virtue of obedience. Now let's take it to a deeper level. *Parental authority is primarily an opportunity for service, and only secondarily and derivatively [consequently] for power,* according to Prof. Oliveros F. Otero, of the University of Navarre.[9] When parents use their authority correctly they teach their children freedom and responsibility. To help parents in this area, Otero lists the steps parents should take in exercising their authority: *To think, to be informed, to decide, to communicate clearly, to lead to accomplishment, are successive phases in the exercise of this authority. To dispense with some or any one of these states may lead to impulsiveness or inconsistency and, consequently, to sheer authoritarianism or an arbitrary exercise of authority demanding a more or less blind compliance* (the example of Maria Von Trapp.)*; or to the attitude of "giving in to everything" and hence to a despairing abandonment or to indifference—the non-exercise of authority* (the example of Martha Washington).

Parents have, among other rights and duties, the power (the right and the duty), to make influential decisions and to sanction negatively or positively, that is, to mete out rewards or punishments. Used as a service for the proper education of children, authority and power do not contradict each other. Power that is soberly and correctly exercised forms a necessary and legitimate part of authority.[10]

To handle authority in a just manner, parents should take to their daily examination of conscience the question, *Am I trying to raise my children to be responsible, independent adults or am I trying to dominate them?* Our role is to raise our children to be independent adults, not dependent, boomerang adults. Parents who dominate use their power

[9] Prof. Oliveros F. Otero, "Authority in the Education of Children," Instituto de Ciencias de la Educación, Universidad de Navarre, 1982, p. 1.

[10] *Ibid.,* pp. 1-2.

and money to impose their will, not only on their teens, but also on their adult children, thereby stunting their children's psychological maturity. Parents who dominate are usually either immature themselves or possess *sheer callous insensitivity. This not uncommon hard-heartedness is evident in parents who look upon their children as their property, who display them like possessions, or simply think of them as projections of themselves.*[11] Besides, as Dr. Allers notes, *simply to assert authority is rather a way to make the young people more resistive and more disinclined to listen or to obey. The adolescent is no longer like the child who...trusted implicitly, and therefore obeyed...The adolescent is impressed only when authority either defends ideas akin to his own...or when he can be made to see the rights and the necessity on which such authority is predicated.*[11A]

Our authority is to be cloaked in the love of Christ. Christ Himself linked love and obedience. Our children should obey us out of love, not fear: ***If you love Me, you will keep My Commandments*** (***John*** 14:15). This concept should be taught to our children from little on. Teens are to obey out of love for God and love for their parents. This was the obedience of the saints towards their parents. This was the obedience of Bl. Pier Giorgio Frassati when he broke off his romance with Laura. Recall the betrayal of Peter toward Jesus. Before Jesus gave him the keys to the kingdom of God Christ asked Peter three times, ***Do you love me*** (***John*** 21:15-17)***?*** Before we hand over the keys to the car, pay college tuition, or do anything major for our teens we should also ask them that question. It should stimulate some spirited conversation as well as reflective thought!

Prof. Otero asks parents to consider these points before giving commands: 1. Is it good for the child/teen or is the command based on my personal whim or caprice? 2. What is my motive for giving the command? Is it rational or based on personal convenience? *Your goal is not "peace and quiet"*

[11] *Ibid.*, p. 2.

[11A] ***Forming Character In Adolescents***, *Op. Cit.*, p. 65.

but rather their own strength of character, notes James Stenson. *Correcting for the sake of your convenience leads to unclear standards, inconsistent punishment and rewards, and an over-influence of sentimentalism in children's consciences.*[12]

There is another dimension to the problem of domination. Prof. Oliveros observes, *...[O]ne spouse sometimes winds up being dominated by the other, and he or she compensates by dominating the children in turn. It also happens on occasion that when a person is dominated by someone in, say, his place of work or in his social relations, he in turn tries to dominate his own family.*[13]

When conflicts arise, it is important to step back and remember our own journey through adolescence. Memories of our own periods of rebellion should provide us with patience toward our children! *Try to understand the aspirations of young people and follow them along the new ways in which they legitimately express themselves, but without accepting the frivolities and errors to which they are nowadays exposed. They [parents] should be brothers and friends of theirs, and at the same time bearers of a more lofty truth and ideal.*[14]

St. Josemaría Escrivá told a reporter: *Parents should also endeavor to stay young at heart, so as to find it easier to react sympathetically toward the noble aspirations and even the extravagant fantasies of their youngsters. Life changes, and there are many new things which we may not like. Perhaps objectively speaking they are no better than others that have gone before; but they are not bad. They are simply other ways of living and nothing more. On more than one occasion conflicts may arise because importance is attached to petty differences that could be overcome with a little common sense*

---

[12] Notes by James Stenson from his lecture on "Peer Pressure." Audiotape available from R.B. Media, Inc.

[13] "Authority in the Education of Children," *Op. Cit.*, p. 2.

[14] The Sacred Congregation for Bishops, Directory ***Ecclesiae imago***, February 22, 1973, no. 154.

and good humor.[15]

Concentrate on the important issues and let matters of personal taste or unimportant matters slide. If you give everything equal importance, your teen will begin to completely ignore you. But use the virtue of fortitude to stand firm on fundamental points.

Developing a friendship with one's teens helps to moderate their rebellion. But this friendship is not one of equals. You must maintain your authority. Teens need to be able to confide in their parents and, at the same, to be taken seriously by them. This is the type of friendship that is necessary. Unfortunately when a teen feels in the mood to talk, many times the parents are "too busy" or concerned with their own problems to take the time to listen. Also, what appears to the parent as silliness, to the teen can be a matter of grave worry or of great importance. St. Josemaría Escrivá counseled parents not to quarrel with their teens but instead to listen to them. He suggested that parents make the time to individually talk with them with affection and understanding. He believed that if you meet your teens half-way you will end up on good terms with them.[16]

Parents also need to develop prestige in the eyes of their children. St. Thomas Aquinas points out that *the respect that one has for a rule flows from the respect that one has for the one who gives it.* This means that as parents we have to develop the qualities/virtues of naturalness, optimism, serenity, and trustworthiness. When our children were little our authority rested solely on the fact that we were mommy or daddy. With teens parental authority rests on the moral worth of the parents. Again, think about the example of Maria von Trapp. *Constant cantankerousness or ill-humor...is detrimental: it not only ages the person concerned, but detracts from his ability to influence for good and makes him lose his good standing in the bargain.*[17]

---

[15] ***Conversations With Msgr. Escrivá*** (Dublin: Scepter, 1969) #100.

[16] St. Josemaría Escrivá in a get-together with parents.

[17] "Authority in the Education of Children," *Op. Cit.*, p. 3.

Serenity is based on flexibility and good sense. *Naturalness rests upon consistency of conduct...The most influential parents are those who are understanding and flexible, and at the same time capable of being firm in what is most important. Glum looks, histrionics, censoriousness, lamentations, and wildly erratic judgments are all opposed to naturalness, and cannot help but damage parental prestige.*[18]

The prestige of parents is also based on how we fulfill our work obligations, strive to improve ourselves, respect others, live our faith and live the virtue of friendship. Parents who are critical or judgmental toward others will lead their children to feel that they will likewise be criticized in a similar manner when problems arise.

The three areas indicated so far in which efforts must be made to maintain one's prestige are:

1. One's own disposition in general, and towards the family in particular;
2. One's attitude towards one's work and one's children; and
3. One's manner of behaving in social situations, with friends, neighbors, relatives or associates.[19]

Again we see that to keep our prestige in regard to authority over our children we have to continually grow in virtue ourselves! **Each parent should build up the other parent in the eyes of the children. This fosters love and respect for the parent. If you never or rarely praise your spouse to your children, the children will not have a high regard for that parent. As a result that parent will lack prestige in their eyes. They may even become indifferent, insulting, or abusive toward that parent.** Should we criticize our spouse to our children, we erode our spouse's authority over them. The parents' loving attitude or lack of love toward one another influences the children/teens as to how they will obey or disobey each parent.

---

[18] *Ibid.*

[19] *Ibid.*, p. 5.

Disobedience results from a lack of respect toward a parent. Archbishop Sheen points out that *the rise of juvenile delinquency is in direct proportion to the decline of moral values among parents. [W]hen parents set a worthy example for their children, obedience is not rendered by the children because of a fear of punishment, but rather because they would not hurt those whom they love. The commandment of God: "Thou shalt honor thy father and thy mother," implies honor in the parents. Honor is a recognition of the excellence of someone.*

It would be quite wrong always to blame the children for failure to honor their parents. Honor and dishonor, love and aversion, respect and disgust are born in them, according to what they see in the parents.[20]

St. Josemaría adds: *The children also have to play their part. Young people are always capable of getting enthusiastic about great undertakings, high ideals, and anything that is genuine. They must be helped to understand the simple, natural and often unappreciated beauty of their parents' lives. Children should come to realize little by little the sacrifices their parents have made for them, the often heroic self-denial that has gone into raising the family. They should also learn not to over dramatize, not to think themselves misunderstood; nor to forget that they will always be in debt to their parents. And as they will never be able to repay what they owe, their response should be to treat their parents with veneration and grateful, filial love.*[21]

Why Do Teens Rebel?

Why is teen rebellion universal? This natural rebellion is triggered by your child's growing *self-affirmation, spirit of independence, and the desire to conquer the world, emotionally speaking.*[22] Teens want to make their own

---

[20] ***Children and Parents,*** *Op. Cit.*, pp. 78-79. [21] ***Conversations***, *Op. Cit.*, #101.
[22] Dr. Ana Maria Navarro, "The Awakening of a Sense of Intimacy In the Adolescent," Instituto de Ciencias de la Educación of the Universidad de Navarre, p. 2.

decisions in all areas while lacking the experience and the power to reason correctly. Parents suffer from the effects of this maturing process but we have to remember God experiences the same thing with us! Vatican Council II boosts our spirits by telling us that *it is only within freedom that man can turn himself towards what is good.*[23] By keeping alert, we can help our teens foster respect and familiarize themselves with this gift of growing freedom. *In an atmosphere of love, children learn more quickly the true scale of values.*[24]

One of the first signals of this phase of development is the desire of the child to be alone...to have his own room, to spend time thinking, as well as a reluctance to always be part of family activities. This reaction of your teen of wanting to be alone is not antisocial behavior but rather the beginning of the development of intimacy, which we'll discuss in more detail later in this chapter. Dr. Ana Marie Navarro writes that *this taste for being alone, which is a consequence of self-affirmation, should be remembered when we are considering the manifestations of modesty, shyness, and sensitivity which are so common in adolescence. [While] it is true that this shyness may be a product of an awareness of one's own shortcomings...it is generally more accurate to regard it as a defensive attitude arising when people who perhaps would not appreciate [the teen's] new inner world threaten to lay it bare.*[25]

Adolescents are terribly sensitive. St. Thérèse's mother, Venerable Zélie Martin, suffered deeply during her youth. Writing to her sister, Zélie discloses: *My childhood and youth were shrouded in sadness; our mother...did not know how to treat me, so ...I suffered deeply.* St. Thérèse herself relates that she was hypersensitive in her autobiography, ***Story Of A Soul***.

---

[23] Vatican Council II, Past. Const. *Gaudium et spes,* no. 17.

[24] *Ibid.,* no. 61.

[25] "The Awakening of a Sense of Intimacy In the Adolescent," *Op. Cit.*

Rapid physical growth makes teens physically awkward, extremely hungry all the time, and very tired. Hormonal growth makes them emotional and self-conscious. A skin eruption, having to walk in front of a group of people, clothes not quite "in", no date for homecoming or prom, parents who are too loud or jovial, all mortify teenagers because of their heightened sensitivity. Avoid doing anything that will embarrass or humiliate your teen, especially in front of his friends, siblings or other people. When correcting teens, do it privately. Teasing or ridiculing teens causes them <u>tremendous</u> suffering.

Show unconditional love toward your teen but also let your teen know that although you love him unconditionally you do not accept certain conduct or opinions. It's the "hate the sin, love the sinner" concept.

Teens communicate their self-affirmation by showing off through "brave" exploits that we term brainless such as driving too fast, accepting dares, drinking, premarital sex, or showing off their father's guns. Teens also showoff to call attention to themselves through their possessions, excessive make-up, hairstyles, jewelry, hair color, body piercing, and weird clothing. They want to try the "new" and "unusual" which is conveniently found *in products of the consumer society.*[26] Dr. Navarro reflects: *This whole range of exaggerated attitudes, whether lacquered elegance or affected forwardness, is an expression of this desire to attract attention;...boys and girls...are alike in seeking admiration.*[27] As your teen becomes more difficult, increase your affection toward him with hugs, kisses, and compliments to boost his self-esteem even if he pretends he does not like the show of affection. Your teen needs your love and affection even more than your baby. Ask his advice about different things to show that you value his opinions. If you withdraw or distance yourself from your child, he

---

[26] Dr. David Isaacs, "The Education of Intimacy," Instituto de Ciencias de la Educación, Universidad de Navarre, 1989, p. 1.

[27] "The Awakening of a Sense of Intimacy In the Adolescent," *Op. Cit.*, p. 3.

will turn to less desirable avenues for affection and self-affirmation.

You just don't understand me! is a normal teen lament. It is difficult to understand teens because many times they don't understand themselves! This is where the virtue of patience is needed. Try to listen before reacting to a situation. Permit your teen to express himself but only in a respectful manner. Do not permit swearing or crude language. If the teen is too emotional to be respectful, calmly tell him that you will be willing to discuss the matter when he is able to talk to you in a calm, respectful manner. **Accepting abusive language violates your intimacy**. When your child calms down, listen to his side of the issue. If you were wrong have the humility to admit you were wrong. Remember that disillusionment is also part of adolescence. Up to this time you were perfect in the eyes of your child. Now your child sees all your defects and vices. Show your teen that **a mature person admits when he is wrong and apologizes for hurting another.** *Sadness and disillusionment were the most prominent characteristics of the start of adolescence...Perhaps this experience is paralleled by that of birth: as crying is generally the first way in which the newborn baby expresses itself, so gloominess, sadness, disappointment characterize the stage at which the child is reborn as an adolescent.*[28]

The behavior of teens is usually guided by their volatile emotions. If you try to reason with them, in the midst of an argument, you will hit a brick wall. Dr. Allers explains that *reason, even the most convincing, seldom overcomes emotion and mood all of a sudden. It is only by repeated attacks that the fortress of mood may be taken by reason. Inefficient though logic may prove at first and even for quite a long time, it is nevertheless the only means we have at our disposal to make the adolescent "see reason."* Yet on the other hand,...*There is no way of becoming aware of truth other than through reason. Truth is not "felt," and it is not grasped by some*

[28] *Ibid.*, p. 5.

mysterious instinctive faculty; it is seen in the cold and clear light of rational analysis.[28A] Hang in there. Persist in using reason and logic but use them when the teen is calm and ready to listen rather than at the height of an argument. Better to walk away in a heated discussion saying, "Let me know when you calm down. Then we will discuss this issue."

When a teen gets into some type of trouble or disobeys in a serious matter, confront him by asking why he did the act or deed. What was his motive? Did he realize what he was doing was wrong? Did he understand the consequences of what he did? If so, why did he still do it? Make him reason out his actions. This will in time wake him up to the seriousness of what he did. On the other hand, he may not have realized the serious of his deed. This will give you a chance to help your teen see the serious consequences that could occur or did occur. Dr. Allers notes: *To punish someone for something he did not know to be bad or as bad as it objectively is, would be a very great mistake which cannot but increase the distance between the young person and the educator [parent]. To diminish this distance is, however, one of our most important tasks, since this is an indispensable condition for gaining the necessary influence and authority over the adolescent.*[28B]

*Stubbornness and unwillingness to see another's point of view, the more or less arrogant upholding of their own ideas and similar traits, are very common in adolescents...When he finds that he cannot rely on reasons, he may try to avail himself of more or less sophistic arguments; but if these too prove useless there remains but the way of stubbornness, of impenetrability, or apparent lack of understanding, of outbreaks of temperament, in which some insignificant detail is emphasized which supplies a pretext for becoming angry...*Furthermore, *adolescents have a trick of saying yes, while letting the other person see that he has not made any real impression and that the assent is made only for the sake*

[28A] **Forming Character In Adolescents**, *Op. Cit.*, p. 79.

[28B] *Ibid.*, p. 107.

of getting rid of an annoying situation...[O]ne has to be careful of what one says, and not to give the adolescent an opportunity of evading the issue. If he tries to fly off at a tangent, one has to bring him back, firmly but without wounding his susceptibility, to the matter under discussion, warns Dr. Allers.[28C]

On your part, resist the temptation to prophesy a dire future for your teen if he doesn't shape up: "You'll be dishing up food on the tray line the rest of your life if you don't start hitting those books" or "you'll end up in prison if you don't straighten out." Teens are aware of their inadequacies, failures, and inabilities. Such prophecies will simply further crush their fragile self-image.

As mentioned in ***Raise Happy Children...Teach Them Virtues!*** if you make threats but do not follow through you diminish your authority. Never threaten what you do not intend to do.

Don't Fence Me In!

As the teen develops his own resourcefulness, his desire for independence grows, fueling his rebellion and separation from his parents. The teen longs to be completely independent but he is not physically, mentally, or financially capable of being so. This triggers frustration that erupts in emotional outbursts.

College students experience a safe "independence." They are living on their own, selecting their own classes, dorm or apartment and friends. But they are still financially dependent on their parents. The fun of this type of independence ends in their senior year when the realization hits that they will be completely independent upon graduation. This causes almost a paralyzing fear. Questions of future ability torment seniors. *Can I find a job? What if it's not a good job? What if the job is in another city where I don't know anyone? Will the job support me? What if I fail in*

[28C] *Ibid.*, p. 108.

the real world? These serious questions cause an emotional upheaval for college seniors. Young adults without the virtue of fortitude can turn into perpetual students because university life is a safer environment than the real world.

As the teen rejects his parents, he at the same time develops closeness to his grandparents who in turn can influence the teen for the good. Wise parents make the effort to cultivate the relationship of their children with their grandparents from little on so that when the teen years "strike" the grandparents can step in to positively influence the teens. If the grandparents do not share your values or will not work with you this natural affinity will cause you additional problems. In one family a college coed wanted to live in the same city as her fiancé. For numerous reasons her parents did not think this was a prudent idea. They insisted that she continue to live at home but suggested the couple could commute on the weekends to see each other since the distance was not great. The parents felt that their daughter could stay with her grandparents when she traveled to see her fiancé while he could stay with her family when he came down to court her. The daughter appealed to her grandparents. They took their granddaughter in over the objections of her parents. This triggered a family feud that lasted until the couple married.

The Awakening of Intimacy

What actually is intimacy? Dr. David Isaacs explains that *intimacy refers to aspects of one's own feelings and thoughts, to one's own soul, and to aspects of one's body.*[29] It is the beginning of one's personality...apart from the family. The teen begins to question, *Who am I? Why am I here? What are my responsibilities?* To be fully human one must understand the purpose of life, which is to give glory to God so as to spend eternity with Him. Once a person understands his purpose in life then he has the obligation to live with dignity so as to achieve that exalted purpose.

[29] "The Education of Intimacy," *Op. Cit.*, p. 1.

Unfortunately, teens and many adults are misled into thinking that working to make money is their only purpose. This concept leads to frustration and unhappiness.

But let's backtrack a bit. At the age of three, children discover their "self." It is at this point that they discover they are different from their parents or siblings. *As soon as a child can say that something belongs to him, or that he was not treated like his brothers and sisters, the self has been discovered.*[30] But this self is completely external. Intimacy is actually born in adolescence. Dr. Ana Maria Navarro insists that intimacy *is the prerequisite of inner life, of the ability to live in a way that is independent of the external world.* Dr. Navarro continues: *This may perhaps startle people who are familiar with the religious life of children. Do children not have any inner life? ...[W]hen a child makes his first confession, does he not contemplate his inner world when he examines his conscience [?] He seems to, but when the child examines his past for sins, he does so with special reference to external objects. I hit so-and-so, I said rude words, I stole sweets from my mother. From adolescence onwards we look at ourselves in order to see inside. The external objects melt away and our own desires, ambitions, joys take shape behind them, as part of ourselves which exist and operate within ourselves in a positive or negative way.*[31]

The teen's awareness of his intimacy is linked to your child's change in temperament from being carefree to sad, disillusioned or sullen. This inner turmoil causes the emotional ups and downs. At the same time that teens are going through their emotional upheaval, parents can be going through their own midlife crisis or menopause making family life challenging at best.

Teens want to be mature, to act like adults, but as yet they do not have the ability to reason things out clearly. When a mature person uses his mind well, the person is happy. When the mind is not working well, as is the case in

[30] "The Awakening of a Sense of Intimacy In the Adolescent," *Op. Cit.*, p. 5.
[31] *Ibid.*, p. 6.

adolescence, the teen is not only unhappy but suffers. *Make clear to older children (10-17) that you trust their integrity, but you must withhold trust of their judgment,* advises James Stenson. *Your control over them has to be inversely proportional to their experience and manifested sense of responsibility. Point out that kids usually get into trouble through bad judgment and inexperience, not dishonesty. You will give more freedom when kids display mature, responsible judgment—not before.*[32]

As the teen matures through the years, his mind will work better because he will learn to contemplate. The more the teen contemplates, the happier he becomes. But in the beginning of the teen years, with all the physical, psychological and emotional changes occurring, teens become fixated on their body rather than the mind. *Am I handsome? Am I beautiful? Am I too fat? Do I have a nice figure? What should I do with my hair?* Clothes, hygiene, and acceptance become the center of their world. This leads the teen to be self-centered. (This self-centered phase can re-emerge with women during pregnancies.) The self-centered attitude combined with a lack of self-discipline as well as being afraid of the nasty world causes internal turmoil that manifests itself in sullenness and emotional outbursts.

To possess oneself, one has to know oneself. To know oneself, one has to have opportunities to think about life, to contemplate how one acts and why one acts. Why do I think the way I do? Why do I feel this way? What is my motivation? To think, a person needs time to be alone, to screen out the noise of the world. This is why teens tend to withdraw into solitude, to get to know themselves. That is why they want to be alone, to have the privacy of their own room, to do things by themselves. Teenage girls express their innermost feelings by journaling in their diaries.

Unfortunately, modern man is afraid of being alone with himself because of what he might find. Instead, we immerse

[32] "Peer Pressure," *Op. Cit.*

ourselves in incessant activity combined with constant noise. The TV, radio, headphones, or CDs are constantly on. Wireless telephones interrupt solitude everywhere. Why do we fear silence? [W]*hen a person is in silence and when he is not doing something, he tends to think of aspects of his own intimacy. And in doing so he notices many things that he does not like—unless his conscience is totally damaged. Upon noticing these things, he has two choices. He can assume responsibility for what he has discovered, by striving to improve. Or he can avoid the responsibility. The easiest system is the use of noise.*[33] Be creative and find opportunities for your teen to enjoy solitude, with the radio off. But here again, you have to lead by example. If the TV or radio are always on in your home, your teen will not know how to function in silence. It was this ability to reflect that converted the youthful Augustine from his life of sensuality to become a Father of the Church. It never ceases to startle me to be invited to friends' homes only to compete with the TV in order to talk! In situations like that I politely ask if they could please turn off the TV since I find it so distracting.

Help your child to discover his worth. Point out to your teen his good points, talents, and abilities. Guide your child to use his talents to help another or for a worthwhile cause. Place your child in a situation in which your teen can feel fulfilled be it making a delicious dinner for the family, sitting for a friend's children, doing artwork for some organization, singing in a choir or doing a charitable work.

Invite your teens to walk with you in the country to sample the peace of nature. It is in a quiet woodland walk that one can think and experience one's emotions. But only if you leave the Walkman home! Instead of commercial noise, listen to various birdcalls, the wind rustling the leaves, the lap of waves against the shores of a small lake, the crunch of your steps along a path. Smell the air. Note the numerous shades of green. Watch for chipmunks, squirrels, and other

[33] "The Education of Intimacy," *Op. Cit.*, p. 3.

small animals. Admire the sunsets, or the sunrises if you are an early riser. A walk in nature awakes the five senses. *Children need their parents to teach them to recognize what these senses are, how to develop them, and how to master them. If the children do not realize that they have these senses, any person can exploit them by means of, for example, selling pornographic products.*[34]

Parents need to respect the privacy of their teens. If a diary is left out, it is not to be read by you. Avoid eavesdropping on phone conversations or reading your teen's mail. Knock on closed doors just as you expect your children to knock on your closed door. Only violate this privacy if you fear excessive moral or physical danger to your child. Explain why you violated your teen's privacy: *I, as your parent, have the duty before God to lead you to the best possible development. This person/situation does not do this.*

While we do have to respect our child's intimacy we likewise have a duty to provide situations in which our teens can discuss their problems, their friends, their worries, their dreams, their desires as well as aspects of their intimacy. Specifically, how can you work this in with your family? Make specific, concrete plans.

Teach your child to protect his intimacy through modesty in dress, language and conversation. Explain to your teen that his personality is composed of his temperament, his ideas, emotions and body. When he shares any of these carelessly, he loses his personality. Clarify for your teen that to protect his intimacy he must think before speaking and be prudent about what he discloses about himself. That is why the virtue of sincerity needs to be learned before the teen years. Recall that sincerity is telling the appropriate person at the right time objective truth. We do not tell everyone everything. *[E]ach one should share aspects of his intimacy while seeking orientation to improve personally and to help another person to improve.*[35]

[34] *Ibid.*, p. 5.

[35] *Ibid.*, p. 7.

Generally people today lack intimacy. Complete strangers casually divulge their mortal sins to you over dinner. Store clerks divulge the most sordid details of their private lives to customers. At one business dinner to meet a new colleague of my husband, the gentleman's wife told a group of us that their daughter "shacked up" with a guy before she married him. Why did we need to know her sins? At another business dinner, a doctor and his wife discussed how they honeymooned *before* their drive-through wedding in Las Vegas. Under pressure from their parents, they eventually married in the Catholic Church. Personally, I find listening to people flippantly discussing their mortal sins distressing. Yet these same people refrain from frequenting confession. Why do people prefer to confess to groups of people socially rather than in the privacy of the confessional where their sins will be forgiven? Their dinner partners cannot give them absolution! Teach your teen to reserve his sins for the confessional so as not to promote scandal. Discussing one's sins improves no one unless it is done in confidence to prevent another from falling into the same sin. Explain to your teen that there are topics to be discussed only within the family, others just with close friends, and still others with one's confessor/spiritual director. Not everyone should know everything about him.

As with every vice there are the two extremes. From the extreme of telling everything to everyone, the other extreme of intimacy is not sharing one's thoughts with anyone. If your child tends toward the latter, find opportunities to invite confidences. Sometimes working together on a task or a fun outing can loosen up the teen, providing an opportunity to confide in you.

There is also the physical aspect of intimacy. Explain to your teen that surrendering one's body to another is done *exclusively* in marriage, even if "everyone else" is promiscuous. To do so outside of marriage is to rob one's personality as well as to kill the grace in one's soul. In helping your teen to understand this concept draw parallels to eating and sleeping. What is the purpose of each, pleasure or to maintain the body? Then ask what the function of the sexual act is. *To find pleasure? Evidently, not. The function of the sexual act is to create children but God has wanted to put pleasure in the act to lead the person to fulfill the function. Thus it is a matter of surrendering the body at the right moment and to the right person in order to create children. That is, to the spouse, after marriage.*[36] We will discuss this more in Chapter 4 under the virtue of chastity.

Commitment is another problem area for teens because of their emotional instability. This can be very annoying as well as frustrating. One day they will be excited about doing a project, taking a job, or joining a club but the next day forget to do the project, reject the job or skip the club meeting. While this is typical, work with your teen to follow through on all commitments. If you don't, you teen will grow into an adult who does not honor commitments. As I related in ***Raise Happy Children...Teach Them Virtues!*** last Fall I was struggling with an abundance of weeds in my backyard due to neglect. Just like the Gospel passage it looked like an enemy had sown cockle among my flowers. At the same I was trying to tackle the backyard, I was trying to finish book three to get it to the printer, make audiotapes to fill orders, then to complicate matters millions of large, colorful leaves fell or were blown into our front yard burying the grass and flowerbeds. I only had two weeks to get the leaves and yard waste bagged for the pickup or I would have to store it all until Spring. Panic set in. How was I going to get everything done by myself? My husband has severe rheumatoid arthritis in his hands and wrists so I did not want to cause him additional pain by letting him help me. As I started to rake the leaves in front I saw a teenage neighbor playing basketball by himself so I walked over to ask if he was interested in a job of doing my leaves. He jumped at my offer, was thrilled with the hourly rate I offered, then promised to be over to begin the next day right

[36] *Ibid.*, p. 9.

after school. That was a year ago. I'm still waiting. After a week of watching him play ball in the street and being told he would be over the next day, I used the yellow pages to hire a landscaping crew to help me out. This young man, coming from a twice divorced situation and living with his father, was not getting the supervision he needed to learn to live his commitments. Contrast this example with another neighborhood teen, Zack, who volunteers to help me with R.B. Media to fulfill his service hours for high school graduation. Zack arrives promptly each day at 3:30 PM or calls to let me know he will be late because he has to take the bus home from school. He learns fast, works swiftly but carefully, and is responsible. It's a pleasure to have his help. Zack's parents take teaching their sons responsibility and virtues very seriously. Their efforts show. Even our mailman comments to me what fine boys these parents are raising.

Instruct your teen as to the importance of making a commitment...be it to a job, a social event or to a spouse. Rather than taking, we are to give ourselves totally through commitments. The lack of commitment is a rampant disease. Look at the number of adult males who have good jobs, own their own homes but cannot commit themselves to a wife. Without commitment, one can never achieve happiness. Consider the staggering divorce rate which is now approaching 60%. This also demonstrates a widespread lack of commitment.

In ***Raise Happy Children...Teach Them Virtues!*** we discussed how to be demanding of your children. When the teen years hit, shift your focus. Emphasize to your teen the importance of thinking before making a decision. *It means giving the children information which should normally be short, concise and clear and then change the subject...It does not mean simply to demand, coldly. It must go together with understanding full of affection and cheerfulness. In this way the young person feels that he is supported in his difficult* *task of assuming the responsibility of his own life.*[37]

Teens Crave Uniqueness

Prof. Gerardo Castillo warns parents that each teen wants *to be original*, while at the same time fears being an oddball. This is simply part of the development of his personality. *That is why it has been said that adolescence is the crisis of originality. The adolescent wants to be himself and wants to do things by himself. He searches for independence and rejects any aid from adults, (especially that of his parents)...It means confronting a lot of new situations, while lacking experience and resources.*

This lack of resources and experiences could be related to the lack of clear ideas. For instance, the adolescent usually confuses freedom and simple independence (don't give me orders, don't forbid me to do anything). Also, they mistake freedom for the most pure spontaneity (one should do whatever one wants to do, and whenever one wants to do it). They also confuse their personal desires with reality. On the other hand, they separate what cannot be separated: flesh and spirit, for example, in the concept of love.

We should...take into consideration this lack of maturity which is well manifested in the lack of objectivity and in dogmatic statements, flavored by an emotional charge that clouds all judgment.

The immaturity of the adolescent does not only exist in the mental aspect, but also in the personality. Typical traits are a lack of willpower to start or continue occupations that require some effort; a difficulty in making personal decisions and assuming the responsibility that they entail; a tendency to daydream in order to escape from reality; a desire to belong to the crowd; a special need where the peer group is concerned to be "in" in everything concerning fashions and customs; a ready susceptibility to suggestion; and a search for novelty.[38]

[37] *Ibid.*, p. 6.

[38] Prof. Gerardo Castillo, "The Influence of Ideologies in the Adolescent," Instituto de Ciencias de la Educación, Universidad de Navarre, 1992, pp. 1-2.

The uniqueness that teens crave is actually found *in serving and loving others. When does a teenager become more conscious of his personality than after he has forgotten it by volunteering in a hospital, teaching dropouts, cleaning up slums and mowing the old widow's lawn? When his heart says, "I want to be for others," that is the moment when his sense of dignity and worth is at its peak. The happy teenager is the one who balances this tendency to be absorbed in the lives of others, with the opposite drive to emerge as a unique person. This happens when teenagers are open to insights which persons other than their peers may give them about themselves.*[39]

Due to the characteristics of adolescence, teens are easily attracted to ideologies because *an ideology is a system of ideas that tries to explain reality while ignoring it.*[40] Likewise ideology *tries to mold reality to the conception that it advocates.*[41] Sound like your teen? Ideologies are not concerned with truth, neither are adolescents. *That is why a coherent and mistaken person can greatly influence them,* according to Prof. Castillo. We see this in the case of Senator Hillary Clinton whose direction in life was changed by her Marxist youth minister.

Ideological persons, not interested in the spirit of service, seek instead to dominate, control and grab power. An ideology can cause student uprisings on university campuses or fuel violent demonstrations. This correlates with the adolescent's drive for independence regardless of the consequences.

Liberalism mistakes license for freedom. So do teens. This leads to permissivism that separates the spiritual from the body abandoning *the flesh to the instincts. Isn't this the same disassociation that we find in the adolescent?*[42] This combined with the collective mentality of ideologies corresponds with the "herd" mentality of teens. *Everyone*

---

[39] *Children and Parents, Op. Cit.,* p. 71.
[40] "The Influence of Ideologies in the Adolescent," p. 2.
[41] *Ibid.,* p. 2. [42] *Ibid.,* p. 3.

is doing it. Everyone is wearing that. Teens fear being the "oddball." Reiterate to your teens, *Be yourself!* Challenge them to put their idealism and spirit of sacrifice at the disposal of God rather than false ideologies. Prof. Castillo warns parents: *Ideologies influence adolescents because they are a network of ideas that coincide with the adolescent's mentality. They constitute a back-up and a strategy for the adolescent to remain indefinitely...immature. That is why we can talk about complicity, the renouncement of the rational, the lack of willpower, and the denial of the possibility of personal growth, as is needed in order to mature.*[43]

Ideologies, whether political, secular or cult-based use fraud and manipulation to dominate. To counter this serious threat to your teens, develop in them the capacity for critical thinking.

The Generation Gap

Prof. Gerardo Castillo believes that the generation gap is caused by three factors:

1. The adolescent's personality;
2. Certain attitudes and reactions on the part of the parents;
3. Negative social factors which may adversely affect the behavior of parents and children alike.[44]

A teen, with the development of intimacy, has new needs:

1. To be himself (personal identity);
2. To be alone (intimacy);
3. To value himself for himself (self-esteem);
4. To be able to choose and decide (independence);
5. To be successful (security);
6. To love and be loved (acceptance).[45]

These needs, while normal, precipitate rebelliousness,

[43] *Ibid.*, p. 3.

[44] Prof. Gerardo Castillo, "The Generation Gap, and Trust Within the Family," Instituto de Ciencias de la Educación, Universidad de Navarre, 1988.

[45] *Ibid.*, p. 2.

contradiction, an insistence on "freedom," and the rejection of advice from elders. This becomes a delicate balancing act for parents. We must begin to treat adolescents as young adults. Allow your children to grow up. Encourage them to be responsibly independent. Allow them solitude and privacy. Trust your teens but punish them firmly when they betray your trust. Then make them re-earn your trust. Give reasons for your directives and commands. Avoid being arbitrary. Develop a friendship with each child. You do not want your relationship to be based on punishments and "don't dos." Never prohibit your child from doing something that you do. It makes you a hypocrite. An example would be forbidding your child to see R-rated movies while you view them. How can you forbid your child to smoke if you do? Explain to your teen that the age for "drinking" is mandated by law. Drinking prior to 21 years old can cause portions of the brain to under develop. Heavy drinking under age 21 can lead to alcholism because of the inability of the immature body to handle liquor.

Strong authoritarianism can lead to run-away teens. Refrain from viewing your teen's friends as rivals. It is normal for them to prefer their friends to family during this stage of their development. By the early 20's family will again take precedence over friends unless the teen is of a strong sanguine temperament.

If you worked to instill virtues in your children when they were young, the teen years will have a much smoother transition. Dr. Rudolf Allers has many useful insights in his book, ***Forming Character In Adolescents,*** but the depth of problems he deals with in the book are not found in teens who have a faith and virtue foundation.

Prof. Castillo advises parents to work on communication with their children from their earliest years by incorporating the following points in your family:

1. Make the effort to communicate and develop close contact between parents and children;
2. Encourage children to take part in household activities in various ways (keeping them informed about family projects and worries; asking for their opinion, depending on their age, before making decisions which affect them; asking for their help with certain household tasks, and so on);
3. Create an atmosphere of understanding and trust, in which the children get used to talking naturally about their own matters and to confiding in their parents on personal issues;
4. Keep an eye on what the children are doing during their spare time (what they are reading, who their friends are, how they spend their time, etc.) and giving them guidance as to how they can use that time profitably.[46]

Once a child reaches the teens, Castillo advises parents that teens need:

1. To be allowed to do things on their own;
2. To have possessions and activities of their own;
3. To make their own decisions on certain aspects of their lives;
4. To have friends (without incurring parental suspicions);
5. To have a free run of the house (without the restrictions imposed on younger children);
6. To dress according to their own personal taste;
7. To be able to follow their own hobbies and take part in their favorite sports.[47]

Again, as with everything in life the above points must be in the realm of the reasonable. A teen is still a child in a maturing adult body. The decisions they make must be suited to their capability. They are not capable of deciding which high school to attend. The school must meet the

[46] *Ibid.*, p. 4.

[47] *Ibid.*, pp. 4-5.

parents' criteria, not the teens. The same applies to s[illegible] a college although your teen should be permitted to decide his field of studies. Remember, you cannot morally send your child to a school that will harm his faith or morals. On the other hand, it is not right to force a child to go to your alma mater solely because it is your alma mater. Should your child be unsure as to what field he wants to study, let him work a year until he decides or let him take classes at the local junior college.

A teen should be free to select his friends unless you see that the friends selected have a negative influence on your child. If this is the case, you have a duty to tactfully work your child out of that group and into another group. Dress is another area of concern. While the teen should be allowed to select the styles that he is comfortable with there are criteria to be considered. The clothing should be modest, clean, pressed, and appropriate for the occasion and the season. Jeans or shorts are not appropriate for Mass. Sandals are not appropriate in January unless you live in Florida or Southern California.

Discuss with your teens the concepts of freedom, love and authority so peers or other groups will not manipulate them. *Make clear to children that you <u>want</u> them to grow up,* counsels James Stenson. *You do not want them to remain "protected" and "innocent" little children. You expect them to mature, as soon as possible, into strong men and women before they are out of their teens. You are confident that, with God's grace, they will be responsible adults who live by Christian principles, who have strength to serve God and other people.*[48]

Dr. Ana Maria Navarro believes that *[f]ailure in life can be caused in two different ways. There is the inner emptiness of the fool, who does not know how to find the joy and beauty of the inner life, or of the coward, who does not dare to face up to his own shortcomings. And there is the tragedy of the embittered or resentful person, who does not adapt his dreams*

[48] "Peer Pressure," *Op. Cit.*

to reality. A life can be regarded as successful when external matters are a means of enriching our inner life, and when we relate to the world and perform external activities by throwing ourselves into them body and soul, that is, not remaining on the level of superficial contact, but drawing on our inner life to give them meaning.[49]

The Emotions...

"We control the emotions by refusing to be subject to our moods." Dom Hubert Van Zeller

Since teens are enmeshed in emotions let's briefly consider them. First of all, personality and temperament type influence one's emotional makeup. If you were diligent in teaching your children the foundation virtues as well as how to do mortifications (sacrifices) it will be easier for them to control their emotions that trigger their moodiness. If this is your first exposure to teaching children virtues, talk with your teens about the lives of the saints and how they made small and large sacrifices to control their impulses. For instance, one day St. Francis of Assisi experienced strong temptations against chastity so he threw himself into a snow drift to achieve control of himself. Your teens can practice self-control by limiting their phone conversations, not snacking between meals, drinking water instead of pop, remaining silent rather than answering a parent back, etc. These little actions will buildup self-control making it easier to control one's emotions.

Dom Hubert Van Zeller, a monk at Downside Abbey, explains: *There are the deep emotions—theologians call them passions—and there is the top-soil stuff....It is the deeper level that we have to care about: what is on the surface we must learn to laugh at. An emotional man is not necessarily one who shows his feelings, whose heart is on his sleeve. An emotional man is simply a man of acute sensibility: if this comes much to the surface he is a superficial man. It is*

---

[49] "The Awakening of a Sense of Intimacy In the Adolescent," *Op. Cit.*, p. 7.

therefore our business to keep emotions well down. At times they will work upon us so powerfully that we shall feel our anchorages to be giving way...It is then that we shall need the strength which the life of grace has built up. It is then that our characters are tested....Emotional people are all too seldom told how vital it is for them to cultivate an intellectual background: they cannot, and should not, live in the emotions, and if they have nothing to fall back upon when the emotions dry up they will find themselves at the mercy of suicidal depressions which tend to drag on until the next emotional upheaval takes place (editorial emphasis).[49A]

While each of us has highs and lows, the object of controlling our emotions is to make them balanced so that while we are experiencing happiness we are not in a silly ecstasy nor when we experience stabs of sorrow are we in the depths of despair (which is sinful). We are to moderate our reactions so that our personality is basically level in happiness or in sorrow. When I first began spiritual direction in my early 20's my confessor told me one day, *Mary Ann, you are either flying high or sunk to the depths. You have to work on being always on an even keel.* This was the first time anyone had explained to me that emotional reactions have to be controlled. I simply thought that was my personality so my job was to live with it, not change it. St. Josemaría also was telling me that I had to change when I read point #4 in his book, ***The Way:*** *Don't say, "That's the way I am—it's my character." It's your lack of character...Be a man!* We cannot simply go with the flow of our reactions. We need to practice self-control.

What about the highs and lows of life? Moments of happiness come but just like time, we can't hold on to them. Dom Van Zeller advises that happiness *is too big a thing for that. We can't enjoy it all at once; it has to be spread out. The experience of happiness is progressive...We are given the faculty of remembering, and that is quite enough to go on*

[49A] Dom Hubert Van Zeller, ***We Die Standing Up*** (NY: Sheed & Ward, 1949) pp. 62-63.

with in this life. Indeed happiness grows, matures, takes on new color as it is remembered...Real happiness stands outside time...Memory is part of the joy, it is an extension of happiness itself...The moment of happiness that we look back upon with pleasure was only the beginning: the happiness itself is not finished yet....and the other moods, those that plunge us into the depths, are to be thought of in the same way. They cannot, may not, last. Sadness never represents the real man for any length of time because it is more in the nature of man to be happy than to be miserable. Grief can be agonizing in its intensity: it can reduce a soul to bitterness, to sin, to madness, even to death; but it can never so overwhelm a man's spirit as to involve him in a settled unhappiness unless he deliberately indulges it. There is the danger: hugging one's sorrow until it becomes part of oneself. Thus, as long as we have the sense to take our moods of misery as moods, we are in no real danger of falling into a self-pitying decline. Our glooms need never reveal our real selves; they are more often physical reactions than natural tendencies.[49B]

Pessimists are not born but made, usually in the mid to late teens. It begins as cynicism and mockery. If it isn't eradicated early on, it can take over one's nature, becoming ingrained, sometimes turning to bitterness. *Sorrow can reduce us for a while, but if we indulge our sorrow it can become the weakness of a lifetime. Even resentment, so long as it is a spasm and not a fostered grudge, is natural enough—we can no more help being hurt by the sting of malice than by the sting of a bee—it is when it becomes a drawn out quarrel with existence, it is when we find ourselves at variance with life that we need to take ourselves in hand.*[49C] St. Paul tells us: ***In all things we suffer tribulation, but we are not distressed; we are sore pressed, but we are not destitute; we endure persecution, but we are not forsaken; we are cast down, but we do not perish...***(2 *Cor.* 4:8-9) Why is this so? St. Paul answers: ***knowing that affliction produces endurance, and endurance, proven character,***

[49B] *Ibid.*, pp. 63-64.

[49C] *Ibid.*, p. 72.

***and proven character hope, and hope does not disappoint, because the love of God has been poured out...* (*Romans* 5:3-6).**

Emotions, like any other talents, are to be trained. The training and direction will require delicate handling...If we fail to master our moods, our moods will master us...Perhaps it wouldn't matter so much if man could keep his disillusion to himself, but there is in him always the tendency to infect others...Insufficiency of love is at the root of all cynicism, and this insufficiency drains the energy out of others. Cynicism can be as subversive as any sin. I have seen more wreckage done among the innocent by the man who sneers at virtue than by the man who solicits to vice, reveals Dom Van Zeller.[49D] With this knowledge you can survive the teens!

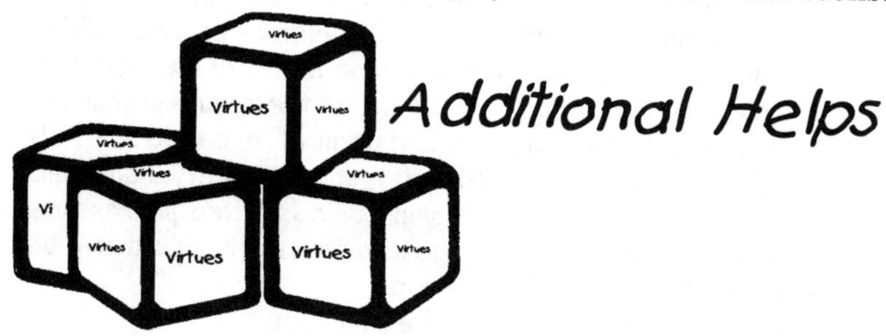

Additional Helps

- ✓ Look up the April 8, 2003 *Wall Street Journal* article entitled "The 'Re-Engineered' Child" by Andrea Petersen.
- ✓ If you or your teen has questions about the faith, check out the website http://www.pretionline.it There are 800 priests on line to consult from Italy. Hopefully some of them speak English.
- ✓ Looking for good films for your family? Contact Feature Films For Families at 1-800-Family-TV (1-800-326-4598). Address is: PO Box 572410, Murray, Utah 84157-2410. For Canadian readers the address is PO Box 88 Barrie, Ontario, Canada L4M 4S9.
- ✓ A great film is *Rigoletto*. On the back cover there is a parents' guide for family discussion questions.

[49D] *Ibid.*, p. 73.

- ✓ Why don't you and your older teens read Leo Tolstoy's ***Anna Karenina*** then discuss it? This book shows how one's right to be "happy" can lead to despair then self-destruction.
- ✓ For parents with little children get the book ***The 7 Lonely Places, 7 Warm Places*** by April Bolton. This is a book on virtues for children.
- ✓ For Preteens call and order a copy of the Bethlehem Books catalogue. They have wonderful books that spotlight virtues in the characters. You can reach them at 1-800-757-6831 or www.bethlehembooks.com
- ✓ Check out NestFamily Distributors. They have animated video hero classics featuring Edison, Washington, Tubman, Columbus, Franklin, Bell, Pasteur, Wright Brothers, Keller, Da Vinci, Joan of Arc, Marco Polo, Galileo, Marie Curie; a bible series; and an American history series; an inventor's series; an artist series; and an adventure series. While I have not viewed these videos the material on them looks excellent. Under each video they list the virtues promoted in the film. For example, under Joan of Arc is listed faith, reverence, obedience, integrity, courage, patriotism, honor and leadership. Under Marie Curie is listed selflessness, sacrifice, love, kindness, generosity, work, education, and enthusiasm. 1-800-988-6378 or www.nestfamily.com/mediamission
- ✓ For more information on teens, you might want to read ***Forming Character In Adolescents*** by Rudolf Allers, M.D., Ph.D., published by Roman Catholic Books. The section on sex education is outdated since this book was written in 1940.

CHAPTER 2

HOW TO TEACH THE VIRTUES OF TEMPERANCE AND MODERATION

Virtues For Teens

As the former headmaster of two prep schools, James Stenson found that *psychological and social development seems to be cyclical with the odd-numbered years (11, 13, 15, 17) being awkward. Teens oscillate between being outgoing, sociable, intellectually inquiring, curious, eager to please [to being] withdrawn, emotional, quiet, critical of self, critical of*

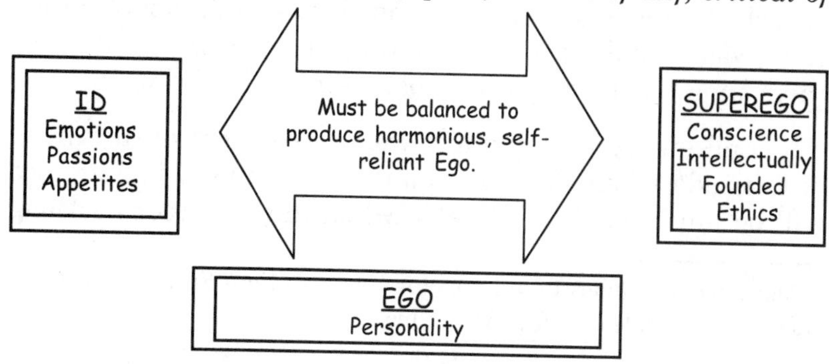

of self, critical of parents, critical of environment, inconsiderate, having only one or two close friends.[1]

Stenson writes that the Id and the Superego must be balanced to fully develop the personality of teens. He believes that *intellectually founded ethics, is derived principally from the father and other legitimate authority. Social forces today positively stimulate the Id, which is intensifying [in the teen anyway]. Parents have to compensate, and even overcompensate, for this pressure; otherwise, children grow off-balance. [When] they learn, through experience, that feelings are criteria for what is "good," [they develop short term] habits of irresponsibility, avoidance of effort, pleasure-seeking, gratification of appetites. Long-term results [are] difficulties in studies, difficulties in professional work, difficulties in marriage—life in 20's characterized by narcissism (no concern for either parents or children) and "prolonged adolescence."*[1A]

For this reason teens need to develop the cardinal virtue of temperance, which is self-mastery/self-control. This virtue aids the teen in controlling his passions due to the rapid development of his *body, intellect, emotions, imagination, and will.*[2] This virtue is crucial since our culture invites our teens to live hedonistic lifestyles. Don't be naïve! Their friends are already experimenting with drugs, alcohol and sex. When our youngest daughter returned home after her freshman year in high school she was eager to rekindle friendships from her Catholic grade school. She was sickened to find that 40% of her 8th grade class was sexually active while the ones who were not spent their time together talking about the ones who were.

If children are initiated into the development of the virtue of fortitude when they are young, the virtue of temperance will be much easier to develop when they are teens. Along

---

[1] James Stenson, notes from lecture on "How To Be A Successful Father." Audiotape available from R.B. Media, Inc.

[1A] *Ibid.* [2] *Ibid.*

with temperance, the virtues Dr. Isaacs recommends for teens ages 13-15 years old are listed below. These are the virtues that pertain to our relationship with others as well as oneself.

Temperance
Moderation
Modesty
Chastity
Sociability
Hospitality
Friendship
Respect for others
Simplicity
Patriotism

Living the Virtues of Temperance and Moderation

"Always remain in the state of grace...and enjoy life as much as you can!"

St. John Bosco

For some, St. John Bosco's advice may seem contradictory yet if one is in the state of grace, life is so much more enjoyable. Living the virtues of moderation and temperance makes food taste better, leisure time more relaxing and purchases guilt-free. There is order to life as well as purpose. James Stenson brings up an interesting link with temperance—*the welfare of others, not ourselves. Self-controlled people are other-directed. Your children need to see this in the way you deal with your family and friends. <u>And you need to explain it</u>* (editorial emphasis).[3] This last sentence is very important. You must discuss with your teens the importance of self-control in all the aspects that will be covered in this chapter as well as in Chapters 3 and 4. Why? Self-control, restraint, self-discipline, willpower, and moderation fly in the face of our overly self-indulgent culture. Your teens will fall victims to self-indulgent

[3] James Stenson, ***Lifeline—The Religious Upbringing of Your Children*** (NY: Scepter, 1996) p. 117-118.

lifestyles unless you instruct them how to act contrary to what society and peer pressure present as acceptable.

At World Youth Day 2000 in Rome, John Paul II told the young people: *Dear Friends: to believe in Jesus today, to follow Jesus as Peter, Thomas, and the first Apostles and witnesses did, demands of us, just as it did in the past, that we take a stand for Him, at times almost to the point of a new martyrdom: the martyrdom of those who, today as yesterday, are called to go against the tide in order to follow the divine Master.*

Perhaps you will not have to shed your blood, but you will certainly be asked to be faithful to Christ! A faithfulness to be lived in the circumstances of every life: I am thinking of how difficult it is in today's world for engaged couples to be faithful to purity before marriage. I think of how the mutual fidelity of young married couples is put to the test. I think of friendships and how easily the temptation to be disloyal creeps in.[4]

The Holy Father is speaking about the practice of the virtue of temperance, the virtue of self-control. This virtue is key for teens because self-discipline is essential for developing character and controlling those raging passions within their bodies. St. Bernard led an extremely austere life leading some historians to complain that his actions impeded his natural gifts. But Daniel-Rops found just the reverse in his study of St. Bernard: *The farther he traveled on the road of self-renunciation, the greater became his influence for good. The more firmly he controlled himself, the more truly human he was found to be...from whatever standpoint his personality is viewed.*[5] The same will be said of your children if they live the virtue of temperance well.

Dr. Alexis Carrel, who won the Nobel Prize for developing the method for suturing blood vessels, writes: *A mode of life which imposes on everyone a constant effort, a*

---

[4] World Youth Day Rome Aug. 19, 2000.

[5] **Cathedral And Crusade**, *Op. Cit.*, p. 87.

psychological and moral discipline and privation, is necessary. He then brings out an interesting point: *An ascetic and mystical minority would rapidly acquire an irresistible power over the self-indulgent and spineless majority.*[6] This is how the early Christians conquered the Roman Empire! In other words, a minority of people practicing self-discipline can bring our unhappy world back to Christ! What an exciting thought that your children can be part of this cultural revolution. Carrel adds that ***without moral self-denial, intelligence becomes feeble.*** Doesn't this explain why so many people enjoy watching the trash on TV; why trying to work with people today is so difficult because so many lack the ability to think clearly?

The Virtue of Temperance

"Why should you invest your life, or any part of it, in anything of doubtful value?"

Actress Dale Evans Rogers

Specifically, what is **temperance**? Joseph Malaise, S.J., in his book, ***Know Yourself***, writes: *Temperance is the moral virtue that moderates the inclination towards sense-pleasure, especially the pleasure of the palate and the flesh, and keeps it within the proper limits of propriety.*[7]

The ***Catechism Of The Catholic Church*** expands on Fr. Malaise's definition:

> **#1809 Temperance is *the cardinal moral virtue that moderates the attraction of pleasure and provides balance in the use of created goods. It ensures the mastery of the will over instinct, and keeps natural desires within proper limits.***

Temperance has many aspects. Besides the use of food, drink, and chastity, it should moderate our use of TV, radio,

[6] From ***Uncommon Friends*** by James Newton (NY: Harcourt, Inc., 1987).

[7] Joseph Malaise, S.J., ***Know Yourself*** (San Francisco:University of San Francisco Press, 1939) p. 152.

phone, electronic gadgets, entertainment, the car, and the Internet, as well as our talking, temper, activities, goals and the purchasing/acquiring of items.

James Stenson gives some wonderful examples of temperance but also a thought provoking examination of conscience for our teens and us:

1. Temperate people...are patient with themselves and others.
2. Temperate people...can delay gratification at will; they can casually take or leave enjoyable goods.
3. Temperate people know how to concentrate on a task.
4. Temperate people...have the practiced power to work quickly without hurrying, and carefully without dawdling. They set and meet their own deadlines.
5. Temperate people make good bosses and get promoted. They are assertive but not obnoxiously aggressive...They take responsibilities seriously, but they are good humored.
6. Temperate people put people ahead of things.
7. Temperate people are not coarse in speech, for such talk is a kind of impulsive self-indulgence and shows disrespect for one's company.
8. Temperate people habitually are courteous to everyone, even in the face of provocation...They are not interrupters. They are slow to anger, quick to forgive and forget.[8]

The Virtue of Moderation

"I believe He [Jesus] expected us to use our God-given talents to make as good a living as we can, to acquire and use our possessions well, but never to make possessions the great goal of life."

Actress Dale Evans Rogers

Associated with the virtue of temperance is the companion

[8] ***Lifeline...***, *Op. Cit.*, pp. 104-105.

virtue of **moderation**. Without developing the virtue of moderation one cannot live the virtue of temperance. What is moderation? Dr. David Isaacs defines the virtue of moderation thus:

> **[Moderation]distinguishes between what is reasonable and what is self-indulgent and makes reasonable use of...senses,...time,...money,...efforts and so on, in accordance with true and upright principles.**[9]

To live a truly Christian life we have to be able to say "no" to ourselves. The virtue of moderation controls our food and drink intake, our sex drive, our spending, our talking, as well as the use of time. Time is a gift from God to be used in His service, in a manner pleasing to Him. We lack moderation when we have the TV or radio news on all day or even for several hours a day; when we spend our free time only on pleasure; when we purchase items that are not needed; when we seek after luxuries and worldly success. Remember, when we are in the state of grace our bodies are temples of the Holy Spirit. As such, we are obliged to treat our bodies with moderation and respect.

James Stenson points out that *temperance also means enjoying the good things of life in moderation, never to excess. It means being on top of life, living life as richly and beautifully as God intended when he made us...Temperate people enjoy all the good gifts of life in balanced moderation. They like food, drink, entertainment, recreation, work itself. They are confident people, so they do not overindulge in these things. (Insecure people are the ones who overeat, addict themselves to pleasure, and work to excess from unreasonable fear of failure.)*[10]

On the other hand, the lack of moderation creates for us a host of problems that start out small but grow like a

[9] Dr. David Isaacs, ***Character Building*** (Dublin: Four Courts Press, 1984) p. 255.

[10] ***Lifeline—The Religious Upbringing...***, *Op. Cit.*, p. 104.

snowball rolling downhill. Overindulging in alcohol leads to drunkenness, possibly alcoholism, weight gain, driving under the influence, sometimes an early death. Overeating leads to weight gain as well as health problems. The lack of sexual restraint leads to promiscuity, adultery, life threatening diseases, and dysfunctional lives. Overspending leads to debt. Workaholism destroys marriages and makes spiritual growth impossible. Overindulging in anything is a vice because it is a lack of self-control.

The idea behind moderation is that there is a higher purpose to life than simply pleasure for pleasure's sake. Since God loves us so, He sprinkles pleasures throughout our day and life but we are to use these pleasures in moderation. They cannot become our gods. When we overindulge in any area we wander off the narrow path that Christ says leads to heaven. The Israelites wandered in the desert for 40 years. Haven't you ever wondered why it took them so long to travel from Egypt to the Promised Land when it is simply a two-week hike? It was because they refused to follow the will of God! Don't let your teens waste their lives going in circles like the Israelites. Help your children to live moderation so that they can keep on the narrow path that leads to happiness on earth as well as unity with God in eternity. Just as we need to live temperance and moderation to get to heaven, it is difficult to do so without a vibrant, living Christian faith that is infused with graces continuously.

Marist Father Thomas Dubay, in an interview on his new book, ***Happy Are You Poor,*** claims that living these virtues involves a *free will. Unfortunately, there are people who so cling to their pleasures and luxuries that they have decided that anything that interferes with their lifestyles is going to get little to no attention.*[11] That includes the practice of their Catholic faith. Fr. Dubay continues: *Fyodor Dostoyevsky ...put on the lips of a character the fact that if a person does not worship the real God, he will bend his knees before things*

[11] Zenit, Oct. 9, 2003.

created and finite. There are, he added, no atheists—they are really idolaters...That, of course, is true. Everyone has one or more consuming concerns. It's either the real God or money, power, pleasures, lust, pride in its various forms and so on. One or more of these latter becomes idols, as the man who rejects the only God centers his thoughts, desires, aspirations, worries and concerns on his idol. They are gods to him...Avarice enslaves a man in a multitude of ways...Vanity about possessions is much like vanity about accomplishments and bodily beauty—one is held in bondage to the minds of other people...St. Paul puts the matter positively in **1 Corinthians** *10:31:* ***"whether you eat or drink or do anything else, do all for the glory of God."*** *All created goodness and beauty is meant to bring others and us to the unspeakable enthrallment of the beatific vision in the risen body. To willingly cling to anything merely created for its own sake reminds me of Dostoyevsky's analysis: It is either idolatry or it tends in that direction.*[12]

Give your child clear principles or criteria for practicing moderation. But remember, in most instances there is no uniformity in practicing this virtue. What may be gluttonous for a woman to eat may be physically needed for a teenage boy. This is why giving principles is important so that your teen can apply them to his circumstances or situation. Remember, family unity depends on common principles. Unless family members agree on the same principles there will be ongoing conflicts.

Moderation in Use of Money

"Shrouds have no pockets."
Proverb

In the Gospel of St. Matthew Jesus makes some rather dreadful prophesies about the rich. For emphasis Jesus repeats His statement twice. Read this passage slowly and meditate upon it: ***Amen, I say to you, it will be hard for***

---

[12] *Ibid.*

one who is rich to enter the kingdom of heaven. Again I say to you, it is easier for a camel to pass through the eye of a needle than for one who is rich to enter the kingdom of God (19:23-25). Why is this? Money itself isn't evil. It is the misuse or selfish use of money, due to the lack of the virtues of temperance and moderation, that is sinful. These vices lead us along the path to hell rather than to heaven. Take the example of the many emperors, empresses, kings and queens that are canonized saints. They possessed great power and wealth but used both in moderation. A recent example of this is Karl, the last Emperor of Austria, who was born in 1887 and who died at the age of 35 in 1922 while in exile. The initial steps for his canonization have been completed. In contrast there are even more emperors, empresses, kings and queens who were in the same situation as the saints but lived lives of vice rather than practiced virtue.

Everyone is familiar with the von Trapp family depicted in the famous movie and play, *The Sound of Music*. But few people realize that although they had status, wealth and prestige they also carefully practiced the virtues of temperance and moderation. They were only able to live these virtues because they had acquired fortitude as well as the other foundation virtues. For this reason, let's use the von Trapp family and their actions as a case study for many of the virtues that we have already discussed or will discuss in this book.

Let's begin this study with a little history to give it background. To cripple Austria, Hitler closed the country's borders. This destroyed the country's main source of income, tourists, resulting in financial repercussions which led to bank closures throughout the country. Prior to this event, the Baron von Trapp had invested his fortune in England but when a bank owned by an esteemed and intelligent friend, Mrs. Lammer, was in danger of failing, von Trapp came to her rescue by withdrawing his fortune from his

English bank to deposit in her Austrian bank. His actions temporarily saved her bank, but over time it too collapsed. His fortune was lost. This was the start of the family's financial hardships. (He was living the virtues of temperance, moderation, charity, flexibility, generosity, friendship, understanding, loyalty, patriotism and optimism.)

Although their fortune was gone, they still had their estate, some money, and valuable possessions that could be sold off. On March 12, 1938, Austria became part of the "Third Reich." This began a tense six month period of veiled Nazi threats for the von Trapps. It began when the Baron was "asked" by the Gestapo to hang the Swastika flag from one of his balconies to celebrate the arrival of Hitler into Salzburg. He replied that he could not afford to purchase a flag. After giving him a flag, the Gestapo asked him if he would now hang it out. *I don't think so. You know, I don't like the color. It's too loud. But if you want me to decorate my house, I have beautiful oriental rugs. I can hang one from every window.*[13] (In this instance von Trapp practiced the virtues of sincerity, fortitude, simplicity, patriotism and loyalty.)

Next, Maria was warned by her daughter's first grade teacher that little Lorli harbored a negative attitude toward the Third Reich. She refused to sing the Nazi anthem. When asked why she refused to sing, Lorli told the class *that her father had said he'd put ground glass in his tea or finish his life on a dung heap before he would ever sing that song.*[13A] (Lorli was living loyalty, patriotism and struggling to live sincerity. She did not blurt out her opposition to the song but only explained when asked. Still, she was too little to understand that sincerity means making a full disclosure only to the right person when appropriate. Disclosing her father's comments to a Nazi sympathizer was the wrong

---

[13] Maria von Trapp, ***The Story Of The Trapp Family Singers*** (NY: Scholastic Book Services, 1971) p. 139.

[13A] *Ibid.*, p. 140.

person. It could have cost her father his life.) After this incident, her parents emphatically stressed that she was not to disclose any of their conversations at school because if she did her family could be put into concentration camps. Several days later Maria was again called to school by Lorli's teacher. This time the little girl refused to give the new greeting, "Heil Hitler." She had to be asked repeatedly why she refused to give the greeting. Under relentless pressure Lorli finally broke down saying, *Mother said if I tell in school what is going on at home, Father will be put in a concentration camp, and Mother, and all my sisters and brothers!*[13B] (Lorli again practiced loyalty and patriotism while valiantly struggling with the virtue of sincerity. She was too young to practice the needed virtue of intimacy discussed in the last chapter.)

The Captain was "invited" by the Third Reich to take over the command of one of their new submarines. In time he would be expected to establish bases in the Adriatic and Mediterranean Seas. Although the idea of again commanding a submarine was tempting, he told Maria, *No, I can't do it. When I took my oath on our proud old flag, I swore: "With the Emperor, for God and my country." This would be against God and against my country. I'd break my old oath.*[13C] (In this situation he was practicing the theological virtues of faith and charity as well as the natural moral virtues of temperance, moderation, patriotism, prudence, loyalty, justice, responsibility, and fortitude.)

Pressure continued to mount on the family. Their eldest son, Rupert, a newly graduated doctor, received "an invitation" to take an important staff position in a hospital in Vienna. *Of course I can't accept...They'll be quite offended. I'd have to consent to all kinds of treatments and manipulations which I am not allowed to as a Catholic—and as a man.*[13D] (Rupert was practicing the theological virtues of faith and charity along with the natural moral virtues of temperance, moderation, loyalty, charity,

[13B] *Ibid.*, p. 141. [13C] *Ibid.*, p. 146. [13D] *Ibid.*, p. 147.

patriotism, prudence, respect for others, justice, responsibility, and fortitude.)

That same week the family received a call from Munich requesting that they sing for Hitler on his birthday. If they consented to sing for the Füehrer their fortune would be guaranteed. That evening, after the smaller children were put to bed, the Baron called the rest of the family together. It was time to make a decision but he did not make the decision for his family alone. Just as Prof. Castillo advises parents in Chapter 1 to keep teens informed in regard to family worries and to ask their opinions before making decisions which will affect their lives, the Captain called the family together. He outlined the flattering offers he and Rupert had received as well as the prestigious invitation to sing for Hitler. Then the Captain asked for the children's comments. After silence came the questions. *Will we have to say, "Heil Hitler" then? Will we have to sing the new anthem on the stage? How about Father Wasner? The Nazis don't like priests."* (Fr. Wasner was their choral director.) *In school we are not permitted to sing any religious songs with the name of Christ or Christmas. We can hardly sing any Bach for that reason."* Another commented, *I am sure we'd have a tremendous success in Germany with our program, but will it be possible to keep up our ideals and remain anti-Nazi while we take their money and their praise?"* Another inserted, *We just can't do it.* (The children were practicing the theological virtues of faith and charity as well as the natural virtues of temperance, moderation, loyalty, sincerity, fortitude, freedom, responsibility, justice, charity, simplicity, patriotism, prudence, understanding, and loyalty.)

Then their father began to speak saying: *Now we have to find out what is the will of God. Do we want to keep our material goods we still have--this our home with the ancient furniture, our friends, and all the things we are fond of? Then we shall have to give up the spiritual goods: our faith and our honor. We cannot have both any longer. We could all make a lot of money now, but I doubt very much whether it would make us happy. I'd rather see us poor but honest. Listen, you can have money today and lose it tomorrow. The very same day you can start all over again, and that can happen more than once to you in your lifetime. But once you have lost your honor or your faith, then you are lost. If we choose this, then we have to leave...soon. You can't say no three times to Hitler--it's getting dangerous. Do you agree?*[13E] The decision was unanimous. They would leave. (The family was practicing the theological virtues of faith, hope, and charity besides the natural virtues of sincerity, simplicity, fortitude, generosity, freedom, responsibility, justice, charity, temperance, moderation, respect for others, patriotism, prudence, flexibility, understanding, loyalty, audacity, humility, and optimism.)

There was no real question what God wanted. As a family it was decided that we wanted to keep Him. We understood that this meant we had to get out...Overnight we had become really poor; we had become refugees, relates Maria von Trapp.[13F]

Their decision was heroic, not just from a material point of view but more importantly it would be life-threatening for Maria since she was at this time a high risk pregnancy. This occurred because shortly after her marriage Maria contracted scarlet fever which left her kidneys badly damaged. Experiencing kidney problems during her pregnancy, her husband took her to Munich to see a specialist who told them that an abortion was necessary to save Maria's life. When the von Trapps refused to even consider an abortion, the doctor told them that the baby for sure would be stillborn, and *I just hope I shall be able to save the life of the mother. She has to go to bed and stay, and keep a very strict diet...Keep her absolutely quiet--no*

[13E] *Ibid.*, pp. 148-149 plus [13F].
[13F] Maria von Trapp, ***Maria*** (Carol Stream, IL: Creation House, 1972) pp. 67-68, 70.

excitement--the blood pressure is very high.[13G] To flee through the mountains at this time took the theological virtues of faith and hope as well as the natural virtue of fortitude. Not only did Maria survive this adventure but she safely gave birth later to a healthy baby.

Once out of Austria, to support themselves they turned their hobby of singing into concert engagements throughout Italy but vicious rumors accused them of being Nazi spies. Maria recounts that *nobody seemed to be able to believe that one would voluntarily leave everything behind only and solely for one's conviction. And, sure enough, Italy told us to get out.*[14] This occurred because the people suspicious of the von Trapps were not themselves living the virtues of moderation and temperance in regard to their money or possessions. If they had been, they would have understood the position of the von Trapps. For now we will leave the von Trapps but will meet them again in later chapters.

The Misuse of Money

In the parable of the sower found in ***Mark*** 4:1-20, Christ warns us how destructive the love of money and possessions can be. He equates it with the seed that falls among the thorns. The seed represents God's grace. Let's read what happens when grace falls among the thorns of "love of money": ***And others are the ones sown among thorns: they are those who hear the word*** [the Gospel, the truth, the teachings of the Church]***, but the cares of the world, and the delight in riches, and the desire for other things, enter in and choke the word, and it proves unfruitful.*** Not only can it render a person unfruitful, it can be the cause of one's loss of faith.

The misuse of money can cause long term suffering for families. Too much affluence, not wisely controlled, can ruin the characters of the children, as well as the parents. We read this in the biographies of the rich and famous.

[13G] ***The Story Of The Trapp...***, *Op. Cit.*,p. 142. [14] ***Maria,*** *Op. Cit.*, p. 70.

Another misuse of money is spending large sums of money for tickets to rock concerts, sporting events, the theatre, or hotel accommodations. I have read of teens paying $700 to scalpers for a Michael Jackson concert. This is morally wrong. *The Wall Street Journal* had two recent articles dealing with excessive waste of money. An article entitled "The Big Picture" discussed the growing trend with families to install home theaters to watch movies in their homes. They spotlighted one family from Alpharetta, Georgia who spent $500,000 *to build an 18-seat theater...including features such as faux-finished Greek columns with gold-leaf trim and a stage with lights that illuminate the screen.* This excess breeds selfishness. When a friend asked the owner if he could *invite nine friends over to screen a home movie made by his nephew and expected Mr. Ames to provide the snacks, [Mr. Ames declined saying] "It was ridiculous."*[14A] In an article on Talbots' merchandising practices, writer Shelly Branch described a 40th birthday party held at a Pennsylvania branch of Talbots, Inc. A husband invited 12 of his wife's closest friends, had a gourmet lunch catered into the store for the women and for their "goody bags" they all shopped at the store with him picking up the $3,000 tab for their purchases.[14B] My favorite vacation is touring the South during spring. This year when I tried to make reservations in Asheville, the cost of the hotel we hoped to stay in was doubled because it was peak season. So we are going to Charleston instead. In conscience I could not pay the doubled price. Families reveal that they pay $500 per night for the concierge level at Disney World. This is a needless extravagance as well as the misuse of money. In addition, the virtue of poverty is not being lived. One has to also question, are these families just as liberal in the Sunday Collection as well as to charities? Observing the collection at Mary, Queen of the Universe Shrine in Orlando I see lots of $1 bills which wouldn't even purchase a soft drink in the city.

[14A] "The Big Picture," *The Wall Street Journal,* Jan. 30, 2004.

[14B] Shelly Branch, "Long Used to Getting Full Price, A Retailer Faces New Pressures," Feb. 3, 2004.

Likewise, overspending leads to debt, foreclosures, repossession of cars and goods. This is not a recent problem. The famous writer, Charles Dickens, was the victim of parents who squandered their money until they were deeply in debt. Dickens said that his father couldn't hold onto a penny even if it was stuck to his hand! Dickens was only twelve-years-old when his parents were hauled away to debtors' prison. He not only had to find a means to support himself, but he also had to find a way to pay his parents' debt. He resented his parents for the burden they had thrust on his young shoulders. When he began to write his books he further showed his resentment by writing them into his novels as despicable characters. ***David Copperfield*** is autobiographical. If you reverse the initials of this book you will get Dickens' initials.[15]

Dale Evans Rogers, actress and wife of cowboy star Roy Rogers, wrote an interesting little book entitled ***No Two Ways About It!*** Living in the affluent area of Hollywood she first addresses the issue of money. Dale reminds us that money is simply a medium of exchange. Acquiring it should not become the goal of our lives. Then she asks some pointed questions: *What was the status of Jesus Christ in Palestinian society? How much did He have in the bank when He died?...Does it strike you as odd that most of the greatest men in human history have been the poorest?...Why are we all so anxious to keep up with* [the Jones] *and not at all anxious to keep in touch with God?...* Living among the affluent, Dale found that *as a rule, the more wealth and fame you get the more worry and responsibility you get, the less privacy you have and the more frustrated you become...*[16]

Living in a consumer society we have to educate our children to differentiate between needs and wants so as to use money correctly. Judas is mentioned in Scripture twice

---

[15] Gerald Charles Dickens, great-great grandson of Charles Dickens, in his performance in *Mr. Dickens is Coming*, Nov. 22, 2003, Springfield, IL.

[16] Dale Evans Rogers, ***No Two Ways About It!*** (New Jersey: Fleming H. Revell Company, 1968) pp. 12-13, 14, 15, 16, 17, 32.

in relation to his lack of temperance toward money. He resented the fact that Mary of Bethany spent large sums of money on ointments to anoint Jesus at the dinner. As keeper of the purse, he wanted that money in his possession so that he could spend it. Each lack of temperance fueled the growth of vice until Judas sold his God for 30 pieces of silver, the going price for a slave.

A recent news story stated that the year 2003 saw the greatest number of filings for personal bankruptcy in the history of the U.S.[17] There were more filings that year than during the years of the Great Depression. At the same time we are told by the *Wall Street Journal* that this is the "Golden Age" due the affluence of the West. Professor Darrin M. McMahon claims that *70% of Americans now own the place they live, as opposed to fewer than 20% a century ago. Their homes and apartments are larger and more comfortable...with once rare...amenities like central heat and air conditioning.*[18] Anyone can be part of the "jet set" flying around the world to vacation in exotic places by charging the fees and hopefully being able to pay for it later. But living beyond one's means leads to paying high interest rates that prevent families from ever becoming debt free. The more debt one incurs, the harder it becomes to pay it off while maintaining the same lifestyle. Eventually bankruptcy is the only option. This is the fruit of vice. (Please note that all bankruptcies are not due to excess expenditures. Some occur through catastrophic illness, death, loss of income, or other unforeseen circumstances.)

Discuss financial expenses with your teens. Show them how much everything costs. Explain a budget. Teach them how to design a personal budget around their allowance, if they receive one. Consider giving each child an allowance to teach the good use of money. Studies show that children who receive an allowance spend less money while saving more than children who are handed money on demand.

[17] WGN TV, Dec. 4, 2003.

[18] Darrin M. McMahon, "Disgruntled in the Midst of Plenty," *The Wall Street Journal,* 12/4/03.

Teach your children the value of things by encouraging your teens to spend their summer working so they can help with school tuition or things they truly need. A free ride does not teach the value of money or appreciation for the financial sacrifices of parents. Talk to your teens about the importance of using their money for others less fortunate to counter the teenage tendency to take, rather than to give.

Explain to your teens that *the evil in the love of wealth lies in the* intention *with which we seek it. It is wrong to seek wealth for its own sake as an end in itself, or for a purpose which we consider as an ultimate end, for instance, honors and pleasures. This is what is called the worship of the golden calf,* warns Fr. Joseph Malaise, S.J.[19] If teens don't learn this lesson from you they may even be drawn to extremes such as the practice of Wicca to acquire money and riches. Carlo Climati, the author of ***Young People and Esotericism: Magic, Satanism and Occultism*** explains in a Zenit interview that Wicca *is a mixture of paganism, magic and superstition. They practice a series of magic rites: from enchantments of love to ceremonies to become rich or "attract money"...In some cases, it suggests rituals that seek to exercise power over people.*[20]

Financial tycoons made their appearance in the beginning of the 11th century. One of the first was St. Godric (or Goodrich) of Finchale. *He made a fortune in the coasting trade along the shores of England, Flanders, and Denmark, as well as by lucky speculation, but was then touched by grace, gave his goods to the poor, and became a hermit.* He had it all but realized it did not make him happy. He finally discovered that only God could fill the emptiness in his heart.[20A]

---

[19] ***Know Yourself,*** *Op. Cit.*, p. 45.

[20] Zenit, April 1, 2003.

[20A] ***Cathedral and Crusade,*** *Op. Cit.*, p. 273

Moderation with Possessions

"One's life does not consist in the abundance of possessions." Jesus Christ

In 2002 one of the most talked about scandals was that of the lavish lifestyles of chief executive officers of major corporations. At that time it was reported that *the average CEO earns roughly 400 times as much as the average production worker, compared with a ratio of 42-to-1 two decades ago...*[21] With this wealth let's see how some of the CEOs wasted it. The CEO of Tyco spent $15,000 for an umbrella stand for his office, $6,300 for a sewing basket, $2,200 for a wastebasket, $5,960 for two sets of sheets, $445 for a pincushion, $1,650 for a notebook and $2,900 for coat hangers. When he was indicted for evading $1 million in sales tax on his art purchases he had to give up plans to purchase a $17.8 million yacht. The CEO of General Electric, in addition to his retirement package of $880 million in GE shares, received $2-$2.5 million in annual benefits that even included opera tickets. These two examples expose excessive greed which is a serious moral vice.

John Paul II in his message for Lent 2003 addressed the virtue of temperance and moderation in regard to possessions. He writes: *Our age, regrettably, is particularly susceptible to the temptation toward selfishness which always lurks within the human heart...the spirit of the world affects our inner propensity to give ourselves unselfishly to others and drives us to satisfy our own particular interests. The desire to possess ever more is encouraged* (editorial emphasis). *Surely it is natural and right that people, by using their own gifts and by their own labor, should work to obtain what they need to live but an excessive desire for possessions prevents human beings from being open to their Creator and to their brothers and sisters. The words of Paul to Timothy remain relevant in every age:* ***The love of money is the root of all evils; it is through this craving that some have***

[21] Zenit, Sept. 29, 2002.

wandered away from the faith and pierced their hearts with many pangs (*1 Tim*. 6:10)![22]

In 1923 Harry Emerson Fosdick observed: *Great possessions only throw a man back upon himself. For there is an important difference between possession and ownership: possession is having things; ownership is the enjoyment and appreciative use of things...Possession concerns what a man has in his hands; ownership concerns what a man is in himself...Possession is having a morocco-bound copy of Wordsworth that you never look at; ownership is having a Wordsworth, it may be in paperback, a source of inextinguishable delight. Possession is having a house; ownership is having a home. Possession is material; ownership is spiritual. A man may possess millions and own nothing. How much a man owns depends on the height and breadth and the depth of his mind and soul.*[23]

Instruct your children as to the danger of coveting money for the purpose of "instant gratification." Be careful how much material goods you lavish on your children as well as your own spending/acquiring habits. Many times parents, unwilling to give of themselves and their time to their children, heap upon them abundant possessions as a substitute. For a parent to do this is morally wrong for two reasons: 1) The parent is living a life of vice by not fulfilling his/her responsibilities; and 2) The parents are ruining the character of their children/teens.

During the Sermon on the Mount Christ listed seven expected behaviors for His followers along with the reward for living in that manner. One pertains particularly to this topic of possessions. Christ tells us, ***Blessed are the poor in spirit, for theirs is the kingdom of heaven*** (***Matt***. 5:3). By living temperance/moderation in regard to possessions we are promised heaven! That's some promise! Those who are "poor in spirit" realize that everything one has not only

[22] John Paul II, Message for Lent 2003, Vatican, Jan. 2003.

[23] Harry Emerson Fosdick, ***Twelve Tests of Character*** (NY: George H. Doran Company, 1923) p. 97.

comes from the hand of God but belongs to God. We are simply the stewards of our possessions. Therefore we are to be detached from them as we practice austerity in their use. Teach your teens this lesson well.

Beware of becoming attached to your possessions. We can easily become attached to a possession without even realizing it. Some years ago we purchased a new family car which turned out to be a lemon. Since I do a lot of long distance traveling alone, after a couple of months we realized that we had to get rid of it. Unable to afford another family size car we ended up with a cute, white 240 Nissan sports car. (This is what they mean about turning lemons into lemonade.) The type of car that I drive has never really interested me as long as it is dependable. My husband, on the other hand, has always wanted a sports car but when we purchased the Nissan, he insisted that I drive it. I thought that was rather silly since he was the one who liked sports cars. It was only later that I learned that he did it as a mortification. I drove the 240 for about six months. Then one weekend Bob took it to drive our youngest daughter to her summer job at the hospital. On the way they were hit by a woman who ran a red light. The woman, turning to discipline her children in the back seat, did not see the light change. My car was totaled but fortunately Bob and Mary Terese escaped the accident without even a bruise. When I arrived at the accident scene and viewed the wreckage I felt two emotions: thanksgiving for protecting my husband and daughter then rage at the destruction of my car. My emotion of rage stunned me. I had no idea that I had become so attached to that car. But my struggle over attachment wasn't over. When the insurance company replaced the car with a red 240 Nissan my husband gave me the keys to the old family car but took the keys to the Nissan. That was a bit of an unwelcome surprise! God knew that the accident had not completely detached me from that silly car so He had to remove the replacement from my grasp as well. But a lesson learned can easily be forgotten. This past summer we had to replace Bob's car. He did all the research, the trial drives, etc. I was completely uninterested in what type of car he got. When he purchased the car he told me that it was mine. I protested, refused, but when I got up in the morning to go to Mass, my car was gone and in its place was the new car. Irritated by this silliness I drove the new car to the hospital, found my car, and exchanged cars. The next day, my car was again gone and the new one was left in its place. (My husband is even more stubborn then me.) The rest of the week I drove the new car. It was rather fun. On Thursday I drove it to a Day of Recollection. The topic was making our possessions our god. The priest even mentioned among a list of items new cars. It never clicked that I was becoming attached to a car again. That evening over dinner Bob told me he decided that he would drive the new car. I was dumbfounded. Too ashamed to admit that I had become attached to another silly car in four days, I said nothing but interiorly I was fuming—fuming at myself for my attachment but also fuming at the loss of the object of my attachment. See how easy it is to become attached and not know it?

To illustrate this point to your teens, ask them to write down a list of things that they are attached to. If they protest they are not attached to anything, go down a list of things they possess and ask if they are willing to give them away. That's the key. If we are unable to live without, do without, or give them away, we are attached. Just like the rich young man in the Gospel, we can become attached to something as little as a pen or as great as our wealth. Everyone has to battle with attachment, even the saints. St. Josemaría wrote frequent letters to his spiritual sons but had difficulty during the Spanish Civil War finding pens that would write with broad strokes, which he preferred. When he found a pen he really enjoyed writing with he would use it for a while then give it away to fight his attachment to it.

Let's face it, the more people have, the more they want. While the thought of possessing an item may be exciting, once it is possessed it is no longer interesting. Rather, it leaves an emptiness that causes one to yearn for something else. Also, desire creates unnecessary needs. A three-year-old girl was shopping with her mother. Seeing something that she desired, she demanded, *I want it!* *You have one of those,* her mother replied. *I want that one,* persisted the little girl. *I don't have the money,* replied her mother. *Charge it*! the child shouted.

Explain to teens the importance of avoiding all impulse buying. Try to instill in your teen that if an item is not on the "need" list to wait several days before purchasing the item, and then only after reflection and prayer. Ask them to consider:

- Why do I want this item?
- Will it help me to be a better person?
- Is this item a need, a want, an impulse item?
- What would God say about this purchase?
- Is it prudent for me to use my money in this manner?

Point out how easy it is to waste hundreds of dollars a year on fast food snacks or small, impulse buys. Spending $5 a week on needless items costs $260 per year!

Dr. Isaacs notes that *some people acquire property in order to show off, to be in fashion, just for a change, to compensate for some inner dissatisfaction or to fill some kind of vacuum in their lives. Yet other people always want new things...*[24] The two vices attached to this aspect of moderation are **consumerism** and **avarice.**

Let's consider these vices a little deeper. What is **consumerism**? An article in *The St. Louis Post-Dispatch* gives a clear understanding of this vice in its covering of the opening of a new mega-mall in the area. The picture accompanying the article showed a shocked woman looking

[24] ***Character Building***, *Op. Cit.*, p. 117.

into her van filled with purchases totaling $4,000. As the first person to arrive at the mall, she recounts: *"I cut the ribbon because I was first in line, and then I did damage." Seven hours and $4,000 later, she loaded up to go home. Her purchases...filled four shopping carts and included clothes, furniture, a grandfather clock and a cello.* Clerks at one store in the mall said that customers *were tearing (the shoe department) apart.* One of those customers purchased 10 pairs of Prada and Gucci shoes saying, *I'm a crazy shopper when it comes to shoes.* A clerk told how he had just rung up a single $4,000 item. Another customer talked about a $651 Gucci tote that was on sale for $329. *That's really a good deal.* In another part of the mall a customer told how he shops *the malls every week after work.* People even took off from work to attend the mall opening. The final comment in the article was from a woman who told the reporter, *We're going to spend the day here. We left our husbands at home, and we have the credit cards. We're on.*[25] Months after the grand opening Bob and I were down in St. Louis so we decided to checked out this new mall. After walking through the whole place we could not figure out how the women quoted in the article could spend so much money there. They had to be buying just to be buying since we found little to even tempt us.

The Friday after Thanksgiving 2003 saw consumerism at its worse. People actually lined up at 4 a.m. in the morning to buy items when the store opened at 7 a.m. At a Best Buy a woman was trampled and left unconscious draped over a $29.99 CD player. At toy stores shoving occurred as well as fights broke out over people jockeying for a better position in line. A friend, nursing a terrible cold, boasted to us that she was in line at 4:45 a.m.to get a flat screen for her third computer. She has no reason to possess three computers and four screens. This is excessive as well as a lack of temperance and moderation. It is sinful to be so obsessed by possessing something that one deprives onself of sleep

[25] Thomas Lee & Lisa Jones Townsel, "Shoppers make a run for the Mills," St. Louis Post-Dispatch, Nov. 14, 2003, Section C, p. C1, C19.

by standing in line to be one of the first into the store. This is the vice of consumerism.

Example again plays an important role in teaching our teens. What a terrible example these adults are giving our youth! If our teens see us spending money on whims or excessive entertainment they will likewise imitate us.

Train your teens to avoid temptation by steering clear of window-shopping or cruising the Mall on weekends. Show them how to toss catalogs away *without* reading them. Catalogs only create needs. Discourage your teens from subscribing to teen magazines unless they are Catholic publications. Teens are major targets of advertisers because they have too much "spending money."

One of the most difficult times of the year to live moderation in regard to possessions is Christmas. The love we feel for our family wants to spill out into piles of prettily wrapped packages that will delight one and all on Christmas Day. Betty & Ralph Thomm of Coal Valley, Illinois, solved this problem: *We ask for only three things on our Christmas list because Jesus received three gifts. That cuts down on the widespread materialism of the holiday, especially with younger children who are influenced easily by television commercials.*[26]

A good indication that a family is acquiring too many possessions is when that family has a yearly garage sale! In addition to the questions for teens to ask themselves, mentioned earlier, here are some other questions to consider before making a purchase:

- ✓ Think before making a purchase. Is this a need or a want?
- ✓ How often will I use it?
- ✓ Am I buying this just because it's on sale?
- ✓ Check out the quality of the product before purchasing.

---

[26] ***We Are Family,*** Office of Family Life, Diocese of Peoria, 1992.

- ✓ Check out specific features of the item.
- ✓ Price the item at three different stores for the best price.
- ✓ Is it a fad that will diminish in value?

Only purchase items of good quality that will be durable. White carpeting is beautiful but not if you have a houseful of active teens or toddlers. Wait until they are adults to purchase your white carpeting. Just because you were pleased with a previous brand appliance or model does not mean that the current model or appliance is the same quality. I went through an iron a year until I purchased an expensive brand that was recommended to me. It was great. When it gave up the ghost I replaced it with the same brand, at the same high cost, and it's a piece of junk. We had a similar experience with a car and a duplicator. Just because the product was great in the past does not make it great today. Check out *Consumer Reports*, Internet reports, and the experience of friends before purchasing high cost items.

Teach your teens and children to care for your and their possessions such as furniture, clothing, appliances and vehicles so that they will last longer. I know several people who replace their furniture every two years because they allow their children, and now their grandchildren, to abuse it. This is a lack of virtue.

Isaacs encourages parents to teach their children the following:

1. To value what they have and what they might have.
2. To control their whims and to do so cheerfully.
3. To think about their reasons for spending money.
4. Not to be attached to pleasure.
5. To identify the appetites that should be controlled.
6. To have high ideals that will give them deep satisfaction, rather than seeking superficial pleasures.[27]

The other major vice opposed to temperance and moderation is **avarice**. ***Avarice*** *or* ***covetousness*** *is the*

[27] ***Character Building***, *Op. Cit.*, p. 120.

inordinate love of money and earthly goods. The avaricious man desires both to get and to keep; the covetous man desires to get something away from its possessor, explains Fr. Joseph Malaise, S.J. He continues, ***Miserliness*** *and* ***niggardliness*** *are avarice in the expenditure of money and earthly goods. Miserly and niggardly persons seek to increase their possession by mean and petty savings; the miserly by stinting themselves, the niggardly by stinting others, even those of their own household. Persons afflicted with this vice are hardhearted and pitiless towards others, and hold tight all they get, and when they give they do it grudgingly. There are others who are covetous, not so much for the sake of the money, but because it gives the means for sensual living. They selfishly and lavishly spend everything upon themselves and close their heart to the dire needs of their neighbor* (editorial emphasis).[28]

St. Basil adds: *Avarice fills homes with secret thieves, markets with deceit and fraud, the halls of justice with false witnesses, the homes of the poor with indigence, the eyes of orphans with tears, the heart of widows with grief, the prisons with malefactors, and hell with damned souls.*[29]

Christ sums up the topic of avarice by counseling, ***Avoid greed in all its forms. A man may be wealthy, but his possessions do not guarantee him life*** (***Lk*** 12:15). Our Lady of Fatima told Bl. Jacinto that *people should avoid luxury.*[30] A final thought to share with teens: We are going to have to give an account to God of how we have used the money entrusted to us. Just as we read in ***Luke*** 16:2, Christ is going to ask us: ***Give an account of your stewardship.*** How will you and your teens answer?

Moderation in Seeking Success

"You must take great pains to please God."

St. Alphonsus Rodriguez

Dale Evans Rogers not only discusses money in her book

[28] ***Know Yourself***, *Op. Cit.*, p. 40. [29] *Ibid.*, p. 43.
[30] Bro. Francis Mary Kalvelage, F.I., "Fatima Seers, Models for All."

but tackles the issue of success which turns people into workaholics. A successful actress herself, she discloses that *success is spiritual. I believe that if you work hard and sincerely and stay humble* [we'll be talking about humility in a later chapter], *you're a success...If, though you do your best, and you still do not reach the top rung on the ladder, but manage to hold fast to faith in God and man, you are a success. For my part I'd rather be successful as Micah describes it than to have all the gold in Fort Knox or top billing in everything I attempt.* Mrs. Rogers then describes how she has seen the passion for success *ruin the characters and careers of many...I've watched them make the first tiny, deadly compromise, and then another, and another, until there was nothing left in them but a ruthless, profane lust to "succeed"—to get their names up there in lights, to be a star, to be on top.* In this quest for success or to pay for their excessive luxurious lifestyles the actors or actresses accept roles that are *morally or spiritually degrading...*[31]

Dale's husband, Western star Roy Rogers, played only wholesome, decent roles. When he was given a script to play a drunken character, he refused. The movie producers threatened him with the loss of his contract if he refused the role. Roy again refused the role, told them he no longer had a contract with them, then walked off the lot. The producers did call him back but from that time on only offered Roy decent roles. Roy was unwilling to trade his ideals for success or money. He practiced temperance and moderation in his career/profession. This is an important lesson that we must teach our teens. If the parents of our so called "Catholic" pro-choice politicians had taught their teens this lesson, this disgraceful group of politicians would not exist today.

Recently, my city of Springfield, Illinois made national news when seventeen-year-old football star Nate Haasis, wrote to the Central State Eight Conference director to ask that his 5,006 pass record be removed from the record book.

[31] ***No Two Ways About It!***, *Op. Cit.*, pp. 12-13, 14, 15, 16, 17, 32.

Why? With less than a minute remaining in Nate's final high school football game, his coach, a friend since seventh grade, made a deal with the coach of the opposing team to let Nate break the passing record. Late in the game Coach Taylor calculated how much yardage Nate needed to break the passing record. *He then moved to a spot on the sidelines to mark the yardage needed for the record.* Later the receiver would run *out of bounds at the coach's feet.*[32] This was the deal: Southeast High's coach would allow Cahokia to score another touchdown if Cahokia would allow Nate his record breaking pass. Cahokia's coach agreed. Right before the play began, Nate's coach yelled across the field, *This is for you, Nate!*[33] Uncertain what his coach meant by that remark, Nate soon noticed that something was wrong as the ball snapped. *The opposing players simply lined up and watched the snap—not even getting down in a crouch at the line of scrimmage. They made no effort to tackle the receiver.*[34] Nate recalls: *I noticed that something was a little fishy when I saw that Cahokia defenders were not even paying attention to the play, talking to each other, not even paying attention to what I was doing.*[35] After the game Nate, still puzzled by what had transpired, told a reporter that his record breaking pass *means a lot to me—a lot.* But integrity meant more than success. That is why he sent his letter saying that the record *would have been great...something to share with my teammates. While I admittedly would... like to have passed the record, as I think most high school quarterbacks would, I am requesting that the Central State Eight not include this pass in the record books. Reaching 4,969 yards required a lot of cooperation and hard work from my teammates. I do not wish to diminish the accomplishments that were made in the last three years.*[36]

---

[32] David Kindred, "A record given back sets QB in Illinois apart," *The Sporting News,* Nov. 16, 2003.

[33] *The Eagle,* "A lesson in integrity by a young player, Nov. 9, 2003.

[34] Associated Press, MSNBC, "High schooler declines tainted record."

[35] ABC News.com, "Winning Values," Nov. 7, 2003.

[36] "A record given back sets QB in Illinois apart," *Op. Cit.*

Now for the reaction of the coaches. Coach Taylor of Southeast High School, who stands to lose his job because of the rigging, said that he was *just sick about this. My intention was just to get Nate's name in the record book. It was just an attempt to do something good. And no good came of it.* Coach Golliday of Cahokia, *was surprised by the reaction.*[37] Aren't you disappointed by both of these coaches? One rationalized his actions. The other is clueless as to the gravity of his deed. It leads one to think that cheating to succeed is acceptable. Success is more important to these two men than integrity. The teen had more sense then the coaches combined! This situation evolved because these coaches lacked the virtue of moderation. What was further disheartening in reading the various news reports of this story were references to other similar acts of dishonesty for the glory of success. Ted Schurter of the *Springfield State Journal-Register* writes that this case is *[s]orta like the deal UConn reached with Villanova to let injured Nykesha Sales score an uncontested basket so she could become UConn's all-time leading scorer. Sorta like Green Bay quarterback Brett Favre letting New York Giants defensive end Michael Strahan sack him so Strahan could set the NFL's single-session sack record. Sorta like Cleveland's Ricky Davis trying to get a triple-double by shooting and missing on purpose so he could grab his 10th rebound. (But Davis shot at the wrong basket and wasn't credited for taking a shot).*[38] Another writer, Rich Mies, recollects an even uglier scenario to the "success at any cost" philosophy when he writes about *the situation at Baylor this summer, replete with lies, murder and corruption…I wondered if we had sold the souls of our future for the glimmer of gold and the bright lights of success.*[38A]

Crispin Sartwell, the author of ***Extreme Virtue:***

---

[37] "High schooler declines tainted record," *Op. Cit.*

[38] Ted Schurter, "Kid's integrity shines after unwise, but heartfeld decision by coach," *Springfield State Journal-Register, USA Today.*

[38A] Mies, Rich, Editor-In-Chief. "A Touchdown for Integrity," www.totk.com/article-print.asp?articleid=49817

Leadership and Truth in Five Great American Lives asserts that *we can become so focused on the glory that the process itself becomes largely irrelevant...The goal is, finally, of no value unless the process of reaching it is a true process...If the process is false, the achievement is reprehensible...The great trope for this in the Western tradition is "selling your soul to the devil." You exchange who you are for what you want. Inevitably, as in the Faust stories, you discover that what you wanted is valueless because the self that wanted it has disappeared. It is a characteristic delusion, one of the simplest and most destructive ways to make yourself over into something evil. It is a temptation, but like all temptations it can be resisted.*[39]

Moderation in Food

"Whereas undernourishment was common until recently, today our biggest problem with food is that we eat too much of it—and for much too long." Author Darrin M. McMahon

Temperance and moderation in regard to food is one of the most neglected areas today. Instead, overweight people are in the spotlight today due to health concerns rather than spiritual concerns. WGN TV did a story on overweight children claiming that 25% of Chicago children ages three to seven are overweight! What to do? The reporter recommended that parents include more fruit in their children's diet while cutting TV and Internet time so children get more exercise.[40] What about teaching children to deny themselves snacks and pop as well as train them to eat smaller portion sizes?

A Surgeon General's Report claims obesity has reached epidemic levels. In fact, in 2000, 300,000 people died from causes related to obesity. Nationwide 13% of children and 14% of teenagers are overweight compared to 5% and 7%

[39] Crispin Sartwell, "Distant Star," www.crispinsartwell.com/passingrecord.htm
[40] December 3, 2003.

respectively, in the 1970's.[41] In addition, 26% of the adult population is in the obese category. To counter this trend, Congress is considering taxing junk food and demanding specific labels for high fat and high sodium products. Food manufacturers fear lawsuits similar to the ones the tobacco industry faced. In fact there is a lawsuit against McDonald's by Caesar Barber who blames them for his 300 pounds. He claims the company should have warning labels on their food. Few people connect this growing health concern with the lack of self-control. Fortunately, there are still some sane people around. The letters to the editor, in *Reader's Digest,* put the blame where it should be. Mark Hines of Waco, Texas writes: *I'd always assumed I was 50 pounds overweight because I didn't exercise self-control. This lawsuit opens up a whole new world for me. Perhaps I could sue my mom, who made the food taste so good initially. Then, of course, I'd have to sue my wife. Please don't blame us poor victimized gluttons for our weight problem.*[42]

Dr. Scott Gottlieg, an internist, writes in the *The Wall Street Journal* about the "Fat Liberation Activists" who *want to classify obesity as a disease and give weight-loss treatments and diet plans special tax benefits...By codifying obesity this way, the fat activists have taken the individual out of the equation, making weight gain another one of the "it's not my fault" maladies and Krispy Kreme a kind of disease transmitter...Despite what the authors of fad diets would have us believe, there is no such thing as bad food, just bad eating habits. You get fat by ingesting too many calories. The war on fat might begin with this simple truth. Indeed, it can end there, without lawsuits, feelings of victimization, diet plans or stomach staples.*[43]

Thin people can also lack moderation in food by overeating. It simply doesn't show on them! A lack of temperance

[41] Shelly Branch, "Is Food the Next Tobacco?" *The Wall Street Journal.*

[42] Mark Hines, "You Said It," *Reader's Digest,* Feb. 2003

[43] Scott Gottlieg, "Fads and Big Fat," *The Wall Street Journal*, Aug. 2, 2002, p. 25.

includes those who are anorexic, bulimic, snackers or picky eaters. Overeating is eating anything we do not need such as ordering appetizers when the meal size is adequate or taking large portions of food, a second serving, a desert when one feels full, or eating two candy bars rather than one. Sometimes we can be tempted to not live temperance because we want "to finish something" off such as the last piece of candy in a large box or the last slice of pie or piece of cake so we "can wash the pan." These instances give us golden opportunities to practice as well as develop the virtues of moderation and temperance. Don't let them escape! Teach teens to eat what is placed before them and to limit, even avoid, snacking between meals.

Two popular weight control programs, The Light Weigh (Catholic) and the Weigh Down Workshop (Christian) are *based* on the principles of living the virtue of temperance. While the world tells us to "super size" our intake, the Christian focuses instead on cutting down his portions. In fact, Suzanne Fowler of The Light Weigh program shocks beginners by explaining that the stomach is the size of one's clenched fist or a coffee mug. Eat just the amount that fits into the mug and you will never gain weight while those with excess weight will drop it. Gwen Shamblin's Weigh Down Workshop asks her participants to first halve their portions then later in the program cut their portion size again. Surprisingly, if you try these methods, which are basically the same, you can eat whatever you want until you reach full but not beyond full. Super size portions do not lead to happiness but only to super sized bodies! St. Bonaventure insists that we have to fight gluttony *for this is the first victory we must gain if we desire to overcome all our vices. He who is mastered by gluttony is too weak to resist any other vice.*[43A]

Parents unwittingly teach their children to be gluttons by insisting that they eat everything on their plate. Children are born with an internal stomach shut-off. By

[43A] St. Bonaventure, ***Meditations on the Life of Christ*** (St. Louis: B. Herder, 1934) p. 107.

forcing them to eat past full, you are stretching their stomachs. This leads to gluttony, one of the deadly sins, as well as overweight children. If you avoid giving them candy, juice and snacks during the day, they will eat what their body requires at each meal. When they are not hungry, do not force them to eat. *It may be hard to believe that the health decisions you make for a five-year-old today will still count when he or she is 50. But a growing body of evidence shows that childhood is actually the best time to start protecting an aging body, buckling it in for a lifetime of good health. Many studies now show that adult afflictions like heart disease and high blood pressure clearly have their origins in early childhood,* writes Tara Parker-Pope in *The Wall Street Journal.*[44] She then goes on to say that *in some cases, childhood presents the* <u>*only*</u> *window of opportunity to markedly influence certain aspects of adult health. Growth and cell division in many parts of the body occur only in childhood, which is why the foods and nutrients children consume in their early years can influence lifelong health—a concept known as "metabolic programming." [A] woman's risk for osteoporosisis is almost entirely decided by the end of adolescence, which is why calcium intake in kids and teens, and exercise in young girls, is so important. And many experts believe that if obesity occurs in childhood, when the number and size of fat cells is largely determined, a child is saddled with far more fat cells for life than she would have developed had she stayed slim into young adulthood. Eating behavior and food preference, perhaps the biggest determinants of long-term health, are primarily decided in childhood and adolescence...[E]ating habits and obesity can affect risk for premature cancer, diabetes, liver and heart disease, and many other health problems.*[45] The lack of temperance and moderation will impact your teen's future health.

Watch portion sizes at home as well as when eating out.

[44] Tara Parker-Pope, "How to Give Your Child A Longer Life," *The Wall Street Journal,* Dec. 9, 2003.

[45] *Ibid.*

A recent survey of restaurant portions disclosed that a restaurant portion exceeds the amount of food that a person needs for a **day** (editorial emphasis). Snack times should be a set part of the routine, for instance, when the teens come home from school, so that teens are not snacking from sunup to sun down. It is important to remember that temperance in food and drink leads to temperance in all the other areas of our lives.

Rev. Winfrid Herbst, S.D.S., suggests *[a]ll can be on their guard against the following defects in eating and drinking: 1. Taking too much. 2. Eating too hastily or out of the proper time [snacking between meals]. 3. Eating too delicately. 4. Studiously seeking only agreeable food.*[46]

To feed the wandering Israelites, God sent them manna from heaven for food. He told them to gather each morning just what they needed for that day. They were to trust He would provide more food the next day. Those who disobeyed and kept extra manna found they could not eat it anyway because it turned wormy! Teach your children that when they overindulge in food they are also showing a lack of trust that God will feed them their next meal.

Professor Hugh McDonald of Niagara University wrote an interesting essay that Zenit nicknamed "We Are What We Watch And Read." While we will consider his essay a little later under "Moderation in the Use of Time", Professor McDonald touches on the point of moderation in regard to food. Consider what he is saying very carefully. He is explaining a profound reality. *The level of sensation present in our lives affects our intellectual judgment. Thomas Aquinas discusses two related cases of intellectual debility arising from an imbalance in the sensory realm. The first is dullness of the intellectual sense, which arises from immersion in the pleasures of food. The second is intellectual blindness, which arises as the result of excessive sexual pleasures. The*

[46] Rev. Winfrid Herbst, S.D.S., ***Follow The Saints*** (NY: Benzinger Brothers, 1933) p. 70.

dulling of the intellectual sense still leaves a functioning intellect. However, what a pure heart can see quickly, the dull of sense must labor to see. The intellect is lacking in penetrative power. In the case of intellectual blindness, the intellect is completely unable to consider spiritual realities (editorial emphasis).[47] Please reread the above again slowly, then explain this to your teens. Intellectual dullness and intellectual blindness are epidemic today. It is our duty to reverse this trend. Next read with your teens ***Ecclesiasticus*** (***Sirach***) 31:12-29 but explain that verse 25 does not apply to Christians. Temperance forbids us from ever eating to the point of sickness.

Before leaving this section it is important to remind ourselves and teens that we are never to judge people, particularly in regard to their practice of the virtues of moderation and temperance, simply because they are heavy. Thyroid problems, chemical imbalances, and various medications can all contribute to unwanted weight gain. Or it can be a cross that God wishes a person to carry despite his best efforts to shed weight. St. Padre Pio existed on half a cup of cold coffee and a half slice of toast daily yet he was plump. Bl. Isnardo of Chiampo also lived a very austere life yet was plump. There are other saints as well that appeared overweight but not due to overeating.

Moderation in Drink

"Drunkenness excites the stupid man to a fury to his own harm; it reduces his strength while leading to blows." Ecclesiasticus (31:40)

Drinking is another area in which our teens are called to practice temperance. As a young girl, St. Monica was given the task of drawing the wine for the meals. Even though she did not especially care for the taste of wine, she would

[47] Hugh McDonald, excerpt from "Ascetiscism and the Electronic Media: Technophilia and Technophobia in the Perspective of Christian Philosophy," Zenit, July 21, 2001.

sample it. Each time she did her task she drank more and more of the wine until she was drinking goblets each time she went to draw it. A female slave catching her called her a winebibber. We would say alcoholic. Humiliated, she knew the servant spoke the truth. Monica used this example to teach her son, Augustine, how easy it is to fall into vice. Tell your teens this story as well as the story of Blessed Matt Talbot, an Irishman, who was a drunk but overcame his addiction.

Alcohol is a serious problem for adolescents since very few escape the teens without violating the underage drinking law. If friends are not finding ways to obtain illegal alcohol, their parents are. A friend told me how her daughter attended a post prom party at the home of a nationally known politician. He provided alcohol for his teen's party. In another incident, a prestigious north shore public high school in the Chicago suburbs made national news over a hazing that was triggered by liquor purchased by one of the girls' parents.

Talk to your teens about the moral seriousness of underage drinking. Explain clearly that drunkenness is a mortal sin. Tell them that teens can develop into alcoholics by drinking since their developing bodies cannot metabolize alcohol as an adult body can. Drinking leads to reckless behavior such as promiscuity or drunk driving. Don't be naïve thinking this could never happen to your teen. These tragedies happen in the nicest families now and in past history. The youngest son of Founding Father John Adams became a drinker. Adams found out from his daughter-in-law that his son Charles *had disappeared, was bankrupt, faithless, and an alcoholic.* Adams, writing about his son, said that he was *a madman possessed of the devil. I renounce him.* His wife Abigail wrote: *when I behold misery and distress, disgrace and poverty brought upon a family by intemperance, my heart bleeds at every pore.* She considered her son *a graceless child.*[48]

[48] David McCullough, ***John Adams*** (NY: Simon & Schuster, 2001) pp. 529-530.

In 1832, the famous Black Hawk War that encompassed Illinois, Southern Wisconsin, parts of Missouri, and Iowa was ignited by drunken American soldiers. The ambitious Governor Reynolds of Illinois was commanded by President Thomas Jefferson to call up the militia to join the U.S. army in taking the Illinois and Southern Wisconsin land from the Sac and Fox Indian tribes. Black Hawk, working to form a coalition of tribes to stand against the Whites, was unsuccessful. Promised British help never materialized and the Indian tribes in the loose federation panicked, leaving Black Hawk and his tribe defenseless. His only recourse was to surrender to the Americans. He sent three Indians, one of whom could speak English, bearing a large white flag of surrender to the U.S. army encamped about five miles from his village. Prior to the arrival of the surrendering Indians, the soldiers had set up camp. Since the soldiers had been marching hard the previous day and their *whiskey ration had not been consumed...the troops were imbibing heavily and with great gusto on the detachment's thirty-gallon liquor supply—a five gallon keg of it in each of the six commissary wagons.*[49] Due to their inebriation the soldiers were intellectually dull. When they spied three mounted Indians slowly approaching their camp, it did not register that there were only a couple of Indians; that they were carrying a flag of surrender; that their horses were walking, not galloping; that they were not painted for war; that they did not have weapons in their hands. The drunken soldiers mistook it for an Indian attack. Soldiers mounted their horses and circled the Indians, shrieking at them. *One of the more inebriated runners stumbled and fell, accidentally firing his rifle when he hit the ground. No one was hurt by the errant ball, but the gunfire caused others to haphazardly fire their weapons too, mainly into the air, as they approached or circled [the Indians]...Sagano [the Indian who spoke English] kept crying, "Wait, we talk! We talk!" but no one was listening...They were merely a shouting, shrieking,*

[49] Allan W. Eckert, ***Twilight of Empire*** (Boston:Little, Brown and Company, 1988) p. 248.

cursing, whiskey-inspired mob galvanized into a disorganized group effort to do exactly what it was they had all joined this-here army to do in the first place...One of the militiamen who had just reached the scene, Thomas B. Reed...threw his rifle to his shoulder, took deliberate aim, and sent a lead ball...into the left forehead of Sagano in the midst of his still crying, "Wait! Wait!," smashing him off his horse and lifeless to the ground.[50] When Black Hawk saw with disbelief what had happened to his offer of surrender, he told his braves: *The war we no longer wished has been brought upon us. We have no more choice. They have spilled Sac blood. They have demanded our vengeance. Now they shall have it!* [51] Numerous whites and Indians were killed because these soldiers did not live the virtues of temperance and moderation. How different history may have been if they had done so! Interestingly, following this episode the U.S. army abolished its practice of giving soldiers a daily liquor ration.[52]

But alcohol is not the only drinking problem we have. We are a nation addicted to soft drinks, coffee and tea. One survey found that teen boys consume 12 cans of coke a day while girls consume 8 cans. Don't you find that shocking? But sippy cups have also made toddlers into perpetual drinkers throughout the day and even at night in bed. It has become so common to have little ones sucking on these cups all day that writer Jonathan Eig says that *some pediatric dentists say they are beginning to see more cavities among children who use sippy cups as if they were baby bottles—sucking milk, juice and other sugary drinks for hours...*In addition, speech pathologists find that children who use the cups have difficulty pronouncing the "th" and "st" sounds. Gail Smith, a director of a pre-school in California states that *articulation for young children has totally disappeared.*[53] Tara Parker-Pope of *The Wall Street*

---

[50] *Ibid.*, p. 249. [51] *Ibid.*, p. 251. [52] *Ibid.*, p. 658.

[53] Jonathan Eig, "What's Next? Blankie? The Beloved Sippy Cup Comes Under Attack," *The Wall Street Journal*, Feb. 13, 2002.

Journal adds, *Most parents think juice, packed with vitamin C and other nutrients, is good for kids. But...juices are still mostly sugar, and many experts put them in the same category as sugared soft drinks, which have clearly been shown to contribute to obesity...Parents should switch kids to water and low-fat milk..[L]iquid calories don't fill us up, so sugared juice and carbonated drinks simply add calories on top of those we'd eat anyway.*[54] Can you see how anything in excess causes problems? Jonathan Eig's article goes on to say that sippy cups in some form have been around for 50 years but were used infrequently compared to their constant use today. Previously parents used the cups at meal time and for fast drinks of water during the day. Children did not walk around with them all day long nor take them to bed with them.

When people get adequate sleep at night, a pot of coffee during the day is not necessary. Excessive coffee is only needed to help those who lack the self-control to get to bed at a reasonable hour. This does not apply of course if your lack of sleep is due to a crying baby, sick children or other situations outside of your control. Teach your teens to live temperance by limiting beverages to meals. Insist they drink water the rest of the time.

Moderation In Use Of Time

"The fault, dear Brutus, is not in our stars, but in ourselves..." Shakespeare

Moderation must also be lived in regard to the good use of time. Time is a gift from God to be used in His service, in a manner pleasing to Him.

The old adage that *if you want to get something done ask a busy person* is true because that person has learned order and self-discipline. If we live moderation in regard to time, our phone calls will usually be limited to ten minutes or less. Luncheons will not last all afternoon. The Internet

[54] "How to Give Your Child A Longer Life," *Op. Cit.*

will be used for business rather than for "killing time." When we kill time we injure our souls. Evenings will be spent doing something productive. Rest is not doing nothing but rather a change of activities. Busyness or activism is also a lack of moderation. Time should be spent fulfilling a specific purpose not simply doing to be doing. *We constantly have to distinguish between what is necessary and what is merely desirable, between high priority matters and things which can be left aside. People say they have time only for important things, but in deciding what is important they are experts at deceiving themselves so that what they really want is to find excuses to do what they really like doing rather than what they should do... In many human undertakings, we can be satisfied with an adequate standard, below the level of perfection, so as to go on to other things which are also important...There is only one area in which we must achieve the highest possible perfection, and that is in loving God and others.*[55]

Teach your teen how to schedule his day with a planner so he can develop a routine for homework, chores, and outside activities. Have set times for bedtime and rising. Limit leisure time for watching TV or videos. This teaches temperance. Set curfews and change them only for special occasions.

Having a problem with bored teens or children? *Boredom nearly always derives from stagnancy. That is, some power of the mind or body is going unchallenged and unexercised.*[56] Stenson's response to boredom is the "job jar." Put the chores or repairs that need to be done on slips of paper, and then place them in a jar. When a child complains of boredom, allow him to select several slips (2 or 3) from the jar. From his selection he can chose which one he wants to do. This should solve the boredom problem!

---

[55] Dr. David Isaacs, "The Education of Moderation," Instituto de Ciencias de la Educación, Universidad de Navarre, 1984, p. 6.

[56] ***Lifeline...***, *Op. Cit.*, p. 111.

In ***Raise Happy Children Through A Happier Marriage,*** I addressed the problems with TV viewing but since TV is a big attraction for teens let's address the topic just a little further since there are a quarter of a million TVs produced each day which is roughly the same number of births per day.

In Professor Hugh McDonald's essay on TV he reminds us that *the brain waves of a television viewer are altered ...without regard to the content. The measurable effect of television was the same whether the person was viewing programming or commercials...*[It has] *a narcotic effect on the abuser.*[57] Fr. Stephen Valenta adds, *I wish to alert you to still another danger to you; this to your mind. It takes the mind a few seconds to complete the process of the eye seeing something and what it sees to be impressed upon the mind. What is being offered both in general programming, as also in advertising, on TV is a bombardment of ten to fifteen images in rapid succession, too fast for the mind to cope with. What this does to the mind is that it attacks its power of comprehension and concentration. In your viewing, your mind can become so deranged that its health and strength fall to the degree that you become like a zombie.*[58]

Recent studies indicate that *young children who watch television face an increased risk of attention-deficit problems by school age.* The study found that *TV might overstimulate and permanently "rewire" the developing brain. For every hour of television watched, two groups of children—ages 1 and 3—faced a 10% increased risk of having attention problems at age 7...Problems included difficulty concentrating, acting restless and impulsive, and being easily confused...Other studies have shown it to be associated with obesity and aggressiveness...*[58A]

While this may sound extreme consider this fact. A

[57] "Ascetiscism and the Electronic Media:..." *Op. Cit.*

[58] Fr. Stephen Valenta, Hearts to heart Ministries, Dec. 2003.

[58A] "Toddlers Who Watch TV Risk Attention Problems, Study Finds," *The Wall Street Journal,* April 5, 2004.

British study found that *a third of children under 3 have a television set in their bedroom.* In the U.S. 25% of children under two have TVs in their rooms. In Britain a survey found that one third of children under the age of six watches 2-6 hours of TV daily. Children—*aged 4-15—spent 2 hours and 23 minutes a day watching TV. Only half an hour was dedicated to children's programming; the rest went to soap operas and other [adult] entertainment programs.*[59]

Other objections about TV center not only on the sexual and violent content of the programming but also on the *affluence portrayed on television [which] can make people dissatisfied with their material condition.*[60] Then there is the impact of TV on fashion. The sleazy fashions are enthusiastically embraced by clothes conscious teens. The street walkers now reside in our own homes!

TV also contributes to weight gain in teens and children. In one study it was found that teens and children who watch TV are heavier than those who do not. Why? Teens and children eat, especially high-fat foods, in front of the TV. The items they snack on throughout the day are also influenced by what they see on TV.[61]

Let's consider some other studies on the effects of TV viewing. A French government commission found that *violent programs have a decided effect on the behavior of adolescents.* In Spain it was found that the *average Spanish child had seen 8,000 TV homicides before reaching the end of primary school.* In the U.S., a study showed that *children who watch violent programs are more likely to be aggressive as adults...Men who liked television shows with violent scenes as children were much more likely to have shown aggression toward their spouses, shoved someone who insulted them... or been convicted of a crime. Women who enjoyed violent shows were four times more likely to have thrown something*

---

[59] Zenit Feb. 7, 2004.
[60] "Ascetiscism and the Electronic Media:..." *Op. Cit.*
[61] "How to Give Your Child A Longer Life," *Op. Cit.*

at their husbands, shoved or punched someone else...or committed a crime.[62] At least five children died as a result of copycat violence seen in professional wrestling shows.[63]

Violence in music is another concern. *Experiments involving over 500 college students found that violent lyrics in songs increase aggression-related thoughts and emotions and could indirectly create a more hostile social environment...*[64] In England parents are suing the band Slayer for the murder of their 15-year-old daughter. *[S]he was slain in a ritual inspired by the band's songs. The three boys guilty of her murder are now in prison.*[65]

John Paul II expressed concerned about the influence of TV and the media in his 2004 World Communications Day letter. He points out that while there is good in the media the *media also have the capacity to do grave harm to families by presenting an inadequate or even deformed outlook on life, on the family, on religion and on morality...[T]he family and family life are all too often inadequately portrayed in the media. Infidelity, sexual activity outside of marriage, and the absence of a moral and spiritual vision of the marriage covenant are depicted uncritically, while positive support is at times given to divorce, contraception, abortion and homosexuality. Such portrayals, by promoting causes inimical to marriage and the family, are detrimental to the common good of society.* The Holy Father furthermore reminded parents that *as the primary and most important educators of their children, [they] are also the first to teach them about the media. They are called to train their offspring in the "moderate, critical, watchful and prudent use of the media" in the home (**Familiaris Consortio**, 76)....Even very young children can be taught important lessons about the media: that they are produced by people anxious to communicate messages; that these are often messages to do something—to buy a product, to engage in dubious behavior—that is not in the child's best interests or in accord with moral*

[62] Zenit, June 21, 2003.
[63] Zenit, Feb. 2, 2001.
[64] Zenit, June 21, 2003
[65] Zenit, Feb. 2, 2001.

*truth; that children should not uncritically accept or imitate what they find in the media...Parents also need to regulate the use of media in the home. This would include planning and scheduling media use, strictly limiting the time children devote to media, making entertainment a family experience, putting some media entirely off limits and periodically excluding all of them for the sake of other family activities. Above all, parents should give good example to children by their own thoughtful and selective use of media...*In addition, *[f]amilies should be outspoken in telling producers, advertisers, and public authorities what they like and dislike.*[65A]

Fr. Peter Harman, a moral theologian from Springfield, Illinois, also expressed his concern about the content of many programs. He adds that *much of what is portrayed depersonalizes our sexual nature. Any time that we view content of a questionable sexual nature, either by image, description or innuendo, we become a kind of third party to what God has given us for the relationship of two persons. Since the greatest sexual energies come from the mind, when we exercise that imaginary realm of fantasy, we separate the pleasures (real or imagined) from the reality. We weaken our resolve to follow what is right, and more importantly, after being berated by these images, we gain the impression that what is portrayed is what is commonly held and accepted. In short, we gain pleasure by seeing or imagining that sexuality can be used for whatever purposes we want, and can be turned off and on at will without consequences ...We are also subjected to stories and images that undermine the dignity and value of life...When doing so in a disinterested fashion, we cannot but lose perspective and become another member of a society that is callous to violent acts...*[66]

Video games and cartoons are also an area of concern. Monitor them as well as limit them. Spending more than 30 minutes playing video games a day has led to children

[65A] Zenit, Jan. 25, 2004.

[66] Father Peter Harman, "Taking personal responsibility for morality and media," *Catholic Times,* June 3, 2001, p. 6.

having problems interacting with "real people." In addition, Professor McDonald points out that watching TV or spending much time on the Internet *upsets normal community and family relations based on physical contact and proximity...People in their relations are reduced to being pieces of disembodied information without context or substance...The media would not continue to grow unless there were an immense appetite for knowledge. Such as it is today, that appetite is disordered* (editorial emphasis).[67]

Here is an example of what Professor McDonald means. On a town on the East coast, Peggy called her friend, Nicole, to say she could not meet her for lunch because of a serious family situation. A distraught Peggy then launched into a detailed explanation of the problem. *I'm so tired of dealing with this problem that simply grows worse and worse. I'm just lying on the couch watching the news. I can't deal with anything else.* When Nicole suggested that she should switch off the TV and start praying, Peggy grew defensive. Peggy insisted that she had to watch TV to keep abreast of the news. The more Peggy defended her TV viewing, Nicole began to realize that her friend was addicted to TV. It also began to dawn on Nicole the correlation between Peggy's intemperance with TV and the Internet and the serious family problems dealing with intemperance in moral areas. Mentally Nicole began to question if the mother had learned the virtues of temperance and moderation when her children were younger then taught her children these virtues, could the serious problems they now faced been avoided? Probably.

One of my West coast readers called to take issue with my strong objections to the content of TV programs. I suggested that he turn off the TV for one month during Lent and spend his regular TV time reading good, morally uplifting books. A month later he called back to tell me that turning off the TV was one of the most difficult things he did in recent years. He realized at that point that he

[67] "Ascetiscism and the Electronic Media:..", *Op. Cit.*

was addicted to TV but he persevered in his resolution. At the end of the month, he returned to watching his favorite programs but to his surprise he found the content completely objectionable. The content had not changed but he did discover that his frequent viewing of immorality desensitized him to the evil he was seeing. When he turned the TV off for the month, then filled his mind with truth and moral beauty, when he returned to viewing the evil, he was shocked. As he ended his phone call he disclosed, *I've decided to strictly limit my TV viewing but keep up my reading. It was a sobering lesson for me.*

Over lunch a friend who is equally concerned about addictive TV told me about her neighbor who lives behind her. *Their TV is on all day long. The big screen is so clear that I can see their programming across two yards and even from my second story bedroom window! Even at night when the big screen is turned off, the TV in their bedroom goes on. I can see its glow when I get up in the middle of the night. It appears that they have a TV on 24-7.* These people lack the virtues of temperance and moderation.

Professor McDonald points out that *[e]ach person has but one mind, and that mind can only know one thing at a time...In knowledge itself, there is a hierarchy of values. The highest value is to know God, and other values in knowledge come below that. A mind distracted by lesser things cannot know God...[T]he mere quantity of information may distract us from knowledge which is of true value.*

The most dangerous attitude is that of one who sits in front of the television set or computer terminal without a critical attitude. Since the machine is on, he takes up a passive and receptive stance. The Christian practices of fasting and abstinence are perhaps easy compared with consciously limiting our use of the media, yet that is required for mental and moral health.[68]

In addition, when a person is surrounded with constant

[68] *Ibid.*

stimuli be it TV, radio, Internet, gameboys, CDs, etc., God's inspirations cannot penetrate that person's mind. God tries to speak continuously to us but we cannot hear His quiet inspirations when surrounded by noise. Share this information with your teens! Encourage them to have set quiet periods in their day as you do. As part of the plan of life in Opus Dei we are encouraged to keep from noon until 3:00p.m. a period of quiet since that was the time Christ died for us. At first it was so difficult for me because I love listening to music. But after a while, the period of quiet has actually expanded throughout my day. This gives me an opportunity to think problems through, understand situations better, and pray. Besides, we work better and more efficiently when there is silence. When I first started writing I listened to classical music. Surprisingly I found that I made more typos and errors when I listened to music so I turned off. I don't need any extra help in making mistakes! Last week I had a teen send out a mailing for me. She had to put on the address labels, but before stamping them, sort the postcards in piles for U.S., Canada, and foreign countries. The U.S. cards she put stamps on. After doing this one afternoon, she asked since it was such a repetitive task if she could bring her walkman to listen to music. I thought it would be a great test to make my point. The cards she sent out the first day had no errors. The days she used her Walkman I had cards returned for insufficient postage. The music distracted her from checking all the addresses so she mailed Canadian and European post cards with the wrong postage.

The Internet can also be a great time-waster. In one parish down South there is a religious priest who helps out on Sundays. When he first arrived the parishioners found his sermons and homilies spiritually dynamic. Then little by little they grew lukewarm. Lately parishioners complained that they don't even make any sense. Then in one sermon he mentioned that he spends his free time cruising the Internet reading the sample chapters of books on

Amazon.com. That explained it all.

Each April there is an annual TV-Turnoff Week sponsored by the Washington-based TV-Turnoff Network. If temperance in viewing TV is a problem in your family consider taking part in this national effort. You will be joined by more than seven million people. Get out the games, fun books, and see how the atmosphere in your home improves. Note that quarreling decreases. Another positive feature is that your teens and children will have fewer "wants." One mother turned the TV off for good after Christmas. The next year the children's wish lists were much smaller. *They actually had to think about what they wanted, which was a wonderful surprise to (the parents).*[69] You will find that you have more time to do fun, productive activities. You can learn more about this by checking out www.tvturnoff.org. You will be glad you did!

Moderation in the use of time also limits the length of our phone calls, visits with friends, and activities. We can become "so busy" doing wonderful things for our community, schools, country, Church, and pro-life movements that we have no time to fulfill our responsibilities toward God, our spouse, or family. Several months ago I gave a lecture in Iowa. After the lecture a mother came up to me to complain about my strong warning against children involved with too many activities. She disagreed with me strongly. She then went on to tell me all the activities her teenage daughter is in. It's a wonder the girl has time to sleep! It is excessive. Yes, it would be great to be involved in everything but that is not the practice of the virtues of temperance or moderation. In the good use of time one must pick and choose. Excessive activism is a vice no matter how morally good the activity is.

Sue Shellenbarger, writing in *The Wall Street Journal,* explains how kids need a balanced life. In her research she found that *[m]ore than 20 hours a week of paid work is linked*

[69] Matthew Dietrich, "Unplugged," *The State Journal-Register*, April 22, 2001, pp. 19-20.

to delinquency, drug use and school misconduct...Don't forget family time. Connecting with family is more than a moral obligation. The largest teen study, the National Longitudinal Study of Adolescent Health by the University of Minnesota and the University of North Carolina, found closeness with family was linked to less smoking, drinking, drug use and early sex. The study involved 90,000 adolescents.[70]

Stephen Covey's son, Sean, has authored a book entitled ***The 7 Habits of Highly Effective Teens***. He stresses four cornerstones for teen lives. He asks them: *Physically, how do you feel? Mentally, are you growing and developing and reading? Socially, are you overbalanced or about right? Spiritually, are you seeking meaning and purpose, and finding ways of serving other people? It's like four tires on a car. If one tire is low, all four will wear unevenly.*[71]

Encourage your teens to give their tremendous energy and idealism to helping others by volunteering for food pantries or kitchens, visiting nursing homes or pediatric wards at hospitals, helping with Habitat for Humanity, and other worthwhile endeavors. At our local Catholic high school a program of service hours has been implemented and I have become a grateful beneficiary. Zach, a freshman who lives several doors away, volunteers after school to fill orders and make audio tapes for my apostolate. He is so intelligent and efficient that he is taking over many of the business aspects for me. His help allows me the time to write this book. Encourage your teens to help others in a similar manner.

Moderation In Talking

"Great virtue undergoes a test in little things."
St. Valerian of Cimiez

Talking is another area in which we must live the virtues of

[70] Sue Shellenbarger, "Work & Family," "Making Time to Veg: Parents Find Their Kids Need Life Balance as Well," *The Wall Street Journal,* Sept. 26, 2002. [71] *Ibid.*

temperance and moderation. Encourage your teens to spend time with their friends in person but to keep phone conversations short and to the point.

Teach your teens that when they are with a friend or in social situations not to monopolize the conversation. Give each person a chance to talk by drawing them out through questions. Talking too much can turn to gossip or possibly slander. Talking to be talking can unintentionally hurt the feelings of others and leave the talker with guilt feelings of "why did I say that?" or "I shouldn't have told such and such," etc. Besides, excessive talking is not only annoying to others but a waste of everyone's time.

Likewise, stress to your teens that in church there is not to be any talking. Talking in church in our diocese is getting so extreme that people actually talk throughout the whole Mass, even right after coming back from receiving the Holy Eucharist. Twice in the last several weeks a friend told me that she had to correct adults who could not control their mouths for 45 minutes during Sunday Mass.

Moderation in Appearance

Dress as well as appearance is still another area in which moderation and temperance need to be lived. Clothing should be neat, pressed, modest, and lacking all extremes. Torn clothing is not "hip." Rather it shows that the person wearing it has little respect or dignity for himself or those who have to look at him.

Clothing should be appropriate for the occasion. For example, jeans and tee shirts are not appropriate for Holy Mass, weddings, or other festive occasions. See ***Raise Happy Children Through A Happier Marriage*** for more specific guidelines. Hair should be a natural color rather than that of the rainbow. Haircuts should be masculine for guys and feminine for gals. Jewelry should be worn in good taste, never excessive. Piercing should be limited to the ears, preferably, of girls. Remember, everything in moderation. Fr. John Dietzen who writes a column for the Catholic News Service warns that body piercing *risks the transmitting [of] hepatitis, HIV, and other disease-causing organisms.* He adds, *[a] resolution of the American Dental Association opposes piercing in or around the mouth as a particularly serious public hazard. The New York Times quotes the president of the ADA: "To have a needle—clean or dirty-stuck through a vascular part of your body in that way, the risk of diseases has to be immense, and there can be nerve damage that affects the way you talk and swallow."*[72]

Talk to your teens about the dangers of disfiguring their bodies with tattoos. Why get one? It's done to call attention to themselves, a sign that they lack temperance and moderation. Besides, it is displeasing to God. Show your teens this passage from Scripture: ***you are not to tattoo yourselves. I am Yahweh*** (***Leviticus*** 19:28).

The Issue of Drugs

Discuss with your teens the seriousness of experimenting with drugs. Explain that taking drugs is not only a grave sin, it is a mortal sin. In December of 2001 the Pontifical Council for Health Care Workers published a manual entitled, ***Church, Drugs, and Drug Addiction***. In this document the Holy Father fingers drug use as one of the main threats facing teens and young adults. *To use drugs, notes the Pope, is always illicit because it involves an unjustified and irrational abdication of our capabilities to think, choose and act as persons. It's also false to speak of any "right" to drugs, because we never have any right to abdicate the personal dignity that God has given us. Using drugs, John Paul II has said, not only damages our health but also frustrates our capacity to live in community and to offer ourselves to others...Legalizing drugs would be a serious blow to potential users, damaging their health and stunting their lives.*[73]

[72] Fr. John Dietzen, "Body disfigurement by tattoo or piercing practices," *Catholic Times*, June 3, 2001, p. 7. [73] Zenit, Dec. 22, 2001.

Research conducted by the National Institutes of Health showed that the *use of marijuana adversely impacts concentration, motor coordination, memory, lungs and reproductive and immune systems.*[73A]

Reinforce the importance of practicing the Catholic faith to your teens. *A Columbia University research report states that people with religious faith are markedly less likely to abuse alcohol and illegal drugs than nonbelievers...Among teens, those who never attended worship were twice as likely to drink and smoke as those who were regular worshippers. Teens who considered religion unimportant were nearly three times likelier to drink, to binge drink, and to smoke; almost four times likelier to use marijuana; and seven times likelier to use other illicit drugs.*[74]

Another important topic to address with your teens is smoking. Several studies show that teens are influenced to smoke by the example of family members who smoke. *[T]he vast majority of addicted smokers started the habit in their teen years.*[75] Not only can smoking cause cancer but it can cause behavioral problems to children born of smoking mothers. Dr. Michael Weitzman, professor of pediatrics at the University of Rochester, New York, points out: *No one has clearly explained the link between maternal smoking and behavior problems but I can tell you there are more than 2,000 chemicals in cigarette smoke. And when a pregnant woman smokes, the concentration of nicotine is higher in the baby's blood than it is in the mother's. And nicotine concentrates in the fertilized egg within days of conception, even before it implants in the uterine wall. We know that nicotine contracts blood vessels in the placenta, it increases the amount of carbon monoxide in the mother's and baby's blood and it reduces oxygen supply.*[76] Research found that mothers who smoked two or more packs *of cigarettes a day during or after*

[73A] Zenit, Nov. 8, 2003. [74] Zenit, Nov. 18, 2001.
[75] "How to Give Your Child A Longer Life," *Op. Cit.*
[76] Deborah Rissing Baurac, "Mothers' smoking tied to behavioral problems in children, doctor says," *Chicago Tribune*, no date.

pregnancy are twice as likely to have children with behavioral problems...[A]s described by their parents, the misbehaved children were occasionally or continually destructive, cruel or mean, caused trouble at school and with friends, and weren't sorry for their misbehavior.[77] To learn more information about the effects of smoking, contact the American Cancer Society, either locally or nationally at (404)320-3333.

Methods to Teach Temperance

"A man buys hell here with so much pain, that he might have heaven with less than half the amount." St. Thomas More

Use the seasons of Lent and Advent as opportunities to teach and to develop temperance in your teens and self. Limit secular entertainment during those two seasons. Many people refrain from watching TV, going to plays or parties to grow in the virtue of temperance since the purpose of Lent and Advent is to develop a deeper interior conversion toward God. Thirteen-year-old Michael Wolf of Monson, Massachusetts has given up TV for Lent for eight years. He began this sacrifice when he was five-years-old. Besides giving up TV, Michael attempts to read a book a week as well as cleaning up his room. In explaining why he makes this sacrifice, Michael admitted, *I think that TV isn't that great all-around. And I think when you give it up it kind of helps you become a better person...Lent is a time of sacrificing something you may enjoy doing but it's not necessarily good for you. It's a chance to thank God and do a little bit of what Jesus did when he fasted in the desert for 40 days. I think it's kind of trying to make yourself a better person by giving up things that aren't good for you.*[78]

The Holy Father asks us to make *a serious examination of conscience*. We do this by prayerfully looking for the

[77] *Ibid.*
[78] *Catholic Times,* "Fifth-grader gives up TV for Lent, for seventh year," March 11,2001, p. 16.

obstacles between God and ourselves, then working to eradicate these obstacles through the means of fasting, prayer, and almsgiving. It takes temperance to fast from foods or activities that we enjoy, to use our time for God, and to give our money to charity.

Although we have discussed mortifications in the previous books in the ***Raise Happy Children Series***, I want to touch on this topic again because it is so important. Share this information with your teens. St. Clement of Alexandria claims that St. Matthias, the disciple chosen to take Judas' place as an apostle, emphasized the necessity of self-denial and mortification. This was a lesson Matthias learned from the example of Jesus Himself. St. Francis of Assisi found that *[i]n the battle of the spirit against the flesh one of the very best weapons is fasting.*[79] Theologian Fr. Thomas Spidlik points out that *fasting is prayer of the body.* The Fathers of the Church taught that *[i]f you do not fast, you cannot pray well. If you are unable to give up something, how can you say that your words to God are sincere?*[80] Mortification and self-denial reap many benefits for us:

1. By it we avoid the sin we would have committed.
2. It purifies the soul.
3. It procures grace and spiritual strength.
4. One act enables us to perform another.
5. It lessens our suffering in purgatory.
6. It calms the passions which cloud the soul and brings interior light.
7. It brings great interior peace.
8. It helps the soul to advance in the spirit of prayer.
9. It gives edification.
10. It increases our future happiness and glory.[81]

Several other reasons for mortifying ourselves are:

11. To show that we love Jesus.
12. To atone for our sins and those of others.

---

[79] ***Follow The Saints,*** *Op. Cit.,* p. 48.
[80] Zenit, Dec. 9, 2001.
[81] ***Follow The Saints,*** *Op. Cit.,* pp. 32-33.

13. To imitate the self-sacrifice of Christ.
14. To help us fulfill all of our duties.
15. To help us to subdue our body.
16. To help us to grow spiritually.
17. To help the apostolate to grow.
18. To help us attain human happiness by purifying our senses.[82]

Fasting does not always require bread and water. One can fast from a soft drink, an extra cup of coffee or tea, salt or sugar or simply eating smaller portions. One can fast by passing up seconds, drinking water, leaving the last bite of dessert on your plate or turning off the radio or TV. Help your teens to develop this spirit of self-sacrifice.

In the Martin family, Zélie and Louis taught their daughters to make little sacrifices (mortifications) to the Child Jesus so that they could add pearls to their crowns in heaven. They used "sacrifice beads." Sacrifice beads are a string of ten beads or more that can be slid down the cord to count one's sacrifices (mortifications). There is a crucifix at one end and a medal of St. Thérèse at the other. Make or purchase a set of sacrifice beads for each of your children. Teach them how to count their sacrifices and mortifications (acts of temperance) during the day as offerings to Jesus. It's a great tool for adults too.[83]

St. Thérèse' sister, Marie, recalls her first mortification at the age of four or five years old. She had asked her father to make her a saucer out of her orange peel. When she showed it to Pauline *...it made you envious and, to have a pearl in my crown (that was the way mother used to make us do things) I gave it to you. It seemed to me that I was accomplishing an heroic act, because that famous orange skin seemed all the more precious to me because you wanted it.*

---

[82] Fr. Jay Alvarez, Day of Recollection, 2000.
[83] Instructions on making sacrifice beads can be found in the set of books ***Catholic Children's Treasure Box*** edited by the Maryknoll Sisters published by Tan Books (written in 1957) or can be ordered from The Mustard Seed (319-337-6893) or Leaflet Missal Company (800-328-9582).

Then, running quickly towards mother, I said: "Mama, if I gave my orange skin to Pauline, will I go to heaven?" Mother smiled and answered: "Yes, my little daughter, you will go to Heaven." That hope alone was able to console me for the loss of my fortune.

When Grandfather Guerin died, nine-year-old Marie Martin offered up the mortification of going to the dentist in the hope of getting her grandfather out of Purgatory.

At Fatima, on July 13, 1917, Our Lady of Fatima showed Jacinto, Lucia, and Francisco a vision of hell telling them that *many souls go to hell because there is no one to pray and make sacrifices for them.* Teach your teens to offer their practices of temperance and moderation for specific intentions such as the conversion of family members, friends, sinners, for concerns close to their hearts. After this vision the three children gave their lunches to poor children. On hot days they avoided drinking water. They even wore a penitential rope around their waists. If these little ones could do such heroic sacrifices, surely our teens can give up salty snacks occasionally, dessert, pop, and other things that they enjoy. When Francisco was dying from complications of the flu he offered up eating food that he detested and the horrible tasting medicines he was asked to ingest. Our teens can eat what's placed before them...and cut back on seconds. My niece decided to give up chocolate until her friend begins practicing her faith again. It's been several years and this teen is still faithfully avoiding chocolate.

Bl. Jacinto of Fatima, shortly before her death, told Mother Godinho some of the instructions she received from Our Lady: *I ask you as an act of charity to make it known to the women throughout Portugal and the whole world, that our Lady requires mortification with regard to food, dress, the eyes, the will and their person...Not to speak ill of anybody, not to murmur...Let men avoid persecutions, greed, lies, envy...Our Lord and Our Lady are very offended with people because they do not obey the pope, nor the bishops, nor the priests...Penance is necessary. If people amend their lives, our Lord will even yet save the world, but if not, punishment will come.*

Maria von Trapp recounts a charming recollection about her son, Johannes, the baby of the family. Each day when the von Trapp family went to Mass little Johannes felt left out. From the time he was three years old he begged to receive the Blessed Sacrament. *When he was told that he must wait until he was able to make real sacrifices to show his true love, he wanted to know what a sacrifice was. "Do something you don't want to do, like eating your spinach without yelling..." "Or don't do something you want to do; for instance, leave those candies for me." And the little fellow set out on the road to perfection by trying to curb his likes and dislikes.*[83A] With permission he received his First Holy Communion on Corpus Christi when he was five.

Mortification, penance and sacrifices are necessary for spiritual wellbeing and even little ones can do these. They strengthen one's character so that when sufferings, setbacks, and contradictions occur, one has the spiritual courage to endure that suffering. Dr. Bengt Safsten recently gave an interesting paper at a Vatican Conference. A member of the Department of Internal Medicine at the University Hospital in Uppsala, Sweden, Dr. Bengt's topic was "The Suicide Crisis". In his conclusions he stressed: *Children and youngsters especially must be taught successful coping skills for difficulties later in life.*[83B] A spirit of mortification and self-control (the virtues of moderation and temperance) are the coping skills needed.

A teen who is permitted to satiate his senses cannot handle problems and sufferings. Hence the increase in adolescent suicides. Suicide is the third leading cause of death for ages 15 to 24.[84] *Suicide claims more adolescents than any disease or natural cause, and still there occur far more suicidal attempts and gestures than completed suicides.*

[83A] ***The Story of the Trapp Family Singers,*** *Op. Cit.,* p. 319.
[83B] Zenit, Nov. 24, 2003. [84] "How to Give Your Child...Life," *Op. Cit.*

Approximately 1 million people will commit suicide annually according to statistics from the WHO. In the last 45 years suicide rates have increased by 60% worldwide. One suicide is committed every 40 seconds around the world.[84A] Do you realize that *about 5,000 people commit suicide every day?*[85] Sound high? In the last several weeks an employee at Bob's hospital committed suicide, a reader called to say her sibling had attempted suicide several times, and a Christmas letter arrived telling of the suicide of an uncle that friends were caring for.

Suicide is increasing at a staggering pace because people cannot accept suffering. Teach your teen to take each suffering and turn it around to use for a special intention. Use it for good, rather than for self-pity. Father Arnaldo Pangrazzi, deputy director of the International Institute of Pastoral and Health Theology highlighted the *increase in the suicide rate of adolescents in countries with a high standard of living such as Germany, Denmark, Finland, Austria, and Switzerland.* He claims that *precisely the life of young people accustomed to well-being is exposed to this risk because of their inability to suffer pain. This fragility explains the difficulty to face disappointments, conflicts, interior and spiritual emptiness, lack of ideals and life plans.*[86] If the teen acquires temperance and moderation, suicide will not even be an option.

Pandering to our senses does not make us happy nor give us a sense of achievement. If it did, the rich and the famous would not be abandoning their jet setting lifestyle to enter the convent. *Talk Magazine* dedicated six pages to the phenomenon of high society women leaving the world to enter the convent. The article entitled "Italy's La Dolce Vita Nuns" relates why the daughters of Roberto Gucci, of the Marchionesses Rossi di Montelera, and of Della Chiesa (who is the sister of Princess Barberini) found their ultimate happiness not in the world but in God. Antonella Moccia, the world famous fashion model, last year left fame, wealth

[84A] Zenit, Nov. 25, 2003. [85] Zenit, May 21, 2003. [86] Zenit, May 21, 2003.

and an exciting career to enter the convent. The Italian publishing house, Mondadori, published her book, ***I Chose God***.[87]

During the conversation at the Last Supper (***John*** 13:36-38), Jesus told His apostles that He was going away and they could not follow Him until later. Impetuous Peter piped up asking, *Why can I not follow you now? I will lay down my life for you.* Looking directly at Peter, Jesus questioned him, *Will you lay down your life me?* Each opportunity God gives our teens and us to practice the virtues of temperance and moderation, He is looking directly into the eyes of our souls and asking, *Will you lay down your life for me?* We have the free choice to say yes, or deny him as Peter did.

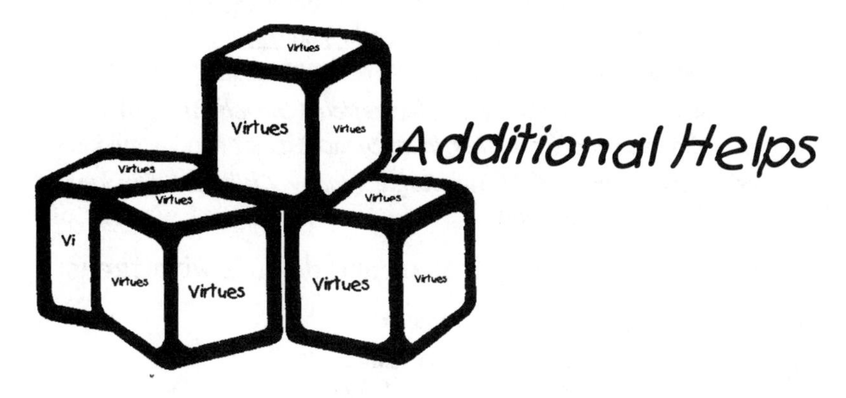

- ✓ View the video/DVD *The Scarlet and The Black* with your teens. Then discuss it. Or read the book, ***The Scarlet Pimpernel of the Vatican*** by J. P. Gallagher.
- ✓ View the black and white video *The Devil and Daniel Webster*. Discuss the vices and virtues in the film. Then view the video *Scrooge*. My favorite version is the musical with Albert Finney, a Fox Family Feature.
- ✓ Other videos to view with your teens for discussion on the virtues in this chapter are: *The Sound of Music* and *Brigadoon*.

---

[87] Zenit, March 14, 2000.

- ✓ Read and have your teens and preteens read: ***Maria*** and ***The Story Of The Trapp Family Singers*** by Maria Augusta Trapp. These book are out-of-print but readily available in used book shops. Then discuss the books together.
- ✓ Other authors to read to discuss virtues and vices are Faust, Dickens, and Dostoyevsky.
- ✓ Consider purchasing ***Know Yourself*** by Fr. Malaise, S.J. on audio tape from R.B. Media, Inc. (the book is out of print).
- ✓ Read ***Fortitude and Temperance*** by Josef Pieper or listen to it on on audio tape from R.B. Media, Inc. It's excellent!
- ✓ Read and have your teens read Father Thomas Dubay's book, ***Happy Are You Poor,*** published by Ignatius. Fr. Dubay explains how to live temperance and moderation in today's society.
- ✓ Websites to teach money lessons:
  www.familyeducation.com ; www.kidsmoney.org
  www1.stock.com ; www.cibc.com/smartstart
  www.kidsenseonline.com ; www.tomorrowsmoney.org
- ✓ Read with your teens ***Ecclesiasticus*** (***Sirach***) 31:25-42. (It's time to read ***Ecclesiasticus*** (***Sirach***) if not read previously.)
- ✓ Reread pp. 139-146 in ***Raise Happy Children Through A Happier Marriage!***

Scripture passages to look up and discuss with teens:

For Temperance:

Is. 22:13
Wisdom 4:1
Tobit 8:9
1 Cor. 10:7
1 Cor. 10:13

Greed & Avarice:

Ecclus. 10:10
Proverbs 1:19
Esth 14:15
Matt. 13:22
Matt. 19:21
Matt. 6:20
Matt. 26:15
Mark 10:24
Luke 16:2
Luke 12: 13-21
1 Tim. 6:9
1 John 3:17
Eph. 5:5
Acts 20:35
Psalm 61:11
Ecclus. 31:8
1 Tim. 6:17

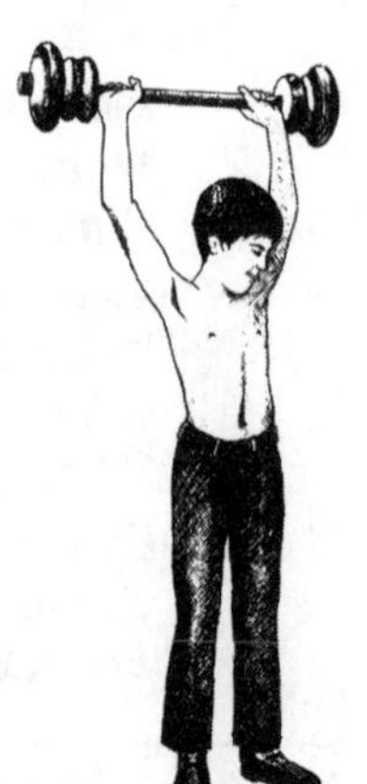

CHAPTER 3

HOW TO TEACH THE VIRTUE OF MODESTY

"At [my daughter's] high school, I'd swear I was walking through the red-light district."
Charlie Solis quoted in *The Wall Street Journal*

Hopefully I caught your attention with the above quote because this chapter is a vital one. A person's dignity depends upon living in a manner that will achieve the purpose for which he was created. Since we were created to be sons and daughters of God, if we live in a manner pleasing to God we have dignity. If we don't, we lack dignity. This is why the virtues of modesty and chastity are so important. **The vices associated with these virtues are immodesty, immorality and prudishness.** But neither modesty nor chastity can be lived without also living the virtues of moderation and temperance discussed in the last chapter.

Christ established common laws for all, wrote St. John

Chrysostom. *I don't forbid you to marry, nor am I opposed to your having a good time. But I would like you to do so with temperance, not with immodesty and countless faults and sins. I don't propose as a law that you go to the mountains and desert, but rather that you be good, modest and chaste living in the middle of the cities.*[1]

The virtue of temperance needed for living the virtue of modesty is unique among the cardinal virtues because *it...operates solely on the person practicing it.*[2]

What exactly is the virtue of modesty? The ***Catechism of the Catholic Church*** teaches that

> **#25221 Purity requires *modesty*, an integral part of temperance. Modesty protects the intimate center of the person. It means refusing to unveil what should remain hidden. It is ordered to chastity to whose sensitivity it bears witness. It guides how one looks at others and behaves toward them in conformity with the dignity of persons and their solidarity.**
>
> **#2522 Modesty protects the mystery of persons and their love. It encourages patience and moderation in loving relationships; it requires that the conditions for the definitive giving and commitment of man and woman to one another is fulfilled. Modesty is decency. It inspires one's choice of clothing. It keeps silence or reserve where there is evident risk of unhealthy curiosity. It is discreet.**
>
> **#2523 There is modesty of the feelings as well as of the body. It protests, for example, against the voyeuristic explorations of the human body in certain advertisements, or against the solicitations of certain media that go too far in the exhibition of**

---

[1] ***In Matthaeum homiliae*** 7, 7.
[2] J. Pieper, ***Prudence and Temperance*** (Madrid, 1969) p. 121.

intimate things. Modesty inspires a way of life which makes it possible to resist the allurements of fashion and the pressures of prevailing ideologies.

#2524 The forms taken by modesty vary from one culture to another. Everywhere, however, modesty exists as an intuition of the spiritual dignity proper to man. It is born with the awakening consciousness of being a subject. Teaching modesty to children and adolescents means awakening in them respect for the human person(editorial emphasis).

Dr. David Isaacs adds:

A modest person recognizes the value of his own privacy and respects that of others. He protects his privacy from the gaze of others; he rejects anything which might encroach upon it and relaxes this practice only in circumstances which can be of benefit to him or others.

From these definitions we can see that there are four areas in which we have to consciously work to live the virtue of modesty. They are

1. **Custody of the eyes.**
2. **Manner of speaking.**
3. **Manner of dress.**
4. **Manner of acting, motions, walking, gesturing and touching.**

St. Augustine warned: *Take care that all your actions and movements be ordered in such a way that none may be offended, but all edified.*[3] A modest person edifies everyone who comes into contact with him. Modesty not only edifies but tells others how we value our interior worth by the way we dress, talk, and act. This is important because people cannot read our hearts. They can only judge us by externals. St. Francis taught a friar this lesson by taking him out "to

[3] St. Alphonsus Rodriguez, S.J., ***Practice of Perfection And Christian Virtues, Vol. 2*** (Chicago: Loyola U. Press, 1929) p. 105.

preach." The two walked around the city then returned home. The friar, puzzled by St. Francis' actions, inquired, *But father, are we not preaching?* Smiling, St. Francis replied, *We have already preached.* How did they preach without speaking? They preached by the way they were dressed, their courtesy to the people they met, and their serenity. Their actions taught more than words could. St. Alphonsus Rodriguez, S.J., writes, *This is a sermon in action, more effectual than one in word.* [4] We and our teens are called to this type of daily evangelization also. Furthermore St. Alphonsus contends that *outward modesty and composure is a great argument and sign of inward recollection and of virtue and spiritual advancement to be found within, as the hand of a clock tells of the harmonious movement of the wheels.*[5]

St. Alphonsus also believed that *[a]s an ill-regulated and ill-kept exterior is a mark and sign, an evidence and token, of fault in the interior, so is modesty and due composure a sign of virtue within, and that is why it so much edifies and impresses men.* He continues, *[T]he soul that loves to see, hear, and say things, will never gain perfection or purity of heart.*[6]

When we live the virtue of modesty we set the tone in our relationship to others. People are careful as to how they act and dress in our presence. They watch their language and the subject matter. They unconsciously know that swearing, blasphemy, gossip or "dirty jokes" are to be avoided when they are with us. This positively changes as well as lifts the tone at family affairs, social events, political events, and business meetings because it unconsciously puts people on their good behavior. It is sort of like children playing raucously until a parent walks in. Then everything settles down. Christ calls you and your teens to be the salt of the world, the leaven in society, the light before men. You can only fulfill your calling if you live this virtue in all its aspects. Just seeing St. Lucian the Martyr moved pagans

[4] *Ibid.*, p. 106. [5] *Ibid.* [6] *Ibid.*, p. 115.

to convert to Christianity. Simply hearing that St. Bernardine was coming was enough to motivate his friends to be good. Can the same be said about you and your family? Do you and your teens bring out the best in people? Scripture tells us, ***By the movement of the eyelids a man is known for what he is. The look of the face reveals him who is sensible and judicious: a man's dress, his way of covering himself, of laughing, of walking, discover at once what he is*** (*Ecclus*. 19:26).

As you read through this chapter, stop to consider what your dress, speech, actions, gestures, etc. say about you and your family. Make concrete resolutions as how to change any negatives and accentuate the positives. If you find yourself fighting these suggestions remember these words of St. Alphonsus: *[O]n the soul's journey, when we begin to taste God and the things of virtue, and one is becoming a spiritual man and a perfect man, one feels no pain in foregoing these sensible pleasures and satisfactions which one enjoyed...as one imperfect in virtue...If you have a relish for pieces of childishness, for giving free vent to your senses, for feasting your eyes, going about and looking at curious and vain things, and your ears in hearing all that goes on, and your tongue in idle and useless talks and conversations, you are...imperfect, since you have a taste for the pastimes and amusements of...imperfect people. He who is a spiritual person...ridicules and scorns them...and would blush to take part in them* (editorial emphasis).[7]

I. Custody of the Eyes

"The face is a mirror that reflects the soul; and according as eyes are modest or loose and wanton, they reveal the inmost secrets of the heart."

St. Jerome

The eyes are the windows to the soul. As such it is important to guard them. *Guard your eyes, since they are the windows*

[7] *Ibid.*, pp. 115-116.

through which sin enters into the soul, cautioned St. John Bosco. St. Alphonsus warns: *They who keep the gates of their senses well guarded will live in peace and recollection; but they who take no care of this will have no peace or quiet of heart.*[8] Other saints have similar advice. Why? What we can see can come back to haunt us in the form of temptations. St. Benedict, while in Rome, met a beautiful young woman who captivated him. The thought of her was such a strong temptation that *it nearly overpowered his virtue,* writes Fr. Michael Morris,O.P. *In this conflict of desire, Benedict solved the crisis by rushing one day from his cave. He tore off his habit and rolled in a thicket of briars and nettles until blood flowed. He was so scratched and torn over his whole body that the pain in his flesh quelled the wound in his spirit. He was never again assailed by lustful temptations, but other challenges awaited him.*[9]

St. Bernard advises, *[e]yes on the ground are a great aid to keeping the heart ever in heaven.* St. Dorotheus adds, *[a]ccustom yourself to keep your eyes modestly cast down, and not go looking about at useless and vain things...* This does not mean we have to stumble around because we aren't looking where we are going. It means to practice self-control in what we view. For instance, a teen walking in the mall realizes that Victoria's Secret is several stores ahead. Rather than gawking at the soft porn ads or the window display, he averts his gaze to something in the distance or in the other direction. At the check out counter in the grocery store one pays attention to the checker rather than reading the screaming headlines of sensational tabloids. Likewise, one does not subscribe to magazines such as *Cosmopolitan, Playboy, Penthouse*, or any others that promote sensuality and eroticism. One avoids reading newspaper articles on erotic topics. St. Peter Julian Eymard teaches, *[w]e must see things without staring at them or looking fixedly...If a child looks intently on a bad picture*

---

[8] *Ibid.*, p. 110.

[9] Michael Morris,O.P., "Saint Benedict," *Magnificat*, July 2002, Vol. 4, No. 5, p. 111.

without yet understanding what it is all about, even he will later on feel early memories stir in him, and his evil look of younger days will come back to torment his imagination. Let us therefore close our eyes and stop our ears.[10]

Custody of the eyes means carefully checking out plays, movies, DVDs, and books **before** viewing or reading them. Why? Because as Fr. John Hardon, S.J., insisted, what we see becomes memorized and *what you memorize literally becomes part of your brain.*[11] St. Dominic Savio, a student of St. John Bosco, fiercely corrected his fellow students when they passed around dirty magazines or pictures. Seeing such material in the hands of his friends he remonstrated them, *Poor us! Did God give us eyes to look at such things as this? Are you not ashamed?* When the boys countered with, *Oh, we were just looking at these pictures for the fun of it.* He ended the conversation by saying, *Sure, for fun and in the meantime you are preparing yourselves to go to hell!* When another lad asked, *Oh, what is so wrong about looking at these pictures anyway?* Dominic retorted, *If you don't see anything wrong, this is even worse. It means you're used to looking at shameful things!* [12]

Recently Cirque du Soleil presented a new Las Vegas production entitled "Zumanity." The title is perfect because it flaunts the dignity of humanity. *The New York Times* headline is telling: "After Nice, A Return to Vice." Joey Arias, the transvestite moderator of the production, explains the goal of this show: *We're playing with gay, straight, bi, drag, bondage...But it's really about the animal drive inside of you...The goal is to have everyone leave the theater so excited they want to go home and make love. But only after they make a stop at the slots.*[13] The show is designed to

[10] St. Peter Julian Eymard, ***In the Light of the Monstrance***, Vol. 9 (Cleveland, OH: Emmanuel Publications, 1947) p. 82.

[11] "Call To Holiness News," Vol. 5, No. 1, p. 8.

[12] Fr. Robert J. Fox, ***Saints & Heroes Speak Vol. Three*** (Alexandria,ND, Fatima Family Apostolate, 1996) p. 119.

[13] Guy Trebay, "After Nice, A Return to Vice," *The New York Times,* June 8, 2003.

sexually arouse the viewers so they will act on this arousal when they leave the show. Hugh Hefner, at the opening performance, was asked for comments. *[H]e leered, "I'd like to think I helped to start it all."*[14] Yes, he did play a large role in the destruction of the virtues of modesty and chastity in the 20th century. In this same news article the reader is told that *Zumanity is filled with the kind of stuff you'd have trouble explaining to your kids—or to your parents.* Prices for this view of hell start at $55 and go on up to $195. Each week there are ten performances with the erotically designed theatre holding 2,000 patrons with *never an empty seat.*[15] In a Reuters review we are told that *Vegas is the perfect place to combine art, sex and money under one big top. Says Cirque's Creative President Lyn Heward: "It is a place we can leave our money, and also part of our soul."*[16] How telling is that comment! Despite this, *audiences are still pouring in. The two nightly performances over the last month have helped raise casino revenue by 30 to 40%.*[17] At a Web site where people can rate and comment on shows, 54% of the 26 reviews on Zumanity were negative saying it was a *bad show. Save your time and money.* Rob Lowman, entertainment editor of the *Los Angeles Daily News* points out that this is not a departure for Cirque du Soleil. He insists that *there has always been a slightly naughty undercurrent to Cirque du Soleil. Oh, parents might ooh and aah along with their children at some gravity-defying feat, but for some adults, watching a beautifully graceful physical specimen—male or female—contort into some impossible position has undoubtedly triggered an erotic image or two. The customers may have quickly banished it from their minds—or at least hidden it away—but it was there nevertheless.*[18] Lowman is very perceptive. We have to be

[14] Richard Ouzounian, "Hypersexual circus for grown-ups," *Toronto Star* (Canada), Sept. 22, 2003, p. B04.

[15] Richard Ouzounian, "Oh, the Zumanity Cirque du Soleil reinvents eroticism," *Toronto Star,* April 5, 2003, p. H01 Arts Section.

[16] Peter Henderson, "Cirque du Soleil Bares All in New Vegas Erotic Show," Reuters, Sept. 29, 2003.

[17] *Ibid.*

[18] Rob Lowman, "Oh the 'Zumanity!', *Los Angles Daily News*, Nov. 2, 2003.

so very careful what we see and what we take our children to see. In view of this, might it not be a good idea to boycott all productions of Cirque du Soleil? Teach your teens to avoid all entertainment that is morally objectionable. St. Peter Julian Eymard points out: *The distractions which disturb our peace of mind come to us only through that which we have seen; and the imagination, an organ of the body, is but a low traitorous copier. We must keep watch over our senses. The thought or the bad image which has not originated in an evil look will not last long; but if the eye has taken pleasure in fixing an impure object, the imagination constantly brings it before the mind until the remembrance of it has completely vanished. That will go on for months, perhaps for years.*[19]

Explain to your teens that another reason we have to be careful as to what we see is the good or bad example that we give to others. By being seen in public viewing a morally objectionable play or movie, we give it a stamp of approval that will be used to encourage others to view it as well. I love to go to the theatre. An acquaintance, knowing this, offered me four complimentary tickets to see *Miss Saigon* suggesting that Bob and I take a young couple as our guests. Tactfully I refused thanking her for her gracious offer but explaining that due to the immorality in the play we really couldn't go and at the same time we would not want to give bad example to this young couple by inviting them. The woman countered my objections by saying, *Yes, the play is racy but the _______ Sisters went to see the play and enjoyed it.* The bad example of the religious was used to try to convince me to see the play. See how careful one has to be in one's actions? People are watching what we are doing then using our example to persuade others to do the same. St. Paul reminds us: ***Let your moderation be known to all men*** (***Philippians*** 4:5).

Having a difficult time keeping your teens from seeing objectionable films with their friends? There are two

---

[19] ***In the Light of the Monstrance***, *Op. Cit.*, p. 81.

companies based in Utah trying to clean up Hollywood's films. A software company, ClearPlay, Inc., founded by a Mormon father of seven and former sports producer cleans up films for customers by cutting the *sex and gore.*[20] Another company, CleanFlicks, *edits nudity, profanity and violence out of major-market films...* [21] Their films are carried in 20 states with 76 outlets with plans to open 3-5 new outlets each month. They also sell their edited films on their Web site. Trilogy Studios, also in Utah, sells software that allows you to cut unwanted scenes via your computer. How does this work? According to the Wall Street Journal, *Trilogy users rent ordinary DVDs at their video store and play them on their computers, or on TV sets that have been hooked up to computers. Trilogy's Movie-Mask software, pre-programmed for specific films, deletes offensive sounds and images in accordance with a user's selected taste.*[22] They have since improved this technology to be able to even put clothes on the actors. One of the editors for Trilogy describes how he chopped quite a bit from the opening scenes of *Saving Private Ryan* but found that *it's just amazing how little of it is crucial to the flow of the story.*[23] Supporters of Trilogy are Marie Osmond, talk-show host Larry King and his wife, and U.S. Senator Orrin Hatch of Utah.

Strangely enough *the film industry is challenging CleanFlicks in court on grounds of copyright and trademark violations.*[24] One would think the movie studios would be happy that CleanFlicks increased the number of their viewers. But they aren't. Why is it so important to them that filth, profanity and violence remain in their films? Is it the purpose of these studios to destroy morals and Christian culture? These are questions that all parents should be addressing to the studios in Hollywood. In the book, ***Kate Remembered,*** author A. Scott Berg relates how

---

[20] Rebecca Buckman, "A Cottage Industry In Utah Cleans Up Hollywood's Act," *The Wall Street Journal,* Sept. 19, 2002, p. 1.

[21] *American Free Press*, Jan. 6 & 13, 2003, p. 2.

[22] "A Cottage Industry In Utah Cleans Up Hollywood's Act," *Op. Cit.*

[23] *Ibid.* [24] *Ibid.*

Warren Beatty wanted Katharine Hepburn to play the elderly aunt in *Love Affair,* the remake of the film *An Affair To Remember.* Katharine was eighty-five at the time. After vacillating whether or not to do it, she finally agreed. Once into the shooting of the film, Beatty wanted her to say a crude expression, "_____ the duck." Berg told Beatty that the phrase was pointless, tasteless and not even funny but Beatty was insistent that the line be in the movie and said by Katharine. In the end she said the line.[25] Why was it so important for Beatty to have that crude phrase in his film?

Another area where custody of the eyes needs to be practiced is in regard to the Internet along with its deluge of pornography. With the abundance of spam, despite federal laws to protect consumers, the pornographic spam and Web sites are proliferating. Purchase software to filter out spam and porn. Teach your teen to avoid cruising the Web. Insist that he use the Internet only when he has a specific purpose. Warn him about the dangers of pornography. It is addictive. More money is spent in the U.S. on pornography *than all the performing arts combined, the London Times noted.*[26] This $10 billion industry not only destroys the soul but it destroys marriages. Francis Cardinal George of Chicago, writing in his diocesan newspaper *The New World* warned Catholics in his diocese that *mildly pornographic material can be found in newspapers and TV programs. Advertising often exploits the human body. Many songs and music videos are designed to arouse people sexually. Most recently, the Internet has begun to furnish a steady supply of pornographic images...The studies that are available show that the use of pornography tends eventually to lead to sexually aggressive action towards others. The sexual abuse of minors is often preceded by a predator showing a child pornographic films or pictures. Pornography separates flesh from the spirit. It destroys the personal modesty that protects human intimacy*

[25] A. Scott Berg, ***Kate Remembered*** (NY: G. P. Putnam's Sons, 2003) p. 341.

[26] Zenit, April 27, 2002.

and that allows men and women to grow in mutual respect. It frees lust from moral scruple and from the control of conscience, and it becomes easily addictive. It isolates those addicted to it. It subverts family life and personal integrity.[27] Morality in Media has a Web site to help you curb Internet pornography. If you receive porn spam or come across obscene sites go to www.obscenitycrimes.org Follow the instructions. Your complaints will be sent to the U.S. Justice Department in Washington, D.C. as well as federal attorneys.

Where we vacation is also important in regard to custody of the eyes. We should avoid any place that could be an occasion of sin such as topless beaches or pools, nude beaches, and other locales that cater to sensuality such as Las Vegas. Signs in the city claim, *Sin City Has Found Its Soul.* Oscar B. Goodman, the mayor of Las Vegas, promotes his city based on immorality and immodesty. *"The new brand we're creating is one of freedom based on sensuality." Under Mayor Goodman, the city adopted a new ad campaign that turns on a kind of licentious koan [word means abandoning reason]: "What Happens Here, Stays Here." "The bottom line is that people can come here, go to the brink of whatever's legal without having anyone look over their shoulder."*[28]

Remind your teens that since the eyes are the windows to the soul, others will be able to discern the type of person they are by looking into their eyes. In the previous books in the ***Raise Happy Children Series*** we mentioned Julian the Apostate. Read what St. Gregory Nazianzen has to say about him. *[W]hen I set eyes on him and conversed with him at Athens, I knew what sort he was. I never saw any mark of goodness in him. His stiff neck, shrugging shoulders, his eyes lightly rolling in every direction, his fierce look, his nostrils ever ready to sneer or scorn, his feet never still, his tongue practiced in malice and buffoonery, his boisterous laugh, his readiness in allowing or denying the same thing with the same breath, his remarks without order or reason,*

[27] Zenit, Dec. 20, 2002.
[28] "After Nice, A Return to Vice," *Op. Cit.*

his ill-timed questions, his unmeaning answers...Before his works, I knew him...Seeing in him such indications, I burst out into the exclamation: "Oh, what a poisonous serpent the Roman Republic is rearing for herself."...[A]t the same time [I] heartily wished I might be mistaken; and without doubt it had been much better that I had been so, since then we should not have seen those evils which have set the whole world on fire.[29] Last year I had a chance to closely observe Hugh Hefner, of *PlayBoy*, at one of MGM's theme parks in Orlando. He was touring the almost empty park the same day as our family. From his restless actions, body language, way of speaking to his companions and just looking into his empty eyes, one can tell he is a most unhappy, miserable individual. Vice does not pay back in happiness or joy.

2. Manner of Speaking

"Beware of talking much, for it is a hindrance to the holy thoughts and desires and inspirations that come from heaven." St. Dorotheus

Although we discussed "talking" under the virtue of moderation in the last chapter, the topic of talking is related to the virtue of modesty so let us go deeper into this subject. Fr. David P. McAstocker, S.J. insists that *the proper use of speech indicates greatness of soul. Obviously strength of character is implied when a person (systematically and religiously) makes a dangerous and venomous instrument like the tongue behave and obey. A man who daily bites his tongue will seldom be seriously bitten by it.*[30]

Listen to what St. Jerome says about talking: *A word coming out of the mouth is like a stone flung from the hand—you cannot stop its going its way and doing mischief; wherefore you must ... look well at what you have to say before letting it pass your lips.*

---

[29] *Op. Cit.*, p. 107.

[30] David P. McAstocker, S. J., ***The Little Virtues*** (Milwaukee: The Bruce Publishing Company, 1940) p. 174.

Various saints point out that God made us with one mouth but two ears. We are to listen twice as much as we speak. St. Bernard and St. Basil counsel the value of cultivating silence: *Continual silence, and removal from the noise of the things of the world and forgetfulness of them, lifts up the heart and makes us think of the things of heaven and set our heart upon them.* Not only Christian writers but the great pagan philosophers also counseled silence. In fact, Pythagoras insisted that his disciples keep silence for five years. Why? St. Alphonsus explains that *speaking well depends on so many circumstances; and we have such a bad habit of blurting out, regardless of these circumstances, just what comes into our head and whatever it pleases us to think, and that in any tone we like to take, without order, without consistency. Two things, mainly necessary for anyone to know how to speak, are achieved by silence. The first thing is that by dint of much silence we forget the evil style of conversation that we brought with us...The second thing is that by this silence we find...time to learn the right style of conversation.*[31] When a person listens rather than speaks, one learns quickly what not to say!

St. James, the author of one of the strongest epistles, is not afraid to "tell it like it is." He warns us *if any man thinks he is religious, and restrains not his tongue, he deceives himself, and his religion is in vain* (1:26). Next he describes the perfect person: *If any man offends not in word, he is a perfect man* (3:2).

St. Paul teaches, ***Let your speech, while always attractive, be seasoned with salt, that you may know how you ought to answer each one*** (**Colossians** 4:5-6). How does one learn to speak well? Begin by training your children that attractive speech does not monopolize conversations. **Talkativeness** is a craving for attention, the opposite of the virtue of modesty. It's a way to grab and keep the attention of others. **Bragging or boasting** is also a vice opposed to the virtue of modesty which

[31] ***Practice of Perfection And Christian Virtues, Vol. 2,*** *Op. Cit.*, p. 118.

St. Paul finds reprehensible. The vice of **complaining** is not only annoying but it draws attention to the fact that the complainer lacks the spirit of self-sacrifice. Those with a **critical spirit** also lack the virtue of modesty. Rather than criticizing, teach your teens to turn critical thoughts into thoughts of helping others. For example, if your teen criticizes someone for being a poor dresser suggest that your daughter offer to take the other girl shopping with her. If someone is doing poorly in school, encourage your teen to offer to help them. *Jack, I see that you have trouble with geometry. Can we do our homework together? Maybe I can help you.* Another is doing a job poorly. *Ann, can I help you with that project?*

A virtuous person refrains from being sharp, rude, or crude. Instead, he speaks and replies with kindness, gentleness, with affection, while listening with attention to others. To listen attentively, one has to focus completely on the person speaking, by looking at the speaker rather than looking around or at one's watch. By thinking before speaking one avoids hurting, wounding, or offending. Guide your children to speak with respect rather than sharply or in a raised voice. At times this will be difficult when one becomes upset unless your teens have developed charity in speech through a close friendship with Christ. If one is not growing spiritually it will be difficult not to be rude, hurtful, talkative or offensive in speech.

Teach your teens that loquaciousness keeps us short of time since we waste time talking. ***Proverbs*** tells us: ***He who guards his mouth, guards his soul*** (13:3). ***He who talks much will do hurt to his soul*** (***Ecclus.*** 20:88). ***He who talks much will go wrong on some point*** (***Ecclus.*** 5:2). ***There will not fail to be sin where there is much talking*** (***Prov.*** 10:19). ***As a city open and without circuit of walls, so is the man who cannot restrain himself in speech*** (***Prov.*** 25:29-28). ***There is a time to speak and a time to be silent*** (***Ecclus.***3:7). Living the virtue of modesty means knowing when to speak and when to keep silent. It would be wrong to keep silent when we need to speak out. But we should think before speaking. St. Vincent says *that we should make as much difficulty over opening our mouth to speak as over opening our purse to pay.*[32] St. Bonaventure agrees. He says that one should be as miserly with one's words as one is with one's money. St. Alphonsus counsels us to speak with reluctance, *looking first to see if you ought to speak at all, and then what you ought not say, and whether you are not saying more words than you ought...St. Ephrem says: "Before you speak, communicate first with God what you have to say and the reason and cause for saying it, and then speak as one who is fulfilling the will of God, Who wishes you to say what you do say"*(editorial emphasis).[33] Fr. McAstocker adds, *And if by some miracle of grace talkativeness does not cause us to fall from the Master's favor, it nevertheless has another bad effect: It consumes the priceless time we should be using for His honor and glory.*[34]

To whom we speak also dictates how we speak and what we say. Explain to your teens that they cannot speak to priests, religious, their parents, teachers and adults with the same familiarity in which they speak to their friends. Rather they are to speak with respect, in a low voice, never shouting or yelling at their parents or elders. St. Paul warns teens, ***Scold not an elder, but entreat him as a father*** (1 ***Tim***. 5:1). Scripture tells our youths, ***Be not talkative in a gathering of ancients*** (***Ecclus***. 7:15). St. Alphonsus Rodriguez writes: *It is a mark of good breeding and reverence to be silent in the presence of elders and in the presence of priests. St. Bernard says that youths honor their elders by silence—a good way of showing reverence and recognition—and by yielding them the precedence.*[35] This also means that youths should not interrupt adults who are speaking unless there is an emergency.

Timing is also important. There is a time to talk, to ask

---

[32] *Ibid.*, p. 131. [33] *Ibid.* [34] ***The Little Virtues,*** *Op. Cit.,* p. 190.
[35] ***Practice of Perfection And Christian Virtues, Vol. 2*** *Op. Cit.,* p. 132.

questions, or to relate events. One must be prudent in picking when to talk and when to listen or refrain from speaking. Modesty, as an aspect of intimacy that we discussed earlier, also relates to what we discuss and with whom we discuss it. Likewise, the virtue of modesty prevents us from prying into matters that do not concern us while modesty also obliges us to protect our privacy from nosey people. Again Scripture instructs us: ***The wise and prudent man will be silent and bide his time; but the foolish and indiscreet has no eye for time and opportunities*** (***Ecclus***. 20:7). One of the times we are to refrain from talking is when another is speaking. To interrupt is rude. St. Alphonsus adds that it shows a lack of humility on the part of the person who interrupts. This advice is also found in Scripture: ***While another is speaking, interrupt him not. Answer not until you have heard to the end what they are saying to you: for that is showing oneself a fool and worthy of confusion*** (***Prov***. 18:13). St. Basil gives further advice about answering questions: *If another person be asked, be you silent. And when there are many together and they are told to speak their mind on a question, if they do not ask you in particular, it shows a lack of humility to seek to make yourself the spokesman and take the matter up in the name of all. Until they tell you in particular to speak, be silent.*[36]

How we speak in regard to our tone of voice and manner is also important if one is to live the virtue of modesty. Refinement dictates that we refrain from shouting, yelling, screaming, using bad or crude language, taking the name of God, Jesus, Mary, or the saints in vain. We are never to discuss subjects opposed to modesty and chastity. St. Maria Goretti, while she was in town one day, overheard a couple speaking in a suggestive manner. Upon returning home she related the conversation to her mother. Upset by what her daughter had overheard, the mother told Maria that she was never to stay and listen to such talk but rather flee

---

[36] *Ibid.*, p. 133.

from the situation. Impress this same lesson on your teens.

We are not to be loud in our conversation. We are to keep our voice low so as not to disturb others around us. If we have to speak to someone in another part of the house or at a distance, rather than yelling we are to perform the sacrifice of going to them. Likewise St. Bonaventure counsels us to speak with serenity at all times, to avoid angry facial expressions or body language. When we have to correct another, St. Ambrose advises, *[w]arning and admonition must be without roughness and without offense.*

The virtue of modesty is not lived when we gossip or are uncharitable in our speech. St. James tells us, ***[d]o not backbite one another, brethren*** (4:11). St. Paul insists: ***Detractors are abhorred of God*** (***Rom***. 1:30). St. Bonaventure teaches us that *[y]ou should speak of the absent as you would if he was present; and that which you would not dare to say to his face or within his hearing you should not say behind his back.*[37] St. Bernard adds, *[n]ot only ought we to beware of saying what is objectionable, but also for giving ear to it, since a willing listener provokes the speaker, and also because it is a shameful and unseemly thing to give ear to matters evil and unseemly.*[38] To hurt another's reputation by speaking ill of the person can be a mortal sin. Likewise, the listener who encourages a person to speak against another can also be guilty of a mortal sin.[39] This would also be a sin against the virtue of justice.

Teach your teens to walk away from gossips or those who delight in talking about unchaste subjects. They can also change the subject or show by stern facial expressions that the information or subject is not acceptable. St. Josemaría disclosed, *when I have met people who make sex the central topic of their conversation and interests, I have felt they were abnormal, wretched people, even sick perhaps. And I would add (and the young people to whom I was speaking would burst out laughing at this point) that these poor things made me feel as much pity as would the sight of a deformed child*

[37] *Ibid.*,p. 140. [38] *Ibid.*,p. 142. [39] *Ibid.*

with an enormous head, one yard round. They are unhappy individuals. For our part, besides praying for them, we should feel a brotherly compassion for them because we want them to be cured of their pitiful illness. But what is quite clear is that they are in no way more manly or womanly than people who don't go around obsessed with sex.[40]

The virtue of modesty prohibits us from exaggerations or certitudes. St. Bernard advises, *[n]ever affirm or deny with unmeasured assertion and certitude that you know, but speak always with...the grace of some doubt saying for instance, "I think it is so," or "If I am not mistaken, it is so," "I fancy I have heard it said."* By not coming across as opinionated, we are also living the virtue of humility.

The virtue of modesty likewise prevents us from teasing, sarcasm, or malicious humor at another's expense or being the class clown. St. Bernard and St. Bonaventure suggest that *when we go out to converse with our neighbor, we should have ready certain good and profitable things to say to them; and when they speak of idle and vain things, we should promptly put in things of edification to cut short and change the conversation...*[41]

To sum this section up, teach teens to think before they speak. Copy the following list for them then ask your teens to reflect on these points before speaking.

Think Before Speaking

- ✓ What am I going to say?
- ✓ Why am I going to say this?
- ✓ Is what I'm going to say necessary?
- ✓ Will I be bragging, boasting, bossy, exaggerating, complaining, criticizing, gossiping, or slandering another?
- ✓ Will my conversation hurt or offend another?
- ✓ How am I going to say it?
- ✓ Is my speech free from profanity, blasphemy, impurity?

[40] St. Escrivá, ***Friends of God***, #179.

[41] ***Practice of Perfection And Christian Virtues, Vol. 2,*** *Op. Cit.*, p. 156.

- ✓ What tone of voice am I going to use?
- ✓ To whom am I speaking?
- ✓ Am I showing respect in my words and tone of voice to my parents, priests, religious, teachers, and others in authority?
- ✓ Is what I'm going to say rude, crude, disrespectful, impure or improper?
- ✓ Is what I'm going to say necessary?
- ✓ How can I say this concisely without rambling on and on?

3. Manner of Dress

"I cannot and will not cut my conscience to fit this year's fashions." Lillian Hellman

Modesty in dress begins with privacy. Privacy begins manifesting itself in young children when they want the bathroom door closed or are uncomfortable taking their clothes off for the doctor. Promote the development of the virtue of modesty by not permitting small children to run around naked after their baths or in the morning when they are getting dressed. If older children bathe the younger ones, girls should help the little girls and boys help the boys. Anyone can change diapers!

Insist that your children and teens walk around the house fully clothed for the sake of other family members. Besides, one never knows when someone will drop in. Explain to your children that "delicate" matters should be discussed privately with the parents, not in front of all the family. Teach your children never to barge into a room with a closed door. Explain that they are to knock first then wait to be summoned in.

Fr. John Hardon, S.J., writes that *modesty in dress is the best line of defense of the virtue of chastity.*[42] Why? Clothing protects our privacy. It sends the message that our body is

[42] John Hardon, S.J., "The Front-Line Defense of Chastity," Eternal Life Publications, Vol. 3, No. 1.

not available to anyone but to our spouse. Unfortunately, many devout people, even people who go to daily Mass and Holy Communion, are caught up in our culture, permitting their children and teens to dress immodestly **even** for church with micro mini skirts or shorts, tight fitting tops, see-through blouses, low-rise slacks with midriffs showing, plunging necklines that expose cleavage, spaghetti strap tops, tight pants, or tank tops. Dannah Gresh, the author of ***And The Bride Wore White: Seven Secrets to Sexual Purity*** revealed that *more and more teen guys are saying they are tempted by the way girls dress IN CHURCH. They are careful to include those two important words—IN CHURCH—because they feel so vulnerable in a place they should feel safe. Girls strut into church dressed in the name of fashion. I don't think they realize that they are actually creating such temptation.* ***Proverbs*** *5:18-19 tells us that a woman's body is intoxicating. The Hebrew writer told the male reader 'may you be intoxicated by her sex.' That speaks to the power of a woman's body. That same verse is talking about one man and one woman. This is consistent with scripture's admonition that the sensual gifts of our body are to be saved for one person. When we use that power to intoxicate many men by the way we dress, it is sin.*[43]

Sadly, these teens, and their parents who permit them to dress in this manner, have not developed the virtue of modesty. As I write this section there is a pile of newspaper clippings on my desk detailing the problem of immodest clothing. Let's examine some of the headlines: "Now There's Something New for Back-to-School: Racy Underwear" is a headline in the *Wall Street Journal*. "Thongs, Bust-Enhancing Bras Are a Hit with Some Teens: Walking the Sassy-Sexy Line" reads the subhead.[44] The headline in the *St. Louis Post Dispatch* is equally disgusting, "Schools update dress codes as near-naked fashions hit the halls." The subhead reads "Principals ask parents to help keep skin

[43] www.ridingthewaves.com/article17.htm

[44] Erin White, "Now There's Something New for Back-to-School: Racy Underwear," *The Wall Street Journal*, Aug. 3, 2002.

covered." In this article the mother interviewed was telling of her difficulty shopping for her daughter's wardrobe. *Everything is low-cut, slit up the side and too short. The materials are so flimsy. But that's all there is in the stores these days.* The mother was returning a dress her daughter, Ashley, purchased because it *clings to her too much.* Ashley told the reporter that the girls at her school were *competing to wear less and less.* At one St. Louis high school things became so out-of-hand that female students went to the principal to ask him to put a stop to the barelook. A principal at another school cited the concern of teachers about what girls are wearing to school. *They are observing males respond to the dress in a manner that is not appropriate and that girls should not think it is appropriate. Let's just say the comments are not ladylike at all.* What is even more distressing is that the article goes on to say, *It's not just the high schools. Middle school students, even elementary students in some cases, are coming to school in clothing considered inappropriate.*[45]

This raises two questions. Why are parents permitting their daughters to dress in this manner? Where are they getting their inspiration to dress this way? Dr. Janet Kuebli, professor of psychology at St. Louis University, blames the media. Both parents and the media are to blame. **Parents need to exercise the virtue of fortitude *and just say no* while at the same time turning off the TV and forbidding their teens to see objectionable films that inspire this type of dress.**

Dr. Janet Kuebli also suggests: *Parents should talk to kids about their motivations for dressing like this. I'm not sure all girls are knowledgeable about how males and older men react to that kind of dress. If you just tell teen-agers no, it's often not effective.* This story concluded with a coed saying, *Some girls wear really short skirts...They'll push it to the limit. That's how girls are.*[46] The next story is from the

[45] Michelle Meyer, "Schools update dress codes as near-naked fashions hit the halls," *St. Louis Post Dispatch*, Dec.12, 2001, p. 1.

[46] *Ibid.*

Wall Street Journal and its headline reads: "The Pared-Down Prom Dress." The subhead is worse: "Skimpy Styles Are in Vogue, But Backlash Is Brewing; A Mixed Blessing for Boys." This article explained the problem teens were having with the raunchy fashions. The reporter interviewed one teen looking for the perfect prom dress. *All the dresses left her feeling, well, undressed. Too-low-cut in front, and she couldn't bend over. Too low-cut in back—she'd be blushing all night. Too tight, and she couldn't dance.* From the male point of view, *with so many strapless or spaghetti-strap dresses, few boys bother to offer the traditional pin-on corsage. Others aren't sure where to place their hands while dancing, some girls report.* Commented one senior boy, *"I think a girl should look more princess-like. The pictures would look better with a nice full dress."*[47] When prom time arrives, mothers of sons voice their concern about the type of dress their sons' dates wear. Some mothers encourage their sons to take specific girls to the prom because the moms feel these girls will dress modestly.

Low-rise pants are another modesty problem. In the article "Darts and Shoelaces Cure a Downside To Low-Rise Pants," writer Suein L-Hwang's front page article in the *Wall Street Journal* discusses the lack of comfort in wearing this fashion. The subtitle is: "When Sharron Senter Felt A Breeze, She Knew She Had to Watch Her Back." The article goes on to say that *Ms. Senter says she has perfected a way of bending over that helps keep her pants from starting that scary slide. Like squats at the gym, it requires that she keep her back straight and her head forward at all times. "Look down and you're exposed."...Ms Senter says that vigilance is so ingrained she automatically turns her back to the wall before attempting to reach under her daughter's stroller...If you want to be fashionable, you've got to practice socially responsible bending.* The article continues: *Not since the streaking craze of the 1970s have so many backsides been on*

[47] Amy Merrick, "The Pared-Down Prom Dress," *Wall Street Journal*, May 11, 2001.

public display. But this time it's usually unintentional....If you aren't very careful, you end up showing too much. And while that might be just the ticket for some, it's a problem in need of a solution to women with even a modicum of modesty. In addition to being immodest, this fashion craze emphasizes a woman's hips making even thin teens and women look fat. How did this fashion craze start? *For years, the phenomenon was popularly associated with overweight workmen who fasten their toolbelts below their stomachs.*[48] Why imitate this? The writer than interviews various women to find out how they deal with sitting at bars (stand), sitting in a restaurant (get a booth or wear a long sweater), general problems (put in darts, hold the back of pants when bending, get longer shirts). For this foolishness women can pay over $100 for a pair of these pants. But the idiocy doesn't end there. I learned first hand that "fashion designers" provide low-risers for the diaper set when I tried to get a pair of pants on my granddaughter but they didn't fit over her diaper. It made me question whether these "designers" were depraved or simply morons. Since women complain that they cannot find "normal" pants anymore maybe it's time for women to return to the wearing of skirts. That would send a clear message to the designers! Just some trivia about fashion: did you know that it was actress Katharine Hepburn who started the custom of women wearing pants? Katharine wore pants because she wanted to be a man. She even nicknamed herself "Jimmy." She was a vocal supporter of Planned Parenthood, abortion rights, contraception and euthanasia.[48A] Is she really someone women should imitate?

What can you do to change the fashion climate? Complain! Complain to the buyer at your local store. Write letters to the designers. Designer Jessica McClintock *says that some customers think the cleavage-baring styles are stepping over the line. "We got an awful lot of letters from parents and kids*

---

[48] Suein L-Hwang, "Darts and Shoelaces Cure a Downside To Low-Rise Pants, *The Wall Street Journal*, July 25, 2003, p. 1.

[48A] ***Kate Remembered,*** *Op. Cit.*

who said, 'You know, we were looking for something simpler.'"[49] In Kansas *a group of about 20 high-school girls got so fed up with the lack of modest choices that one complained to customer service at a Nordstrom, Inc. store in Overland Park...Nordstrom executives invited them to explain what styles they would like. For four months, the girls—all members of a Kansas City area church youth group—combed through magazines and even sketched their own designs. Some asked seamstresses to make the gowns...Most of the designs were long gowns with covered shoulders, higher necklines and low or no slits...[T]he Nordstrom executives told the girls...that their buyers would look for more demure styles. "I think they had a lot of great ideas," says Lynn Brooks, a regional merchandiser who attended the [girls'] presentation.* The clothes were "*trendy but maybe not so bare and strappy." As word of their presentation spread, the girls say they received hundreds of letters and e-mails in support.*[50] Why not help your daughter to gather a group of friends to likewise complain and you can get a group of your friends together too. If you can't get a group, write letters of complaint yourself. Ask your high school principal for a "prom dress code." Other schools across the country are doing this. If all else fails, teach your daughter to sew so that she can sew her own clothes or find a friend or seamstress who will make chic but modest outfits for her.

You and your daughters dictate fashion trends by your clothing purchases. Designers want to sell their clothing to stores while at the same time stores want to make profits on the clothing they sell. If immodest clothing is not purchased, stores will no longer buy from those designers. The ultimate guilt for immodesty is on those who purchase these items then wear them.

Teach your daughter to make her own modest fashion statement. Point out that not all models follow the sleazy

---

[49] "The Pared-Down Prom Dress," *Op. Cit.*
[50] *Ibid.*

fashion designers. Turris Eburnea Association, an organization of fashion models, tries *to project the idea that a woman's external beauty is a reflection of her internal dignity.* One of the model members, 17-year-old Elena, explained, *this is not just about fashion parades but also ideas. To be modern, to be well groomed, is not opposed to our search for interior growth. We do not portray hollow mannequins but integral women who are enriched by values.*[51]

What does the Church say about fashion? St. Paul firmly stated:***...I wish women to be decently dressed, adorning themselves with modesty and dignity...***(1 ***Tim***. 2:9). St. John Chrysostom writes: *that out of foolish vanity and pride we have made another sin in his heart...we, by our manner of dress, carry our snare everywhere and spread our nets in all places.* Pope Pius XII in 1957 in an address to the Congress of the Latin Union of High Fashion stated: *An excess of immodesty in fashion involves, in practice, the cut of the garment. The garment must not be evaluated according to the estimation of a decadent or already corrupt society, but according to the aspirations of a society which prizes the dignity and seriousness of its public attire.* In ***Familiaris Consortio***, John Paul II points out: *The practice of decency and modesty in speech, action and dress is very important for creating an atmosphere suitable for the growth of chastity...parents should be watchful so that certain immoral fashions and attitudes do not violate the integrity of the home.* The Congress for Catholic Education put out a publication entitled *Educational Guidance In Human Love* in which it was explained: *Parents should teach their children the value of Christian modesty, moderate dress and, when it comes to trends, the necessary autonomy characteristic of a man or woman with a mature personality.* The Pontifical Council for the Family in its document, *The Truth and Meaning of Human Sexuality* #55 teaches, *[a]lso of importance [in the education for purity] are what Christian*

[51] Zenit, Oct. 31, 2001.

tradition has called the younger sister of chastity (modesty, an attitude of sacrifice with regard to one's whims), nourished by a strong faith and a life of prayer...Respect for privacy must be considered in close connection with decency and modesty, which defends a person who refuses to be treated like an object of pleasure instead of being respected and loved for himself or herself (#57).

Bl. Jacinta Marto, the visionary of Fatima, was told by Our Lady right before her death, *Woe to the women wanting in modesty!...Women are worse than men on account of the fashions.*[52] At another time Our Lady told her: *Fashions will be introduced which will offend Our Lord very much. People who serve God should not follow these fashions.* Even as she was dying in a hospital in Lisbon, Bl. Jacinta would point out to visitors and her nurses how offended Our Lady was by their low cut blouses and uniforms. Likewise it was at Fatima that Our Lady said that most people go to Hell because of sins against the flesh. Sister Lucia of Fatima told one American couple, *When I think of the United States, I think of this: One of the things which Our Lady especially asked was for modesty in dress. There seems to me not too much modesty in the life of the women of your country. But modesty would be a good sacrifice to offer Our Lady. If the Catholics in your country could establish a league for modesty in dress, it will greatly please Our Lady.*[53]

If your daughters are still not convinced, use quotations from Scripture such as ***Matthew*** 18:6, ***Matthew*** 5:8, ***1 Corinthians*** 6, ***Colossians*** 3: 5-6, ***Matthew*** 5:29-30 to prove your point. Teach your teens the words of St. Paul: ***For you know what precepts I have given to you by the Lord Jesus. For this is the will of God, your sanctification; that you abstain from immorality; that every one of you learn how to possess his vessel in holiness and honor, not in the passion of lust like the Gentiles who do not***

---

[52] Fr. Robert J. Fox, ***Saints & Heroes Speak Vol. 1***(Alexandria, Fatima Family Apostolate, 1996) p. 130

[53] Bro. Francis Mary Kalvelage, F.I., "Fatima Seers, Models for All to Imitate," p. 4.

know God...For God has not called us unto uncleanness, but unto holiness. Therefore, he who rejects these things rejects not man but God, who has also given his Holy Spirit to us (*1 Thessalonians* 4:3-8).

Spell out to your teens the importance of modesty in dress. Instinctively we women know that men are visually oriented while we are stimulated by touch, "sweet nothings" and tenderness. We inherently know the power our body has in attracting men. That is why women spend billions of dollars a year to look as lovely as we possibly can. Beauty elicits compliments, attention, and our way with men.

Sometimes we can get a little carried away with this desire for "attention" from the male sex by drawing attention to our body rather than ourselves by wearing that "itty-bitty bikini," tankini, a décolleté dress, tight sweater or other revealing clothing. Unfortunately this manner of dress arouses men to lust, not love. When your daughter insists on wearing immodest clothing ask her, *Do you really want a guy to be interested in you as a sexual object? Wouldn't you rather have him interested in you as a person he could love as his wife? Why advertise what is not for sale? Save the gift of self for your husband. Remember, nice guys are not attracted to loose looking women. Do you really want to give scandal, which leads another into temptation?*

Teach your daughters that a coed in a scanty outfit can easily find a guy looking for a quick romp, but turn off a "nice guy" with husband potential. But it's even deeper than that. Each male that passes you on the street, sees you in class, or works with you could become sexually aroused. This arousal could trigger sinful, lustful thoughts that could become mortal sins...serious sins that destroy the man's relationship with God. Should any of these men die in an accident in this state of mortal sin without time to repent, he will go to hell. But that's his problem, you say? No, it's also the problem of the woman who led him into temptation. She also sinned through her immodesty in dress. Point out to your daughters that their dignity rests on the fact that they are daughters of God, temples of the Holy Spirit. Dressing modestly shows a chaste, pure heart and high self-esteem. Warning his flock of the powerful temptations against the virtue of chastity, St. Ulric, bishop of Augsburg, advised, *Take away the fuel, and you take away the fire.*[54]

Next quote Katherine Kersten, chairman of the Center of the American Experiment, who points out: *If you want to date and marry a really good man, remember that modesty is a virtue that will be noticed as much as any "sexy" outfit. By dressing modestly, we can make a difference. You can be an example of purity to your family, friends and the men who see you. You'll feel better about yourself as you spend more time working on your inner beauty. You'll also greatly increase your odds of meeting a good man who will love you for your virtuous character than a man who thinks of you primarily as a "sex object". Modesty is a great way to stand out as a shining star in an impure world.*[55]

Monica Lewinsky used her thong to attract former President Clinton. In the beginning of their relationship he did not even know her name, or even *care* to know it. She was merely a body to be used for sexual gratification. She was dumped when she became a political liability. Using sex to get love never works. It leads to heartbreaking disasters such as unintended pregnancy, abortion, sexually transmitted diseases, depression, suicide, low self-esteem, adultery, and divorce. But even worse, spiritually it results in a complete break in our relationship with God. Besides, excessive sexual pleasures cause intellectual blindness in which *the intellect is completely unable to consider spiritual realities.*[56]

---

[54] Rev. Hugo Hoever, S.O. Cist., Ph.D., ***Lives of the Saints Illustrated Part I*** (NJ: Catholic Book Publishing Co., 1999) p. 282.

[55] Katherine Kersten Commentary, "Cosmopolitan's Philosophy of Unfettered Freedom," *Star Tribune*, June 11, 1997.

[56] Hugh McDonald, "We Are What We Watch and Read," Zenit, July 21, 2001.

Katherine Kersten adds: *In the delicate arena of male-female relations...we cannot do without limits and constraints. These used to be supplied, in part, by a general regard for modesty—decency in dress, speech and behavior, so as not to suggest ready sexual availability...Why is modesty important? Because it channels sexual desire—potentially one of the most selfish of human passions—into the selfless and productive context of marriage and family. Modesty rejects instant gratification. Instead, it promises gratification in harmony with society's central priorities—the procreation and rearing of children, and the successful transmission of culture to the next generation.*[57]

From the male viewpoint, Author Ron Hutchcraft contends that *many young women are naïve about the messages they are sending by what they wear and how they move.*[58]

Only when we rediscover the virtue of modesty ourselves can we then pass it on to our children beginning at a young age. Avoid two-piece bathing suits, even for preschoolers. Steer your daughter away from short shorts, minis, crop sweaters, anything that displays midriff, tank tops, spaghetti straps, anything low cut, sleazy prom dresses, see-through blouses, sleeveless tops, low-rise pants, slits above the knee, tight or form hugging clothing. Should your daughters protest, remind them that Pope John Paul II called the youth of the world to a "new martyrdom," to go against the tide of immorality and immodesty which chokes the goodness out of our world.

Explain to your teens that how we dress has consequences. It advertises our morals, or lack of morals, our values, or lack of values, and even how we feel about those we are with, not to mention how we feel about ourselves. When we wear immodest/seductive clothing we advertise that our body is available for the touching, either visibly or

---

[57] "Cosmopolitan's Philosophy of Unfettered Freedom," *Op. Cit.*
[58] Ron Hutchcraft, ***5 Needs Your Child Must have Met At Home*** (Grand Rapids: Zondervan, 1994) p. 57.

physically. With such a blatant sexual invitation is it any wonder that immodest clothing can not only lead to the loss of chastity but could trigger date rape? Writer Mary R. Andras notes: *Provocative exposure of the human body is at first attention getting. But it soon degenerates into arousing precisely the kind of aggressive and violent behavior which so often plagues today's society. Dressing with taste and simplicity beautifies the person and makes life more pleasant. Fashion should be an aspect of human life that leads us to God.*[59]

How did some well known parents deal with the issue of modesty in dress? When the von Trapp family performed, they always wore their native Austrian costumes. When asked why, Maria said that it saved money; they did not have to deal with the fashions of the day; but most of all *no nightmarish evening gowns which suffer from lack of material somewhere can haunt us.*[60] Gwen and Jerry Coniker, the founders of the Apostolate for Family Consecration, were also firm in regard to modest clothing. Daughter Maureen recalls, *I was now twelve and starting into the rebellious state. At that time short skirts were in style, but Mom and Dad had a seamstress make our skirts go below the knee. I was furious and cried for a couple of weeks. But Dad did not give in. Skirts were short then but not as short as they used to be, just above the knee. Thank goodness a year later the style was again below the knee. Now, however, I would never change to above the knee. As Dad always insisted, it is more modest. I remember how hard it was facing all that peer pressure. Now, I never regret what my parents did to teach me what was right, no matter if it meant being different.*[61]

Several months ago I attended a lecture by Annie Lang, a Fashion Consultant, who is presenting fashion curriculum in schools as well as giving seminars on fashion for mothers

[59] Mary R. Andras, "Fashions and their Effect on Society," *Catholic Position Papers,* No. 305, March 2001, p. 3.
[60] ***The Story Of The Trapp Family Singers***, *Op. Cit.*, p. 333.
[61] Peter Lappin, ***Challenge and Change*** (Bloomingdale, OH:Apostolate for Family Concentration, 1999) p.124.

and teens. Impressed by her ideas, I asked if she would share them with you. She graciously agreed.

TEENAGE GIRLS AND FASHION

By Annie Lang

As a fashion consultant, I receive numerous questions on how to handle teenage girls and their choices in fashion. The immodest and suggestive fashions that are prevalent in the media, in magazines and on television have an incredible impact on our young girls, who often lack sound judgment and objective criteria when selecting apparel. I have witnessed many arguments in the dressing room between mothers and daughters. All too often, most likely out of frustration and exhaustion, I see mothers reluctantly giving in to clothing that is immodest or too form fitting.

I share the concerns of mothers and other adults over the current trends in fashion for teens. Often teenagers do not understand that immodest and suggestive apparel is not only unattractive, but is also causing serious harm to themselves and society. The idea that self worth lies primarily in how physically beautiful you are or in how much of your body is exposed has so permeated the minds of our teenagers (and a large portion of our society as well) that it can be extremely difficult to convince a teen that she shouldn't walk out the door in many of the current fashions.

Having a teenage daughter myself, I know what a challenge this is. I remain optimistic, however, because I do think there are practical things we can do to help our teens make better choices. I have come up with a list of some positive steps you can take to help your daughters make good choices in the area of fashion.

1. Moms – Evaluate YOURSELF in the Area of Fashion !

What? You must be kidding, right? No, I am not kidding and let me explain. I was blessed with a grandmother and mother who paid close attention to fashion and the care of their appearance. While never overindulgent or vain, they both presented an excellent example to me of the importance of taking care of yourself and of your appearance. Because of this, they were excellent role models for me in the area of fashion.

I know of many teens that don't consider their mother as a good resource when choosing clothing. Unfortunately, many moms have put this area of their life on the back burner and therefore their daughters don't see mom as someone who cares about fashion or would have good advice or suggestions to give.

I recognize that staying up to date and fashionable is a real challenge for most women. So many demands on our time, limits to our budget, and those unwanted curves that arrive with the baby often make putting a polished look together difficult. Some women I talk to also worry about vanity and feel that putting emphasis on their appearance is wrong and displeasing to God.

If you identify with any of these challenges, I would like to ask you to look at your appearance and fashion from another point of view. What a beautiful act of charity it is when you dress not for yourself, but for all of those you will come in contact with throughout your day – your children, teachers, coworkers, and most importantly, your spouse. Think of how much time and effort you put into how you looked when you were dating. We keep the love in our marriages alive when we struggle to do the same throughout our marriage. In doing so, you are telling your spouse that you love him, as much or even more than you did when you were younger.

You also send a powerful message to your daughter, like my mother and grandmother did. If mom pays attention to how she looks, then your daughter is much more likely to listen to you when you have advice or suggestions on her appearance.

2. Say YES to Whatever You Can !!!

I have made this a real priority with my daughter. Not taking offense at her preference for chunky shoes, leopard belts, sweats, jeans and sparkly eye shadow have left me a lot of room to object in the areas that are really important to me, like immodest or tight clothing.

Just remember for a minute what it was like to be a teen. We all wanted to fit in. My mother tells a humorous story about wearing dog collars when she was a teen. She had every color she could find, with jewels and studs, and wore them with great pride because that was "in" then. Her mother did not make a big deal about that and she eventually replaced them with pearls and scarves.

I am also enjoying watching my own daughter evolve in her sense of style. At *almost* 16 she is showing less preference for "trendy" teen styles and is moving towards more sophisticated pieces. She recently purchased a handbag that was remarkably stylish. I was really impressed with her when she chose it and am trying to figure out if she would consider letting me borrow it! Be careful not to "nitpick". Choose your battles wisely.

Mothers should also recognize that *your* style might not be *her* style. For example, my mother has always chosen romantic fashions for herself. Her closet is filled with florals, embroidered pieces and pastels. I remember as a teen having a big argument over a lacey blouse she purchased for me that I absolutely refused to wear – not because *she* had purchased it for me, but because I absolutely hated lace! My personal style is classic with solid colors and simple designs being my fabrics of choice. However, my mother never realized this and often ended up hurt or frustrated when I did not appreciate her gifts.

Find out your daughter's style and purchase things that she will feel comfortable wearing. This will help her to see that you don't want her to dress like you, but in a manner consistent with her dignity.

3. Never Underestimate the Influence of DAD

I can honestly say that my daughter does not tend to want to purchase immodest clothing. We rarely fight in the dressing room or have arguments over clothing that is revealing or tight. Because this is so abnormal for a teenager, I began asking myself how could this be, given the culture she has grown up in. However, by observing the way my husband has related to my daughter from the time she was a baby, I think I have come up with one possible theory.

My husband is a very affectionate person by nature. He loves our six kids incredibly and is the kind of father that would rather spend time with his kids than do just about anything else. And being that he was blessed with only one girl (our other five children are boys!) he has lavished loads of affection and attention on her. While the boys' idea of spending quality time with dad is playing catch or watching a ball game, our daughter prefers sitting on the couch with her head on her father's shoulder and his arm around her.

By nature we all seek human affection. I have heard from more than one expert that women and girls need this human affection shown in a more physical way due to our unique psychological makeup. Which brings me to my theory. Perhaps because my daughter has received such a generous dose of affection from her father during her childhood years, she does not feel the need to look overly suggestive or provocative to attract the opposite sex.

And while the desire to attract the opposite sex is a normal and healthy part of God's designs to bring men and women together for the good of the human race, I would like to suggest that immodest dress could very well be a sign that a girl is looking for a disordered level of attention from the opposite sex – attention that should be coming from her father in her formative years. I encourage fathers to spend a lot of quality time with their daughters. It's one piece in the puzzle, but perhaps the most important one.

My husband also feels it is extremely important that my daughter and I not argue over clothing that I find objectionable. He has made it a priority to be the final say on questionable items. During the times when we have disagreed, as soon as I ask her what she thinks her father would say, the argument fizzles out quickly. She seems to know instinctively that, if she would be embarrassed to wear it in front of dad, she shouldn't purchase it at all. Knowing that I will be working with my daughter on most of her fashion choices, and his desire that we maintain a positive relationship in the area of fashion, my husband feels he can easily assume the role of "bad guy" if needed.

4. Be REASONable

Believe it or not, teens do have some capacity to reason things out. However, you need to look for creative ways of helping them come to their own conclusions about immodest apparel.

One technique that has worked very well for me when I present seminars on fashion to teenagers is to show them photographs of girls dressed both modestly and immodestly. Having them guess which girls are more likely to succeed in life has been enlightening. Inevitably the girls choose the ones who are more modestly dressed as those who are more successful, and those that are immodest are typically viewed in a negative light. This exercise proves to them that people judge by appearances, like it or not. If they acquire a negative impression of a person entirely based on their appearance, then people also do that with them. This is a great time to help them reflect on what they want to communicate to others with their appearance. Get them thinking!

Knowing some dressing strategies can also be helpful. For example, horizontal lines, whether in stripes or in clothing that pulls because it is too tight, emphasize and add weight. If your daughter is squeezing into a tight pair of jeans, they will pull at the hip area and make her look heavier than if she purchased the next size up. The larger size will actually make her look slimmer. Giving solid and factual information like this can help your daughter make better choices based on her figure type.

Most importantly, stay calm when you talk to your teens about clothing. Getting overly upset and arguing rarely solves anything. Let them know you admire their interest in fashion and looking their best. These are positive attributes that will serve them well throughout their life. Have patience, because like most phases in their life, this one will likely pass. Given an interested mother, solid support from her father and credible information, your daughter will have all the tools she needs to make better choices now and as she moves into full maturity.

Annie Lang presents fashion seminars for teens, women and corporations. She also has a curriculum on Leadership and Fashion for schools. What a great apostolate it would be to bring her into your parish or town![62]

While this section addressed the clothing for teen girls, modesty is likewise important for males. Tight fitting pants, bikini swimsuits, etc. are just as objectionable for boys as they are for girls. While it is not immodest for males to be topless, just out of a sense of refinement encourage your sons and husbands "to keep their shirts on".

In the area of dressing, as in every other area, the good example of the parents is primary. If mothers dress immodestly, their daughters will imitate them. Several months ago I attended "A Festival of Faith Conference" put on by the archdiocese of Chicago. Because of the large crowds huge TV screens were set up throughout the conference center so everyone could clearly see the altar for Mass. One of the readers, a woman in her late 60's or

[62] Annie Lang, Fashion Consultant, 2 Little Meadow Road, Wexford, PA, 15090, (724) 935-0995, talang@connecttime.net

early 70's, certainly old enough to know better, walked forward from the audience to make her way to the podium to read. When I saw her outfit on the screen I was so scandalized I gasped out loud, *Oh, no!* Her floor length, beaded gown was extremely low cut. The slit in her skirt looked like it came to her underwear line. Sitting on the altar watching her approach were eight bishops, many priests and the Cardinal! What a scandal this woman was to all the people attending, and she was clueless! A story is told about Bl. Pope John XXIII when he was a papal nuncio. At a state dinner he attended he was seated next to a woman wearing a low cut evening gown. On the table was a bowl of fruit. The papal nuncio took an apple from the bowl and offered it to the woman next to him. She declined the apple. *Please take the apple and eat it. It was only after Eve ate the apple that she realized she was naked*, explained Bl. John XXIII.

Along with how we adults dress, we also have to remind our pastors and bishops that we want the subject of modesty in dress addressed not only from the pulpit in church but also in our Catholic newspapers. In our diocesan paper there was a cover story on the Holy Father meeting with youth in Rome. The headline reads: "Be chaste, use summer vacation to boost prayer life, pope tells youth." The accompanying picture that takes up half the page is a rear view of three teenage girls sitting on a barricade looking up at the Holy Father. Two of the three girls are wearing skimpy spaghetti strap tops with one of the girls' bra straps visible. All three have their back midriffs showing and one's underwear is even showing above her low-rising pants. The editor of the paper did not catch the incongruity of the picture and the Pope pleading for teens to live chastity and modesty![63] Sadly, we have become insensitive to living the virtue of modesty in dress. It is time to turn this situation around. Start by considering, what do your daughter's clothes say about her?

---

[63] *Catholic Times,* "Be chaste, use summer vacation to boost prayer life, pope tells youth." July 13, 2003.

4. Manner of acting, gesturing walking, sitting, and touching.

"As clear water reflects the countenance of them that look into it, so the prudent man knows the hearts of men by the cast of their exterior."
Proverbs 27:19

Remember the adage, "Actions speak louder than words"? It is true. Point out to teens that all their actions should be modest, refined, and Christ-like. This includes dancing. They should never move or act in a manner that would be suggestive or erotic. From dancing let's make the leap to "Living together." Whether the couple plans to play house or simply to save money by sharing an apartment it is morally wrong and a mortal sin opposed to the virtue of modesty. It likewise gives scandal.

Recall the song, "There's a kind of walk you walk when you're feeling happy. There's a kind of walk you walk, when you're feeling blue"? This is also true. A person can simply walk or slink. One can stroll or titillate with bumps and grinds. Check out your daughter's walk. Help her to modify it if it is suggestive.

Explain to teens that no matter how upset they get with someone whether during an argument or when driving, they are not to use obscene gestures or foul language.

The simple action of bending over or stooping to pick something up can cause unwelcome exposure for women even in modest tops or dresses. Encourage your daughters to check in their mirror what happens when they bend over. Exposure can be avoided by putting one's hand on the top of the shirt or dress and holding it until the bend or stoop is completed. A heroic example of modesty is St. Joan of Arc when she was wounded by an arrow to the chest in one of her major battles. Surrounded by men on the battlefield, she refused to permit any of them to remove the arrow. Instead, she painfully removed it herself to protect her modesty. St. Joan, a lovely young teenager, not only cut her beautiful long hair but she wore men's clothing so that she could modestly lead her soldiers. She realized that dressed as an attractive young woman she might be a possible temptation against the virtues of modesty and chastity for her soldiers. So she dressed as a young boy.

We can sin against the virtues of modesty and chastity in our choice of profession. WGN TV ran a story about Catholic parents who owned a "Gentlemen's Club" in the Chicago area. This is a euphemism for a sex club. The mother wanted to run for the Catholic school board but her pastor refused her permission because of their business profession. The parents were so angry at what they perceived as an injustice that they pulled their child out of school and told the TV reporter they are leaving the Church.[64] This family made their living from the vice of lust. This is a mortal sin. They were no longer practicing the Catholic faith when they opened that club.

The issue of how one looks while sitting also impacts the virtue of modesty. If skirts are worn, they should come to the knee when sitting. Check out how far shorts ride up when one sits. Strive to purchase longer Bermuda shorts to avoid the short, short look when sitting. How one sits is equally important. Legs should be kept together. If legs are crossed, women should not cross their legs in the same manner as men even if they are wearing slacks.

Modesty insists that we treat everyone with dignity which means keeping one's hands to one's self. Couples can hold hands, or put an arm around a shoulder if it stops at that, (but not in church). Anything else is off limits. A quick kiss is acceptable but passionate kisses, French kisses and "too close for comfort" positions are neither modest nor chaste for the single.

---

[64] WGN TV April 15, 2002.

Make clear to your teens that an action always precipitates a reaction. Take for example this news story from Philadelphia: *A man described by authorities as a known sexual offender was chased through the streets of south Philadelphia by an angry crowd of Catholic high school girls, who kicked and punched him after he was tackled by neighbors, police said Friday. The 25-year-old man, who has exposed himself to teenage girls on as many as seven occasions outside St. Maria Goretti High School, struck again on Thursday just as students were being dismissed, police said. But this time, a group of girls in school uniforms angrily confronted the man with help from some neighbors, police said. When the man tried to run, more than 20 girls chased him down the block. Two men from the neighborhood caught him and the girls took their revenge....Police said he would be charged with 14 criminal counts including harassment, disorderly conduct, open lewdness and corrupting the morals of a minor.*[65]

The Role of Privacy in Modesty

As we said at the beginning of this chapter, modesty begins with privacy. Dr. David Isaacs notes three signs that indicate a child values his privacy:

1. They begin to shut others out from certain spheres of their life, to do with their body or their emotions.
2. They are capable of remaining silent and alone for certain periods.
3. They keep their private matters safe by seeking guidance from an appropriate person.[66]

Our home is not only our castle but a place of privacy where we retreat to reflect, to relax, to be ourselves. It is a private place to invite a friend to share confidences. While the home is our private domain, our children also need a private space of their own. For little children it may simply be a dresser,

65 "High school girls pummel flasher," *State-Journal Register*, Nov. 1, 2003.
66 ***Character Building,*** *Op. Cit.,* p. 107.

or toy box or even a drawer in the child's room. Adolescents need more private space. If a private room is not possible, can part of a bedroom be portioned off? Can a basement corner be turned into a teen hangout so that your teen can have a place to take his friends when they come over? By making space available for your teen and his friends you will get to know the friends as well as the influence they have on your teen. When your teen begins dating, you want him to feel comfortable bringing his date home to watch a video, play cards, games, or pool. If the teen feels he cannot invite his date home, he will look for someplace "private" outside the home such as his car or a bar with their associated risks.

Dr. Isaacs reminds parents: *The proper sphere of intimacy for two young people who are still far from being able to think of marriage is an area involving discussion of ideas, thoughts and plans, sharing some kind of activity such as study, practicing some hobby, going for a walk or to the cinema, for example. If the youngsters have developed a proper sense of modesty they will see how far they should and should not go in this kind of intimacy and they will behave accordingly. Modesty will draw a veil of respect over any premature physical outbursts or over inappropriate revelations on matters affecting the deepest recesses of the human heart.*[67]

A Final Thought

Super Bowl 2003 showed families the power they have to transform our culture when they speak out to demand change. When Janet Jackson and Justin Timberlake pulled their obscene publicity stunt during halftime, the FCC was immediately flooded with email complaints. This led to apologies from the head of the NFL football league, CBS, and the culprits personally involved. Apart from Jackson's sleaze, the show itself was debased. The public outcry made other events reevaluate their proposed entertainment. The Pro Bowl scheduled for the following week canceled their

[67] *Ibid.*

planned entertainment bringing instead native dancers and conch blowers. It was the first time I saw hula dancers wearing black teeshirts with their grass skirts! The NBA basketball officials went over the words for all the songs planned for their extravaganza. They cut out two songs even though the composer offered to change the objectionable words. They were not going to take any chances. Teach your teens never to accept the role of being a "victim" of the times. Teach them to speak out, to complain verbally, to phone in complaints, fax complaints, email complaints, and write letters to the companies involved as well as letters to the editors. Speak out! You and your teens can make a difference!

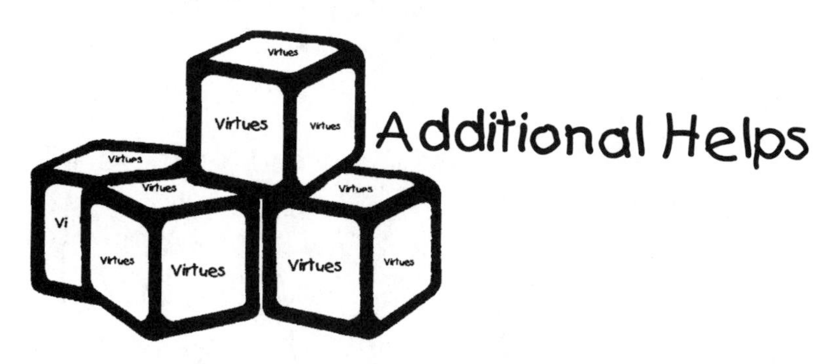

- ✓ Read the Scepter Booklets "With Respect To Sex..." #158 by Dr. Daryl Glick and "Sex and The Education of Our Children" #170 by William J. Bennett online at Scepter Publishers Or Listen to these booklets on audiotape from R.B. Media, Inc.
- ✓ View Radix's video, *How Far Can You Go? Unpacking the Sixth & Ninth Commandments* from St. Joseph Communications (800) 526-2151 with your teens. It's excellent.

Scripture verses for modesty in speaking:

Matt. 12:34
James 1:19
Tit. 2:7-8
1 John 4:5
Psalm 3, 38:2

Ecclesiastes
7:15; 20:22; 21:29; 22:3; 28:28; 29:13; 7:20; 41:15

Proverbs
21:23; 22:1; 24:9; 25:11; 25:22-23

CHAPTER 4

HOW TO TEACH THE VIRTUE OF CHASTITY

"Two roads diverged in a wood. And I took the one less traveled by and that has made all the difference." Poet Robert Frost

Imagine my shock the day I opened my latest copy of *Food and Wine* magazine to read the following editor's column: *My first encounter with wine country was a romantic one—and the association has remained. After college, I headed to Napa Valley with a friend, hoping a little alcohol and a change of scenery might change our status from friends, to, well, more than friends. We went from winery to winery...then returned to our (shared) room in a lazy, hazy way. But it was the love affair with the vine, not the guy that lasted.*[1] This woman made sure there was no doubt in her readers' minds that in search of romance she shared a room with a guy by emphasizing the fact with parentheses. Why did she think it was important for thousands of readers to know she committed a mortal sin? Disclosing her lack of chastity caused her no shame or embarrassment. Why not?

[1] Dana Cowin, "from the editor", *Food & Wine*, Oct. 2002, p. 25.

How about this article? *Pageant bureaucrats ordered Miss America, Erika Harold, to say no more about the virtue of virginity. Miss America was furious. Public ridicule blossomed. Within hours, pageant bureaucrats said it would be OK, after all, for Miss America to continue promoting sexual abstinence among teens.*[2]

Another article reveals that in Canada the number of married couples increased by 3% since 2001 but the number of cohabiting couples increased by 20%. This is 1.2 million people living in grave mortal sin. This same survey found that 40% of couples ages 30 to 39 chose cohabitation as their first union. *For women aged 20 to 29, the percentage is estimated to reach 53%.*[3] In England and Wales, four out of ten children are born outside of marriage. In Ireland, one out of three children is born outside of marriage. In 1999 49% of births in Norway were outside of marriage. For Iceland the figure was a shocking 62%. France showed a 41% illegitimacy rate.[4]

Robert Frost's lines above could easily be applied to the **virtue of chastity**. It is the road less traveled today but if one is striving for happiness, joy, and eventually eternity with God, it is the **only road to travel**. It is the "yellow brick road" to peace and serenity. Yet John Paul II says that *[i]t is hard, for the uncommitted mentality that invades a good part of society and the culture of our time, to understand the beauty and value of chastity...[S]exuality [is] a factor that affects all the aspects of a person and hence, must be lived with an inner attitude of freedom and reciprocal respect, in the light of the original plan of God. In this perspective, the person discovers himself or herself as the object of a gift and is called at the same time to become a gift to the other.*[5]

What do the saints say about this virtue? St. Caesarius of Arles stresses: *[b]ecause Christ is both truth and justice,*

---

[2] "Virginity Scores," *American Free Press,* Oct. 21, 2002, p. 2.

[3] Zenit, July 20, 2002. [4] Zenit, July 20, 2002. [5] Zenit, July 8, 2002.

whenever either justice or truth or chastity is in difficulty, you will receive the reward of the martyrs if you have defended it with whatever strength you possess...Let us with God's help strive to preserve bodily chastity and purity of heart. Christ commends chastity to you for the few days in which you live in the world in order that He may make you like the angels in heaven. Bl. John XXIII insisted that *[p]urity of heart, carefully and constantly guarded, becomes the rule, and the radiance, of our whole life, and of every word and deed.* Bl. Jacinta of Fatima told the nun who was caring for her during her final illness, *[t]o be pure in body means to preserve chastity.*[6] Bl. Pierina Morosini, who died protecting her virginity in 1957, prayed, *May I never allow myself even the smallest compromise with sin, whether in dress, speech, reading, looks, or entertainment.* St. Peter Julian Eymard points out that *as long as a man is not master of his body, he is neither holy nor really pious. He may perform good actions, but he is not in a state of solid and lasting piety.*[7]

Before we delve deeply into the virtue of chastity, Father Jack Kubeck of the Prelature of Opus Dei put together thirteen points for us to consider. Please share these points with your teens.

LOVING CHASTELY

Learning to love others as persons—human beings—composed of body and soul.

1) Attraction to the opposite sex is neither evil, nor the result of original sin, but a divine gift to each human person, male and female, for the purpose of increasing the family of God's children.

2) However, this attraction—good, and even holy, in itself—must be clearly and decisively distinguished from the disordered lust of concupiscence.

---

[6] Msgr. Joseph A. Cirrincione, ***Ven. Jacinta Marto of Fatima*** (Rockford,IL: Tan Books & Publishers, Inc., 1992) p. 55.
[7] ***In the Light of the Monstrance,*** *Op. Cit.*, p. 77.

3) This is accomplished—with the constant aid of divine grace—by always striving to *see* the person made visible in each and every body, i.e., each and every body is always a unique, individual person.

4) A further consideration, in this regard, is to make the decisive effort to always look at everybody precisely as a whole human being, a human person. (See no. 11 below.)

5) We readily tend to focus upon a person's body considering it apart from the whole of what they are as a human being. In this situation the person's body readily becomes a mere object, an object of lust for us, while the person to be loved is lost sight of, being reduced to this falsifying abstraction.

6) By viewing the human person as the whole reality that they are —made up of body and soul— we can then come to *see* every human body as a human person.

7) Every human person needs encouragement, support, correction, material assistance, spiritual esteem, companionship, affection and understanding; and this can be supplied only by another person.

8) Lust artificially and cruelly separates the 'components' (the 'body' from the 'soul') of the human person and rivets its exclusive focus on the body as a mere object (turning it into an abstract "article"), while disregarding the person —whose body we see— as a subject to be loved!

9) The only appropriate response, therefore, to another human being —as a person— is to love him/her.

10) As we begin to *see* human beings as whole persons (creatures made up of 'body—'soul', incarnate spirits), the process of destroying lust in ourselves begins and continues to wane until it ultimately disappears in the next life (but never entirely in this life).

11) In this life, however, all the ascetical practices needed to live chastely must be employed—i.e., keeping custody of our eyes, imagination, memory, etc.. Only in this way can we ultimately begin to see other human beings in their fullness, as beings made up of 'body'—'soul'—as incarnate persons.

12) Each created person is meant by God to be—literally—a gift to every other created person—a loving subject to be loved by another loving subject. We mirror, reflect or imitate, in this way, the intimate life of the Holy Trinity.

13) Celibacy is not a sacrament, because it is not just a sign of our ultimate union with the Triune God in Christ Jesus. It is already the dawning within us of that ultimate loving union of Christ, the Bridegroom, with his Bride, the Church. And all of those who are learning (persons struggling on earth) or have learned (the saints triumphant in heaven) to love chastely are incorporated into that Church.

What Is The Virtue Of Chastity?

"Every human life is really a personal decision of what we do with our bodies. Do we allow the power of sin or the power of redemption to hold sway?" Msgr. Vincent Walsh

The virtue of modesty protects the major virtue of chastity which comes under the cardinal virtue of temperance. Sometimes people interchange chastity and purity. But *purity is a general attitude of mind, rather than a "virtue"*[8] ...while chastity is the virtue. Chastity is called the "angelic virtue" which makes us like the angels. What precisely is chastity? The ***Catechism of the Catholic Church*** teaches:

> **#2345 Chastity is a moral virtue. It is also a gift from God, a grace, a fruit of spiritual effort. The Holy Spirit enables one whom the water of Baptism has regenerated to imitate the purity of Christ.**

---

[8] Rev. E. C. Messenger, Ph.D., ***Two In One Flesh, Vol. 2, The Mystery Of Sex And Marriage*** (Westminster, Maryland: The Newman Press, 1948) p. 117.

#2337 Chastity means the successful integration of sexuality within the person and thus the inner unity of man in his bodily and spiritual being. Sexuality, in which man's belonging to the bodily and biological world is expressed, becomes personal and truly human when it is integrated into the relationship of one person to another, in the complete and lifelong mutual gift of a man and a woman.

The virtue of chastity therefore involves the integrity of the person and the integrality of the gift.

#2339 Chastity includes an apprenticeship in self-mastery which is a training in human freedom. The alternative is clear: either man governs his passions and finds peace, or he lets himself be dominated by them and becomes unhappy. "Man's dignity therefore requires him to act out of conscious and free choice, as moved and drawn in a personal way from within, and not by blind impulses in himself or by mere external constraint. Man gains such dignity when, ridding himself of all slavery to the passions, he presses forward to his goal by freely choosing what is good and, by his diligence and skill, effectively secures for himself the means suited to this end."

Put more simply, Rev. E. C. Messenger, Ph.D., writes that *[c]hastity...is the virtue which prescribes due moderation in the exercise of the sex appetite, confining it within the bounds of right reason....Chastity is quite compatible with the use of sex within the married state. But chastity obviously excludes the exercise of sex outside that state.*[9] Furthermore, *chastity is a recognition that both the physical and emotional dimensions of our sexual nature are too important to be left to any passing whim,* writes Fr. Peter Harman of the Springfield, Illinois Diocese. He adds, *[i]t is more than saying "no" to some actions depending upon our state in life.*

[9] *Ibid.*, p. 10.

It is an understanding of why it might be good to do so. But it does begin with knowing the proper boundaries for how to develop such understanding.

That chastity would mean abstinence before marriage and complete fidelity during marriage may seem to be too demanding. But in a real way, it frees us from so much confusion and pressure. It allows a couple to become closer for the right reasons, and to communicate at the proper levels, and not be overwhelmed or pressured into a marital decision.[10]

Sins opposed to the virtue of chastity are lust (thoughts, words, actions, or desires), masturbation, fornication (living together outside of marriage which Christ calls *the unclean spirit* in the Gospels), pornography, prostitution, rape, homosexual acts, polygamy, incest, pedophile acts, adultery, contraception, sterilization, free unions, trial marriages and divorce. Sins against chastity are mortal sins.

Fr. Joseph Malaise, S.J. points out that *[t]here is an innate inclination to sexual pleasure in human nature, which begins to manifest itself normally at the age of puberty, and increases in intensity during the age of adolescence. This sexual tendency is not of itself sinful, since it is in us by nature, as long as we do not yield to it. But it is grievously sinful to seek even slight unlawful venereal pleasure, or to consent to it deliberately even when it has not been directly sought.* He continues: *To control this sexual tendency is a virtuous act, very meritorious in the sight of God. It contributes more than anything else in the building up of a good character...There is no vice more disastrous to the physical, mental, and spiritual welfare of man than the vice of lust.*[11]

Explain frankly to your teens that slipping seriously just once by not living the virtue of chastity can have lifetime repercussions. A child can be conceived panicking the parents into getting an abortion. The anguish, the guilt,

[10] Fr. Peter Harman, "Freedom of chastity allows loving relationships," *Catholic Times*, Springfield, IL, Jan. 6, 2002, p. 6.

[11] ***Know Yourself,*** *Op. Cit.*, pp. 81-82.

possibly medical problems in the future or the inability to conceive a future child can result from that sequence of events. Or, the mother may elect to keep her baby but that child is raised in a single parent home without the benefit of a father. It may be difficult for the mother to find a good husband because chaste guys are not attracted to girls who show poor judgment as well as the lack of self-control. Another scenario, the mother is unable to finish school or to go on for a higher degree. She is stuck at the poverty level with little hope of bettering herself and her child. Even if none of the above happens, in an article entitled "A Lot of Groping, Yes, but Not Much Happiness", in the *The Wall Street Journal,* Dr. Gareth Leng of the University of Edinburgh says that *[t]his type of intense contact does change us.*[12] Researchers at the University of Edinburgh found that *during sexual intimacy, a woman's brain releases a chemical "love potion" that alters her brain's hormonal reactions. Not only does the release of this chemical, oxytocin, create for her a bond with her mate but it appears that the more sex the couple has, the deeper her sense of commitment and love will become. Men's brains—surprise!—do not work the same way. Which suggests that if you wanted to devise a prescription for sexual misery and social wreckage, 30 years of frantic, indiscriminate coupling would pretty much be it.*[13] Fr. Winfrid Herbst, S.D.S.,laments that, *[i]t is often truly said that the greater part of mankind spends the first years of life to make the last miserable.*[14]

The Culprit...Original Sin

How did we reach this moral low? It all began with original sin, when our first parents rebelled against God. Fr. Messenger points out that *we can distinguish two special results of human sin. One is the progressive darkening of man's intellect so far as his knowledge of God is concerned. This has led to the abandonment or the overclouding...of*

[12] Meghan Cox Gurdon, "A Lot of Groping, Yes, but Not Much Happiness, *The Wall Street Journal*, Oct. 25, 2001. [13] *Ibid.*
[14] ***Follow The Saints,*** *Op. Cit.*, p. 53.

...belief in one God...Side by side with this degeneration in religious ideas, we find a corresponding corruption in sexual morality. The primitive monogamy was abandoned quite early in human history in favor of polygamy...and side by side with all this there has been a still worse tendency towards sexual immorality of various kinds outside the marriage bond. Another remarkable and significant feature is that these two lines of development in human thought, religious and sexual, have had repercussions upon each other.[15] We see this clearly today. **If people are unwilling to live morality according to the teachings of the Church neither are they likely to believe in the other teachings of the Church such as belief in the Real Presence, infallibility, etc. This leads to a falling away from the Catholic faith.**

The lack of chastity has caused problems throughout the centuries. Let's consider several Scripture examples. Herod Antipas, the son of Herod the Great, is our first example. If you recall, it was Herod the Great who had all the male children two-years-old and under killed in the Holy Land for fear that baby Jesus would usurp his throne. Herod Antipas, his son, had St. John the Baptist arrested because John publicly condemned him for living openly in sin with his brother's wife, Herodias. Herod, although fascinated by John, could not stand John's constant appeals to his conscience. His mistress, Herodias, hated John's constant reminders that they were living in sin. When an opportunity arose she seized it. She told her daughter, Salome, to ask for the head of St. John. The lack of chastity led to murder. Herod's end was pretty awful. He was eaten alive by worms.

This isn't the first time we read in Scripture how the lack of chastity led to murder. In the Old Testament, King David, looking out from his roof top, saw a beautiful woman, Bathsheba, bathing. He was not practicing custody of the eyes that we discussed in the last chapter. Even after learning that Bathsheba was married to Uriah, a member

---

[15] ***Two In One Flesh...***, *Op. Cit.*, p. 56.

of his military, he still lusted after her. He knew that adultery was punishable by death according to the command of God in the ***Book of Leviticus***. Lacking the virtue of chastity, he slept with Bathsheba anyway. When she became pregnant David panicked. He had Uriah called home from the battlefield hoping he would have relations with his wife. When that failed, he sent Uriah back to the battlefield with a letter telling his commander to put him in the thick of the fighting so he would be killed. He was. After the required period of mourning, David married Bathsheba. The prophet Nathan rebuked David telling him that although David's life would be spared, God will ***stir up evil for you out of your own House...[B]ecause you have outraged Yahweh by doing this, the child that is born to you is to die*** (***2 Samuel*** 12:11-25). David plunged himself into prayer and fasting hoping to change God's mind. But God was firm. His life grew more miserable after the death of his child. His firstborn son, Ammon, raped his own sister, Tamar. Absalom, another brother, killed Ammon in revenge. Next Absalom attempted to dethrone his father David but is killed. Read with your teens ***2 Samuel*** starting at chapter 12 verse 11. The lack of the virtue of chastity in this case leads to adultery, murder, rape, intrigues, and many more murders. But it also formed a very dysfunctional family similar to the abundance of dysfunctional families we see today.

In ***Genesis*** we read how God punishes homosexual acts which are also offenses against the virtue of chastity. God told Abraham and his nephew, Lot, to leave their homeland. Due to their vast combined herds the two separated, with Lot settling in the Jordan plain which was ***irrigated everywhere—this was before Yahweh destroyed Sodom and Gomorrah—like the garden of Yahweh or the land of Egypt, as far as Zoar...Lot settled among the towns of the plain, pitching his tents on the outskirts of Sodom. Now the people of Sodom were vicious men, great sinners against Yahweh*** (***Genesis*** 13:10-13). When God told Abraham that he was going to destroy Sodom and

Gomorrah because of their sins of homosexuality, Abraham began that famous passage in Scriptures where he bargains with God to save Sodom if fifty or even ten good men are found there. Ten good men could not be found so the town was destroyed (***Genesis*** 18:16-33). But before it was destroyed, the men of Sodom surrounded Lot's home demanding that he hand over the two angels who came to lead him and his family to safety because the townsmen wanted to sexually abuse them. When Lot refused, they tried to kill him as they attempted to break into his house to grab the male looking angels. ***Yahweh rained on Sodom and Gomorrah brimstone and fire...He overthrew these towns and the whole plain, with all the inhabitants of the towns, and everything that grew there...Rising early in the morning Abraham...saw the smoke rising from the land, like smoke from a furnace*** (***Genesis*** 19:1-29). The irrigated garden that Lot chose for his portion was destroyed because of the sins committed against chastity by the inhabitants. Even to this day the land in that area is incredibly desolate. Little grows but scrub. Archeologists believe that Sodom and Gomorrah are buried under the silt of the Dead Sea. The chemicals in the water are so intense that once a person begins to swim or float it's almost impossible to stand in the water due to its buoyancy. The mud found in various pockets in the Dead Sea is known for its health benefits but it is so chemically rich that if you leave the mud on your skin for more than 10 minutes the skin will sustain a burn. God explained why He took such strong action toward Sodom and Gomorrah in the ***Book of Leviticus***: ***You must not lie with a man as with a woman. This is a hateful thing*** (***Leviticus*** 18:22).

Haven't you wondered why God commanded the Israelites to kill all the inhabitants of a city or plain, even the women? The answer is found in ***Leviticus*** 18 where God gives the Israelites a long list of sins against chastity that He will not tolerate. He warns them: ***Do not make yourselves unclean by any of these practices, for it was by such things that the nations that I have expelled to make***

way for you made themselves unclean. The land became unclean; I exacted the penalty for its fault and the land had to vomit out its inhabitants. But you must keep my laws and customs, you must not do any of these hateful things...If you make it unclean, will it not vomit you out as it vomited the nation that was here before you? Yes, anyone who does one of these hateful things, whatever it may be, any person doing so must be cut off from his people. Keep to my rules; do not observe the hateful practices that were observed before you came, then you will not be made unclean by them. I am Yahweh your God (***Leviticus*** 18:24-30; editorial emphasis). Does this give you an idea how God views "gay marriages" and gay acts?

Let's digress briefly. My intention was not to get deeply into the subject of homosexuality but as I was writing this section I stopped briefly to meet a friend for lunch. Over lunch she brought up the topic then revealed a startling ignorance of the whole issue. For this reason I decided to briefly tackle this subject using the Statement issued by the Catholic Medical Association which was adapted by Zenit in two parts, April 18 and April 20, 2003. Please check out the Web site listed in the footnote for the complete statement. It is required reading.[16]

The statement begins:

The Catholic Medical Association (CMA) supports the teachings of the Catholic Church as laid out in the revised version of the ***Catechism of the Catholic Church***, in particularly the teachings on sexuality: ***All the baptized are called to chastity*** (***CCC***, no. 2348): ***Married people are called to live conjugal chastity; others practice chastity in continence*** (***CCC***, no. 2349); ***tradition has always declared that homosexual acts are intrinsically disordered... Under no circumstance can they be approved*** (***CCC***,

[16] http://www.cathmed.org/index.html

no. 2333).

It is possible, with God's grace, for everyone to live a chaste life including persons experiencing same-sex attraction, as Cardinal George, Archbishop of Chicago, so powerfully stated in his address to the National Association of Catholic Diocesan Lesbian & Gay Ministries: *To deny that the power of God's grace enables those with homosexual attractions to live chastely is to deny, effectively, that Jesus has risen from the dead.*

There are certainly circumstances, such as psychological disorders and traumatic experiences, which can, at times, render this chastity more difficult and there are conditions which can seriously diminish an individual's responsibility for lapses in chastity. These circumstances and conditions, however, do not negate free will or eliminate the power of grace...This in no way implies a genetic predetermination or an unchangeable condition. Some surrendered to same-sex attractions because they were told that they were born with this inclination and that it was impossible to change the pattern of one's sexual attraction. Such persons may feel it is futile and hopeless to resist same-sex desires and embrace a "gay identity"...The research referenced in this report counters the myths that same-sex attraction is genetically predetermined and unchangeable and offers hope for prevention and treatment...A number of authors have carefully reviewed these studies and found that not only do the studies not prove a genetic basis for same-sex attraction; the reports do not even contain such claims...There are, however, ongoing attempts to convince the public that same-sex attraction is genetically based. Such attempts may be politically motivated because people are more likely to respond positively to demands for changes in laws and religious teaching when they believe sexual attraction to be genetically determined and unchangeable. Others have sought to prove a genetic basis for same-sex attraction so that they could appeal to the courts for rights based on this "immutability."

Healthy psycho-sexual development leads naturally to attraction in persons of each sex for the other sex. Trauma, erroneous education, and sin can cause a deviation from this pattern. Persons should not be identified with their emotional or developmental conflicts as though this were the essence of their identity. It is, therefore, probably wise to avoid wherever possible using the words "homosexual" and "heterosexual" as nouns since such usage implies a fixed state...

Individuals experience same-sex attractions for different reasons...In the histories of persons who experience same-sex attraction, one frequently finds one or more of the following:

- ❑ Alienation from the father in early childhood because the father was perceived as hostile or distant, violent or alcoholic.
- ❑ Mother was overprotective (boys).
- ❑ Mother was needy and demanding (boys).
- ❑ Mother emotionally unavailable (girls).
- ❑ Parents failed to encourage same-sex identification.
- ❑ Lack of rough and tumble play (boys).
- ❑ Failure to identify with same-sex peers.
- ❑ Dislike of team sports (boys).
- ❑ Lack of hand/eye coordination and resultant teasing by peers (boys).
- ❑ Sexual abuse or rape.
- ❑ Social phobia or extreme shyness.
- ❑ Parental loss through death or divorce.
- ❑ Separation from parent during critical developmental states.

In some cases, same-sex attraction or activity occurs in a patient with another psychological diagnosis, such as:

- Major depression
- Suicidal ideation
- Generalized anxiety disorder
- Substance abuse
- Conduct disorder in adolescents
- Borderline personality disorder
- Schizophrenia
- Pathological narcissism

In a few cases, homosexual behavior appears later in life as a response to a trauma such as abortion, or profound loneliness.

Same-sex attraction is preventable. If the emotional and developmental needs of each child are properly met by both family and peers, the development of same-sex attraction is very unlikely. Children need affection, praise and acceptance by each parent, by siblings and by peers. Such social and family situations, however, are not always easily established and the needs of children are not always readily identifiable.

Some parents may be struggling with their own trials and be unable to provide the attention and support their children require. Sometimes parents work very hard but the particular personality of the child makes support and nurture more difficult. Some parents see incipient signs, seek professional assistance and advice, and are given inadequate, and in some cases, erroneous advice.

The Diagnostic and Statistical Manual IV of the American Psychiatric Association has defined Gender Identity Disorder (GID) in children as a strong, persistent cross gender identification, a discomfort with one's own sex, and a preference for cross sex roles in play or in fantasies. Some researchers have identified another less pronounced syndrome in boys—chronic feelings of unmasculinity. These boys, while not engaging in any cross sex play or fantasies, feel profoundly inadequate in their masculinity and have an almost phobic reaction to rough and tumble play in early childhood often accompanied by a strong dislike of team sports. Several studies have shown that children with Gender Identity Disorder and boys with chronic juvenile unmasculinity are at-risk for same-sex attraction in adolescence.

Early identification and proper professional intervention, if supported by parents, can often overcome the gender identity disorder. Unfortunately, many parents who report these concerns to their pediatricians are told not to worry about them. In some cases the symptoms and parental concerns may appear to lessen when the child enters the second or third grade, but unless adequately dealt with, the symptoms may reappear at puberty as intense, same-sex attraction. This attraction appears to be the result of a failure to identify positively with one's own sex....[I]t is important to note that a significant percentage of these children do not become homosexually active as adults....The labeling of an adolescent, or worse a child, as unchangeably "homosexual" does the individual a grave disservice. Such adolescents or children can, with appropriate, positive intervention, be given proper guidance to deal with early emotional traumas...

When Catholic parents discover that their son or daughter is experiencing same-sex attractions or engaging in homosexual activity, they are often devastated. Afraid for the child's health, happiness, and salvation, parents are usually relieved when informed that same-sex attraction is treatable and preventable. They can find support from other parents in [the organization] Encourage. They also

> need to be able to share their burden with loving friends and families.
>
> Parents should be informed about the symptoms of Gender Identity Disorder and the prevention of gender identity problems, encouraged to take such symptoms seriously and to refer children with gender identity problems to qualified and morally appropriate mental health professions.

This is only a small portion of the report. I urge you to read the full report.

Father John Harvey, the author of a book published by Ignatius Press entitled ***Same-Sex Attraction: A Parent's Guide***, is also the founder of Courage, a Catholic apostolate for adults with same-sex attractions. In an extensive Zenit interview January 24, 2004, Fr. Harvey discussed this serious topic. He concluded his interview by noting: *It's a long process to heal sexual identity. It doesn't take place all at once. It can start at 3 or 4 years old—when kids start showing signs of same sex attraction—and can go through the teen-age and adult years. It has to be put in a larger perspective. I find two factors helpful for teen-agers: professional therapy with a good therapist who is faithful to the Church's teachings; and spiritual direction and prayer.* Fr. Harvey then discussed other aspects of the problem. *One of the ways that homosexual activity is "learned" is when a person is introduced to that form of activity by another person. There are other ways that one may learn homosexual activity, such as through the things that they watch or read. However, the homosexual condition itself generally develops involuntarily.*

I don't believe that anyone chooses to have same-sex attractions. The homosexual condition has emotional roots and is influenced by attitudes in the mind that come about because of various external events. However, it is not a real choice because that person usually didn't have control over the circumstances and traumas that influenced the development of same-sex attractions. Real choice involves full knowledge and advertence in the mind and freedom in the will.

The evidence leans heavily on the fact that same-sex attractions are due largely to environmental causes. There is no evidence of inborn homosexuality—it doesn't exist. There is a hundred years of evidence that same-sex attractions are related to environmental factors and psychological influences. All the evidence before 1973 pointed to environmental factors. Then came the idea that it is related to genetics. So far, there is no evidence that it is genetic...

Please review pp. 341-368 in ***Raise Happy Children... Raise Them Saints!*** as to the influence of schools and teachers toward the homosexual lifestyle. Be alert to the type of programs your school presents as well as "gay" clubs. In the U.S. there are 1,144 such clubs in middle and high schools across the nation.[17] Inquire if there is such a club at your school. Warn your teens to avoid such clubs. Do you know your teen's friends? Be aware that "gay" friends can introduce your teen to the "gay lifestyle." Check out the books your teens are required to read for school as well as the speakers your teens are required to listen to...even in Catholic schools. There are examples I could give as to speakers and required reading but these are too disturbing to put in print.

How To Protect One's Chastity

"Fear is the foundation of our salvation. By fearing we shall be on our guard, and by being on our guard we shall be saved..." Tertullian

Teach your children the importance of keeping their minds and bodies pure. Explain to preteens and teens that the word sex can be used as a noun or a verb. When it is used as a noun the word "sex" denotes the gender of the person.

[17] "GLSEN web site lies about number of homosexual clubs," *Choice 4 Truth,* Jan-April, 2004, p. 1.

When the word "sex" is used as a verb (as to have sex) the word denotes intercourse or coitus. The verb sex is *not* part of the dating scene. Sex is to be reserved exclusively for marriage. If you wait to explain this to your children until they are in junior high it is too late. Map out for your teens what is proper conduct on a date and what is sinful. There is to be no necking, petting, passionate kissing, French kissing, or impure touches. The use of alcohol (it breaks down one's restraint), music that appeals to the passions, and strobe lighting can endanger the virtue of modesty leading to the loss of the state of virginity. Warn your teens of these dangers before they become potential victims. Do not permit your teens to date at a young age. Jason and Crystalina Evert of Catholic Answers insist that teens should never date before the age of 16. They also tell parents to forbid daughters to date older guys.[18] Encourage them to go out with a group rather than singly. Stress they are to avoid cozy, secluded places that could tempt them to be intimate. Review the section on Marriage and Dating in ***Raise Happy Children...Raise Them Saints!*** pages 307-317. Share this material with your teens. Before sending teens off to college ask them to read ***Raise Happy Children Through A Happier Marriage*** so they understand the seriousness of selecting the correct spouse.

Another way to protect the virtue of chastity is to insist that all teen parties your teen attends be chaperoned. **Never permit your child to participate in coed prom "sleepovers" be they in a home or a hotel...even if everyone else is going!**

Scholastic Choices Magazine reported that *[i]n a study by University of California, Los Angeles researchers, more than half of the teen boys and almost half of the teen girls surveyed thought it was [okay]...for a boy to force sex on a girl if she excites him sexually.*[19] This study was done 14 years ago.

[18] Zenit, Dec. 12, 2003.

[19] Jenna Zark, "Date Rape, What You Need To Know," *Scholastic Choices Magazine*, Feb. 1990, pp. 7, 10.

In the permissive sexual climate we live in the percent has probably gone up appreciably. *Scholastic Choices Magazine* also reported a survey by Mary Koss, professor at the University of Arizona Medical School's Psychiatry Department. This survey found that in the U.S. *[o]ne woman in four over age 14 has been the victim of rape or attempted rape...*[20] Guard your children and teens by telling them how to protect themselves from child abuse, incest, date rape, sexual harassment, and rape:[21]

- Avoid dark, lonely, questionable, and strange places either outdoors or in.
- If at all possible go to public restrooms with a companion.
- Refuse to give strangers information on the phone or through email.
- Never let anyone touch you improperly in the area of your private parts.
- Do not answer doors to strangers when parents are not home.
- Do not let strangers get into your car.
- Should a stranger call you to his car, ignore and keep your distance.
- If strangers approach you, keep a set distance away.
- If something does not seem right to your child or teen tell them to come to you to discuss it. They are never to feel ashamed to talk about anything with you.

The Christian use of sexuality cannot be achieved without effort, an effort that at times has to be heroic. This applies especially to young people in whom the strength of the sexual tendencies combined with immaturity of personality make a more rigorous struggle necessary...One of the firmest

---

[20] *Ibid.*, p. 10.
[21] Some of this material was taken from a handout marked DEY/ Almost EVERYTHING

foundations for the sexual aspects of education is to strengthen an awareness in young people that human life can be fully lived only as a struggle.[22]

St. Alphonsus relates how in the beginning of the apostolate of the Society of Jesus, when the first priests were all young, a group of them was sent to escort the Portuguese Princess Doña Maria to Castile, Spain, to marry King Philip II. At the court of King Philip they heard the confessions of all the ladies of the court. He relates that the court was stunned by the conduct of the young Jesuits saying *[s]uch youth with such chastity. [T]hey were seen in the midst of so many dangerous occasions, and on the other hand with such an aroma of chastity about them. This became the talk of the court.* One day King Philip II asked one of the priests, Fr. Araoz, if it was true that they *carry with them an herb that has the virtue of preserving chastity.* The priest replied, *Your majesty's story is true. "For the life of you tell me what the herb is,"* asked the king with curiosity. *"Sire, the herb which the members of the Society carry about with them to preserve chastity is the fear of God."*[23] Scripture assures us: ***Upon him that fears the Lord no harm shall come, for God will preserve him and deliver him from all evil*** (**Ecclus**. 33:1). St. Gregory stresses that *[f]ear is the safeguard of virtues.* Educate your teens in the fear of God. This "fear of God" that I am referring to is not terror of God but rather "fear of offending such a loving Father." St. Josemaría would say he could not understand any fear of God except the fear of displeasing our Father God. Our love of God should be so deep that we do not want any of our thoughts, words, actions or omissions to be hurtful toward God so as to cause Him any sorrow, suffering, or disappointment. This is the "fear" you need to teach your children and teens.

---

[22] V. García Hoz, "Contestación a una pregunta en una entrevista" in *Palabra* (Madrid), March 1972, p. 11.

[23] St. Alphonsus Rodriguez, S.J., ***Practice Of Perfection and Christian Virtues, Vol. 3*** (Chicago: Loyola University Press, 1929) p. 265.

The immorality encouraged by our culture has no benefits. The National Marriage Project at Rutgers University headed by Barbara Dafoe Whitehead and David Popenoe found that *since young men are able to indulge in a sexually active single life—often with a live-in girlfriend—they "are in no hurry" to marry* (editorial emphasis). On the other hand the report found that marriage has a host of benefits.

- Married men live longer than single men.
- Married men live a healthier lifestyle than single men.
- *Marriage has some kind of profound effect on human beings, because it reduces stress levels in some way and protects against illness.*
- Married men eat healthier and drink less alcohol.
- Married couples by sharing worries have lower stress levels.
- Married couples cared for each other better.
- Married men make $4,700 more than single men.
- Those who stayed married were less likely to die from various causes compared to those who divorced.
- There is less domestic abuse in marriage.[24]

When people are married, they make an investment in each other's lives, said Jennifer Marshall, director of the Family Resource Council's family studies department. *When you're in a less-committed relationship, it can get volatile because these kinds of relationships don't carry the same commitment.*[25]

Aside from heartbreak and abuse, there is also the serious matter of living in the state of mortal sin. The seriousness of sins against the virtue of chastity becomes even more apparent when we understand that *Our Lord atoned for the concupiscence of the flesh with the austerities and the sufferings of His whole life, but especially with the sufferings of His Passion. We wonder how the Father could condemn our Lord to torments as cruel as those of the Passion: He had to, in order that our sensuality, our sins of the flesh might be*

[24] Zenit, July 20, 2002.

[25] *Ibid.*

expiated, relates St. Peter Julian Eymard...*He required every bit of the Passion as a reparation for the sins of sensuality. Some saints say that our Lord atoned for the sins of thought especially during His agony of blood in Gethsemane. These sins must then be very grievous!...There is often more sensuality in thoughts than in actions; we can renew the thoughts and dwell on them without interruption, whereas we commit the actions only occasionally. That is why our Lord bore this crucifixion of soul for three hours. As for impurity of action...He, purity itself, is led into the presence of the incestuous Herod...Jesus submitted to the shame of nakedness, of being entirely stripped before these wretches...And see what reparation He makes for sensual vanity, for vanity of the body....Our Lord's head is pierced with a crown of thorns and His cheeks are covered with spittle. The feet which are shod so daintily to lead us to sin and the hands which are kept white and delicate to commit it, do you see them pierced with nails in our Lord? His whole body is torn with wounds because we are vain and sensual in all our members.*[26] To understand this more fully see Mel Gibson's movie, *The Passion of The Christ.*

Author Hutchcraft emphasizes, *According to the Bible, sexual purity is more than just another social viewpoint—it is "God's will." Sex outside of marriage is much more than a physical or romantic act—it is a violation of the laws of* God. *Society has changed its mind about sex; the Creator has not.*[27]

How Far Can One Go?

"The women of any period [of time] are the true gauge of its moral standards."

Church Historian H. Daniel-Rops

St. Alphonsus Rodriguez, S.J., counsels: *You cannot use such language as this in the matter of chastity: "I will go so far, but not a step further;" for when you think it least, you will go*

---

[26] ***In the Light of the Monstrance,*** *Op. Cit.*, pp. 78-80.
[27] ***5 Needs Your Child Must have Met At Home***, *Op. Cit.*, p. 67.

where you never thought to go. He who casts himself down a slippery descent thinks only to go as far as the particular spot which he has marked; but the weight of his body and the smoothness of the rock makes him go further, though he had no such intention when he started. So it is here; this is very slippery ground, and the weight or inclination of our flesh downwards is very great.[28]

When Jason and Crystalina Evert of Catholic Answers begin their chastity ministry to teens, they begin by addressing "how far is too far". Cleverly, they answer the question with another question: *how far [do] you want someone to go with your future spouse?*[29]

Tell your daughters firmly that it's the girl who sets the tone. It is her responsibility to quickly diffuse any potentially dangerous sexual situation. She sets the tone for dates by scrupulously following the rules of modesty in her dress, actions, conversation, and refraining from touching her date in any manner that could arouse him. Tell her to keep her hands to herself. My mother used to tell me, *People who keep their hands to themselves never get into trouble!* Sexual attraction should never be used to tease a male. The root cause of all the promiscuity in our culture is because girls have agreed to allow guys to use them sexually outside of marriage. Why would they be so foolish?

1. Contraception and abortion have psychologically "taken the fear of getting pregnant" out of premarital sex.
2. Girls hunger to be loved.

When a large segment of teenage girls refuse to be "live-ins" or pay for dates with sex, the climate will change. This will only happen when parents begin to teach the importance of the virtue of chastity along with the importance of spiritual growth.

Keep your teens spiritually growing to protect their chastity. *A survey commissioned by the National Campaign*

---

[28] ***Practice Of Perfection and Christian Virtues, Vol. 3,*** *Op. Cit.*, p. 234.

[29] Zenit, Dec. 12, 2003.

to Prevent Teen Pregnancy found that 39% of teens said that "morals, values and/or religious beliefs" were the most important factors affecting their decision about whether to have sex...That's more than double the second most popular answer, concern about sexually transmitted diseases which was cited by 17%.[30] Another survey found that *conservative Protestant and Catholic girls delay sexual activity longer than their less religious cohorts. Moreover, it is religious activity and parental influence that has the greatest effect on teenagers, not advice from the clergy.*[31]

Fr. Lawrence Scupoli wrote a wonderful book in 1589 entitled ***Spiritual Combat*** that has become a spiritual classic. In protecting one's chastity he suggests that we use special tactics. Along with his suggestions I am including additional helps from other sources:

1. *Before the time of temptation we must avoid all persons and occasions* [and things] *that would expose us to sin.*
   a. *Be cautious.* Fr. Malaise, S.J., adds: *Avoid undue familiarity especially with persons of the other sex, and all inordinate friendship and affection.*[32]
   b. *Avoid idleness.*
   c. *Obey your superiors promptly; do what they command.*
   d. *Never judge others rashly, particularly in regard to impurity. (For if you permit yourself the liberty of severe judgments on your neighbors, God will permit you, for your punishment and amendment, to fall into the same faults...in order that by such humiliation you may discover your own pride and rashness, and then you can find proper remedies for both...*[33]
   e. Live the virtue of modesty well. (Review the chapter on modesty.)
   f. Practice acts of self-control such as mortifications and fasting. St. Thomas Aquinas says that *chastity is*

---

[30] Zenit, March 23, 2002.

[31] "Media Ignore Survey On Religion And Teen Sex," *Catalyst,* Nov. 2001

[32] ***Know Yourself***, *Op. Cit.*, p. 85.

[33] Fr. Lawrence Scupoli, ***The Spiritual Combat*** (Westminster, Maryland: The Newman Bookshop, 1947) pp. 53-56.

so called from chastisement, because its vice must be restrained by chastisement of the body.[34]

2. When troubled by a temptation ignore the thought by distracting yourself with some activity. St. Jerome took up the study of Hebrew to distract himself from temptations.[35] Say aspirations to Our Lord and Our Lady. Or, look at a crucifix as you meditate on the Sorrowful Mysteries of the rosary. Bless yourself with holy water if possible, then sprinkle it around the room. *Like Joseph and Suzanna* [in Scripture] *we should say whenever we are tempted: "How could I dare commit such a sin in the presence of Him Who is to judge me?*[36]

3. If the temptation was given consent, confess it in confession as soon as possible since sins against the sixth and ninth commandments (chastity) are usually mortal sins. Be delicate in confessing the sin by saying, *I sinned against the virtue of chastity in my thoughts,* or *words*, or *actions.* Never conceal anything from the priest because of shame.

Let me add one additional point:

4. Should you fall into sin consider how you can be more vigilant in the future to avoid falling into the same sin. Ask the priest in confession how to avoid temptations or the giving in to temptations. Remember that the sacrament of confession confers graces to help you. Also the graces of frequent reception of Holy Communion will protect and give you strength to fight temptations.

A story is told that a holy hermit was taken by an angel to see a monastery and the nearby town. When he looked down at the monastery it was filled with what looked like flies but were actually devils in every part of the monastery. Then the angel took the hermit to town where he saw just one devil in the town square with nothing to do. Asking the angel the meaning of this, the angel replied that *those people in the city all did what the devil wanted, and therefore one devil was enough for all; but in the monastery all were doing their best to resist the devil, and that was the reason why so*

[34] ***Practice Of Perfection and Christian Virtues, Vol. 3,*** *Op. Cit.,* p. 249.

[35] *Ibid.,* p. 251.

[36] ***Know Yourself,*** *Op. Cit.,* p. 86.

many devils were at them to tempt them and make them fall.[37] See why the graces of frequent confession are so necessary?

Chastity Pluses

Tell your teens that chastity is fashionable, not only with God but also with teen idols. Recently *Us* Magazine published a list of stars who intend to stay chaste until marriage. Among them are tennis player Leelee Sobieski, 17; the star of the mini-series "Joan of Arc"; and Jonathan Jackson, also 17, of the soap "General Hospital."[38] There are also a host of crowned beauty queens that not only proclaim that they are living chastity but are promoting abstinence publicly to teens. Miss America 2003, Erika Harold, is one who was mentioned at the start of this chapter. Others are Miss Illinois 1999, Jade Smalls; Miss Kankakee Country 2000, Maggie Johnson; Miss Wisconsin 1999, Mary-Louise Kurey; Miss Missouri USA 2002, Tara Bollinger; Miss District of Columbia 2000, Rashida Jolley; Miss Lanston University/Okahoma, Nitia Harris. This is just a sampling. Miss Wisconsin 1999, Mary-Louise Kurey, even wrote a great book for teens entitled, ***Standing With Courage: Making Tough Decisions About Sex*** (Our Sunday Visitor Press).

Chastity Clubs are growing in the U.S. *An estimated 3 million teen-agers have signed pledges since campaigns such as True Love Waits began a few years ago.*[39] Teens take a pledge, then wear a ring given to them by their parents. The chastity ring is worn until it is exchanged for a wedding ring. Baptist Reverend Richard Ross in Nashville, Tennessee began this movement in 1993. The concept rapidly spread to other churches, schools and communities. "Next Generation," "Best Friends," "Girls, U.S.A.," and "Choose," are Catholic chastity groups. You can do something similar in your area or school. Why sign a pledge? Signing an agreement is more binding than a verbal

---

[37] ***Practice Of Perfection and Christian Virtues, Vol. 3,*** *Op. Cit.,* p. 271.
[38] Zenit, Feb. 21, 2000. [39] Zenit, March 23, 2002.

agreement.

Steve Habisohn, the founder of The Gift Foundation, began his apostolate because he found that *problems in marriage often stem from a family's lack of pursuit of holiness.*[40] Next Habisohn launched e5 Men named for ***Ephesians*** 5 where St. Paul tells men to ***love their wives as Christ loved the Church.*** Each of the more than 5,500 registered members fasts on the first Wednesday of the month for 24 hours on bread and water *for the benefit of his bride, whether that be his wife, his fiancée or his future, unknown bride and for the e5 Women who have registered. A celibate man can fast for Christ's bride, the Church.* Why fast for women? Habisohn explains that *many men, whether married or unmarried, have caused much harm to women. Therefore, a great reason to fast for women is for reparation for the sins committed against women by men—for both their own personal sins and the collective sins of men. I even recommend to single men that they fast for past girlfriends first before fasting for their future bride.* In addition, Habisohn feels that *the practice of sacrificial love before marriage helps reorient a single man toward love and not self-love. Even good Catholic single men are so affected by our culture that they form deep habits of self-love. Fasting for a future bride and for other women that need it reorients them toward making a total gift of self when the time arrives, whether in the married or celibate vocation. There is one e5 Man who is only 12-years-old who has received permission from his parents to abstain from certain things for the sake of his future bride.*[41] This would be a great father-son activity.

Regaining Secondary Virginity

Make clear to your teens that should they have the misfortune to lose their virginity they can regain a secondary virginity through the practice of chastity after first making a good confession. Use St. Augustine as such an example. He had a mistress while in his teens who bore him a child. Although he eventually wanted to live a chaste life, he

[40] Zenit, Oct. 29, 2003.

[41] *Ibid.*.

prayed: *Grant me chastity and continence, but not yet!* He confesses: *I feared my pleas would be too quickly answered and I would be too soon healed of this sickness of concupiscence, for I preferred to satisfy it than to see it extinguished.* Finally, "tomorrow" came for this man and he became the greatest doctor of the Western Church. He comforts those who may have fallen into the same trap as he by saying *a long practice of chastity counts for virginity.*[42]

St. Margaret of Cortona, at the age of 17, fell in love and became the mistress of a young nobleman. For nine years she lived in sin with him until he was killed. When Margaret found his decomposed body, it was covered with maggots. It was with shock that she realized her soul looked like his putrid body. She cooperated with God's grace and converted. She threw herself into arduous penances. When her confessor protested she insisted: *Father, do not ask me to come to terms with this body of mine, for I cannot risk such a compromise. Between me and my body there must always be a struggle until death.* This is the same struggle we and our teens have to wage, in our culture that exalts the sins of the flesh.

St. Mary of Egypt, who lived in the mid 300's, is another such example. At the age of twelve Mary ran away from her home to live in Alexandria. It was there that she lost her innocence. Fr. Herbst tells us that for seventeen years *she reveled in all the abandonment of shameful and public immodesty—all to gratify an unbridled lust.*[43] Then one day she started to walk into a church in Jerusalem but an unseen hand refused to let her enter. That was the moment of her conversion. Mary later explained that seeing a picture of Our Lady painted on the church, *I addressed myself to that holy Virgin, begging of her, by her incomparable purity, to succor me, defiled with such a load of abominations, and to render my repentance the more acceptable to God.*[44] After making a good confession, attending Mass, and receiving the Holy Eucharist, Mary left the city to spend forty years alone in the desert doing penance for her sins. Remember

[42] ***Follow The Saints,*** *Op. Cit.*, p. 55. [43] *Ibid.*, p. 54. [44] *Ibid.*

how we said in the last chapter that images are burned into our imaginations? Mary had to fight the images from her sordid past. She recounts, *Seventeen years I passed in most violent temptations and almost perpetual conflicts with my inordinate desires. But weeping, I begged the Blessed Virgin to obtain my deliverance from the affliction and danger of such thoughts...She has never failed to show herself my faithful protectress.*[45]

Explain to your teenagers that even if they safely navigate the teens chastely they must still be vigilant throughout their lives. St. Alphonsus Rodriguez tells the story of St. James, the hermit. For forty years he practiced extreme penances. He worked miracles and was known for successfully casting out devils. When he was sixty a girl was brought to him who was possessed. He successfully cast out the demon, but the people who brought her to James were afraid to take her back home fearing the devil might attack them. James let the girl stay. *For his trusting and presuming on himself God permitted him to fall into sin. And because one sin calls on and invites another, he did a stupid thing—he murdered the girl and threw her body into a river...[I]n despair of the mercy of God, he determined to return to the world and give himself wholly over to that course of vice and sin which so late in life he had entered upon.*[46] God did not desert him. James came to his senses, did ten years of rigorous penance, and was canonized after his death.

The Education of Human Love

"A child whose innocence has been preserved through good instruction is a treasure more precious in God's eyes than all the kingdoms of this world." St. Anthony Mary Claret

Dominican Brother Nicholas Lombardo, who has been involved in youth ministry since 1997 and served as a

[45] *Ibid.*
[46] ***Practice Of Perfection and Christian Virtues, Vol. 3,*** *Op. Cit.*, p. 261.

theological consultant to the YOUTH 2000 movement, has prudent advice for parents: *Church teaching on sexuality seems burdensome and unattractive when it is presented as a list of sins to avoid. On the other hand, when we present chastity as a choice for self-respect, love, healthy relationships and happiness, and as the embrace, not the denial, of sexuality and the body, youth respond very positively.*[47] John Paul II presents chastity to youth as *the safeguard of love.*

St. Josemaría Escrivá reminds us: *We have been created by God and endowed with an intelligence which is like a spark of the divine intellect. Together with our free will, another gift of God, it allows us to know and love. And God has also placed in our body the power to generate, which is a participation in His own creative power. He has wanted to use love to bring new human beings into the world and to increase the body of the Church. Thus sex is not a shameful thing; it is a gift, ordained to life, to love, to fruitfulness.*

This is the context in which we must see the Christian doctrine on sex. Our faith does not ignore anything on this earth that is beautiful, noble and authentically human. It simply teaches us that the rule of our life should not be the selfish pursuit of pleasure, because only sacrifice and self-denial lead to true love. God already loves us; and now He invites us to love Him and others with the truthfulness and authenticity with which He loves.[48]

A person who lacks purity, chastity and modesty cannot live a Christian life. This is why educating your children in human love is a delicate but necessary duty. To leave this responsibility to others, no matter how much you trust them, is a sin of omission. Once I took a group of high school girls to a high school retreat where I planned to also attend a retreat for women in another building on the same grounds. After the priest gave the meditation on chastity and how it must be lived to the teens, my daughter, Marianne, sought me out to ask if I could talk to the daughter of one of my

---

[47] Zenit, May 9, 2003.

[48] St. Josemaría Escrivá, ***Christ Is Passing By*** (NY: Scepter, 1982) #24.

friends who was distraught by the meditation. At the time she was taking a moral theology class given by a priest-friend of her family. It was her understanding from this class that premarital sex was permissible if the couple "loved each other." She was torn between the two priests. Who was right? The priest who is a good friend of her family or the priest on retreat? (Answer: priest on retreat.)

Parents have the grace of the Sacrament of Matrimony to explain the "facts of life" in a prudent manner, at the appropriate time. *The family is the best atmosphere to fulfill the duty of ensuring a gradual education in sexuality. It has the affective reserves needed to facilitate the assimilation of even the most delicate realities without traumas, and their harmonious integration in a balanced and rich personality.*[49] The appropriate time is when the children ask questions or situations arise in which children may be given harmful information. Fr. Thomas Gerrard stresses that *knowledge should never be thrust into the child's mind before it is asked for. The state of innocence or ignorance, whichever we like to call it, is better kept untouched as long as possible...To put sexual images into a child's mind before due time is to start a tendency towards precocity and moral depravity.*[50] Should a child or teen ask a question but you ignore it out of embarrassment, an opportunity is missed to give sound, moral information while at the same time the child's or teen's curiosity is intensified leading him to question someone else who may not handle the answer in a moral, delicate manner.

When parents asked St. Josemaría how and when to teach their children the mystery of life he would say that the parents are to instruct their children. If the father does not speak to the boys they will go to shameless friends who will not treat the subject with dignity. This will lead them to look at their parents with disgust. Mothers should speak

[49] Congregation for Catholic Education, *Educational Guidelines for Human Love,* Nov. 1, 1983, #48.
[50] Rev. Thomas J. Gerrard, ***Marriage and Parenthood*** (NY: Joseph F. Wagner, 1911) p. 142.

to their daughters frankly and clearly. *Tell them that God has used you to bring them into the world, that they are the fruit of your love, your self-giving, your sacrifice.*

To a newspaper reporter, St. Josemaría urged parents to befriend their children so the children are comfortable talking with them, *making it easy for them to talk about their small problems, also makes it possible for the parents to be the ones who teach them gradually about the origin of life, in accord with their mentality and capacity to understand, gently anticipating their natural curiosity. There is no reason why children should associate sex with something sinful or find out about something that is in itself noble and holy in a vulgar conversation with a friend.*[51]

To permit your child to attend sex education in school is to endanger his chastity. Why? Fr. Thomas J. Gerrard explains that *the mind and the senses, the brain and nerves are so related to each other that they act and react on each other. So intimate and organized is this relationship that conversation or reading about sexual matters tends to excite the sexual functions. Even though the conversation and the reading may be justified and done with a right intention, it is, nevertheless, fraught with certain dangers. It emphasizes images in the imagination which may become temptations to sin, when the brain is tired or the mind off its guard.*[52] Abstinence-based programs are usually acceptable but check them out first before permitting your child to attend. This program can never replace your responsibility to educate your children in this area.

If you haven't done so already, now is the time to read the Pontifical Council for the Family document, *The Truth and Meaning of Human Sexuality* published in 1995. This document was published specifically to help parents: *...[T]he virtue of chastity is found within temperance—a cardinal virtue elevated and enriched by grace in baptism. So chastity is not to be understood as a repressive attitude. On the*

[51] ***Conversations,*** *Op. Cit.,* #100.
[52] ***Marriage and Parenthood,*** *Op. Cit.,* p. 140.

contrary, chastity should be understood rather as the pure and temporary stewardship of a precious and rich gift of love, in view of the self-giving realized in each person's specific vocation. Chastity is thus that "spiritual energy capable of defending love from the perils of selfishness and aggressiveness, and able to advance it toward its full realization"...

In the framework of educating the young person for self-realization and self-giving, formation for chastity implies the collaboration first and foremost of the parents, as is the case with formation for the other virtues such as temperance, fortitude and prudence. Chastity cannot exist as a virtue without the capacity to renounce self, to makes sacrifices and to wait.

Prepare yourself by reading books on the topic and talk to other parents for tips on how to handle the subject. Pray for light from the Holy Spirit for the correct timing and the words to say by avoiding excessive explicitness yet insufficient detail. While it is imprudent to delay this talk with your children, answer only the questions young children ask without going into more detail than their minds can accept.

Fr. Henry Sattler, C.SS.R. asks, *Does the boy or girl know when the sexual functions are to be exercised? Do they know what is right or wrong concerning sex? Have they learned self-control? How does the growing girl feel about motherhood? Does the boy look upon the girl merely as a source of physical pleasure, or as a future mother, companion and helpmate? The correct answers to these...will indicate whether one is* ***educated*** *in this matter. Mere instruction on the "facts of life" may take but a few minutes. Sex education takes the whole lifetime of the child from its earliest years up to maturity.*[53]

Explain that love is different from sex. Love develops in the heart and will while sex is a physical attraction. When

[53] Henry V. Sattler, C.SS.R, Ph.D. ***Parents, Children and the Facts of Life*** (NJ: St. Anthony Guild Press, 1952) p. 5.

a person loves, he is interested in the good of the other, what he can do for the beloved, how he can help the beloved. In love the self is sacrificed for the other. In sex, the questions are *what can I get from that person? How much pleasure can I count on? How long can I use that person?* St. Josemaría explained: *Chastity—not just continence, but the decisive affirmation of a will that's in love—is a virtue that maintains the youthfulness of love in any state of life.*[54]

Describe premarital sex as a form of murder, or thievery. It is counterfeit because it is based on physical attraction rather than love. It not only kills the soul, but forever psychologically injures the couple involved because it is not simply a physical act but a total act of giving that involves the body and the soul. When a teen gives himself or herself in casual sex, he/she has nothing unique to give to a future spouse. The couple becomes "used material." Their dignity has been defiled. They rob each other of what is most private, most personal...their intimacy and virtue. Archbishop Sheen believes that *[s]ex is not wanted primarily; something else is wanted, and sex is the substitute for that other thing. It is not the other person who is wanted, but some fleeting seconds of escape, thanks to the other person.*[55] Sheen continues about premarital sex: *Over stimulated, and wrongly stimulated, they cannot later respond to normal marriage relations and the chances of compatibility are poor. Any divorce of the sexual experience from the spiritual experience is bound to create a disturbed mind. As one doctor put it, "Promiscuity makes people lose the greatest experience in life, love."*

Premarital experience also destroys certain inhibitions in the young, which prepares them for infidelity later on in life.[56] On the other hand, Jason and Crystalina Evert, newlyweds who speak on chastity to over 10,000 teens for Catholic Answers, say that *the peace and joy that comes from*

[54] Salvador Bernal, ***A Profile Of Msgr. Escriva, Founder Of Opus Dei*** (NY: Scepter Press, 1976) p. 55.
[55] ***Children and Parents,*** *Op. Cit.,* p. 90.
[56] *Ibid.,* p. 87.

a lifestyle of chastity is worth more than all the pleasures in the world.[57]

When sex is divorced from love, which is tied to commitment and concern for the other, it leads to cohabitation. **Make it plain to your children that you will not accept cohabitation before marriage** even if 4.2 million couples cohabit. Of couples marrying today, 50% lived together before marriage. Clarify for your children that you will not accept this situation because it is a terrible offense against God, it is a mortal sin, and it will destroy their future happiness. Point out that 50% of married couples who cohabited before marriage have marriages that end in divorce. University of Chicago sociologist Linda Waite, in her book, ***The Case For Marriage***, found that *[c]ohabiting changes attitudes to a more individualistic, less relationship-oriented viewpoint* making them less committed to their spouse because these couples enter marriage without commitment. Karen S. Peterson, interviewing Waite, learned that *live-ins are less happy than marrieds, less sexually faithful and less financially well-off. Cohabiting and being married are not the same...people who cohabit are less likely to marry their partners than in the past...Cohabiting may be a better deal for men than women. Women can end up with the responsibilities of marriage but without the legal protections. Researcher Susan Brown at Bowling Green (Ohio) State University finds that women who cohabit are more prone to depression than married women, especially if children are involved. If such women constantly feel the union could dissolve at any time, "the instability is terribly detrimental to their psychological well-being."*[58] Then there is the issue of children born out of wedlock. What about their future, their happiness, their souls? How can these children be taught the faith by parents who are not living it?

---

57 Zenit, Dec. 12, 2003.

58 Karen S. Peterson, "Changing the shape of the American family," *USA Today,* April 18, 2000, Section D.

The continual changing of sexual partners leads not only to sexual diseases, some fatal, but also broken hearts, broken lives, depression and suicide. Last night I read the obituary of a man in his early thirties. He was the father of three young children. No wife or "partner" is mentioned. His mother's name is given along with "her companion." His father's name is given along with "his companion." What a messy family situation! Why does the lack of chastity hold such a grip on our society when it leaves nothing but pain and sorrow in its aftermath? Point this out to your teens.

Inform your teens that oral contraceptives do *not* prevent pregnancy. The ***British Medical Journal*** found that 50% of teenage girls on contraceptives became pregnant.[59] But actually the rate is much higher because contraceptives do not prevent pregnancy but keep the embryo from implanting thus resulting in spontaneous, possibly monthly abortions. Contraceptives not only kill the soul, they kill the body by causing blood clots and breast cancer.[60] David Paton, of Nottingham University Business School, found *[i]t seems family planning seems to encourage more people to have sex...The availability of the morning-after pill seems to be encouraging risky behavior.*[61] This morning-after pill will be available shortly over the counter. Warn your daughters about it.

Condoms are likewise not fool proof. Use of them leaves the male and the female susceptible to HIV and other sexually transmitted diseases (STDs) if either partner is infected. Cardinal López Trujillo, president of the Pontifical Council for the Family in an interview on Vatican Radio stated that *[o]ne cannot speak of "safe sex," leading people to believe that the use of condoms is the formula to avoid the risk of HIV and thus to overcome the AIDS pandemic. Nor*

---

[59] Zenit, Aug. 23, 2000.

[60] For a deeper explanation of the problems of contraception see ***Raise Happy Children Through A Happier Marriage*** (book one in this series). pp. 71-90.

[61] Zenit, March 23, 2002.

should people be led to believe that condoms provide absolute safety. They do not mention that there is a percentage of grave risk, not only of AIDS, but also for the different sexually transmitted diseases, and that the rate of failure is quite high....We also received news of a study report of groups representing 10,000 doctors accusing the Centers for Disease Control in the United States for covering up the government's own research which showed the "ineffectiveness of condoms to prevent the transmission of sexually transmitted diseases."[62]

Mexican Cardinal Javier Lozano Barragán, who heads the Pontifical Council for Health Care Workers, noted: *One of the practices for which the Church has been maligned in the fight against AIDS is the teaching that condoms, as contraception, are forbidden. They say the Catholic Church is the greatest killer for this teaching but this is a misconception. If you look at Botswana for example, a rich African country, 39% of its population is infected with AIDS, but it has the highest distribution of condoms. People think condoms means "safe sex." But the facts do not bear this out.*[63] The National Director of the Society for the Protection of Unborn Children, John Smeaton of Britain, pointed out in an interview that *even the makers of Durex condoms say quite clearly that "for complete protection from HIV and other [sexually transmitted infections], the only totally effective measure is sexual abstinence or limiting sexual intercourse to mutually faithful, uninfected partners."*[64] Smeaton pointed to the African country of Uganda as *perhaps the biggest success story in the fight against AIDS and much of its achievement is because of changes in sexual behavior, particularly emphasis on abstinence and fidelity...[A] USAID [report] on Uganda found that condoms were not a major factor in the decrease in HIV transmission. In fact, the decline...began before the widespread promotion of condoms....[I]t was noted that fewer than 5% of 13- to 16-year-olds were sexually active in 2001 compared with 60% in 1994, a significant change in sexual behavior achieved in*

[62] Zenit, Nov. 11, 2003. [63] Zenit, Nov. 6, 2003. [64] Zenit, Nov. 21, 2003.

just seven years.[65]

The Southern African Bishops, faced with an AIDS epidemic, issued guidelines. Due to the confusion in regard to the morality of condoms I think it is important to share with you the message of these bishops. *Many people and especially governments promote condoms for preventing AIDS. This is a matter of deep concern for us in the Church. The bishops regard the widespread and indiscriminate promotion of condoms as an immoral and misguided weapon in our battle against HIV/AIDS for the following reasons:*

- The use of condoms goes against human dignity.
- Condoms change the beautiful act of love into a selfish search for pleasure—while rejecting responsibility.
- Condoms do not guarantee protection against HIV/AIDS.
- Condoms may even be one of the main reasons for the spread of HIV/AIDS.
- Condoms...contribute to the breaking down of self-control and mutual respect.
- Condoms as a means of having so-called "safe sex" contribute to the breaking down of the moral fiber of our nations because it gives a wrong message to people. What it really says is this:
    1. It is alright to sleep around as you like even if you are still young—as long as you do not contract HIV/AIDS.
    2. There is no need for training yourself in self-control.
    3. There is no need to prepare yourself to be faithful to a future spouse.
    4. It is all right to use another person for selfish pleasure.

What undermines the morals of our countries?

1. It is lack of self-control and lack of respect for others.
2. It is unfaithfulness and irresponsible sexual behavior.
3. It is loose living, which destroys human dignity...and self respect.

---

[65] Zenit, Nov. 21, 2003.

This is our conviction as Catholic Bishops of Southern Africa. We proclaim our message loud and clear, a message which will strengthen again the moral fiber of our countries:

1. "Abstain and be faithful" is the human and Christian way of overcoming HIV/AIDS.
2. Abstain from sex before marriage and be faithful to your spouse in marriage—this is the answer which Christ gives us.

The bishops next addressed youth:

Dear young people, we are well aware that you are searching for real love, happiness and meaning in your lives. God says, **"I am offering you life or death, blessing or curse. Choose life, then, so that you and your descendants may live" (Deuteronomy** 30:19). *Make sure you choose life by accepting God's way.*

Do not allow yourselves to be misguided by people who show you the wrong way by offering you condoms. Abstain from sex before marriage and be faithful to your spouse in your future marriage—this is the way Christ shows us.

We often hear people saying, "Condoms save lives and therefore they should be promoted." Our answer is, "If we follow Christ's way, we shall save far more lives and encourage people to grow in self-control and responsibility for others."

Dear young people, you should not say: "It is impossible to abstain." You must prove to yourselves that abstinence is possible and that lust is not love. There are many groups of young people who help one another in their struggle to live chaste lives...Yes, it is difficult to abstain, but it is not impossible with God's help, which we obtain through prayer. Do not listen to people who say, "You will go mad if you do not have sex!" In fact, you will be very healthy in mind and body...

We call on young men: Respect girls and young women

and relate to them without making sexual demands of them. St. Paul says, "God wills you all to be holy. He wants you to keep away from sexual immorality" (1 ***Thessalonians*** 4:3)...

So often we blame God or other people for what happens to us. Instead we have to take responsibility for our actions before God. This involves listening to God's word and to the teachings of the Church so that we can have informed and mature consciences. The message of the Gospel is very different from that which we receive from television, videos, Internet, newspapers and magazines, which so often promote uncontrolled sex and infidelity. Dear People of God. We have to solve our problems in this "Kingdom Way." Therefore let us heed the call of Christ to return to the way of self-control and fidelity. St. Paul encourages us to shine among corrupt people like stars lighting up the sky as we offer them the message of life (see ***Philippians*** 2:15-16).[66]

When adolescents treat sex casually rather than as something sacred to be shared only in marriage, STDs leave individuals sterile, victims of cancer or dying with AIDS. *Ten thousand teens per day contract a sexually transmitted disease. Nationally, one in four Americans has an STD.*[67] On the other hand, those who live chaste lives remain physically healthy and psychologically balanced. Another consideration is the experience of your teen's peers. *Reliable surveys find that eight out of 10 girls and six out of 10 boys wish they had not had sex when they did.*[68]

Should your teen give you the line, *I have the freedom to follow my own conscience,* use these words of Bishop Victor Galeone of St. Augustine, Florida: *Yes, that's true [that one must follow one's conscience] provided that it's a properly formed conscience. Specifically, we must all conform our individual consciences to the natural law and the Ten Commandments, just as we have to adjust our clocks to sun time...[T]o say that we must accommodate our individual conscience to behavior that clearly contradicts God's law is*

[66] Zenit, Aug. 3, 2001.
[67] Zenit, Interview with Connie Marshner, Jan. 31, 2002. [68] *Ibid.*

to say that we must rule our lives by the clock, even when it tells us that night is day (editorial emphasis).[69]

John Paul II in his ***Letter to Families*** written February 2, 1994, explains the dangers of "safe sex." *So called "safe sex", which is touted by the "civilization of technology", is actually, in view of the overall requirements of the person, radically not safe, indeed it is extremely dangerous. It endangers both the person and the family. And what is this danger? It is the loss of the truth about one's own self and about the family together with the risk of a loss of freedom and consequently of a loss of love itself.* ***"You will know the truth"****, Jesus says,* ***"and the truth will make you free"*** **(*Jn* 8:32)*: the truth, and only the truth, will prepare you for a love which can be called "fairest love"*** (cf. ***Sir*** 24:24).

What Happened To Romance?

"Chastity is a richness that proceeds from the abundance of love and not from a lack of love."
Rabindranath Tagore, poet

Up until the late 1950's the term "dating" was used to define an opportunity to meet many different people in various settings in order to find one's spouse. Couples were not exclusive. Suddenly, the term "dating" took on a different connotation. It signified that couples were "going steady," an exclusive relationship symbolized by the exchange of class rings or fraternity pins. Today, Dr. Janet Smith, a consulter to the Pontifical Council on the Family, stated that *[t]here is basically no such thing as dating and courtship except in the smallest of religious circles. Now there is "coupling" and "hooking up" and "living together," but little really careful selection of dating partners followed by a slow and careful process of getting to know the other and to let oneself be known.*[70] Author Connie Marshner agrees. She finds that the term "dating" *is little more than a euphemism*

[69] Zenit, Nov. 8, 2003. Adapted from "Good Work," The Dorothy Day Book (Templegate).
[70] Zenit, Oct. 17, 2003.

for serial sex partnering. Every public high school student knows that to be "dating" somebody is to be sexually active—with a few prominent exceptions, such as Mormon or Muslim students.[71] (Don't you find it disturbing that Catholics are not mentioned in that exclusion?) Marshner, the author of ***Decent Exposure: How to Teach Your Children About Sex***,[72] explained that *sex is viewed by the younger generation—at least in the U.S., and probably most of the West [as] not something special or private, let alone sacred: it is really regard as little more than a rite of passage, something you do to prove you're grown up...Meet, sleep with, break up—over and over again, that is the cycle of dating in America, from junior high around age 12 until marriage around age 25. It doesn't prepare anybody for marriage. It prepares them for divorce!*[73] Dr. Janet Smith believes that contraception *has greatly increased the incidence of sex outside of marriage. Certainly very few people marry as virgins. Many people start having sex early in a relationship.*[74] One mother told me of taking her engaged daughter to her gynecologist for a checkup prior to her wedding. Afterwards the doctor told the mother, *your daughter is a very unusual young woman. You are very lucky.* The mother, puzzled by the doctor's comments repeated the doctor's words to her daughter then asked what he meant. *Oh, I guess he's not use to seeing virgins or having brides decline contraceptive prescriptions,* her daughter replied.

Dr. Smith recounts the pattern of marriage in the U.S.: *multiple sexual partners before marriage; a two-or three-year period of cohabitation, all the while contracepting; two or three years of contracepted sex after marriage; suspending with contraception for a short period of time in order to conceive the first child; return to contraception; suspending contraception to conceive the second child; then the wife or husband get sterilized; then they get divorced.*[75]

Sadly, Catholic guys and gals who live chastity are saddled

---

[71] Zenit, Jan. 31, 2002. [72] Legacy Communications, 1994.
[73] Zenit, Jan. 31, 2002. [74] Zenit, Oct. 17, 2003. [75] *Ibid.*

with the exclusive label if they are seen together frequently which prevents other guys from asking the girl out. A guy who wants to play the field will be considered "weird" and avoided by everyone. Marshner points out that such an attitude *severely limits the range of a girl's association, to say nothing of programming repeated emotional crises. Under these rules, the only way a girl can hope to have a range of friends through her college career is to not date anyone at all, but to always be part of a group. Our sons and daughters should get to know each other naturally, as siblings of friends, as co-workers on practical projects, as partners in academic projects, in groups, mainly through normal activities. It is through shared work and activities that a person gets to see many different facets of another...[I]n the exclusive dating game each wears a mask that is designed to achieve a certain response.*[76] Dr. Smith adds, *[a]bstinence before marriage permits the couple to get to know each other without the confusion and premature bonding of sexual involvement; they can get out of relationships that aren't leading to marriage without severe heartbreak and disruption to one's life. They develop a wide range of methods of expressing their love for each other, and when they begin their sexual relationship after marriage it is the proper "seal" to put on a relationship they have already established and intend to nurture for a lifetime.*[77]

How can the current "dating" situation be changed? Marshner suggests that this situation could be reversed by a large number of students at a campus or in a school who are willing to boycot the rules of "serial exclusivity." *But it would have to be a critical mass—enough girls in enough different cliques to simply say, to every boy, "We're not going to go steady with anybody"; enough boys willing to have real friendships with a number of girls at the same time, rather than one semi-marriage with one girl at a time. The alternative norm is this: Exclusive, one-on-one unstructured dating should be viewed as preliminary to a proposal of*

[76] Zenit, Jan. 31, 2002.

[77] Zenit, Oct. 17, 2003.

marriage. And until a couple is contemplating marriage, the mode for male-female relationships should be fraternal friendship.[78]

The Passion of Love

"Love is the chiefest and strongest of the passions, and the passion most difficult to withstand." St. Alphonsus Rodriguez,S.J.

Morally, the most dangerous time for teens is when they "fall in love." If they are not well grounded in faith and morals, with a growing relationship with God, their chastity will be endangered. Once passionate love takes over the will it is difficult to reason with the person. Teens and young adults refuse to see the dangers involved in the relationship. For this reason, all safeguards have to be established before they fall in love. St. Augustine, a Father of the Church, held the opinion that original sin entered our world because of the passionate love Adam had for his wife Eve. While this is his opinion, not the teaching of the Catholic Church, I thought you would find his viewpoint interesting. Augustine believed that Adam was not deceived by Satan. He simply wanted to please the wife he loved. *He had conceived such love and such affection for his wife that, not to vex her, he did what she asked. This is the way that Adam was deceived; it was love that deceived him—not that he was overcome by sensuality and concupiscence of the flesh, says St. Augustine, for at that time there was not that rebellion in it; but he was carried away by love and good will of friendship, by which, sometimes, to please a friend we displease God. Thus it was by love that sin entered into the world and with it death and all evils and afflictions.*[79] Teach this example to your teens so that when a date proposes doing something immoral and prefaces it by saying, "If you love me..." your teen will be warned that this is simply a repeat of the temptation of Adam. Remind him/her that

---

[78] Zenit, Jan. 31, 2002.

[79] ***Practice Of Perfection and Christian Virtues, Vol. 3,*** p. 241.

real love wants and expects a lifelong commitment.

There is another such example in Scripture, King Solomon. Solomon is reputed to be the wisest man ever to have lived yet he became an idolater because of the passionate love he bore for his pagan wives. Each pagan wife wanted her own shrine so he built each of them a shrine then went with each wife to offer incense to the idol. Being so wise, he knew the idols were not God but Scripture tells us that ***He loved with a most passionate love idolatrous women*** (***3 Kings*** 11:1-2). He did this *because he was overcome and blinded by love, and was loath to displease the objects of his affections, and wished to give pleasure and satisfaction to those whom he loved so much. Love perverted his heart.*[80]

Falling In Love

"How can a youth remain pure? By behaving as Your word prescribes." ***Psalm 119***

The common sense of humanity has always considered love to be an absolutely necessary element of happiness, writes Fr. Cormac Burke. *Love involves an attraction between two persons which unites them in a desire to share major aspects of life. There is the love of friendship by which, if it is genuine, each friend not only enjoys the companionship of the other but also desires what is good for him or her.* This type of love does not require any commitment. Friendships can endure for decades or for short periods of time. We will discuss this further in the next chapter. *Married love, in contrast, goes much farther. The person who marries chooses not only to love, but to do so with a distinctive love that is committed, exclusive and permanent...Loving someone means coming out of oneself and being prepared to share. To be loved is to be treated as an exception with special consideration. To fall in love, perhaps against one's deliberate will, can release him or her from the trap of self-sufficiency. When love is reciprocated, we can speak of two freedoms that*

[80] *Ibid.*, p. 242.

meet in a movement toward mutual gift and acceptance of each other. To fall in love means to realize that one is incomplete, and cannot be whole or happy without the loved one. And to <u>*want*</u> *to fall in love, even when one does not yet feel attracted to any concrete person, is equally a sign of the sense of incompleteness.*

A sign of true love is the new joy toward life that it induces...Love gives meaning to life...What the person in love fears, is not the loss of freedom but the loss of love... It is true that love is normally accompanied by feeling. But, more importantly, it is always—if it is authentic—an operation of the will.[81] *"[T]herefore it can be corrected, increased, perfected. This conclusion is not in fashion: nevertheless it is based on reality. If love were only a feeling, an inner sense of the variations of joy or exaltation, etc., one would have to say that love goes and comes as it wants, that we are not free in its regard, since it overpowers us and we can do nothing to defend ourselves from it."*[82]

Fr. Burke stresses that love resides in the will not in feelings. Our culture, on the other hand, prefers to think love is a feeling so when the "feeling leaves" we can divorce and switch partners. *But this modern argument is so often the cloak of selfishness...a society not prepared to accept this principle would gradually become inhuman. But love, in the precise sense of wishing well to another, is due in strict justice in many situations. Thus parents have a duty to love their children, just as children owe love to their parents; felt affection may dwindle or disappear, but love—as Aristotle defines it: "To love is to wish good to another"—can and ought to be maintained.*

A strongly felt attraction toward another can be easily mistaken for an outward-going and truly...self-giving love, whereas all it may want is its own satisfaction, without being prepared for any commitment that could break the bonds of attachment to self—a necessary condition if one is to

[81] Fr. Cormac Burke, ***Christian Anthropology Workshop 2002,*** pp. 71-73.

[82] Rojas: Una Teoria...p. 94.

experience the liberating openness of true love.[83] This selfish love that refuses commitment is responsible for "living together," trial marriages, and the general promiscuity we see all around us. Tens of thousands of chaste young men, who have a vocation to marriage, put it off until their late 30s or 40s for fear of making a lifelong commitment. A large percent of these selfish men never marry. Instead they string a girl along building her hopes that someday they will be ready to marry but the day never comes. In the meantime their monopoly of her time has prevented her from finding another guy who is willing to commit to marriage. Suddenly all the available guys are married and she is left on the shelf.

Explain to your teens that exclusively dating one person means courtship. Courtship should lead to engagement within six to 12 months of exclusive dating. Marriages should take place within six to 12 months of the engagement. If an engagement does not take place within this time period the relationship should be broken up so that the individuals can move on to meet other possible spouses. Start talking to your sons and daughters about this when they are in junior high. If you don't, you all are in for a lot of heart break down the road.

True love wants to do the will of the beloved. *He comes out of himself so as to find what he wants. True love, while wishing to possess the other, not only respects him or her, but is uplifted and opened out to other people and to all values. When the opposite occurs, love has been more egoistic than real...The opening out from self involved in true love, enables one to see not just the loved one but others too with new appreciation, while the absence of love darkens and warps one's outlook towards life and one's fellow-creatures.*

To be bound by love to someone else can give a needed sense of completion, and a new happiness. It is true that the bond with the other links one also with his or her sorrows, and so enlarges our possibilities of suffering.[84]

[83] ***Christian Anthropology Workshop 2002,*** *Op. Cit.*, 73. [84] *Ibid.*, p. 74.

For those of you who have married children, help them to understand the depth and commitment they made to love. Should they come to you saying *"I cannot love this person"...This may be a handy formula which in the end simply means, "I am not prepared to make the effort, if not to love, at least to accept or forgive him or her." One can allow that acceptance or forgiveness may be difficult; but then it is a difficulty, not an impossibility, one is faced with. This can also be true in the case of an apparently opposite affirmation: "I cannot help loving this person", used perhaps as a justification for a relationship that is considered immoral (love for someone already married; certain ways of expressing love in extra-marital relations, etc.). Unless a person knows how to govern love, he or she cannot claim the power to love, and will not be capable of persevering in love.*

Love has many types, and many counterfeits. In the end, it is the most definitive measure of personal worth, for the person is most genuinely revealed in the kind of love he is capable of: "each one is worth what his love is worth".[85]

What does a parent do when his child "falls in love"? This is a normal consequence of maturing because each person feels a sense of incompleteness. *But physical union of itself does not necessarily bring completeness, for even after the most intense physical union, there can be a deep sense of separateness and aloneness,* writes Archbishop Sheen. Sheen suggests parents ask their child to consider the following questions, then discuss each with them:

1. "Am I in love with a person, or am I in love with love?"
2. "Do I realize that sex is replaceable, but love is not?" The mere enjoyment of passion as such can be indifferent to persons in its grip, but love can never be indifferent."
3. "Do I think that the passion and the romantic feeling I have for a 'steady' now will endure with ever-increasing depth and intensity?"...[B]iological and erotic accompaniment of love decreases. Therefore, one has to make sure that it is a person and not a "thrill" that one loves.

[85] *Ibid.*, p. 75. Mouroux, ***Sens Chrétien***...p. 131.

4. "If I fall in love with an 'ideal,' will I marry a 'fact'?"[86]

I encourage you to reread pp. 307-317 in ***Raise Happy Children...Raise Them Saints!*** then utilize that material as well.

Besides teaching your children faith and morals, talking with them, counseling them, encouraging them, what else can you do as parents to help your teens practice the virtue of chastity? Jason and Chrystalina Evert ask parents to:

- Pray for their children. *The offering of Masses, rosaries and days of fasting should not be seen as a backup plan when all else fails, but as a parent's most powerful tool.*
- *Chastity...like all virtues is easier caught than taught. When a married couple practices chastity, their purity of heart, reverence and sacrificial love is obvious.*
- Do not use contraceptives in your marriage. If you do use them you teach your teen that *[y]ou need to follow the Church's teachings on sexuality outside of marriage, but you don't need to follow them inside of marriage.* (Sadly, 90% of all married couples contracept at some point in their marriage.[87])
- Protect teens from online pornography.
- Be a *parent first, and not a buddy. We have lots of buddies, but very few parents.*
- *Should a child make some mistakes, parents must be patient and not blame themselves. After all, who is the best parent in the universe? The Heavenly Father. Now look at the mistakes his children make. See His mercy as a model of patience.*[88]

Those Who Gave Their Lives To Protect Their Chastity

"I would rather die than lose holy chastity."
St. Casimir of Poland

Should your teen contend that chastity is too difficult to

[86] ***Children and Parents,*** *Op. Cit.*, pp. 80-82. [87] Zenit, Nov. 8, 2003.
[88] Zenit, Dec. 12, 2003.

live, give him the examples of the saints. All the saints practiced this virtue, some through the discipline of their bodies and intense prayer, like Mary Magdalen, others through martyrdom. When St. Thomas Aquinas announced that he planned to join the Dominican Order his family was terribly upset. When he left home, his brothers captured him and imprisoned him in the family castle for two years. Unable to dissuade him from his vocation, they employed a prostitute to tempt him to sin. When she was brought to his room, he took a red-hot fireplace poker and chased her out of his quarters. Then he branded his door with a cross. His family, realizing he was serious about his vocation, relented. For this reason he is known as the "Angelic Doctor of the Church." Due to his dedication to live the virtue of chastity perfectly he was able to write thousands of pages on God some of which are known today as his ***Summa Theologica***. Only one so pure and chaste could give us such a profound knowledge of God.

Other saints subjected themselves to more sensational penances such as throwing themselves into thorn bushes or into a river in the middle of winter.

Youth, raised on the blood and gore of such movies as *Braveheart* and *The Patriot*, should be able to relate to the following saints who heroically sacrificed their lives to protect their chastity.

In 303, although St. Agnes was only thirteen years old she had already made a vow to remain a virgin. When she refused to marry a prominent young man who had fallen in love with her, his father denounced Agnes to the Roman authorities as a Christian. As she was being led to her death the young man boldly approached her only to be struck dead by God. His father pleaded with Agnes to restore his son to life promising to stop her persecution. Her prayers restored the young man to life. Immediately upon his return to life he became a Christian. But his father could not stop the angry mob. Agnes was cast into a fire but the flames attacked the spectators instead. Again she prayed and the fire was stopped. Finally Agnes was beheaded.

Bl. Laura Vicuña, at the age of twelve, offered her life to save her mother from the life she was living as the mistress of a wealthy hacienda owner. In 1901, in a drunken rage, the man who her mother was living with beat the very ill Laura into a coma. Her mother, on learning of her daughter's sacrifice, left her life of sin and returned to the Church.

Bl. Teresa Bracco was a victim of Nazi brutality in 1944. A daily communicant, she was one of three young women dragged into the woods as retaliation against the resistance movement. Resisting the soldier's attempted rape, she told him, *I would rather be killed than give in.* The soldier choked then shot her. John Paul II, at her beatification, said: *To young people in particular, I hold up this young woman whom the Church is proclaiming blessed today so they may learn from her clear faith, witnessed to in daily commitment, moral consistency without compromises and the courage of sacrificing even life if necessary, in order not to betray the values that give it meaning.*[89]

A year later Bishop Vilmos Apor, of Hungary, was declared blessed. He was martyred by Russian troops when he refused to turn over the hundred women and girls hiding in his cellar. Shot by a Russian officer, he did not die instantly. Instead he lingered from Good Friday until Easter Monday. The sacrifice of his life saved the women and girls he was protecting.

Bl. Maria Nengapete of Zaire was a young professed sister when military troops invaded her area in 1964. A colonel, attracted to her, made advances. When she refused him in the name of Jesus, he murdered her.

Bl. Pierina Morosini of Fiobbio, Italy, was born in 1931. She was the eldest of nine children. At the age of fifteen as a skilled seamstress, she took a job at a cotton factory to support her family when her father became disabled. Before

---

[89] Matthew, Margaret, Stephen Bunson, ***John Paul II's Book Of Saints*** (Huntington: Our Sunday Visitor, 1999) p. 347.

work each day she attended Mass, said the rosary as she walked to work and at lunch time she made visits to the Blessed Sacrament. As head of her parish's Catholic Action, she attended the canonization of St. Maria Goretti. After her pilgrimage to Rome she told her brother, Andrew, *I'd rather be killed than commit a sin.* Walking home from work in 1957 she was attacked. Protecting her chastity, she was fatally wounded. She died two days later.[90]

A soon to be declared Blessed, Alessandrina Maria da Costa of Portugal, was only fourteen in 1918 when she jumped out of a window to preserve her virginity. As a result of her actions, she was gradually paralyzed. *From her bed she carried out a precious apostolate of prayer and advice in favor of the numerous persons who visited her, attracted by her extraordinary virtues and charismas.*[91] Alessandrina died in 1955.

And of course, everyone knows the story of eleven-year-old St. Maria Goretti who Pope Pius XII called a *little and gentle martyr of purity.* Maria or Marietta, as she was familiarly called, was attacked by Alessandro Serenelli. When she fought off his attempts to rape her, Alessandro stabbed Marietta multiple times. She died days later in 1902. Alessandro's actions were fed by his addiction to pornography. While serving his 27-year jail sentence Alessandro was converted by a vision of Maria while he was in jail. Immediately upon leaving prison he went to beg pardon from Maria's mother. He spent the rest of his life working as a gardener in the Capuchin monastery of Macerata. When Maria was canonized, Alessandro attended her canonization with her mother. In honoring St. Maria, John Paul II told the youth of the world that *true happiness calls for courage and a spirit of sacrifice, the rejection of any compromise with evil, and readiness to pay in person, including with death, for one's faithfulness to God and His commandments. Today, pleasure and egoism, or even immorality, are often exalted, in the name of false ideals of*

---

[90] *Magnificat*, April 2002, Vol. 4, No. 2, p. 195. [91] Zenit, Dec. 22, 2003.

freedom and happiness. It is necessary to reaffirm with clarity that purity of heart and body must be defended, because chastity safeguards authentic love. May St. Maria Goretti help all young people to experience the beauty and joy of the evangelical beatitude: "Blessed are the pure of heart, for they shall see God." Purity of heart, like every virtue, calls for daily training of the will and constant interior discipline. It requires, above all, assiduous recourse to God in prayer.[92]

Our teens may never become red martyrs but if they hope to protect their chastity they will certainly become white martyrs as they resist peer pressure, the media, the advice of school counselors, doctors, and the immoral propositions of a boyfriend or girlfriend.

Other Examples Of Chastity

The Servant of God, Archbishop Fulton J. Sheen provides several interesting quotes, one from Mozart and the other from Victor Hugo when they were teens. Mozart in a letter to his father noted, *Nature speaks in me as loudly as in anyone else, and I believe with greater force than in the uncultured and gross. Nevertheless, I refuse to regulate my conduct on the same basis as some young men of my age. On the one side, I have a spirit sincerely religious; I have too much honor and too much love for my neighbor, to deceive any innocent creature. On the other hand, my health is infinitely too precious to hazard it in any passing fancy. I can swear before God that I can reproach myself with no failure.*

Writing to his fiancée in 1820, Victor Hugo reassures her: *It is my desire to be worthy of you, that has made me so severe on myself. If I am constantly preserved from those excesses too common to my age, and which the world so readily excuses, it is not because I have not had a chance to sin; but rather it is that the thought of you constantly preserves me. Thus have*

[92] Zenit, July 6, 2003.

I kept intact, thanks to you, the sole treasures I can offer you on the day of marriage; a pure body and a virginal heart.[93]

But lets look at some more contemporary examples. Loretta Young, a successful actress in the mid 1900's, was under contract to a studio to do whatever films they selected for her. After receiving the lead in a film that glamorized adultery she went to Louis B. Mayer, the head of her studio, and told him courageously, *I find this script immoral. I don't want to do it.* She then asked if he had read the script. When he replied in the affirmative she asked, *Well, if your daughters...were actresses, would you want either of them to play this role?* Mayer thought for a moment then replied, *No, I wouldn't. And you don't have to either.*[94]

When Miss Young ventured into TV her goal was to have a weekly show where she *could get one wholesome and positive idea into the mainstream of life each week.*[95] *She would then play the lead role, and return at the end to deliver "a thought for the evening," something patriotic, character-building or spiritual.*[96] Although she won an Emmy for her program and was named TV's Most Important Female Personality, her sponsor, Proctor and Gamble, was less than pleased. She was told by them *to tone down your moral standards, and stop doing shows involving priests and nuns.*[97] She refused, thereby losing them as her sole sponsor. When things looked bleakest, God sent her two sponsors to replace Proctor and Gamble so the show could go on.

Catholic actor Jim Caviezel, who starred in the film *The Count of Monte Cristo* and was Christ in *The Passion of The Christ*, refused to do a love scene with Jennifer Lopez until she covered up her chest.

Anna Nobili began disco dancing at the age of 19 and danced until she was 21. *They were three very intense years,*

[93] ***Children and Parents,*** *Op. Cit.*, p. 58.
[94] Joan Wester Anderson, ***Forever Young*** (TX: Thomas More Publishing, 2000) p. 170.
[95] *Ibid.*, p. 183. [96] *Ibid.*, p. 190 [97] *Ibid.*, p. 211.

during which I got lost. I used to go to discos every night and would stay there until 8 in the morning. I used to dance in the club from midnight until 4 a.m. and from 4 to 8 a.m. I would dance nonstop in another disco. I would even go to places outside Milan, for example, Amsterdam, where I would stay for four or five days. I looked for the most popular discothèques; and from there I got involved with men and alcohol. It happened that at a certain point I was in church for no particular reason. I began going to church on Sunday. In church, I cried continuously, aware of a different Presence. I saw young people who loved each other with great simplicity and were happy—in a real world, not a false one like the one I was involved in. Anna decided to make a retreat. One evening during the retreat she was gazing at the sky in St. Clare's Square in Assisi. Suddenly, *my heart was filled with an indescribable joy. I began dancing, but this time not to attract men, but to thank God and praise Him. I found what I was looking for.* The disco dancer became a nun. Anna joined the Sister Workers of the Holy House of Nazareth that works with the less fortunate, such as former prostitutes and immigrants. From her previous life experience Sister Anna points out that *the problem is not so much to go or not to go to discothèques, but to let yourself be caged in by unsatisfactory human relationships. Let's go to discothèques but with Jesus. It is normal that young people go in search of sensations and that these are stronger in the night, but often night life is lived out as a rebellion that leads to perversion.*[98]

Blessed Pope John XXIII, when he was but sixteen wrote in his journal, *Through the grace of God and the intercession of my Mother Mary most holy, I am convinced of the inestimable worth of holy purity and of my own very great need of it, called as I am to the angelic ministry of the priesthood.* He made ten resolutions. Below are seven of the ten resolutions that we can certainly teach our teens:

1. To pray to the Lord every day for the virtue of holy purity,

[98] Zenit, March 9, 2003.

especially at the time that I receive Our Lord in Holy Communion. I promised to offer the first decade of the rosary for holy purity and to ask St. Joseph to help me.

2. I resolved to mortify my own feelings to keep them within the bounds of Christian modesty; to this end I promised to guard my eyes.
3. I resolved to take care, when passing through towns or places full of people, never to look at posters or illustrations, or visit shops that might contain indecent objects...
4. At table, whether speaking or eating, I resolved never to be greedy or immoderate: I would always find an opportunity for a little mortification; as regards the drinking of wine, I promised to be more than moderate, because in wine lies the same danger as in women: "Wine and women lead intelligent men astray..." (*Sirach* 19:2)
5. I resolved to observe the greatest modesty with regard to my own body at all times and in every movement of my eyes, hands, mind etc., both in public and in private. At night I would place the rosary of the Blessed Virgin around my neck, fold my arms crosswise on my breast...
6. In everything I would always remember, I resolved that I must be pure as an angel...
7. I resolved not to forget that I am never alone, even when I am by myself: God, Mary and my guardian angel, I knew, would see me. When I was in danger of sinning against holy purity, more urgently then ever I would appeal to God, to my guardian angel, and to Mary with my familiar invocation, "Mary Immaculate, help me." Then I would think of the scourging of Jesus Christ and of the four last things, death, judgment, heaven, hell, mindful of the Holy Spirit's words, "In all you do remember the end of your life, and then you will never sin" (*Sirach* 7:36).[99]

Promoting Chastity in Society

In our recent mayoral elections in Springfield, a city where Catholics predominate, there were four contenders, all Catholics, in the primary. The weekend before the primary,

[99] Fr. Robert J. Fox, ***Saints & Heroes Speak, Vol. Four*** (Alexandria: Fatima Family Apostolate, 1996) pp. 65-66.

"Catholic" candidate "A" announced, *I don't want to alienate my Catholic friends, but I've been experimenting with Abundant Faith, and I like it a lot.* He then explained that he and his "Catholic" wife attend the non-denominational, black, evangelical church. My husband and I felt terrible that he, a fellow parishioner, had left the true faith. Despite his apostasy from the Catholic faith, he won the primary in a predominantly Catholic city. (Why would Catholics vote for him? If he can't keep his promises to God he's not going to keep his promises to the electorate.) Then, four days before the April election, in a very tight race, we received a letter from this same gentleman addressed to "Dear Fellow Catholic," telling us how, *Over the years, I have served the Church as an altar boy, a lector, and a Eucharistic minister. I am currently a member of Blessed Sacrament Parish [the neighboring parish].* He then goes on to tell about his pro-life involvement. Candidate A needed the black vote in the primary but the Catholic vote in the main election so he traded his soul back and forth for votes that would lead to power. His main opponent was no better. Candidate B, another "Catholic", lied that he had a college degree while at the same time promoted the fact that he is a member of the Knights of Columbus although he refused to divulge his stand on the abortion issue. After his primary victory he disclosed in the area newspaper that he left his wife several years ago for another woman, who he continued to live with in adultery. The Catholic population of Springfield elected him mayor!(If he could not be faithful to his wife how can he be faithful to the electorate?) Pressure placed on him forced him to give up living openly with his mistress but she publicly accompanies him to civic functions and is flaunted in public introductions. Catholic candidate C who lost the primary was a practicing Catholic, faithful to his wife of 40 plus years, and had proven his integrity and character when he served as mayor 20 years earlier—but he lacked the duplicity of the other candidates. He honestly addressed the issues telling people what they should hear, maybe not what they wanted to hear.

Catholic apathy is not limited to my city. Studies show that Catholic voters in the U.S. are responsible for electing **all** the pro-abortion politicians. At the Festival of Faith in Chicago a participant asked Cardinal George about Senator Kennedy and other "Catholic" pro-abortion politicians. Cardinal George threw the question back to the audience saying, *I don't vote for those people. Why do you continue to vote them into power?* Think about it. There are 400 "Catholic" pro-abortion politicians nationwide that Catholics have elected to represent them.[100] This is morally wrong. When you cast a vote for such individuals you are casting a vote against God as well as the virtue of chastity. This is not something you want on your résumé when you stand before God at the moment of death. Furthermore, everyone, not only God, but your friends, business acquaintances, family members, the saints and everyone in the world is going to know how you voted at the final judgment. Are you willing to possibly lose your soul for the sake of voting for a certain party? Vote for candidates that stand for life, for morality, for marriage, for family values. Build up the culture of life! Don't cast your vote for the culture of death. Moreover, how can people living chaste personal lives vote for candidates who are unchaste? It is segregating our lives into one part chaste and one part unchaste and the result is the destruction of our culture and government.

Remember...**sin darkens the intellect.** Fr. Messenger pointed this truth out earlier in the beginning of this chapter but it bears repeating here that *we can distinguish two special results of human sin. One is the progressive darkening of man's intellect so far as his knowledge of God is concerned. This has led to the abandonment or the overclouding...of...belief in one God...Side by side with this degeneration in religious ideas, we find a corresponding corruption in sexual morality*. This means that a person in the state of mortal sin (one who is living in adultery, fornication, contracepting, or promoting abortion in some

[100] ALL press release 11/12/03.

manner, and "gay marriages") will not have the gifts of the Holy Spirit which are wisdom, understanding, counsel, fortitude, piety and fear of the Lord. Without these necessary gifts, how can a public official exercise his governmental power in a manner that will benefit citizens? He cannot. It would be like a dog trying to drive a car. It's beyond his capability. Furthermore, by refusing to live Catholic morality this person is rejecting the teachings of Christ as well as defying God. By doing so he/she is helping to destroy our culture and our government.

Our government representatives should be held to the same high standards that we demand of ourselves. Or is that the problem? Is it because we don't live the virtue of chastity that we are so comfortable with political candidates who have the same vices as ourselves? People called to be canonizable saints, and that is us, cannot support immoral candidates. We must expect and demand political candidates to be men and women of virtue, (particularly the virtue of chastity), responsibility and character. Only then will we have a chaste culture.

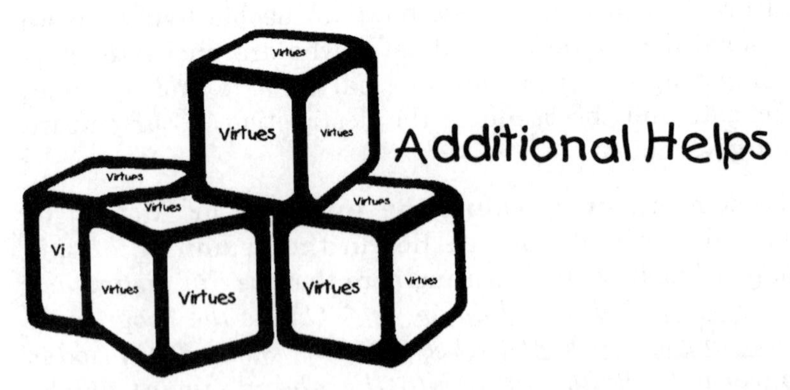

Additional Helps

✓ Read the Pontifical Council for the Family Document, ***The Truth and Meaning of Human Sexuality*** published in 1995. It can be ordered from CNS Documentary Service at (202) 541-3290.

- ✓ Read ***Parents, Children and the Facts of Life*** by Henry V. Sattler, C.SS.R., Ph.D. printed by St. Anthony Guild Press, 1952 or the shorter booklet entitled "Sex Education In The Catholic Family" by Rev. H. Vernon Sattler, C.SS.R. from Christendom Publications, Route 3, Box 87, Front Royal, Virginia 22630.

- ✓ Dr. Colleen Mast has a parent guide, student workbook and teacher's manual for both ***Love and Life: A Christian Sexual Morality Guide for Teens*** and ***Sex Respect: The Option of True Sexual Freedom.*** Mast also has a variety of videos. Check out her website www.sexrespect.com Get her free sheets for parents of 10-year-olds (one for boys, one for girls) on what to tell them to develop virtue without giving away the mystery. They are called the *6 M's For Girls* and the *7 C's For Guys.* Her address is Respect Incorporated, PO Box 349, Bardley, IL 60914. Her phone is (815) 932-9398. Listen to her show on Catholic radio.

- ✓ Abstinence-based curriculum can also be obtained from Project Reality (847) 729-3298 or (847) 729-3308. They have an excellent workbook for teens entitled, ***Weaving Character Into Sex Education*** by Pat Socia. This book demonstrates how *Virtue is the fabric of our lives. It details how character and virtue can be woven into the fabric of sexuality education...* Project Reality also has a *Parent Power Initiative, Game Plan Abstinence Program, I Can Do That! Character Education Program* and *Navigator Life Skills Abstinence Program* in English and Spanish. The address for Project Reality is PO Box 97, Golf, IL 60029-0097.

- ✓ To learn more about homosexuality in schools check out the following web sites: www.missionamerica.com; www.Choice4Truth.com; and www.truthatschool.org

- ✓ Give your teens the book ***If you Really Loved Me*** by Jason Evert published by Catholic Answers.

- ✓ I recommend getting books by Mary Beth Bonacci, Dr. Janet Smith and Molly Kelly. There are also wonderful programs by the Couple to Couple League, Family Honor and Family of the Americas to help you.

- ✓ Chris West gives an excellent explanation of John Paul II's

Theology of the Body. Listen to Chris' audio tapes.

- ✓ Read ***The Theology of the Body—A Simplied Version*** by Msgr. Vincent Walsh. This book is published by Key of David Publications.
- ✓ Ask your teen to read ***Standing With Courage: Making Tough Decisions About Sex*** by Miss Wisconsin 1999, Mary-Louise Kurey. Her book is published by Our Sunday Visitor Press.
- ✓ Subscribe for your teens to *Reality Check* ($12 per year) published by the American Life League. *Every issue is designed to educate, energize and equip pro-life teens with the truth about life.* To subscribe call (540) 659-4171 and ask for Jason.
- ✓ Have your teens read ***Confessions*** by St. Augustine.
- ✓ Have your teens read the book ***Natural Family Planning and the Christian Moral Code*** by Jeanne Dvorak. It can be purchased from the Priory of St. John the Baptist (502) 637-3839.
- ✓ A great four-year religion series for teens is published by C.R. Publications (781-762-8811). Titles include: ***Catholicism & Reason, Catholicism & Life, Catholicism & Society, and Catholicism & Ethics.*** The books are only $9.95 each and the Catechist' Manuals are $4.95 each.
- ✓ Are your young adults frustrated at not being able to find a chaste, committed Catholic? Consider having them checkout the web site AveMariaSCOL.com This web site has produced 43 marriages and 29 engagements.
- ✓ Read the ***Catechism of the Catholic Church*** #2331-2400.
- ✓ Read ***Talking to Youth About Sexuality*** by Mike Aquilina. This is published by Our Sunday Visitor (1-800-348-2440).

Note: I have not personally checked out the Abstinence Programs listed. I am relying on the good reputation of the authors. Remember, what may be a good program for one family may not be suitable for yours. Please check all material before handing it on to your teens.

Scripture Verses for Chastity

Proverbs 5:26; 6:32
Ecclus. 7:40;19:1;33:29
Matthew 5: 27-32
Romans 1:24-32; 7:14-18; 8: 13; 12:1; 12:10; 16:17-19
1 Corinthians 5: 11-13; 6:9-11; 6:13-20; 7:9-16; 10:6-11; 15:33
Galatians 5:13-26; 6:6-10
Ephesians 5:3-14
Colossians 3:5-11
1 Thessalonians 4:2-8
1 Timothy 5:6; 5:23
2 Timothy 3:1-9; 4:3-5
Titus 2:11-13
2 Peter 2:4-10; 3:3-4
Jude 1:16-19

Fear of the Lord

Proverbs 14:26; 15:27
Ecclus. 1:11-13; 2:6; 20; 24:16; 25:13-15; 24:16; 34:19
Judith 16:19
Job 4:6; 28:28
Psalm 24:14
Isaiah 33:6
Luke 1:50

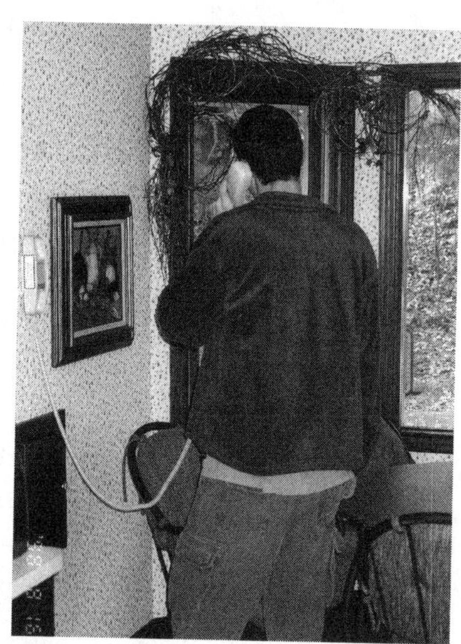

CHAPTER 5

HOW TO TEACH THE VIRTUES OF SOCIABILITY, HOSPITALITY, FRIENDSHIP AND RESPECT FOR OTHERS

The virtue of sociability, which is connected to the virtue of charity, lays the groundwork for the virtues of hospitality and friendship. Besides contributing fun, excitement and zest to life, people who practice the virtue of sociability also add years to their lives. The *Harvard Women's Health Watch* notes: *the more we socialize, the longer we're likely to live and to have our wits about us.* Research found that *a decline in social activity increased the risk of cognitive decline or death...[E]vidence indicates that it [socialization] has a host of other benefits—a reduced risk of colds, depression, and even death.*[1]

---

[1] *Harvard Women's Health Watch*, Volume VII, No. 4, Dec. 1999.

The Virtue of Sociability

"You will have found Christ when you are concerned with other people's sufferings and not your own." Flannery O'Connor

How does one live the virtue of sociability? Dr. David Isaacs explains:

> **The social person makes good use of and discovers ways of getting together with different people; he manages to communicate with them through the genuine interest he shows in them, in what they say, in what they do, in what they think and feel** (editorial emphasis).

Sociability is actually the virtue that helps us to grow in various other virtues. How? We need other people in order to grow in virtue (to improve) and others need us likewise to improve (and grow in virtue). St. Josemaría explains: *You clash with the character of one person or another...It has to be that way—you are not a dollar bill to be liked by everyone. Besides, without the encounters which arise in dealing with your neighbor, how could you ever lose those sharp corners, those edges—imperfections and defects of your character—and acquire the smooth and regular shape, the firm mildness of charity—of perfection?*[2]

Let's begin with the aspect of communication. But by communication I do not mean talkativeness, which we learned is a lack of the virtue of temperance. True communication is sharing our thoughts and concerns with another but **if one does *all* the talking there is no communication only a speaker and a listener.** We cannot help another unless we know their needs and they cannot help us unless they know our needs. **Vices** opposed to this virtue **include indifference and excessive sociability**. We practice this virtue with co-workers, acquaintances, friends, extended family members, and people we simply

[2] ***The Way***, *Op. Cit.*, #21.

run into day to day. A shocking example of the vice of indifference is found in the following newspaper article: *A 60-year-old tax official in Finland who recently died at his desk while checking tax returns went unnoticed by 30 of his colleagues for two days, reported a Finnish newspaper.*[3] Don't you find such gross indifference toward another person disturbing?

Teaching Sociability

The first step to socialize your children is to get them together with other children their age even if they do not at first play together. Small children play alone rather than with each other although they may be in the same room. They may watch each other but they do not as yet have the ability to interact together. Eventually the children will realize that they need each other to play house, have a tea party or play a game. This begins communication. Interaction will point out different qualities in each child that will attract or repel your child. **The next step is selection.** Your child will favor some children based on how likeable the child is or how good the child is in a certain activity. You will also notice that your child will avoid other children. **Mutual likeability leads to friendship between the children while admiration for mutual skills leads to sociability.** It's the same with adults. When your personality clicks with another, friendship blossoms. On the other hand, you may enjoy bowling or playing bridge with people simply because they are good at it but you do not consider them " friends." They are just people to have fun with, not share intimacy. Sociability leads us to take an interest in others by helping them with a project or concern or learning from them such things as how to do a hobby better, improve a skill or play a sport.

In teaching children this virtue, do not always invite the children to your home. Rotate homes so that one child does not become the "boss." Each home has its own set of rules

[3] "News You May Have Missed," *American Free Press,* Feb. 9, 2004.

so by rotating homes for play little children learn that while they may be the boss in their home they are certainly not the boss at the other homes!

In the chapter dealing with perseverance in ***Raise Happy Children...Teach Them Virtues,*** we discussed the importance of learning rules of the games and keeping them. This ability aids in the growth of sociability. A child will readily socialize with strangers if a parent or teacher warmly introduces the child to the group, and then explains the rules of the game or the expectations for the project. **Meeting new people in different situations is difficult for every age, not only children**. A new school, a new job, a new neighborhood, new parish, social events are stressful for everyone. **But one has to fight one's natural fear and shyness by focusing on the others rather than self.** Build up your child by pointing out the things that he can accomplish, has accomplished and what he can do in the new situation. If a child has to change schools, point out the child's assets and how they can be used at the new school: *You're an excellent musician. Why don't you join the band or chorus at school? You have a talent for writing. Why don't you volunteer for the yearbook or school paper? You seem to grasp subjects well. Why don't you volunteer to tutor slower students? You enjoy sports. Why not try out for basketball or softball? Why don't we invite all the girls (or boys) in your class for a pizza party so you can get to know them?*

Older children may have sociability problems because they are overly shy or refuse to play by the rules. If your child has one of these problems, work hard to help him to overcome it because a life without socializing and friendship is a lonely, unhappy life. Besides, the child needs to be involved with other children, to be concerned about them, and interested in them for him to mature properly. Try to discern the problem. Pray for insights on how to handle the situation. Try to find a group or activity that your child enjoys, or some children who are in similar need of companionship. Invite the families over to socialize. Suggest outings that you can all go on. Enroll your child in classes such as swimming, gymnastics, dance, or science.

Teach your child how to ask questions. It is through questioning people that we learn what they are doing, what their opinions are, what they have experienced. Few people cultivate this aspect of sociability. It occurred to me years ago to try an experiment. Rather than volunteering any information about my life or family, I would wait until someone asked. Instead I would listen and question people (this also comes from being a reporter!). It was amazing to find that some women could call and carry on an hour-long monologue. I knew everything, and I mean everything, going on in their lives, but they knew nothing about what was going on in my life. Next I tried the technique on extended family either listening or questioning them with pretty much the same results. Those experiences gave birth to my infamous Christmas letter, which is my way of sharing my life with others.

Train your children to ask the questions that reporters ask: who, what, where, how, when, and why. Everyone is interesting. Everyone has interesting aspects to his life or is involved in interesting pursuits. Show your children how to draw people out by asking appropriate questions. *What is your name? Where do you live? Have you lived there long? What school do you go to? How many brothers and sisters do you have? What are their names and ages? Do you like sports? What are your favorite teams? What type of music do you like?* People love to talk about themselves when asked. If your children are going to a social event, use role playing to practice with them until they feel comfortable. If they learn this social grace they will be welcomed into every social situation because people are charmed by people who are interested in them. My husband, Bob, told me that what impressed him the first time we met was the fact that I kept asking him questions about himself, that I truly seemed interested in his life, what he was doing, his goals. Actually, I was just trying to think of ways to keep the conversation going! It worked and I got the catch of a lifetime. (Bob's a close second to St. Joseph.) There *have* been occasions when I have been on the receiving end of the questions. The most memorable was when I flew to Ann Arbor, Michigan to interview Mr. Tom Monaghan for ***Raise Happy Children...Raise Them Saints!*** It had been twelve hours from the time I left Springfield to the time I sat down to a private dinner hosted by Mr. Monaghan. During that time I was unable to eat because of plane cancellations, flight problems, running late, frazzled nerves and then trying to do the interview before the dinner party. As the caterer served the first of eight dinner courses, I was stunned to discover that *I* was the guest of honor. As such the other guests directed their questions to me rather than vice versa. The questions lasted through the first six courses. As hungry as I was, there was only time to sample part of each course between the questions and my answers. Fortunately the questions ran out just as the main course was served. Isn't life either feast or famine?

Communication though is more than just questioning as I learned. The other party has to express an interest in you and your activities. Also, help your child to keep up on current events. Expose him to cultural interests. Encourage him to read good books on a broad range of topics. These will all help him to become a good conversationalist. In addition, reading books will also increase your child's vocabulary. People who can only recount TV shows tend to be boring conversationalists. When conversation lags teach your teen to have a bombshell topic to drop that will stimulate conversation on an important current affair or moral issue. It gets people thinking about issues rather than self.

Coach your teen to have the humility to share his views,

interests and concerns with others without being boorish or overbearing. I mention humility because **shyness is an aspect of pride that fears rejection or embarrassment while boorishness is pride of authority.**

Allowing each child the opportunity to talk and to be listened to are important aspects of the family dinner hour. This teaches the child how to express himself in a friendly setting. Use the dinner hour conversation to help children learn to read body language...arms crossed may mean disagreement. Flushed face may mean anger rather than a temperature. Without the ability to read body language and facial expressions your teens will not only make social blunders but could unknowingly make many enemies. This is a learned skill that many people have not developed because they lack sensitivity toward the feelings of others as well as empathy, appreciation, and congruence which were discussed in Chapter 4 in ***Raise Happy Children Through A Happier Marriage***. They may be hypersensitive themselves but insensitive toward others.

David Isaacs lists the following points for parents to work on with their children:

1. Talking too much or too little through lack of vocabulary or not thinking enough;
2. Always talking about one's own interests without taking others peoples' interests into account;
3. Keeping quiet out of shyness or pride;
4. Not knowing how to ask questions;
5. Not knowing how to keep conversations going;
6. And not knowing how to bring up subjects which are interesting in themselves.[4]

When your children hit the teens their circle of socialization expands when they attend high school. Most likely they will be invited to parties at friends' homes. Keep tabs on whether chaperones are available. When your teen hosts parties keep an eye on the tone as well as the volume

---

[4] ***Character Building,*** *Op. Cit.*, p. 228.

of the party.

The virtue of sociability grows from one's respect and charity toward others. Unfortunately this is one of the forgotten virtues. People are reluctant to socialize. At weddings or other social events, people eat fast then run for the exit rather than staying to talk with others or dance. People may accept social invitations but not show up or cancel at the last minute. Besides a lack of commitment, it almost seems that people are afraid to have to communicate with others. What is the cause for this lack of virtue in our culture? Is it pride, laziness, the unwillingness to cultivate conversation or simply fear? Author Alan Ehrenhalt observes, *[S]cholars of modern American life...have been warning for years that simple sociability has been waning in this country and that there are bound to be consequences—ranging from the weakening of the democratic process to a worsening of middle-class mental health.*

...Robert Putnam, the Harvard political scientist...traced the erosion of social life across a wide range of categories, from the decline in church attendance to the reduced membership rolls of the Shriners and the Jaycees to the shrinking number of Americans who attend neighborhood meetings or other community events. But the statistic that struck him hardest was the change in American bowling habits. He noticed that people were going to bowling alleys as much in the 1990s as ever, but they weren't joining leagues as they once did. They were doing it solo.

...Ray Oldenburg, a sociologist at the University of West Florida...wrote... "In this culture we have come to totally devalue idle talk. We consider it a waste of time..."

...James Milam...looks out at the empty park in the center of town. "We're a lot closer together in communication, but we don't communicate all that well. People don't talk as much."

And the reason they give is nearly always the same: not

enough time. Life is too fast, too hectic, too full of activities, to permit much in the way of informal social life.

..."People don't have time to do anything but go to work, take care of the house, and go to bed."

...Sociability exists, but it must consist of planned events that have a beginning and an end, concluding promptly so that participants can move on to the next event in their lives...The sociability problem...comes not from an absence of relationships, but from a decline in the number of opportunities to nurture those relationships.[5]

Unless these vices are overcome the virtue of friendship is impossible.

St. Francis Xavier used the virtue of sociability to convert pagans in addition to bringing back lapsed Catholics. In his first missionary assignment in Goa, India, a Portuguese friend introduced him to Antonio Silva who did not appreciate the priest's long sermons. *Father Xavier began some noncommittal talk. At first Antonio said nothing...But the priest directed an occasional remark at Antonio, and he was obliged to answer. The priest was gracious, witty and always smiling. Antonio went unconsciously from silence to monosyllables, to grudging smiles, to awakened interest, finally to whole-souled conversation...Xavier kept on until he saw that his new acquaintance was fairly well thawed.* He then nurtured this relationship until Antonio eventually invited him to dinner. When he arrived at Antonio' luxurious home he was captivated by the man's charming children but troubled by the absence of a wife. *"Too bad they have lost their mother so young. It must be a great anxiety to you to care for them alone," purred Xavier consolingly... "Their mother is not dead, Father. She is right here in the house..." "Tell her to come in...Surely you want to introduce me to your wife...for...I am anxious to meet her."* St. Xavier knew the couple was not married. At the

[5] Alan Ehrenhalt, "The Empty Square," *Preservation,* March/April 2000, p. 46, 48, 50, 51.

conclusion of the meal, St. Xavier told Antonio that he and the mother of his children were to plan to be married the following day in the rectory. In saying good-bye he told Antonio, *"What is the use to be friends, if you won't let me help you, Antonio? There is a fine woman whom you are not treating properly. You could not have a better wife. And there's your own soul. Are you treating it right? Don't expect me to be satisfied until I get you straightened out. What kind of friendship would that be?"* [6]

Another aspect of the virtue of sociability is keeping in touch with friends and acquaintances through notes, letters, emails, Christmas cards, phone calls and visits. We live in a highly mobile society. Due to this, we and our teens have to make an effort to keep in touch with people who move away. What to say? Take a tip from St. Josemaría who was a master at writing letters to his spiritual children. Although written in the third person, the saint was really explaining how he wrote letters: *You praise very highly the "letter-writing apostolate." You wrote: "I just can't manage to fill the pages if I only talk of things that can be useful to the friend to whom I am writing. When I begin, I tell my Guardian Angel that all I hope from my letter is that it may do some good. And even though I may write only nonsense, no one can take from me—or from him—the time I have spent praying for whatever is most needed by the one to whom my letter is addressed."* [7]

The Virtue of Hospitality

"The social person makes good use of and discovers ways of getting together with different people..."
Dr. David Isaacs

The virtue of sociability has a sister virtue, hospitality. People who practice the virtue of hospitality eagerly plan events as well as occasions to get together with other people

[6] James E. Walsh, Titular Bishop of Sato, ***Tales of Xavier*** (NY: Sheed & Ward, 1946) p. 57, 59-61.
[7] ***The Way***, *Op. Cit.*, #976.

either at their home or invite people to join them in various activities outside the home. They are just as busy as everyone else but they make the time to practice the virtues of sociability and hospitality. Why do they put themselves out in this manner? Dom Van Zeller explains, *[i]t is the expansive, outgoing, hospitable people who are the happiest.*[8]

James Stenson points out the practical benefits of living the virtue of hospitality:

- Teens will learn from you how to be a good host.
- Teens will see the joy and laughter that results from friendships.
- Teens will see that friendships keep us young in spirit.
- Teens will see how adults respect you.
- Your friends' esteem for you will enhance your teens' pride in you.
- This will enhance your effectiveness as a parent.[9]

St. Padre Pio said that many sins are forgiven through the exercise of the virtue of hospitality. St. Josemaría writes: *"The apostolate of the dinner table!" It is the old hospitality of the Patriarchs, together with the fraternal warmth of Bethany. When we practice it, can we not picture Jesus there, presiding, as in the house of Lazarus?*[10]

The Virtue of Friendship

"He who walks with the wise grows wise, but a companion of fools suffers harm."

Proverbs 13:20

From the virtues of sociability and hospitality flows the virtue of friendship. From practicing those virtues we meet or are introduced to a variety of people from which we can select those we would like to befriend. Dr. David Isaacs explains how the virtue of friendship works:

Through friendship a person, who already knows

---

[8] ***We Die Standing Up,*** *Op. Cit.,* p. 143.

[9] ***Lifeline,*** *Op. Cit.,* p. 118.

[10] ***The Way,*** *Op. Cit.,* #974.

certain other people through shared interests in work or leisure, has regular personal contact with them which stems from mutual rapport, each interesting himself in the other person and in his improvement (editorial emphasis).[11]

We meet people at work, church functions, social functions, neighbors, newcomers, etc. Friendship has the same mysterious quality as love. Why is a certain person attracted to another? A person is attracted by a specific quality, interest, or value held by the other person. This grows into an acquaintanceship when each enjoys the other's company and qualities. *[T]he two do a lot of laughing and talking; they never feel bored; they learn—without the conversation ever becoming particularly personal or intimate—a great deal about each other.*[12] Once common interests and values are discovered, potential friendships are developed by the reciprocal practice of the virtue of hospitality (inviting people over and being invited back). It is from this more intense contact that friendships develop based on mutual rapport and common interests with the idea of enjoying, helping and improving each other. At this first stage of friendship, the relationship has not been tested. The next phase, Dom Van Zeller explains, is similar to marriage. The honeymoon is over and the relationship can seem flat with strained conversation. *This is the point at which many [potential] friendships disintegrate; these are the lean months...But now precisely is the time to hang on...The relationship entered upon a new phase...a necessary one and ...a temporary one.*[13] During this phase the individuals learn to adjust to each other's temperament, idiosyncrasies, moods, and tastes. The acquaintance is blossoming into a friendship in which confidences are shared, help given and received, sorrows shared, and the good of each advanced by the other.

---

[11] Dr. David Isaacs, "The Education of Friendship," Instituto de Ciencias de la Educación, Universidad de Navarre, 1981, p. 1.

[12] ***We Die Standing Up,*** *Op. Cit.*, p. 137.

[13] *Ibid.*, p. 138.

One of the aspects of friendship is helping our friend to improve, to grow in character and in virtue. How can this be done? By introducing him or encouraging him to grow more in holiness and in culture through our conversation, the sharing of our values and inviting our friend to accompany us to spiritual formation such as retreats, days of recollection, confession and cultural activities. St. Josemaría adds: *You cannot just be passive. You have to become a real friend of your friends. You can help them first with the example of your behavior and then with your advice and with the influence that a close friendship provides.*[14] Why should a person want to help his friend grow in holiness? As we have learned in previous books, only if a person fulfills the purpose for his life can he be happy. A true friend wants his friends to be happy. Our friends can only be happy if they live as children of God. St. Augustine uses this example: *Suppose you saw someone walking in the dark and you knew of an open well into which he might fall and didn't warn him—you would rightly be held an enemy of his soul. And yet, if he fell in, only his body would die. If you see him falling into sin, and you chuckle over it—what then?* As for cultural activities, they help to refine us as well as round out our personality.

A true friend can never accept or encourage a friend to do anything immoral or illegal. St. Josemaría cautions: *If your friendship is brought down to such a level that you become an accomplice in the wretched behavior of others, it will have been reduced to a sad confederacy which deserves no esteem whatsoever.*[15] Even if speaking out costs you your friendship, you must always exhort your friends to strive for the good, the better, the moral, the truth and all things holy. John Paul II insists, *a failure to speak the truth because of a misconceived sense of compassion should not be taken for love.*[16]

Explain to your teen that although he may give a friend

[14] ***Furrow,*** *Op. Cit.*, #731. [15] *Ibid.*, #761.
[16] Zenit, March 28, 2003.

advice or direction he must also be willing to accept the fact that his friend may chose freely to disregard it. *Where there is no freedom there is no true friendship.*[17] One can never force or dominate a friend.

Ron Hutchcraft advises teens: *You should not pick your friends based on who are the easiest friends to make (often they are the kids who are living for nothing) or the most influential (what makes you popular in high school is often what will cost you happiness for the rest of your life). You should choose your companions based on these two questions: "Where do I want to end up as a person?" and "Who is going in that direction?"*[18] This is because true *friendship arises out of virtue and it grows as virtue grows*, insists Dr. Isaacs. *This growth, in turn makes the person more lovable and more capable of loving.*[19] Can the converse be said as well? If one party continues to grow in virtue while the other falls more and more into vice can the friendship endure for long? Probably not. It will drop back into acquaintanceship.

Bertha Conde takes the relationship of virtues and friendship one step further: *Every friendship that lasts is built of certain durable materials. The first of these is truthfulness* (editorial emphasis). *If I cannot look into the eyes of my friend and speak out always the truthful thought and feeling with the simplicity of a little child, there can be no real friendship between us. Friends who have to be "handled" or "managed," or with whom we take refuge in fencing or posing, do not know the love that casts out fear.* Another view holds that: *"Trust is the first requisite for making a friend,"* says Hugh Black, *"faithfulness is the first requisite for keeping him"; and trust and faithfulness cannot endure without truthfulness* (editorial emphasis).[20]

Once a teen discovers his intimacy he can learn to share

---

[17] ***We Die Standing Up***, *Op. Cit.*, p. 100.
[18] ***5 Needs Your Child Must Have Met At Home,*** *Op. Cit.*, pp. 96-97.
[19] "The Education of Friendship," *Op. Cit.*, p. 1.
[20] Bertha Conde, ***The Business of Being A Friend*** (NY: Houghton Mifflin Co., 1916) "Truthfulness."

it cautiously with those who are trustworthy. When your child chooses his friends, *whether you judge those friends to be winners or losers, greet them, talk to them, feed them, drive them, get to know them. Every friend should feel important at your home.*[21] Include your children's friends in some family activities. Be careful not to negatively judge a person by dress or behavior. Remember that the psychology of teens (self-affirmation and independence) drives them sometimes to outrageous ends. If your child has been taught the virtues throughout his childhood, when he hits the teens he will be naturally drawn to similar companions. The guy or girl your child befriends may look extreme on the outside but may be rock solid within. Diamonds are not mined looking beautiful. They are usually hidden in chunks of coal that need to be cut, then polished to perfection.

Also remember that your teen can positively influence his friends by passing on the formation he has been given by you. While I do not have an extreme example to share, the following is an example of how your teen can influence friends for the good. Our daughter Mary Kate had a cute high school chum, Chris, who did not want to go on to college. The young woman was perplexed about her future. Chris was an excellent cook and a talented seamstress with a bubbly personality. When Katie learned about Lexington, a two-year college in the hospitality industry in Chicago (it is now a four-year college) she urged Chris to apply because she felt this was an area in which Chris could excel. Chris did attend Lexington and it launched an exciting career in food design and the food industry for the young woman. Now she's going to night school to complete her college degree while working a job she loves during the day. Her skills are in such demand that companies are vying to employ her.

John Paul II turned one of his most vocal critics into a friend. Domenico del Rio, a laicized priest, was a correspondent for the *La Repubblica* newspaper. He

[21] ***5 Needs Your Child Must Have Met At Home,*** *Op. Cit.*, pp. 96-97.

sharply criticized the Pope's trips abroad as "triumphalism" rather than evangelization. Due to his hostility he was barred from traveling with the Holy Father to Latin America in 1985. *That "punishment," as it was interpreted by his colleagues, changed del Rio's life. John Paul II met the journalist personally after the incident, and in that encounter del Rio began to discover the Pope's personality.* This led del Rio to dedicate himself *to researching the Pope's life, [which led to] writing five books* [on the Pope] *the last of which is* ***Karol the Great.*** As del Rio was dying in the hospital, a friend asked if he could pass any messages on to other friends. Del Rio replied, *[t]o the Pope! I would like you to tell the Pope that I thank him. See how you can say it to him. Tell him that I thank him, with humility, for the help he gave me to believe. I had many doubts and many difficulties to believe. I was helped by the strength of his faith. Seeing that he believed with so much strength, then I also found strength. I received this help when watching him pray...*[22]

Who Can Be Friends?

Children and parents can be friends, spouses should be friends, and boys and girls who are not romantically attracted can be friends. *Friendship is a free spiritual union of mutual, expansive and creative human love; it is a connection different from sex or the instincts of the flesh.*[23]

Dr. Isaacs writes about the parent-child friendship: *[T]he parent who takes an interest in what his child is doing, who talks to him, who gives him real support, but who does not seek—or does not find—a reciprocal response in this relationship: this parent is developing a relationship different from friendship.*

[P]arents can give their children friendship only in so far as the parent manages to get his child to respond in some way: the child has to seek the parent's good. When a

[22] Zenit, Jan. 28, 2003.

[23] A. Vazquez de Prada, *Estudio sobre la amistad,* Madrid, 1975, p. 188.

son really takes an active interest in his father, he can do so as a son or as a friend. The two roles are complementary, but it is worth emphasizing that the son continues to be a son of his father even if he does not become his friend.[24]

Grade school children interacting with classmates learn sociability but are actually too immature to have a real "friend." Any child who interacts with another child in some interest is loosely considered a "friend" for this age group. *The most problematic children in this stage are shy ones, who are afraid to take part in a group, and spoilt children, who often have a very bad time because suddenly they discover that others are not inclined to indulge their whims.*[25]

Other children who appear shy may simply be handicapped in some manner such as a hearing or vision loss that goes undetected or a speech impediment that triggers ridicule. Check your children's vision and hearing regularly. If a speech impediment is a problem, take your child to the area public school for speech evaluation and free speech therapy.

Pre-adolescents, while still members of a clique, begin to seek out a special friend to confide in, to express their feelings to. This companion is still not technically a "friend."

The Qualities of a Friend

"Do I not destroy my enemies when I make them my friends?" Abraham Lincoln

Did you realize that thieves cannot become friends? Recall the saying, *There is no honor among thieves*. Likewise, other people who are steeped in vice cannot become friends. Why? Dr. Isaacs explains:*...**there is no friendship where there is no virtue**. Therefore, the development of the whole range of human virtues is essential for friendship...Loyalty is a virtue which helps a person to accept the bonds implicit in his attachment to his friend;...it strengthens and protects the series of values that go to make up friendship. Generosity*

[24] "The Education of Friendship," *Op. Cit.*, p. 3. [25] *Ibid.*, p. 6.

makes it easier for a friend to help another, taking into account what is useful and necessary for his improvement. Modesty will control the extent to which he surrenders certain aspects of his intimacy. Understanding will help him to recognize the various factors which affect his situation. Trust and respect lead a person to show interest in his friend: to show that he believes in him and in his ability to improve. We could say, therefore, that a good friend is someone who tries to surpass himself in a whole series of virtues (editorial emphasis).[26]

In addition, friendship is the giving of oneself to another. In friendship a person sacrifices himself for the other. Also through friendship one shares the joys and sorrows of life with his friend. **If one gives and the other only takes, the friendship is strictly one sided and will crumble shortly. If a child is always taking from the parent, friendship between the parent and child cannot develop. If the parent lacks interest in the child, friendship between the parent and child cannot develop.** If in-laws lack interest in each other, friendship cannot grow between the two. Friendships between boys and girls are possible but there is the added dimension of sexual attraction. Between a boy and a girl of upright character, the desire for mutual self-giving leads to marriage rather than premarital sex. St. Josemaría sums this up by saying: *You consider yourself a friend because you say nothing bad. That is true, but I see in you no sign of giving good example or service. This kind makes the worst friends.*[27]

To make friends rather than acquaintances one must be selfless rather than selfish. *You can make more friends in two months by becoming really interested in other people, than you can in two years by trying to get other people interested in you,* says Dale Carnegie. *Which is just another way of saying that the way to make a friend is to be one.*

In addition, teach your child how to be a friend. Friendships take work to cultivate, and work to maintain.

---

[26] *Ibid.*, pp. 6-7.

[27] ***Furrow***, *Op. Cit.*, #740.

It takes a spirit of sacrifice and spirit of service to nurture friendships. To be a friend means to put oneself out, to be inconvenienced, to personally suffer in order to help our "friend." Our "me" and "mine" society is practically friendless because it's self-based rather than other-based as in the following example. Beth received a call from a woman who hadn't been in contact with her for several years. She asked if Beth would throw a bridal shower for her daughter. At the same time she apologized for asking her to do this since Beth had already thrown a bridal shower for her first daughter but *I don't have any other friends to ask.* A friend does not ignore a friend for several years nor call only to get, not to give. Totally enmeshed in her own family and concerns, this woman makes no effort or sacrifice to become part of other people's lives. Ralph Waldo Emerson reminds this woman, *[t]he only way to have a friend is to be one.* Dr. Samuel Johnson adds, *If a man does not make new acquaintances through life, he will soon find himself left alone. A man...should keep his friendships in constant repair.*

Explain to your teens that friendship involves giving not just taking. It means fulfilling personal commitments rather than pushing them off on the other. It means putting up with the moods and quirky personality traits of the other. St. Josemaría must have heard lots of complaints from friends about friends for he writes: *You say that he is full of defects. Very well...but, apart from the fact that people who are perfect are found only in Heaven, you too have defects, yet others put up with you and, what is more, appreciate you. That is because they love you with the love Jesus Christ had for His own, and they had a fair number of shortcomings. Learn from this.*[28] *You complain that he shows you no understanding. I am certain he does as much as he can to try to understand you. But what about you? When will you make a bit of an effort to understand him?*[29]

Let's face it, we all have some quirks! Friends do not nurse grudges, hold resentments, gossip about the other, envy the

[28] *Ibid.*, #758.

[29] *Ibid.*, #759.

other, and refuse to forgive real or imagined injuries. A friend is there when the other is in need, despite his own personal concerns and obligations. Friends are never "too busy" to help. Alfred Adler believes that *[i]t is the individual who is not interested in his fellow man who has the greatest difficulties in life and provides the greatest injury to others. It is from among such individuals that all human failures spring.*[30]

The virtues teens must cultivate to make and keep friends are:

- Loyalty
- Generosity
- Modesty
- Understanding
- Trust
- Respect
- Spirit of sacrifice
- Truthfulness (simplicity)
- Commitment
- Service
- Compassion

We have discussed or will discuss all of the virtues listed above with the exception of compassion. Compassion is empathy for the sorrows or worries of another. *So deeply can some natures feel the miseries of others that often the elicited sorrow is more agonizing than the evil which causes it. A man may suffer more over a friend's distress than the friend does,* writes the monk, Dom Hubert Van Zeller. *[W]hether it is over a sin or a sickness, a disillusion or a defeat, the fact of having to play the part of passive spectator to another's drama is an experience so purifying that fortunate are they who have been given the grace to endure it. They will never be quite the same again... When we grieve together with the members of Christ's Mystical Body we grieve with Him; when we comfort them we comfort Him. That is what our emotions are for—to be used for other people. But used wisely. We may not parade our emotions—even sympathy can become sticky and tiresome when overdone—but the more altruistic they become, the better. The more lively of our emotions are to be used for jollying up other people, the deeper ones for bringing them what we have to offer* (editorial

[30] Hallmark Editions, ***The Treasure of Friendship***, (KC, MO, 1998) p. 61.

emphasis).[31]

All writers on the virtue of friendship stress that having a friend is a privilege. As such *[t]he choicest gift that any man can give his friends is himself at his best. Most people are willing to give almost anything rather than that. Even fathers and mothers will give their children things in lavish and sometimes smothering abundance, but themselves at their best in intimate companionship—for the lack of that bestowal homes go to ruin.*[32]

Warn your teens against the natural tendency to want to possess a friend exclusively. *If we are greedy for the other's affection, demanding a monopoly and constant attention, then of course we shall try and run our friend. The manager-companion is an abomination... Possessiveness can spoil everything—not only the quality of the relationship but also the plan of God.*[33]

Teens tend to collect and discard "friends" easily because they *don't think about what they want or expect of others. Friendship implies service. A child who has not learned to serve others will only with difficulty develop a friendship based on mutual improvement.*[34] Dr. Rudolpf Allers believes that teens *form friendships because they are in need of someone to cling to, and they abandon their friends because these prove to be incapable of supplying the security for which they long.*[35]

Socrates advises: *Get not your friends by bare compliments, but by giving them sensible tokens of your love. It is well worthwhile to learn how to win the heart of man the right way. Force is of no use to make or preserve a friend, who is ...tamed but by kindness and pleasure. Excite them by your civilities, and show them that you desire nothing more than their satisfaction; oblige with all your soul that friend who*

---

[31] ***We Die Standing Up***, *Op. Cit.*, pp. 67-69.
[32] ***Twelve Tests of Character***, *Op. Cit.*, p. 98.
[33] ***We Die Standing Up,*** *Op. Cit.,* p. 99.
[34] "The Education of Friendship," *Op. Cit.,* p. 8.
[35] ***Forming Character In Adolescents***, *Op. Cit.,* p. 35.

has made you a present of his own.[36]

Teach your teen how to be a friend through your example. They must see that we value the virtue of friendship. Do we invite friends to our home frequently? When friends are sick, do we bring over meals, visit them in the hospital, send cards or flowers, have Masses said for their recovery? When a friend is suffering some hardship, do we devote our time and energies to be with them, to listen, to help in whatever needs to be done? Do we keep in contact with friends? *Children should see in their parents people who are ready to commit themselves, to help, to give, even if it costs an effort, because that is what makes friendship such a great thing. Parents who concentrate their friendships on superficial social activities lead their children to think that friends are tools for making life pleasant for oneself. Inviting people home, behaving nicely towards them, and then criticizing them behind their backs gives a child a totally wrong idea of his duties to his companions.*[37]

Once we live the virtue ourselves then we can encourage our teen to live the virtue of friendship by urging him to visit his friend *when he is sick, cheering him up when he is a bit gloomy, going with him when he has some job to do, sharing this intimacy as far as makes sense. And making an effort to keep in regular contact not only during the normal times, such as [school], but also during holidays, by sending postcards or phoning him. It is this effort to keep in touch that enables some people to stay friends, even to the end of their life, with someone they knew in childhood.*[38]

Select Friends Carefully

"There can be no genuine friendship between Christians unless Christ comes in to make a third." St. Aelred

During adolescence, the greatest influence on teens is their friends so teach them to select their friends wisely. The

---

[36] ***The Treasure of Friendship***, *Op. Cit.*, p. 52.
[37] "The Education of Friendship," *Op. Cit.*, p. 11.
[38] *Ibid.*, p. 9.

people we associate with have a great impact on our lives. If we associate with good people, we will be influenced for the good. If we associate with holy people, we will grow holier. If we associate with worldly people, we will grow worldlier. If we associate with evil people, we become corrupted. St. Paul, quoting a line from a popular play at that time entitled "Thais" written by Menander, insisted that ***evil companionship corrupts good morals*** (*1 Cor*. 15:33). Why are we so strongly influenced by friends? We want to please those we love. One of the most disturbing blows a person can receive is the disapproval of a friend or family member. For this reason Author Harry Fosdick warns: *When, therefore, conflict comes between our best conscience and the general average of our inner social group, we face the need for courage in its acutest form. We know then that to possess the strength of will to live above the average is one of the primary and most searching tests of character.*[39] That is why fortitude needs to be developed prior to the development of the virtue of friendship.

In researching this series of books I found it interesting how the saints were friends of other saints. One example is Ven. Louis of Granada who was the good friend of St. Charles Borromeo. St. Francis de Sales explains why: *Perfection consists not in having no friendships at all, but in having none except such as is according to God.* St. Thomas Aquinas adds: *Since genuine friendship is founded on virtue, anything good intensifies it...perfect friendship cannot extend to many persons.* Dom Van Zeller explains what St. Thomas means: *St. Thomas means...that though a man may have many true friends he will only once or twice in a lifetime know the joy of perfect friendship...God is the basis of all love, and is therefore the source of true friendship.*[40] An outstanding example of saintly friendship is found in the friendship of St. Basil the Great and St. Gregory Nazianzen whose feasts and friendship are celebrated on the same day, January 2nd. These two saints were born around 330 in Cappadocia. Both

[39] ***Twelve Tests of Character***, *Op. Cit.*, p. 140.
[40] ***We Die Standing Up,*** *Op. Cit.*, p. 129.

went to Athens to be educated then returned home to join monastic life for several years. Their personalities were very different. Gregory was a poet and a contemplative while Basil was an organizer and leader. Both were ordained bishops. St. Basil, the dynamic one, spread and defended the faith through his preaching, interventions, and writings. St. Gregory was appointed bishop of a small diocese then promoted to the see of Constantinople. Beloved by the people for his fatherly care and his faith filled sermons, he could not cope with the factions caused by the Arian crisis. After eighteen months he stepped down as bishop and retreated to the monastery where he was known as "the Theologian", while his friend Basil is known as "the Great."[41]

Teens & Friends

Teens, in a quest to distance themselves from their parents, develop lots of acquaintances whom they refer to as "friends." *The more he matures, the more selective he becomes in these relationships, distinguishing between a general sort of relationship and one which calls for commitment on his part. It is not very usual for a person to have many friends*(editorial emphasis).[42] We may have many acquaintances but few real friends—soul mates. The book of ***Sirach*** (6:5-17) gives advice in this regard: ***A kind mouth multiplies friends, and gracious lips prompt friendly greetings. Let your acquaintances be many, but one in a thousand your confidant. When you gain a friend, first test him, and be not too ready to trust him. For one sort of friend is a friend when it suits him, but he will not be with you in time of distress. Another is a friend who becomes an enemy, and tells of the quarrel to your shame. Another is a friend, a boon companion, who will not be with you when sorrow comes. When things go well, he is your other self, and lords it over your servants; but if you are brought low, he turns against you and***

[41] *Magnificat*, Jan. 2003, Vol. 4, No. 12.

[42] "The Education of Friendship," *Op. Cit.*, p. 6.

avoids meeting you. Keep away from your enemies; be on your guard with your friends. A faithful friend is a sturdy shelter; he who finds one finds a treasure. A faithful friend is beyond price, no sum can balance his worth. A faithful friend is a life-saving remedy, such as he who fears God finds; for he who fears God behaves accordingly, and his friend will be like himself.

Friendship is not simply based on mutual interests, friends, or tastes but a friend *must sympathize with him and tolerate him, but it will be enough if he shares my enthusiasms and loyalties. I don't ask that he should understand the things that I like but I insist that he should understand my liking them. His principles must be my principles but I can't see that his appreciations need be mine; it will help, though, enormously if they are. What is more important than having the same likes and dislikes is having absolutely no secrets about them...I must trust my friend sufficiently to let him see the flaws in my composition. Besides seeing my weaknesses and putting up with my failures this friend of mine must be ready also to look for any good that there may be in me.*[43]

A good friend can help and comfort you; a bad friend can hurt or destroy you. Thomas Alva Edison went into business with a close friend, Ezra Gilliland, who betrayed him in the end. We are told of St. Patrick that *[t]he bitterest blow of his life, [was] his betrayal at the hands of his dearest friend.*[44] St. Patrick in his ***Confessions*** explains how he was being considered as a candidate for bishop of Ireland. St. Patrick did not think he was a worthy candidate but his friend did, arguing with Patrick to agree to the office. His friend also spoke out in St. Patrick's behalf before ecclesiastic authorities as to Patrick's worthiness for the office. Then to these same ecclesiastic authorities this friend revealed a mortal sin that Patrick had confided in him over 30 years before. St. Patrick expresses his grief at the betrayal of his

---

[43] ***We Die Standing Up,*** *Op. Cit.,* pp. 130-131.
[44] ***The Wisdom of St. Patrick,*** *Op. Cit.,* p. 59.

friend: *But how, then, did it occur to him so soon afterwards to shame me in public, in the presence of everyone, good and bad, to heap upon me disgrace for an offense that he had willingly and gladly forgiven—just as had the Lord, who is greater than all men?*[45] Patrick then explains the situation he found himself in: *After the lapse of thirty years they [these Churchmen] found a charge against me, raising the words of a confession that I had made just before I was ordained a deacon. When in a state of worry and sadness, I had privately confided to my dearest friend a sin I had committed one day in my youth—in fact, in a single hour of weakness. I cannot say for certain—if I had yet reached the age of fifteen, and I was still, as I had been since my childhood, not a believer in the living God.*[46]

Another interesting friendship is that between John Adams and Thomas Jefferson. In reading ***John Adams*** by David McCullough, John Adams was the true friend whereas Thomas Jefferson was the type that the ***Book of Sirach*** warns against. Even after Jefferson betrayed him, Adams retained his goodwill toward him writing: *I do not believe that Mr. Jefferson ever hated me. On the contrary, I believe he always liked me: but he detested Hamilton and my whole administration. Then he wished to be President of the United States, and I stood in his way. So he did everything that he could to pull me down. But if I should quarrel with him for that, I might quarrel with every man I have had anything to do with in life. This is human nature...I forgive all my enemies and hope they may find mercy in Heaven. Mr. Jefferson and I have grown old and retired from public life. So we are upon our ancient terms of goodwill.*[47] Adams considered Jefferson a friend for life. He mourned the loss of companionship when they were estranged. Adams was the type of friend praised in the ***Book of Proverbs***: **He that is a friend loves at all times.** *All times. Not when it suits him or when there is nothing to prevent it, but when he*

---

[45] *Ibid.*, p. 207.

[46] *Ibid.*, p. 206.

[47] ***John Adams,*** *Op. Cit.*, p. 632.

feels the thing to be crumbling, when he is puzzled by the behavior of his friend, when other people oppose the relationship...when he has been treated abominably or casually or maddeningly...these are the times when his loyalties must remain fixed and unquestioned. Patience...call it constancy, longsuffering, magnanimity, or simply generosity—that is friendship's particular virtue. Heroic endurance is sometimes required to put up with misunderstandings...One of the saddest things in life is to watch the inability of one or the other in a friendship to meet the price which his privilege demands.[48]

Explain to your teens that sometimes someone who causes us pain, suffering, or intense dislike can over time actually become a great friend. Such was the case with St. Bernward and St. Willigis. Archbishop Willigis had ordained Bernward. After Bernward was raised to the episcopacy an ill-natured sister superior drew him into a jurisdictional conflict over her convent with Archbishop Willigis. The conflict became so contentious that the pope finally intervened on Bernward's behalf. *Willigis repented of his own impetuous conduct, expressing his recognition of Bernward's authority over the disputed convent by placing his crosier into Bernward's hand. The two bishops thereafter remained friends.*[49]

Thomas Edison and Henry Ford became close friends when Ford sought Edison's advice on his mechanical design for the car. We are told that *their friendship was a driving force behind their bright ideas. As business partners, friends and neighbors, Edison & Ford put the wheels of progress in motion...moving society toward a brighter future.*[50]

During the War of 1812 John Kinzie was a successful trader in Chicago. His lifelong honesty toward the Indians not only made him wealthy but it had earned their friendship. Because of this friendship, several prominent

[48] ***We Die Standing Up***, *Op. Cit.*, p. 133.
[49] *Magnificat* Nov. 2002, Vol. 4, No. 9, p. 303.
[50] Brochure from the Edison Ford Estates.

Indian chiefs traveled great distances to warn Kinzie of the planned slaughter of whites as they evacuated Fort Dearborn in Chicago to move to Fort Wayne, Indiana. The Indians convinced Kinzie to send his family away by boat but were unable to convince him to join his family. Kinzie, friend to many of the people in the town of Chicago and at the fort, hoped that his presence might prevent the attack on the whites. So for friendship's sake he resolved to stay behind and risk his life. At the same time, John Kinzie as well as several Indian chiefs warned the commanding officer of the fort, Captain Heald, not to leave Fort Dearborn but Heald's pride refused to allow him to believe the Indians. Kinzie as well as the Indian Agent William Wells were both warned a second time: *Be wary as you leave this place in the morning.*[51] *An attack will occur tomorrow morning after the march begins. It will be very bad.*[52] Unable to convince Kinzie to escape, the night before the Fort Dearborn Massacre Black Partridge warned the chiefs of the attacking tribes: *Many of you know Shawneeawkee [Kinzie] by sight. Those who do not must have him pointed out to them. His family will not march with the others; they will be in a boat and two of Topenebe's warriors will be with them. They are not to be harmed. The Shawneeawkee will be with the marchers, but he is not to be harmed.* ***Hear me well!*** *If one drop of blood is spilled from Shawneeawkee or any member of his family, we three here will personally kill those responsible, even should they turn out to be friends who have done it.*[53]

Other whites who had befriended Indians were grabbed by the Indians prior to the attack then told to run into the woods and hide. On August 15th, 1812, only a half hour after the whites abandoned Fort Dearborn, they were attacked by several hundred Indians as they marched along the shore of Lake Michigan. In the midst of the battle Kinzie was grabbed from behind by a group of Indians. He was told not

[51] Allan W. Eckert, ***Gateway To Empire*** (NY: Bantam Books. 1984) p. 572.
[52] *Ibid.*, p. 573. [53] *Ibid.*, p. 580.

to struggle but to stay with the band of Indians brought to safeguard him. When Kinzie asked the leader, Siggenauk, why he was protecting him since *I have not known you much, Siggenauk, and have done little for you.* The Indian replied: *You have been fair with us always and do you remember a summer ago when you stopped the Frenchman who was drunk from killing the young warrior who had no weapon? That was my son.*[54]

Margaret Helms, the wife of Lieutenant Helms and the step-daughter of Kinzie, was also placed under protection by the Indians. After the massacre, the boat occupied by the rest of the Kinzie family was returned to Chicago so that the whole family could be reunited at the Kinzie home where they were placed under protective guard. But as the days passed, hostile Indians began outnumbering the friendly Indians. Just as a band of painted warriors approached the Kinzie home to murder the family two influential aides of the Warrior Chief Tecumseh, Chaubenee and Sauganash, arrived just in time to save the lives of the Kinzies. Chaubenee and Sauganash asked the hostile Indians: *Why have you blackened your faces? Is it that you are mourning the friends you have lost in battle? Or is it that you are fasting? If so, ask our friend here and he will give you food to eat. Perhaps you have never met him before, and it is good that now you have at last. The Shawneeawkee is the Indians' friend and never yet refused them what they have need of. Friends such as that always deserve the utmost of protection from those who have benefited from such kindness. It is a policy that our chief—and close friend—Tecumseh has always observed.*[55]

From Chicago Kinzie moved up to Detroit where he had lived previously. There he was arrested as a spy twice but again through the intercession of Chaubenee and Sauganash he was released.[56]

The few whites who survived the massacre were awarded

[54] *Ibid.*, p. 625. [55] *Ibid.*, p. 671. [56] *Ibid.*, p. 688.

as prizes to the different tribes. Lieutenant Helms, the son-in-law of John Kinzie, was taken to Pittsburgh by Chief Mittatass. When Black Partridge learned of his fate he ransomed Helms with his own horse, rifle and the gold nose-crescent he had worn for years.[57]

How can you ensure that your children will select "good" friends? The selection of good friends depends on the values and virtues you have taught your children from little on. If you have trained them in goodness, goodness will attract them. If you are immersed in worldly concerns your children will be attracted to worldly people. *If the children have had a soft life, going always after superficial pleasures, it is quite likely that the child will look for friends among people who can give him the same sort of pleasure...*[58]

If your child is not home schooled, select your child's school carefully because it will be at school that your child develops friendships. A school that lacks values and ignores God will attract like-minded students for the most part. Check the values and moral beliefs of coaches or the leaders of clubs and other organizations that your child wants to join. Avoid those groups or activities headed by morally questionable people. In one family the youngest daughter wanted to take ice-skating lessons from a person she considered to be the best skating instructor in town. Her parents said "no" when they learned the instructor was a homosexual activist. The parents definitely did not want him influencing their daughter.

Help your children and teens to meet good friends by organizing clubs and fun, adventurous activities with families who have children and teens the same ages and who hold similar values. Another idea is to begin a boys' club or girls' club, a cooking club, a hobby club, a sportsman's club, a nature club, or put together a summer day camp.

When is a friend a bad influence? A friend is a bad influence on our children or us if his influence *tends to favor*

[57] *Ibid.*, p. 687.

[58] "The Education of Friendship," *Op. Cit.*, p. 8.

the development of vices rather than virtues.[59] Isaacs warns parents: *...[T]he most dangerous friendship a person can have is a relationship based on dependence of one person on another where the young person allows this influence to be exerted on him and makes no use of his own principles. Parents should keep a careful eye on the so-called friendships between their as yet immature children, and people who are very sure of themselves but whose principles are all wrong.*[60]

A friendship of this type could be with a teacher, coach, youth minister, employer, or older student. Dr. Isaacs also warns parents to keep an eye on friendships that develop, not based on personalities, but on the attraction our child has for the possessions of "the friend" such as cars, electronic games, a vacation home, horses, CDs, etc. Excessive possessions on the part of the friend indicate a lack of moderation on the part of the friend's parents and the friend. This friendship can lead to the growth of the same vice in your child. In other cases, a "friend" may have a beautiful sister or handsome brother who attracts your child. *The love of friendship should be gratuitous,* according to St. Augustine. *You ought not to have or to love a friend for what he will give you. If you love him for the reason that he will supply you with money or some other temporal favor, you love the gift rather than him. A friend should be loved freely for himself, and not for anything else.*

Through friendship there is a comfortable understanding and usually shared principles. Friends enrich one's life. Friends bring joy and happiness in shared activities or a common cause, along with consolation and support in times of trouble. To grow, friendship must be flexible, respectful, with a deep desire for the good of the other. Jealousy or envy destroys friendship. *A good friend makes demands on his friend, is understanding with him, is an example to him, gives him what he needs—neither more nor less—and finds time to spend with him.*[61] Bl. Mother Teresa of Calcutta adds: *The true way and the sure way to friendship is through*

[59] *Ibid.*, p. 7. [60] *Ibid.* [61] *Ibid.*, p. 12.

humility—being open to each other, accepting each other just as we are, knowing each other. That knowledge leads to great love, and love leads to great service, giving to each other. For me, that is friendship—that knowing each other, accepting each other just as we are, so that we can love one another and so fulfill the words of Jesus: ***"Love one another as I have loved you—as the Father has loved me."***[62]

A friendship in which one party is growing in virtue and the other is not usually drops down into the category of acquaintanceship. Take care of your friendships! A life devoid of friendship is not only unhappy, it is lonely.

Like everything else in life, friendships can suffer from overexposure. That is why it is important to help teens broaden their base of friends and acquaintances.

One of the heartaches of life is the loss of a friend for whatever reason. Be compassionate toward your adolescents when they lose friends. It's a wrenching experience at any age, but particularly during the emotional teens. St. Jerome, himself betrayed by people he considered friends, insists that *[f]riendship that can cease was never friendship.*

James Newton, the close friend of some of the greatest men of the 20th century observes: *As I think about each of those five men—Thomas Edison, Henry Ford, Harvey Firestone, Alexis Carrel, and Charles Lindbergh... [k]nowing them did much to shape my life. Edison, who never gave up, but turned a thousand failures into a triumph; Ford, with his imagination constantly grappling with new ideas; Firestone, who maintained a rock-like integrity amidst the shifting sands of business expediency; Carrel, who could lift you in a single conversation from the street to the stars; and Lindbergh, never content to pursue one great purpose, but constantly reaching for ever more challenging goals...They not only challenged my life, but they changed the life of everyone living in this century...And their greatest legacy to*

[62] Sean-Patrick Lovett, ***The Best Gift Is Love*** (Librerie Vaticane, 1982).

us would still be their faith, expressed by each in his own way, that we place our body, mind, and spirit at the disposal of our Creator, who will use them to fashion mankind in ways beyond our wisdom or imagination (editorial emphasis).[63]

Friendship is not only a privilege, a gift, and a virtue but *[f]riendship is an expansive spirit that overthrows vindictiveness and takes in enemies, overpasses jealousy and embraces rivals. Such magnanimous friendship is an elemental test of character. Such undiscourageable good-will is the indispensable foundation for the brotherhood of man.*[64]

The Virtue of Respect for Others

> *"The person who has respect for others acts or refrains from acting so as not to harm, and indeed so as to benefit, himself and others, according to their rights, status and circumstances."* Dr. David Isaacs

To practice the virtue of respect, one must love and one must practice the virtue of charity. St. Paul tells us that ***love* (charity) *is patient, is kind; love does not envy, is not pretentious, is not puffed up, is not ambitious, is not self-seeking, is not provoked; thinks no evil, does not rejoice over wickedness but rejoices with the truth; bears with all things, believes all things, hopes all things, endures all things*** (***1 Cor.*** 13:4-7). This is how one practices the virtue of respect for others. Until our teens acquire this type of love they will have difficulty practicing the virtue of respect.

Respect is shown to each person because that person is a child of God. In the second place respect is shown to people because of the person's status. The virtue of respect has a hierarchy. Teach your children and teens that they have an obligation to respect first God, then their parents not

[63] ***Uncommon Friends***, *Op. Cit.*, pp. 355-357.

[64] ***Twelve Tests of Character***, *Op. Cit.*, p. 179.

only when living under their parents' roof but throughout the life of their parents. They are also to show special respect to priests, religious, teachers, law enforcement officers, elders, siblings, relatives, bosses, fellow employees, neighbors, and anyone in a position of authority.

Parents, no matter what age or personal qualities/defects, will always be their children's superiors. The respect we have for our parents must be based on love and justice. Why? Because our parents brought us into the world, cared for and educated us. While we can never repay our parents we can make life more pleasant for them through our respect and love. This virtue in fact helps us to live the fourth commandment.

When we hurt them, cause them worry or sorrow, ignore them, manipulate them to suit our whims rather than for their good, we lack the virtue of respect. The ***Catechism of the Catholic Church*** points out:

> **(#2188)** ***Children sin against the respect they owe their parents by speaking unkindly to or about them, by striking or insulting them, and being ashamed of them.***

Additional sins against parents include **unkindness, disrespect,** and **neglect** of their needs. **Disobedience** is the main sin of children of minor age. As children mature and leave home, they are still bound to listen to the advice, accept corrections, and anticipate the wishes of their parents. The book of ***Proverbs*** teaches: ***a wise son hears his father's instruction, but a scoffer does not listen to rebuke*** (***Prov***. 13:1).

As parents age it is the obligation of children to give moral, physical and financial support when needed. We should be with them when they are ill, lonely or upset. The book of ***Sirach*** reminds us: ***Whoever honors his father atones for sins, and whoever glorifies his mother is like one***

who lays up treasure. Whoever honors his father will be gladdened by his own children, and when he prays he will be heard. Whoever glorifies his father will have long life, and whoever obeys the Lord will refresh his mother (*Sir*. 3:2-6).

This virtue not only obliges us to show affection and gratitude toward our parents but also toward our ancestors. It promotes harmony rather than rivalry among siblings. Respect is also owed to those from whom we received the gift of faith and the sacraments. This may include grandparents, other family members, pastors, priests, teachers, godparents or friends.

Parents assume that this virtue is infused into their children, that they will naturally practice it. Wrong. Original sin did a number on this virtue as it did on all the others. It must be cultivated and learned just as all the other virtues. But isn't it prideful for parents to insist on respect? No. If you don't teach this to your children and teens who else will? Furthermore, if your child does not learn to respect you, he will neither respect God nor anyone else.

How is the virtue of respect taught to children? *Responsible parents frequently draw their children's attention to the greatness of the other spouse,* James Stenson points out. *Children need to be reminded: Mom and Dad honor each other. Mom says, for instance, "See how patient and dedicated your father is, how much he loves us; see how he goes off to work even when he is tired or has a headache." Dad, in turn, says, "Your mother is a great woman. See how she never stops serving us, doing countless things for our happiness, no matter how tired she is. She deserves the best that we can give her."*

If children respect their parents, they will unconsciously imitate them. A huge part of that respect (as with any respect given another) derives from one's "reputation." So each parent works, on purpose, to reinforce the other's "reputation"—the high esteem earned by personal excellence.[65]

The converse is also true. Should we tear down our spouse in front of the children they will learn disrespect toward that parent. Other tips:

1. Do not permit your children to yell at or talk back to you or your spouse.
2. Present a united front to your children even if you disagree with your spouse on an issue that involves the children. Resolve it away from their prying eyes and ears.
3. Do not permit vulgar, coarse language or swearing in your presence or in the home.
4. Exercise your authority consistently.
5. Do not permit your children to bully or manipulate you.
6. Never take your child's side in opposition to your spouse.
7. Do not give in to the pressure of your children when you know what they want is wrong.

Sometimes parents neglect to teach their children the virtue of respect toward them because they "feel" that it is more important for their children *to like them* then respect them. This attitude smacks of the vices of pride, intemperance, cowardliness, and selfishness as well as the excessive vice of groveling for the regard of others.

After parents, children must be taught to respect others no matter what their race, religion, occupation, nationality or political persuasion. The "respect" that is flung around quite loosely in our society is actually disrespect. Some groups want "respect" for their position but refuse to grant that same "respect" to others. The pro-choicers are the darlings of the media while the pro-lifers are the villains. Society expects us to "respect" the free expression of art even though it is disrespectful as well as insulting to Catholic beliefs. This is actually disrespect and bigotry. The true virtue of respect means that we do not harm nor attack

---

[65] ***Lifeline,*** *Op. Cit.*, p. 96.

another person or another's belief. When the Church is attacked through radio, TV, films, articles or art this is disrespectful. We cannot ignore nor tolerate these attacks on the Catholic Church which Christ founded. The practice of the virtue of respect is to act in a positive manner to prevent or end disrespect. One of the main activities of the Catholic League is to see that this virtue is lived in the public arena. Do support this organization.

The virtues of sincerity, which we discussed in ***Raise Happy Children...Teach Them Virtues!*** and prudence, which we will discuss later in this book, also play a part in the practice of this virtue. If news reporters lived this virtue they would give both sides of the issue rather than censor the news to suit their agenda. The virtue of respect insists that people have a right to the truth.

Respect For People Vs Animals

It seems ridiculous to discuss this topic but last year while my family was vacationing at the Portofino Bay Hotel in Orlando, Florida, my youngest daughter, who was pushing her three little girls in a stroller, pointed out to me a woman pushing an umbrella stroller. In the stroller was a poodle! Is that not insane? But then society kills babies through abortion yet feverishly works to protect baby whales. Our culture does not respect the person but exalts animals. Consider this news story. *The British Daily Guardian reported Oct. 23 that the country's censors have approved, uncut, the rape scene portrayed in Gaspar Noe's film "Irreversible "...The author of the article, who defends the use of the scene, notes that the film "has been described as misogynistic, repulsively sensationalist, gratuitous and grotesque example of 'directionless machismo.'" In an Oct. 21 press release, the British Board of Film Classification justified allowing the rape scene saying it "contains no explicitly sexual images and is not designed to titillate."* Yet at the Cannes Film Festival, viewers were so shocked that

250 walked out and 20 people fainted during the scene and had to have oxygen administered to them. This same British Board of Film Classification was upset over a scene in "The Dancer Upstairs" which shows how the Maoist guerrillas in Peru attached explosives to animals so they could be blown up in crowded areas. *The board was particularly worried about two scenes in the film, showing a chicken and a dog with fake sticks of dynamite tied to them. The animals are shown walking into the crowds, but the film changes scene before the explosions commence. The board said the animals were "clearly distressed," and that it would not grant a certificate unless both scenes were cut. The Telegraph noted it was curious that the board made no complaint about other scenes in the film depicting children similarly strapped with explosives...After a long debate, the board approved the film, without cuts to the animal scenes.*[66]

There is another disturbing article detailing the fact that only half of the children in sub-Saharan Africa have been immunized. This accounts for the fact that 700,000 children die each year there from preventable diseases. The same day that this report came out there was an announcement by Associated Press of the debut of a glossy magazine for pets in Palm Beach, Florida. The purpose of the magazine is *to chart the season's biggest canine social events, the latest designs in dog beds and the general comings and goings that make pedigreed purebreds the talk of weekly grooming sessions.* But it doesn't end there. We are told that there are *lavish $1,000 plus birthday parties* for pets who wear $75 designer collars, diamond and pearl jewelry and $100 sweaters. A new business bringing in $222 million gross is pet insurance. In the same article *The Narragansett Times* of Rhode Island covered a story on the views of biomedical ethicist Dan W. Brock who *contended that society might be better off if it prevents the birth of blind and severely disable children. He justified aborting children by saying it would result in "less suffering and loss of opportunity in the world."*

[66] Zenit, Dec. 14, 2002.

Compare this to the last news story in this article that reported that the *Scottish Society for the Prevention of Cruelty to Animals, hoping to reduce the spread of the phocine distemper virus, had organized six marksmen to shoot the sick seals. The idea was to kill the animals before they could infect other seals.* The animal rightists learned about the plan and successfully stopped the action.[67] Our culture needs to learn the virtue of respect for other people!

Respect for Possessions

Young children base their respect for others by how these people treat them as well as the possessions (toys in most cases) the other child owns. Teens base their respect on the possessions, intelligence, and attractiveness of others. This is a false, superficial type of respect. No one should be judged except as a son or daughter of God.

In order to teach respect for the possessions of others, each family member should possess his own clothes, own toys, etc. as was discussed in the virtue of generosity in ***Raise Happy Children...Teach Them Virtues!*** In addition there should be family items that everyone is free to use such as scissors, tape, hammers, etc. Respect is taught by explaining to each child the difference between personal items and family items. *You can use the scissors because it is a family item. Everyone can use it but you must return it to its place when you are finished using it so when someone else needs it he can find it.* If the child refuses to respect these directions, penalize him in some manner such as an extra chore or not allowing him to use the item again. Make it very clear that personal items can only be used if the owner's permission is obtained first. It is wrong to take an older sister's sweater when she's out of town or to wear a brother's jacket without asking. When an owner gives permission for an item to be used, it must be returned in the same condition as well as to the same place it was taken from. It can't be dropped on the floor or rolled into a ball

[67] Zenit Nov. 30, 2002.

then thrown under a bed.

Watch little children carefully when they play with toys. For example, ask your daughter, *Did you ask Susie if you could play with her tea set? If you did not ask her, put it back. That is not yours to play with.* Avoid allowing pre-school children to play with their older siblings' things while they are at school unless the pre-schooler asked for permission from the brother or sister first. If you work on this aspect of the virtue of respect when the children are young, when they hit the teens clothes won't be missing from your closets!

It takes the practice of fortitude on the parents' part to stay on top of the development of this virtue in children and teens. It is much easier to give in to the teen's lack of respect by giving the item outright to the teen than to keep harping, *ask before using, put back the item where the item belongs!* But that would not be teaching your teens virtue. Besides the vice of selfishness, it is also a lack of fortitude on the part of the teen who takes items without permission or fails to return items after using them. Teach your teens that their actions have consequences. Point out how selfishness and the lack of respect causes others problems or hardships. If the teen can't seem to learn this lesson penalize him to get his attention.

Treating Others with Respect

The virtue of respect also pertains to the feelings of others. We are not to incite people to anger, hatred, envy, jealousy or revenge. To practice this we have to **think** before we act or talk. *How will this person react to what I have to say? Will he take this in the wrong way? How can I say it in a manner that he will accept? Is the timing right?* The virtue of respect is also linked to the virtues of meekness and benevolence. Fr. Joseph Malaise, S.J., explains that *[m]eekness is the virtue by which we control anger, bear with* *our neighbor in spite of his defects, and treat him with kindness. Meekness requires self-mastery, which forestalls and checks the impulse of anger. It requires tolerance of the failings of others, which demands patience. It requires benevolence, namely good will towards all, which demands a readiness to forgive and forget. It brings peace with our neighbor because it makes us bear with his faults, and enables us to remain on good terms with others; and it helps us to remain unruffled when others are provoked at us.*[68]

As for the virtue of benevolence, Fr. Malaise, S.J., teaches that it is *good will towards others, feeling glad of any good they happen to have, and not feeling bitter towards them because of their advantages.* It also involves sympathy: ***Rejoice with them that rejoice; weep with them that weep*** (***Rom***. 12:15). Furthermore he counsels: *Christians therefore must combat every impulse of hate, envy, and jealousy that rises in the heart. Benevolence brings superiors and inferiors, rich and poor, master and servants into a closer union of friendliness and makes them all children of the same Father in Heaven.*[69]

To practice the virtue of respect, the virtue of courtesy is also necessary. Fr. David McAstocker, S.J., defines courtesy as *an act of kindness performed with politeness...No cordon of police was needed to hold back the curious when St. Elizabeth of Hungary went about her task of aiding the poor and ill. For in those days such acts were common occurrences. People demonstrated their love then in deeds rather than in words. But now prominent personages must be photographed when visiting a settlement project...*

Courtesy should be the badge of all, both high and low...[But] courtesy no longer flourishes in urban localities...Strong men and hardened women push and jostle until they have thrust aside weaker people...Then the mad scramble to secure a seat...Where is the welcoming nod, the respectful tipping of the hat?

---

[68] ***Know Yourself***, *Op. Cit.*, p. 167.

[69] *Ibid.*, p. 173.

In defining charity, St. Paul tells us that it seeks not its own, and in another passage he speaks of fervent Christians as being the good odor of Christ. In these two ideas we have the essential characteristics of genuine courtesy. It is disinterested, self-forgetting, altruistic; and besides it is the exquisite perfume that emanates from a noble, gallant life...Courtesy...is alluringly attractive. It draws souls from far and near...Courtesy presupposes an unfaltering habit of self-denial, of thinking about the other fellow at every turn of the road, and even when you are off the road and camped about the fire at night.[70]

Courtesy is holding doors, greeting people with a smile, offering seats, returning phone calls, answering letters promptly, being kind and thoughtful toward everyone we come into contact with even when we are driving. Sadly, courtesy has been relegated to the Middle Ages when knighthood was in flower. People push and shove, slam doors in your face, snarl their misery, and use obscene gestures while driving. One of the saddest displays of lack of courtesy happened during a novena my husband and I organized, with the help of friends, for the diocese each year. Since the novena was during Advent and during Advent we are encouraged to give alms, we thought it would be a good idea to take up a collection to help the people in an Honduran diocese who suffered great loss and poverty from Hurricane Mitch. Each night we would hand out a sheet explaining about the collection and where they could send their check if they wanted to send it direct, along with the novena songbooks. The people who came for the nine evenings of the novena were "good" Catholics but many of them were not "nice" Catholics. As I handed them the slip of paper with the information some people actually yelled at me for taking up a collection "to help foreigners." Others threw the sheet back at me in anger. It was very disturbing to see the lack of courtesy, the lack of respect as well as their lack of charity toward their suffering brothers and sisters in Central America.

[70] ***The Litle Virtues,*** *Op. Cit.*, pp. 3-11.

Another virtue needed to practice the virtue of respect is the virtue of tact. Tact is a combination of patience, fortitude, and at times courage as well as self-denial so one can bring happiness to others. *In a hundred and one different ways this virtue may be daily brought to the front. We may exercise it by...arranging a nosegay in the room of a sick person, by a word of praise, by a wave of the hand to a friend, by writing a note to one in distress, by adroitly defending the absent, and so on...[T]here is an inherent quality which sets them apart from all others; the genuine thoughtfulness and interest, namely, which you have manifested in performing them...Our pet peeves really are petty, and when we lose our temper, we actually lose much more besides—our self-respect, the friendship of others, and innumerable opportunities of benefiting our neighbor spiritually.*[71]

To practice the virtue of respect towards others these virtues must also be exercised:

- Charity
- Courtesy
- Tact
- Meekness
- Benevolence
- Sincerity
- Kindness
- Thoughtfulness
- Prudence

More Tips

Little children, not having developed intimacy yet, can only live respect if it is tied to the virtues of obedience and fortitude. Begin the foundation of this virtue by teaching your child and teen that:

1. Everyone is different so each person must be treated differently.
2. Do not upset anyone by taking his or her things without asking.
3. Do not upset anyone by being unkind.
4. Do not criticize others.
5. Look for the good in people.

[71] *Ibid.*, p. 132, p. 142, p. 143.

6. Act positively toward others.
7. Show gratitude when others help you.[72]

I wish to add:

8. Return phone calls promptly.
9. Treat everyone politely.
10. Be courteous to everyone.
11. Write thank you notes for gifts, favors extended, dinners or weddings attended.
12. R.S.V.P. immediately to all invitations.
13. If you promised to attend a party or event follow through on your commitment unless you are on your deathbed.
14. When you commit to help, follow through.
15. Rearrange your schedule so that you can be present at the important events in your family and friends' lives such as birthdays, christenings, First Communions, weddings, confirmations, graduations, and family reunions.

If you and your children live the above you have a solid foundation in the virtue of respect for others. If not, get to work! The *Wall Street Journal* ran a distressing article on the problem of getting people to respond to invitations: *"Staggering, the number of people who have no respect," says Memphis socialite Pat Kerr Tigrett...In the old days, everybody responded to R.S.V.P.'s Now she and her social set figure they are lucky to get a 75% return...*

Hosts say their desire is simple: They want the head count. Caterers need it. Seating charts require it. Too often, guests treat hosts' homes, parties and weddings like bars; drinks and eats provided if they feel like dropping by. Such ingrates don't have "that higher level of morality," says Helen Meldrum, an associate professor of communication and psychology at a Boston-area college...

Consider Jennifer Kisyh of Gilbert, Ariz., who with her husband throws three big bashes a year. After attracting only about a 50% response rate...Ms. Kish, a violinist, pulled out all the stops on her latest invitation: "Please call me if

[72] ***Character Building,*** *Op. Cit.*, p. 87.

you CAN make it. Do not use the excuse that you are too busy for a two-minute phone call."[73]

That article shows how firmly our culture is in the grip of personal selfishness with its accompanying vice of the lack of respect for others. But the lack of respect is not limited to responding to invitations. **Once committed to attend a function the person also has an obligation to follow-through by attending that function**. One of my friends entertains during the Christmas season. Last Christmas she invited 83 people. After having to follow-up by calling the ones who did not have the courtesy to R.S.V.P., the day of her party 41 of the people who committed to come either called to cancel right as the party began or simply did not show up. The expense and the preparation for 41 no-shows were very costly, well over $100, as well as time consuming. These people lacked the virtues of respect, sociability, charity, courtesy, justice, responsibility, kindness, thoughtfulness, etc. You get the idea. Once a commitment to attend a function is made only the stomach or intestinal flu, hospitalization or death excuses you. Excuses such as: *I'm too tired; I don't feel like going*; *I'm angry with my spouse*; *No one will miss me;* are not options. In addition, explain to your teens that when they are invited to a private home for a party or a visit, the virtues of respect for others, courtesy, sociability, and hospitality oblige them to reciprocate by inviting the host within a short period of time to their home for a party or to visit. This is how the virtue of respect for others helps one to also practice and grow in the virtues of sociability and hospitality.

Another problem is a person committing to attend a wedding reception then not showing up. Weddings are costly with each plate costing between $50-$100. Typically 20-30 people commit to attend but are no-shows. This is a waste of food, which has to be thrown out, as well as a needless financial loss of $1500-$3000. Besides a lack of

---

[73] Christina Duff, "It's My Party, I'll Cry If I Want to, Cry if I Want to, Cry if I..." *The Wall Street Journal,* no date.

virtue, God is offended when we waste food needlessly. Think how careful Christ was with the food He multiplied. He told his apostles to collect the left over food into baskets. Likewise, think how you would feel if you personally suffered the loss of $1500-$3000. You would feel crushed and angry over the thoughtlessness of the wedding guests. Still not convinced of the importance of following through on commitments made? Read the parable of the wedding feast in ***St. Matthew*** 22:1-14. If you are a no-show your host would must likely want to throw you into the darkness ***where there will be the weeping, and the gnashing of teeth.***

The Catholic Church has always been in the vanguard of teaching people the virtue of respect. Even today in reading the writings of Pope John Paul II he always underlines the importance of respect for the individual as well as respect for various peoples. In reading Church history I have been so impressed how the Catholic Church has always taught respect for others. As early as the fifth century the Church *began to protest against the iniquity of slave-owners, and at least fifty regional councils between 451 and 700 enacted canons for the protection of slaves. Many bishops refused to allow them on their estates, and urged their masters to enfranchise them; while a council held at Toledo was obligated to check the zeal of certain holy prelates who were on the way to ruining their dioceses in order to meet the cost of manumission.*[74] From the twelfth century onwards various councils forbid slavery. It was the Protestant countries who allowed the slave trade to flourish. Remember it was Protestant England who brought the slaves to America.

Along with fighting slavery, the Church took up the cause of the serfs. *The serf was in no sense a slave; he was treated not as an animal but as a person; he possessed his own family, home, and plot of land, and he was quits with his master once he had paid his dues.*[75] But until that time the serf was tied to that land. Also, the serf was not permitted to

[74] ***Cathedral And Crusade,*** *Op. Cit.,* p. 264. [75] *Ibid.,* p. 264.

marry outside the fief. If he left the land, the lord could bring him back by force. When he died, the lord could seize all his goods. Furthermore, the lord could sell a serf and the property he worked thereby separating spouses. The Church stepped in to stop these abuses.

Then there is the case of Galileo Galilei. Pope Urban VIII, concerned about Galileo's failing health, wanted his case to be resolved promptly. Here is his actual story: "*When, in 1610, Galileo published "Sidereus Nuncius," in which he upheld the centrality of the sun in the universe, he received the applause both of Johannes Kepler, the great astronomer, and of the Jesuit Clavius, the author of the Gregorian calendar," [said] Archbishop Amato. "He even had great success among the Roman cardinals. In fact, all of them wanted to look at the sky through his famous telescope. Those who opposed him were above all the philosophers, especially those of the peripatetic school of Pisa, who were inspired by Aristotle, and they started to bring sacred Scripture into play. Because of these pressures, the Holy Office intervened." Archbishop Amatao called for an end to the legend surrounding Galileo, "transmitted by a false iconography according to which Galileo was incarcerated and even tortured so that he would abjure. When he resided some 20 days in the Holy Office, his room was the apartment of the attorney—one of the highest officials of the inquisition—where he was assisted by his own servant. During the rest of his stay in Rome he was the guest of the Florentine ambassador at the Villa Medici"...Cardinal Poupard said that "of course, Galileo suffered much; but the historical truth is that he was condemned only to 'formalem carcerem'—a kind of house arrest. Several judges refused to endorse the sentence, and the Pope at the time did not sign it. Galileo was able to continue to work in his science and died on Jan. 8, 1642, in his home in Arcetri, near Florence. Viviani, who stayed with him during his illness, testified that he died with philosophical and Christian firmness, at 77 years of age."*

The Vatican commission that served to rehabilitate Galileo stated that "the abjuration of the Copernican system by the scientist was due essentially to his religious personality, which tried to obey the Church even if the latter was in error. Galileo did not want to be a heretic; he did not want to be exposed to eternal damnation and therefore accepted the abjuration so as not to sin," Archbishop Amato said.[76] Galileo heroically lived the virtue of humility in this instance. We will study the virtue of humility in a later chapter.

There are many stories of saints showing heroic human respect. St. Patrick had such a refined sense of respect for others that he asked God not to judge harshly those who attacked him saying: *And when I was attacked by certain of my elders, who came forward and brought up my sins against [as a challenge to] my hard-won episcopate, I was truly on that day so cast down that I might have fallen, now and for all eternity. But the Lord spared His disciple, who has chosen exile for His name's sake, and He came strongly to my aid during this time of humiliation. And since I did not fall badly into disgrace and reproach, and no harm came to me, I pray to God that it will not be reckoned against them [who brought these charges] as a sin.*[77]

St. Hallvard, a Norwegian Sea trader, was on his ship about to leave the wharf on a business trip one day in 1043 when a pregnant woman begged him to take her aboard for protection. She told Hallvard that she had been falsely accused of stealing. Before Hallvard could cast off with the woman aboard, the men who accused her arrived at the wharf demanding that Hallvard hand the woman over. When he offered instead to pay the amount the men accused the woman of stealing, the accusers used arrows to shoot and kill Hallvard and the woman.[78]

Living respect for others does not have to involve a bloody martyrdom. It can simply be changing our plans to make

[76] Zenit, Aug. 21, 2003.
[77] ***The Wisdom of St. Patrick***, *Op. Cit.*, p. 177.
[78] *Magnificat,* May 2001, Vol. 3, No. 3, p. 211.

life easier for others. When Ronald Reagan was president, rather than going home to California for Christmas he *had Christmas Day in the White House so the security agents wouldn't have to leave their families.*[79] Several days after President Reagan was shot, while staying in the hospital he got out of bed to go to the bathroom. He was feeling poorly so he slapped some water onto his face but in doing so, he splashed some on the floor. Just then an aide came in to check on the President. When he saw Reagan wiping up the floor he said, *Mr. President, what are you doing? We have people for that.* Reagan replied that he did not want any nurse to have to clean up his mess.[80]

Francois Michelin, who headed the Michelin Tire Group for 51 years, spoke at a conference *which highlighted the importance of Catholic culture in valuing the person.* Michelin is presently the firm's honorary president. He stressed that *a true businessman responds to the client, and this is why he is always looking for a product of better quality that can be offered, while controlling the price.* Michelin pointed out that it is *[v]ital for a well functioning business to bring out into the light the diamond that is in each person. In this connection, Michelin said that one of the people who contributed most to the development of tires was a worker who had been hired as a printer. Eventually, the personnel office realized that he had many other qualities, such as imagination and the ability to do research. "Every human being is unique, irrepeatable. Functions and labels don't count, the person does. Both in the factory as well as in society, life is possible only if we listen to and understand the other's reason. To love is to see in people what they are."*[81] It was his company that aired those cute tire commercials with babies.

The virtue of respect for others also means faithfully living our vocation by being honest toward God and others. The story is told of the famous French artist Millet who gave us

[79] Peggy Noonan, ***When Character Was King*** (NY: Viking, 2001) p. 113.
[80] *Ibid.*, p. 187.
[81] Zenit, Sept. 1, 2003.

the painting "The Angelus." At his wedding dinner, his grandmother reminded him of this obligation: *Remember, my Francois, that you are a Christian before you are a painter...Never sacrifice on the altar of Baal.* Millet replied, *[e]ven if they cover the canvas with gold then ask me to paint a "St. Francis possessed by the devil," I will promise you never to consent.*[82]

For several years Bob and I attended Saturday evening Mass at the priests' retirement home for our Saturday Mass. Fr. Frank Sheahan turned the standing room only congregation into a large, affectionate family through his practice of the virtue of respect for others. His warmth, affection, thoughtfulness, and concern touched everyone's heart. So much so that people came 20 minutes early in the hope of chatting with him before Mass or possibly going to confession. No one left Mass early out of respect for him. They waited until he entered the sacristy so they could exchange pleasantries with him as they left. When the retirement center closed last year and Fr. Sheahan left the city, the group as whole was devastated. One of the women who attended that Mass called today reminiscing: *How I miss our Saturday evening Mass because Fr. Sheahan made us into a family. How I miss seeing everyone weekly.* See the power of living the virtue well?

Author André Nguyên Vãn Châu recounts in his book on Vietnamese Cardinal Francis Xavier Nguyên Vãn Thuân: *What struck me most whenever I saw Thuân was his great courtesy. He showed respect to all who crossed the path of his life, including those who betrayed, persecuted, or tortured him.*[83]

Respect was ingrained in all the family members of Vãn Thuân's family by his grandparents. As a result, his uncles and aunt made great contributions to Vietnamese culture and society. His uncle, Archbishop *Thuc, became founder and chancellor of the University of Dalat, the first Catholic*

[82] ***Twelve Tests...***, *Op. Cit.*, p. 131.

[83] ***The Miracle Of Hope***, *Op. Cit.*, p. xvii.

university in Vietnam. [Another uncle, President] *Diem worked tirelessly to develop the national education system, and founded the University of Hue. Nhu became the soul and mind behind the philosophical movement of Christian personalism in Vietnam. Luyen was instrumental in improving the mapping of Vietnam.*[84]

What happens when the virtue of human respect is not lived? It can cause divisions in a family, it gives bad example, it can lead to murder and even topple governments. Now let's consider the damage that can be done by one person who does not live the virtue of human respect. Into this model Catholic family, Cardinal Thuân's Uncle Nhu married a woman who did not live this virtue. She is the infamous "Madame Nhu" who made headlines in the 1960's with her rude, outspoken comments. She not only caused tension in the country of Vietnam but also within the family she married into. *The family's indivisibility seemed no longer to be possible...there had come between them a constant irritant: Nhu's wife, Le Xuan. The irresponsible improprieties... committed by Le Xuan, known to the family and public as Madame Nhu and to the press as "the first Lady," was making it difficult for the family to remain united. Her imprudent and thoughtless actions and words, especially her insulting remarks about the Buddhist who protested against Diem* [her brother-in-law and President of the country] *also jeopardized Diem's political standing by making him seem anti-Buddist himself.* (Madame Nhu held the position of first lady since President Diem was unmarried. Unbeknownst to his family or countrymen he had become a Catholic monk in France during the period of time when he left Vietnam prior to his presidency.)

Annoying incidents constantly marred the atmosphere at major family events. When the family gathered at mealtimes, Madame Nhu made sure that her children sat with President Diem. By doing so, Diem's brothers and sister could not be at the same table...[They] did not mind...but this prevented them from discussing together important family or political

[84] *Ibid.*, pp. 28-29.

matters. Diem fumed over the selfishness that forced their separation. Not knowing what to do, Nhu, looking guilty and helpless, sat by and did nothing. He did not have the courage to interfere with his wife's actions...Later [Cardinal] Thuân wondered...if Madame Nhu's ambitions and extravagances, as well as the anti-Buddhist cloud of suspicion that she personally had caused to hang over the family, had not played a major role in the Ngo Dinh clan's eventual downfall.[85] President Diem and his brother Nhu were eventually murdered in a coup believed to be instigated by the U.S. government. Other members of the family fled the country or were imprisoned by the Communists when they took over Vietnam. Cardinal Thuân was one of the members imprisoned. The way the virtue of human respect is lived can have international repercussions.

Teens & Respect

With the development of intimacy teens, wanting to be respected themselves, are more inclined to understand the concept of respect toward others. While they understand the notion plus demand respect for themselves, it does not necessarily mean they live the virtue themselves! Unfortunately, teens have an eschewed view of the virtue of respect. They feel that "respect" restrains them from helping another. To help another in the teen mentality is to "butt in," to interfere. Take the example of a teen who has an indication that another teen is threatening to shoot a fellow student, commit suicide or engage in premarital sex. Rather than utilizing the virtue of respect to stop the student from harming himself and others, the teen neglects his duty by remaining silent. Teach your teens that the virtue of respect is a duty to help others to be better. When students are harassing a friend or acquaintance, the virtue of respect insists that the teen step in and defuse the situation or get an adult on the scene. The virtue of fortitude that they should be deepening at this same time will fortify the virtue of respect.

[85] *Ibid.*, pp. 145-146.

Does respect mean that we have to accept everyone's ideas? No. Isaac writes: *We must distinguish between each person's right to his own opinion and the right of others to be told the truth and have whatever information they may need in order to improve. There is no lack of respect involved in showing another person that his opinion is mistaken; it is precisely our respect for the truth that obliges us to clarify matters.*[86]

Sometimes living the virtue of respect for others can lead to collapse of a friendship. Rather than feeling guilty about the loss of a friend console yourself with the fact that the friendship would have eventually ended because the other party is apparently unwilling to grow in virtue.

Pope St. Leo the Great reminds us that the virtue of respect is also tied to the virtue of charity. He urges us never to look down on anyone, never to judge, never to give up on a soul: *We know that many have gone into good lives from bad, have become sober from being drunken, merciful from cruel, generous from avaricious, chaste from promiscuous, peaceful from fierce. As the Lord said, however,* ***I came not to call the virtuous, but sinners,*** *and to no Christian is it permitted to hate anyone, for no one is saved except by the remission of sins. We do not know how priceless the grace of the spirit is going to make those whom worldly wisdom has debased.*[87]

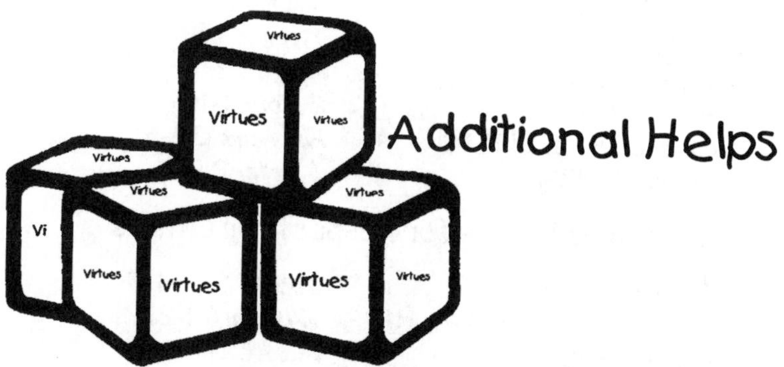

Additional Helps

✓ Review Chapter 4 in ***Raise Happy Children Through A Happier***

[86] ***Character Building,*** *Op. Cit.*, pp. 88-89. [87] *Magnificat,* May 2001, p. 185

Marriage! particularly pp. 158-160 and pp. 172-178. Also review the pages on courtesy: p. 144, pp. 241-244, p. 261.

✓ Plan to practice the virtue of hospitality at least once a month. Discuss with your teens how you are going to live it this month.

✓ Encourage your teens to read ***Uncommon Friends*** by James Newton; ***The Miracle of Hope, Life of Francis Xavier Nguyen Van Thuân*** by Andre Nguyen Van Châu; and ***Gateway To Empire*** by Allan W. Eckert (This book is out of print so try the library or second hand book stores.)

✓ Consider purchasing a book on courtesy for your children. Karen Santorum authored a book entitled ***Everyday Graces: A Child's Book of Good Manners.*** You can order the book at 1-800-5266-7022 from ISI Books.

✓ ***A Book of Courtesy*** originally written by Sister Mary Mercedes, O.P., in 1910 and updated recently is available from HarperSanFrancisco.

✓ View the movie *Ben-Hur* with your teens and children. Which vices destroyed the friendship of the two main characters?

Scripture Verses for Sociability

Proverbs 27:17 ***Tobias*** 11:18-20 ***John*** 2:1-12

There are too many to cite in the New Testament. What other examples can you point out in the New Testament?

Scripture Verses for Hospitality

Judges 7:6-7; 19: 1-30
Tobias 7:1-10
Mark 6:10-11
Luke 10:38-41; 14:7-14
Romans 12:13
Tit. 1:8
Heb. 13:2
2 John 1-10
Hebrews 13:1-6
1 Peter 3:9

Scripture Verses for Respect for Others

Proverbs 27:11
Eccles. 7:1-9:1-23; 4:12-6:17
Lev. 17: 9-10
Tobias 12: 1-22
Job 32:6-33:1-7
Wisdom 6:1-27
Mark 6:17-29

CHAPTER 6

HOW TO TEACH THE VIRTUES OF SIMPLICITY AND PATRIOTISM

The Virtue of Simplicity

"Better a poor man living an honest life than the adept at double-talk who is a fool."

Proverbs 19:1

The virtue of simplicity is simply refined naturalness...being completely genuine. Dr. David Isaacs points out:

> **A simple person ensures that his normal ways of acting—his speech, the way he dresses, the way he behaves—is consistent with what his real motives are; he allows other people to know him accurately: he is what he seems.**

To live this virtue we must be truthful and upright in our thoughts, words and actions. This virtue requires the virtues of humility, which we will discuss in a later chapter, and sincerity, which we discussed in ***Raise Happy Children...Teach Them Virtues!*** At the same time, sincerity lays the foundation for the virtue of humility.

John Adams, the second U.S. president, is referred to as the "always truthful Yankee patriot." What an outstanding compliment! He writes to his wife Abigail: *Let us have ambition enough to keep our simplicity, our frugality, and our integrity, and transmit these virtues as the fairest of inheritance to our children.*[1] Adams' view of the importance of the virtue of simplicity never changed. Writing to his grandson, John, he asked: *Have you considered the meaning of that word "worthy"? Weigh it well...I had rather you should be worthy possessors of one thousand pounds honestly acquired by your own labor and industry, than of ten millions by banks and tricks. I should rather you be worthy shoemakers than secretaries of states or treasury acquired by libels in newspapers. I had rather you should be worthy makers of brooms and baskets than unworthy presidents of the United States procured by intrigue, factious slander and corruption.*[2]

Cardinal Thuân's father, Thaddeus, and paternal grandfather, Dieu, were renowned builders and businessmen. Although known and successful, in the Vietnamese caste system they were regarded as commoners. When Thaddeus fell in love with the daughter of a Mandarin, Elizabeth Hiep Ngo Dinh, his father doubted that Elizabeth's father would accept his son's marriage proposal. Not only was there a difference in their castes but Elizabeth was the confidante and favorite of her father. Despite Thaddeus' urging his father to ask for Elizabeth's hand in marriage, his father procrastinated. Finally his son's pressure pushed him to seek an audience with Elizabeth's parents. He found that her parents lived simplicity in a refined manner. *Dieu*

---

[1] ***John Adams,*** *Op. Cit.*, p. 238. [2] *Ibid.*, p. 608.

was cordially welcomed into the home of the Ngo Dinh family. Upon [learning] *the reason for his visit, Kha said in all simplicity: "My wife and I have always had a profound respect for your father Vong and grandfather Danh. We would be honored to join our two families together. After all, both our families are descendents of martyrs."*[3]

The virtue of simplicity must also be lived in politics and society. Former President Reagan was criticized for his famous Evil Empire speech in which he condemned the Soviet Union. When asked why he used that term, Reagan replied: *I wanted to do some things differently, like speaking the truth about [the Soviets] for a change, rather than hiding reality behind the niceties of diplomacy.*[4] Peggy Noonan, who worked as a special assistant to President Reagan, writes: *Ronald Reagan loved the truth...He thought that by voicing it you were beginning to make things better. He thought the truth is the only foundation on which can be built something strong and good and lasting—because only truth endures. Lies die. He thought that in politics and world affairs in his time there had been too many lies for too long, and that they had been uniquely destructive. And so his public career was devoted to countering that destructiveness by speaking the truth, spreading it and repeating.*[5]

Vices Opposed To Simplicity

The vices opposed to simplicity are duplicity, insincerity, lying, dishonesty, finickiness, and contemptuousness. The excess vice is naivety that is a deficiency in prudence, wisdom or informed judgment.

Duplicity, the major vice opposed to this virtue, **is** best explained as **saying or thinking one thing but doing another**. It was the vice of duplicity used by Satan that tempted Adam and Eve to sin. Satan presented himself to

---

[3] ***The Miracle Of Hope,*** *Op. Cit.*, p. 22.
[4] ***When Character Was King,*** *Op. Cit.*, p. 201. [5] *Ibid.*, p. 200.

Eve as someone concerned for her welfare while his intention was to move her will to sin. Note also the lack of the virtues of respect and simplicity in the "Parable of the Two Sons" (*Matt.* 21:26-32). ***A man had two sons; and he came to the first and said, "Son, go and work today in my vineyard." But he answered and said, "I will not"' but afterwards he regretted it and went. And he came to the other and spoke in the same manner. And this one answered, "I go, sir"; but he did not go. Which of the two did the father's will?***

The first son lacked respect but rectified his actions. The second son lacked simplicity. He told his father what the father wanted to hear but had no intention of following through on his request. We are like the second son when we tell people what they want to hear rather than what they should hear. When a friend asks our opinion, we have to have the virtue of simplicity supported by the virtue of fortitude to rise above human respect to speak the truth even if the truth angers our friend causing a break in our relationship. Relationships can only be built between people practicing the virtue of simplicity. Without being able to trust that what a person says is what the person believes, the relationship collapses. For a person who lacks the virtue of simplicity future friendships cannot be built and sociability becomes difficult.

Mentioned in the last chapter was the friendship of St. Martin de Porres and Bl. John Massias. One day a boy in his early teens volunteered to take a letter from St. Martin to Bl. John. Once the boy set out, his curiosity got the better of him so he opened the letter to see what St. Martin had written. Then he carefully folded it up as it had been given to him. *Even before Brother John took the letter into his hands he said to the boy, "Son, don't you know it is wrong to read a letter entrusted to you? Curiosity can lead one into serious sin."* The boy did not deny he had read the letter. Bl. John answered the letter sending it back with the same teen after forgiving him his transgression and giving him a peach. Half way back to the convent, the boy's curiosity got the best of him again. Did Brother John tell Brother Martin what he had done? So again he opened the letter to read it. When he gave the reply letter to Brother Martin, Martin told the boy: *So, once wasn't enough! You had to repeat the offense. Child, what's going to happen to you if you keep repeating faults?*[6] That teen finally learned to live the virtue of simplicity but it took an embarrassing lesson to instill it.

Let's look at an historical incident involving duplicity on the part of the U.S. government which contrasts with the simplicity of the Ngo Dinh family. Following the assassination of two of Cardinal Thuân's uncles, President Diem and Nhu, his uncle Can took refuge in the American Consulate. He was put on an American plane after being promised safe conduct out of Vietnam. *However, when the plane landed, he was turned over to Vietnamese generals in Saigon. He was immediately jailed pending his trial by a military court. His fate was sealed...The generals told Hiep [Cardinal Thuân's mother] that they would spare Can's life if the family paid them a huge sum of money. But the family did not have money for the ransom. Ironically, had Diem and his family been corrupt, as some accused, they might have had hidden resources to redeem Can's life. The military's search for the "treasures" belonging to Diem, Nhu, and Can turned up nothing. The alleged foreign bank accounts and properties were pure fabrication. Any money Thuân's parents had saved had been invested in the restoration of the Phu Cam Cathedral...*

Pope Paul VI then personally intervened on Can's behalf. In a private audience with the pope, Henry Cabot Lodge promised that Can would not be killed. But the generals and the Buddhist leader Thich Tri Quang, who had long been opposed to Diem, encouraged by Lodge's subsequent silence,

[6] Eddie Doherty, ***Bl. Martin De Porres***, (St. Paul: Catechetical Guild Educational Society, 1953) pp. 45-46.

condemned Can to death and had him shot on May 8, 1964...[7]

As for the vice of naivety, it can get a person into a lot of trouble. Maria Von Trapp recalls how when they escaped Austria they became a family without a country. They toured Europe giving concerts, then came to the states for concerts but were not permitted to stay. When their visas expired they had to return again to war torn Europe. After another tour abroad they were invited back to the U.S. Relieved to be back in the states, when the Immigration Officer asked her how long she would be in the country she impulsively answered: *Oh, I am so glad to be here—I want never to leave again!*[8] She was supposed to say she had a six month visa. Her wrong answer landed the family on Ellis Island for four days. It took Congressional help to get them released!

Dr. Isaacs warns parents about the **vice of craftiness**. A teen is crafty when he **uses sly, cunning, or manipulative means to get something** he wants. This vice is most difficult to conquer because the teen lacks the will to fight the vice.

The Importance of Simplicity

How important is this virtue? St. Peter Julian Eymard believed that *[o]ne of the characteristics of holiness is simplicity, whereas one of the chief signs of spiritual decay is duplicity.*[9] He then points out Our Lady as a perfect example of simplicity in her actions, piety and virtues. *<u>Mary is simple in her exterior</u>. She is characterized neither by the severity of demeanor nor by an affected negligence. Her spirit is humble and gentle like that of Jesus. Everything that is hers bears the mark of her low station and places her among the women of the common people. In like manner should we wear the insignia of a humble rank: neither too much nor too little.*

<u>Mary is simple in the world.</u> She will readily sacrifice her

[7] ***The Miracle Of Hope,*** *Op. Cit.*, p. 158, p. 163.
[8] ***The Story Of The Trapp Family Singers***, *Op. Cit.* p. 200.
[9] ***In The Light Of The Monstrance,*** *Op. Cit.*, p. 129.

retirement...to go far away to her cousin Elizabeth so as to congratulate her and wait upon her...Whenever the glory of her Son will demand it, she will appear in public. She will say nothing in self-praise, will take advantage neither of her dignity as mother of the Messiah nor of the power and glory of her Son to gain prominence in the eyes of men.

Mary is simple in her duties. Mary fulfills her duties with meekness, without haste, ever content with what happens to her, ever ready to take up a new task. She fulfills them all with an evenness of temper...and seeks no consolation, which catches the attention of no one because everything is natural and nothing is overdone.[10]

If our goal is holiness we need to be straightforward toward God and others. St. Josemaría writes: *Naturalness and simplicity are two marvelous human virtues which enable men to take in the message of Christ. On the other hand, all that is tangled and complicated, the twisting and turning about one's own problems, all this builds up a barrier which often prevents people from hearing our Lord's voice.*[11]

The ***Book of Sirach*** teaches: ***When a sieve is shaken, the husks appear; so do one's faults when one speaks...the fruit of a tree shows the care it has had; so too does one's speech disclose the bent of one's mind. Praise no one before he speaks, for it is then that people are tested*** (27:4-7).

Christ tells us to have the simplicity of children if we hope to get to heaven: ***Amen I say to you, whoever does not accept the kingdom of God as a little child will not enter into it*** (***Lk*** 18:17). Most of the time we know exactly what is on a child's mind because they speak out, many times without thinking of the consequences: *Why does that man have a sore on his face? Why is that lady so fat? I don't like this food! Johnny broke the lamp!* This is not simplicity but rather a lack of tact. Simplicity is being truthful while being tactful. Teach your children and teens right behavior and

[10] *Ibid.*, pp. 130-131.

[11] ***Friends of God***, *Op. Cit.*, #90.

refined conduct. Original sin makes this a difficult virtue even in little ones. When parents ask children, *what are you doing?* Children reply, *nothing.* When we ask who did something, the reply is *I didn't do it.* There is a wonderful poem entitled "Mr. Nobody" that explains who is doing all the mischief around your home. Unfortunately I cannot recall the author but look it up if you have a chance because it will give you a chuckle. One day my one-year-old granddaughter, Noelle, found her way into the kitchen, pushed a chair over to the counter, then climbed up to help herself to some cookies. When her mother discovered the cookie thief, Noelle turned toward her mother, putting her hand with the cookie in it behind her back. As her mother was correcting her, Noelle would sneak a turn to take a bite of the cookie behind her back. The lack of simplicity begins young!

Dr. Isaacs reminds us: *Doing things with simplicity does not mean, therefore, doing things spontaneously, if this spontaneity goes against truth, beauty, goodness or order. To have the virtue of simplicity a person needs to use his mind and his will in the right way.*[12]

We practice the virtue of simplicity by being ourselves, not trying to be someone else in our lifestyle, dress, speech, activities or behavior. Teens show their lack of simplicity when they insist on following fads such as body piercing, tattooing, and boys bleaching their hair blonde. Following are some more traits that indicate a lack of simplicity:

- ✓ Wanting to be like someone else; trying to imitate that person; tossing one's own convictions aside;
- ✓ Expressing oneself in a dishonest manner;
- ✓ Thinking one is superior, inferior or simply different to what one really is, and acting in keeping with this false image;
- ✓ Spending one's time in superficial environments where there is little chance to express one's true self, because of the influence of others;
- ✓ Wanting to hide one's real intentions.[13]

---

[12] ***Character Building***, *Op. Cit.*, p. 215. [13] *Ibid.*, pp. 217.

Teens and children may lack simplicity simply because they want to be accepted, to be popular, to be seen as outstanding in some manner. When I was in first grade I took piano lessons because all the popular girls took piano. There was no love of music in my motivation just a wish to be part of the "in group." After a couple of months of this, my music teacher and I decided it wasn't worth the effort. It was an expensive and possibly frustrating experience for my parents but it taught me that life was easier when I was simply myself, not trying to be someone that I wasn't.

Teens, looking for respect and self-affirmation, sometimes go to extremes in their lack of simplicity. When my eldest daughter, Mary Kate, graduated from high school, tradition mandated floor length white dresses. Imagine the stir when one of the graduates flaunted tradition by showing up in an exotic black gown. While the teen and her parents thought this was a great joke on the school, it indicated a whole list of virtues the girl and her immature parents lacked. Rather than helping their daughter to grow in maturity and virtue, her parents were reinforcing her defects. Think before you permit your children to rebel against authority. It's a dangerous precedent to set.

Another example of the lack of simplicity is adults dressing or acting like teens or children dressing like adults. When we try to be something that we are not we become eccentric or odd.

Simplicity helps a person to live the virtue of responsibility. If a commitment is made, it is completed. This virtue helps a person to develop spiritually as well as to develop all the other virtues.

Obstacles to the virtue of simplicity are:

- ✓ Dress: wanting to seem better off, poorer, younger, older or, simply different.
- ✓ Speech: wanting to appear more intelligent by using

complicated words: pretending that one does not have qualities which one obviously does have; quoting writers one has not read, to appear well read; appearing to be better off or better educated through one's tone of voice or the "experiences" one tells; pretending to be revolted when one is not; making oneself out to have abilities one does not have; etc.

✓ Behavior: trying to project a false image; pretending one has a lot of work to do when that is not so; organizing one's life in such a complex way that one has no time for the things that really matter; reading everything, looking at everything, listening to everything on the excuse of wanting to be up to date, instead of trying to get a better grasp of the more important things; spending one's time, money, effort in a frivolous way, in order to show off, etc.[14]

The virtue of simplicity even affects the way we listen to people. Do we pretend to listen while we eavesdrop on another conversation, or glance around the room to see if something more interesting is going on, or try to watch TV while the other is talking? If we do any of these things we lack simplicity. This virtue is lived well when we give our full attention to the person speaking to us no matter how boring the conversation becomes. Rather than chaffing to disengage from the speaker see Christ in the other person. Consider how the conversation can be turned to bring the person closer to God. What can you interject to raise the tone? Pope John Paul II lives this virtue heroically. As part of the group of pro-lifers who fought for life at two UN Conferences, I was invited to a private audience with the Holy Father. In the room there were people from all over the world. As the Pope went from person to person he rapidly changed languages to speak to each in his own tongue. When it was my turn to kiss his ring and speak to him, I was so nervous that I spoke too rapidly for him to catch what I said since he had just been speaking Croatian but had to switch to English to understand me. Since the room

---

[14] ***Character Building***, *Op. Cit.*, p. 219.

was filled with people he still had to greet, the Pope could simply have smiled at me then moved on. I would never have known he did not understand what I said. Instead, he very kindly asked me to repeat what I had said slowly so that he could grasp it. That detail of love and kindness left such an impression on me. He was interested in the thoughts of a complete stranger. He truly sees Christ in each individual he meets. This moves him to show each person great respect.

Cardinal Albino Luciani, known to the world as Pope John Paul I, whose cause for beatification is progressing, was known for his simplicity. Although the patriarch of Venice, he walked the streets of the city dressed as a simple priest. Known to be timid, *when the truth had to be told, there was no timidness able to silence him. Albino Luciani had a sense of humor...[He] used to say that the not-so-interesting homilies he had given as a priest, automatically became brilliant and exciting for the people the moment he was consecrated bishop.*[15]

Bishop Jorge Carvajal of the Colombian diocese of Zipaquira, was kidnapped by Columbian rebels. Upon his release he displayed simplicity when he stated: *I owe my release from the rebels to prayer and to the Virgin, Mother of God.*[16]

And then there is the simplicity of Fr. Mieczyslaw Malinski, a friend of Pope John Paul II's from youth. *At a Mass celebrated in the Polish College in Rome on August 25, 1978, shortly before the conclave that would elect John Paul I, Fr. Malinski prayed for an intention during the Prayer of the Faithful: "Let us pray so that our Cardinal Karol Wojtyla will be elected Pope." Everyone at the Mass was stunned. After hesitating for a moment, Fathers Stanislaw Dziwisz, then secretary of the archbishop of Krakow, and Stanislaw Rylko, the current president of the Pontifical Council for the Laity, responded in a timid voice: "hear us, we pray." Cardinal Wojtyla, the main concelebrant, did not respond.*[17]

[15]Zenit, Aug. 25, 2003. [16]Zenit, Jan. 31, 2003. [17]Zenit, Oct. 17, 2003.

John of Fidenza, born in 1221 of a noble Tuscan family, is known to the world as St. Bonaventure. St. Francis of Assisi gave him that name when the saint cured John from a deadly disease when John was a child. It is said of St. Bonaventure, a Franciscan, that he projected *a picture of refinement, of exquisite and unequalled sensibility, together with a kind of supernatural radiance.*[18]

St. Bonaventure's friend was St. Thomas Aquinas, a Dominican. They both taught at the University of Paris. Thomas, also an Italian, came from the noblest of noble families. *As a layman he would have been entitled to bear four or five royal quarterings on his shield.*[19] His uncle was Emperor Barbarossa and his cousin, Frederick II. Yet he lived simplicity with refinement. He was a huge man whose face had the appearance of being absent-minded. As a student of St. Albert's at the University of Cologne *[w]ith his incredible tranquility and his astonishing gift of remaining silent, he appeared to his fellow students so dull-witted that they nicknamed him "the dumb ox". But on one occasion, during a debate, the ox broke loose, and with ten words silenced all his adversaries...[A] day came when the Master* [St. Albert the Great], *echoing their sarcasm, cried out: "Dumb ox if you like, but I tell you that he will bellow so loudly that the whole universe will be amazed!"*[20]

A lack of the virtue of simplicity is demonstrated by the national corruption scandal in Mexico where *political leaders have been taped and shown on television receiving money from an Argentine businessman...or planning deals with federal lands in the tourist region of Cancun...Bishop Martin Rábago appealed to corrupt politicians not to accuse others of their own guilt... "That is our tragedy, always trying to look for solutions to the problem of corruption and morality outside ourselves, and not beginning by the most difficult part, which is oneself...Something more is need than a change of laws, something more is needed than simply the force to*

---

[18] ***Cathedral and Crusade***, *Op. Cit.*, p. 327. [19] *Ibid.*, p. 329. [20] *Ibid.*

change. Evil is very often within the heart, and it is from there that social evils spring." [20A]

What are the benefits of living the virtue of simplicity? This virtue keeps us patient, optimistic, respectful rather than argumentative; humble, gracious, thankful, complimentary when appropriate; and aware of our relationship with God. It also protects one's government from corruption when practiced by politicians. In which areas do your teens need to grow in this virtue?

The Virtue of Patriotism

"Remind people to be loyally subject to the government and its officials, to obey the laws, to be ready to take on any honest employment."
St. Paul (*Titus* 3:1)

Patriotism is exemplified in the words of the Patriot Nathan Hale who told his British executioners, *I only regret that I have but one life to lose for my country.* Let's consider how Dr. David Isaacs defines a patriot:

A patriotic person recognizes what his country has given him and is giving him. He pays it due honor and service, thereby supporting and defending the values it stands for, while also making his own the noble aspirations of every country in the world.

Author Alan Ehrenhalt writes: *a direct link exists... between sociability and democracy. Those societies whose members retreat into their private lives eventually encounter a depletion in the stock of social capital they need to thrive over time...Oldenburg wrote in 1989... "The grass roots of our democracy are correspondingly weaker than in the past, and our individual lives are not as rich."*[21] See how necessary the virtue of sociability is to live the virtue of patriotism?

[20A] Zenit, Mar. 16,2004
[21] "The Empty Square," *Op. Cit.*, p. 46.

Patriotism Needs Moral Values

"Liberty permits us to freely pursue virtue or vice. People need limited government to have liberty. The right use of freedom develops virtue." Fr. Robert Sirico

Along with the virtue of sociability, patriotism likewise needs moral values founded on a belief in God. Consider the concern of John Adams upon learning about the French Revolution. As Author David McCullough explains, Adams *could not accept the idea of enshrining reason as a religion, as desired by the philosophers. "I know not what to make of a republic of thirty million atheists."*[22] In his retirement from politics, John Adams read a book entitled ***French Revolution*** with which he totally disagreed. On a blank page in the book he wrote his comments: *If [the] empire of superstition and hypocrisy should be overthrown, happy indeed will it be for the world; but if all religion and all morality should be over-thrown with it, what advantage will be gained? The doctrine of human equality is founded entirely in the Christian doctrine that we are all children of the same Father, all accountable to Him for our conduct to one another, all equally bound to respect each other's self love.*[23] These thoughts were echoed earlier in his life when he dedicated Washington, D.C., as the permanent seat of government. At that august occasion he told those gathered: *It would be unbecoming the representatives of this nation to assemble for the first time in this solemn temple* [the unfinished Capitol] *without looking up to the Supreme Ruler of the universe, and imploring His blessing. May this territory be the residence of virtue and happiness! In this city may that piety and virtue, that wisdom and magnanimity, that constancy and self-government, which adorned the great character whose name it bears, be forever held in veneration! Here, and throughout our country, may simple manners, pure morals, and true religion flourish forever!*[24]

---

[22] ***John Adams,*** *Op. Cit.*, p. 418. [23] *Ibid.*, p. 619. [24] *Ibid.*, p. 554.

A hundred and fifty years later a Frenchman, Dr. Alexis Carrel, who gave us modern surgery techniques, agreed with Adams. Carrel believed that the religious faith of people strongly impacted the positive workings of democracy. He worried that *the democracies seemed to have discarded faith, and there lay the cause of their weakness and inefficiency.*[25] Today, Cardinal Angelo Sodano, the Vatican secretary of state, insists that *a democracy without values is weak, very weak! In order that it be just, it must be cemented on a firm rock.*[26] For this reason the Holy See has been waging an intense, several-year-long campaign to include "religious heritage, especially Christian," in the European Constitution. *Archbishop Jean-Louis Tauran, Vatican secretary for relations with states [said that] rejection of the proposal...would involve "rewriting European history."* Which it would. See the interplay of the virtues we are discussing?

According to St. Thomas Aquinas the virtue of patriotism is linked to the virtue of justice as well as the virtue of piety. We mentioned previously that the virtue of piety relates to one's parents, families and country. How are they linked? *[O]n the basis of birth and upbringing, parents and country are the closest sources of all our existence and development; as a consequence everyone is indebted first of all under God to his parents and fatherland.*[27] How does this work? Our parents gave us life, cared for us and educated us. Our country provides us economic opportunities in which to survive, commerce, protection, socialization, a system of law and order, monetary exchange, intellectual stimulation and a host of other services. **Vices that undermine the virtue of patriotism include nationalism and indifference**. Another vice that undermines this virtue of patriotism is known today as "**the one-world government" or the "new world order**." This is a concept that creates certain

[25] ***Uncommon Friends,*** *Op. Cit.*, p. 137.
[26] Zenit, Dec. 11, 2002.
[27] ***Sum. Th.*** II-II, q. 101, a.1.

indifference toward one's country and the common good. It **emphasizes personal gain at the expense of one's countrymen**. We saw this in the last Olympic Games when a German skier won three gold medals for Spain and a Russian ice dancer won a gold medal for France.

The Role of the Church in Politics

"Statesmen may plan and speculate for liberty, but it is religion and morality alone which can establish the principles upon which freedom can securely stand. The only foundation of a free constitution is pure virtue." John Adams

Let's not forget that *a government's first duty is to labor for the world's salvation* according to historian H. Daniel-Rops.[28] All power to rule comes from God. Politicians and the people who elect them are answerable to God for the exercise of that power. For this reason while the Holy See is not a political power it is *a moral power that gives voice to the conscience of people*, stressed Archbishop Tauran.[29] A country can never legislate the acceptance of abortion, gay marriages, cloning and other moral aberrations and expect Christians to accept such legislation or legal rulings because they are opposed to the natural law of God. Neither can we say, "it's my country right or wrong." *Leo XIII, in his encyclical **Immortale Dei** of 1st November 1885, expressly declared that the temporal and the spiritual power are sovereign, each in its own sphere which is bounded by clearly defined limits* (editorial emphasis).[30]

In the Vatican II document, ***Gaudium et spes*** we read: *Citizens should develop a generous and loyal devotion to their country, but without any narrow-mindedness. In other words, they must always look simultaneously to the welfare of the whole human family, which is tied together by the manifold bonds linking races, peoples and nations.*[31]

---

[28] ***Cathedral And Crusade,*** *Op. Cit.*, p. 184.
[29] Zenit, May 25, 2003.
[30] ***Cathedral And Crusade,*** *Op. Cit.*, p.186.
[31] No. 75.

For this reason, politicians cannot leave their Catholic faith at home when they legislate for the common good. It is gravely, sinfully wrong for them to say, *I'm a Catholic but pro-choice* or *I'm personally opposed to____ but...* Former Italian President Oscar Luigi Scalfaro who headed that country from 1992 to 1999 believes *the problem of Christians' involvement in politics lies in their lack of formation.* Scalfaro points out that *the right/duty of forming a citizen corresponds, in the first place, to the parents. How many parents are capable of giving this formation? From my point of view, very few. When a young person is studying, his parents do everything possible to dissuade him from making political commitments. And when he begins to work, they say to him: "If you go into politics, you will get into problems. You will be fired from your work!" The other entity that has the right/duty to form, by divine reason, is the Church. It has the right to form the Christian as an individual person, as a member of a family, as a man who works, studies, enjoys himself, as a man who participates in the community in which he has rights and duties.*

What is of interest to me is that each Christian citizen lives his condition of citizen as a Christian. This is what really interests me, as the Lord will not judge a people, but persons individually. And I will not be able to say: "As no one got involved, I didn't get involved either." What is important for the Lord is if I do my duty...The Gospel is valid for all persons and for all peoples. It is valid for states and governments. It is valid for international organizations...The Gospel has the capacity to resolve international or national problems of all types.[32]

Across the ocean in the U.S., Archbishop Charles Chaput of Denver, Colorado, speaking at a Rotary Club meeting stressed additional points. He quoted philosopher Hugo Grotius *who once said that, "A man cannot govern a nation if he cannot govern a city; he cannot govern a city if he cannot govern a family; he cannot govern a family unless he can*

[32] Zenit, May 23, 2003.

govern himself; and he cannot govern himself unless his passions are subject to reason." And I'd add that a man's reason can't truly serve him or anyone else until he roots it in a moral conscience.

As a citizen, I think one of the worse moments in recent political history was when John F. Kennedy promised a Texas audience that he'd keep his Catholic faith out of his public service. I think all Americans—not just Catholics—have been paying for that mistake for 40 years. It's one of the turning points in our community life where this unhealthy fracture between public behavior and personal belief began to grow.

I want my elected officials to inform their actions with their religious and moral beliefs, even if I don't agree with them. I want them to do it prudently and in a spirit of reasonable compromise—but on the hard issues, I want them to act on their principles, because then I can respect them. I can't respect and I can't trust an elected official, or any other leader, who claims that he or she personally believes one thing, but then publicly does another.[33]

The Congregation for the Doctrine of the Faith published an 18-page document on January 16, 2003, entitled "Doctrinal Note on Some Questions Regarding the Participation of Catholics in Political Life." This document was signed by Cardinal Joseph Ratzinger and approved by John Paul II. Later, in the same year, in July, 2003, the Holy See published an additional document dealing with the moral problem of legal recognition of same-sex unions. The first document *highlights the current "cultural relativism" that advocates "ethical pluralism," namely, the rejection of absolute truth as "the very condition for democracy... [S]uch relativism, of course, has nothing to do with the legitimate freedom of Catholic citizens to choose among the various political opinions that are compatible with faith and the natural moral law...Catholic involvement in political life cannot compromise on 'the principle of respect for the human person,' because otherwise the witness of the Christian faith*

[33] Zenit, Oct. 24, 2002.

in the world, as well as the unity and interior coherence of the faithful, would be nonexistent." The note further makes it clear that Catholics can never collaborate with those laws that attack the person..." The document demands utmost respect of the human embryo and the family, based "on monogamous marriage between a man and a woman, and protected in its unity and stability in the face of modern laws on divorce. In no way can other forms of cohabitation be placed on the same level as marriage, nor can they receive legal recognitions as such" (editorial emphasis). *Catholic lawmakers must also defend "the freedom of parents regarding the education of their children... [as well as the] protection of minors and freedom from modern forms of slavery (drug abuse and prostitution, for example)."*

This document also notes that in *recent years, there have been cases within some organizations founded on Catholic principles, in which support has been given to political forces or movements with positions contrary to the moral and social teaching of the Church on fundamental ethical question. Such activities, in contradiction to basic principles of Christian conscience, are not compatible with those who...define themselves as Catholic"* (editorial emphasis).[34]

Since this document is so important let us look at other key points in it:

- It is not the Church's task to set forth specific political solutions—and even less to propose a single solution as the acceptable one—to temporal questions that God has left to the free and responsible judgment of each person. It is, however, the Church's right and duty to provide a moral judgment on temporal matters when this is required by faith or the moral law.
- Democracy must be based on the true and solid foundation of non-negotiable ethical principles, which are the underpinning of life in society.
- The democratic structures on which the modern state is based would be quite fragile were its foundation not the centrality of the human person. It is respect for the person that makes democratic participation possible.

[34] Zenit, Jan. 16, 2003.

- [T]he lay faithful are never to relinquish their participation in "public life", that is, in the many different economic, social, legislative, administrative and cultural areas, which are intended to promote organically and institutionally the common good.
- [T]hose who are directly involved in lawmaking bodies have a grave and clear obligation to oppose any law that attacks human life. For them, as for every Catholic, it is impossible to promote such laws or to vote for them (Editorial emphasis).
- When political activity comes up against moral principles that do not admit of exception, compromise or derogation, the Catholic commitment becomes more evident and laden with responsibility. In the face of fundamental and inalienable ethical demands, Christians must recognize that what is at stake is the essence of the moral law, which concerns the integral good of the human person.
- [N]o Catholic can appeal to the principle of pluralism or to the autonomy of lay involvement in political life to support policies affecting the common good which compromise or undermine fundamental ethical requirements.
- Those who, on the basis of respect for individual conscience, would view the moral duty of Christians to act according to their conscience as something that disqualifies them from political life, denying the legitimacy of their political involvement following from their convictions about the common good, would be guilty of a form of intolerant secularism. Such a position would seek to deny not only any engagement of Christianity in public or political life, but even the possibility of natural ethics itself. Were this the case, the road would be open to moral anarchy...The oppression of the weak by the strong would be the obvious consequence...The marginalization of Christianity, moreover, would not bode well for the future of society or for consensus among peoples; indeed, it would threaten the very spiritual and cultural foundations of civilization.
- ...[A]uthentic freedom does not exist without the truth. "Truth and freedom either go together hand in hand or together they perish in misery." In a society in which truth is neither mentioned nor sought, every form of authentic exercise of freedom will be weakened, opening the way to libertine and individualistic distortions and undermining the protection of the good of the human person and of the entire society.[35]

[35] Zenit, Jan. 16, 2003.

Ten months later, on October 13, 2003, the U.S. bishops came out with "Faithful Citizenship: A Catholic Call to Political Responsibility." In this document the U.S. bishops told Catholics that they *need to take the demands of their faith seriously when they vote in elections.* The major points stressed are:

- [A] new kind of politics—focused on moral principles not on the latest polls, on the needs of the poor and vulnerable not the contributions of the rich and powerful, and on the pursuit of the common good not the demands of special interests.
- The most important challenges we face are not simply political, economic, or technological, but ethical, moral and spiritual.
- Catholics [are] to act on our faith in political life.
- How will we protect the weakest in our midst—innocent unborn children?
- How can our nation help parents raise their children with respect for life, sound moral values, a sense of hope, and an ethic of stewardship and responsibility?
- A Catholic moral framework does not easily fit the ideologies of "right" or, "left," nor the platforms of any party. Our values are often not "politically correct." Believers are called to be a community of conscience within the larger society and to test public life by the values of Scripture and the principles of Catholic social teaching.
- Our responsibility is to measure all candidates, policies, parties, and platforms by how they protect or undermine the life, dignity, and rights of the human person—whether they protect the poor and vulnerable and advance the common good.
- We need more, not less engagement in political life. We urge Catholics to become more involved—by running for office, by working within political parties; by contributing money or time to campaigns; and by joining diocesan legislative networks, community organization, and other efforts to apply Catholic principles in the public square.[36]

In other countries bishops are likewise urging Catholics

[36] Zenit, Oct. 13, 2003.

to become more involved. On April 16, 2003, the seven members of the Scottish bishops asked Catholics to *consider how each party addresses issues such as faith schools, abortion and contraception. They explained that it is not the task of the Catholic Church to propose a particular ideology or political manifest. But they added: "The Church does however present the transcendent values and principles, which provide criteria for evaluating particular political choices. The state runs campaigns against smoking and drunken driving because of the high social cost of these behaviors. Why, then, do our policy makers take fright at conveying similarly bold messages in drug and sexual health campaigns? Why do they instead bend over backwards not to be judgmental? A failure to set these issues in a moral context can lead to a behavioral free-for-all, creating a moral vacuum in which many, especially impressionable young people, crave guidance and absolute truths only to receive platitudes and a seemingly endless array of choices."*[37]

Within days of the Holy See's publication of the Doctrinal Notes the bishop of Sacramento, California, Bishop William Weigand *called on Governor Gray Davis to either renounce his support of legal abortion or stop receiving Holy Communion. "As your bishop, I have to say clearly that anyone—politician or otherwise—who thinks it is acceptable for a Catholic to be pro-abortion is in very great error, puts his or her soul at risk, and is not in good standing with the Church. Such a person should have the integrity to acknowledge this and choose of his own volition to abstain from receiving Holy Communion until he has a change of heart.*[38] Governor Davis defied Bishop Weigand but shortly after that lost the governorship unfortunately to another pro-abortion "Catholic," Arnold Schwarzenegger. Bishop Robert Carlson of Sioux Falls, South Dakota, wrote Senate Minority Leader Tom Daschle telling the Democrat *to remove from his congressional biography and campaign documents all references to his standing as a member of the*

[37] Zenit, Oct. 4, 2003. [38] Zenit, May 24, 2003.

Catholic Church. "Daschle's consistent political opposition to Catholic teachings on moral issues—abortion, in particular—has made him such a problem for ordinary churchgoers that the Church must deny him the use of the word 'Catholic.'"[39] On January 8, 2003, Bishop Raymond L. Burke of La Crosse, Wisconsin, wrote a canonical notification to pro-abortion "Catholic" politicians telling them they could not receive the Blessed Sacrament as long as they held pro-abortion views. It was only after he was named archbishop of St. Louis that pro-abortionist lawmakers leaked their private letters to the press. In this letter Bishop Burke explained: *A Catholic legislator, who supports procured abortion or euthanasia, after knowing the teaching of the Church, commits a manifestly grave sin which is a cause of most serious scandal to others. Therefore, universal Church law provides that such persons "are not to be admitted to Holy Communion" (**Code of Canon Law**, can. 915). ...Therefore, in accord with the norm of can. 915, Catholic legislators, who are members of the faithful of the Diocese of La Crosse and who continue to support procured abortion or euthanasia may not present themselves to receive Holy Communion. They are not to be admitted to Holy Communion, should they present themselves, until such time as they publicly renounce their support of these most unjust practices.*[40] This was followed up with instructions to priests, deacons, and extraordinary ministers in the diocese not to distribute Holy Communion to these politicians. Shockingly, some Catholics have protested this action. To protest is to show ignorance in matters relating to Catholic doctrine. Only a person in the state of sanctifying grace can receive Jesus in the Blessed Sacrament. A person in the state of mortal sin is never to receive Holy Communion. To do so would be an additional sin of sacrilege and a terrible offense against God. This compounds the enormity of the sin. St. Paul reiterates: ***Therefore whoever eats this bread or drinks the cup of the Lord unworthily, will be guilty of the body and the blood of the Lord...for he who eats and drinks***

[39] *Ibid.* [40] *St. Louis Review,* January 30, 2004, section 3, p. 23.

unworthily, without distinguishing the body, eats and drinks judgment to himself. This is why many among you are infirm and weak, and many sleep [die] [*1 Cor*.12:27-31]. Anyone in the state of mortal sin is not permitted to receive Holy Communion...and that includes politicians.[41] The bishop of New Orleans took this additional step telling Catholics in his diocese that they commit a serious sin if they vote for pro-abortion candidates. A **serious sin is** a **mortal sin**.

Problem "Catholic" politicians are not limited to the U.S. President Hugo Chávez of Venezuela has attacked the Catholic Bishops and Catholic institutions since his election. Thrown out of office by a coup, he ran to the Cardinal for protection. Once again back in power, his attacks on the Church intensified. In Canada, Paul Martin, hoping to succeed current Prime Minister Jean Chrétian *took care not to miss Sunday Mass. "And yet despite that strict adherence to Catholicism, Mr. Martin gives virtually no public utterance of his faith as he campaigns to become the 22nd Canadian prime minister." In an interview, Martin explained that he believes a politician must be able to separate his religious convictions from public policy stands. Martin said that while he does not like abortion, he defends "a woman's right to choose." Prime Minister Chrétian, also a declared Catholic, is firmly pro-choice on abortion. He is also strongly supporting legislation to allow same-sex marriage and stem cell research on human embryos.*[42]

In Hong Kong, Bishop Joseph Zen is fighting to preserve the civil liberties there. When Hong Kong was returned to Communist China by the British it had been agreed by Beijing that while it would now be part of Communist China there would be two systems within the one country—one Marxist and the other democratic. Beijing had promised to protect Hong Kong's way of life. Now the government has

[41] To learn more about mortal sin read ***Looking for Peace? Try Confession!*** by this author.
[42] Zenit, Sept. 15, 2003.

proposed a national security bill *that many view as a dire threat to Hong Kong's civil liberties. Seeing Beijing's determination to enact it, [Bishop Zen] has made himself the most outspoken voice of warning. "I'm sorry, I could not keep quiet. When I read the document, it was terrifying"...[T]he security law...would impose heavy penalties for what Beijing defines as subversion, sedition or treason...Bishop Zen sees the fight to preserve liberty in Hong Kong, particularly religious freedom, as part of a wider struggle to end the suffering of China's Catholics. "At the moment, we are the only ones who can speak the truth, both for China and ourselves. If we don't speak now, I think history will hold us guilty."* Bishop Zen is fortunate because *[w]hat gives Bishop Zen clout is the fact that he leads a Church that has penetrated deep into the social fabric of Hong Kong...the Catholic Church built strong links with the local community through its schools and charities. Decades later, Catholics or the products of Catholic schools are strongly represented in the city's elite.* The story goes on to point out that the head of the 180,000-strong civil service is a devout Catholic and the most popular government official. Other senior officials, especially in the police force, and the head of the democratic newspaper are also strong Catholics.[43]

To help Catholics implement the directive from the Holy See, former U.S. ambassador to the Vatican Raymond Flynn has formed a nonpartisan political movement called Your Catholic Voice. Flynn explained that: *We understand that faithful Catholics of good will, through prudential judgment, may disagree over different policies to accomplish similar objectives. For that reason, Your Catholic Voice will only focus on those issues on which the Church's teachings are so abundantly clear that there is no room for misunderstanding...Your Catholic Voice....is to both cultivate and activate Catholics for a response to the call of faithful citizenship...We seek neither popularity nor recognition. We do intend to restore credibility, dignity and respect for the*

[43] David Lague, "The Catholic Voice Leading Hong Kong's Opposition," *The Wall Street Journal*, no date.

values and principles of our Catholic Faith.[44] Have your teen search for this Web site. After studying the material, discuss how you can support this effort as a family.

Living the Virtue of Patriotism

"Man cannot be separated from God, nor politics from morality." St. Thomas More

Parents instill the virtue of patriotism by first teaching their children about their city, state (province) and finally the country as a whole. Take your children to see the historic sites in your city. If there are books on your city or famous people who lived there check them out of the library and read them to your children. Tour the area museums, archeological digs, and historic forts. Stroll through the older parts of the city to show them the architecture. Attend civic festivals and parades. Celebrate national holidays. Rather than using national holidays to catch up on chores or shop, make them festive by celebrating them with family and friends with a cookout or potluck. Introduce them to the folk dances of your area and music. Sample the food specialties. When guests visit from out of town, let your children explain the history of the area and serve as tour guides. Moving to the hometown of President Abraham Lincoln, our three daughters gave so many Lincoln tours to our guests that they could give a better tour of the city than the paid guides!

Display your country's flag on national holidays. Lisa Beamer, the wife of 9-11 hero Todd Beamer, recalls how important it was in her family home to fly the flag: *Both Dad and Mom had relatives who had died in World War II, so we always displayed a flag in front of our house on Memorial Day, Flag Day, Independence Day, and Veterans Day. We often celebrated the Fourth of July with our extended family...and then returned with a load of firecrackers, which we loved to set off in our driveway.*[45]

[44] Zenit, Aug. 26, 2003.

[45] Lisa Beamer, ***Let's Roll!*** (Wheaton, IL: Tyndale House Publishers, Inc., 2002) p. 55.

Next introduce your children to the historic sites in your state/province. Read the biographies of your state heroes. Make a weekend visit to your state capitol or visit during the week and observe your government in action. Visit your representative at his office. Tour historic mansions and graveyards. So many of the old grave markers tell the story of the family. Take scenic rides along the river, ocean, through the city, in the mountains, etc. People who have never left Springfield to see Chicago or other points north or even south amaze me. What a stifling life they have!

As the children grow older tour different parts of your country to introduce them to the varied accents, styles of food, types of architecture, music, and historical sites that tell the history of your country. Let them experience the different climates and scenery. Take them to see battlefields so they learn to appreciate the sacrifices others have made so that your family can live in freedom. Read historical biographies of your national heroes to them. As a family, watch films that depict <u>authentic</u> history, not a revisionist version. Teach your children your national anthem. Not only will they feel proud to be part of such a country but they will be willing to make their country even better in the future.

Explain that since this is your country, you have to take pride in keeping it clean by throwing trash in the garbage, not in the street. Teach them to respect public property. It is not to be defaced or subjected to graffiti. Attending the UN Conference in Copenhagen, Denmark, I was appalled to see that beautiful city defaced by graffiti everywhere. What an ugly impression that city left on me! Likewise, garbage and graffiti litter Jerusalem and the country of Israel. There is very little beauty anywhere...just partially built buildings or partially torn down buildings. It shows a lack of public pride and love of country.

Point out how you keep up your home by painting it, raking

the leaves, cutting the grass so that your home looks nice which in turn makes your neighborhood look clean and inviting. This is all part of the virtue of patriotism...to care for one's country.

The role of parents is also to teach their children their civic duties as well as how to live them. Teach your teens the obligations of a citizen: to work for the common defense, to pay taxes, to obey just laws, to work responsibly performing our duties for the common good.

Have your children accompany you when you go to vote. One of the earliest memories I have is going with my mother to vote. Discuss political issues and how morality must be considered in resolving issues. Debate the pros and cons of candidates over dinner. Point out the difference in platforms, character, and programs. Talk about why you are supporting a specific candidate. Teach your children how to research political stands and issues. Encourage them to join the debate club at school or start a debate club. As electives in college suggest they take some political science courses to better understand the workings of government. Encourage teens to consider a political career. Two seventeen year old cousins in Central Illinois, Stuart and Andrew Schmadeke, founded *the Illinois League of Young Voters*, a nonpartisan group dedicated to informing young people about politics and helping raise awareness of youth issues. They are using as their main draw a unique online survey that matches people to candidates. Check out their Web site with your teens, *www.leagueofyoungvoters.com*. It may encourage your young adults to get politically involved.

Make clear to your teens that **Christians do not base their vote on a specific political party but rather on specific moral issues.** Tell them that as citizens they will have to make sacrifices such as becoming involved in the political process by campaigning for moral, upright politicians, as well as fighting immoral or unjust legislation or laws. Let them see you working to support good candidates. Take them to your statehouse when you are supporting a bill or protesting a bill. Seeing you promoting moral issues in government will leave a profound impression on your teens. Get your children and teens involved stuffing envelopes, passing out campaign literature, making calls, and raising money by having a garage sale, selling lemonade or doing odd jobs for neighbors.

Volunteer as a family to work for pro-life and pro-family issues. Call or write congressmen to express an opinion when important bills are before the legislature. Take your children to the March for Life in Washington, D.C. that is held each January.

If the 62 million Catholics in the U.S. would cast their vote based on the law of God our country would be transformed. Besides the important area of right-to-life, the gay marriage issue, and the various other moral/ethical issues, another area for immediate attention is the reduction of the tax burden on families. As one editorial explained: *Although government cannot compel people to be responsible parents, it can certainly promote policies that make it easier for them to take care of their children. One such policy is to alleviate the economic pressure on families by reducing their heavy tax burdens...[M]ore and more families are finding it necessary to have two incomes in order to pay their bills...It is unfair that families with young children have the lowest per capita incomes yet are saddled with such high tax burdens. Rather than taxing them further, the government should let them keep more of their own earnings. That is one sure way to strengthen the family.*[46]

If our children and we abdicate our civic responsibilities we have only ourselves to blame for the problems in our country. Surveys taken after President Bill Clinton's election showed that large numbers of Catholics voted for this pro-choice president. St. Josemaría, speaking to lay

[46] *State-Journal Register*, Springfield, IL, Feb. 22, 1991, p. 6.

people, told them that their faith has to guide them in forming judgments on world situations and events. Although Catholic doctrine does not impose specific solutions to problems that are temporal, we are to resolve them in a responsible, Christian manner.[46A]

Explain that it is the Christian's moral duty to participate in government. Christ says, ***Render, therefore to Caesar the things that are Caesar's, and to God the things that are God's*** (***Mk.*** 12:17). If Christians do not make their voices heard, the things of God will be taken over by Caesar. This is the growing problem we are faced with today. But when Christians get involved, with God's help they can move mountains. Tax-law professor, Susan Pace Hamill took a sabbatical from her divinity school to change the tax structure in the State of Alabama. She found that *[t]he Alabama code requires families of four earning as little as $4,600 to pay income tax, the nation's lowest threshold. It charges a higher sales tax on baby formula than on cattle feed and permits timber interests to pay relatively meager property taxes compared with homeowners.* During her sabbatical she wrote a paper entitled "An Argument for Tax Reform Based on Judeo-Christian Ethics." Her reason for doing this? *"How could we, in a free society of a bunch of Christians, have the worst, most unjust tax structure that you could ever have dreamed up?" asks Ms. Hamill.*[47] Her campaign to change the tax structure has caught the eye of the governor and legislators. See how one person can make a difference?

Other areas that Christians need to address are the free trade treaties that cost millions of jobs in one country to establish sweat shops in third world countries.

As Christians our interest is not limited to our own country. We are interested in and concerned for our brothers and sisters around the world. When tragedies

[46A] *Letter*, Oct. 15, 1948, No. 28.

[47] Shailagh Murray, "Seminary Article Sparks Alabama Tax-Code Revolt," *The Wall Street Journal*, Feb. 12, 2003.

strike we are called to help through prayers as well as financial and material support if possible. Teach your children about the different cultures, their languages, customs, music, form of government, and geography. If expenses permit take them to different countries even if it is simply the country next-door. It will keep your children from having a provincial outlook. Every country has something to offer. St. Josemaría writes: *To be "Catholic" means to love your country and to be second to no one in that love. And at the same time to hold as your own the noble aspirations of other lands—so many glories of France are glories of mine! And in the same way, much that makes Germans proud, and the peoples of Italy and of England... and Americans and Asians and Africans, is a source of pride to me also.*[48]

Examples of Patriotism

"Our obligations to our country never cease but with our lives." John Adams

Let's begin in Rome in 174. Marcus Aurelius and his Twelfth Legion composed mostly of Christian soldiers were suddenly surrounded by the Germanic Quadi tribe of Moravia. Rations and water were running low. The situation looked hopeless. *Thereupon the Christian troops knelt to pray for the deliverance of the emperor and themselves. Their prayer was quickly answered when a violent thunderstorm came over the battlefield, unleashing strong winds and blinding lightning that dispersed the Quadi forces. The emperor later admitted in an edict that his deliverance was due "to the shower obtained, perhaps, by the prayers of the Christians."*[49]

Saints have always been patriotic. *St. Isidore of Seville exalted the patriotism of his people...and in England, the extremely sagacious [St.] Bede was equally enthusiastic in his efforts to encourage his fellow countrymen to be proud of*

[48] ***The Way***, *Op. Cit.*, #525.

[49] *Magnificat*, January 2003.

being different from other nations.[50] Joan of Arc became a saint because she lived patriotism heroically. St. Thomas More is not only a canonized politician but he is the Patron of Statesmen and Politicians. St. Thomas à Becket was the devoted minister of King Henry II of England. Cultured, intelligent, and highly experienced, he possessed what some said was a "subtle pride". When Henry decided he needed a friend he could control in the highest position in the Catholic Church in England, he appointed Becket as the Archbishop of Canterbury. Becket protested. He did not want the job but Henry insisted. *[I]n spite of ecclesiastical opposition, Becket, the one-time politician, underwent a psychological transformation due to the promptings of divine grace. He was now a churchman, and devoted himself body and soul to the interests of the Church; henceforward the royal tyranny would have no more able or more zealous an opponent.*[51] Henry couldn't believe the change in his devoted minister. Rather than working together for Henry's best interest, the two were locking horns on a variety of issues. In a rage Henry bellowed one day: *What! is there no one among all these cowards whom I support that will rid me of this wretched priest?*[52] Thomas à Becket was killed at Henry's instigation in 1170 at the foot of his altar. Daniel-Rops notes: *We may compare the martyrdom of St. Thomas à Becket with that of St. Stanislaus of Cracow, who fell victim to Boleslav II of Poland in 1079.*[53] It was Archbishop Langton who forced the Magna Charta on despotic King John in 1215.

St. Louis of France, who ruled from 1226 until 1270, was a man of integrity whose spirituality enhanced his ability to rule well. It is said that his reign was "one of the happiest in French history." In counseling his son and heir he told him: *You must see to it that your people, who are your subjects, live under your rule in peace and equity."*[54] Not only did Louis ransom prisoners, practice all the works of mercy, founded hospitals, orphanages, guest-houses, and other charitable institutions, he likewise founded colleges,

[50] ***Church In The Dark Age***, *Op. Cit.*, p. 244.
[51] ***Cathedral And Crusade***, *Op. Cit.*, p. 216.
[52] *Ibid.*
[53] *Ibid.*
[54] *Ibid.*, p. 294.

student residences and the Sorbonne University. He initiated the emancipation of serfs; he personally judged legal cases for common people as well as for the high born. He also sentenced the guilty to death, even members of the aristocracy who murdered. He was careful to appoint only good judges. These judges *were obliged to take an oath to receive neither gold nor silver nor any other fee from interested parties, and forbidden to frequent taverns or to play at dice.*[55] He leveled no unfair taxes nor used the services of moneylenders. *St. Louis enjoyed universal respect because he was a thorough-going Christian. This much is evident from the fact that he was called upon as "elder statesman" to arbitrate between one nation and another...*French historian Joinville wrote that his *throne shone like the sun which sheds its rays far and wide.*[56] *Many priests and prelates might envy the king his manners and his virtues.*[57]

John Adams, while he was in France on behalf of the new U.S. government, told a French banker and his wife that *in some cases it was the duty of a good citizen to sacrifice his all for the good of the country.*[58] He was describing his life. He had left his successful law practice and his family back in the states, to help form a new country with support from France.

Hundreds of years later in Vietnam, another family echoed the same sentiments as Adams. Cardinal *Thuân would sometimes speak of his family's "political spirituality," which he shared particularly with Hiep* [his mother] *and Diem* [his uncle]. *For his family it was a given that Christians made God's will the foundation of their political thought and action...All of Ngo Dinh Kha's children* [Cardinal Thuân's maternal uncles and his mother] *strongly believed that their dedication to the liberation of Vietnam and the welfare of its people was God's will. Their sense of justice, their righteousness, their humanity and heroism would make them*

[55] *Ibid.*, p. 296. [56] *Ibid.*, p. 291. [57] *Ibid.*, p. 292.
[58] ***John Adams***, *Op. Cit.*, p. 206.

some of the most tragic and misunderstood yet exalted figures of Vietnam's modern history.[59] Let's consider just a brief segment of this tragic story.

With the power of the Viet Cong in North Vietnam growing along with U.S. control of South Vietnam, Cardinal Thuân's uncle, President Diem, felt that the sovereignty of his country was threatened from both sides. He explained to his nephew: *I must tell you that we are now caught up in a fight for our very survival. I am not overly concerned about the [Viet Cong]....We simply have to make it impossible for their troops to assemble and launch attacks. The other front is more dangerous. The Americans want us to accept their advice and personnel. They want us to immediately adopt their form of democracy. They want us to include in our government structures, elements, that so far have only worked for their own personal interest. They want me to submit to their ambassador. But I am the head of state; if I submit to the will of the U.S. ambassador, South Vietnam will have lost its national sovereignty...I cannot allow any encroachment upon our national sovereignty. I will do what I believe is the right thing and I am ready to pay any price for that.*[60] He gave his life.

Cardinal Thuân eventually became the president of the Pontifical Council for Justice and Peace. Prior to his sudden death he had published a compendium of social doctrine requested by the Holy Father. In explaining what it means to work toward peace and justice, the Cardinal pointed to the beatitudes *as a moral guide for those in politics. "Blessed will be the politician who is responsible and honest, who works for the common good and is consistent and open to dialogue, who is committed to change with an evangelical perspective and who listens to the people, his conscience and God. Blessed too is that politician who is not afraid of truth, and who does not allow himself to be conditioned by the media.*[61]

---

[59] ***The Miracle Of Hope,*** *Op. Cit.*, p. 17.
[60] *Ibid.*,p. 154. [61] Zenit, May 6, 2002.

Recently in Rome the process of beatification began for Fr. Luigi Sturzo (1871-1959), the founder of the Italian Popular Party which is now known as Christian Democracy. As a young priest Fr. Sturzo promoted Pope Leo XIII's social teachings in ***Rerum Novarum,*** particularly the teachings on labor. In 1919 with the Fascist threat mounting and Catholics excluded in Italy from the democratic process, *Fr. Sturzo founded the Italian Popular Party, "Lay and non-confessional," which was rooted in the Christian view of man. The Popular Party for years was one of the few forces capable of opposing Benito Mussolini's Fascism. In 1924, at the request of the Holy See, Father Sturzo resigned as party secretary. He was asked to concentrate his energy on ethical and spiritual advice to politicians.* Forced to leave Italy due to threats on his life he went to London until war broke out there. He found refuge in the U.S. for six years.While there he founded the American People and Freedom Association for Catholics. Upon returning to Italy he *refused to re-enter politics, despite being named senator-for-life by President Luigi Einaudi in 1952.*[62] Fr. Sturzo saw a political need and devoted his life to fill it.

In ***Raise Happy Children...Raise Them Saints!*** we saw the strong, self-sacrificing patriotism of the Kolbe family (pp. 66-80). Another such patriotic Polish family was that of Archbishop Zygmunt Felinski (1822-1895) of Warsaw. The third of six children, his father died when he was eleven. When he was sixteen, *his mother was arrested by the Russians and sent into exile in Siberia for her involvement in patriotic activity. Her patriotic activity was working for the improvement of the social and economic conditions of farmers.* Prior to his ordination Felinski took part in the unsuccessful revolt of Poznan in 1848. After his ordination Fr. Felinski concentrated on founding the Felician sisters as well as a charitable organization. The year he was appointed Archbishop of Warsaw, 1862, the Russians took control of the city by siege. His attention turned to *the systematic elimination of government interference in the*

[62] Zenit, May 5, 2002.

internal affairs of the Church...He made every effort to free imprisoned priests. He encouraged them to proclaim the gospel openly, to catechize their parishioners ...In political action he tried to prevent the nation from rushing headlong into a rash and inconsiderate position. As a sign of his own protest against the bloody repression by the Russians of the "January Revolt" of 1863, Archbishop Felinski resigned from the Council of State and...wrote a letter to the Emperor Alexander II, urging him to put an end to the violence. He likewise protested against the hanging of the Capuchin Father Agrypin Konarski, chaplain of the "rebels." His courage and interventions quickly brought about his exile by Alexander II. The next 20 years he spent in Siberia. Through negotiations between the Holy See and Russia he was finally released to semi-exile in the Krakow region of Poland.[63] At his beatification John Paul II pointed out that: *Archbihsop Felinski gave himself fully in defending the freedom of the nation. This is necessary today also, when different forces—often under the guidance of a false ideology of freedom—try to take over this land. When the noisy propaganda of liberalism, of freedom without truth or responsibility, grows stronger in our country too, the Shepherds of the church cannot fail to proclaim the one fail-proof philosophy of freedom, which is the truth of the Cross of Christ. This philosophy of freedom finds full motivation in the history of our nation.*[64]

Fr. David P. McAstocker, S.J., admonishes us, *if we continue to remain as spectators in the game of life and allow a chosen few actively to control the sport—what is to prevent their making sport of us? Nero did just this. And so acts many a modern Nero on the world's stage today. A democracy demands that the people rule; and where they do not, or apathetically turn their obligations over to others, there we find not a democracy, even though the name still remains. In fact, external manifestations of a democracy may be highest when that form of government is actually falling to ruin and decay, as a peach tree will shower the ground with*

[63] Zenit, Aug. 19, 2002.

[64] Zenit, Aug. 18, 2002.

a wealth of blossoms just before it withers and dies.[65]

And In Summary...

We have just considered the virtues to be instilled at the beginning of the teen years. As you have probably noted, each virtue builds on the other to mature our teens into responsible young men and women. But before we end this section, Archbishop Fulton J. Sheen gives two simple rules for teens that <u>if followed</u> will guarantee them happy lives:

1. *Your conscience is like the carburetor [of a car]. God put into your conscience certain directions for leading a happy life, but if you heed others who tell you to follow them instead of your conscience, you will feel an inner unhappiness...Go on rebelling against the inner voice which is the voice of God, and you will feel frustrated, miserable, unhappy, and wish you were dead!*
2. *"Get out of your teenage nest as fast you can..." [Adolescence] is a transition period, not a career...One...is a teenager as long as he fails to mature into an acceptance of responsibilities. All those who are destined for greatness get out of the period of immaturity as soon as possible...[Y]ou are not here to have the world serve you, but for you to serve the world...*[66]

THE TEEN YEARS: AGES 16-18

"By seventeen generally the character of most youths is formed."

Servant of God Archbishop Fulton J. Sheen

During the critical years of sixteen to eighteen, values are set, vocational choices made, and one's path in life is on the way to being decided. Archbishop Sheen points out: *A well-*

---

[65] ***The Little Virtues,*** *Op. Cit.*, p. 137.

[66] ***Children and Parents,*** *Op. Cit.,* pp. 76-77.

known biographer of Napolean stated that at fifteen "he was already formed; true, life had something to add to it, but all the defects and good qualities were there in his fifteenth year." Mussolini, fighting with his classmates when he was fifteen, had manifested the same characteristics that he manifested later on. He himself wrote, "I was then formed. I fear that the influences I underwent then were decisive." If one puts garbage into the stomachs of children, it will be easy to forecast their health; if moral garbage is put into the minds of children, it is easy to predict how these ideas will become acts.[67]

For this reason, the virtues that Dr. David Isaacs finds important for this age group pertain to the ability to reason in an intelligent manner. Blaise Pascal, a world-renowned mathematical genius by the age of sixteen, penned the following words when he was but a teen! *There is a God-shaped vacuum in the heart of every person, and it can never be filled by any created thing. It can only be filled by God, made known through Jesus Christ.*

It is evident that this age group, if spiritually well formed, has tremendous potential not only for deep interior spiritual growth but also as a powerful force for changing the world through evangelization. John Paul II told the Pontifical Commission for Latin America that he wants this potential tapped: *I would particularly like to mention the evangelization of young people. On them are based the hopes and expectations of a future of greater communion and solidarity for the Church and the societies of America...The last World Youth Day, celebrated in August of the Jubilee Year, underscored how young people are a powerful force for the evangelization of the world today. They must be evangelized in-depth, starting from their resources of generosity, openness and intuition.*[68] This is your responsibility, parents!

On Palm Sunday in 2001, the Holy Father blessed the cross that toured Canada, in preparation for World Youth

[67] *Ibid.*, p. 59. [68] Zenit, April 8, 2001.

Day 2002. At that time he told the youth of the world that Jesus is the only *way to reach the triumphal palm branch on the day of resurrection. Jesus did not live His own earthly life seeking power, as a career toward success, as a will to control others. On the contrary He gave up His privileges of equality with God, and took on the condition of a slave, becoming like men. He obeyed the Father's plan all the way to death on the cross. Thus he left his disciples and the Church a precious teaching: "Unless the grain of wheat falls on the ground and dies, it remains alone; but if it dies, it produces much fruit."...[R]enew your own fidelity to Christ the Lord. Fidelity to Christ, this is my invitation to all English-speaking pilgrims.*[69]

The importance of the formation of this age group cannot be emphasized enough. Recall how in earlier chapters we discussed how many of the saints found their vocations at this age. The Little Flower, St. Thérèse, had already been in Carmel a year when she turned sixteen. During this critical adolescent phase many teens develop a desire to become priests, religious, missionaries, convert to the Catholic faith, or decide to live a celibate lay vocation to serve God. These vocations need to be fostered by you. As mentioned in ***Raise Happy Children...Raise Them Saints!*** Ted Turner, not known for his love for Christianity, wanted to become a missionary in his teens. If this had been cultivated by his parents what a positive influence he would have exerted on our world! Tom Monaghan, as you recall, tried the seminary in his teens. Jasmine,[70] a former Muslim who lived in England, spent her adolescence pondering a conversion to Catholicism. *She was attracted by Jesus and His promise to save all, men and women alike, who are equal in dignity and value, in His sight. She was also attracted to the idea of service to the weakest.* When she told her parents of her decision to convert, they beat and insulted her. When she converted despite her family's protests, the Muslim community in England threatened and humiliated her family. Disgraced by Jasmine's actions, her

[69] *Ibid.*

[70] For her protection no last name can be used.

father abandoned his family. Her mother and the rest of the family were forced to move frequently to evade threats and persecution from fellow Muslims. Jasmine, now a missionary nurse, ministers to the poor and African refugees in Egypt.[71]

Ven.Cardinal John Henry Newman, maintained that his *first conversion* was at the age of 15.

Cardinal Juan Luis Cipriani Thorne, Archbishop of Lima, Peru, a national basketball star in his youth, reminisces how *when I had my 18th birthday, an Opus Dei priest asked me if I thought of the possibility of following God. I answered yes, but the truth is I hadn't thought much about it...[W]hen I was asked this question, I realized what it meant for the first time. I realize that I have received the grace not to be afraid every time the Lord has asked me to take another step. Therefore, when God willed it, He came close and knocked on my door.*[72]

As Cardinal Theodore McCarrick of Washington, D.C., told a group of young adults at a Theology on Tap session held at a D.C. bar: *You have to make the effort to take control of your life and make sure that you are becoming all that God wants you to be, all that you can be. It is possible to rush through all of this [life] and end up with nothing.*[73] He speaks from experience. When he was in junior high, he recalls parish priests asking his class: *Who wants to be a priest? Eighty percent of us raised our hands. We all wanted to be like them.* In high school the dating scene interested him more until his senior year in high school when he started thinking, *maybe God will allow me to become a priest.* After a year of study in Europe with a friend he was convinced of his priestly vocation.[74]

Cardinal Avery Dulles, the son of a politically famous Presbyterian family, converted to Catholicism while attending Harvard University. He relates that *I learned my*

[71] Zenit, March 7, 2001. [72] Zenit, Feb. 27, 2001.
[73] Zenit, March 14, 2001. [74] Zenit, March 5, 2001.

Catholicism mostly from books. Upon deciding to convert to the faith he went to a Catholic bookstore and asked: *How do I get into the Catholic Church?* They told him that he would have to be instructed by a priest. He replied, *I've never met a priest. How will I find one?* The bookstore clerk found him a Jesuit graduate student who asked Avery point blank if he was truly serious about converting. *I don't have time to waste on someone who is merely curious. I indicated that yes, I was serious about it—that I was seriously thinking about becoming a Catholic.* When his six weeks of instructions were completed he told his family about his decision to become a Catholic. His grandmother, the wife of a Presbyterian minister, was dying at the time so his parents asked him to postpone his conversion until after her death. *Well, I was a rather impatient young fella, and I said, "No, I wouldn't delay it." I had the grace to do it now. What would happen if I didn't use the grace of the moment?* Dulles converted with his grandmother's blessing, eventually becoming a Jesuit theologian and recently a cardinal.[75]

The Associated Press and *Sporting News* named Catholic football star, Josh Heupel, player of the year. Heupel, as quarterback for the Oklahoma Sooners, won the prestigious Walter Camp player of the year award and was the runner-up for the Heisman Trophy. When he was only in second grade he told his mother, *Mom, I know what my mission in life is...to help kids that get into trouble. You know I'm going to be a football player, Mom, and pro-football players make a lot of money. That's how I'll do it. That's what God wants me to do with my life.* As a senior in high school he reiterated this same goal telling his mother, *I don't know exactly what I'm going to do, but I know what my mission in life is. It's to help at-risk kids and to help people who are disadvantaged and homeless.* Josh began his mission while still in high school by organizing a food drive in connection with the school's football games. Despite the distractions of college,

[75] Zenit, Feb. 22, 2001.

his campaign provided Thanksgiving for 250 families. Later in the season his efforts provided Christmas for 14 elementary school children. As his college career peaked, Josh launched a charitable organization using his famous jersey number, 14. *I think the Lord has blessed me tremendously throughout my life. I'm thankful, so I want to give back to people who aren't as fortunate as I have been. It's something that I enjoy and will continue throughout my life,* reflects Josh. But when Josh was injured, his priorities changed: *God wasn't No. 1 in my life. Things weren't going along the way I planned. My first year in college I allowed other things to become No. 1. I had to give God complete control over my life.* Zenit reports that Josh *credits a close relationship with his parents, sister and relatives for his growth as a Christian, a leader and a giver. My parents were both leaders in their fields. They are great human beings who genuinely care about the well-being of others. I saw the commitment they made to each other, but also to other people. They instilled those values in me.*[76]

From sixteen to eighteen years old is your last opportunity to instill virtues and faith in your children before they leave home, many for good. Make heroic sacrifices to provide opportunities for your children to grow in the Catholic faith. One opportunity that was briefly mentioned before is World Youth Day. Cardinal Francis James Stafford, president of the Pontifical Council for the Laity explains that *World Youth Day opens the most profound feelings...to youth, which, at a time of advanced technology, are often obfuscated* [obscured/confused]. *The participants make a kind of journey of return to the sources of Christian life, thus living—in the ambit* [in the sphere of influence] *of a community of disciples—a journey of love and friendship, of prayer and contemplation. Many experience the wisdom of Christian humanism for the first time. The young people walk and pray together. They perspire together and together receive water and what is necessary to refresh themselves*

[76] Zenit, April 2, 2001.

along the way. They feel hungry. At the end they gather around a guitar and sing traditional songs or religious hymns. [In this atmosphere the Pope exhorts them to] *have the courage to believe in the good news in the life that Jesus teaches in the Gospel.*[77] In preparation for the next World Youth Day the Holy Father gave young people *five specific counsels to help them make room for Jesus in their lives: "Prayer, hearing the Word of God and meditation, the Mass, Eucharistic adoration and the sacrament of confession..."* Reminding the youth that it is *not easy* to be a Christian, he told them: *To proclaim and witness to the Gospel entails many difficulties. Yes, it is true: We are living at a time when society is influenced by models of life that place having pleasure and appearance, in the egotistical sense, in the first place. The missionary determination of believers must confront this way of thinking and acting. However, we must not be afraid, because Christ can change man's heart and accomplish a "miraculous catch" when we least expect it.*[78]

Consider sending or taking your teens to a World Youth Day. Do a Web search for information.

To focus the idealism of your teen supernaturally, make the financial sacrifices to send your teens not only to World Youth Day, but also on pilgrimages to Rome, shrines of Our Lady, to yearly retreats, and the other means of spiritual formation. If you make the effort to give them the truth of the Catholic Faith, other ideologies will have no appeal. When one knows Jesus, *nothing* else is attractive. What a thrill for the teens present at World Youth Day in Rome to hear John Paul II tell them: *Don't ever think, then, that you are unknown to Him, as if you were just a number in an anonymous crowd. Each one of you is precious to Christ, He knows you personally, He loves you tenderly, even when you are not aware of it...[T]he journey of faith is part of everything that happens in our lives. God is at work in the concrete and personal situations of each one of us: through them, sometimes in truly mysterious ways, the Word "made flesh," who came*

---

[77] Zenit, March 16, 2001. [78] Zenit, April 5, 2001.

to live among us, makes Himself present to us.

If you begin teaching the faith to your children when they are little, they absorb it as naturally as a sponge absorbs water. But if you are new to the realization of the importance of teaching your children the faith and your children are in their teens you must proceed prayerfully, delicately and cautiously. Appeal to their intellect and reason rather than using dogmatic force. Force only causes resentment or alienation. Recently one of my husband's directors converted to the Catholic faith in his mid forties. He had never even been baptized. At a social gathering he told us that when he was a teen, a Baptist minister came to his home preaching hell and damnation if his family did not consent to be baptized that very evening. Everyone in the family agreed to be baptized but Phil. Despite the minister's threats and his mother's tears he resisted being bullied into a religion. He married a practicing Catholic, raised his children Catholic, attended Sunday Mass with his family but never considered converting to Catholicism until he moved to Springfield. After his conversion he sent a note to my husband saying that Bob had helped to influence his decision to become a Catholic by his example, along with the fact that he never pressured Phil religiously.

Dr. Ana Maria Navarro reminds parents that *it is the responsibility of education* [given by parents] *to ensure that the values which are chosen and adopted by adolescents are correct, good and genuine ones.* The virtues Dr. Isaacs recommends specifically for this age group are:

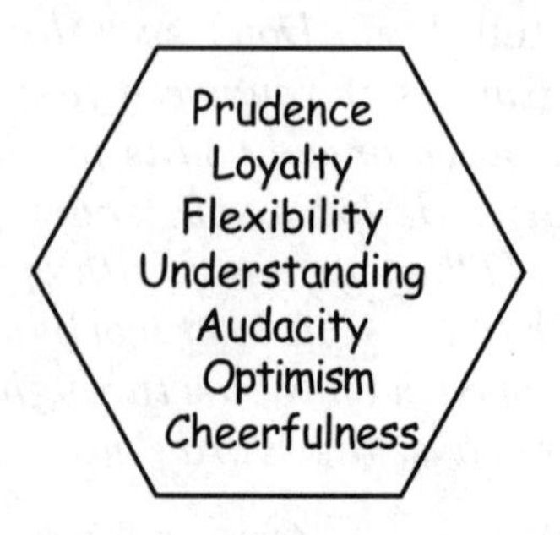

Younger teens, those between the ages of thirteen and fifteen, need to develop the virtues that control their passions. These we discussed in the previous chapters. Older teens, in addition to the virtues that control passions, need another set of virtues...those that control their idealism. In Chapter 1 we discussed why teens are attracted by ideologies. Without the virtues we are discussing in this chapter and the following chapters, idealistic young people could very well become involved with cults, radical causes or fundamentalist religions. If my parents, particularly my mother, had not developed in me such a tremendous love for the Catholic faith and truth, my passion for politics and political action could easily have led me into Marxist causes, so enticing in the '60's. When my husband proposed in college, accepting meant putting my political aspirations on hold since neither of us believed in working mothers. But that strong idealism was still there. How I burned to make the world better through politics. It took until my mid-twenties and two children before I woke up. It was while campaigning for a presidential candidate that the realization hit me that *only* God can change the world for the better because He changes hearts and souls. This discovery led to a prayerful search to find a spiritual path that united prayer with action. When an acquaintance invited me to an Opus Dei retreat one Lent, it took just one meditation by the priest to show me that I had *found* the narrow path that would give my life meaning, purpose, and joy. It proved to be the path not only for me but also for my husband, Bob, and our daughter, Marianne. Help your teen to discover the correct spiritual path that will lead him or her closer to God. This will ensure your child's happiness and joy in this life and eternity with God in the next.

Within the Catholic Church God has a variety of ways and paths to lead us to Him...one for every kind of temperament or aspiration! You and your children are free to select any spiritual path that will give your lives meaning, purpose and joy. Or, the Church in her goodness allows you to start a new path under her benevolent guidance. But without the foundation of the virtues we are discussing your teen will not be motivated to seek any spiritual path. Why do we need a specific path? Can't we get to heaven by ourselves? It is difficult, if not impossible, to grow holy on our own because we lack objectivity. On a business trip to Rome I had the great blessing to speak privately for an hour with Fr. John Hardon, S.J. Among the topics we discussed were the interior life and the struggle to grow in holiness. Looking me directly in the eye he emphatically said: *You cannot become a saint by yourself.* His adamant observation was not just addressed to me alone but also to you and your children. Look for some concrete means to help youself and your children to grow in holiness.

The virtues we will be discussing in the next chapters are all attached to the cardinal virtue of prudence and the theological virtue of hope. Prudence helps your teens to discern correctly. **Flexibility** helps them to apply moral criteria to different situations. **Audacity** united with prudence helps them to use their talents for God. Prudence directs them as to what and to whom **loyalty** should be accorded in addition to helping them to live **understanding**, **humility, cheerfulness** and **optimism**. All in turn are based on our hope and trust in God.

In addition to the idealism of youth, their natural audacity and optimism compels them to throw themselves wholeheartedly into anything they believe in. Make sure their energies are directed toward pleasing God. St. Thérèse, at fifteen years old, begged her bishop to allow her to enter Carmel *now* rather than at the customary age of twenty-one. When he said *no*, St. Thérèse went on pilgrimage, with her father and sister Celine, to Rome. Before entering the audience with Pope Leo XIII the pilgrims were told not to speak to the Holy Father, as this would prolong the audience. Encouraged by Celine to pursue her plan, Thérèse shocked the assembly by pleading with the Holy Father to give her permission to enter Carmel early. Rapidly she presented her arguments to the Pope as two Swiss Guards, each grabbing an arm dragged her away, but not before the Holy Father blessed her and told her to obey the will of God. Teenage Thérèse refused to take "no" for an answer.

Blessed Pedro Calungsod, a Philippino teenager, left his homeland and family to accompany a Spanish missionary priest, Blessed Diego Luis de San Vitores, to the Mariana Islands to evangelize the natives. As the seventeen-year-old Pedro was teaching catechism to a group of children and adults in Guam, an ex-Christian slaughtered him.

Blessed Pauline Visenteiner, an Italian by birth, was raised in Brazil. A*t the age of fifteen, she and a companion moved into a shack to look after a woman dying of cancer. The Daughters of the Immaculate Conception, founded by Pauline, grew out of that first act of mercy...*[79] She died in 1942.

We spoke earlier about Bl. Pier Frassati who died at the age of twenty-four, in 1925, from polio. Caring for an abandoned person with polio, he contracted the deadly disease himself. Even as he lay dying, he begged for medicine for a destitute friend who was likewise dying from the same disease. John Paul II at his beatification noted: *The power of the Spirit of Truth, united to Christ, made him a modern witness to the hope which springs from the Gospel and to the grace of salvation which works in human hearts...Thus he became a living witness and courageous defender of this hope in the name of the Christian youth of the twentieth century. Faith and charity, the true driving forces of his existence made him active and diligent in the milieu in which he lived, in his family and school, in the university and society; they transformed him into a joyful, enthusiastic apostle of Christ, a passionate follower of his message and charity. The secret of his apostolic zeal and holiness is to be sought in the ascetical and spiritual journey*

[79] ***John Paul II's Book Of Saints,*** *Op. Cit.,* p. 323.

which he traveled; in prayer; in persevering adoration, even at night, of the Blessed Sacrament; in his thirst for the Word of God, which he sought in Biblical texts; in chastity lived as a cheerful, uncompromising discipline; in his daily love of silence and life's "ordinariness." It is precisely in these factors that we are given to understand the deep wellspring of his spiritual vitality.[80]

Additional Helps

- ✓ View the DVD *Miracle* by Disney with your teens. This recounts the quest for a USA gold medal for hockey in the 1980 Olympics. After the film note in the credits what each of the players is now doing. Discuss the film and how it influenced the future of each of the players.
- ✓ Borrow from an interlibrary exchange the history of the Church by H. Daniel-Rops. Read the books with your teens.
- ✓ Read Pope Leo XIII's encyclical, ***Rerum Novarum.***
- ✓ Encourage your teens to read ***John Adams*** by David McCullough.
- ✓ If you have not viewed these films with your teens yet consider doing so now: *The Lion In Winter* and *A Man for All Seasons.*
- ✓ Read and discuss with your teens the "Doctrinal Note on Some Questions Regarding the Participation of Catholics in Political Life." You can find it on the Vatican web site.

Scripture Readings

1 Corinthians 6:11-20; 7:10-16
2 St. Peter 2:4-22; 3:3-13
1 Timothy 3:9-11; 5:6-7; 5:22-25
1 St. Peter 2:11-25
Psalm 12
Ephesians 5:5-20
James 3: 1-10

[80] *Ibid.*, p. 334.

CHAPTER 7

HOW TO TEACH THE VIRTUES OF PRUDENCE, LOYALTY, FLEXIBILITY, UNDERSTANDING & AUDACITY

The Virtue of Prudence

"Walk in wisdom as regard outsiders, making the most of your time. Let your speech, while always attractive, be seasoned with salt, that you may know how you ought to answer each one."

St. Paul (*Col.* 4:5-6)

Prudence is the virtue that directs all the other moral virtues. Unless one cultivates the virtue of prudence, the other virtues are in the state of flux going from one extreme to the other. Prudence is needed for stability in the practice of all the other virtues. For this reason St. Bernard taught that *prudence* is the *guide of every good habit.*[1] This virtue also prevents us from working on some virtues to the neglect of others.

The dictionary defines prudence as *the ability to govern and discipline oneself by the use of reason.*

The ***Catechism of the Catholic Church*** gives this virtue one of the longest definitions in the ***Catechism.*** Space only permits me to quote parts of it so please read the whole quote on your own:

> **#1806 Prudence is the virtue that disposes practical reason to discern our true good in every circumstance and to choose the right means of achieving it...It is prudence that immediately guides the judgment of conscience. The prudent man determines and directs his conduct in accordance with this judgment. With the help of this virtue we apply moral principles to particular cases without error and overcome doubts about the good to achieve and the evil to avoid.**

St. Thomas adds that prudence is right reason in action.[2] How does a person know he is prudent? Dr. David Isaacs explains:

> **In his work and in dealings with other people the prudent person gathers information which he assesses in the light of right standards: he weighs the favorable and unfavorable consequences for himself and others prior to making a decision and then he acts or refrains from acting, in keeping with the decision he has made.**[3]

Sound judgment (prudence) and conscience, according to

[1] St. Bernard, *Sermones in Canticas Canticorum,* 49, 5 (PL 183, 1018).
[2] St. Thomas Aquinas, STH II-II, 47, 2.
[3] Dr. David Isaacs, "The Education of Prudence," Insituto de Ciencias de la Educación, Universidad de Navarre, 1984, p. 1.

James Stenson, is *right reasoning about people, events, ourselves; the ability to make the great distinctions in life—truth from falsehood, good from evil, the beautiful and noble from the squalid.*[4]

St. Thomas Aquinas reminds us that we also need this virtue, as well as our young adults, *in order to be just, in order to live charity, and to give good service to God and to all our fellowmen. Not without good reason prudence has been called...the mother of the virtues.*[5]

The virtue of prudence is the companion of wisdom. ***Webster's New Collegiate Dictionary*** defines wisdom as *insight, judgment,* and *good sense.* In addition, it is *a wise attitude or course of action.* As Catholics we are so blessed because we do not have to rely only on natural wisdom that is acquired many times in the "school of hard knocks." With the reception of the sacraments we receive an infusion of sanctifying grace which includes the gift of wisdom. This gift, if we are responsive to it, helps us to view everything with the mind of God.

Theologian Fr. Gregory D. Gaston, of Manila in the Philippines, explains that the gift of wisdom which *accompanies sanctifying grace, makes a person well disposed to receive the inspirations and movements of the Holy Spirit, and completes and perfects the virtues of those who receive them. What is specific to wisdom is that it makes the soul responsive to the Holy Spirit in the contemplation of divine things and in the use of God's ideas* <u>*to judge both created and divine matters*</u> (editorial emphasis). *It effects a filial fear of God, as well as a welcome peace in the heart of man...We ask for the gift of wisdom not only for special undertakings, but to follow God's will, which is a continuous task for the Christian..[W]e should never cease to ask the Almighty for the gift of wisdom in the struggles of every day* (see **Wisdom** *9:10). With this gift we constantly use God's standards and not ours. Or better still, we try to make our standards conform*

[4] ***Lifeline,*** *Op. Cit.*, p. 26.
[5] St. Thomas Aquinas, *In III Sententiarum,* dist. 33, a. 2, a. 5.

to God's...in such a way that a prior conformity to God's will makes us always will what is good.[6]

Wisdom, King Solomon tells us, ***will never make its way into a crafty soul or stay in a body that is in debt to sin*** (***Wisdom*** 1:4). ***Wisdom is...found by those who look for her. Quick to anticipate those who desire her, she makes herself known to them...In her company all good things came to me, at her hands riches not to be numbered...In each generation she passes into holy souls, she makes them friends of God and prophets; for God loves only the man who lives with Wisdom...[O]ver Wisdom evil can never triumph... [V]irtues are the fruit of her labors, since it is she who teaches temperance and prudence, justice and fortitude; nothing in life is more serviceable to men than these*** (6:13-17; 7:7, 11, 27-28. 30; 8:7).

Another gift of the Holy Spirit is the gift of counsel. This is likewise infused into our souls along with sanctifying grace. Theologian Alfonso Carrasco Rouco, of Madrid, Spain, explains: *The gift of counsel also perfects what is known as the moral virtue of prudence, which guides man, advising him to the extent that reason is capable of understanding things. Human reason in fact is unable to grasp the singularity and the contingency of beings and events; it needs therefore to be orientated by God's counsel, to welcome His counsel, like those who accept advice from the wiser, because He knows all things...[W]ith the gift of counsel, reason is instructed by the Holy Spirit in regards to what it must do, prudence is carried to its maximum perfection, and actions are orientated to the ultimate objective of eternal life, moved and guided by the Love of the Spirit.*

St. Louis de Montfort quotes Scripture to explain the connection between wisdom, counsel and prudence: ***"I, Wisdom, dwell in counsel," "He who trusts in himself, trusts in a fool." "The prudent man does all things with counsel."*** *And the great counsel given by the Holy Spirit is*

[6] Zenit, Aug. 30, 2002.

this: Do nothing without counsel and you shall have nothing to regret afterwards. Seek counsel always of a wise man.

Prudence is impossible to instill in our teens if we ourselves lack this virtue. Your teen needs to see you seeking advice, taking advice, weighing the consequences of your actions or they will not learn how to practice prudence. You may have the desire along with the best intentions to raise your children saints but the numerous daily decisions you make negatively or positively affect this goal. Day by day as you tackle each child's problems and personality you are either forming your child or deforming your child. Prudence is the virtue we need if we are to successfully mold the character of our children. Why? The virtue of prudence prevents us from overreacting to situations because we are tired, crabby, unhappy, or stressed out. This virtue helps us think and reflect on the possible consequences of our decision. Will our children become better because of it or worse? This is the virtue that keeps *you* on the path of raising your children saints.

Prudence is one of the last virtues to be taught because to practice this virtue one must have a certain level of intellectual development. *It is a matter of discerning, of having standards, of judging and deciding.*[7] ***Proverbs*** tells us that ***the praise of a man is in proportion to his prudence*** (12:8).

C. S. Lewis humorously describes peoples' misconception of prudence: *Prudence means practical common sense, taking the trouble to think out what you are doing and what is likely to come of it. Nowadays most people hardly think of Prudence as one of the "virtues." In fact, because Christ said we could only get into His world by being like children, many Christians have the idea that, provided you are "good," it does not matter being a fool. But that is a misunderstanding. In the first place, most children show plenty of "prudence" about doing the things they are really interested in, and think them out quite sensibly. In the second place, as St. Paul points*

[7] "The Education of Prudence," *Op. Cit.*, p. 3.

out, Christ never meant that we were to remain children in intelligence: on the contrary, He told us to be not only "as harmless as doves," but also "as wise as serpents." He wants a child's heart, but a grown-up's head. He wants us to be simple, single-minded, affectionate and teachable, as good children are; but He also wants every bit of intelligence we have to be alert at its job, and in first class fighting trim. The fact that you are giving money to a charity does not mean that you need not try to find out whether that charity is a fraud or not. The fact that what you are thinking about is God Himself (for example, when you are praying) does not mean that you can be content with the same babyish ideas which you had when you were a five-year-old. It is, of course, quite true that God will not love you any the less, or have less use for you, if you happen to have been born with a very second-rate brain. He has room for people with very little sense, but He wants everyone to use what sense they have...God is no fonder of intellectual slackers than of any other slackers...Anyone who is honestly trying to be a Christian will soon find his intelligence being sharpened: one of the reasons why it needs no special education to be a Christian is that Christianity is an education itself.[8]

Cardinal Nicolas de Jesús López Rodríguez of Santo Domingo was interviewed at Columbia University about our culture. He stressed that *contemporary man has not grown in moral qualities. He grows in the area of having, of power and pleasure, but not in the area of truth and life. We have an opulent person who enjoys things, but not a virtuous and wise person. There are many educated people, but few who are morally wise. There is an abyss between education and formation, both in the school as well as in society...In history, each culture has opted for different values and proposes to its society the models that best embody them: the Greek hero, medieval mystic, Renaissance and modern philosopher... Contemporary society emphasizes material well-being, pleasure, and sees these fulfilled in the one who possesses*

[8] C. S. Lewis, ***Mere Christianity,*** (NY: Macmillan Publishing Company, 1952) pp. 74-75.

and enjoys them without limits, even if deep down he is a miserable human being.

Contemporary man, equipped with weak reason, has abandoned the great ideals to allow himself to be progressively seduced by the passion of lust, which keeps him enslaved and depraved...[T]o be a person, a minimum of well-being is certainly necessary—we do not dispute this. But even for material well-being, little is needed: health, a modest home, work, food and clothes. One is a person because of one's spiritual dimension, and one grows as a person in the measure that one grows spiritually.[9]

Developing Moral Judgment[10]

"Fools are more to be feared than the wicked."
St. Christina of Sweden

There are six stages of moral development according to Dr. Lawrence Kohlberg. Each person proceeds through the steps at his own pace. As a consequence, age itself is not a reliable indicator of one's state of development in making moral judgments.

Stage 1

In this initial stage, moral judgments depend on one's wants. The same action can be good or bad depending on its consequences for the person who is acting. Eating cake is good if the child isn't caught eating the last piece which mom told him not to eat; it's bad if the culprit who ate it is caught and punished. At this level there is awareness of the importance of obeying authority but the act is seen as right or wrong only in terms of its personal consequences. **Enjoyment is good, punishment is bad!** Dr. Kohlberg claims that some adults never get beyond this first stage of moral development.

---

[9] Zenit, Nov. 23, 2003.
[10] This material is drawn from a handout adapted from ***Sharing the Faith with Your Children—From Birth to Age Six,*** Chapter 15, by Phyllis Chandler and Joan Burney, Liguouri Publications (1984).

Stage 2

In this second stage, the person qualifies behavior by its positive consequences—for himself—rather than by its negative effects. If I do this for dad, maybe he will take me to a baseball game, to the movies or something else that is enjoyable and fun. The person reasons that *doing what those in authority want is good because it gets rewards.* The motivation is focused on the pursuit of pleasure rather than the mere avoidance of punishment. Punishment is rightly understood as the appropriate response to an infraction of the rules. But the good is understood primarily as what immediately benefits me. The motivation for acting well is self-centered and for self-gain. **Obtaining rewards is good, missing out on them is bad.** Dr. Kohlberg claims that many adults never progress past this stage either.

Stage 3

It is during this stage that some standards of behavior are set. *There is now an awareness of, and a concern for, doing what is right.* Unfortunately, the intention motivating the action is wrong. The intention is for oneself to be accepted and approved of, rather than the correctness of the action itself. One acts well because he/she wants to belong, to be liked and to be admired. In this instance, the person is motivated by social recognition—be it of peers or others. Cutting the grass is done because it earns approval. Putting one's heart into winning the game is good because I will be looked up to and thought of as "cool." The correct intention would be to cut the grass because of a sense of responsibility toward the family or win the game so that my team is thought well of. **Esteem is good, non-recognition is bad.** *Most adolescents are at this stage of moral development.*

Stage 4

At this stage, *rules and regulations become the absolute*

criteria for behavior. Dr. Kohlberg refers to this stage of moral development as the stage of "law and order" morality. *Rules are not violated* because the laws are established for the common good. However, *the individual does not* ask *whether* or not *the rule is* good or *just*, this is simply assumed, taken to be a "given". **Order is good, chaos is bad.** Kohlberg believes that the majority of adults reach this fourth stage but few progress beyond it.

Stages 5 & 6

Dr. Kohlberg does not clearly separate these two stages because, in practice, they tend to overlap. *The mature individual makes moral decisions based on principles he or she has internalized.* The deeper this internalization—the greater the identification of the person with the law—the stronger the person's commitment to living by the law. *Laws remain because the person understands the need for them, not just because they exist.* At this level a person makes a decision based on his conscience. *If a mother, for example, was rushing a dying child to the hospital and came to a stop sign, she would make her decision to either stop or not to stop, depending on whether or not traffic was present. If no traffic was present —ignoring the sign— she would continue through the intersection, because she would realize that, in this instance, the saving of a life has greater moral value than the obeying of a traffic law.*

For a Christian, the highest level of moral development is the total identification of one's own will with the will of God—the ultimate Law, the law of Love. For the truly mature Christian—the saint—this identification is complete, for the will of God is both understood and experienced as God's love and God himself. **God, who is love, is good; opposition to God is <u>the only</u> evil.** This is the ideal—a true conscience—for every Christian to strive for.

Exercising Moral Judgment[11]

To develop a child's ability for making sound moral judgments he must experience consistent consequences that result from his behavior.

- ❑ Reward a child's appropriate behavior and suitably punish his unacceptable behavior (through a loss of privileges: by being grounded, limiting phone or internet time, etc.)

- ❑ Be consistent. Don't scold a child for his behavior one day and ignore it the next. This only confuses him. For moral principles to be established, moral habits (virtues) must take root and this requires time and consistent application of principles to many individual cases.

- ❑ Encourage a child to make decisions about the way a person should act. Use stories to illustrate such situations, then ask him such questions as: "Why do you think this little boy got hurt?" "Would this have happened if he had obeyed?" "What would you have done in this case?" This gives you an opportunity to understand your child's moral reasoning while giving him a chance to solve a moral problem or come to a moral decision. Provide your child with alternatives but don't give your child the right answer. The child's decision should be based on his or her level of moral development. Then explain the correct answer as well as why it is correct.

- ❑ Let your child exercise options in real life situations as to how to spend his money—either on a birthday gift for his sister or on something for himself. What options does he have in his purchases? What are the consequences of his expenditures? Discuss the situation with the child.

Dr. Kohlberg points out having religious beliefs and values are not the same thing as acting morally. People can practice their faith but *be immature in making moral judgments.* For example, people can go to church each week and believe in the Ten Commandments but accept the gay lifestyle, abortion and euthanasia. These individuals either were never formed morally or fell victim to situation ethics. On

[11] *Ibid.*

the other hand, there are other people who have no set religious beliefs but adhere with their lives to strong moral and ethical principles. *Religion helps us to be more aware of moral options and offers guidance in decision-making. Alone, however, religion does not provide moral maturity.* This is why in the ***Raise Happy Children Series*** it took two books to discuss the important virtues.

Young children do not understand how their actions impact others. They are just beginning to learn about their responsibility toward God and others. Before the age of reason, a child cannot commit a serious sin because the child *lacks full awareness of the significance of her acts which is a necessary condition* for a serious sin to be committed. For this reason, parents should not be overly troubled if a small child deliberately breaks a minor rule or hurts a friend. Instead, *parents should watch for patterns of behavior that may be signs of serious personal problems. This is why the need for consistent consequences on the part of parents is so needed: to prevent these potentially serious patterns from developing.*

Emphasize the positive aspects of your child's behavior. This will motivate your child to do good because "I am good." Children need to know they are loved even when they make mistakes and do wrong. *[A]s a loving parent you root your discipline in love so that your child grows into a responsible individual. Remember, you're not raising children, you're raising adults—the end product of successful parenting. The Bible story of the prodigal son is a good example of why this security is important to a child. (The prodigal son had the courage to return home, to his father's house, and ask his father for forgiveness because he knew that—regardless of his behavior—he would be loved. We all need to know that we can return to God—no matter what we have done—and that He will forgive us because He is merciful. Children form their image of authority by observing their parents' behavior.)*[11A]

Dr. Kohlberg stresses that *your own moral judgment is a powerful model.* Talk to your children and teens about how you struggle with moral questions and dilemmas at work, with friends, in family situations. *When an elderly member of the family is dying are extraordinary means necessary to keep them alive?* (No). *Should they receive food and hydration?* (Yes). *Should I continue working on this charitable board when the paid employees are fiscally irresponsible and they refuse to work with me to correct the situation?* (No). *A pregnant woman is advised to have a test to see if her child has Down's syndrome. She is also told that the procedure could possibly cause blindness to the baby. Should she have the procedure done?* (No). Since there is no treatment available at this time to correct Down's syndrome, this test is frequently used to encourage mothers to abort their babies. Ask your child what you or he should do if a clerk under or over charges you or him or gives back too much change. Use examples in the newspaper, on TV, in movies as well as situations that come up in everyday living, to discuss how and why a person should act in a moral manner.

In the musical *Les Miserables,* the hero of the story, Jean Valjean, after spending nineteen years in prison, escapes. He was sent to imprison for stealing a loaf of bread which he took to feed a sick child. After escaping, he changes his identity, becomes the mayor of a town and the owner of a factory; in the process he acquires a sizeable fortune. After some years, he learns that another man, whom the police mistakenly think is Jean Valjean has been taken into custody. This innocent man will be imprisoned unless he, the real Valjean, comes forward. His moral dilemma is acute. In his mind he agonizes over what he should do. He rationalizes as to why he should not come forward and give himself up. He is the mayor of the town. He is doing so much good there. He owns the factory where many towns'

[11A] *Ibid.*

people are employed. If he goes back to prison they will lose their jobs and possibly remain unemployed for an unforeseeable future. He agonizingly goes back and forth in his mind over what to do. Finally, he sees clearly that the only ethical solution is for him to give himself up, so that the innocent party may go free. Explain to your teens that there are many everyday situations that depend on them living their moral beliefs to the fullest.

Teaching the Virtue of Prudence

"A prudent man sees danger and hides himself; but the simple go on, and suffer for it."
Proverbs 22:3

Little children cannot practice the virtue of prudence because they lack intellectual development. But if they are grounded in the virtue of obedience, then taught to base decisions on the advice of reputable people, they can begin to acquire some of the basics of the virtue.

Explain clearly to young children in what areas they are free to make choices and in what areas they are to seek advice. Tell them clearly from whom they should seek advice. For example, children can select the toys they want to play with, the playmates to associate with, how they want to handle their "spending money," and what they plan to wear within reason. In the other areas that are too complex or where they lack capability children need to seek advice.

A sense of responsibility is necessary for prudent actions or decisions. A teen needs *to size up a situation accurately, to know the standards which should guide his judgment and make the right decision.*[12] Drum into your teen's consciousness that a mark of wisdom/prudence is to be open to advice and guidance from prudent people, especially their parents. Read the ***Book of Proverbs.*** Then go through it again with your teens. It begins with an explanation why it

[12] "The Education of Prudence," *Op. Cit.,* p. 4.

was written: ***That men may know wisdom and instruction, understand words of insight, receive instruction in wise dealing, righteousness, justice, and equity; that prudence may be given to the simple, knowledge and discretion to the youth-the wise man also may hear and increase in learning, and the man of understanding acquires skill, to understand a proverb and a figure, the words of the wise and their riddles*** (2-6).

Next read ***Ecclesiastes, The Book of Wisdom,*** and finally ***Sirach (Ecclesiasticus)*** with your children. Discuss the books with your teen in regard to how they apply to the teen's life. Relate what you are reading to practical examples so he/she understands. Explain that it is the vice of pride that insists that we "know it all" and do not need to seek or take advice. This form of pride, like pride in all its other forms, leads only to misery. Tina, a young professional, fell in love with a fellow that her family could see was immature and unable to make a commitment. Friends, family members, and siblings tried to point out to Tina that she was wasting her time with this fellow. Stubbornly she resisted all advice thereby wasting six years of her life waiting for him to make a commitment. Finally she woke-up and moved on but only after suffering much sorrow. What grief she would have been spared if she had been open to advice.

How does one make a prudent decision? First one must know all the aspects involved before making a decision. It takes humility to realize one's limitations then seek out all the facts rather than acting impulsively. Teens tend to be impulsive. Teach them to refrain from acting until they have all the necessary information. How many times do we rashly judge people or situations only to find out later that the situation was not what it seemed? Recently I was trying to muster the courage to ask a pastor of a parish for permission to host our yearly diocesan Novena to the

Immaculate Conception. In the past this pastor has not been very friendly. Knowing this, an associate of the pastor offered to secure the permission. Upon returning from vacation, I found a message from the pastor requesting that I contact him. When I did, he was on vacation. For the next week I agonized over what to do *when* he said *no*. The bishop was already tentatively scheduled for the novena. How embarrassing! Wild thoughts were flying off in all directions. All I could think about was *what if…what will I do?* A priest friend cautioned me not to overreact; *the pastor may simply be calling to confirm the novena dates.* It turned out that that *was* precisely the purpose of his call.

Dr. Isaacs recommends that we train our children to mentally run through the following list before making a decision:

1. Has all the information possible been gathered?
2. Is one's information based on fact, opinion or feelings?
3. Are the sources of information credible?
4. Has any doubtful information been checked out?
5. Am I being objective or subjective in my decision?
6. Has advice been sought from competent authorities such as parents, teachers, etc.
7. Has the situation been analyzed?
8. If a commitment is being made, does the teen have the ability to follow through with it?
9. What are the consequences if one acts, if one does not act?
10. How does this relate to past experiences and consequences?

The temptation in seeking advice is to find someone sympathetic to one's point of view rather than to an unbiased source. Some Catholic couples "shop around" to find a priest to give them permission to contracept. Isaacs warns: *It is quite possible to go to a source of information because one is well disposed to it-and not to another source because one is turned off it or because it means making a greater effort. We should seek the most objective, complete, and suitable information available.*[13]

Children develop information by

1. Observing,
2. Reading,
3. Assimilating what is read, and
4. Listening.

Isaacs adds: *By observing, reading and listening he can come to grips with reality, but as we have said it is also a matter of knowing what to observe, what to read and whom to listen to...*[14]

Parents unconsciously teach their children observation skills when they point out the differences in the size, shape, and sounds of different animals. *What does a cow say? What does a horse say?* When small children listen to stories they learn more information about the animals. They learn that cows live in barns, while most dogs live in homes. Children easily assimilate information by listening when you point out the different things the animals do at the zoo or the problems you are having with squirrels or moles. Rather than stopping with animals, help your children to observe differences in nature such as trees, flowers, and water plants. Remember the party game where a tray was covered with a cloth? For three minutes the tray was uncovered displaying a variety of items. At the end of the time, the tray was again covered. The child who remembered the most items on the tray won the prize. This game plus card games, matching games, etc. help children to observe, remember, and learn from experience.

As your children grow older encourage them to research their interests by taking books out of the library and watching TV specials on favorite topics. Critique books and TV programs so that they can learn that people view the same thing in different ways. Introduce fourth or fifth grade students to the original ***Nancy Drew Mystery Series*** (for

[13] *Ibid.*, p. 5.

[14] *Ibid.*, p. 6.

girls) and ***The Hardy Boys Series*** (for boys). Mysteries train the mind to observe, assimilate, and come to a conclusion. When a wrong conclusion is arrived at, mysteries teach the child that his powers of observation are not infallible. Also, it helps him to draw information from various characters (sources) to reach a conclusion. Watch mystery shows or magic shows with your teens. Discuss the program afterwards. Who figured out the mystery or magic trick first? How did the person figure it out? Was the viewer misled by opinions expressed by the characters rather than the facts? In a magic show was the viewer's attention distracted by peripheral activity so as not to see how the trick was contrived?

Encourage your teens to read Agatha Christie mystery novels, spy thrillers written by Helen McInnes,[15] the Sherlock Holmes stories, the ***Father Brown*** series by G. K. Chesterton and the **Mrs. Pollifax** mystery series by Dorothy Gilman. These books will train them to discern between facts and opinions. The books and the films based on the writings of Daphne du Maurier such as ***My Cousin Rachel*** and ***Rebecca,*** and ***Green Dolphin Street*** by Elizabeth Goudge as well as the film *Babbet's Feast* teach interesting lessons in regard to prudence. The objective is to train your children to be *able to judge correctly in accordance with suitable standards.*[16]

Push your teens to read appropriate newspapers such as ***The Wall Street Journal, U.S.A. Today***, ***The Chicago Tribune, The New York Times,*** etc. Caution them to avoid the sensational tabloids that one encounters at the checkout

---

[15] In one of her later books, McInnes alluded to a premarital affair. Do read all material before sharing it with your children. When there is little objectionable material in a book I edit it out with a heavy black marker...even for my married daughters. If a book has an objectable theme, don't read it; shred it. By purchasing inexpensive used books you won't feel so badly about shredding them. I have only read several of the Mrs. Pollifax series and I have not read them in order. Please preview these books before giving them to your teens... just in case.

[16] "The Education of Prudence," *Op .Cit.,* p. 6.

counters. Discuss editorials in the newspapers. Point out how people have different viewpoints on the same issue. Help them to differentiate news articles from biased reporting. What sources are being quoted in the newspaper? Is it a primary source or a secondary source? Explain the difference to your children. Have them read the book, ***Bias*** by Bernard Goldberg. Reading is crucial to the development of prudence. Those who do not read or read little can be handicapped in living the virtue of prudence.

We adults must also be well-informed by reading a variety of sources before making a judgment or voting for a candidate. If we do not make the effort, our judgment may be misguided or imprudent. Doesn't it amaze you that people vote for presidential candidates based simply on what the biased media tells them? Rather then making the effort to think for themselves they soak up the misinformation of some reporter. With the majority of the means of communication centralized in the hands of a few wealthy people, these owners of newspaper and electronic media exploit these tools to distort truth. Without researching issues from alternative sources, your vote will not be based on truth but on what these people want you to believe. This was one of the shocking lessons I learned covering the UN Conferences. What occurred at the Conferences was not accurately portrayed in the news accounts.

Listening is also important in the operation of prudence. Teach your teen how to listen. A clue that your child is not a listener is if the child is disobedient. If he is not listening to you, he will not listen to other authorities or the voice of reason. Listening is a lost art today. Each time Bob and I go out to eat we grade the listening ability of the waitress. He always takes his coffee black. He explains this to each waitress but usually gets cream anyway. When Bob is out of town rather than stopping to make dinner, I will grab a carryout. Each time I ask *please hold the hushpuppies.*

When I get home to eat my carryout the first thing that rolls out are those blasted hushpuppies! Professional people are likewise guilty of not listening. When I was working with the layout designer for my book ***Looking For Peace? Try Confession!*** written instructions were sent along with sample layouts giving specific details. Through numerous phone calls I reiterated exactly what I wanted. Despite all these efforts the layout was done incorrectly because the designer was neither listening nor paying attention to instructions. That experience taught me that I had to do my own typesetting and layouts if I wanted it done a certain way.

To listen we have to stop thinking our own thoughts. We have to stop talking. We have to focus our full attention on the person speaking. Look at the person's face, particularly his eyes, to keep from being distracted. Think about what the person said to you. Turn it over in your mind. Ask questions to be sure you understand. Make a comment to indicate that you heard what the person said. Repeat instructions to be sure you correctly comprehend them. This is how to listen.

Explain clearly to your teen that advice needs to be gleaned from an authority in the field, or from someone with proven maturity and wisdom. Listening to the immature advice of friends is similar to the *blind leading the blind*...they both will fall into a pit.

Dr. Isaacs encourages parents to train their teens to develop the habit of mentally going through the following list to arrive at a prudent decision:

1. What do you know about this topic?
2. Where did you get your information?
3. Are your sources reliable?
4. Are they adequate?
5. Have you already formed an opinion about this matter independently of the information you now have?

6. Are you prejudiced in any way?
7. Are there any gaps in the information you have gathered?
8. How can you supplement this information?
9. Have you sifted this information to distinguish facts from opinions, secondary material from important material?
10. What standards have you chosen for assessing the situation?
11. Are these the right standards?[17]

Help your teen to understand that information has to be gathered to make a "prudent" decision. *What are the facts? Are they really facts or only opinions or an emotional feeling?* Are the facts from a reliable source or the kid down the street? Before being able to make a prudent decision explain to your child that he has to have a standard by which to judge an opinion or action. That is why a solid grounding in faith and morals is key to the practice of prudence. Teach your teens that God has given them a brain with which to think and reflect. Their actions are to be based on the Ten Commandments and the moral teachings of the Church. A prudent person not only puts God first in his life but remembers that Satan is not only alive but is busily working to cause his eternal damnation. Cardinal Dionigi Tettamanzi of Milan, Italy, published a message about our *great Tempter*. In teaching prudence it is wise to teach teens the following ten points to help them withstand the attacks of the devil. Cardinal Tettamanzi writes:

1. Do not forget that the devil exists. The first lie, of which we are often victims, is to make us believe he does not exist.
2. Do not forget that the devil is a tempter.
3. Remember that the devil is very intelligent and astute.
4. Be vigilant since, as St. Peter reminds us, he goes about like *a roaring lion seeking someone to devour.*
5. Believe firmly in Christ's victory over the tempter.
6. Christ makes us participate in His victory.
7. Listen to the Word [Gospel]...
8. Be humble in mortification as temptation is always a call to

[17] *Ibid.*, pp. 7-8.

follow the path of egoism.
9. Pray without ceasing.
10. Adore the Lord our God and worship Him only.[18]

It is these values and beliefs, along with the grace of the Holy Spirit, that instills wisdom into our thoughts, words, and actions. Without these, prudence is inoperable. Teach your children to use these standards to evaluate situations since they are based on Truth. On Holy Thursday, Pope John Paul II reminded priests: *Although it is true that no one can become a saint in someone else's place, it is also true that each one must become a saint with and for others, following Christ's model. Is not personal sanctity nourished by that spirituality of communion, which must always precede and accompany concrete initiatives of charity?*[19]

Reminding your teen of this standard, ask if the film, video, book, or activity he wishes to engage in is going to bring him closer to God or separate him from Him. Ask your teen if it is going to make him a better person. If not, the prudent decision is to avoid the situation. Without clear spiritual standards actions easily become unjust, uncharitable, impatient, intolerable, prideful, slothful, along with all the other vices. Pleasure, fame, money and power become the standard.

What if the situation is morally indifferent? Should this be the case, ask if the time spent on the project could be more fruitfully spent on something else. Viewing a yard blooming with dandelions from my sunroom, I have the choice of digging weeds or completing this book. The dandelions are morally indifferent but how does God wish me to spend my time and energies right how? Prudence dictates that my time during the day be spent on this book but there may be several hours in the early evening that I could use to weed or maybe wait until the weekend. Prudence is setting priorities, then working down the list.

Explain to your children how *you* judge situations and

[18] Zenit, March 8, 2001.
[19] Zenit, April 12, 2001.

events. Clarify what you *actually* mean by the words "good," "excellent," "important," "necessary," or "bad." We understand what these words mean but children and teens have to learn the meaning from us to avoid being confused.

Dr. Isaacs insists, *we parents must steadily give standards to our children, so that they know which standard to use in each situation:*

1. Standards for behavior at home: the relationship between chores, free time, helping others, homework.
2. Standards for evaluating what other people do: the injustice of a companion; who is right in some argument; etc.
3. Standards for judging whether it is good to read some book or see some film.
4. Standards for evaluating social and personal problems;
5. Standards for seeing if one is acting justly, generously, sincerely, respecting others, etc., and prudently.[20]

Help your children to

1. Understand the things they are told to do and why they are to do them.
2. Get your children to act and to do these actions on their own initiative.
3. Help your children to think about the options available to them.
4. Ask them questions to see if they are in fact thinking through their decisions.[21]

The two vices opposed to the virtue of prudence are imprudence (lacking wisdom and discretion) and negligence (inattention to a duty or obligation). Prudence is not only a reflective virtue but also **a virtue of action.** Once we reflect on the situation, we must move our will to the best course of action. If it is a difficult action, the virtue of fortitude, if cultivated beforehand, kicks in to support the exercise of the virtue of prudence. Without fortitude, we will cave in to fear, laziness or the nagging of our teens thereby committing the vice of negligence.

---

[20] "The Education of Prudence," *Op. Cit.*, p. 10. [21] *Ibid.*, p. 11.

Imprudence is the vice by which we neglect to reflect or if we reflect, do not carry out the necessary action. For instance, Molly wants to attend a post prom party at a hotel where her friends and their dates have rented a suite for a night of partying. Prudence tells her parents this is not a good idea because there will be no chaperones and liquor will most likely be served. This situation presents serious moral problems. The daughter contends that her life will be ruined if she is not permitted to go. She badgers, cries, storms, nags and the parents reluctantly give in. This is an example of imprudence. The parents know the right course of action but lack the fortitude (courage/will) to carry it out.

An example of the lack of reflection was the decision of the parents of a young woman to permit her to visit her fiancé, unchaperoned, for a week at his naval base. Rather than sending her sister along or taking her themselves, they readily gave her permission to go alone then dropped her off at the airport. Her fiancé picked her up the airport, took her to check into her hotel and you know the rest. Years later this young woman blamed her parents for what happened. *What were they thinking letting me go alone?* There are prudent ways to handle similar situations. Let me elaborate on a situation that I mentioned in ***Raise Happy Children...Raise Them Saints!*** When I was nineteen and in college, I was invited to attend a ball at a military college in Alabama. My parents were not enthusiastic about my invitation although they had met the cadet previously and his family was reputable. Permission was granted if I met three difficult conditions. The cadet was to make arrangements for me to stay at a neighboring women's college that had a strict curfew. The second condition was that I had to not only pay my own expenses but I had to also pay the expenses of my college roommate, whom they trusted, so she could be my chaperone. If she could not go, I, like Cinderella, would have to stay home from the ball. The third condition was that the cadet was to know that I was coming simply to be his date, that I could not become serious about him since he was Episcopalian. They imposed these conditions hoping to discourage me from going or at least to make me think about the value of what I was doing. It did make me weigh the pros and cons. Their requirements caused complications. Could the cadet find a date for my roommate? Was this ball worth emptying my savings account? In retrospect it was well worth the expense and effort. The weekend opened my eyes to the dangers of a mixed marriage. What a shock it was to attend Easter Sunday Mass, held in a classroom, attended by only six people of which only four were Catholics. Our Protestant dates accompanied us out of respect. It showed me what a lonely road a mixed marriage would be. This was reinforced later the same day when another male friend met us at the airport in Atlanta during our layover. A Presbyterian, his parents were furious that he was meeting a Catholic coed, no less on Easter, at the airport. My weekend in the South convinced me to drop Protestant boyfriends because there were too many difficulties to overcome in a mixed relationship. Unlike Cinderella, I came home from the experience knowing that my "prince" had to be a Catholic. My parents had been prudent by allowing me *limited* freedom but also demanding responsibility. Their delicate balance allowed me to personally observe two situations that made me reevaluate the qualities I wanted in my future spouse. This is the same delicate balance you have to achieve with your teens and young adults. Fear of your teen's displeasure should never intimidate you to the point of falling into the vices/sins of imprudence or negligence. As long as your teen is living in your home and you are paying his expenses (tuition, etc.) you are justified in exercising your authority even over the age of eighteen. Once your child leaves home and is self-supporting you are limited to giving advice.

St. Josemaría reflects: *The difficulties you have met have made you shrink back, and you have become "prudent, moderate, and objective." Remember that you have always despised those terms, when they become synonyms for cowardly, fainthearted and comfort-seeking.*[22] *There are some ways of acting that are so careful that, in a word, they are just pusillanimous* [lacking courage and resolution].[23]

Dr. Isaacs warns: *Imprudence—which includes precipitance* [undue hastiness], *thoughtlessness and inconstancy* [lacking steadiness]*—is very much connected with failure to control one's passions. Imprudence can lead parents to pre-judge their children or pigeonhole them, not realizing that a person is dynamic and changes a little every day. We all have some sort of mania—big or little—and this can influence our objectivity. There are parents who insist blindly on their children following the same career as themselves. Others, through excessive anger or envy, make unjust demands on their children; others, who are very clear on what they want, think that their good ends justify whatever means they use to attain them.*[24]

To act in a prudent manner one must have the right intention, which is to do the will of God. Engrave this belief in your children's intellect! Warn them about the herd mentality. Explain that as sons and daughters of God they are called to lead, not follow. Prepare them to accept the suffering that comes from being virtuous, particularly being prudent: ***Let us lie in wait for the virtuous man, since he annoys us and opposes our way of life, reproaches us for our breaches of the law and accuses us of playing false to our upbringing. He claims to have knowledge of God and calls himself a son of the Lord. Before us he stands, a reproof to our way of thinking, the very sight of him weighs our spirits down; his way of life is not like other men's, the paths he treads are unfamiliar. In his opinion we are counterfeit; he holds aloof from our doings as though from filth; he proclaims the final end of the virtuous as happy and boasts of having God***

[22] ***Furrow***, *Op. Cit.,* n.101. [23] *Ibid.*, n.109.
[24] "The Education of Prudence," *Op. Cit.,* p. 3.

for his father...Let us test him with cruelty and with torture, and let us explore this gentleness of his and put his endurance to the proof (***Wisdom*** 2:12-19). While this passage refers to the Passion and Death of Jesus, as followers of Christ it also pertains to us.

David Isaacs gives tips on how to discern if your child is developing the virtue of prudence:

1. Does your child ask for advice?
2. Does your child look for sufficient sources of information?
3. Does he weigh this information?
4. Does he discuss it with you or other mature people?
5. Does your child have standards?
6. Does he act or refrain from acting after he weighs the consequences?[25]

Did you realize that the Church considers this virtue so important that it is a prerequisite for a bishop being named a cardinal? The Council of Trent set these requirements for a cardinal: he is to be selected from priests who *are outstanding for their doctrine, piety and prudence.*[26]

When our daughter, Marianne, was fifteen, we vacationed with friends at Perdido Key, Florida. It was there that I realized that maybe I had over emphasized the issue of faith to the detriment of prudence when I asked her if she wanted to go shopping with us. She declined saying, *No. Christ called us to be fishers of men so I think I'll go down to the beach and start fishing.*

Flexibility

"Blessed are the flexible for they won't be bent out of shape." Fr. Jack Kubeck

Flexibility is the virtue we appreciate in people we have to work with but is difficult to live ourselves. What precisely is the virtue of flexibility? Dr. David Isaacs explains that:

[25] *Ibid.*, p. 12.
[26] Zenit, Feb. 21, 2001.

A person who is flexible adapts his behavior readily to the particular circumstances of each individual or situation, but without thereby abandoning his own personal principles of behavior.[27]

To live this virtue we have to live by set standards and principles so as to know in which areas we can be flexible and in which areas we have to stand firm. Living the virtue of flexibility does not mean that we give in to others easily but rather it *means learning to say yes and learning to say no at the right time.*[28] To live this virtue, we have to also practice the virtues of patience, perseverance, justice, generosity, temperance, moderation, respect for others, friendship and sociability that we discussed in previous chapters.

Those who practice the virtue of flexibility cannot be "know-it-alls"; they do not pontificate their opinions; they do not force others to do things their way or force others to believe as they do. They do not insist on uniform taste of clothing, style, furnishing, etc. Flexibility is refraining from being dogmatic on topics that are open to opinion. In ***Raise Happy Children...Teach Them Virtues!*** I described Benjamin Franklin's method of struggling to attain virtue. Franklin was a rare genius. Not only was he a great diplomat, he was an inventor, writer, printer, scientist, herb-doctor, postmaster, editor, chemist, political economist, orator, statesman, athlete, philosopher, wit, tinker and self-taught intellectual. When a friend learned that Franklin had put together a plan to eradicate his vices, he bluntly advised him to work on his manner of speaking to people first. Franklin was flexible. Not offended by the fraternal correction, Benjamin diligently worked on changing his tone and manner of speaking to others: *I made it a rule to forbear all direct contradiction to the sentiments of others, and all positive assertion of my own. I even forbid myself...the use of every word or expression in the language*

[27] ***Character Building,*** *Op. Cit.,* p. 124. [28] *Ibid.,* p. 132.

that imported a fix'd opinion, such as ***certainly, undoubtedly,*** *etc. and I adopted instead of them,* ***I conceive, I apprehend,*** *or* ***I imagine*** *a thing to be so or so; or it* ***so appears to me at present.*** *When another asserted something that I thought an error, I deny'd myself the pleasure of contradicting him abruptly, and of showing immediately some absurdity in his proposition; and in answering I began by observing that in certain cases or circumstances his opinion would be right, but in the present case there* ***appear'd*** *or* ***seem'd*** *to me some difference, etc. I soon found the advantage of this change in my manner; the conversations I engag'd in went on more pleasantly. The modest way in which I propos'd my opinions procur'd them a readier reception and less contradictions; I had less mortification when I was found to be in the wrong, and I more easily prevail'd with others to give up their mistakes and join with me when I happened to be in the right.*[29]

Franklin believed this change in his manner of speaking to people along with acquiring the virtue of integrity was responsible for his international success as a statesman and politician. He writes: *And this mode, which I at first put on with some violence to natural inclination, became at length so easy, and so habitual to me, that perhaps for these fifty years past no one has ever heard a dogmatical expression escape me. And to this habit (after my character of integrity) I think it principally owing that I had early so much weight with my fellow-citizens when I proposed new institutions, or alterations to the old, and so much influence in public councils when I became a member; for I was but a bad speaker, never eloquent, subject to much hesitation in my choice of words, hardly correct in language, and yet I generally carried my points.*[30]

Flexibility accepts others as they are as long as they do not infringe on our standards. It is not important if our child cuts the lawn in the opposite direction than we do. It is not

---

[29] Benjamin Franklin, ***The Autobiography of Benjamin Franklin*** (NY: Collier Books, 1962) pp. 89-90.

[30] *Ibid.*, p. 90.

important if someone folds the laundry differently or sweeps the floor in an unusual manner as long as the result is acceptable. Graciously accept how others cook, clean, and generally live their lives. Permit family members to use their creativity freely. Don't stifle them by being rigid. Through inflexibility we demonstrate a lack of tolerance, a strong case of the vice of stubbornness, pride, and in some situations a lack of intelligence.

[T]here are circumstances which are not matters of opinion, and this fact will affect the way we behave in our relationships with others and in our work. When it is a question of objective truth, we cannot revise or change our opinion, although it may well be that we can find a better way of expressing it.[31] In matters of truth, faith, and morality there is no flexibility but we can listen calmly, disagree politely and try to find areas that we can mutually agree upon. Learn how to change topics skillfully. Avoid heated arguments and personal attacks. Refrain from insisting that people have to agree with you. Just as God allows us to utilize our free will, allow others this same right.

Dr. Isaacs cautions parents: *If a parent discusses matters of faith, political questions or cultural affairs with his children and is equally certain in his views on them all or, on the other hand, if he treats all these subjects as equally debatable and open to argument, the children are unlikely to distinguish between what they can simply accept or reject and what is open to discussion. The result will be both confusion and a tendency to go either too far or not far enough in the virtue of flexibility.*[32]

Being dogmatic on all issues causes confusion. Be dogmatic in regard to faith, truth, and morality but be open to discussion on all other topics so your children see where flexibility is to be exercised and in what areas it cannot be exercised.

---

[31] ***Character Building***, *Op. Cit.*, p. 124. [32] *Ibid.*, p. 125.

The virtue of flexibility depends upon the development of the virtue of humility that we will discuss in the next chapter. Humility teaches us that we can always learn something from everyone we meet, from every sermon we hear, from everything we experience. If one has the opinion that he "knows it all" he cannot practice flexibility toward new things, consider new ideas or new approaches. **It is pride that contributes to the vice of inflexibility, which prevents us from growing as a person and learning from others.** Several weeks ago I attended a lecture on growing vines. The speaker is a horticultural expert with impeccable credentials. After his presentation we were walking out together when I asked him some questions about some of the vines he discussed. He heartily recommended growing autumn clematis but warned against planting white honeysuckle vine because it's invasive. He warned gardeners not to waste their time growing wisteria in Springfield unless they want only the leaves since our Spring frosts kill the flower buds. In my yard I have experienced the opposite. My honeysuckle doesn't spread but the autumn clematis is like kudzu choking out my other plants and springing up not only everywhere in the backyard but is also trying to blanket my front yard. Frustrated I asked what I should do about the clematis. Rather than being interested in my experience with this plant, he reacted to my questions as if I personally attacked him. He was inflexible in regard to the growth pattern of these plants! Then I made the mistake of asking about my wisteria that blooms heavily each year. I wanted to know what I was unknowingly doing right so I could continue to do it. He told me in a condescending manner that *if your wisteria has bloomed in the past it was a freak. It certainly won't bloom this year because the severe cold killed the buds.* My autumn clematis continues its stranglehold in my gardens. The wisteria didn't overhear our conversation so it doesn't know it's not supposed to bloom. Again this year the vine is covered with fragile, fragrant lavender flowers. It's more flexible than our horticulturalist! As David Isaacs points out: *Everyone has certain prejudices; we may be ignorant on some points and we may have a "mental" block on others. Flexibility, therefore, means that we should listen, not just to the words, which may be inexpertly chosen, but rather to the person who is speaking, and try to understand what is going on in his mind.*[33]

It is not always easy to be flexible in new situations where we have no experience to guide us in adapting to the circumstances; consequently, we should try to learn from others. That is to say, a flexible person is one who has learned from his own experience and that of others. Hence the importance of observing and listening.

If we are to learn from others, we must believe that what they have to say may be interesting and worthy of our consideration. People are often willing to listen to certain topics but not to others, even when these are open to debate, because they consider themselves "experts" on these subjects or at least they are convinced that they know more than others. This attitude makes it impossible to learn.[34]

Isaacs recommends that we

- ✓ Listen to others with interest.
- ✓ Observe them carefully.
- ✓ Notice if <u>we</u> are talking too much.
- ✓ Note if others have lost interest in what we are discussing. If so, drop the topic and let the other person/persons talk.

Whether we wish to admit it or not, we are easily influenced by what we read, what we see, and what we hear. If you disagree with this statement try this test. Watch the news and note the opinions of the reporters on the major story of the day. The next day ask acquaintances their opinions on the news story. Most of them will parrot the same views as the newscasters! This is what is meant by the media molding public opinion. Be careful not to be swayed by public opinion. This is not flexibility but

[33] *Ibid.*, p. 127.

[34] *Ibid.*, pp. 128-129.

gullibility.

Flexibility pertains to our actions. We may plan on reading a book or watching a recommended video but part way into the book or the video we realize that the material does not meet our personal standards. It is offensive to God. A person with the virtue of flexibility will toss the book or turn off the film. Likewise, we have to practice the virtue of flexibility in morally indifferent situations such as daily schedules, mealtimes, vacation spots, etc. While it is good to have set times for meals, circumstances do arise that make this sometimes impossible. We have to develop the flexibility to adjust to changes. An elderly uncle, who lived with my husband's family while Bob was growing up, refused to eat dinner if it was delayed more than ten minutes. We can be inflexible in regard to favorite pieces of furniture. *That's my chair!* Or we can insist on sitting in a certain position on the furniture. *I like to sit in the middle of the sofa* or *by an arm!* Or every time we go out to dinner it has to be the same place even though our spouse dislikes the restaurant or its food. Accept changes in your routine graciously as mortifications for a special intention or particular person. This will aid in the development of this virtue. Look for ways to change your set habits so as to develop flexibility. Change seats at dinner. Eat your food in a different order. Try a different clothing style or color. Push yourself to do things you fear such as talking to strangers at a social event, trying new foods, reading a different style of fiction or nonfiction, flying on an airplane, attending a cultural event on a week night instead of on a weekend. Don't permit yourself to get into a rut.

Point out to your children that they are inflexible when they have to wear a certain shirt all the time or a special cap; or if they have to have the radio or TV on to do their homework; or if they are reluctant to participate in family gatherings or go on family vacations.

To live the virtue of order we need a daily schedule. The night before put together either a written schedule or a mental schedule for the next day but realize as you do so that life being what it is, *what man appoints, God disappoints.* Be flexible in realizing that while you may plan to accomplish this and that, cheerfully accept changes without becoming unglued. This is living the virtue of flexibility.

Flexibility is lived when we are working on a project, the project is going well but just before we can complete it we have to stop because of a phone call, another commitment or a request for help from someone. St. Thomas Aquinas was plagued with interruptions when he was trying to develop his theological masterpiece, ***The Summa***. He cheerfully accepted each interruption. It was only after his death that people realized what violence he did to himself to be flexible. Although they saw him place his fingers under his desk, people did not realize that he was controlling his aggravation by carving out the underside with his nails!

When we become rigid in some goal we can even drive ourselves to the point of sickness. With Bob on retreat one weekend, I planned to use that time to complete the previous chapter. Come hell or high water that chapter would be completed by the time he returned! So I worked 20 hours a day both Friday and Saturday, completed the chapter but spent the next two weeks quite ill because I had run myself down due to a lack of sleep, flexibility, prudence, moderation, patience and temperance. What had been accomplished in 40 hours set me back two weeks. Not very smart was it?

We also have to realize that things do not have to be done according to our style or way of thinking. Flexibility also means giving up what we want to do to please another. My husband may feel like going out to dinner tonight while it would help me more if we went out tomorrow night. Living flexibility I will go out when it suits my spouse rather than me. Or, I can ask: *Would it be possible to go out tomorrow instead?* He may practice the virtue of flexibility to accommodate me. My spouse may enjoy a quiet vacation lolling on a familiar beach while I may need a more stimulating vacation that includes seeing new places, experiencing different cultures, trying exotic foods. This is where flexibility needs to be exercised by both spouses. We practice flexibility when we change our plans to accommodate the wishes or needs of others who ask for our help.

We exercise flexibility in regard to new experiences such as trying new foods when invited to a friend's home rather than saying: *I don't like that* or *I don't eat that.* Flexibility is practiced when we agree to try or take on something we have never done before. Unfortunately, we can become so comfortable in our routine that new duties, responsibilities, or undertakings send us into a panic. It is so common to hear, *I can't do that. I've never done something like that before!* Remember, life is filled with firsts—first steps, first food, first day of school, first job, first time driving a car, first time away from home, first time having a baby, first time having surgery, first time buying a house, etc. Teach your children/teens to accept rather than decline when they are asked to do something challenging or different. Show them how by *your* example. Each new experience is a chance to practice the virtue of flexibility. Explain that each opportunity that God presents helps the child to mature, to grow in virtues, to use talents that your child may not even know he possesses. God is constantly stretching us because He needs us, His friends, to participate in as many different activities as possible to bring souls to Him. Even though our efforts may seem a failure, a humiliation, a waste of time...in God's hands these labors will bear fruit, not only within our souls, but also within the world.

Only two weeks prior to the UN Population and Development Conference in Cairo, I was invited to attend as a reporter to fight for the "culture of life." It was a costly experience that meant a great financial sacrifice from my husband. Friends and family members willingly jumped in to help. Pat Daily of the St. John Fisher Forum helped me to set up a news service. Dr. David Mack, the father of my graphic artist, donated a laptop computer and paid for private computer lessons for me, while another doctor purchased a portable printer. A friend offered to come in each morning to forward on my news stories to 60 outlets. Fr. Sirico of the Acton Institute offered to be my computer backup here in the states if my computer system at home crashed which was a likelihood. Some of the organizations that I represented paid a small fee to help offset some of my expenses but ***The Wanderer,*** a weekly newspaper that featured my reports, also stipulated that I would have to be a guest speaker at their Wanderer Conference. While I had reluctantly given talks on spiritual topics, never had I addressed a conference before. (Remember, I mentioned that I am a stutterer in ***Raise Happy Children...Raise Them Saints!***) Experience as a foreign correspondent was lacking in my resume. To further complicate matters, I only had two weeks to become proficient in the use of the computer, a laptop, tape recorder, a fax, and the phone system of Egypt. The night before I left for Cairo *none* of my new, expensive equipment worked. The transformer I needed to power my equipment had been sent to Springfield, Missouri, rather than to Springfield, Illinois, where I live. It arrived twenty minutes before my plane departed for New York. There was no one in my traveling group that I knew. Talk about stepping out in faith! It never got any easier. Throughout the whole experience a tape kept replaying over and over in my mind, *I can't do this, I can't do this, I can't do this.* It was truly the most hellish two weeks of my life. Once safely home, preparation had to begin on my address for the conference. But what a lesson in the virtue of flexibility I learned from this experience! In Scripture we are told that God uses the weak to confound the proud. It was astounding to see with my own eyes what God can do with nothing when we allow ourselves to be flexible in His hands. Despite my ineptitude and equipment problems, the daily faxed reports alerted organizations back home to the "culture of death" being proposed by the UN. God not only gave me fluency when I addressed the conference but a standing ovation when the lecture concluded. On the wall in my office hangs a beautifully engraved plaque naming me *Journalist of the Year in 1994* for my coverage of the UN Conference. But my experience was such a diminutive part of the whole. God took the couple of hundred pro-lifers, their sacrifices, and their willingness to serve Him and used them to soundly defeat the evil plans of the thousands of highly paid, highly trained UN delegates. It was exciting to see the might of our God! What God can do if we have the flexibility to say "yes" to His outrageous plans for us! ***Now we know that for those who love God all things work together unto the good,*** as St. Paul tells us. ***If God is for us, who is against us*** (***Romans*** 8:28, 32)*?*

The two vices opposed to the virtue of flexibility ***are rigidity*** **[inflexibility]** *in trivial matters—which is very different from firmness in matters of principle—**and** what we might call **fragility, which means that we let ourselves be carried away by any influence, without reflection on the meaning of what we are doing,*** in other words **to be too open-minded or indifferent.**[35] We can also have a false sense of human respect in that we are so fearful of offending people that we refrain from expressing the truth. We have the *"live and let live" attitude.*

How can you train your children in this virtue? Expose them to a variety of different families from different religious backgrounds, cultures, and interests so that they can observe how different people react, think, express themselves or handle situations. Invite these people to your home then finagle invitations to their homes. Encourage your teens to sit in and join your discussions on religion and politics so they learn what topics they must stand firm

[35] *Ibid.,* p. 130.

on and which topics to let slide. They will also *see that there are different rules and habits in every family...Furthermore, such visits to other families whether they be relatives or not, will help the children to learn the difference between adapting to other people's way of life and giving in on fundamental principles...*[For example if] *the child tells his parents that he has seen several programs which they had forbidden him to watch [h]is parents can only say, "What a pity! You have missed a great chance to give good example to your cousins."*[36]

Suggest they try new experiences, organize a club or become involved in an organized way in some interest they have. Debate clubs are a great means to develop critical thinking and the ability to express oneself clearly and concisely. When we were in high school, my husband took me to a debate at his school. It so impressed me that I asked permission to start a debate club at my high school. The debates between different schools taught me not only how to craft arguments without loopholes but to look for the loopholes in the arguments of others.

Help your teens overcome their fear of inadequacy by skillfully helping them along. *Why don't you organize a debate club at school? I bet Mr. Jones would be a great moderator. Wouldn't it be fun to debate your friends who attend other schools? Why don't you suggest they start a debate club too?* Or, *Why don't you attend this Catholic summer camp for a week? You can meet new friends. You'd have a chance to canoe, design rockets, get to daily Mass. It would be a great experience for you.* Or, *You play the organ so well. Why don't you volunteer to play for the church choir? Why not start a pro-life club at school or a teen club at the parish?*

Teach flexibility by:

1. Introducing your children/teens to families of different religions, cultures, backgrounds.

[36] *Ibid.*

2. Explaining which topics one can compromise and which topics one cannot compromise.
3. Allowing teens and children to sit and listen to your conversations with friends so that they can see how you handle people when controversial topics come up.
4. Encouraging teens to try new experiences by shopping on their own, taking care of their own banking (savings accounts).
5. Urging teens to take on new responsibilities or begin initiatives at school, at home, at the parish, in their community.
6. Teaching teens to accept the idiosyncrasies of others.
7. Practicing with your teens how to express the truth in a polite, kind, considerate manner rather than arrogantly or brusquely.
8. Showing teens through word and example how flexibility covers dress, conversation, management of time, friendship, generosity, school work, chores, relations with siblings, etc.
9. Teaching your teens how to listen, observe and express themselves well.
10. Introducing your teens to foreign languages so they can communicate with other nationalities. The joke at the UN Conferences was, *How can you tell a person is an American? He can only speak English!* People I met from Third World countries could speak at least three languages.
11. Helping your children/teens see that they can learn from any person or from any situation.

When our youngest daughter, Mary Terese, was in fourth grade she asked if she could ride her bike over to meet a friend because the two of them wanted to go to a hobby store. When I told her she could go, she burst into tears accusing me of not loving her. *I could get killed crossing the street. Something terrible could happen to me,* she sobbed. Her real problem was her reluctance to try something new. So I explained to her that she was responsible; she knew how to ride her bike on the sidewalk; she knew how to cross the street at the light and she had a Guardian Angel to protect her. It was time for her to venture out on her own. She dried her tears, thinking I still had it in for her, and then rode away. Later she admitted that she had a great new adventure. Like the ducks and eagles, we have to push our children out of the safety of their nest or they will never learn to soar on their own.

Examples of Flexibility

Consider the flexibility of Our Lady and St. Joseph. Maternity was not in Mary's plans. The greatest exercise of the virtue of flexibility was her fiat, ***be it done to me according to thy word*** (***Lk.*** 1:38), that gave us Our Savior. St. Joseph was going to dismiss the pregnant Mary quietly until an angel told him ***take to thee Mary thy wife, for that which is begotten in her is of the Holy Spirit*** (***Matt.*** 1:20). Without asking a single question he changed his plans. Joseph's life was at the mercy of angels who kept popping up in his dreams, giving him traveling directions, and time lines.

The saints were flexible. St. Francis Xavier wanted to be a missionary to China but he never got there. He died on a beach close to China but not in China. Throughout his life he practiced the virtue of flexibility by accepting God's will in all matters dealing with his life.

When St. Frances Xavier Cabrini was rejected by the religious orders she selected she founded her own order. When it was well established she went to the Holy Father to ask for permission to be sent as missionaries to the Orient. He told her that the Italian immigrants needed her more in the United States so off she sailed to become the first American saint. She did not want to go into hospital ministry but through prayer and discernment she was flexible when she realized that this was God's wish.

St. Elizabeth Seton was very flexible in regard to the

schooling of her sons. She was open to sending them to whichever school would provide the best education. She was flexible toward God's will in her life by accepting the death of her husband; the resentment of family and friends toward her conversion; the directives of her bishop in the founding of her order; and life in general.

St. Louis de Montfort had lovingly and meticulously built an exquisite outdoor Way of the Cross. The bishop had even agreed to dedicate it. Just before the dedication, enemies, who were jealous of St. Louis de Montfort, convinced the bishop that the Way of the Cross had to be destroyed. When St. Louis received word from his bishop to destroy it, he walked all night to the bishop's residence in order to plead his case before the bishop. When the bishop refused to relent, he walked back and destroyed the shrine with his own hands. That's flexibility!

Another person who practiced flexibility was Cardinal Thuân's maternal grandfather. Kha (the grandfather) had been away from home studying to be a priest when there was a raid upon his village with the intent to kill all the Catholics. When the villagers heard about the attack, they did not have time to arm themselves so they ran to their thatched roofed church for refuge. There they were burned alive. Only a few children or people who were away from the village survived the massacre. When the superiors of the seminary learned of the massacre they counseled Kha to return home to marry so his family name could be carried on. *Kha accepted this advice and headed home. He knew that he would have to provide for his ailing mother, now left without any resources.*[37] Kha later became a close adviser to the Emperor.

Cardinal Thuan's paternal grandfather, Vong, married a close relative of a Vietnamese martyr. The newlyweds moved to a village where they met a priest by the name of Fr. Allys who eventually became the bishop of Hue. He

[37] ***The Miracle of Hope***, *Op. Cit.*, p. 8.

asked the young couple to become unique Catholic missionaries. They were to move to a village but Vong was not to preach the Catholic faith. Instead he was to convert the villagers by living a life of Christian virtue. *Once there were enough converts in a village, he was to move on to a new village. This novel evangelization technique took Vong from village to village in a region located more than forty miles south of Hue.*[38] He evangelized in this manner for fifteen years and would have continued the rest of his life but Fr. Allys lent him money to purchase a farm and counseled him to go home to his extended family. Vong eventually became a wealthy farmer, who later made a name for himself in construction. His life is a great example of flexibility.

Cardinal Thuân's goal as a newly ordained priest was to be a country priest, like the Curé of Ars. When his bishop called him in to discuss his new assignment, Thuân expressed his hopes which the bishop immediately dashed: *The Church needs you elsewhere and in other capacities. Erase your dream of becoming a country pastor from your mind. That is not going to happen...I did not send you to Rome for nothing. The Church in Vietnam will need many new leaders, and you will be one of them. Do not let false modesty get in the way of good judgment. You must prepare yourself for a leadership role. And that requires work and prayer...and cooperation with your bishop.*[39] He obeyed and practiced the virtue of flexibility which led him to be selected a cardinal.

Fr. Werenfreid van Straaten, known to the world as the "bacon priest," likewise lived the virtue of flexibility. Born near Amsterdam, he intended to become a teacher but when he heard the call of a religious vocation he was flexible enough to exchange his plans for God's. Only 34-years-old, he wrote an impassioned plea for help *for the 14 million* homeless Germans, expelled from the eastern territories, six million of whom were Catholics. The response was beyond all expectations and marked the start of the

[38] *Ibid.*, p. 12.

[39] *Ibid.*, p. 140.

organization known today as Aid to the Church in Need. He was given the nickname of "bacon priest" because he asked farmers to share their food with the refugees.[40]

The virtue of flexibility can and must be lived in all situations. When the von Trapp Family were permitted to reside in the U.S. on renewable six month visas due to the War, friends purchased them a house in which to live. Maria writes: *With new strength and vigor, we reorganized our life. Johanna took over the kitchen; Hedwig was in charge of the laundry; Agathe started to sew; Maria took charge of the mending and darning; Martina did the housecleaning, the boys brushed the shoes for the entire family and helped with the dishes; George did the shopping; I took care of the correspondence; and Father Wasner did the bookkeeping.*[41] It is pretty remarkable how each member of the family took over a specific task for the good of the others. But even more remarkable is the fact that these children and teens were used to having servants wait on them as well as doing these tasks for them. Their practice of the virtue of flexibility is extraordinary considering their privileged background. The von Trapps' eldest son, Rupert, a skilled doctor, gave up practicing medicine to help his family get established financially by joining them on their concert tours. The family needed his voice and presence to round out the choral group. He cheerfully practiced the virtue of flexibility to help them out. Once the family was financially established, he took up medicine again.

Walt Disney had his first studio in Kansas City where he conceived a series called "Oswald the Lucky Rabbit." In a heated disagreement he lost most of his animators and, through a loophole, his series. Rather than giving up his dream or wallowing in anger or self-pity, he conceived of Mickey Mouse on a train going to Hollywood. He exercised the virtue of flexibility.

Each day we are given numerous opportunities to practice

[40] Zenit, Jan. 31, 2003.
[41] ***The Story of the Trapp Family Singers***, *Op. Cit.*, p. 225.

the virtue of flexibility. It may be as simple as cheerfully taking public transportation when the car won't start, to eating later because of unforeseen circumstances. Flexibility is lived when we accept small and large disappointments or upsetting events. My husband has a magnificent plant in his office which he inherited. Each leaf is a foot and a half long and the plant gracefully drapes across his credenza. He proudly claims his success with the plant is due to his sunny windows and the cold coffee he feeds it. On Valentine's Day this year I decided to surprise him by repotting his plant in a masculine looking container. With Bob standing over my shoulder anxiously watching the procedure, imagine my horror when I broke the plant off at the roots as I tried to repot the root bound plant. Although the plant is the only object he owns that I've ever seen him attached to, he simply said, *Oh, that's ok. It was getting too big for this office anyway.* Now that's flexibility!

The Virtue of Understanding

"Walk with the wise and you will become wise."
Proverbs 12:20

Before we can practice the virtue of understanding we have to understand ourselves. This relates back to intimacy which we discussed in Chapter 1. What causes our mood swings or quirky behavior? Is it a lack of sleep, an oversensitive nature, pride or other vices? Once we understand ourselves, diligently work to improve ourselves, cultivate sincere affection for others, only then can we more easily practice the viture of understanding toward others.

Dr. David Isaacs points out that:

> **An understanding person recognizes the various factors which influence feelings or behavior; he studies each of these factors and how they relate to one another (and encourages other people to do**

the same), and in his behavior he takes these factors into account.[42]

The virtue of understanding is related to empathy which was explained in detail in ***Raise Happy Children Through A Happier Marriage*** (pages 172-173). Review these pages. Some people have this gift while others are clueless. Even if we naturally lack empathy we can work to acquire a certain degree of empathy. It is vital as a foundation for friendship, a satisfying marriage, and a happy family. If the virtue of understanding is not cultivated we will lack friends, make our spouse miserable and our family will grow cantankerous.

Since the virtue of understanding is rooted in intimacy little children cannot practice this virtue. They may cry when a sibling cries, give mom a hug when she's crying or avoid dad when he's angry but this is done either out of affection, a desire to help, or natural fear.

Here are some tips to help you teach your children the basics of this virtue:

1. Teach your children the importance of observing the reactions of people.
2. Explain the moods and the reason for the actions of your spouse. Dad explain to your children why mom is upset, distracted, or worried. Mom explain why dad may be short tempered, tired, or unusually quiet. This helps the children to see cause and effect.
3. Point out the moods and reactions of each brother and sister. Try to explain why each reacts the way he does. Why is Mary happy? Why is Ted cross? Why is Lucy worried? How can we support or help each of them?
4. Train your children to be sensitive as to the best time to ask for help or when they should refrain from bothering someone. If Rick is having a fight with his girlfriend on the phone, it's not the best time for his brother to ask to borrow his car. If mom is talking to dad, the kids are to wait until they are finished talking. If someone is on the phone, they are not to be interrupted. If someone is crying, now is not the

---

[42] ***Character Building***, *Op. Cit.*, p. 240.

time to ask them for help.

5. When a child notices that another is upset or sad, suggest ways that the child can help the other. (A self-centered person is too absorbed with self to help others.)
6. Help your child to view situations realistically rather than emotionally. Is the situation being exaggerated or ignored? What practical steps can be taken to resolve the problem? With God no situation is helpless. Remember the virtue of hope.

[A] child who has learned to have reasonable confidence in his own abilities, in his parents' help and other people's help, and especially to believe in the help of God, is in the best position to try to understand others, writes Dr. Isaacs. The same goes for us in the practice of this virtue.

If we have a critical spirit or tend to be judgmental toward people we cannot develop the virtue of understanding. To live this virtue we are to listen intently, practice patience, carefully observe, then react with kindness. Sarah storms in from school without even a "hello," pounds up the stairs, then slams her bedroom door. We can react to this situation in three ways: we can ignore her; get angry ourselves; or wait until she regains control then knock on her door. Prudence suggests trying the third option. Something caused Sarah acute pain. Her reaction is rage. Only with sympathy and much affection can we help her. *[A] good attitude towards others is serenity, a sense of security, flexibility and good humor.*[43] *Understanding is not just **feeling** for someone, that is to say, sympathy; it is also a matter of seeing things from the other's point of view: empathy. This degree of understanding will develop only if someone realizes the importance of being understood and recognizes that he has a responsibility to help others,* writes Dr. Isaacs.[44]

Help your teen to learn the following points:

✓ People are not all the same. Each person reacts differently to stimuli. Therefore, one should not think that the other

[43] *Ibid.*, p. 243.

[44] *Ibid.*, p. 241.

person is going to feel the same as oneself in a given situation. Adults, too, make this mistake. For example, some people say: *That doesn't annoy me, why should it annoy him?*

- ✓ What people say or what they do is not necessarily a true reflection of their intimate intentions or feelings...[T]ry to see what the facts of the situation really are, not what the person's external behavior *suggests* that they are.
- ✓ It is very easy to be simplistic, thinking that there is only one cause for any given problem. Normally there is a series of causes...
- ✓ In normal situations...the most important thing for the other person is to know that someone is concerned about him and that that person also respects his privacy.[45]
- ✓ We will never understand another completely as we will probably never truly know ourselves.

To live the virtue of understanding we have to be aware of the different factors that influence the moods and dispositions of people. These are the factors that influence us the most according to Dr. Isaacs:

- ✓ Something good or bad has happened in the recent past.
- ✓ Something was left undone that brought about a poor result or causes worry or panic.
- ✓ Another person's action caused pain or hurt.
- ✓ You were depending on another to do something and they did not follow through.
- ✓ It can be something thought, seen, felt or heard.[46]

Once we discover the cause of the problem, we then consider it from the other's point of view, not our own, since everything affects people differently. This is where we have to develop sensitivity toward others. What can keep me tossing and turning for nights on end has no effect on my husband. Once we understand the other person's viewpoint, we can empathize as the person talks out his concerns. Usually people can resolve their own problems without advice if we but listen to them.

---

[45] *Ibid.*, pp. 243-244. [46] *Ibid.*, p. 244.

The understanding that so many people demand of others is that everyone should join their party, writes St. Josemaría in the ***Furrow.***[47] This of course is the vice opposed to understanding. Millions of people around the world are attracted to the writings of St. Josemaría principally, I think, because of his virtue of understanding, not only in matters of faith and morals, but also of the human heart. He confides, *It is true that life, which by its nature is already rather narrow and uncertain, sometimes becomes difficult. But that will help you to become more supernatural and to see the hand of God. Then you will be more human and understanding with those around you.*[48]

The Virtue of Loyalty

"Loyalty to God is alone fundamental."
Fr. David P. McAstocker, S.J.

As with all the other intertwined virtues, the practice of the virtue of loyalty is linked with our set of values plus the practice of the virtues of prudence, respect for others, responsibility, perseverance, charity, friendship and patriotism. But even more than this, to practice this virtue *requires that all the virtues be highly developed...[L]oyalty is a virtue for the mature person.*[49]

Who is a loyal person? Dr. David Isaacs explains the qualities:

> **A loyal person accepts the bonds implicit in his relationship with others—friends, relatives, superiors, his country, its institutions, etc.—so that, as he goes on, he defends and reinforces the system of values which these represent.**[50]

To practice loyalty toward God, the Church, our spouse, family members or friends, one must be prudent in conversation with others. **We must refrain from mentioning anything confidential, critical or**

[47] ***Furrow,*** *Op. Cit.*, #576.
[48] *Ibid.*, #762.
[49] ***Character Building,*** *Op. Cit.*, p. 139.
[50] *Ibid.*, p. 133.

judgmental. We do not gossip about or rip a person to shreds behind his/her back. To be able to act in this upright manner we have to have developed the virtues of friendship, charity, prudence and respect for others. Without charity and respect gossip easily drops into our conversations. If there is a problem with a friend talk the problem out with the person, not with others. It's a terrible feeling of treachery when one discovers his "friend" has betrayed him. Fr. David McAstocker, S.J., reminds us: *Man is the image of the Creator. And the vast majority of our faults and sins of uncharitableness and disloyalty toward our fellow beings occur simply because we forget this central truth.*[51]

For fifteen years Terry and Sally were friends helping each other, concerned about each other, and enjoying each other's company. Terry, because of her profession, gradually became more successful than Sally. She did not realize that Sally had become consumed with envy until she received an e-mail by mistake that Sally intended for someone else. The e-mail not only contained lies about Terry but it was sent in an effort to stir up trouble between Terry and several of Terry's friends. When Terry confronted Sally with the e-mail, Sally's feeble defense was *I didn't really mean what it said. The other person knew what I actually meant.* Sally's lack of loyalty destroyed their friendship. Can such a friendship be repaired? Trust was destroyed. Once destroyed, it is difficult to rekindle. Likewise, it is difficult if the common values and the practice of the virtues that initially attracted the two friends are missing. If the one is unwilling to match the other's higher standards the two can remain acquaintances but no longer friends.

Part of loyalty, as with the other virtues, is mutual help *to behave properly and to improve.*[52] Prudence prevents us from siding with our friend, family member, or spouse out of mistaken loyalty when they plan to do something wrong or are doing something wrong. For example, if a friend is upset over a situation but she is wrong about her reaction,

---

[51] ***The Little Virtues***, *Op. Cit.*, p. 87. [52] ***Character Building***, *Op. Cit.*, p. 137.

you are obliged to explain her error in a kind, charitable manner. If the correction ends your friendship, criteria was lacking in the friendship from the beginning. If a daughter announces plans to move in with her boyfriend, accepting this situation to keep peace in the family is not loyalty but a lack of loyalty. Fornication will not make the daughter a better person. It will kill her soul and harm her body. Or, our spouse comes home from work with a shady business deal that could make the family wealthy. Prudence united with loyalty must move us to do everything possible to dissuade our spouse from participating in this "deal."

The Hierarchy of Loyalty

"God should be loved without thought of reward." St. Bernard

We practice the virtue of perseverance in regard to loyalty when we take care of each relationship, *defending it and reinforcing it.*[53] There is a tendency to think of loyalty in terms of friends, business, and country but there is a hierarchy of loyalty that begins first with God and then works its way down to others:

1. God
2. Spouse
3. Family
4. Country
5. Friends
6. Profession

We are reminded by Fr. McAstocker, S.J.: *Any definition of loyalty must primarily concern itself with our fealty toward the Creator; for here is allegiance at its highest...[O]ur presence here on earth is a particular mark of His loving care over us...He who might have created millions and millions of souls and left us nonexistent, nevertheless chose us to be formed in His image rather than someone else. He whose decrees are from eternity willed that you and I should, at a definite period, be born instead of another person who, possibly, might have served Him more faithfully...Out of countless numbers we were selected...God created us! He*

[53] *Ibid.,* p. 133.

owns us! We are His servants!

In the Roman martyrology we frequently read the account of some young girl or lad in his teens who, when asked to offer incense to idols, refused and, as a consequence, suffered death...Are we not all required under penalty of eternal damnation to do the very same thing? When there is a question of openly professing the Faith, or cowardly denying it—well, there is no choice.[54] This is the first priority of the virtue of loyalty. One priest, meeting a fallen woman, told her: *Don't hurt Jesus!* Those three words changed the woman's life. Teach your teens to use those words also. Should your spouse be opposed to the practice of the Catholic faith, by you maintaining and nourishing your relationship with God, as a Catholic, you practice the virtue of loyalty toward God, in addition to practicing loyalty toward your spouse. Sounds like a contradiction doesn't it? But if you are faithful to God, the graces you receive will help you to become a better person so as to enrich your marriage and family life, which in turn helps you to be loyal to your spouse in the appropriate areas.

Sometimes there is a tug between loyalty toward our spouse and loyalty toward our family. This is a delicate balance. The care of our spouse comes before our parents, siblings, and children but our spouse must also be reasonable as well as virtuous toward the care of our family. If a spouse refuses to attend holiday celebrations or to visit our family he/she is guilty of the vice of injustice as well as other vices. On the other hand, our parents cannot be so demanding of us that our spouse takes second place rather than first place. We practice loyalty toward our spouse when we put the needs of our spouse before those of our friends.

After God and your spouse, how are you caring for each of your other relationships? Are you giving the correct priority to each? How are you defending each relationship? Reinforcing each relationship? How are your teens treating

---

[54] ***The Little Virtues,*** *Op. Cit.*, pp. 71-72, 74, 80.

each of those relationships?

Loyalty toward family means making the effort to phone frequently, visit frequently, and generally care for each member of your extended family, i.e. parents, siblings, etc. Teach this to your teens. Explain that backbiting, jealousies, envies, lack of concern or helpfulness are just some of the vices contrary to loyalty. But even more important than these considerations, if we are loyal to our family we will never shame our parents by our conduct. Our loyalty must be so refined that we refrain from any conduct that would disgrace the good name of our parents. Stress this to your teens. How many good family names are disgraced by the crimes, drugs, violence, or illegitimacy of one's children!

Loyalty is expressed toward our friends when we acknowledge our friendship to other people rather than pretending that we don't know a friend when we are out with others. Sometimes teens and adults segregate friends into the "cool group" and the "not so cool group" and never mix the two. Betty had three separate groups of friends and acquaintances which were divided into levels according to their social rank: A level, B level, and C level. Socially, Betty never mixed the three but seemed to enjoy each of them in their place. When she died, each group was finally united when the top friend from each level did the readings and petitions at her funeral. This is not loyalty.

Other times we can use people who think we are their friends and then drop them when they no longer serve our purpose. We can also refuse to socialize with the friends of our friends thinking they are beneath us or too above us. All these examples lack loyalty.

Loyalty involves being faithful to our word. Explain to your teens that they are only to make promises or commitments that they intend to keep.

Since this virtue also involves knowledge of one's intimacy and intellectual capacity, young children cannot practice it per say. *A child who is helpful to his parents, brothers and sisters is beginning to discover the family as an entity. At the same time, he is helped by the other members of the family and he realizes that in this unity he has found something that cannot be found elsewhere...[W]hat he is aware of is other persons or individuals, and not the value of the relationship as such.*[55] A child may practice his concept of "loyalty" by lying for a sibling or friend. Loyalty, as a virtue, seeks to help the other person to become better; hence lying to protect a chum increases vice in both parties rather than helping the other.

A child may have a sense of loyalty to a team, his school, a sport, etc. but if one of these loses its esteem, the child's "loyalty" may fade. Help your child to develop the foundation for loyalty by persevering rather than giving up on a losing team, sport, etc. Note how little children get discouraged if the team they are playing on loses. They want to switch teams or find a better coach. Instead of complying with their wishes, enkindle their team spirit with pep talks. Encourage your child to practice more, strive harder, and cheer his teammates on. Discuss with him the importance of loyalty. The Chicago Cub fans are famous for their loyalty in the face of persistent loses. Today we have too many examples of the lack of loyalty in business and in sports. Discuss these negative examples with your teens.

Isaacs maintains that there are more important things than winning such as *sportsmanship, playing ability, good humor, helping the others and so on. Once again, we are emphasizing that one of the values of a relationship is the element of improvement for oneself and others; this improvement involves defending and reinforcing other values connected with the relationship, such as justice, respect for others, personal initiative etc.*[56]

Teach your child loyalty by

1. Showing him how he can help others.
2. Teaching him the difference between good and evil then

---

[55] ***Character Building***, *Op. Cit.*, p. 136. [56] *Ibid.*, p. 137.

explaining why the good must always be supported and the evil avoided, not protected.

3. Helping your child to make an effort to always do good and avoid evil.
4. Explaining that part of the duty of a Christian is to help others be good and to improve.
5. Encouraging your children to be honest with you when they break rules. This should teach them eventual loyalty to the rules.
6. Showing your children that these rules are teaching them integrity, justice, respect, etc.
7. Pointing out that they have a duty to improve themselves and help others to improve.
8. Encouraging your children to practice loyalty in the family by not accusing siblings in front of others. They are to take their concerns or problems privately to a parent who will deal with the situation.
9. Helping your child to discern his motives for acting.
10. Explaining the importance of living the virtue of respect for others.
11. Asking your child how he can live loyalty toward his God, family, school, and friends. Give him practical examples on how he can live it toward each.
12. Explaining how a citizen lives loyalty toward his country. Loyal citizens never betray their country.[57]

Since the virtue of loyalty is based on our personal set of values, which is doing the will of God, we can only practice loyalty to those people and organizations that are in harmony with God's law. To practice "loyalty" toward a political party or politician who defies God is morally wrong. *Loyalty to one's country or to one's city will be meaningful only if the people of that country or that city are loyal to themselves, to their basic principles and to truth. Loyalty to these fundamental values is essential in a world which is destroying itself by frantically concentrating on things which are merely transitory.*[58]

Isaacs explains: *Loyalty to one's parents does not mean*

[57] *Ibid.*, pp. 139-142.

[58] *Ibid.*, p. 142.

approving of their behavior even when it is wrong, but rather defending them, protecting their good name against groundless slander and helping them to improve. It also means being sincere and generous with them. Loyalty to one's country does not mean concealing the defects to be found in it or responding emotionally whenever its name is mentioned, but rather defending and reinforcing the permanent values we find there. Only in God is there perfect harmony between His words and His deeds, between what He is and what He does.[59] Mel Gibson was under tremendous personal attack for his film *The Passion of The Christ.* During an interview with Diane Sawyers, Diane tried to create controversy by bringing up some comments that Mel's father had made. Mel immediately cut her off saying: *Give it up, Diane. My father is my father and I love him. I'm not going to talk about this further. Give it up.*[60] Mel was practicing the virtue of loyalty towards his father.

Dr. Isaacs warns us as parents, but also as individuals: *If a child avoids any type of relationship or commitment, he will find himself unable to practice any permanent principle properly. His standards will all be merely provisional and he will end up by adapting to any situation, to the majority opinion and to mere fashion. On the other hand, if he works out the permanent values involved in his relationships, he will find that he has a solid basis on which to base his whole life.*[61]

Examples of Disloyalty/Loyalty

In the Gospels we have three striking examples of disloyalty, not to a mere man but to the Son of God. First we have Judas, a man selected from scores of disciples to be one of only twelve apostles of the Son of God. What an honor to be chosen from millions of possible people to be part of that inner circle! Yet despite the fact that for three years he had been an intimate companion of God; was

---

[59] *Ibid.*, p. 138. [60] TV interview, Feb. 16, 2004.

[61] ***Character Building,*** *Op. Cit.*, p. 141.

present at countless miracles; and was the object of Christ's affection, Judas betrayed Him. To add insult to injury, Judas had listened to the parables and teachings of God's mercy and forgiveness yet he ignored them and committed suicide. When the soldiers came to take Jesus prisoner, He asked them to let His friends go. What loyalty God has! With that, all the rest of the apostles fled the Garden of Olives leaving Jesus utterly alone. This was a significant part of Our Lord's Passion, the disloyalty of his friends. But the night wasn't over. Peter's denials that he knew Jesus were the final blow of disloyalty toward Christ by one of His closest friends. In the Old Testament we have countless examples of the disloyalty of people toward God beginning with Adam and Eve.

Now for some examples of loyalty. In 1617 there was a persecution of Catholics in Japan. Bl. Caspar Hikojiro and Bl. Andrew Yoshida, Catholic laymen, were housekeepers for two priests who were martyred. Following the martyrdom of the priests, the two laymen along with ten others were ordered arrested and executed. *The Japanese authorities were dismayed to see over six hundred Catholics present themselves to them, offering to suffer with the ten condemned men.* What loyalty their fellow Catholics displayed! *On the morning of October 1, they were led out to be beheaded. The authorities' efforts to conduct the men's execution in secret at dawn...failed as thousands of Catholics gathered to pray with the two martyrs before they died.*[62] These Catholics were loyal to the end toward their fellow Catholics. Probably many in the crowd did not even know the men being martyred.

Cardinal Thuân's paternal great-grandparents endured the "phan sap" (divide and integrate) policy/persecution of the Vietnamese Emperor toward Catholics. Under this plan all Catholic families were split up. The husbands/fathers were sent to the country to work as unpaid laborers on large plantations owned by non-Christians. The hope was that

---

[62] *Magnificat,* October, 2003.

poorly fed and poorly treated they would either die or renounce the Catholic faith. The children and wives became unpaid servants in non-Christian households with the hope that they would forget or give up their faith. This would then eradicate the "foreign" religion of Catholicism. Fortunately, many non-Christians were compassionate toward the Catholic slaves. Thuân's grandfather, Vong, who was fourteen at the time, was separated from his parents by six miles since he was forced to work in a rice field. *Vong heard of the terrible conditions his father suffered under his cruel landlord. When Vong learned that his father was being starved, the young boy...approached his own landlord and asked permission to bring food to his father every morning. Vong did not stop to consider that he hardly received enough food to eat himself. Every morning, while it was still dark, Vong woke up, cooked his small ration of food, and carried half of it to his father. He had to run the twelve miles back and forth to be in the rice field on time to begin work...at sunrise. He did this for several years.*[63] What heroic loyalty Vong had toward his father and it was those heroic sacrifices that saved his father's life.

The topic of loyalty comprises a chapter in St. Josemaría's book ***Furrow***. Let's conclude this virtue with some of his profound thoughts: *Loyalty demands a real hunger for formation, because you are moved by a sincere love and you do not wish to run the risk of spreading or of defending, through ignorance, principles or attitudes which are very far from being in accordance with the truth.* (#346)

The disloyal are eager that those who are loyal should remain inactive. (#362)

I have always thought that lack of loyalty out of human respect is lack of love—and a lack of personality. (#370)

Turn your eyes towards the Blessed Virgin and see how she practices the virtue of loyalty. When Elizabeth needs her, the Gospel says that she went...joyfully making haste. Learn from her! (#371)

---

[63] ***The Miracle Of Hope***, *Op. Cit.*, p. 11.

The Virtue of Audacity

"Do not be afraid to go out into the streets and public places, like the first Apostles, who preached Christ and the Good News of Salvation in the city and village squares. This is not the time to be ashamed of the Gospel. It is the time to preach it from the rooftops."
John Paul II, 1993 World Youth Day in Denver

Supernaturally, audacity is the virtue of those so deeply in love with God and truth that they are willing to be daring, to sacrifice, and to suffer in order to accomplish great things for God, their Love. This is the love of the saints! Fr. Jay Alvarez, a priest of the Prelature of Opus Dei, maintains that when we fall deeply in love with God we become powerhouses because love is the strongest passion. It urges us to move out of ourselves, to do great deeds, or to accomplish difficult tasks for the love of God and our fellow men.

Remember, in developing the virtues, we tend to seesaw back and forth between practicing the virtues and falling into the vices until the virtues become stabilized through grace, heroic practice, and the virtue of prudence. Recall St. Peter. He was audacious sometimes but at other times impetuous. We read in ***St. John*** (21:7) that Peter and some of the others were out fishing on the Sea of Galilee: ***Simon Peter therefore, hearing that it was the Lord, girt his tunic about him, for he was stripped, and threw himself into the sea*** he was so eager to reach Our Lord as swiftly as possible. Another time in his eagerness to reach Our Lord, he asked to walk to Jesus on the water then panicked when the waves were rough. When the mob, led by Judas, came to arrest Jesus in the Garden of Olives after the Last Supper, Peter drew his sword cutting off the ear of the high priest's servant. When he was closely united to Jesus, he was audacious. But when he was not close to Jesus things did not go so well. He became cowardly and so do we when we distance ourselves from God. In the ***Gospel of St. Matthew*** we read, ***But Peter was following him at a distance, even to the courtyard of the high priest, and he went in and sat with the attendants to see the end*** (26:58). Note the words ***at a distance.*** Peter's heart was still loyal but when he distanced himself from Jesus his audacity faltered leading him to betray Jesus three times. When we distance ourselves from God through the cares of the world, personal ambitions, or through a "lack of time" (a nice way to express laziness), not only do we betray Jesus but also the mission He has given us in this life. To practice any of the virtues, but especially the virtue of audacity, we need to heed the words of Christ, ***Come follow me,*** which He repeats 19 times in the New Testament. Note how after the descent of the Holy Spirit on Pentecost, Peter's virtues stabilized. He fearlessly evangelized although threatened, punished, and eventually martyred. We likewise need the graces of the Holy Spirit as well as His gifts, fruits and virtues to live the life God expects from each of us.

On a natural level, what qualities does an audacious person possess? David Isaacs contends that

> **an audacious person sets out on and completes courses of action which may appear imprudent, convinced—after calm assessment of the facts and taking account of possible risks—that he can achieve a genuine good.**[64]

The virtue of audacity is linked to the virtues of justice, prudence, perseverance, fortitude, patience, magnanimity and charity. **For our action to be virtuous, it must be based on a noble goal, something good**. After prudent consideration, the person believes it is possible to achieve the noble goal because of God's grace, the supernatural virtue of hope, his own personal knowledge, his past experiences, abilities, potential and the support/help of

[64] ***Character Building,*** *Op. Cit.*, p. 198.

others. **Should we avoid doing a necessary, good action when it is possible for us to try or to attempt it, we are guilty of the vice of injustice as well as the vice of cowardice.** Will we be successful in all our audacious undertakings? Probably not but "success" is a worldly term. Bl. Zefirino Agostini (1813-1896) insisted that *God rewards not according to results, but effort.* Every effort, made with the right intention, brings spiritual growth. While the project may fizzle, we have grown stronger in the virtues of perseverance, courage, patience, long-suffering as well as a host of other virtues. The School of Hard Knocks graduates the greatest movers and shakers of the world. Experience is priceless. Read the lives of the saints and famous people. See how many of their audacious original enterprises failed only to be replaced with greater, more lasting endeavors. Great enterprises are rarely successful on the first attempt. If they were, pride would develop ruining everything.

The degree to which the virtue of audacity is practiced depends upon the *strength of the passion behind it.* *Audacity is a passion of the irascible appetite which sets vigorously about dominating some evil or achieving some good...Passion in itself is blind, and therefore it can lead to rather imprudent results. That is precisely why we are more interested in the virtue than in the passion of daring. A passion is only an instinctive movement, born of an instant realization that something can be achieved, but it can evaporate as quickly as it arises* (editorial emphasis).[65]

The virtue of audacity must be united to a strong passion as well as the virtue of prudence. Without prudence the passion becomes "daring" which sometimes leads to the vice of rashness. Rashness in turn can lead to disastrous consequences.

Audacity increases with good health, energy and youthfulness, writes St. Thomas Aquinas, but this does not mean that you must be young to practice this virtue.

---

[65] *Ibid.,* p.198.

Youthfulness resides more in your spirit than in your body. Look at the example of John Paul II.

The virtue of audacity, which is part of the virtue of magnanimity, helps a person to pursue the good and to set about great undertakings, convinced that he can really achieve something worthwhile, maintains Isaacs. All the great good we see about us such as great literature, the magnificent shrines and churches, our masterpieces of art and music, is the result of people practicing this virtue. There are countless founders of orders, secular institutes and laity who work to better the lives of the poor, to evangelize, to educate, to nurse the sick, to protect life from conception to natural death. On a secular level it was the practice of this virtue that fueled the crusades, the discovery of the Americas, the founding of the United States, inventions, medical research, etc. This audacity is based on the third theological virtue...hope. It is just as alive today as in the past. Look at Judi Brown who founded the influential American Life League; Fr. Paul Marx, O.S.B., Ph.D., the founder of Human Life International; Drs. John & Lyn Billings who have given their lives to refining and teaching natural family planning; Fr. Robert Sirico who founded the Acton Institute which specializes in Christian economics; Eleanor Schlafly who founded the Cardinal Minzenty Foundation to fight the spread of communism; Phyllis Schlafly, her sister-in-law, who founded Eagle Forum, an influencial political force for good; Dr. Colleen Mast who founded Sex Respect to promote abstinence education rather than sex education in schools; Fr. Harold F. Cohen, S.J. who found Closer Walk Ministries and Johnnette Benkovic, founder of Living His Life Abundantly, which are powerful tools of evangelization through TV, radio, and print; Suzanne Fowler, who teaches weight loss through temperance while at the same time teaching catechesis; Rose Marie Rudolph who founded Rose of Sharon Music Ministry; Kathleen Sullivan who founded Project Reality to teach abstinence education in public schools;Christine Vollmer of Venezula who not only organizes international conferences on the family but has put together a course on developing virtues for grade schools and high schools, Catholic and public, in English and in Spanish; Fr. John Hardon, S.J., who founded the Institute on Religious Life, the Marian Catechist Apostolate, The Real Presence Association, *Catholic Faith Magazine*, and authored over 2,000 manuscripts among other activities. We have already previously cited the virtue of audacity in Mother Angelica, Mother Teresa, and Tom Monaghan. My Rolodex is filled with names and address of hundreds of people who live this virtue courageously. It's just not possible to list all of them here. Look around you. See how people in your community are practicing this virtue. The people who begin Right to Life Centers, Medical Ethics Committees, Counseling Centers, Birthright, free health clinics, food pantries, adult daycare, teen clubs, Catholic summer camps, and soup kitchens are all audacious. Point these examples out to your children. Explain how they are likewise called to use the talents God has given them in similar undertakings although it means a time commitment, effort, sacrifice and suffering.

Last year I attended the Catholic Marketing Network Convention in Chicago. It gave me an opportunity to meet many Catholic bookstore owners. These are basically mom and pop businesses energized by couples wanting to spread the faith in their communities. Dr. & Mrs. Karl Ossoinig of Austria began a bookstore apostolate in Iowa City. Dr. & Mrs. Tim Moran began a bookstore apostolate in Sioux City, Iowa, which has grown into a shrine for three states. Dr. David Mack and his wife Elaine, mentioned in my dedication in ***Raise Happy Children...Teach Them Virtues!*** founded a Catholic TV station, three Catholic radio stations, a Catholic bookstore, and numerous other apostolic ventures to spread the faith. Dr. & Mrs. John Dailey founded the St. John Fisher Forum to bring in Catholic speakers to enrich the faith in Central Illinois. Dr. Peter Popovich and his wife, Ange, whom we interviewed in ***Raise Happy Children...Raise Them Saints*** in regard to home schooling, began Perpetual Eucharistic Adoration at their new parish when they moved to Springfield. This was something that no one else in the community had been able to get going. Dr. David Reardon, an engineer by profession, left his secure job to begin the Elliott Institute, which does research on post-abortion syndrome. He has become such an authority in this area that he recently completed a European lecture tour where he presented papers to thousands of people about this growing tragedy.

How does one teach children this virtue? There are thirteen steps:

1. Develop strong passion in your children through the right conditions.
2. Help them to discern worthwhile goals...to see a worthwhile initiative and tackle it.
3. Teach them to make well thought out, consistent decisions.
4. Point out to your child that all decisions should be rooted in convictions, not whims.
5. Show your child his potential by helping him to exercise it so that he develops self-confidence in his abilities. Teach him to not only utilize his talents, but also to make an effort and stick with the effort by employing the virtue of perseverance.
6. Help your child to realize his limitations so as to avoid discouragement.
7. Teach your child self-control. Without self-control passion turns into recklessness or into a search for superficial pleasures.
8. Insist that your child care for his health through proper sleep, diet, and exercise. It is difficult to be audacious, to do good, when one is tired, ill-nourished, out of shape or sick.
9. Ask your child to perform good, difficult actions.
10. The practice of all the virtues increases audacity so help your child to live all the virtues.

11. Encourage your child to be sensitive to the needs of others so as to do things to help out without being asked.
12. Discuss different points of view with your teen to stimulate his intellect so he can defend his views with peers.
13. Support your child in his undertakings. It is difficult to practice audacity without any support.[66]
14. Do not allow your teen to give in to fear.

Let's consider the first two points. The rest are pretty self-explanatory. Developing passion and noble goals are rooted in the unconditional love found in healthy families. It is in such an environment that self-confidence is born. Seeing virtue lived by family members gives the teen a standard not only to live by but also to use as criteria to judge other situations. There is a natural development of knowing what is good or evil, right or wrong, just or unjust. Neither laziness nor escapism is tolerated within a virtuous family. The child learns that *many valuable experiences are disagreeable until one discovers their real meaning... If a person carries out some valuable action, convinced that he will succeed, aware of the means available to him to do it, he is not being imprudent. But if he does not know the value of the action and does not have the resources to do it, he is being imprudent on two scores.* [67]

Normally a human being is able to do much more and much better than he himself thinks, contends Dr. Isaacs. *He continually limits himself, sometimes unconsciously, out of false prudence, laziness, lack of self-confidence, or because he has not developed himself—his body, his mind, his abilities—so as to be able to rise to the opportunities which present themselves.*[68]

Dr. Isaacs also points out: *A Christian should be ready to expose himself to all kinds of risks, because he can count on God's continuous help*.[69]

To live the virtue of audacity one cannot give in to fear.

[66] *Ibid.*, pp. 199-201.
[67] **Character Building**, *Op. Cit.*, pp. 201-202.
[68] *Ibid.*, p. 199.
[69] *Ibid.*, p. 204.

Each time we draw back from doing something out of fear, we grow in the vice of cowardice. People drive to business trips or vacations because they fear flying. This is cowardice. A woman cannot stay overnight alone in her house out of fear. This is cowardice. Some Catholics were afraid to view the film *The Passion of The Christ.* What wimps! While the fear may be natural, it's necessary to fight it. Recall the saying that if you fall off a horse, you have to get right back on that horse to overcome fear. If you experience a car accident, you cannot give up driving. You have to instead push yourself to drive again unless you are physically incapacitated. If you are afraid of public speaking, you have to push yourself to give a talk when asked. Whatever you fear, you must struggle to overcome it. Let your children and teens know how you work to overcome your fears. Likewise, you have to help your children and teens overcome their fears or they will never be able to practice the virtue of audacity. St. Thérèse was afraid of the dark. To help her overcome her fear, her parents sent her to dark rooms to fetch different articles for them. No excuses were allowed. She confides: *I regard it as a real grace that I have been accustomed since my childhood to overcome fear.* St. Frances Xavier Cabrini was terrified of water from childhood. But she had to overcome her fear to travel by boat, the only means of travel at that time, to America to fulfill her calling.[70] St. Toribio Romo Gonzalez (1900-1928) lived in Santa Ana de Guadalupe, Mexico, when the government was persecuting Catholics. Ordained a priest, he *carried out his priestly ministry in secret, making his home in an abandoned factory, and traveling to the faithful by night. He prayed continually for courage in his dangerous circumstances. He confided to his sister Maria, "I am cowardly, but if one day God wants me to be killed, I hope He will give me a rapid death with only the time necessary to pray for my enemies." On February 24, 1928, Maria noticed that her brother was preoccupied with completing all his unfinished tasks, working relentlessly through the night until*

[70] *Mother Cabrini Messenger,* Vol. 64, No. 2, 2002.

four the following morning, the 25th. He had set his altar for Mass before taking a rest. Little more than an hour later, Mexican troops stormed his hiding place, shooting him in his bed. After he was shot a second time, he died in the arms of his sister.[71]

Rashness and cowardice are the vices opposed to the virtue of audacity. Rashness we discussed briefly before. Cowardliness is rooted in the lack of self-confidence mixed with laziness.

Catholic Examples of Audacity

"The Lord commands you, 'Go out into the whole world and proclaim the good news to all creation' (Mk 16:15), but He doesn't issue a timetable or draw up a plan. He leaves the initiative—and the difficulties to overcome—to you. He asks only that you carry the Gospel wherever you go."

Cardinal F. X. Nguyen Van Thuân

St. Patrick, whose mother is believed to be the niece of St. Martin of Tours,[72] spent his life living the virtue of audacity. As a captive of the Irish in his teens he prayed for deliverance from them. Then one night he heard a voice in his sleep telling him that his ship was ready. He successfully escaped from his master then traveled two hundred miles to the port of Wicklow where he saw the ship in his dream. He offered to work in exchange for passage home but the captain refused him. *Disappointed, he went away from the mariners and prayed. Before he had finished his prayer, one of the crew shouted after him, "Come quickly, for they are calling you." The shipmaster had been persuaded to take him aboard.*[73] After other adventures Patrick finally arrived home where his family asked him never to leave them again. But several years later Patrick again had a dream that a man came to him from Ireland

---

[71] *Magnificat*, Feb. 2004. [72] ***The Wisdom of St. Patrick,*** *Op. Cit.*, p. 21.
[73] *Ibid.*, p. 23.

with countless letters. As he read the letters, he could hear the voices of the Irish calling him back: *We ask you, holy boy, come back and walk among us once more.*[74] On a natural level, Patrick did not want to go back to Ireland but supernaturally he knew it was God's will so he applied himself to accomplish his mission.

Bl. Nuno Alvares Pereira, the Constable of Portugal and Count of Ourém, lived in the fourteen century and was knighted by the Queen of Portugal. The nation was plunged into a crisis upon the death of her husband, King Fernando. There was intrigue in the palace and Spain was positioned to invade. In the light of these series problems, the former king's half brother, João, was unsure what to do. Nuno hastened to Lisbon to urge João to act. João accepted the crown and moved to check Spain's expansion. He named the twenty-four-years old Nuno the Constable of Portugal which was the highest ranking military office. Prior to the battle with Spain, Nuno urged all his soldiers to attend the Masses he had arranged and receive Holy Communion. He is quoted as saying: *Whoever wishes to see me defeated in battle let him take away from me the sacred banquet where God, the food of the strong, refreshes men. Strengthened by this food, I have the courage, fortitude, and strength to put down my enemies.* With an image of Our Lady on the King's helmet, and the Portuguese soldiers fighting under Our Lady's banners, they defeated the Spaniards saving the sovereignty of Portugal. *The following day Nuno returned to Ourém to give thanks to Our Lady. The king went, barefoot, to the Shrine of Our Lady at Guimarães; and decreed the building of the Church and monastery of Our Lady of Victories, Battle Abbey, (Batalha).*[75]

San Juan Capistrano is more than the name of a California mission. It is the name of a great saint. St. John was born in Capistrano, Italy, the home of his mother although his father was a German Baron. St. John was intellectually gifted.

[74] *Ibid.*, p. 24.

[75] From a revision of a chapter from the book, ***Our Lady of Fatima***, by Bishop Finbar Ryan, O.P.

He studied law at the University of Perugia and eventually was appointed the governor of the city by the King of Naples. Known for his ability to arbitrate disagreements he was sent to a town to settle a civil disturbance. Instead of listening to his proposals, he was thrown into prison. While in prison he had a vision of St. Francis inviting him to join his order. After ransoming himself at great expense, he renounced his wealth to become a Franciscan. In time he became a great friend and companion to St. Bernardine of Siena, whose cause for canonization he promoted, after his friend's death. *In 1453, the Byzantine capital of Constantinople fell to Mohammed II, and his superior forces were poised to overrun Hungary and Germany. Although [St. John] was seventy years old and worn out from hard work and penitential austerities, [he] scurried all over Europe calling for volunteers to meet the challenge that was now threatening Christian civilization.* (Rememer, this was before planes, trains, buses or cars!) *Filled with confidence in the power of the Holy Name which he bid the soldiers use as their battle cry and standard, he personally led the troops against the larger Muslim army at Belgrade. His courageous mustering of the Christian army which was only one-tenth the size of Mohammed's forces had a decisive effect...On the feast of St. Mary Magdalen in 1456 the Muslims were turned back. Christian Europe was saved.*[76]

Bl. Junípero Serra (1713-1784) of Majorca, Spain, after joining the Franciscan order taught philosophy for twelve years at the University of Padua. He left his teaching position to become a missionary to Mexico City where it is said he baptized over 6,000 Indians. *He founded twenty-one missions, and he is recognized as a builder of the state of California.*[77] Fr. Serra walked back and forth from Mexico City up the state of California founding missions <u>on foot</u>, limping all the way with what is believed to have been bone cancer.

---

[76] Michael Morris, O.P., St. John of Capistrano, *Magnificat,* Oct. 2003, p. v.
[77] *Magnificat*, July 2002.

Bl. Nikolaus Gross (1898-1945), a coalminer active in the Catholic workers' union eventually became the editor of the union's newspaper. Although an activist by nature, Nikolaus put his wife and seven children before his work and other activities. In the evenings he taught his children the Catholic faith. *An early opponent of Nazism, Nikolaus wrote in 1930 that Catholics must reject Nazism not only for political reasons, but more importantly because of "our religious and cultural attitude."* He told his chaplain a month before his arrest in August of 1944: *If we do not risk our life today, how do we then one day justify ourselves before God and our people?* He was hung by the Nazis January 23, 1945.[78]

Fr. Marcial Maciel, the founder of Regnum Christi and the Legionaries of Christ, founded his order of priests while he was only a seminarian. In 1940 he was called home to see his brother who was dying of typhoid. While home he gathered together a group of young boys who wanted to be priests. He had to find the financial resources, a place for the boys to live, ecclesiastic permissions, then faculty to educate his future priests. After facing contradiction after impossible contradiction the only solution available was to speak to the Holy Father but he had no one to give him an introduction. *During a ceremony at St. Peter's I went with my surplice on and stood beside Cardinal Giuseppe Pizzardo as if I were one of his secretaries. When the ceremony was over, the cardinals went to greet the Holy Father before he took the elevator out of the basilica. I kept close to Cardinal Pizzardo and took advantage of the situation to go up to His Holiness: "Holy Father, I am a Mexican priest and have something important to tell you, but I don't have anyone to introduce me." Pius XII turned to Monsignor Callori di Vignale, his secretary at the time, and said, "Tomorrow at twelve."*[79] The rest is history. So many times Fr. Maciel could have given up but he practiced the virtues of audacity and perseverance.

---

[78] *Magnificat*, January 2003.

[79] ***Christ Is My Life***, *Op. Cit.*, p. 40.

The Servant of God, Fr. Walter J. Ciszek, S.J., was born in 1904 and was the seventh of thirteen children. When he was in eighth grade he decided to become a priest. Fr. Ciszek recalls, *My father refused to believe it. Priests, in his eyes, were holy men of God; I was anything but that. In the end, it was my mother who finally decided the issue, as mothers often do. She told me that if I wanted to be a priest, I had to be a good one.*[80] After reading the life of St. Stanislaus Kostka he decided to become a Jesuit even though he really did not want to be a Jesuit because of the long years of study as well as a life of "perfect obedience." He finally decided to become one because the life was hard and he loved a challenge. When he was refused by the Polish providence he took a train from Shenandoah, Pennsylvania to New York, unbeknownst by anyone, to personally meet the American Provincial, of course unannounced. His practice of the virtue of audacity kicked into high gear to the point of offering himself for the new Russian Center that opened in Rome in 1939, to prepare priests to evangelize Russia. He made it to Russia but as a prisoner, not an evangelist. His twenty-three years inside of the Soviet Union, fifteen years of which were spent in prison or prison camps in Siberia, are incredible examples of the practice of the virtue of audacity. Read his autobiographies and encourage your teens to read them also: ***With God In Russia*** and ***He Leadeth Me.*** I recommend reading them together. ***With God In Russia*** gives the physical details of his life while ***He Leadeth Me*** explains spiritually how he survived.

When the Spring Offensive of March 11, 1975, hit the central highlands of Vietnam, it resulted in a massive retreat of South Vietnamese soldiers. In the midst of the chaos of the retreat, along with the critically injured the soldiers were carrying, the refugees ran out of food. When Bishop Thuân learned of the situation he immediately sprang into action. He purchased tons of rice, bread, milk, and medicine, then hired planes to drop the supplies to the

---

[80] Walter J. Ciszek, S.J., with Daniel L. Flaherty, S.J., ***With God In Russia*** (Garden City: Image Book, 1966) p. 19.

soldiers. *He had no doubt that his intervention would incur the wrath of the Communists, but Thuân heard in his mind the voices of his grandfather and uncles saying, "We have to do what is right, and we are willing to pay the price."*[81] He did pay the price. When the Communists took control of the whole country, Bishop Thuân was imprisoned for his actions. Later, while he was in prison he wrote a book entitled ***The Road of Hope***. He wrote his book on scraps of paper smuggled in to him and his writings were smuggled out and passed from person to person to encourage Catholics to continue to live their faith in the face of persecution. On one slip of paper he wrote: *Be prepared to reject wealth and position—even to give up your own life—in order to preserve your ideas, your integrity, and your faith. You must never behave otherwise, for to do so means to lose everything.*[82]

Fifteen-year-old Bl. Ursulina (1375-1410) who lived in Parma, Italy, was told in an interior locution *to admonish the anti-pope in Avignon, France, to renounce his false claim to the papacy. With this mission, she journeyed to Avignon twice, accompanied, as always by her mother. The anti-pope refused to heed her, but in Rome she was able to inform the true pope Boniface IX of her efforts on his behalf.*[82A]

One of the most moving accounts of someone practicing the virtue of audacity is the story of Irene Sendler, a ninety-three-year-old Polish Catholic. She personally saved the lives of 2,500 Jewish children. Her story begins in 1940 when *the Nazis decided to close the Warsaw ghetto, exposing 500,000 Jews to the risk of death from hardships and illness.* Through the help of an old professor of hers, she obtained *nurses' entrance permits for herself and a group of friends. Using funds from the Commune and Jewish humanitarian organizations, Sendler purchased food, essential goods, coal and clothing.* When the Nazis began deporting Jews to concentration camps, Irene developed a plan to save the Jewish children by finding *Christian couples who posed as*

---

[81] ***The Miracle of Hope***, *Op. Cit.*, pp. 183-184. [82] *Ibid.*, p. 199.

[82A] Magnificat, April, 2004.

their parents. "We looked for the addresses of families with children and went to see them, proposing to take the little ones out of the ghetto, to entrust them to Polish families or to orphanages under false names." Jewish parents were at first fearful of sending their children away. Sometimes a mother wanted to send a child away for safekeeping but a father refused to do so. *Nevertheless, the great rescue began. Most of the children were taken in ambulances. They hid at the bottom, covered in bloodstained rags, or were tied inside bags. Others escaped the ghetto in rubbish trucks. The older ones were brought to the ghetto's church: Jewish children arrived and then left with Christian parents to whom they were entrusted. To ensure that Jewish children might someday be reunited with their real parents, Sendler compiled tiny slips of paper, on which every child's name was registered according to his or her real parents. She hid the slips of paper in a glass jar, which was buried in a friend's courtyard.* At the time of Irene's betrayal in 1943 she had already saved 500 children. Although tortured as well as her arms and legs broken, Irene refused to divulge any information on the children When condemned to death, a Jewish organization *paid a huge sum to a Gestapo official* to save her life. *Sendler was released, although officially she was considered dead. Before the war ended, she succeeded in saving another 2,000 Jewish children. Sendler is one of 19,700* people who were awarded the title *Righteous Among the Nations,* [because of] *heroic deeds to save Jews from persecution. Almost all of those so honored are Catholic.*[82B]

More Examples of Audacity

"Audacity is one of man's most precious qualities. If he lacks that, he'll never amount to anything."
Dr. Alexis Carrel

We met John Kinzie and his family at the Massacre of Fort Dearborn in Chicago but the beginning of his life was almost as exciting as his later years. He was delivered by his father,

[82B] Zenit, Jan. 28, 2004.

Captain John MacKinzie on December 27, 1763, in Quebec, Canada. His father was a surgeon with the British Army's Sixtieth Regiment. Shortly after John's birth his father died, leaving his mother, Emily, a widow for the second time. Within a short time she met a widower who was raising four sons on his own. They married. By the time John was ten years old, his stepfather decided to move to Detroit. It was there that John saw his first Indians and trading posts where the Indians traded their furs for the items they needed. It sparked John's interest . That's what he wanted to do when he grew up. The family's stay in Detroit was temporary. They moved on to New York where John was placed in a school that he hated in a city that he loathed. Still ten-years-old, he decided to go back to Quebec, find a craftsman to indenture himself to, save his money, then when the time was ripe he would start his own trading post somewhere in the Frontier. After being dropped off at school, he found a ride to the river where he stowed away on a sloop. On the ship he made friends with a gentleman going to Montreal who promised him transportation to Quebec as well as a letter of introduction to a silversmith who was looking for an apprentice. John obtained the job for three years and at the same time changed his name to Kinzie. After his three years of training were completed, at the age of thirteen he went to Detroit to ask for employment with William Burnett, who was known for running a fair and honest trading post. John wanted to learn from the best. His plan was to work for Burnett to learn the trade then launch out on his own combining it with the silver trade. It was here that he developed a friendship with Topenebe who would later save his life and the lives of his family during the Fort Dearborn Massacre. While working with Burnett, John had a private side business of making exquisite silver bracelets that he sold to the Indians in exchange for furs. The furs he sold for top dollar, stashing the money away for his future trading post. By the time he was seventeen, John owned and ran two trading posts. His honesty and friendship with the Indians made him a wealthy man. Eventually he bought the main trading post in Chicago. That's audacity!

In the War of 1812 General William Hull, the governor of the Michigan Territory, was elevated to brigadier general and given the command of the Northwestern Army. His job was to raise an army of 1200 men, move north, take Detroit from Britain, then from Detroit launch an attack on Canada. He had the advantage. He could have achieved the objective but what President Madison did not know was that General Hull was terrified of Indians, lacked prudence, and possessed no fortitude or audacity. His pride did not allow him to listen or take advice. Although Hull had taken Detroit and begun an invasion of Canada, he, without any reason, began to retreat. When Tecumseh learned of his fear of Indians from confiscated letters taken from dead couriers he used that knowledge to fake large numbers of attacking Indians. This sent Hull into a panic. It is believed that Hull secretly contacted the British commander offering not to shoot at them if the British and Indians did not shoot at the Americans. The Indians staged an attack and Hull rapidly surrendered to the British giving up Detroit and the fort, himself, his officers, his troops and a detachment that was out escorting a supply convoy. It was believed at the time that Hull had secretly asked the British to attack so he would not look bad when he surrendered. Hull was also the coward responsible for ordering the evacuation of Fort Dearborn in Chicago that resulted in that massacre. He was later disciplined by the U.S. government for his cowardliness.

William Henry Harris, Governor of the Northwest Territory, wielded the same authority in the Territory as the President of the U.S. in the states. He sanctioned huge, illegal land grabs from the Indians, taking their hunting areas as well as their agriculture areas pushing them continually west where the means to survive were not adequate. This is what prompted the great Indian warrior, Tecumseh, to unite all the Indian tribes under himself. The Indians wanted their ancestral lands back! This motivated them to become allies of the British during the War of 1812. The battles were bloody on both sides. To spare more bloodshed, Tecumseh sent Harrison an audacious proposal: *We are enemies and we are met here to oppose one another at last. Why should not we, who are the leaders, settle the matter between us alone, so that the blood of our fine young men need not be shed in the fight which presents itself? Meet me in combat on a neutral ground of your choice and with whatever weapon is your choice, or even with none, and I will have the same, or none, and we will then fight this matter out between us until one of us is dead. He who triumphs will then hold this ground and he who has been beaten, his people will immediately return home and remain quiet ever after. My chiefs are in agreement...We are men. Let us meet like men. Let us fight like men. Let us spare our people. I await your answer.*[83] It sounds like a rational proposal to me but Harrison did not have the audacity nor bravery to even reply.

In the chapter on temperance we discussed how the Black Hawk War of 1832 was ignited by drunk U.S. solders and volunteers. The volunteers were given permission to pillage Indian villages, most of which had been abandoned by fleeing Indians. In one village an elderly man was too disabled to leave so he requested to stay behind. When the volunteers discovered the unarmed Indian a cry rose up to kill him although he protested he was a friend to Americans as he produced a safe-conduct pass from the War of 1812. Just as the volunteers were going to run him through a voice stopped them saying: *"Stop! You men back off! He's harmless, and no one's killing him." The words had come from their company commander, Captain Abraham Lincoln. His face was flushed with anger as he stepped between the cringing Pottawatomie and the soldiers. "It must not be," he shouted. "We will not kill this man." "You're a damn' coward,*

[83] ***A Sorrow In Our Heart***, *Op. Cit.*, p. 761.

Lincoln!" a voice cried out, instantly seconded by others. Lincoln smiled mirthlessly, curled his hands into fists at his sides, and replied, "If any man here thinks I am a coward, let him test it right now!" "Damn, you, Lincoln," complained the short soldier who had first raised the cry against the old Indian, "you're bigger'n we are." Lincoln gave him a scornful look and then let his eyes move across the men of his company as he spoke. "You can guard against that very easily," he said. "Any of you. Choose your weapons."[84] With that the men moved off and the Indian was given a safe-conduct pass. It took audacity for Lincoln to step in and save the Indian from the angry, undisciplined soldiers.

In the War of 1812, Fort Stephenson, a small fort with only one cannon, was commanded by a twenty-one-year old Major George Croghan, who had little battle or fighting experience. After testing the defenses of the little fort, British commander General Proctor, with his force of soldiers and Indian allies numbering about 2,000, sent a man to demand the surrender of the fort. He was told: *I am instructed to advise you that the commandant and garrison of this fort are determined to defend it to the last extremity. No force, sir, however great, can induce us to surrender. You may advise your commander that we are resolved to maintain our post or bury ourselves in its ruin.* When threatened with a massacre if they did not surrender, the ensign replied: *Gentlemen, when—and if—the fort is taken, there will be none to massacre. It will not be given up while a man is able to resist.*[85] Through the clever use of their one cannon, the U.S. soldiers inflicted heavy casualties on the British and Indians pushing them to retreat and escape down the river. *Maj. George Croghan's defense of Ft. Stephenson was deemed by a great many as the single most gallant military act of the war of 1812.*[86] It was also pivotal because it handed the British a surprising defeat that destroyed their confidence.

Beethoven, the renowned composer, was completely deaf

---

[84] ***Twilight of Empire,*** *Op. Cit.*, p. 326.

[85] ***A Sorrow In Our Heart,*** *Op. Cit.*, p. 785. [86] *Ibid.*, p. 966.

when he composed his famous work, "Ode to Joy." He never heard a single note of his composition nor any applause when it was performed. You know how he composed it deaf? He cut off the legs of his piano. By putting his ear to the floor he could feel the piano vibrations.

The story of Helen Keller and her teacher Annie Sullivan is an incredible example of the virtue of audacity. Helen, born in 1880, was a very smart little baby who began talking at six-months-old. At nineteen-months she was struck with a fever that left her deaf and blind. The pity and heartbreak of her parents made her a badly spoiled child devoid of any discipline. Annie Sullivan, herself born blind but later given sight through nine operations, had the compassion, empathy, understanding and insight to realize that Helen Keller could become a fully functioning person. Drawing from her own background of being raised in an asylum then being taught Braille at a renowned blind school, she had the confidence that she could release Helen from the prison of her body. And she did. This is truly one of the most amazing examples of the virtue of audacity.

Charles Lindberg recounts in his autobiography, ***The Spirit of St. Louis,*** the dangers of flying the mail between big cities. His run was from St. Louis to Chicago with stops in-between. *Of the first forty pilots hired by the Air Mail Service, all except nine died. Charles Lindbergh was one of the nine survivors.*[87] Every month he faced incidents when his motor would cut out forcing him to land. In bad weather he flew with no visibility. At other times a piece of his plane would fall off causing problems or a crash. Still he says, *I'm here only because I love the sky and flying more than anything else on earth. Of course there's danger; but a certain amount of danger is essential to the quality of life. I don't believe in taking foolish chances; but nothing can be accomplished without taking any chance at all.*[88]

---

[87] Beatrice Gormley, ***Amelia Earhart*** (NY: Aladdin Paperbacks, 2002) p. 128.
[88] Charles A. Lindbergh, ***The Spirit of St. Louis*** (NY: Charles Scribner's Sons, 1953) pp. 243-244.

Amelia Earhart, the famous aviatrix, had her first plane ride in 1920 when she was a college coed. Her father paid Frank Wright, the pilot, the ten dollar fee. Amelia found her vocation that day—flying. She had already taken a course on automobile engines after high school so when she read the owner's manual for the plane she was not frightened by the warning: *Never forget that the engine may stop, and at all times keep this in mind.*[89] Rather than discouraging Amelia, she decided that if she wanted to fly, she would have to learn to fly so well that she could safely make emergency landings. She signed up for 10 flying lessons for $500 without having any money. She took two jobs to pay for her lessons. To get to the airport she would ride the trolley to the end of the line then walk several miles to the airport. By the time she was twenty-four, she put together enough money to purchase her own plane. That's audacity!

Gino Bartali, a tertiary of the Discalced Carmelites and a member of Catholic Action, helped protect the lives of 800 Jews during World War II. Bartali, the winner of the Tour de France in 1938 and the three time winner of Giro d' Italia worked with the *Oblate priests of Lucca, the archbishop of Genoa, Franciscan friars, cloistered nuns, and Catholic politicians to save 800 Jews from extermination. Bartali would make trips between Florence and Rome, carrying valuable false documents hidden in the tube of his bicycle. His role was to take photos and paper to clandestine printing presses to produce the false documents. He was also a guide to indicate the less known roads to arrive at central areas of Italy without being seen. When the police stopped him, he said he was in training. In fact, the fascists of the area had their doubts, but did not dare arrest him, as they ran the risk of causing a popular rising* because of his fame.[90]

How about this for audacity? The Vatican, under Pope Pius XII, commissioned Vittorio de Sica, one of the great Italian film directors, to direct a film entitled, "The Gate of

---

[89] ***Amelia Earhart***, *Op. Cit.*, p. 133. [90] Zenit, July 25, 2003.

Heaven" in 1943. The future Pope Paul VI, Msgr. Montini, was the liaison between the Vatican and the film producer. The idea behind the film was to save the lives of 300 people, many of them Jews. *The film's set was installed in the Basilica of St. Paul Outside the Walls, which territorially belongs to Vatican City. Those working in the film lived there. De Sica and the Holy See had the production of the film last longer than planned, to give refuge to some 300 people who were contracted as extras....Actors—professional and improvised—were sheltered in the Basilica during the March 3, 1944, bombings, which took place on Rome's Via Ostiense. The secret agreement between De Sica and the Vatican was that the film would not end "until the Germans left Rome." De Sica accepted the official commission given to him by the Catholic Cinematographic Center so that he would not have to work for the Italian Fascist government which, together with Nazi propagandist Joseph Goebbels, tried to establish a film production center in Venice...*[91] To practice the virtue of audacity one must also be clever.

Sometimes the practice of the virtue of audacity can lead to martyrdom. In Munich, Germany, in 1942 there was a group of Orthodox, Protestant and Catholic students who called themselves the White Rose Youths. They *understood that [Nazism] represented a great threat and opposed it clearly in six leaflets, taking positions against the deportation of Jews. The leaflets, which they circulated in German cities and universities, were signed with a "white rose." When they were discovered, they were all killed. They were youths rich in faith,* Msgr. Moll of the Cologne Archdiocese insists. He is promoting these youths as models for participants in World Youth Day 2005.[92]

Brother Stablum (1895-1950), proposed for beatification, was a doctor at the prestigious Dermatological Institute of the Immaculate in Rome which was run by his congregation, the Sons of the Immaculate Conception. He took in 51 Jews and politicians sought by the police registering them as

[91] Zenit, Aug. 20, 2003.

[92] Zenit, Dec. 17, 2003.

patients. They were swabbed with special creams when the Gestapo or police visited. Fr. Giovanni Cazzaniga insists: *He made the decision, conscious of the fact that he risked his life; what is more, from that moment he tied his life to the lives of those he helped. Had the Nazis discovered him, he would have been sent to a death camp in Germany.*[93]

Following the end of World War II in 1947, the von Trapp family received a letter from the U.S. General in charge of the occupation of Austria. He told of the thousands of Austrians who were destitute and starving asking if the family could possibly help the Austrian people through their concert tours. The following day the von Trapps incorporated the von Trapp Family Austrian Relief Fund. Maria recalls, *We had never done anything like it before, but when had we ever run a music camp, or a handicraft exhibition, or thought of giving concerts, or started to build a new home? These big assignments had been hurled at us without allowing even enough time to buy ourselves a handbook to look up the "how to."*[94] At each concert they passed out brochures asking for food, clothing and financial donations. The brochure ended with these words of St. Ambrose: *If you know that anybody is hungry or sick, and you have any means at all and do not help, then you will have the responsibility for each one who dies, and for each little child who might be harmed and crippled for life.*[95] When they arrived at a new town, some of the family went to the newspaper to ask for an interview while others in the family went to the radio station. Brochures were handed out with the concert programs. Maria would give a talk about the Austrian relief effort during the intermission. She would plead with the audience to bring donated items the next morning to the hotel where the von Trapps were staying so they could be loaded onto their traveling bus. As the bus traveled to the next city, the family would sort and box up the items to be shipped from the next town's post office and so the routine would begin allover again in the

[93] Zenit, Nov. 27, 2001.
[94] ***The Story Of The Trapp Family Singers***, *Op. Cit.*, p. 341. [95] *Ibid.*

next town. In two years, 300,000 pounds of goods were shipped to Austria. The U.S. army general also asked the von Trapps to find U.S. families to adopt destitute families by agreeing to send aid to them on a regular basis. Fourteen thousand families were adopted by Americans. See what good can be accomplished when the virtue of audacity is practiced?

King Baudouin I, the king of Belgium, opposed *the 1990 draft law on the liberalization of abortion, approved by the Chamber and senate [of his country]. On March 30, the monarch wrote to the prime minister that his conscience impeded his sanctioning that law, as the constitutional system established, before it came into force...[T]he council of ministers considered that by reason of his decision, Baudouin was faced with the loss of constitutional power. In such a case, the Council of Ministers could assume the king's constitutional prerogatives.*[96] That took audacity.

Heather Mercer, who was captured and imprisoned by the Taliban government in Afghanistan, explained that Christ's words in the Gospel: ***But of everyone to whom much has been given, much will be required*** (*Lk* 12:48) motivated her to sacrifice her life for others. As a college coed at Baylor University she prayed: *Lord, send me to the hardest place. Send me where others do not want to go—or are afraid to go. In prayer I felt God ask me if I could do three things: Can you love your neighbor? Can you serve the poor? Can you weep as I weep for poor and broken people? I came to see that God did not need someone with extraordinary gifts and achievements. He just needed someone who could love, share her life, and feel for others as He did.*[97] This is also audacity.

In St. Paul, Minnesota, a group of young adults from the University of St. Thomas' Catholic Studies wanted to become part of the Holy Father's call for a new

[96] Zenit, July 31, 2003.
[97] Dayna Curry and Heather Mercer, ***Prisoners Of Hope*** (NY: Doubleday, 2002) pp. 20-21.

evangelization so they decided to give a copy of the ***Catechism of the Catholic Church*** to students being confirmed. "*You cannot love what you do not know," said Stephen Maas, one of the founders of the group. "We believe the catechism is the first step in fostering a deeper love of the Church, especially in the youth—a generation that is searching for answers".* Already the group known as the Corpus Christi Catechism Fund has given copies of the catechism to sixteen thousand teens in the area.[98]

Seventeen-year-old Fatmir Gjimaraj grew up in Albania. In 1991 he heard *that an Italian military ship and a fishing vessel were close to port. He decided to flee his country. [He] swam two miles to reach the boats, which had not docked at the port for fear of the crowds that wanted to embark.* Once in Italy he traveled from city to city until he found a job as a barber in Trivigno. While there he heard about the Catholic faith and decided to study it. *On Christmas Eve 1992 he was baptized, confirmed and made his First Communion. "I began to live a normal life as a Christian. Increasingly I dedicated more time to discernment and less to amusing myself. I was impressed by a poster of St. Francis' face and the phrase: 'Lord, what do you want me to do?'"*[99] Gjimaraj is now Fr. Gjimaraj. His audacity lead to the priesthood.

Michael Van Hecke, the headmaster of St. Augustine Academy in Ventura, California, practiced the virtue of audacity when he looked over the secular history textbooks and decided that they were not good enough for his students. He founded the Catholic Schools Textbook Project which will publish books for Catholics schools, beginning with a history series. *[T]here use to be whole lines of texts separately produced for the Catholic school system similar to the secular models, but which included the Catholic contributions to history, or literature, or science, as the subject allowed. Yet, this option has disappeared. Some had decided that the secular texts were just fine...We plan on eventually producing texts for all subjects and grades so Catholic schools have a*

[98] Zenit, Sept. 2, 2003.

[99] Zenit, Sept. 21, 2003.

choice.[100] [101]

Another clever use of the virtue of audacity is Mirabilandia, an amusement park in Ravenna, Italy, designed by the Salesians of St. John Bosco. The aim of the park is to combine spirituality with fun events so Sunday Masses and Eucharistic celebrations take place in the park. This is to fulfill their founder's ideal that *Christian life must be a "joyful" service of the Lord.*[102]

Russell Ford, a convict, converted to the Catholic faith in prison due to the audacity of an older Catholic convict. The older convict tried various means to bring Ford to God but was unsuccessful. Finally he challenged his ego. He gave Ford a copy of ***The Baltimore Catechism #2*** then told Ford that he bet he couldn't read the book then answer the questions. Ford rose to the challenge and in the process converted to the Catholic faith. Now he acts as a Catholic catechist and *counts 61 godson converts and has played a direct role in the conversion of nearly 200 other inmates. Perhaps more impressive, the recidivism rate among his Catholic converts is only 1.6% compared to a general recidivism rate between 70 and 80 percent for the state.*[103] If that older Catholic convert had not practiced the virtue of audacity think of all the lost souls!

One of the most impressive examples of audacity is that of twelve-year-old Ryan Hreljac of Kemptville, Ontario, Canada. In 1997, six-year-old Ryan asked his parents for *$70 for poor people in Africa. They don't have clean water to drink. They drink bad water from swamps and streams and get sick and die. We heard about them in school today. My teacher said it would cost $70 to dig them a well. So can I have it?* Ryan's parents urged him to earn money by doing extra chores. When the chores around the house were done,

[100] Zenit, Aug. 21, 2003.

[101] For more information call (866) 458-3332 or see www.CatholicTextbookProject.com

[102] Zenit, Aug. 21, 2003.

[103] Tim Drake, "Reaching Out from Behind Bars," *CMN Trade Journal*, Vol. 7, Issue 1, pp. 30-31.

he offered to do lawn work and other jobs for neighbors and relatives to earn money for his "well project." Each night he prayed to help the people in Africa get clean water. When he saved up $70 he went to donate it only to find out that his money would only purchase a hand pump. He would have to raise an additional $2,000 to drill the well. *That's OK. I'll just do more chores.* He worked for months to earn the money then the media learned of his efforts. With newspaper stories, as well as TV stories, funds started to trickle in. When he had raised $1,000 the Canadian International Development Agency matched his funds. He was allowed to pick the location of the well and selected Angolo Primary School in Uganda. Ryan was told that the well would be dug by hand because a drill costs $25,000. On learning this Ryan replied: *Maybe I can start raising money for a drill so you can build more wells.* His family became more involved with his younger brother stuffing envelopes and licking stamps while his older brother prepared audiovisual equipment for Ryan's presentations. The second grader hit the talk circuit speaking at service clubs around his area. A pen pal system was set up with Angolo School and his class. Two years after he began his project, Ryan learned that the villagers and school finally had water. This fueled a desire to see the well and his pen pals. The family began saving and when Ryan was twelve they traveled to Uganda. Along the road hundreds of people gathered to see Ryan, chanting *Rayan! Rayan! Rayan!* The well was decorated with flowers with the school children dressed in their uniforms flanking it. On the well there was a plaque that read: *Ryan's Well, Funded by Ryan H.* But this did not end his story. Canadian Olympic gold-medalist wrestler Daniel Igali asked Ryan to help him build wells in Nigeria. That began another crusade. To date Ryan is responsible *for raising almost $1 million and building over 70 wells in Africa.* He has attended and spoken at UN Conferences, been on various TV shows but the most thrilling for him was receiving Holy Communion from John Paul II. His mother says, *Ryan doesn't think he's special at all. He says that not everyone is called to drill wells, but everyone is called to make some difference in the world around, by helping a sibling, for instance, in his homework.* Ryan believes: *Getting others to help is "sort of like a dandelion. When the wind blows, the seeds go everywhere. I'm trying to let people know they need to help out, too. God puts us on earth, but he doesn't make us perfect on purpose. If God made us perfect, we wouldn't need to make the world a better place.*[104] Ryan's parents also practice the virtue of audacity. When they learned that Ryan's pen pal was orphaned and had escaped miraculously from becoming a child-soldier for the Lord's Resistance Army, they began a campaign to adopt him. Now Ryan's pen pal is his brother.[105]

One of the most public and recent examples of the virtue of audacity is Mel Gibson and his film, *The Passion of The Christ.* It is the most talked about film in history. As for popularity, five million tickets were sold before it even opened. But to get to this point, Gibson personally financed the film for over $30 million. James Caviezel, the actor who played Christ, did not take any money upfront. Interestingly, Caviezel has the same initials as Christ and was thirty three years old when he portrayed Christ. During twelve of the eighteen weeks of filming, Gibson was afflicted with a serious lung virus and high fever. Then, prior to the debut of the film, harsh critics attacked him and the film. These attacks ranged from the U.S. Catholic Bishops' Conference to Jews with scores of others thrown in besides. In TV, newspaper, and magazine interviews he was accused of being anti-Semitic for portraying Christ's passion. His practice of the virtue of audacity had awakened the sleeping public to Hollywood's control of the film media. Reports are circulating that he will be blacklisted for making this film. Makes one wonder what ever happened to freedom of speech. Apparently it's OK to attack Christ and the Catholic Church in films but to portray our salvation...hey, that takes

[104] Zenit, Oct. 20, 2003.

[105] For more info see www.ryanswell.ca or write: ryan@ryanswell.ca

audacity and a thick skin both of which Gibson has in great supply. Mel accomplished what he felt God called him to accomplish. Hopefully, there will be many more fruits besides a religious revival. One fruit mentioned by two people I talked with on the phone today is this: *Before this film no one talked about religion but now everyone is talking about it.*

To live the virtue of audacity one must be free of a false sense of human respect, that is, worrying about what other people think. **It does not matter what others think. It only matters what God thinks.** Author Harry Fosdick observes that *the majority is almost certain to be wrong...The fact is that in any realm where judgment calls for spiritual fineness only the minority who are above the average are ever right. And because a man is always tempted to live down to the average of his social group, a searching test of character is involved in one's relationship with this dead level of public opinion and practice...[We need] courage to live above the average and ahead of the time.*[106] He adds: *Psychoanalysts tell us that together with the preservation of life and the attraction of sex, this instinct to follow the herd is the most powerful force in our subconscious life...In a day when there is no hope for our civilization except in superior character, Christians should recall that the cross of which they sing means something besides singing—sheer courage to live above the average and ahead of the time.*[107] This is the virtue of audacity! Live it daily and teach your teens to live it as well!

---

[106] ***Twelve Tests of Character***, *Op. Cit.*, pp. 125-126. [107] *Ibid.*, pp. 141-142.

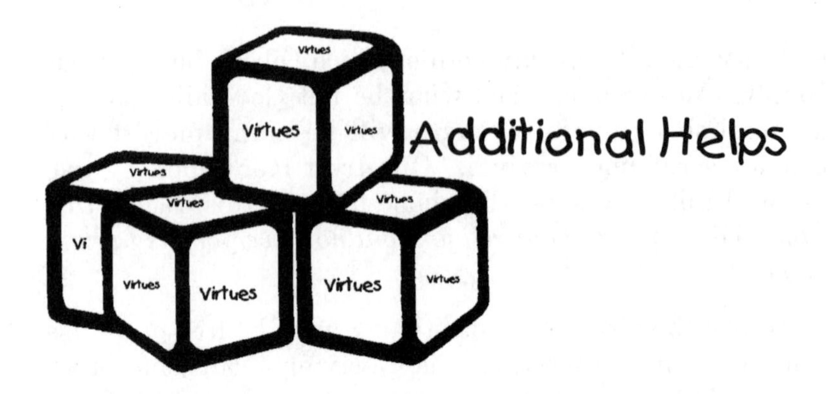

Additional Helps

- ✓ For a fun family exercise (junior high and older) briefly review the virtues and vices mentioned so far in this book. To make it more of a game, give each family member a list of the virtues and vices on a sheet of paper. Watch the film *El Cid.* After each virtue or vice put an incident or character from the film. Note the surprise ending. Isn't it just exactly what this last virtue we discussed is all about? Discuss the film together afterwards.
- ✓ Do the same with the film *My Fair Lady.* Can they point out the 7 Capital Sins in this film?
- ✓ Discuss with your teens the virtue of audacity. Ask them how they are living it daily.
- ✓ Have your teens read, ***With God In Russia*** and ***He Leadeth Me*** by Servant of God, Walter J. Ciszek, S. J. Have them read the books together for a more balanced understanding.
- ✓ Read the revised edition of David Isaacs' book, ***Character Building.*** Each chapter includes a checklist to see if your child has acquired the virtue/virtues.
- ✓ View with your children and teens the movie *The Miracle Worker,* the story of Helen Keller. Discuss the film. In what manner did Helen's parents hurt her? Were her parents disciplined? Then have your teens read ***The Story of My Life*** by Helen Keller. Discuss the book and the movie with your teens.
- ✓ Go online and print out a copy of "We Were There...Catholic Priests and How They Responded" on 9/11. www.usccb.org/vocations

- ✓ Get a copy of and listen with your teens to Russell Ford's audiotape "No Escape" from St. Joseph Communications, Inc. (800-526-22151). Discuss it.
- ✓ Get your teens a copy of the book, ***They Call Me The Bacon Priest*** by Fr. Werenfried Van Streaten. Discuss how they could imitate his example of helping others.
- ✓ Have your younger children read the series of books entitled "Childhood of Famous Americans." Why not begin with ***Amelia Earhart*** by Beatrice Gormley?
- ✓ Have your teens read the Chapter on Loyalty in the book ***Furrow*** by St. Josemaría. It's in Catholic bookstores or you can purchase it from Scepter (800-322-8773).
- ✓ Have your teens read ***The Spirit of St. Louis*** by Charles Lindbergh as well as ***Prisoners of Hope*** by Dayna Curry and Heather Mercer.
- ✓ Read Josef Pieper's book, ***Prudence, The First Cardinal Virtue*** or listen to it on audiotape from R. B. Media, Inc.
- ✓ Listen to the audiotapes of ***The Apostolate of Moral Beauty*** by Henri Morice from R. B. Media, Inc. or purchase a used copy of the book.
- ✓ Reread pp. 115-121 in ***Raise Happy Children Through A Happier Marriage!***

Scripture Verses for Prudence & Wisdom

Prov. 14:15
1 Pet 4:7
James 3: 13-18
Psalm 19

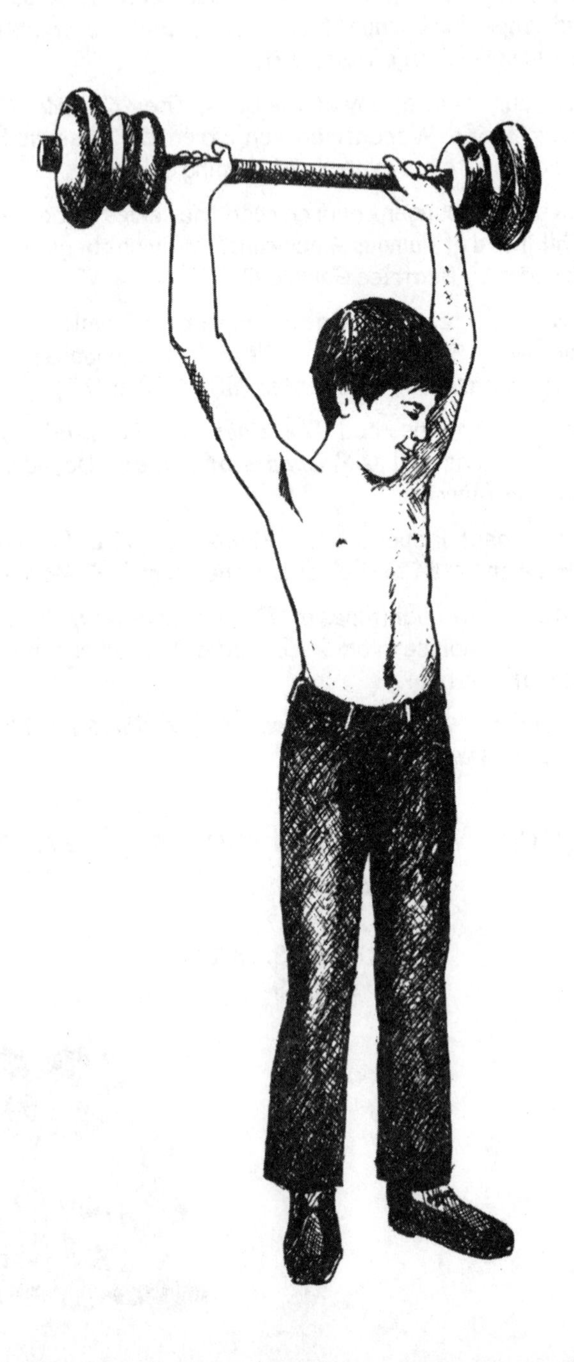

Chapter 8

The Virtues of Humility & Optimism

The Virtue of Humility

"Let no one rate himself more than he ought."

St. Paul (***Romans*** 12:3)

The virtue of humility has taken a bad rap. People think that to be humble one must be mousy or devoid of spunk. This is not true. In the ***Acts of the Apostles,*** St. Paul addressing the Sanhedrin notes that ***Moses was mighty in his words and deeds*** (7:22). Although Moses was mighty, in the ***Book of Numbers*** (12:3), we read that ***the man Moses was very meek [humble], more than all men that were on the face of the earth.*** Humility is strength through virtue rather than power through pride. Fr. Joseph Malaise, S.J., tells us that humility *is related to the virtue of temperance because it moderates the sense we have of our* *own worth.*[1] To practice any of the other virtues we must exercise humility. It is the foundation virtue of our spiritual edifice. Why? The virtue of humility serves two functions. First of all, it speeds us along the path of sanctity. A person without humility cannot grow in holiness because he is too full of himself. The virtue of humility gives us the self-knowledge to know that we are nothing and can do absolutely nothing without God. Secondly, the virtue of humility is required for one to grow in the Catholic faith. St. Alphonsus Rodriguez insists: *Faith requires a humble and submissive understanding...and not only for the reception of faith is humility necessary but also for the preservation of it. It is the common doctrine of doctors and saints that pride is the beginning of all heresies. A man gets such a conceit of his own opinion and judgment that he prefers it to the common sentiment of saints and of the Church and thence he comes to plunge into heresy.*[2] With humility in place as our foundation we, as well as our teens and young adults, can grow steadily in faith, sanctity, happiness and joy.

Humility also plays a role in the development of the theological virtue of hope. When we live the virtue of humility we know that all rests on God, not ourselves. When we neglect to live the virtue of humility, we depend on ourselves. When we cannot handle the problems, contradictions or sufferings in life, we despair, sometimes to the point of suicide.

If we seek happiness we have to imitate Jesus' example of humility. St. Peter Julian Eymard insists *humility is the outstanding virtue of Jesus Christ.* ***"Learn from Me; I am gentle and humble of heart,"***[3] *He said. He makes of humility His distinctive and predominant virtue.*[4] Christ also tells us in the Gospel of St. Mark (10:43-45): ***Whoever wishes to be first among you will be the slave of all. For the Son of Man did not come to be served but to***

[1] ***Know Yourself,*** *Op. Cit.*, p. 158
[2] ***Practice of Perfection and Christian Virtues, Vol. 2,*** *Op. Cit.*, p. 171.
[3] ***St. Matthew*** 11:29.
[4] ***In The Light of the Monstrance,*** *Op. Cit.*, p. 68.

serve and to give His life as a ransom for many. At the Last Supper He gave a visual of this teaching when He washed the feet of each of His apostles. But Christ's example of humility did not begin at the end of His life. Jesus teaches us humility beginning with His Incarnation then His humble birth, His materially poor existence throughout His life, His 30 years of hidden life, His acceptance of the abuse of His detractors, and finally His horrific Passion and Death. But it did not end there. Today He continues to live the virtue of humility in the Blessed Sacrament. He allows imperfect, sinful men to bring Him from heaven to earth at the moment of the consecration of the Mass. Furthermore, He permits sinful people to consume Him in the Holy Eucharist.

Humility is a difficult virtue to develop since it's corresponding vice, **pride, is considered the greatest vice.** Pride is also considered a capital sin or one of the seven deadly sins because it kills the soul. This vice caused Satan's fall as well as original sin. Why? If our ego is too big there is no room for God. In fact, the vice of pride is so strong that St. Josemaría believed our pride dies several hours after we do!

Pride also spawns the additional vices of envy, presumption, ambition, vanity, boasting, ostentation and hypocrisy. St. Augustine writes: *Pride is the great sin, the head and cause of all sins, and its beginning lies in turning away from God. Beloved, do not make light of this vice, for the proud man who disdains the yoke of Christ is contained by the harsher yoke of sin: he may not wish to serve, but he has to, because if he will not be Love's servant, he will inevitably be sin's slave...Because of this great sin of pride, God humbled Himself, taking the nature of a servant, bearing insults and hanging on a cross. To heal us, He became humble; shall we not be ashamed to be proud* (editorial emphasis)?[5]

---

[5] St. Augustine, ***Daily Readings With St. Augustine*** (Springfield, IL: Templegate Publishers, 1986) p. 27.

Pride is wanting to be like God. On the other hand, *humility*, Fr. Frank Pavone says, *is knowing there is a God and I'm not He.* Bl. Mother Teresa insists: *Humility is nothing but truth.* ***What do we have that we have not received?*** *asks St. Paul (1 Cor. 4:7). And if I have received everything, what is it that I have that is mine? If we are convinced of this, we will never lift up our heads with arrogance. If we are humble, nothing will touch us—neither praise nor contempt—for we know what we are.*[6] St. Josemaría tells us to: *Reject from our hearts any pride, any ambition, any desire to dominate; and peace and joy will reign around us and within us, as a consequence of our personal sacrifice.*[7]

Fr. Joseph Malaise, S.J., explains the vices connected to pride. **Presumption** *is an inclination and wish to undertake what is above one's capacity...Presumptuous persons never take counsel with any one...Presumption leads to* ***ambition****, namely to the inordinate striving after honors, dignities, authority and power over others...*[V]***ainglory*** *or* ***vanity*** *is the inordinate striving after the esteem of men...A vain person is not only satisfied with himself and his qualities, but he wants others to admire them. He adores himself and he wants others to adore him...He is vain about his external appearance, about his clothes, his jewelry, or anything that favorably differentiates him from others....Vain persons like to receive the attention of people of quality, but they will not be bothered with the lowly and poor...*[T]*he vain person is deeply chagrined when the praises are not forthcoming from his should-be admirers. Vanity leads to* ***boasting,*** *which is bragging about one's good qualities or accomplishments with a view to gaining the esteem of others...Vanity leads to* ***ostentation,*** *which consists in posing, in putting oneself on display to draw attention and admiration of others by a pompous way of acting, and by distinguished singularity...****Hypocrisy*** *is the feigning of a sort of homage*

[6] Bl. Mother Teresa, ***Heart of Joy, The Transforming Power of Self-Giving*** (Ann Arbor: Servant Books, 1987), p. 133.
[7] ***Christ Is Passing By***, *Op. Cit.*, p. 174.

*that vanity pays to virtue, for vanity likes to clothe itself in the garb of virtue, say humility, in order to get the admiration this virtue creates. Pretense of humility is **an excess of pride.***[8]

Earlier we discussed Benjamin Franklin and his quest to acquire virtue. When he confided his goal to a friend, the friend told him to add humility to his list: *My list of virtues contain'd at first but twelve; but a Quaker friend having kindly informed me that I was generally thought proud; that my pride show'd itself frequently in conversation; that I was not content with being in the right when discussing any point, but was overbearing, and rather insolent, of which he convinc'd me by mentioning several instances; I determined to endeavor to cure myself if I could, of this vice or folly among the rest, and I added* **Humility** *to my list, giving an extensive meaning to the word.*

I cannot boast of much success in acquiring the **reality** *of this virtue, but I had a good deal of success with regard to the* **appearance** *of it...In reality, there is perhaps, no one of our natural passions so hard to subdue as* **pride**. *Disguise it, struggle with it, beat it down, stifle it, mortify it as much as one pleases, it is still alive, and will every now and then peep out and show itself; you will see it, perhaps, often in this history; for, even if I could conceive that I had completely overcome it, I should probably be proud of my humility.*[9]

The Four Types of Pride

"Whoever exalts himself shall be humbled, and whoever humbles himself shall be exalted." Jesus Christ (*Matt.* 23:12)

St. Bonaventure names **two types of pride: spiritual pride and worldly or temporal pride**. Spiritual pride is the more serious of the two. In spiritual pride we credit ourselves with our growth in holiness, in the success of

[8] ***Know Yourself,*** *Op. Cit.*, pp. 22-28.
[9] ***The Autobiography of Benjamin Franklin***, *Op. Cit.*, pp. 89-90.

apostolic endeavors and the touching of souls. In effect we are robbing God of the credit due to Him. To avoid falling into spiritual pride refer all success to God. Remember, God throughout salvation history has chosen the weak to confront the proud. If God chooses us for a specific task it is because we are weak and inept. This will permit His glory to be more visible in the work we do. St. Alphonsus reminds us, *if thou wert possessed of great abilities, perhaps God would not choose thee for the work, because thou wouldst take pride therein, and attribute the doing of it to thyself. It is God's way to choose humble folk, people who attribute nothing to themselves, and by them He wishes to do great things.*[10]

There are **four types of worldly pride**. The first is **pride of authority or arrogance**, according to Fr. Jay Alvarez, a priest of the Prelature Opus Dei. This type of pride projects an overbearing attitude. Symptoms of this type of pride include the repeated use of the words *I, me, mine.* A person in the grip of this type of pride refuses to seek advice. He takes pleasure in belittling or criticizing people, places and things. Although keen on finding fault in others, he must have the last word. He pushes ahead to be first in line or finds ways to call attention to himself. This person will argue in defense of an issue even when he knows that he is wrong. He becomes irritable when his ideas are opposed. *Knowledge is proud that he has learn'd so much; Wisdom is humble that he has learned no more,* writes Cowper.[11] Last weekend we went out to dinner and sat at a table close to another party of four. Due to the closeness of the tables we could hear their whole conversation. One of the gentlemen was an attorney. He argued every topic. It was so obnoxious that when we left the restaurant the waitress rolled her eyes at me. Even she found his conduct a bit much. From his conversation we gathered that this gentleman was a practicing Catholic but he needs to work on this defect because it's a real turn off. ***And all of you practice***

[10] ***Practice of Perfection and the Christian Virtues,*** *Op. Cit.,* p. 186.
[11] W. Cowper, ***The Winter Walk at Noon,*** Bk. VI, line 96.

humility towards one another; for, "God resists the proud, but gives grace to the humble. Humble yourselves, therefore, under the mighty hands of God, that He may exalt you in the time of visitation; cast all your anxiety upon Him, because He cares for you (*1 Pete*r 5:5-7).

John Paul II addressed this form of pride in one of his Wednesday audiences saying that *superficiality and social climbing do not constitute the real good of man and society. Quoting St. Paul, the Holy Father said that "the Kingdom of God is effectively prepared by people who carry out their work seriously and honestly, not aspiring to things that are too high, but turning, in daily faithfulness, to those that are lowly. The "mentality of the world pushes one to stand out, to get ahead, with shrewdness and without scruples, asserting oneself and one's own interests." The "consequences can be seen by all: rivalries, abuses, frustrations." The Kingdom of God, on the contrary, rewards "meekness and humility"...The proof of this is Jesus Himself...Herein lies the secret, "so that every activity, professional or in the home, may be done in an atmosphere of genuine humanity, thanks to the humble and active contribution of everyone."*[12]

The second type of pride is **pride of timidity**. This is fake humility. A person with this pride hides her weaknesses by being shy. She is easily embarrassed, exaggerates weaknesses, and blushes easily. She is also shy about doing things in public. Consider these questions: Do I compare myself to others? Does human respect enter into my daily life? Do I worry about what people are thinking about me? If you answer yes to these questions then pride of timidity is your area of struggle.

The third type of pride is **pride of sensibility**, which is wounded self-love. A person with this type of pride is suspicious of everything that is said. A harmless joke is taken as a personal attack. Feelings are easily hurt. People have to tiptoe around this person because a look, a word, or

[12] Zenit, Sept. 2, 2002.

an action can become offensive due to the person's hypersensitivity. The imagination runs wild making one think that others are willfully hurting me. This type of pride broods.

The fourth type of pride is **pride of concupiscence or vanity**. We long to be praised, to be honored, to be thought well of. *Pride leads one to want to be greater, or to be better at something than other people are.*[13] We can even be vain about our piety criticizing others for how they practice virtue. This pride likes to show off or brag whether it is in appearance, possessions, or talents. The best way to nip this type of pride is to recall that everything we are, everything that we have comes from God. We had nothing to do with the color of our eyes, our talents, our knowledge, or possessions. Each is a gift from God that can be taken away in a moment. If troubled by this form of pride recall the words of St. Benedict Menni, *We are nothing and we can do nothing without God's help.*

Many of the TV talk show hosts display this type of pride. They refuse to allow the guest to complete a sentence or thought. They rudely break in to bring attention back to themselves and to their "intellectual brilliance". If the guest continues speaking they shout over the guest. This isn't simply my observation. *The Wall Street Journal* wrote a column on two "Catholic" commentators—Bill O'Reilly on Fox and Phil Donahue on MSNBC. In speaking about O'Reilly, writer Tunku Varadarajan observes: *He's bloody good at his job, to put it bluntly; and if he struts a bit from time to time, and preens like a prized peacock, it's because he knows that he's the nearest to a ratings gold-standard that we have on grown-up TV today...[H]e's clever...with a charismatic bluster, not to mention an unshakeable faith in his own convictions.* The writer next turns to Donahue: *He believes in himself so completely that any self-doubt might be ascribed to momentary madness. He adores the sound of his own voice, and will, like his competitor on Fox, shout down*

[13] ***Character Building***, *Op. Cit.*, p. 210.

someone with whom he disagrees....And vanity with vanity. You can picture Mr. Donahue saying "You hunk, you!" to himself as he fixes his silvered mane...just as Mr. O'Reilly might say to his own little looking glass, "Who's the blaringest of them all?"[14] Another point to take from this article is the fact that our pride is observed and laughed about by everyone but ourselves. We are usually the last to discover that we are proud!

Another example of this type of pride was a mother who rigged the test results of her six-year-old son so he would be classified a genius. She not only had him memorize the answers to tests but she altered test scores. The mother finally confessed what she did only after her son, now eight, attempted suicide.[15] If you haven't done so yet, now is the time to scrape off your van the bragging bumper sticker about your honor student!

The Wall Street Journal ran another distressing article dealing with the terrible consequences of pride: *Like most chefs and artists, Bernard Loiseau literally lived for praise...Last Monday, after one of those guides, Gault Millau, knocked him down from 19/20 points to 17/20 and proclaimed his cuisine as "hardly dazzling, just simply very well carried out," he took out his hunting gun and shot himself...If a larger message is stewing here, it's not that the guides have too much power, but that France's rigid social structure has trouble digesting competition without suffering a nervous breakdown.*[16] To commit suicide with the potential of spending eternity in hell over two points, is this not pathetic? G. K. Chesterton would have quipped after reading that article: *Angels fly because they take themselves lightly.*

---

[14] Tunku Varadarajan, "Foghorn Phil Joins the Battle With Bawling Bill," *The Wall Street Journal*, July 18, 2002.

[15] "Mom admits falsifying claims son is genius," *State Journal Register*, Mar. 3, 2002.

[16] Willaim Echikson, "Wish Upon A Star," *The Wall Street* Journal, Feb. 28, 2003.

Prideful people can become manipulators, treating people like puppets. *They are experts at projection, that is, blaming others for their problems. They decide their best defense is a good offense—attacking others! They try to rid themselves of their guilty feelings by getting angry and directing the anger, judgment, insults, and jabs at others. They go so far as to slander, sabotage, and lie about people. It is so much less painful to blame our behavior on those around us or even on God,* notes Gwen Shamblin.[17] Let me share this clipping with you. It drives home the various types of pride we just talked about:

What It Means

He who is speaking shouts loudly, means that his arguments are weak.
He who has to speak much, means that his words are of little value.
He who to exalt himself, has to speak ill of others, means that he is of little value.
He who imagines that he is able easily to solve all the problems of a country, means that he has never tried to solve his own problems.
He who sees all the defects of others, means that his eyes have not grown to see his own defects.
He who uses coarse words, means that he did not live a humble life when young or was drunk with his high status.

During our lifetime the various types of pride mix and mingle alerting us that we have to be on our guard at all times. When we do not fight the defects of our temperament and pride, these sins become a spiritual virus eating away at our union with God. My confessor compares it to cancer, which grows slowly unnoticed until it erupts into a deadly, often times terminal illness. Remember how St. Theresa of Avila was shown the place reserved for her in hell if she didn't conquer her defects? Carelessness in committing venial sins eventually leads us to commit mortal sins.

Once we and our teens identify our prideful defects, we need to call in the big guns of penance, mortification, prayer,

[17] Gwen Shamblin, ***The Weigh Down Diet*** (NY: Doubleday: 1997) p. 232.

almsgiving and frequent confession to help us fight them. So as not to become overwhelmed, just pick three areas that you plan to work on like Ben Franklin. Write these down. Next to them write the penance or mortification you plan to utilize to conquer them. Scripture tells us: ***Odious to the Lord and to men is arrogance, and the sin of oppression they both hate. The beginning of pride is man's stubbornness in withdrawing his heart from his Maker; for pride is the reservoir of sin, a source which runs over with vice. The roots of the proud God plucks up, to plant the humble in their place: He breaks down their stem to the level of the ground, then digs their roots from the earth*** (***Sirach*** 10:7, 12-13, 15-16).

St. James also has some pretty strong words about pride: ***God opposes the proud but gives grace to the humble. Submit yourselves, then, to God. Resist the devil, and he will flee from you. Come near to God and he will come near to you. Wash your hands, you sinners, and purify your hearts, you double-minded. Grieve, mourn and wail...Humble yourselves before the Lord, and he will lift you up*** (***James:*** 4:6-10).

We can counter the four types of pride with these acts of humility:

Prayer *is the humility of the man who acknowledges his profound wretchedness and the greatness of God. He addresses and adores God as one who expects everything from Him and nothing from himself.*

Faith *is the humility of the mind which renounces its own judgment and surrenders to the verdict and authority of the Church.*

Obedience *is the humility of the will which subjects itself to the will of another, for God's sake.*

Chastity *is the humility of the flesh, which subjects itself to the spirit.*

Exterior ***mortification*** *is the humility of the senses.*

Penance *is the humility of all the passions, immolated to the Lord.*

Humility is truth on the road of the ascetic struggle, concludes St. Josemaría.[18]

What the Saints Say...

"The great virtue of the saints is humility."
St. Bernard

Let's begin with St. Peter: ***In your relations with one another, clothe yourselves with humility, because God "is stern with the arrogant but to the humble He shows kindness." Bow humbly under God's mighty hand, so that in due time He may lift you high*** (*1 Peter*: 5:5-7). St. Paul adds: ***Do nothing out of selfishness or out of vainglory; rather, humbly regard others as more important than yourselves, each looking out not for his own interests, but also for those of others. Have in you the same attitude that is also in Christ Jesus, Who...did not regard equality with God something to be grasped. Rather, He emptied Himself, taking the form of a slave, coming in human likeness; and found human in appearance, He humbled Himself, becoming obedient to the point of death, even death on a cross*** (***Phil.*** 2:1-11).

St. Augustine points out: *If you ask me what is the essential thing in the religion and discipline of Jesus Christ, I shall reply: first humility, second humility and third humility...Pride changed angels into devils; humility makes men into angels.* He adds: *When pride has crept into a servant of God, straightaway envy is to be found there too. The proud person cannot help being envious. Envy is the daughter of pride; but this mother is unable to be barren; wherever she is, she immediately gives birth.*

---

[18] ***Furrow****, Op. Cit.*, #259.

St. Jerome has much to say about the vice of pride: *The proud...are God's enemies.* ***God resists the proud, but gives grace to the humble.*** *The devil is the prince of the proud.* ***Lest he be puffed up with pride****, says Holy Writ,* ***and incur the condemnation passed on the devil****, for everyone who glorified himself in his heart is partner to the devil, who used to say: "By my own power I have done it, and by my wisdom, for I am shrewd. I have moved the boundaries of people...All other failings deserve the mercy of the Lord because, in humility, they are submitted to the tribunal of God: pride alone, because it honors itself beyond its power, resists God...When pride and inordinate desire for glory raise up a man, they, at the same time, abase him, for by his sin they make him an enemy of God...The sinner who supplicates God merits pardon, but the man who vaunts himself in wickedness is proud, and pride makes God an enemy.*[19]

St. Bernard and St. Gregory explain: *He who seeks to gain virtues without humility, is like one carrying a little dust or ashes in the teeth of the wind; it is all scattered, all blown away by the gale.*[20]

St. Leo the Great counsels: *Let humility be loved. Let every exaltation be avoided by the faithful. Let all prefer others to themselves...That way, when an inclination to do good abounds in us all, the poison of hate might not be found in any one.*[21] St. Thomas More agrees: *Christ the commander teaches by His own example that His soldier should take humility as his starting point.* St. Jane Frances de Chantal explains: *We must serve our Lord according to His liking and not according to our own.* This takes a lot of humility to live. God speaking to St. Catherine of Siena told her: *I am who Am; you are she who is not.*

St. Peter Julian Eymard confides: *Virtues, even the most lovable such as meekness and humility, are very difficult naturally for us to practice. It is not easy to be meek under insult; and I understand very well why a world without faith*

[19] *Magnificat,* Sept. 2002.
[20] ***Practice of Perfection...*** *Op. Cit.,* p. 168.
[21] *Magnificat,* Sept. 2003.

finds Christian virtues disheartening.[22]

St. Teresa of Avila reflected: *I was wondering once why our Lord so dearly loved this virtue of humility; and all of a sudden...the following reason came to mind: that it is because God is Sovereign Truth and to be humble is to walk in truth, for it is absolutely true to say that we have no good thing in ourselves, but only misery and nothingness; and anyone who fails to understand this is walking in falsehood. He who best understands it is most pleasing to Sovereign truth because he is walking in truth. May it please God, sisters, to grant us grace never to fail to have this knowledge of ourselves. Amen.*[23]

Christ told the Servant of God Concepción Cabrera de Armida: *All your ills come from pride and the lack of recollection. In general, your soul is troubled when you are deprived of praise, affection, consideration. These ills also proceed from the fact that you seek the creature, not in order to be led to me, but to satisfy your self-love. And should you not succeed, you are disturbed and uneasy, searching for empty pleasures which can only leave a void in your heart...Make up your mind that in order to be happy it is only necessary for you to disappear...to come down, to detach yourself from yourself and to leave me full scope, for I alone can give you happiness in humiliation and suffering...Humility: that is the remedy if you desire to be healed. Lose sight of yourself. Be convinced of your own nothingness. Endeavor to be the least before men, and the greatest only before God. O Mary, make us humble like yourelf!*[24]

Jesus spoke to Ven. Charles De Foucauld, a mystic who lived in Algeria, about His thirty-three years of humility. He then advised Charles: *Be taken as what I was taken for, my child, unlearned, poor, of lowly birth, also for what you really are: unintelligent, untalented, and ungifted. Always look for the meanest tasks, but cultivate your mind. But do it*

[22] ***In The Light of the Monstrance***, *Op. Cit.*, p. 47.

[23] *Magnificat,* July 2002.

[24] *Magnificat,* November 2003.

secretly. Do not let the world know. I was infinitely wise, but no one knew it. Do not be afraid to study; it is good for your soul. Study zealously to become better, to know Me and love Me better, to know My will and do it more perfectly, and also to become more like Me, who am perfect knowledge. Be very unlearned in the eyes of men, and very learned in the knowledge of God at the foot of my tabernacle. I was lowly and despised beyond all measure. Seek out, ask for, and love those occupations that will humiliate you: piling dung, digging, whatever is lowest and most uncouth. The less important you are in this way, the more like Me you will be. If you are thought a fool, so much the better. Give infinite thanks for it to Me. They treated me as a madman—it is one of the ways I offer you of being like Me. If they throw stones at you, mock you, curse you in the streets, so much the better. Thank Me for it: I am giving you an infinite grace—for did they not do as much for Me? How fortunate you should think yourself when I give you such close resemblance to Me.[25]

The Servant of God, Fr. Walter J. Ciszek, S.J., whom we met earlier, notes: *Learning the full truth of our dependence upon God and our relations to His will is what the virtue of humility is all about. For humility is truth, the full truth that encompasses our relation to God the Creator and through Him to the world He has created and to our fellow men. And what we call humiliations are the trials by which our more complete grasp of this truth is tested. It is self that is humiliated: there would be no "humiliation" if we had learned to put self in its place, to see ourselves in proper perspective before God and other men. And the stronger the ingredient of self develops in our lives, the more severe must our humiliations be in order to purify us...I doubt very much that Peter ever again boasted that he would never desert the Lord even if all others deserted him. I find it perfectly understandable that Peter, in his letters to the early churches, should have reminded his Christians to work out their salvation in fear and trembling. For just as surely as man begins to trust in his own abilities, so surely has he taken the*

[25] *Magnificat,* April 2003.

first step on the road to ultimate failure. And the greatest grace God can give such a man is to send him a trial he cannot bear with his own powers—and then sustain him with His grace so he may endure to the end and be saved.[26]

St. Aloysius Gonzaga warns: *[T]he devil continually attacks you by vanity and self-esteem, and as this is the weak side of your soul, you must the more strenuously and constantly endeavor to resist him by humility, and self-contempt, both interior and exterior. For this end you will propose to yourself some rules to attend especially to the study of this virtue, which have been taught by our Lord and confirmed by experience.*[27]

Ven. Luis de Granada teaches: *If you cannot imitate the virginity of the humble, then imitate the humility of the virgin. Virginity is praiseworthy, but humility is more necessary. The former is recommended to us, the later is an obligation for us; to the former we are invited, to the latter we are obliged....And so we see that the former is celebrated as a voluntary sacrifice, the latter required as an obligatory sacrifice. Lastly, you can be saved without virginity, but not without humility.*[28]

St. Francis of Assisi had a specific barometer for measuring virtues: *When those who should cooperate with you do the exact opposite, then we can tell. A man has as much patience and humility as he has then, and no more.*[29]

What Others Say...

"If you seek an example of humility, contemplate the crucifix."

St. Thomas Aquinas

The virtue of humility, rather than being part of a chapter could easily become a large volume. All serious spiritual writers as well as people of deep moral convictions extol

[26] *Magnificat,* June 2001. [27] *Ibid.*
[28] Ven. Luis de Granada, ***Suma de la vida cristiana***, book 3, part 2, chap. 10.
[29] *FMA*, "Patience and the spirit of God," p. 5 no date.

the importance of the virtue. John Paul II concisely tells us that *God lets Himself be conquered by the humble, He rejects the arrogance of the proud....The Lord of history is not indifferent before the rage of the arrogant who think they are the only arbiters of human affairs: God brings down to the dust of the earth those who defy heaven with their pride.*[30] Cardinal Joseph Ratzinger, the prefect of the Congregation on the Doctrine of the Faith, points out how miserable pride makes us: *Egoism and a genuine love of self are not only not identical, but are also mutually exclusive. It is possible to be a confirmed egoist and, at the same time, to be at odds with oneself. In fact, egoism is often due to one's own inner strife, to the attempt to create for oneself a different I, whereas the proper attitude to one's I grows spontaneously in an atmosphere of freedom from self...[T]o the degree that we seek only for ourselves, to realize our own potential, and are concerned solely with the success and fulfillment of our I, to that same degree this I becomes disagreeable, irritable, and repugnant. It disintegrates into a thousand forms and in the end there remain only a dissatisfaction with self that leads to flight from oneself and a turning to drugs or one of the many other forms of a self-destructive egoism...[O]nly when we have accepted ourselves can we address a genuine yes to anyone else. To accept, to "love," oneself presumes the existence of truth and requires that we never relinquish our quest for that truth.*[31]

Monsignor James Turro who writes for *Magnificat* insists: *Humility says much about a person's refinement of character. "The boughs that bear most hang lowest."* (English Proverb)[32]

Dominican Fr. Sertillanges observes: *Pride aspires to the least height, disdaining to surpass itself; humility is quite ready for the sublimest prospects. Some men would be capable of great things if they did not think themselves great.*[33]

John Adams exhorted his grandson John, the son of President John Quincy Adams: *The Lord deliver us from all*

[30] Zenit, July 23, 2003.
[31] *Magnificat,* June 2001.
[32] *Magnificat,* October, 2002.
[33] *Magnificat,* July 2001.

family pride. No pride, John, no pride. To his granddaughter Caroline he wrote: *You are not singular in your suspicions that you know but little. The longer I live, the more I read, the more patiently I think, and the more anxiously I inquire, the less I seem to know...Do justly. Love mercy. Walk humbly. That is enough...So questions and so answers your affectionate grandfather.*[34]

G. K. Chesterton maintained that humility is the key to contentment. *As for pride, pride doesn't go before a fall. Pride is the fall.* Demosthenes pointed out: *Nothing is so easy as to deceive one's self; for what we wish, we readily believe.* Marie Curíe confessed: *I never see what has been done; I only see what remains to be done.* The famous Michelangelo when complimented on his masterpieces would say, *I am still learning.* Giuditta Tettamanzi, the ninety-three-year-old mother of Cardinal Dionigi Tettamanzi, the archbishop of Milan, told her son when he became a priest and then again when he became a cardinal: *Only with humility will you be able to take souls to God.*[35]

Living Humility

"The way I must take, the right way for me, is that of humility." Bl. John XXIII

The virtue of humility is founded not only on grace but also on self-knowledge. *Humility means looking at ourselves as we really are, honestly and without excuses. And when we realize that we are worth hardly anything, we can then open ourselves to God's greatness: it is there our greatness lies,* writes St. Josemaría Escrivá.[36] In other words, we understand our strong points but also our defects. Humility allows us to be at ease with our abilities without having to thrust them down another's throat. We graciously accept compliments rather than denying our ability in some area. To deny abilities is another form of pride. Isaacs warns: *There is also the vice that has to do with abdicating one's*

[34] ***John Adams,*** *Op. Cit.*, p. 650. [35] Zenit, July 14, 2002.
[36] ***Friends of God***, *Op. Cit.,* No. 96.

honor and good name.[37]

To grow in self-knowledge one needs to cooperate with one special gift of the Holy Spirit—the gift of knowledge. The knowledge that the Holy Spirit gives us is not book knowledge or prophetic knowledge but knowledge about ourselves and our failings. Fr. Gary Devery, OFM, Cap. from Sydney, Australia explains that the *first work of the Holy Spirit is to convince us of our sin...It is a convincing that is not accusative but diagnostic...the Holy Spirit draws us into a journey of conversion...an emptying of ourselves of our egoism...The word of God begins us on the journey of knowing ourselves profoundly. When we are salvifically convinced of our sin we arrive at humility. Living in humility by the grace of the Holy Spirit the Christian journey of permanent conversion can be lived in simplicity. With this self-knowledge revealed by the Holy Spirit the Christian has discernment on his life. Discernment is a principle aspect of the gift of knowledge given by the Holy Spirit.*[38]

Remember, each time we receive the sacraments we receive an infusion of the Gifts of the Holy Spirit. So, to grow in humility, we need the frequent reception of the sacraments to receive the gift of self-knowledge. Teach this to your teens and young adults! In particular, the frequent reception of the sacrament of reconciliation is vital in the development of humility. One indication that you are growing in humility is the frequency of receiving the sacrament of confession. Proud people avoid confession. That is not to say that people who go to weekly confession have achieved high humility. They could be guilty of spiritual pride. See how careful we have to be with this virtue and its companion vices?

How does a humble person react? Dr. David Isaacs points out that:

A humble person recognizes his own

[37] ***Character Building***, *Op. Cit.*, p. 205.

[38] Zenit, Aug. 30, 2002.

inadequacy, qualities and abilities, and presses them into service, doing good without attracting attention or expecting the applause of others.[39]

In addition, humility is the virtue that refrains from purposely exciting jealousy or envy.

St. Peter Julian Eymard taught that *there are two motives and two ways to practice humility: one comes from the realization of our sinfulness, and the other from our love of Jesus Christ humiliated. The first type is negative humility; the second is positive. Both types are found in humility of the mind and in humility of the heart.* To live the virtue of humility, teach your teens to imitate Jesus. Jesus, being God, knew all things, yet He never boasted, bragged, or even indicated that He knew all. Teens, who think they know everything, need to emulate the example of Christ. Christ, being God, could do everything perfectly. Yet He never indicated this in His words or actions. Teens need to mimic Jesus in this as well. *Even in His teachings, He attests that He merely repeats the words of His Father...He never boasted of anything, never sought to shine, to pass for a wit, or to seem better informed than others. Even when He stood in the midst of the doctors in the temple, He listened to them and asked them questions to improve His knowledge...[I]f He is asked for a miracle, He prays to His Father before working it, as if to beg for the needed power,* explains St. Peter Julian. Following Christ's manner, *[d]o not make of God's gifts a subject of personal pride, nor look upon them as your own, as if they came from you, but confess that they come from God. Do not rely on them as if they were part of what is due you by nature, but live a continual and actual dependence on God, never deeming yourself the owner of the gifts you ceaselessly receive from Him.*[40]

St. Bernard broke down the virtue of humility into three stages: **sufficient humility, abundant humility, and superabundant humility**. *Sufficient humility consists in*

[39] ***Character Building***, *Op. Cit.*, p. 205.
[40] ***In The Light of the Monstrance,*** *Op. Cit.*, pp. 70-71.

submitting to him who is one's superior and not imposing oneself on him who is one's equal; abundant humility consists in submitting oneself to him who is one's equal and not imposing oneself on him who is lower than oneself; superabundant humility consists in submitting oneself to him who is lower than oneself.[41] Superabundant humility is the humility of Pope John Paul II and the saints. Research has begun into the possible beatification of John Paul I. His motto was "Humility."

How can we teach our children/teens this virtue? To teach sufficient humility instill the following points in your young children:

1. The foundation of this virtue is the knowledge that one is a son or daughter of God. This is the measure of our true worth.
2. All gifts, abilities, talents, beauty, come from the goodness of God and are to be used for His honor and glory.
3. Point out the areas the child/teen does well in but also, with affection, point out the areas in which the child must improve.
4. Avoid instilling pride in your child/teen by bragging about him to others, exaggerating his abilities, making him self-conscious through excessive compliments about the child's/teen's good looks.
5. Enforce rules and your authority.
6. Insist that blame be correctly placed. If a child runs into a table, the child is at fault, not the table. Everyone makes mistakes. To accept one's mistakes is a sign of maturity/humility.
7. When something wrong is done, insist that the child/teen say *I'm sorry.* This is humility in word and action.
8. Do not praise a child/teen for doing what the child should do. Encourage him but do not praise him.
9. Encourage your child/teen to serve others without seeking compliments.
10. Impress on your child/teen that integrity of character is

[41] *Sententiae,* No. 37, Pl 183, 755.

more important than success.[42]

To teach abundant humility instill the following points in your teens:

1. Teach your teen that God is present in each person. As such we are all equals. We are never superior to another.
2. Everyone has talents and abilities. While our teen's talents may be more noticeable, the talents of others may be more important.
3. Help your teen to appreciate the talents of others by exposing them to music, art, culture, etc. Tell them that they can learn something from everyone they deal with if they focus *on their qualities and forget about their defects.*
4. Explain to your teen the importance of taking an interest in other people. Give practical examples on how to do this. We discussed many of these in previous virtues.
5. Point out examples of prideful attitudes in themselves.
6. Encourage your teen to avoid self-sufficiency that *results in a person being unable to talk about anything but himself*, a refusal to seek advice or guidance which seeks a false sense of freedom/independence.
7. Continually remind your teens of the standards and values they are to live. Without a living faith in God a teen/adult cannot practice humility.
8. Emphasize the importance of self-control. *Show them generous affection so that they learn not to be so boastful about their achievements; to accept other people's ingratitude; to forget themselves, to give themselves generously to the service of others for the love of God.*
9. Teach your teens to avoid being loud; or acting or dressing in an odd manner. All extremes are to be avoided.
10. Help your teen to see the value of accepting corrections.
11. Teach your teen the custom of asking before each action, *will this serve or be pleasing to God?*[43]

The saints advise these practices for your young adults:

1. Think little of yourself.

[42] Thoughts taken from David Isaacs, ***Character Building***, *Op. Cit.*, pp. 208-210. [43] *Ibid.*,pp. 208-211.

2. Do not desire nor seek honors or esteem.
3. Accept with patience the insults, lack of esteem, etc. of others.
4. Do not exalt in the praise of others.
5. Remember your sinfulness.
6. Keep your eyes on your faults, not those of others.
7. Refrain from speaking about oneself.
8. Avoid stubbornness unless the matter deals with truth.
9. Avoid all envy. It is part of pride.
10. Seek and accept advice.
11. Seek and accept corrections.
12. Make use of the sacrament of confession regularly.

The first and final points are key to living this virtue. Dr. David Isaacs insists: *It is very important for everyone to be an achiever and to know he is an achiever. But it is also important for a person to learn to lose, to recognize that he does not do everything right, that he is not indispensable, that the reason he has endowments is that God wanted him to have them. With young people of this sort one has to find ways by which they do experience small failures—and, of course, one has to make more demands on them. A person can only reach the highest level of humility when he realizes his objective personal inadequacy.*[44]

Many of the virtues discussed previously help to instill the virtue of humility such as flexibility, moderation, modesty, gentleness, and studiousness. Gentleness controls one's anger while fostering obedience. *Studiousness will control the appetite [that desires] to know too much out of curiosity.*[45]

The highest level of humility, the humility of the saints, is called superabundant humility. The Holy Father lives this level of humility. The story is told of a priest from the U.S. who was visiting Rome. During his visit he received an invitation to have lunch with John Paul II. Before the luncheon he stopped at a church to make a visit. Going into

---

[44] ***Character Building***, *Op. Cit.*, p. 211. [45] *Ibid.*

the church he was shocked to find a priest from his seminary class begging for food. His classmate, who left the priesthood, was now nothing more than a common beggar. Upset by the encounter, the priest blurted out his sad experience over lunch with the Holy Father. *You and that priest come to dinner tomorrow*, instructed the Pope. The next day the priest searched for the beggar who first refused to go but finally relented. The priest cleaned him up, lent him clothing, and then the two kept their dinner date with the Pope. After dinner John Paul II motioned for the priest to excuse the two of them. Turning to the beggar, the Pope asked him to hear his confession. Dumbfounded the beggar refused saying, *Holy Father, I'm no longer a priest. I cannot hear your confession.* The Pope kindly reassured him, *You are a priest forever. I tell you, you can hear my confession.* So he did. Then the beggar sank to his knees asking the Holy Father to hear his confession. The former priest was restored to good standing and appointed an assistant at the Roman parish where he formerly begged for food. Now he begs God for souls. Teach your teens to imitate the example of the Holy Father.

It takes deep, interior growth to achieve this level. When a person reaches this level he understands that he is a great sinner, that without God he is a nothing, without the grace of God he would be guilty of the worst of sins. This cannot be taught. It must be learned. From whom do we learn it? Fr. Alvarez recommends that we go to Mary, who is the mother of Humility. Christ humbled Himself to take on our human nature while Mary humbled herself to accept her mission from God: ***Behold the handmaid of the Lord; be it done unto me according to thy word* (*Lk.* 1:38).** Note Our Lady's word "handmaid" which is another word for servant. She does not call herself "first lady," "first mother," "queen of heaven," but servant. What humility! Before we leave this section I would like to share with you the following:

A New year's Resolution Prayer

Lord Thou knowest better than I know myself that I am growing older and will some day be old.

Keep me from the fatal habit of thinking I must say something on every subject and on every occasion.

Release me from craving to try to straighten out everybody's affairs.

Make me thoughtful but not moody, helpful but not bossy. With my vast store of wisdom, it seems a pity not to use it at all—but Thou knowest, Lord, that I want friends at the end.

Keep my mind free from the recital of endless details—give me wings to get to the point.

Seal my lips on my aches and pains.

I Dare Not ask for improved memory but a growing humility and a lessening cocksureness when my memory seems to clash with the memories of others.

Teach me the glorious lesson that occasionally I may be mistaken.

Keep me reasonably sweet. I do want to be a saint—but a sour old person is one of the crowning works of the devil

Give me the ability to see good things in unexpected places and talents in unexpected people. Give me the grace to tell them so. Amen.[46]

Examples of Humility

"Virtue—even attempted virtue—brings light; indulgence brings fog." C. S. Lewis

All of the saints imitated this degree of humility. St. Bernadette Soubirous, the visionary of Lourdes, remarked: *The Blessed Virgin used me as a broom to remove dust. When the work is finished, the broom is placed behind the door and left there.*[47] Bernadette was referring to her hidden life in a convent after Our Lady's apparitions to her. It was not the life Bernadette sought but she embraced it out of obedience to the Church authorities.

---

[46] *Apostolate of The Little Flower,* Jan.-Feb. 1987.
[47] ***Lives of the Saints Illustrated Part I***, *Op. Cit.*, p. 75.

When Bl. Francisco, one of the three visionary children of Fatima, was preparing to make his First Holy Communion, he asked his sister, Bl. Jacinta, and his cousin, Lucia, to tell him his faults. He did not want to leave anything out of his first confession. When they reminded him of some of his defects, he gratefully accepted their corrections. Do we willingly ask for or accept corrections or do we instead angrily give excuses for our failings?

St. Francis Xavier became acquainted with St. Ignatius Loyola, the founder of the Jesuits, while he was teaching at the University of Paris. Since Francis was a brilliant young doctor of philosophy, St. Ignatius sent him students to tutor. St. Peter Faber, one of the first Jesuits, protested saying: *With Francis spoiled already by his little success, do you think it is wise to add to it? When a man is full of pride and vanity already, why not leave bad enough alone?* Ignatius smiled, *I admit I am playing a hazardous game. But the stake is worth it. Unless I am entirely wrong, he is too genuine...to be fooled long by a little success. Or even by a big one. The sooner he succeeds, the sooner he will see the futility of succeeding.*

When Francis dreamed dreams of greatness, Ignatius was there to point out reality: *Suppose you did discover a new system [of philosophy], as you call it. What would it mean beyond the praises of a few empty heads? Suppose the greatest success you can imagine. What would it do for you except to expose you to the one great danger, which is pride? "What does it profit a man if he gain the whole world, and suffer the loss of his own soul?"*

It wasn't long before Francis ran out of funds to finance his active social life. Ignatius stepped in with loans to help him out. Again St. Peter Faber protested: *Have it your own way, of course. But I am not at all sure that was wise. On top of everything else you lend him money to continue his foolish running around. More vanity, that's all. What possible good can that do? "It can help to show him the vanity of vanities, perhaps,"* responded Ignatius. *"I know that gratitude is the rarest of virtues, but you must also remember that we are dealing with the rarest of men. Let him once wake up to realities, and you will see a return to my investment."* Ignatius was richly rewarded for his investment. When Xavier finally learned the folly of pride and vanity he threw in his lot with the Jesuits eventually becoming a saint!

But before he did, at the end of the each school year, the University of Paris held an interclass race. The undisputed champion, St. Martin de Tours, a Frenchman, found himself facing off with Francis Xavier, a young Spaniard. A close race, Xavier won it in the last seconds becoming the new champion of the school. Although Francis never bragged about his racing ability nor referred to his win over Martin de Tours, interiorly he struggled violently against prideful thoughts. (We don't have to boast to be prideful. Thoughts also count!) To kill his pride, unbeknownst to anyone, he began to wear tight cords of rope around his ankles since they were the source of his pride. (They had won his race.) In time the tightly tied ropes caused his skin to actually grow over them causing him extreme pain in walking. After seeing the sorry state of Xavier's ankles, St. Peter Faber confessed: *Why, he never said a word about his running, even when he was champion. How could a man be more modest? Of course, he might have had his own thoughts about it. Anyhow, God will surely accept his foolish little sacrifice.* The following day, Xavier admitted his reason for the ill-advised mortification: *Forgive me, Peter. It was on account of winning the races...at school, you know. It was foolish of me, but I had to do something.*[48]

St. Osmund, a Norman, was named bishop of Salisbury, England, in 1078. *His humility can be seen in the way he ended a dispute with...St. Anselm. As Anselm was journeying to Windsor, Osmund came to kneel before him, begging his forgiveness.*[49]

---

[48] ***Tales of Xavier**, Op. Cit.*, pp. 24-35. [49] *Magnificat,* December 2001.

Many Catholic kings and emperors showed humility by offering their countries to God or to Our Lady. The first king of Portugal, Alonso I, offered Portugal as a fief to Our Lady of Clairvaux in 1147. In 1646, following the lead of the first monarch, King John IV of Portugal swore fidelity to Mary under her title of the Immaculate Conception (this was prior to the dogma of the Immaculate Conception). *Since Mary was considered Queen and Patroness of Portugal the Portuguese monarchs never wore the crown. It was reserved exclusively for the Immaculate Virgin.*[50]

St. Magdalen Sophie Barat, born in 1779 in France, became the foundress of the Madames of the Sacred Heart. As a child and adolescent, her older brother Louis became her teacher. When he was ordained, then sent to Paris, he asked his parents to allow Magdalen to accompany him so that he could continue her instruction, particularly in the way of sanctity. Something occurred one day that led him to scold her saying: *You will never be a saint, Sophie!* After the scolding, Sophie reflected on her actions: *I must set myself to be very humble.* This was her personal struggle throughout her life. Upon her deathbed she counseled her sisters: *Be very humble; for, you see, if this step of the ladder is wanting, you will never get to heaven. Please pray for me...The saints have done so much for souls because they made no more account of themselves than of the dust under their feet.*[51]

St. Martin de Porres exercised heroic humility. As a doctor he cared for all the sick brothers and priests in the monastery infirmary. One of the priests resented being cared for by a mulatto. Yelling at Martin he asked: *What are you doing here, Half-Breed? You don't belong in a convent. You belong in a jail! What idiot let you into my room. I'd sooner be touched by a snake than have you put a finger on me.* How would you or your teen act in this situation? This is how Martin reacted. Falling on his knees at the bedside

---

[50] Brother Francis Mary, "Portugal: The Land of Holy Mary."
[51] ***Follow The Saints,*** *Op. Cit.*, pp. 83, 85.

of the sick priest, he told him:*O Father, what keen eyes God has given you! You have seen my sinfulness at a glance! I marvel at your patience with such as me. You speak truly, Father. But for the mercy of God I should indeed be in a penitentiary now.* When other brothers came to Martin's aid he told them: *It is all right. My patient has discovered I am not worthy to kiss his hands. I therefore kiss his feet to show that I agree with him.* Wow! That's why Martin is a saint and we are still struggling. The patients that treated Martin with contempt and scorn, he treated with the greatest patience, attention, and love. Martin also developed the habit of bringing in the sick to the convent and caring for them in his room. The other priests and brothers complained fearing that he would bring in people with diseases that would spread throughout the monastery. His superior placed him under obedience not to bring in anymore outsiders. Shortly afterwards Martin found a bleeding Inca on the street and brought him back secretly to his room where he cured the man through a miracle. His superior was not amused with Martin's disobedience so Martin received a stiff punishment. He humbly received the punishment in silence then faithfully carried it out. Much later the matter must have come up again. At that time Martin explained that he had to make the choice between a man-made rule and the life of a man. *Maybe I was wrong but I knew the Indian would die before I could get him to my sister's home, whereas he might live if I could take him to my cell, which was so much closer. I though that, in this case, obedience should yield to mercy, to charity. Was I wrong, Father?* The superior replied: *You acted in good faith, my son. And perhaps you did well. At any rate, in the future, be guided by your own common sense—and your charity.*[52]

Humility was a virtue instilled in the Martin girls. St. Thérèse recounts that one day her mother said to her: "*Thérèse if you will kiss the ground I will give you a halfpenny.*" "*No thank you, Mamma, I would rather go without the halfpenny.*" Thérèse was too proud to kiss the

[52] ***Blessed Martin De Porres,*** *Op. Cit.*, pp. 24, 27.

ground then but her mother kept trying to teach her humility through different means.[53] Years later in the convent the humility her mother worked so hard to develop bore fruit. Thérèse' cheerful acceptance of unfair blame along with the criticism of Mother Marie de Gonzague, her Mother Superior, found Thérèse kissing the ground each time she ran in to her! She writes: *I see myself subject to many frailties, but they never surprise me...it is so sweet to feel myself weak and little.*[54] When she was dying one of the sisters asked her for a favor. She showed impatience toward the request. Immediately she composed herself then told another sister: *"How glad I am that you have seen my imperfection," she confided to another Sister, "I am strengthened by the thought that that Sister has seen my lack of virtue; I am glad to see myself as I really am."*[55] Then shortly before her death she revealed her superabundant humility: *As for me, the only light I have is to see my utter nothingness...The greatest thing that the Almighty has worked in me, is to have made me see my littleness and my powerlessness for all good."*[56] Why not teach your children, when they are small, to kiss the ground each morning as they say the "Morning Offering"? This begins the day with a beautiful act of humility toward God.

During the Black Hawk War, a large percent of the soldiers fighting came from state militias. Farmers and craftsmen would sign up for tours of twenty days. When their time was up, they simply went home even though the war was still raging. The commanders of each unit would urge their men to reenlist but only a fourth would agree. *Abraham Lincoln, unable to secure enough men to reenlist under him as their company commander, accepted his discharge and immediately reenlisted as a private in the company of his friend, Elijah Iles.*[57] That was an act of humility for Lincoln to do. Few men who hold important positions will volunteer for lesser ones. Only men who are truly great take lesser

---

[53] St. Thérèse, ***Story of a Soul***, p. 21.
[54] *Ibid.*, p. 367.
[55] **Novissima Verba**, p. 91.
[56] ***Story of a Soul***, *Op. Cit.*, p. 154.
[57] ***Twilight Of Empire***, *Op. Cit.*, p. 329.

positions. Lincoln was not the only truly great man in Iles' company. In fact, his company was *made up of privates who were former generals, colonels, captains, and other distinguished men.*[58]

Charles Dickens was a very humble man. Several times he was invited to perform his works before Queen Victoria. Each time he declined. He was not interested in such an honor. Dickens was an actor more than a writer. In fact, an audition had been arranged for him with a famous theatre company but due to illness he missed the tryout. By missing out on the role he had no choice but to turn to writing. His misfortune gave the world cherished literature. After writing ***A Christmas Carol*** Dickens decided to act out the book as a one man play. He wanted each character done properly so he decided to do the play himself. After his first performance a newspaperman complained that one of the characters was not performed as he contemplated the part so Dickens changed his adaptation to suit the newspaperman's concept saying, *whenever I am wrong, I am indebted to the one who tells me.* Once he wrote a scathing criticism of Americans. Later in 1886 while touring the United States he gave a speech retracting his criticism of America. He furthermore asked that this speech be included in each addition of his book entitled ***American Notes*** for prosperity.

Another very humble man was saying his rosary as he traveled by train decades ago. A college student occupied the same coach and thought the man a well-to-do peasant but out of touch with reality since he was praying the rosary. The student interrupted the man saying, *Sir, do you still believe in such outdated things? "Yes, I do. Do you not?" asked the man.* Laughing, the student replied, *"I do not believe in such silly things. Take my advice. Throw the rosary out through this window, and learn what science has to say about it." "Science? I do not understand this science? Perhaps you can explain it to me," the man said humbly with*

[58] *Ibid.*, p. 354.

some tears in his eyes. The student saw that the man was deeply moved. So to avoid further hurting the feelings of this man, he said: "Please give me your address and I will send you some literature to help you on this matter." The man fumbled in the inside pocket of his coat and gave the boy his visiting card. On glancing at the card, the student bowed his head in shame and became silent. On the card he read: "Louis Pasteur. Director of the Institute of Scientific Research, Paris."

In Vietnam it was the custom for the father to reprove his young and adult children yearly in a family session. Part of the purpose of this was to correct while the other part was to instill humility in family members. Upon the death of the father, this responsible fell to the eldest son. But in Cardinal Thuân's family, as his maternal grandfather was dying, he called his family together and assigned Thuân's mother with the task of correcting her brothers on the anniversary of her father's death. It did not matter that her brothers were bishops and political figures. *It was her duty to tell each of them where they had done right and where wrong. He said, "It is only natural that Hiep, who listened to me so well in my life, should speak in my name when I am gone."* Each year *when Hiep addressed the family, they listened with bowed heads and invariably thanked her for her strong and reproving words. The annual ritual...continued until, through a series of tragic events, all of Kha's sons were killed or forced into exile.*

Humility was so engrained in his family that Cardinal Thuân wanted to join a contemplative order to avoid an ecclesiastic career filled with honors. His Cardinal had other plans for him as we saw in an earlier chapter. Later he would write: *True leadership is founded in a spirit of humility and charity as shown in the Gospel.* When Fr. Thuân was appointed bishop of the city of Nha Trang he was disappointed. *Since the death of his uncles, he wanted to lead a life hidden from the public eye. He had seen the price one paid for honors and power, and he wanted none of it.* His mother, rather than proud of her son's new honor counseled him: *A priest is a priest. The Church has honored you and given you a greater mission, but as a person, you have not changed. You are still a priest, and that is the most important thing to remember.* In his book, ***The Road of Hope,*** Cardinal Thuân offers this advice for those seeking to grow in the virtue of humility: *When you assume the responsibilities of leadership, remember that even after you have achieved success in the task at hand, you should still regard yourself as a useless servant and recognize that you still have many faults and failings. And do not be surprised or annoyed when the response to your efforts is only misunderstanding and ingratitude.*

Cardinal Thuân's uncle Diem was offered the office of prime minister by the Vietnamese emperor. Diem did not immediately accept the position. Instead he wanted to be a contemplative Benedictine. In fact, he had taken preliminary vows *at the Abbey of St. Andrew in Bruges, Belgium. He was still a patriot, and he had not forgotten his father's wish, but Diem had begun to think that living the life of a monk could also be a great contribution to his country.*[59] In time, like his grandfather, he left his personal wishes behind to help his country in a role he did not seek. A proud man would have snapped up the title and position in an instant

Peggy Noonan, in her book on President Ronald Reagan, confesses: *I think his character is the least criticized of any great political leader of the century.* She explains how she searched for stories that would give a completely balanced picture of him but found it difficult to find anything negative. *[T]he stories are almost invariably about his graciousness, generosity, good humor.* The only negative story she did find ended in an act of humility. It appears that Reagan made a reservation at a popular restaurant for himself but when he arrived there was no record of his reservation.

[59] ***The Miracle of Hope,*** *Op. Cit.,* pp. 17, 94, 111, 143, 168.

Reagan lost his temper,...berated the man, was rude and impatient and left. But the next morning he went back to apologize to the man. Peggy, in her research, found that *[h]e was not given to conceit, didn't play with people when he had the chance, didn't show up places late because he's the most important and interesting man invited, so the fun will have to start when he gets there.* When he was sworn in as President of the United States, he had his mother's Bible opened to ***2 Chron.*** 7:14: ***If my people, which are called by my name, shall humble themselves, and pray, and seek My face, and turn from their wicked ways; then will I hear from heaven, and will forgive their sin, and will heal their land.*** Next to this verse his mother had earlier written: *A most wonderful verse for the healing of the nations.* When Reagan entered the Oval Office for the first time, he stopped to pray first. He had the humility to know Who was the power in control of the world and it wasn't him. When he left the office eight years later he summed up that timeframe:*...I never thought it was my style or the words I used that made a difference: It was the content. I wasn't a great communicator, but I communicated great things, and they didn't spring full bloom from my brow, they came from the heart of a great nation—from our experience, our wisdom and our belief in the principles that have guided us for two centuries. They called it the Reagan revolution. Well, I'll accept that, but for me it always seemed like the great Rediscovery—a rediscovery of our values and our common sense.*[60]

Henry Ward Beecher, a famous author and minister, lived in Brooklyn, New York. It became a proverb in the area that *[i]f you want a favor from Beecher, kick him!* The nastier people were to Beecher, the kinder he was toward them. That's humility![61]

Are teens really capable of practicing humility? Yes. I've seen them do it. At a family party my niece was receiving a

---

[60] ***When Character Was King***, *Op. Cit.*, pp. 83, 133, 161, 315.
[61] ***Twelve Tests of Character***, *Op. Cit.*, p. 162.

great deal of attention because of her newly discovered acting and singing talents. Her older brother was standing in the group listening with interest to all his sister's accolades. I finally turned to him asking how school was going. We chatted for about fifteen minutes with me digging for information until I finally pulled out of him that he had recently won two first place medals in cross country. My father, overhearing our conversation, added that these were in addition to the collection of medals he already had. Tom, rather than basking in our praise, instead turned our attention to his sister Kathryn, telling us that she also had a collection of first place medals. These teens have been trained by their parents to do the best they can in everything they do but never to brag about their successes.

Examples of Pride

"The perfect man never speaks of self."
Aristotle

Scripture is filled with examples of pride. We have the pride of Satan, Adam and Eve, the builders of the tower of Babel, the Israelites, King Saul, even the apostles who argued over who was the greatest. St. John the Baptist was killed by the pride of Herod. Herod was glowing over his generous offer to his niece until she demanded the head of John on a platter. Suddenly Herod found himself trapped in the vice of human respect. While he did not want to kill John he likewise did not want to look foolish in the eyes of his banquet guests. Better to be a murderer than a fool!

Another example of pride is found in Franciscan Roger Bacon. Bacon was a brilliant man capable of great sanctity but his pride got in the way. Born in 1214, he hungered for truth throughout his life. When he was thirty-seven he became a Franciscan in the hopes of satisfying *his intellectual hunger...[T]he Poverello's* [St. Francis of Assisi] *meekness did not sink very deep into his heart; for Bacon hurled himself with unrestrained ferocity upon all whom he suspected of upholding erroneous opinions. [St.] Albert [the*

Great] came under fire, as did St. Bonaventure, the master general of his Order. He caused trouble everywhere, even among his own brethren. Nay, he went so far as to cast the horoscope of Christ, maintaining that God could not have saved the world except by virtue of certain heavenly conjunctions! It took the intervention of two popes to save him from himself. Yet he was a brilliant man. *There is scarcely a science which Bacon left untouched: mathematics, optics, and medicine were but three...His book on The Secrets of Art and Nature is filled with visions of the future—steamboats, railways, balloons, cranes, submarines, microscopes, telescopes, and the terrible effects of gunpowder. In optics, long before Galileo and Newton, he formulated the laws of the reflection and refraction of light. It was he who suggested to Clement IV a reform of the Julian calendar, though this was not done until three centuries later...This great scholar...helped to found the rational method...Though a Christian genius, Roger Bacon carried within himself forces that were hostile to his faith.*[62] His brilliance did not make him a saint!

Theodosia, the daughter of Aaron Burr, was jealous of her father's attention. She disliked the fact that he traveled between Philadelphia, Washington and Albany, New York pleading law cases. She wanted him home with her since her mother was dead and her older brothers were away as well. Her peevishness led to her neglecting her studies much to the chagrin of her tutor. Her father, learning of the situation, sent her a strongly worded letter attacking her pride:...*I am sorry, very sorry, that you are obliged to submit to some reproof. Indeed, I am afraid that your want of attention and politeness require it...A moment's reflection will convince you that this conduct will naturally be construed into arrogance; as if you felt that all attention was due to you, and as if you felt above showing the least to anybody...I believe you will in the future avoid it. Observe how Natalie [her friend] replies to the smallest civility offered to her...*

---

[62] ***Cathedral and Crusade,*** *Op. Cit.*, pp. 342-343.

Receive with calmness every reproof, whether made kindly or unkindly; whether just or unjust. Consider within yourself whether there has been no cause for it. If it has been groundless and unjust, nevertheless...we must learn to bear these things; and, let me tell you, that you will always feel much better, much happier, for having borne with serenity the spleen of anyone, than if you had returned spleen for spleen.

You will, I am sure, my dear Theodosia, pardon such two grave pages from one who loves you, and whose happiness depends very much on yours. Read it over twice. Make me no promises on the subject. On my return, I shall see in half an hour whether what I have written has been well or ill received. If well it will have produced an effect...[63]

One of the most puzzling events in life is to see people with little wisdom, few virtues, little common sense, no humility, and in many cases scant intelligence achieve high positions in business, politics and other positions of authority. Could God plan this to teach those under these people patience and long suffering? Whatever the reason, history is filled with such examples. In the previous chapter we met Brigadier General William Hull during the War of 1812. Prior to the declaration of war, Hull commissioned a schooner to take excess baggage and nonessential personnel up north toward Detroit. His son, not known for sobriety or intelligence packed up *his father's papers, orders, notes, correspondence, accounts and field reports. Since it was the end of the month, he also thoughtfully included the up-to-date muster rolls for the whole army, company by company.*[64] A delegation of officers asked him to reconsider doing this since war may have been declared already and the schooner could be captured by the British who also prowled the lake. Hull was too proud to listen to advice or reconsider. The officers were correct. War had been declared and the British captured all of Hull's orders and information on the strength

---

[63] Anne Colver, ***Theodosia*** (NY: Holt, Rinehart and Winston, 1962) pp. 35-36.
[64] ***Gateway To Empire***, *Op. Cit.*, p. 504.

of the U.S. army. As mentioned before, it was also from his correspondence that the British learned of his morbid fear of the Indians. Hull, when he learned that war was declared, *neglected to inform Fort Mackinac, Fort Dearborn, and Fort Wayne.*[65] He was too upset over the loss of his private papers to the British due to his pride, to focus on his responsibilities. This left the three forts vulnerable to attacks. When Hull finally wrote to the forts ordering them to prepare to defend themselves, he neglected to send the orders. If the commander of Fort Dearborn had received that order there would not have been an evacuation of the fort that resulted in the ensuing massacre.

At the Massacre of Fort Dearborn in Chicago the commander of the fort refused to heed the advice and information given to him by the Indians, Indian agents and the traders. The fort had enough food, provisions, and arms to out last any Indian attack. In fact, before they vacated the fort, the soldiers spent the whole night disposing of the arms so they wouldn't fall into Indian hands. The commander refused to believe the Indians would attack after the whites left the fort. It was pride alone that was responsible for the massacre. Then once the attack began, the commander again refused to heed the advice of friendly Indians and Indian fighters on how to repulse the attack. He insisted on doing things his way. His pride cost most of the lives under his protection although he personally escaped death. While the prideful cause suffering and death to others, they seem to have a knack for surviving. Meanwhile, up in Detroit, where Hull was snugly in control, a small force of British demanded that he surrender Detroit. *Initially flabbergasted at the unmitigated gall of the inferior force demanding the surrender of a superior force safe within its fortifications, the American troops finally burst into laughter...But then, when Hull remained closeted with the two British officers...the laughter dwindled away and was replaced by a faint but growing apprehension. Surely the*

[65] ***A Sorrow In Our Heart***, *Op. Cit.*, p. 692.

general couldn't possibly even consider such a demand![66] Not only did he consider it, he surrendered against the strong advice of his officers. Look at the high cost of pride!

Prior to the start of the Black Hawk War, Illinois governor Reynolds decided to make a national name for himself. He had been ordered to raise a state militia then join his militia to the regular U.S. army under General Atkinson who would command both. Reynolds and his men were eager for action so Reynolds disobeyed orders, drew up orders as though they came from the U.S. army then had a brigade major sign them. He lacked the virtues of obedience, sincerity and humility.[67] In the chapter on temperance we learned that it was his militia that triggered the Black Hawk War when the drunk soldiers opened fire on the surrendering Indians.

Probably one of the most famous symbols of the vice of pride is the ring in the book ***Lord of the Rings*** by J. R. R. Tolkien. Joseph Pearce, writing on the book, explains that *the character of Gollum is debased by his attachment to the Ring, the symbol of the sin of pride. The possessor of the Ring is possessed by his possession and, in consequence, is dispossessed of his soul. The wearer of the Ring always becomes invisible to those that are good but at the same time become more visible to the eyes of evil.*[68] Encourage your teens and young adults to either read the book or see the DVD. Then discuss the film/book together.

The Virtue of Optimism

"The Christian idea has not been tried and found wanting. It has been found difficult, and left untried." G. K. Chesterton

During the hormone-laden emotional ups and downs of adolescence, the practice of the virtue of optimism is a welcome virtue. But this virtue, like all the rest, is

[66] ***Gateway To Empire***, *Op. Cit.*, p. 675.
[67] ***Twilight Of Empire*** *Op. Cit.*, p. 242. [68] Zenit, Nov. 15, 2001.

necessary through all of life's stages since *life is a never-ending road to Calvary,* so well put in the musical *Les Miserables.* Who is an optimist? Dr. David Isaacs explains:

> **An optimist has confidence, based on reason, in his own abilities, in the help which he can obtain from others and in the ability of others: thus in every situation, he can identify, first of all, the positive elements and the opportunities for improvement which it offers and secondly, the difficulties and obstacles in the way of such improvement; he takes advantage of everything favorable and faces up to the rest in a sportsmanlike and cheerful manner.**[69]

Optimism can be a virtue, part of one's temperament or based on past successes. When it is simply part of one's temperament one can see the bright side of life either realistically or unrealistically. My father is optimistic by nature but he also practices the virtue of optimism. No matter how troubling a situation can be he tries to find a happy conclusion. It can be pouring rain on his picnic but he's positive it will stop shortly so the picnic can continue. If it's bitterly cold, he finds it *bracing...perfect for snowmobiling.* The virtue of optimism *involves being realistic and consciously seeking the positive aspects of a situation before looking for the difficulties.*[70] When the rain continues to wash out my father's picnic despite his optimistic forecast of sun, the virtue of optimism kicks in. He skillfully organizes a way to continue the party by using the covered decks for eating and the other rooms in his country home saying, *at least we won't have to battle the mosquitoes outside.*

Or it may mean trying to see what can be gained from the difficulties in themselves.[71] What to do with a houseful of adults and 30 children of all ages stuck in the house together? *Why we can all can play charades, card games, or simply talk together. We can "bond" which isn't possible*

[69] Dr. David Isaacs, "The Education of Optimism," Instituto de Ciencias de la Educación, University of Navarre, 1986, p. 1.
[70] *Ibid.* [71] Ibid.

when the kids are playing outside, swimming, fishing, or exploring. My father's practice of the virtue of optimism turns rainy afternoons into a fun memories for everyone.

A person whose optimism is based on past successes is living on borrowed time. Nothing, including success, lasts forever. That is why cultivating the virtue of optimism is necessary for the happiness of our children as well as for ourselves.

The vices contrary to the virtue of optimism are pessimism and naiveté.

To practice the virtue of optimism, one must develop confidence in one's own abilities and those of others. *It presupposes reliance on our own well-developed fortitude and the security and knowledge that others are willing to act in our favor. If it is to be meaningful,* Dr. Isaacs notes, *confidence must be based on reality, but always allowing for the possibility that the other and we may improve.*[72] For the most part, when we need urgent help in some matter, people are usually willing to help either through their own good will or by the prompting of their guardian angels. Next we need trust in God and in others. *[O]ptimism which is not based on confidence in God, on the conviction that He always helps us and acts for our good, is fragile and indeed may lead to either naivety or pride.*[73] When we run into difficulties but try to solve the problem completely by ourselves this is usually the vice of pride. *[O]ptimism does not invariably lead to outward jubilation...what optimism gives us is inner peace...For instance, when a near relative dies, we may be optimistic [the person died in the state of grace] yet sad at the same time. Optimism overcomes depression and downheartedness but it is fortitude that conquers sadness.*[74]

To learn the virtue of optimism oneself and to teach it to your teens you must:

---

[72] *Ibid.*, p. 2. [73] *Ibid.* [74] *Ibid.*, pp. 2-3.

1. Be realistic. What can be expected from my abilities and the abilities of others; my character and the character of my companions?
2. Learn to take personal responsibility for one's own life.
3. Allow your teens to make the effort to solve their own problems. Only step in should things get out of hand.
4. Show great affection and loving support toward your teens in success and in failure.
5. Encourage your teen to make good use of his talents, abilities and qualities.
6. Teach your teen to ask help from qualified people in a rational manner.
7. Help your teen to seek the positive aspects of all situations.
8. Train your teen to analyze the difference between an opinion, fact or feeling before reacting. Are the facts objective or subjective?
9. Give pointers to your teen how to resolve obstacles...If a plan does not work, how can it be revised so it will work?
10. Help your teen to see the difference between the important aspects and the trivial aspects of the project. Just because one aspect failed does not mean the whole project is doomed. Just because one person failed in fulfilling his part, someone else or oneself can still complete the project.
11. Point out what can be gained from difficulties (growth in virtues, etc.).
12. Teach your teen to accept suffering and disappointment as steps to human and spiritual maturity.
13. Develop confidence in your teen based on reality. Guide him to try the possible rather than the impossible.
14. Train your teen to trust in others, particularly God. Remind your child that prayers will only move God to do what is best for him rather than satisfying his goals or desires.
15. Serve others to develop optimism. Serving oneself develops pessimism.
16. Put God first to foster optimism.
17. Promote a cheerful atmosphere in your home.
18. Avoid overprotecting your children.
19. Foster the virtue of generosity to increase optimism in your

teen.

20. Help your teen to avoid being critical and judgmental.
21. Teach your teen to concentrate his efforts on helping those around him rather than on trying to change the world. He will have more success!
22. Remind your teen that *optimism and fortitude lead to inner peace and joy.*[75]

Have you noticed that many of the methods used to teach a specific virtue apply to the other virtues as well? It is simply the focus that changes a bit.

Teach your teen to put on a happy face, to accept the contradictions and sufferings of life (and everyone has them) with a cheerful smile rather than a "woe is me" attitude. Fr. David McAstocker, S.J., writes: *Christianity and joy are interchangeable...Cheerfulness, then, is an offshoot of goodness and of grace. It supposes the friendship and love of Christ...No one can consistently go along in a buoyant, lighthearted manner without possessing valor and courage in no small degree. The temper and outlook of a man who is in the world and of the world rises and falls as a barometer in variable weather. He has no settled standards; no anchor to steady him. But it is far otherwise with the saints of God...*

The great spiritual forces, the forces of the heart, are the ones which make for prosperity, contentment, and happiness. And when these springs cease to flow, verily all our coaxing and efforts are in vain...And those private springs which make for the happiness of the individual—courage, faith, and cheerfulness—these are likewise drying up in America...As we see the picture, then, courage and a joyous acceptance of the crosses of life are woefully lacking in the ordinary person we casually meet...

It is, however, in the family circle that the absence of buoyant optimism and joy are chiefly noted. Trial marriages multiply,

---

[75] These are thoughts compiled from Dr. David Isaacs' article, "The Education of Optimism," Instituto de Ciencias de la Educación, University of Navarre, 1986.

divorces increase, and cynics lash out against marriage itself because so many are cowards...

It is especially in pursuit of personal holiness that the importance of cheerfulness is apparent...One of the pet methods employed by the evil one to break down the morale of beginners is to inject into their souls large quantities of discouragement and sadness...We are not called upon to face the work of a whole life at any one moment. Were this the case, the strongest man would fail. But because our tasks are divided into fragments the weakest may carry the load. Even trials and crosses do not come en masse...Hence our part is not such a difficult one. It is to strive to cultivate a cheerful, hopeful, buoyant temper, to refuse to see the dark side of things or to be conquered by the oppression of work or to sit sadly down under the shadow of possible calamities.

There are some who confuse mirth with cheerfulness. The former is brief and transitory...while the latter has a permanency and a serenity all its own. Holy Scripture makes mention of the oil of gladness; and a joyous soul possesses just that. He has the lubricant which makes the machinery of life go along smoothly and quietly...[T]he more one gives of joy, so much the more peace and happiness return to the giver...[76]

Dr. Isaacs warns parents: *If a child tends to be intelligent, good at games and sociable, he has every reason to be optimistic, because everything he does works out well and he finds [superficial] satisfaction...*The danger with such a child is that he can become totally self-reliant. *[I]f he has not learned to rely on others and even need them, especially God, this [superficial] satisfaction will certainly not last, because it is unrelated to the importance of [difficult] personal effort and a recognition of the fact that he is a child of God. This kind of child should be made to face difficulties, to enter into undertakings requiring more effort but which can be achieved, so that he will learn to accept defeat cheerfully*

---

[76] ***The Little Virtues***, *Op. Cit.*, pp. 23, 25, 29-30, 34-35.

and to discover the positive aspects of situations which at first seem hopeless. It is not a question of teaching children simply to be successful, but rather to make the best of every situation, relying on their own abilities, the love of their parents and the love of God.[77] If a naturally successful child is not taught this lesson, when he faces his first failure in life he will not have the capability to handle it. On Ivy League campuses following exams, brilliant students have been known to commit suicide simply because they found out they were not quite as brilliant as other students or they failed to achieve their customary straight "As." I have a friend who never completed college because she was afraid she might not get her customary straight "As." So she would rather not have the degree than achieve it with lesser grades. During the financial crash of 1929 millionaires who could not face losing their wealth jumped out of windows to their deaths. The above examples exhibit the vices related to the virtue of optimism.

At the other extreme are the children, teens and adults who lack self-confidence due to continual failure or the lack of support from parents or friends. For these people, the theological virtue of hope is needed if they are to develop the virtue of optimism. Hope in God's love, hope in God's help, and the hope of struggling daily to do God's will can build this virtue in spite of the natural problems of this group of people. A lavish love helps these people regain their lost confidence in themselves as well as getting them to see that others need them. Rather than trying to convince an unsuccessful person that he is successful, focus instead on creating *situations where he can succeed and, consequently, gain confidence in himself and in them. What we are really suggesting is that parents have to encourage the virtue of fortitude, for the child needs the experience of having tried hard and actually achieved what he set out to do: this will teach him self-confidence. He needs to have benefited from the help of his parents in order to gain confidence in them. However, if children concentrate merely*

[77] "The Education of Optimism," *Op. Cit.*, p. 4.

on achieving certain unimportant objectives, they will not gain that total confidence which fosters the love of God. The important thing is to combine success in trivial matters, with help and support at times of failure and a gradual realization that every individual, however limited, has an inalienable mission to glorify God.[78]

When feeling discouraged about your teens, consider these remarkable observations of Bishop Rylko on World Youth Day: *These young people are different from those of the past: mostly in their 20s, they are truly the sons and daughters of John Paul II's pontificate. They are on the same wavelength as the Pope—they follow him and trust him...Looking at youth today, from the standpoint of Saturday night car crashes, drugs, and delinquency, one would be tempted to paint a sad picture, with no future. However, in my opinion, this is only a partial picture or, rather a false one. Here is a new wave of young people, different from those portrayed by the media and even their parents. Many World Youth Day participants are children of nonbelievers. This new generation is discovering something their parents failed to discover or appreciate. The generation of '68 has been overtaken by the John Paul II generation...*

A new generation is growing, a generation in search of the Lord and of those who have found the Lord; young people who regard the Church as their home, and John Paul II as their spiritual guide, whom they love and trust.[79]

The saints were all optimists, but their optimism, for the most part, was that of the virtue rather than from their natural temperament or success in life. Few saints knew outstanding worldly success. If they were successful, they were usually stripped of it before they died, yet they still died optimistically like St. Thomas More, St. Elizabeth of Hungary, and Venerable Louis Martin. When St. Thomas More's family was pleading with him to save his life by signing the document the king demanded, he told them: *One*

---

[78] *Ibid.*, p. 5. [79] Zenit, August 16, 2000.

can't get to heaven in a feather bed.

An optimistic temperament is usually associated with the sanguine temperament but while there are some saints of this temperament, most of the saints appear to be a combination of the choleric and melancholy temperaments...not strongly optimistic by nature. The optimism of the saints was founded on the fact that they were children of God. They trusted in His divine providence. As they struggled daily to do the will of God they practiced the virtue of hope. Venerable Charles de Foucauld notes, *When I am sad, discouraged about myself and about others, I must think of Jesus in His glory, sitting on the right hand of the Father forever, and rejoice. I should at these times say the glorious mysteries of the Rosary, so as to bathe my spirit in their joy.*

Our Lord speaks, "Never worry about small things. Break away from all that is small and mean, and try to live on the heights, not from pride, but from love.

"You must break with all that is not me. Make to yourself a desert where you will be as much alone with me as Mary Magdalene was alone in the desert with me. It is through detachment that you will attain to this, by driving out all mean thoughts, all littlenessess, which are not evil in themselves, but which succeed in scattering your mind far from me, when you should be contemplating me from morning to night. Fix your mind on me as you work, as you pray; contemplate me unceasingly and give all the time you can to prayer and holy reading, which will unite you to me and through which I will speak to you as I spoke to my parents..."[80]

Sometimes the virtue of optimism is crushed by fear of God or fear of one's past life. St. Maria Faustina Kowalska writes in her diary: *Let no soul even the most miserable, fall prey to doubt; for, as long as one is alive, each one can become a great saint, so great is the power of God's grace. It remains*

[80] Charles de Foucauld, ***Meditations of a Hermit*** (London: Burns and Oates, 1974).

only for us not to oppose God's action.[81]

St. Josemaría points out: *Have you seen how water is stored in reservoirs against a time of drought? In the same way, to achieve that even character that you need in times of difficulty, you have to store up cheerfulness, clear insights and the light which the Lord sends you.*[82] The cheerfulness that he speaks about is based on the virtue of optimism. But life being what it is, we are going to be slammed frequently against the wall. Each slam makes the virtue of optimism difficult to live so it's important to learn some tricks to pick up one's spirits when they are crushed. Besides increasing prayer, using holy water, spending more time before the Blessed Sacrament, I also use the following methods. You may have others but it's good to have a plan in mind when optimism is at low ebb.

- Play peppy, upbeat music such as musicals, folk music, (The Kingston Trio, The Limelighters), Irish music (River Dance, Irish Rovers, Clancy Brothers) and/or Christian pop. My favorite song to play is "I hate that word 'down'" from *The Unsinkable Molly Brown*.
- View a humorous or uplifting film. I favor musicals while my husband favors *Patton*.
- Read a humorous or lighthearted book such as one by Bill Cosby or Erma Bombeck.
- Plan something fun to do such as seeing a play, touring a museum or going for a ride in the country or for a walk in the woods.
- Be sure to get lots of sleep. The lack of sleep makes one pessimistic.
- Develop friendships with cheerful, upbeat people. Avoid the "Eeyores" who will only pull you down with their "woe is me" attitude.
- Develop a hobby that you can retreat to for short periods of time when life is rough.
- Read jokes. *Reader's Digest* is filled with funny ones.
- Read an adventure or clean romance novel for a short escape.

---

[81] St. Maria Faustina Kowalski, ***Diary, Divine Mercy in My Soul*** (MA: Marians of the Immaculate Conception, 1987) #283. [82] ***Furrow***, *Op. Cit.*, #788.

Examples of Optimism

"If you think you can or you think you can't, you are right." Henry Ford

During the American Revolutionary War, the situation became very grim. When the British fleet was sighted in the Chesapeake Bay, American hopes for independence began to sink. To counter the widespread pessimism, *Washington paraded his troops through Philadelphia, every man wearing a sprig of green as an emblem of hope.*[83] That bit of optimistic show was enough to lift the hopes of the soldiers and civilians to persevere in the effort to win their independence. The rest is history.

Bl. John Munden (1543-1584) not only lived optimism but he died optimistic. Denied a fellowship at Oxford because he was Catholic, he simply became a school teacher. Then in 1580 he went abroad to study to become a priest. Two years later he was ordained in Rome then returned to England to minister to the persecuted Catholics. A year later he was capture and imprisoned. *At his trial and sentencing to death, Father Munden was so cheerful that some observers mistakenly thought he had been acquitted.*[84] This is the type of optimism we want to teach our young adults.

President Ronald Reagan's mother was an optimist. When Reagan tried to get a job running the sports department at Montgomery Ward but failed he was devastated. He needed that money to help support his family. His mother just took him aside to explain that God has a plan for everyone's life. If you try and don't succeed, that wasn't part of God's plan for you. Try something else. *Later on, she said, something good would happen and you'd find yourself thinking, "If I hadn't that problem back then, then this better thing would not have happened to me."*[85] Following his mother's example,

---

[83] ***John Adams,*** *Op. Cit.*, pp. 172-173. [84] *Magnificat,* Feb. 2004.
[85] ***When Character Was King,*** *Op. Cit.*, p. 40.

Reagan worked hard to cultivate the virtue of optimism. In the White House, *[h]is days always began, and in time this became famous, with jokes. He had a repertoire of them, perhaps a thousand on call in his head at any time...*[86] Reagan could lighten the most serious situations with a joke. After he was shot, he was in critical condition floating in and out of consciousness. At one point he awoke to find a woman holding his hand. When he asked who she was, the nurse did not reply. Before slipping back into unconsciousness again he quipped, *Does Nancy know about us?*[87] The first time Nancy was allowed in to see him he lightened the situation by telling her, *Honey, I forgot to duck.*[88] When the medical team informed him that they were going to have to operate on him, he found the strength to jokingly say, *I just hope you're all Republicans.*[89] When he was told about the medical progress of those who were shot along with him, he quipped: *That's great news. We'll have to get four bedpans and have a reunion.* When he finally left the hospital he told the doctors: *If I had this much attention in Hollywood, I'd have stayed there.*[90] Now it's your turn to be upbeat!

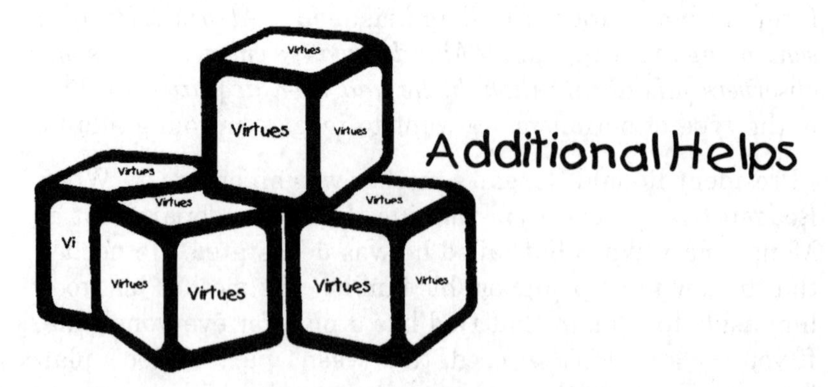

Additional Helps

- ✓ Have your teens read the chapter on humility in ***The Way*** by St. Josemaría Escrivá (Scepter Press 800-322-8773).
- ✓ Have your teens read ***The Practice of Humility*** by Pope Leo XIII (Pauline Books). This is a short, easy to read book.

---

[86] *Ibid.*, p. 162. [87] *Ibid.*, p. 174 [88] *Ibid.*, p. 185 [89] *Ibid.*, p. 186.
[90] ***How An Ordinary Man...***, *Op. Cit.*, p. 206.

✓ Preteens and Teens will enjoy reading ***Johnny Tremain*** by Esther Forbes. Read the book first and then discuss it with your teens afterwards. Point out the vices and virtues, particularly humility and pride. But also point out to your children the discrimination against Catholics as well as the Masonic Lodge used as a meeting place. Explain clearly that Freemasonry is not only opposed to Catholicism but its goal is to destroy it.

Scripture Verses for Humility

Genesis 11:1-9
Deut. 1:17
Sir. 3:20; 4:11-19
Ecclus. 5:2-3;11:2; 19:23
Wisdom 1:1-7
Psalm 4:3;44:14; 87:16
Is. 2:11
1 Kings 16:7; 18:7
Ag. 1:6
Luke 14:11
John 15:5
1 Peter 3:3; 5:1-4
Coloss. 3:17
1 Tim. 6:3-10;
2 Cor. 10:17
Phil. 2:3,12
Galatians 1:6-10; 6:1-10
Proverbs 3:5; 3:7;13; 18:12; 22:1; 27:2; 29:33
Matthew 5:16; 6:1, 5, 8, 16; 23:4, 7, 12, 27-28
1 Cor. 1: 28, 29, 31; 2:6-16; 10:12,31
James 1:2-18; 2:2-4; 3:13-18; 4:6

Scripture Verses for Envy

Gen. 37:3 ***Wis.*** 2:23-24 ***1 Cor.*** 12:312
How many more verses can you find?

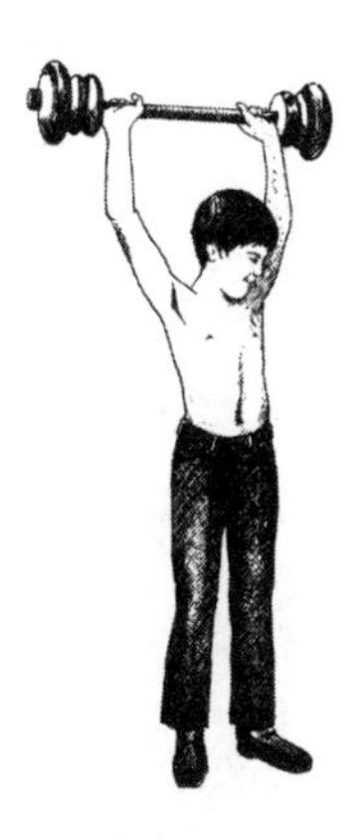

CHAPTER 9

LET'S TALK HAPPINESS & JOY

"Joy is the echo of God's life in us."
Bl. Dom Marmion

Growing up in the Chicago suburbs, I found it easy to recognize fellow Catholics. It wasn't a medal hanging around the person's neck, or a rosary falling from a purse, but rather the person's ability to laugh at the little tragedies of life, to see the humor in the mundane.

Much has changed since then. Technology is advanced. People are more affluent. I have been told that the average American family has more luxuries than most medieval kings! What used to be considered luxuries are now part of everyday living but **suddenly the laughter has stopped...even among our children.** It has been replaced by forced chuckles, rueful smiles, and perpetual whines.

Even TV has to have a "laugh-track." My growing concern about our unhappy culture was confirmed when a wealthy woman in town, who lives a storybook life, shocked me by saying, *I envy your ability to laugh!* But her comment was not an isolated one. Shortly after we moved to Springfield, a friend from the Chicago suburbs accompanied her husband on a business trip to Springfield so that we could meet for lunch. We had such a fun afternoon talking and laughing. When it came time to leave, our waitress lingered at our table to say, *it was great to hear the two of you laughing so much. It's so rare to hear customers laugh. It brightened my day hearing the two of you having so much fun.* Anne Marie looked at me in surprise. Laughter comes easily to the people we know.

Italian Economist Stefano Zamagni discovered through research that *beyond a certain income, an increase in consumption leads to a loss, rather than an increase, of happiness.*[1] How can this be? Venerable Zelié Martin, the mother of the Little Flower, writing to her sister the Visitandine nun explained, *it is certain that unvarying prosperity draws men away from God. Never does He lead His chosen by that road; they must first pass through the crucible of suffering in order to be purified.*[2]

Greg Easterbrook even wrote a book on this topic entitled ***The Progress Paradox.*** Professor Darrin McMahon in his review of the book asks the question: *But if the evidence for a revolution in living standards is really so overwhelming—and it is—then why aren't people happier?... [T]he number of people in America who describe themselves as "very happy" has decreased slightly since 1950 (to 6% from 7.5%) and the percentage of those who consider themselves "happy" has remained at 60%. Meanwhile,the incidence of depression seems to have increased sharply, which leads Mr. Easterbrook*

---

[1] Zenit, Dec. 21, 2000.

[2] Fr. Stéphane-Joseph Piat, O.F.M., ***The Story Of A Family*** (Rockford: Tan Books & Publishers, Inc.1994) p. 143.

to the paradox referred to in his title: Life gets better; people feel worse. The author of the book draws on *a new discipline known as Positive Psychology—the study of what makes people happy, not sad—to offer suggestions for improving the way we feel...To make ourselves feel better, he says, we might begin by making the world better.*[2A] Isn't this what Christ teaches us?

Talking about depression, the 18th International Congress on Depression was hosted by the Vatican November 13-15, 2003. After studying the illness that affects 340 million people in the world today, the Congress concluded: *Individualism, unemployment, divorce, insecurity, the absence of a genuine education, the lack of the transmission of learning, of culture, of morality, and of the religious life, and ethical relativism's negligence of objective norms, weaken people who feel uprooted and unstable in life...To recreate a genuine social bond, beginning with a complete change in man's behavior, it is necessary to value the principles of morality again, which are able to "affect" a profound change in the spirit of the depressed person and uplift him, restoring, at the same time both the person and society*(editorial emphasis).[2B]

Prosperity contributes to unhappiness but the loss of faith triggered by *the loss of a sense of sin* confers misery. Mrs. Martin continued, *True happiness is not to be found in this world; we waste our time seeking it here.*[3] Why? Fr. Jack Kubeck, of the Prelature of Opus Dei, told women attending his retreat: *Happiness is simply fulfilling the will of God. If we are moody or lack serenity it means that we are not doing what God expects of us. Stop whining and listen to God!* That triggered a chuckle from the women. St. Peter Julian Eymard seconds Fr. Jack: *The only real happiness of a soul is to live according to the holy will of God.*

[2A] Darrin M. McMahon, "Disgruntled in the Midst of Plenty," *The Wall Street Journal,* Dec. 4, 2003.

[2B] Zenit, Nov. 23, 2003.

[3] ***The Story Of A Family***, *Op. Cit.*

St. Augustine advises, *he who wills nothing but what God wills is always happy; for, as everything happens by the will of God, the soul has always that which it wills.*[3A] John Paul II insists *the deepest reason for happiness a person can have is to know he is loved by God with a mother's love.*[3B] *To know that God is not far but close, not indifferent but compassionate, not a stranger but a merciful Father who follows us lovingly while respecting our freedom--all this is reason for profound joy that different daily events cannot affect. An unmistakable characteristic of Christian joy is that it can coexist with suffering, because it is totally based on love. In fact, the Lord who is at hand, to the point of becoming man, comes to infuse in us His joy, the joy of loving. Only in this way can one understand the serene joy of the martyrs even in the midst of trials, or the smile of charity of the saints before those who are suffering: a smile that does not offend but consoles.*[3C]

Hopefully you and your children have learned from the ***Raise Happy Children Series*** of books that happiness, true happiness, comes from uniting our will to the will of God. This means sacrificing what I want, to do what God wants me to do. This may mean having to put aside your busy schedule to attend a rally in the cold or pouring rain at your capitol to support the sanctity of marriage. It may mean working late at night, when you are tired or want to simply relax, stuffing envelopes to support a pro-life, pro-marriage politician. It may mean agreeing to host a meeting or a dinner at your home for a good cause when your schedule is already overbooked. It's doing the things you would rather not do because God wills it of you. It could mean visiting relatives for a holiday when you would rather stay home and just celebrate it with your family. In the words of St. Francis of Assisi, *to live in virtue one must die to oneself.* At a dinner party a friend explained how life was easier now that he was praying more. The actual key to his easier life is the fact that he is no longer trying to force God to do his bidding. Now he is content to do God's will.

[3A] St. Alphonsus de Liguori, ***The Incarnation, Birth And Infancy of Jesus Christ*** (St. Louis:Redemporist Father, 1927) p. 109.
[3B] Zenit, July 16, 2003. [3C] Zenit, Dec. 14, 2003.

When we reach the same spiritual maturity as my friend, sufferings and sorrows will not destroy our cheerfulness. Sadness occurs when we cannot manipulate God to do our bidding.

Speaking to the youth, John Paul II told them: *Never forget: Christ needs you to carry out His plan of salvation! Christ needs your youth and your generous enthusiasm to make His proclamation of joy resound in the new millennium...People are made for happiness. Rightly, then, you thirst for happiness. Christ has the answer to this desire of yours. But He asks you to trust Him. True joy is a victory, something which cannot be obtained without a long and difficult struggle. Christ holds the secret of this victory.*[3D]

In the Old Testament we are scolded for our self-centered conduct: ***Had you walked in the way of God, you would have dwelt in enduring peace*** (***Bar.*** 3:13). St. Maximilian Kolbe insists: *The source of happiness and peace is not outside, but within us. Let us use every opportunity to make our soul exercise patience, humility, obedience, poverty, and the other virtues of the religious life, and our cross shall not be so heavy.*[3E]

In 1854 Fr. Frederick W. Faber, D.D. wrote the following. It is so apropos for our topic: *[W]e stand in need of cheerfulness to face the long outstretching desert that lies before us; and nothing keeps alive in us a holy joy more effectually than fidelity to grace and our appointed observances. The sense of wretchedness which follows frequent or habitual laxity drives us to seek consolation from creatures, and to re-enter the world that we may have the pleasure of forgetting ourselves there awhile, and hiding ourselves from the merciful persecution of exciting grace. Besides, which the formation of virtuous habits is interrupted by our unfaithfulness and this weakens our whole position, and makes our future harder, while actual ground also is lost by the intermission. In a word, fidelity is the raw material of perseverance; and to perceive this, is to see that*

[3D] Zenit, July 26, 2002. [3E] *Magnificat*, Oct., 2002.

its importance cannot be exaggerated.[3F]

During his visit to the U.S. in 1979, John Paul II reminded us that *we are an Easter people and "Alleluia" is our song. With St. Paul I exhort you:* ***"Rejoice in the Lord always, I say it again, rejoice"*** (***Phil.*** 4:4) *Rejoice because Jesus has come into the world! Rejoice because Jesus died upon the cross! Rejoice because He rose again from the dead! Rejoice because in baptism, He washed away our sins! Rejoice because Jesus has come to set us free! And rejoice because He is the master of our life!*

Then he proceeded to explain why people have stopped laughing: *How many people have never known this joy? They feed on emptiness and tread the paths of despair.* ***"They walk in darkness and the shadow of death"*** (***Lk.*** 1:79). *And we need not look at the ends of the earth for them. They live in our neighborhoods, they walk down our streets, they may even be members of our own families. They live without true joy because they live without hope. They live without hope because they have never heard, really heard the Good News of Jesus Christ, because they have never met a brother or sister who touched their lives with the love of Jesus and lifted them up from their misery.*[4]

The Holy Father ended with a challenge to us: *I encourage you, be men and women of deep and abiding faith. Be heralds of hope. Be messengers of joy.*[5]

The Formula For Happiness

"We are responsible...for the things we ought to have uprooted and left to grow; for the things we ought to have planted and did not plant."

Cardinal Pole (1545)

To be the messengers of joy that the Holy Father has asked us to be, we have to unite the virtues of faith, hope and

[3F] ***Growth In Holiness***, *Op. Cit.*, p. 46.

[4] John Paul II, *The Pope's Challenge* (NY: Scepter, 1979) pp.55-56.

[5] *Ibid.*, p. 56.

optimism with a sense of humor. This comes from the cultivation of the virtue of cheerfulness. To acquire the virtue of cheerfulness recall the formula for happiness devised by Dr. David Isaacs that was mentioned in ***Raise Happy Children Through A Happier Marriage!***: **Happiness = pleasure + suffering.** Without the combination of suffering and pleasure we cannot be happy. Pleasure sweetens life, while suffering matures us by directing us toward correct priorities. Once we accept the formula for happiness, the virtue of cheerfulness becomes second nature.

Cardinal Schönborn gave an outstanding address entitled "Christian Vocation: Call to Happiness". Let's consider his profound words: *We have been created to be happy. The desire for happiness is given to us by the Creator and it is written in the heart of every man. It represents an end to which the Creator has destined us. For many, the search for happiness is deceptive and is manifested in such things as drugs, fame, success or sex. All are actions that can give momentary pleasure and satisfaction, but they do not guarantee happiness. Instead, the "little happiness"—little gestures that give a bit of light to daily life—is the way to come closer to the great happiness. One depends on the other, they belong to one another...This disdain for little happinesses is, in fact, profoundly inhuman and finds tragic applications in history where the political power arrogates to itself the task of creating the great happinesses on earth. In fact, whoever is unable to appreciate little joys, mentioned even in the biblical book Ecclesiastes, will not be aware of the great happinesses either. The real search for happiness in the Christian sense is translated in the Magisterium of the Catholic Church in topics such as peace, the defense of life, respect for human rights...Without these topics there is no room for the happy life.*

The "little" and "great happiness" have their roots in the gift of self, in fact the key to happiness lies in giving oneself for the good. Padre Pio certainly made many people happy. He freed them from sin, he bore their faults, and he led them to conversion. Padre Pio was a man full of sufferings, but he was not unhappy.

For her part, St. Thérèse of Lisieux, of delicate health and "queen of tears", is the example of the gift of self for an end. She showed the way to follow: self-forgetfulness to please God.

And John Paul II has stressed that "man cannot find himself completely if it is not through the gift of himself." In no realm of life can the Holy Father be described as an unhappy man, even when we know what he suffers.

The sincere gift of self finds its supreme fulfillment in the gift of Christ on the cross...[5A]

St. Josemaría explains to us: ...*The Holy Spirit helps us to realize with certainty that we are children of God. And, being children of God, how can we be sad? Sadness is the end product of selfishness. If we truly want to live for God, we will never lack cheerfulness, even when we discover our errors and wretchedness. Cheerfulness finds its way into our life of prayer, so much so that we cannot help singing for joy. For we are in love, and singing is a thing that lovers do.*

If we live our lives in this way, we shall be bringing peace to the world. We shall be making God's service attractive to others, because ***"God loves a cheerful giver"*** (***2 Cor***. 9:7). *Christians are ordinary people, but their hearts overflow with the joy that comes when we set out to fulfill, with the constant help of grace the will of the Father. Christians don't see themselves as victims, underrated, or restricted in their behavior. They walk head held high, because they are men, and children of God.*[6]

Our cheerfulness is a visible indication of our friendship with God and our love for Him. *Christian cheerfulness is not something physiological. Its foundation is supernatural,*

[5A] Zenit, Aug. 29, 2003.

[6] ***Friends of God***, *Op. Cit.*, #92, #93.

and it goes deeper than illness or difficulties...True cheerfulness is...something within: something that keeps us peaceful and brimming over with joy, explains St. Josemaría.[7]

Cheerfulness is the virtue that helps us to keep our life on track despite the potholes that develop along our way, and there are large and small potholes in everyone's life. Cheerfulness united with the virtue of optimism lifts everyone around us. The more joy that we give, the more peace and happiness come back to us. St. Josemaría explains: *Your charity should be likeable. Without neglecting prudence and naturalness, try to have a smile on your lips for everyone at all times, though you may be weeping inside...*[8]

My friend Joyce lives that advice well. Each time she picks up the phone she has a cheery "hello." No matter when you meet her, she has a smile on her face. Yet she faces complex problems. When asked why she puts on such a good "front," she replied, *just because I'm having a hard day, doesn't mean that I should pass my misery on to others.*

Cheerfulness is mandatory for Christians for four reasons:

1. We are to be cheerful to please God. No one likes a long face...that includes God.

2. Cheerfulness gives honor and glory to God. To do His will in a sullen manner shows our displeasure. It conveys the impression that we *are doing a great deal and that we are ready to burst with the effort, and that we can scarcely bear the burden of its being so great and heavy; and this attitude is thankless and offends.*[9]

3. Cheerfulness gives good example to our neighbor. It demonstrates that Christianity is a positive force in our lives. If we are trying to bring souls to God, we have to exhibit the joy of being in love with God. Sullenness repels while a smile attracts. People surmise that Christianity is not worth the effort if we are always

[7] St. Josemaría Escrivá, ***The Forge*** (NY: Scepter, 1988) #520.
[8] *Ibid.*, #699. [9] **Friends of God**, *Op. Cit.*, p. 464.

complaining, sullen, or irritable. If people see that we are happy they will be eager to imitate us in striving for holiness.

4. Work cheerfully done has greater merit and value. *The cheerfulness and relish with which a work is done gets it done to perfection, while sadness spells bad work,* maintained Aristotle. St. John Chrysostom explained that cheerfulness and satisfaction of souls gives strength and sustenance to work. Our work goes easier with less effort. We feel less tired. There is a direct correlation between the rise in unhappy workers and poor workmanship.

How To Develop The Virtue of Cheerfulness

"The thing to acquire is true virtue, not a show of virtue."

St. Marcellina to her little brother, St. Ambrose

How can you and your children develop cheerfulness? First develop the previous virtues we discussed in ***Raise Happy Children...Teach Them Virtues!*** as well as the virtues discussed in this book. As you develop these virtues teach them to your children and teens. The word "holiness" comes from living the virtues daily. Through the development of the virtues you and your children truly become whole, more human. Your personalities and characters become more attractive to others. Not only does one become whole in personality but also holy spiritually. Christ told Gabrielle Bossis: *Seek perfection. Aim at perfection in each one of your actions. At first it seems difficult. Then you learn to recognize the fact that all happiness is in this. The joy of having more of Me brings about all other joys.*[9A]

St. Alphonsus Rodriguez gives us five other reasons to practice the virtue of cheerfulness:

1. The Lord so requires it.
2. It redounds much to the glory and honor of God.

[9A] Gabrielle Bossis, ***He & i*** (Sherbrooke, Quebec: Editions Paulines, 1985) p. 65.

3. It gives good example to our neighbor.
4. Work done cheerfully has greater merit.
5. Cheerfulness shows perseverance in striving for holiness.[9B]

To live the virtue of cheerfulness begin by seeking, then accepting, the self-knowledge that comes from your mental prayer and the cultivation of the virtue of humility. Ask the Holy Spirit to enlighten you to know in what areas you need to strive for cheerfulness. If you neglect daily mental prayer you will flunk the virtue test! Ask your teens and yourself these questions: **Do I always talk about myself? Is my conversation centered on complaining... about my health, family members, spouse, work, etc? Am I always criticizing others? Do I judge others? Is my conversation filled with pessimism?** Once you lock in on the specific defect that kills your cheerfulness, take that as your particular examination of conscience. Each night go over your day to see how your struggle to kill the defect and replace it with cheerfulness went. If you are by nature optimistic, you can build on that. If on the other hand, you tend to be pessimistic, begin by thinking positive thoughts rather than critical ones. Look for the possible good in the problems. For example, the car breaks down. Maybe by the car breaking down you avoided a car accident. The sale of your house fell through. Maybe your next offer will be higher. Sickness prevented you from attending a family event. Maybe that sickness prevented you from an unforseen family conflict or argument. The job you did not get may have ended with you being laidoff in the near future. Remember it was Charles Dickens' illness that turned him into a successful author rather than an actor. As an actor he would be forgotten today. As a writer his work still influences lives. Teach your teens to look for the positive in disappointments. My daughter, Mary Terese, applied for a specific industrial engineering co-op job but the company instead offered her a different job. Disappointed, she declined that company's offer to take her second choice job with a consulting company. This created problems finding

[9B] ***Practice of Perfection And Christian Virtues, Vol 2,*** *Op. Cit.*, pp. 463-467.

summer living arrangements two hundred miles away as well as having to borrow my car for three months. It was difficult for all of us. As she drove away, I tried to make light of a difficult situation by saying, *maybe you will meet your husband there.* As she drove north she thought my parting words were really stupid since the people she met during her interview process were all middle-aged, married men. Her first day on the job she met her wonderful husband, Jeff. If she had landed her first choice job there would not have been a bride for my ***Raise Happy Children Through A Happier Marriage*** cover.

Remind yourself that it is impossible to smile on the outside while thinking or speaking negative thoughts. Try to see the good, the beautiful, the possible, the positive in everything. In God's plan <u>everything</u> works for the good. When tempted to be negative, say an aspiration such as *Sacred Heart of Jesus grant me peace* or *I believe, help my unbelief.*

Once you develop positive thoughts and words, begin to work on the "smile mortification" together with your children. Smile at everyone you meet from the clerk in the store, to your spouse, to your boss or that obnoxious person you have to deal with. Put a smile into your voice when you answer the phone. Write upbeat thank you notes, letters, e-mails. If smiling does not come naturally, try to smile at everyone in the morning. When that becomes second nature, try to smile at people in the afternoon and so on until it becomes part of your personality. At times it can be heroic to smile. Bl. Mother Teresa of Calcutta once said, *I sometimes find it difficult to smile at Jesus...He might be very demanding sometimes, and it is then that we have to see Christ in that distressing disguise also, and accept and smile at Him then more than before. The same thing in our own homes.*[9C]

The acceptance of suffering is another aspect of happiness

[9C] Zenit, Oct. 8, 2002.

and cheerfulness. Christ again tells Gabrielle Bossis: *When the love of the cross sinks deep into a person, he lives in a joy that the world can never know. For the world has only pleasures, but joy belongs to Me and Mine, My friend.*[10]

If you or a child projects a lack of cheerfulness, impose a penance. Anyone with a long face gets no dessert at dinner tonight. Or, a specifically distasteful chore can be assigned to the moody and the whiner such as cleaning the toilets. You know what will work best in your home. The object is to make it quite clear that moodiness, grumpiness, testiness or scowling are not acceptable for Christians. Carol Kelly, a friend, has a sign in her kitchen that reads: *If you are grouchy, irritable, or just plain mean, there will be a $10.00 charge for putting up with you.* Maybe you could have a "whiney/moody" money jar where unhappy people have to pay a quarter per mood or whine.

For cheerfulness to become a virtue, we have to also use the spiritual means. A child who is unhappy lacks a living faith even if he or she goes through the motions. Teach your child to bring his struggle for cheerfulness to God in his daily prayer. The grace of daily Mass and Holy Communion gives sufficient help to keep us smiling through all difficulties. Encourage your children to go to weekday Mass with you or on their own. Without that daily infusion of grace it is difficult, if not impossible to stay upbeat. Even the rich and famous are discovering this fact. Faye Dunaway, a Hollywood star for the last 30 years, told Esquire magazine, *I'm a new Catholic. I love the Church; I love Mass. I go every morning at 6:30. When I'm on the right track spiritually and emotionally, things happen in my life. It's mysterious.*[10A] Your confessor can guide you and your child/teen in this struggle during weekly confession. Remember, a spotless soul lightens the heart and gives joy.

Dr. Ana Maria Navarro, of the University of Navarre, has four points for helping you and your teens develop happiness:

[10] ***He and i,*** *Op. Cit.*, pp. 64-65. [10A] *On This Rock,* September 1999, p. 8.

1. Educate your children's/teens' intellects with clear criteria.
2. Educate their will in virtues. If they develop humility they will look for advice when confused rather than relying on feelings.
3. Teach the correct meaning of freedom—to choose the best things even when they are difficult. Your teens need a strong relationship with God to be truly free.
4. Keep your family life stable. Divorce causes unhappiness for spouses and children.[10B]

Msgr. Luigi Giussani, the founder of the Catholic organization Communion and Liberation, insists: *To affirm Christ is to affirm objective beauty that gives us a passion for life and everything becomes transparent to our eyes. It is no coincidence that gladness visible on the face is the main argument for Christian witness in the whole world, before everyone. The gladness of your heart, the older you get, as time passes, is the confirmation to ourselves of what we say and what we believe in.*[10C] He adds: *Joy alone is the mother of sacrifice, because sacrifice is not reasonable if it is not attracted by the beauty of the truth. It is beauty—"The splendor of the truth"—which calls us to sacrifice...[T]his joy, this gladness lies even at the depth of the most acute sorrow, a sorrow which at a certain point cannot be avoided: sorrow at one's own evil.*[10D]

The great Russian author Tolstoy wrote in his diary: *The means to gain happiness in life is to throw out from oneself in all directions like a spider an adhesive web of love, and to catch in it all that comes: an old woman, a child, a girl, a policeman.*[10E]

Cardinal Ratzinger encourages us to read a great how-to-learn-happiness book. The title? The ***Catechism of the Catholic Church.*** *"The primordial impulse of man, which*

[10B] Dr. Ana Maria Araujo, "The Denial of Happiness," audiotape.

[10C] *Magnificat,* July, 2002. [10D] *Magnificat,* Sept., 2002.

[10E] ***We Die Standing Up,*** *Op. Cit.,* p. 101.

no one can deny, and which in the ultimate sense no one can oppose, is the desire for happiness for a fulfilled, complete life." Explaining the third part of the ***Catechism****, dedicated to Christian morality, the cardinal said that it "is the doctrine of the fulfilled life, the illustration, so to speak, of the rules to attain happiness. The book relates this innate tendency in man with the beatitudes of Jesus, which free the concept of happiness of all banalities, give it its real depth, and, in this way, allow one to see the connection between the absolute good, the good in person—God—and happiness.*[10F]

THE DANGER OF SADNESS

"Every evening I turn my worries over to God...Because He's going to be up all night anyway!" Sign in a store

We have to be wary of the **vice of sadness. It is one of contrary vices of cheerfulness. The other extreme vice is silliness**. While silliness does not need to be dwelt upon, the vice of sadness does. It's a dangerous enemy that strikes unexpectedly killing our spiritual life. Sadness, which is opposed to happiness, cheerfulness and joy, comes from Satan. In the ***Book of Ecclesiasticus*** (30:24) we are warned: ***Put sadness far from you for there is no profit in it, and it has been the death of many.*** This same book also tells us: ***All evils come from sadness*** (25:17). Sadness destroys our will to spiritually struggle. When we become sad it becomes too difficult to do our mental prayer so we avoid it. It disturbs our ability to comprehend our spiritual reading so we give it up. We become so absorbed in our misery that we skip the rosary. It becomes too great an effort to attend daily Mass or frequent confession. ***Psalm* 28** well describes this scenario: ***My soul has fallen asleep for weariness.*** Our interior life dies when we give in to sadness which triggers the vice of spiritual sloth [laziness].

Sadness affects our personalities and our relationships. St. Alphonsus Rodriguez writes: *Cassian,*

[10F] Zenit, Oct. 8, 2002.

an early Christian writer, tells us that it makes us disagreeable and rude. St. Gregory says that sadness moves us to anger and peevishness. We become easily irritated and have an outburst of temper at anything that comes in our way. It makes us impatient with our work, suspicious and evil-minded.[10G] This is the cause of most estrangements between family members--someone is sad so he/she takes it out on the other members of the family. Sadness can even make us irrational. It fills us with melancholy and despondency. We can no longer do any good works because we have allowed our will to grow weak. The next step in the spiritual backslide is the sin of despair. *St. Francis warned his followers that the devil rejoices over a sad heart because he can plunge it into gloom and despair or turn it to worldly pleasures.*[10H]

Sadness is triggered by a loss of the virtue of hope, which in extreme cases can lead from depression to despair then possibly to suicide which we see in the example of Judas. If our love of God is rock solid, it must be manifested in our cheerful and joyful attitude toward life and people no matter what our lot in life may be. Consider the cheerfulness and joy of the saints who underwent terrible tortures or illnesses.One such saint was twelve-year-old Cyril who lived in the early Church. His pagan father was horrified when he discovered his son had become a Christian. To force him to renounce his new-found faith his father whipped him bloody. When that did not convince Cyril to apostasize, his father disowned him, throwing him out on the street bleeding and penniless. Rather than becoming sad and discouraged, Cyril was cheerful and happy. His cheerfulness angered the pagan populace. They brought him to court yet he told them: *I rejoice when unfriendly hands treat me in unfriendly ways; for then God will receive me with greater friendliness still. I rejoice to be banished from my father's house; in its stead I shall receive one much more beautiful. I rejoice to be poor, in order that I*

[10G] ***Practice of Perfection And Christian Virtues*, Vol. 2,** *Op. Cit.*, p. 460.
[10H] *Ibid.*, p. 461.

may possess eternal riches. And why should I fear a happy death,—I who await a better life?[10I] Granted, at times we will be plagued with discouragement but by saying frequent acts of hope we can restore interior joy.

Sadness can be caused by pride eating away within us as well as by troubles or disappointments. St. Bonaventure believed that *sadness is apt to arise from some trouble befalling you, or from your not having some object of your desire. St. Gregory and St. Augustine and other saints also specifiy this cause, and say that the sadness of the world springs from a man's being attached to worldly things...But he who shall be loosened and detached from all things of the world, and put all his desire and contentment in God will be free from the sadness of the world.*[10J]

Sadness denotes a lack of faith, a spiritual sickness epidemic in our culture. Archbishop Shimamoto Kaname of Nagasaki, Japan contends that Japanese society is a culture of *anxiety and sadness. The president of the nation's bishop's conference said the myth of materialism, and the pursuit of pleasure, productivity and technology, have robbed Japan of its soul. After World War II, Japan gave priority to economic development. By 1987 it was the richest country in the world...However, many human values were sacrificed in the pursuit of economic development, including the weakening of family ties.*[11] Contrast this with a 20 year study done by a communist "think tank" in China. Stephen Uhalley, in his book ***China and Christianity***, discusses how this group wanted to find out the cause for the greatness of the West. They studied in depth our economic system, our political system, our labor and business practices. After studying for decades all aspects of our culture they came to the conclusion that Christianity was responsible for our greatness! The converse is also true. Each time some parcel of Christianity is stripped from our government, culture, and laws, our greatness decreases. British Cardinal Cormac

[10I] ***Follow The Saints,*** *Op. Cit.,* p. 86.
[10J] ***Practice of Perfection And Christian Virtues, Vol 2,*** *Op. Cit.,* p. 472.
[11] Zenit, March 30, 2001.

Murphy-O'Connor furthermore points out *that the Christian faith has been a primary influence in the development of Western culture over 2,000 years, and that it has also been the key to human flourishing. The living traditions of the Church still have an enormous amount of wisdom to offer.*[11A]

Sadness causes illness. The leading incapacitating illness by the year 2020 will be psychological depression, according to Juan José López-Ibor, president of the World Psychiatric Association.[12] By 2010 over 386 million people will suffer from this disease! Canadian Jean Vanier left his brilliant military career to study philosophy and theology which led him to found the Faith and Light Lay Movement, now in 72 countries. This movement helps the mentally handicapped. Recently he wrote a book on depression entitled ***Depression: Way to Healing***. In an interview with Zenit he disclosed his findings about this illness: *People are aware of the chaos in themselves: violence, banal sexuality, inability to forgive. Men are more aware of the wounds they carry within. Before, living in the domain of morality and will, many people were able to bear difficulties, although their reasons were not always pure. Today confusion prevails...As I don't feel love, I submerge myself in a political project or even in consumerism.*

[Depression is typical of the so-called developed world] because people don't know what to do with their leisure. There are no amusements in Africa; one struggles to survive and to eat. All one's energies are in the service of life; and, when one works, there is no depression. Instead, free time is the ambit for family conflicts, and the lack of creativity [is due to]... television. In this environment, one wonders about the meaning of life.

[W]e don't know how to use [our free time]. The people who know how to exploit it discover the fruitfulness of loving, of caring for the elderly, of being concerned for others. [If] it is an encounter with the other, an exchange of love, then it

[11A] Zenit, Feb. 20, 2004.
[12] Zenit, April 5, 2001.

becomes communion and confidence that can heal our wounds.

Unbridled individualism gives birth to depression. Of course, we must not underrate physical and genetic causes...I always say that three things are necessary, in order to have valid psychotherapy: a good community, a job we like, and faith. On the contrary, today many individuals no longer have a family or friends, or a worthy job, nor the faith that allows them to put reality into perspective. Then, not even the best therapy works. Depression is normal; it often happens between 40 and 55 years of age, the midlife crisis. People must be helped to understand that it is a period of change, that spring can follow winter. There are even well-motivated people, priests and religious who lose their enthusiasm in midlife. This happened to Tauler [mystic, disciple of Meister Eckhart] in the 14th century.

What is necessary is a greater number of priests able to listen to men who have become fragile due to sadness. Confession is... a meeting with someone who can listen to another's sufferings and difficulties, not only to console him but to help him understand the meaning of depression.[13]

Being in the state of mortal sin is another cause of sadness. St. Diadochos of Photiki maintained that when the Holy Spirit withdraws from a person because of mortal sin *He leaves the intellect without the light of spiritual knowledge, dark and full of gloom.* This triggers, among other things, pessimism. A pessimist, according to Fr. Jay Alvarez, looks at the Land of Milk and Honey but sees only calories and cholesterol!

St. Alphonsus Rodriguez relates: *St. Francis [of Assisi] greatly disliked seeing any such sadness among his friars; and said to one of his companions who was looking sad: "a servant of God ought not to be sad except for having committed some sin; if you have committed one, repent and confess it, and beg God's pardon and mercy, praying with the prophet*

---

[13] Zenit, March 26, 2001.

that he will restore to you your former joy (***Psalm*** 1:14).[14] Teach your teens that sadness, *born of waywardness and distance from God, obscures and causes damage* while joy and optimism *is a stimulus and an encouragement for others.* [15]

St. Josemaría Escrivá confides: *The more you belong to Christ, the more grace you will obtain to be effective in this world and to be happy in eternity. But you must make up your mind to follow the way of self-surrender: The Cross on your shoulders, with a smile on your lips, and a light in your soul.*[16] St. Josemaría taught that joy has its roots in the cross: *You should realize that God wants you to be glad and that, if you do all you can, you will be happy, very, very happy, although you will never for a moment be without the Cross. But that Cross is no longer a gallows. It is the throne from which Christ reigns. And at His side, His Mother, our Mother too. The Blessed Virgin will obtain for you the strength that you need to walk decisively in the footsteps of her Son.*[17]

This is the lesson we have to instill in our children when they are little so that they persevere cheerfully in the practice of their faith during the wretched trials of adolescence or their first taste of "freedom." The sufferings of life "prune" us spiritually. They teach us empathy, compassion and humility. They mature us. They are like the wild fires that consume the mountains leaving everything in the fire's path ashes. Yet over time a new lushness emerges from the destruction. Almost magically the mountains are reborn in a burst of wildflowers carpeting the slopes. Next a patchwork of plants sprout up that in time become towering trees providing protection and food for birds and animals. From the ashes comes beauty. Or, we can compare suffering to the metal mesh that blankets some mountains to prevent boulders from crashing onto the highway injuring someone. At first it appears that the mesh

[14] ***Practice of Perfection And Christian Virtues, Vol. 2***, p.468
[15] Francis Fernandez, ***In Conversation With God #2*** (NY: Scepter, 1989) pp. 300, 302.
[16] St. Josemaría Escriva, ***The Way of the Cross*** (New York: Scepter, 1983) p. 32.
[17] ***Friends of God***, *Op. Cit.*, No. 141.

not only disfigures the beauty of the mountains but also appears to kill the vegetation beneath it. In actuality the mesh anchors the flowering trees and rhododendrons into the rocky crevices adding beauty in places where it never could have survived before. Similarly sufferings could be called our intimate, spiritual boot camp. They prepare us for the mission God has entrusted to our lives.

St. John Henry Newman explains: *I will trust Him...If I am in sickness, my sickness may serve Him, in perplexity, my perplexity may serve Him...He does nothing in vain...He may take away my friends. He may throw me among strangers. He may make me feel desolate, make my spirits sink, hide the future from me. Still, He knows what He is about.*[18]

John Paul II echoed these same sentiments: *When He [Christ] said:* ***"He who loves his life loses it, and he who hates his life in this world will keep it for eternal life,"*** *He was not only addressing the disciples but everyone* (**John** 12:25).

The fact is that, contrary to the false teachers of yesterday and today, Christ does not deceive. He knows the human creature profoundly and knows that in order to reach life, [the creature] must complete a "transition," a Passover, precisely, from the slavery of sin to the freedom of the children of God, denying "the old man" to give way to the new man, redeemed by Christ.

"Whoever loves his life loses it." *These words do not express contempt for life, but, on the contrary, genuine love for it. A love that does not desire this fundamental good just for itself and immediately, but for all and forever, in sharp contrast to the mentality of the "world." In reality, life is found in following Christ on the "narrow road" whereas, whoever chooses the "wide" and comfortable road, exchanges life for ephemeral satisfactions, being contemptuous of his own dignity and that of others.*[19]

---

[18] St. John Henry Newman, ***Meditations and Devotions.***
[19] Audience, March 4, 2001.

Christ is demanding with his disciples, and the Church does not hesitate to propose again to you also His Gospel "without discounts." Those who join the divine Master's school lovingly embrace His Cross, which leads to the fullness of life and happiness. Isn't it, perhaps, precisely the Cross that has guided, the last 15 years, young people's pilgrimages on the World Youth Days?[20]

Besides sadness, **the vice of fatalism is another destroyer of happiness**. Dr. Ana Maria Navarro, of the University of Navarre, points out that people who fall into fatalism depend on God to do everything for them rather than using their God given wills and abilities to work out their problems. Teach your teens and young adults to take responsibility for their life and actions.[20A]

As for sadness...what can we and our teens do if we find ourselves sad even though we are trying to be cheerful? St. James exhorts us: ***Is any of you sad? Let him pray*** (5:13). When we feel down, a chat with a friend usually picks up our spirits. The best friend to chat with is God. If we take the time to sit and chat about our problems with Him, we will soon find our sadness replaced with peace and consolation. If circumstances permit, talk to Jesus before the Blessed Sacrament at church. At times there's nothing like a good cry in front of Jesus in the Holy Eucharist to lighten the heart. You will find that there is a palpable feeling of peace and calm praying before the Blessed Sacrament. You think things are bad? Meditate on the passion and death of Our Lord. Nothing in life is as grim as what He faced. Another remedy is to use holy water frequently. Since sadness is a tool of the devil, holy water sends him packing. Aspirations can also help us to get back on track. Also consider if you and your children have been to confession lately. The graces received in this great sacrament are a wonderful picker-upper.

Besides the supernatural means, it is important to use

[20] John Paul II, audience, April 1, 2001.

[20A] "The Denial of Happiness" audiotape, *Op. Cit.*

the natural means also. Are you getting enough sleep? Are you eating correctly? Too much sugar can cause the blues. Allergies to foods or molds can affect us mentally. Medications can cause depression or a hormonal imbalance. Should this be the case, consult with your doctor.

Put on upbeat music to lift your spirits such as the scores from musicals, inspirational music such as Dana's, folk music or any type that you particularly enjoy. Sing along. It's hard to be sad when you are singing a happy song. Music can positively influence our mood. Weather also influences us making us happy or depressed. If the dreary weather has you down, turn on the lights to brighten the day and your work area. St. Augustine adds: *Whatever you do, do it with joy. Then you do good and you do it well. If, instead, you act with sadness, even if through it you do good, it is not you who do it.*

Proverbs (13) tells us ***a joyful heart makes a cheerful face.*** What good we can do with a cheerful face! St. Josemaría writes *I am every day more convinced that happiness in Heaven is for those who know how to be happy on earth.*[21]

When tempted to give in to sadness, recall the song from the musical, *Bye-Bye Birdie* and "Put On A Happy Face"!

Let's Talk Hope

"You will live in my love if you keep my commandments...that My joy may be yours and your joy may be complete." Jesus Christ (***John*** 15:11)

Reading the newspaper or watching the news can tempt us to despair unless we cultivate the virtue of hope. John Paul II urges us to cross ***The Threshold of Hope***! Hope is *the* virtue for the new millennium.

[21] ***The Forge***, *Op. Cit.*, #1005.

As one of the three theological virtues that you received at baptism, hope is the virtue that you must live daily to become a saint. Fr. James Meyer, O.F.M., explains: *To be perfect is in effect the same as to be just or righteous, to be holy, to be a saint, or also to be good, to be pious...[T]o be pious means...to act the part of a dutiful child toward God. To be good means truly giving God the honor, love and service due to Him while pleasing others under God's pleasure. To be saintly or a saint means to be in a state approved by God. To be holy means to be in a condition which is spiritually complete, healthy, vigorous, and not sickly or dead. To be just or righteous means to measure up to what God has a right to expect of us, to be "just right" with the standards of God.*[22] Part of this standard is the practice of the virtue of hope.

St. Zeno, the bishop of Verona, Italy in the 300's wrote that three things are fundamental for Christian perfection—faith, hope and charity. He explains: *These three virtues are so interwoven with one another that each one is necessary for the others. If one does not progress in hope, of what use is faith? If one does not have faith, how can hope be born? And if one's faith and hope are denied charity, each will be useless, for faith does not operate without love, nor hope without faith. Consequently, the Christian who wishes to be perfect has to be well grounded in the three: if one of them is missing, he will not attain perfection in his work.*[23]

Are you aware that hope is the basis of most of your actions? The breadwinner works hard everyday in the hope of receiving a paycheck. You pay your bills in the hope of paying off your debts. You clean your home in the hope that it will look nice. Your children go to school in the hope of learning. You read this book because you hoped to learn how to teach your children and teens virtues.

The infused theological virtue of hope, received at Baptism,

[22] James Meyer, O.F. M., ***A Primer of Perfection for Everybody,*** (Chicago: Franciscan Herald Press, 1946) p. 2.
[23] Claire Russell, ***Glimpses of the Church Fathers*** (NY: Scepter, 1994) p. 122.

grows through the channels of grace, which include prayer, reception of the sacraments, and acts of hope that you say throughout each day. Spiritually, it is the virtue of hope fueled by the virtue of faith that assures you that your sins are forgiven in the Sacrament of Reconciliation. When illness, financial problems, family problems or tragedy strike, it is the virtue of hope that helps you to accept the suffering, which at the same time keeps you from despairing. Hope impels you to turn all your problems over to a loving God. You pray in the hope of pleasing God. You do not fear death because you hope in God's promise of eternity in His Presence if you are faithful.

As St. Zeno notes, to have hope, we have to also cultivate the virtue of faith. This faith must be deeper than external actions. We can go to Sunday or even daily Mass, say our daily rosary, use sacramentals but unless these are building up a vibrant, living faith in God, they are just external actions. A living faith is one in which whatever happens to us we accept God's will, cooperate with the graces He sends, and offer our sufferings for the conversion of souls, for the souls in purgatory or in reparation for our own sins. If our faith is not a living faith, we will turn on God when we experience suffering or misfortune. Two contrasting examples come to mind. In ***Raise Happy Children...Raise Them Saints!*** I explained how Ted Turner, of CNN, lost a younger sister to a serious illness. Before his sister's death, he wanted to be a missionary. Following her death, he turned his back on God using his media to attack the Christian faith. His faith was external rather than internal. He never developed the virtue of hope. His reaction contrasts sharply with the reaction of a family that was part of a pro-life mini conference in Rome several years ago. A Mormon family, the Goodmans of Utah, had twelve children. They promoted the beauty of large families by attending UN Conferences to lobby delegates to promote life issues. They also had a singing ministry similar to the von Trapp family singers. This family, beautifully dressed with smiling, radiant faces, serenaded the Holy Father with the Irish blessing. It was thrilling to see and hear them. Shortly after their arrival home following the audience with the Holy Father, part of the family was in a fatal car accident. Three of the children ages 10, 11, and 12, died instantly when they were thrown from the car. In a matter of seconds a fourth of their family died. The father and two other children were left in critical condition with severe head injuries. The mother, Claudia, came upon the accident right after it occurred. Her faith in God and the cultivation of the virtues of faith and hope sustained her. Only God knows why this happened and the purpose it will serve.

To cultivate the virtue of hope, our faith must be unshakably centered on God and His will—never questioning or fighting His actions in our lives. In addition to faith, we must live charity toward God and our neighbor. Charity is another word for "love." If we are consumed with self-love, which is self-centered and selfish, hope will elude us. We will whine, complain, and drown in self-pity when misfortune comes our way. In addition, we will spread despair like the flu to everyone we come into contact with. People will avoid us like the plague. Their hearts will sink when they hear our voice on the phone.

Charity comes from living a mortified life—a life that is at the disposal of the spirit of service—thinking of God and others first, ***even as you wish men to do to you, so also do you to them*** (*Lk*. 6:31). A mortified life is developed by silently offering up the daily inconveniences, disappointments, physical discomforts, and problems we all encounter without letting those around us know our misery. If we do not develop the habit of constantly mortifying ourselves in this manner, we become moody, embittered and temperamental despite going to daily Mass and praying frequently. Without the spirit of mortification, we cannot accept draughts, cold food, hot weather, difficult people, bad news, flooded basements, rolling blackouts, children with stomach flu, babysitters who cancel out, discomforts or disappointments, the usual daily crosses that give color to our days. Without the spirit of mortification, our faith is externalized by going through the actions of a practicing Catholic, but it is not internalized so as to do us any spiritual good. In other words, it does not influence our behavior or reactions toward other people. When our faith is only externalized through actions, we tend to view everything from a physical or material standpoint rather than with the eyes of faith. For example, the young mother of a large family stopped by to visit a woman injured in an accident. Despite the demands on her, this woman had taken the time to make a dinner for the injured woman. After she left, a friend of the patient commented on what a thoughtful person that woman was. Rather than agreeing, the patient criticized the young mother's appearance. There was no gratitude for the kindness shown to her.

We can lose the virtue of hope through despair. This was Judas' sin. St. Peter also denied Our Lord, but he repented rather than despaired. His example should be our model. No matter how badly we may fall into sin, if we repent God forgives us through the Sacrament of Reconciliation. There is nothing God will not forgive if we just ask Him. Fr. Meyer explains, *...to give up hope is as bad as to renounce the Faith and to turn charity to hatred. There is one sin worse than piling all other sins together: it is doing God the culminating indignity of giving up trust in His goodness and promises after He has in so many almighty and boundlessly bountiful ways deserved our utter reliance on Him and His word.*[24]

We can lose hope through our pride of self-reliance simply by relying on ourselves rather than God. *In prosperous and in less prosperous times we must not forget our dependence on God. We must seek from Him and ascribe to Him all success, in virtue and in achievement.*[25] If we

[24] ***A Primer of Perfection for Everybody,*** *Op. Cit.,* p.140.
[25] *Ibid.,* p. 171.

find ourselves saying, *I did this...I achieved this...*rather than giving God the credit, we are guilty of pride of self-reliance.

Fr. Meyer also addresses our struggle for perfection: *More common is the fault of those who devote their time to God and the affairs of their soul...seeing no results...begin to ask, "What is the use?"*

This form of despairing pride is dangerous...[and] has proved fatal, leading to complete refusal of effort and to final hardness of heart. The cure for it is generous acts of faith and hope. Our holy Faith teaches us that not a single good deed or prayer or pious exercise is lost: each has its resulting or additional grace...

Whether we see external results or not...we must live on trustingly, in the fullest confidence that what God tells and promises us in the Faith is being realized in us.[26]

What about praying for special intentions but receiving no immediate answer? As creatures, we cannot manipulate God. **Hope tells us that God will do what is best for our souls.** At other times, He will answer our requests but not before we develop the virtue of perseverance in prayer. Recall the example of St. Monica. *We owe God so much reliance on His word that we firmly believe that they are being heard and are going to be rewarded in the way that is best.*[27]

As you can see the virtue of cheerfulness is a crucial virtue. The ***Book of Proverbs*** tells us: ***A joyful heart makes a cheerful face*** (15:13). St. Alphonsus Rodriguez explains: *As sadness of spirit redounds also upon the body, drying it up and consuming it, even to the very flesh and bones—**a sad spirit dries up the bones*** (15:13)—*so inward cheerfulness of heart redounds also upon the body and is shown in the countenance. So we read of many saints that there appeared in their face cheerfulness and serenity which bore witness to the cheerfulness and inward peace of their*

[26] *Ibid.*, p. 172. [27] *Ibid.*, p. 173.

soul. That is the cheerfulness that we want.[27A]

Now to Live All These Virtues!

"My supreme prayer for my family, my wife, my child, and grandchildren, is that they will persevere in the faith." Bl. Frederick Ozanam

Raise Happy Children...Teach Them Virtues! and ***Raise Happy Children...Teach Them Joy!*** focused on helping you to lay the foundation of virtues in your children and teens as well as living the virtues yourself. As you work on each virtue, remember that this is simply that, a foundation. From this foundation your child and teen can then build a life of heroic sanctity using God's grace and the gift of his free will. As you plod along on this tedious task (nothing good comes easy!) *[c]onsider how great and noble virtue is in itself, how it elevates the soul which it adorns; and, on the contrary, how vile and dishonorable vice is. This thought will lead you to make every effort to cultivate virtue, and to shun every occasion of vice,* writes St. Vincent Ferrer, O.P.[27B]

But it isn't only the saints who write about the importance of developing virtues. We discussed the strenuous efforts that Benjamin Franklin employed to become virtuous because he knew that they not only made him more pleasing to God but their fruits brought joy not only to him but to those who associated with him. A sinner like the rest of us, he discovered that practicing virtues is like having the Midas touch! Franklin writes, ...*[N]ow I speak of thanking God, I desire with all humility to acknowledge that I owe the mentioned happiness of my past life to His kind providence, which led me to the means I used and gave them success.*[27C]

Even today prominent people are recognizing the importance of virtues in making life happier and more fulfilling. Best selling author Jan Karon is just one of these

---

[27A] ***Practice Of Perfectoin And Christian Virtues, Vol. 2,*** *Op. Cit.*, p. 486.
[27B] St. Vincent Ferrer, ***Treatise on the Spiritual Life*** (Westminster, MD, The Newman Book Shop, 1944).
[27C] ***The Autobiography of Benjamin Franklin,*** *Op. Cit.*, p.17.

people. *Jan Karon's Mitford novels...about an Episcopal priest's good works in a fictional North Carolina town, entered The Wall Street Journal list at No. 1, beating out Danielle Steel's new bed-hopping drama for the top slot.*[27D] The Mitford Series by Jan Karon actually provides discussion questions for groups at the end of her first book. One question lists the cardinal and the theological virtues then asks readers to name the virtues the main characters exemplify. The characters are not perfect but realistic. They grapple with their vices and defects as they struggle to improve.

Employers are now actually listing virtues as part of the job requirements. One job in the Chicago suburbs requires that the applicant *must have the ability to control emotions and maintain composure under stress, using tact and good judgment.*

During the first week of March 2004 Zenit printed new stories dealing with the importance of three groups of people living virtues: families, businesspersons and bishops. The March 1, 2004 article began with families due to the release of the document *Family, Become What You Are!* by the Bishops of the Americas. We are told: *Through words that teach and by daily gestures of kindness, tenderness and forgiveness, parents cultivate in their children the authentic freedom of God's sons and daughters. Thus children grow in respect for others, a sense of justice, cordial openness, dialogue, generous service, promoting justice, peace and solidarity. This is the task God gives Christian parents, often helped by grandparents who can be so vital in the transmission of faith and values.*

On March 5th, 2004 the Holy Father addressed business ethics by *pointing out the virtues that should characterize the Christian businessperson: "diligence, industriousness, prudence in undertaking reasonable risks, reliability and fidelity in interpersonal relationships, and courage in carrying out decisions which are difficult and painful.*

[27D] Elizabeth Bukowski, *The Wall Street Journal,* "Her Bestsellers Are Rated G For Godliness," May 1, 2001.

On March 9th, the final group to be addressed were bishops when the Holy See announced the publication of the *Pastoral Directory for Bishops.* This document insists that bishops must be men of virtue. *The theological virtues and human talents are listed that must support the bishop in the pastoral ministry: pastoral prudence, rich humanity, humility, chastity, goodness, sincerity, ability to listen and to dialogue, a heart open to all. No one is excluded from the bishop's heart.* In addition it insists that *some principles that must guide the bishop's pastoral governance: "the principle of truth, of collaboration, of respect for competencies, of the right person for the right post, of justice and legality."*

Another group that is regularly encouraged to practice virtues by the Holy See are politicians and government employees.

Why this growing interest in virtues? People are looking for happiness, peace, goodness, and good employees. These qualities are rooted in the practice of virtue. Consider the thoughts of St. Mark the Ascetic: *The self-controlled refrain from gluttony; those who have renounced possessions, from greed; the tranquil, from loquacity; the pure, from self-indulgence; the modest, from unchastity; the self-dependent, from avarice; the gentle, from agitation; the humble, from self-esteem; the obedient, from quarrelling; the self-critical, from hypocrisy. Similarly, those who pray are protected from despair; the poor, from having many possessions; confessors of the faith, from its denial; martyrs, from idolatry. Do you see how every virtue that is performed even to the point of death is nothing other than refraining from sin?*[27E]

Raissa Maritain, the wife of the famous political philosopher Jacques Maritain, expressed in her journal the development of the virtues within her: *I seem to realize that for some time a certain work has been going on in my soul, which, if I obediently cooperate with it, will lead me to the total abandoning of all my will to God. The things I read, fortuitously, revolve round this, at the very same time that*

[27E] Mark the Ascetic, ***Philokalia*** compiled by St. Nikodimos and St. Makarios.

my personal plans are regularly thwarted...

To sum up, this year I have been led to be vigilant above all about humility, charity towards my neighbor, the abandoning of my own will to the will of God. A feeling which opens the heart towards God is good. That is why true friendship is good.[27F]

Consider this profound inscription written on a Catholic Bishop's tomb in Westminster Abbey in London:

> *When I was young and free and my imagination had no limits, I dreamed of changing the world. As I grew older and wiser, I discovered the world would not change, so I shortened my sights somewhat and decided to change only my country. But it, too, seemed immovable.*
>
> *As I grew into my twilight years, in one last desperate attempt, I settled for changing only my family, those closest to me, but alas, they would have none of it.*
>
> *And now as I lie on my deathbed, I suddenly realize: If I had only changed my self first, then by example I would have changed my family. From their inspiration and encouragement, I would then have been able to better my country and, who knows, I may have even changed the world."*

Take these words of the great French spiritual writer Bossuet to heart: *It is a common failing of men to give themselves entirely to what is outside and to neglect what is within; to work for mere appearances and to neglect what is solid and lasting; to think often of the impression they make and little of what they ought to be. That is why the most highly esteemed virtues are those which concern the conduct and direction of affairs. The hidden virtues, on the contrary, which are practiced away from the public view and under the eye of God alone, are not only neglected but hardly even*

[27F] Raissa Maritain, ***Raissa's Journal*** (NY: Magi Books, Inc., 1974).

heard of. And yet this is the secret of true virtue...a man must be built up interiorly in himself before he deserves to be given rank among others; and if this foundation is lacking, all other virtues, however brilliant, will be mere display...they will not make the man according to God's heart. Joseph sought God in simplicity; Joseph found God in detachment; Joseph enjoyed God's company in obscurity.[27G]

The founder of the Community of the Cenacle in Italy, Sister Elvira Petrozzi, adds her thoughts to this discussion: *Every defect that weighs on our conscience is an open wound that bleeds. If we don't accept the help of others, who see and suffer from our defects every day, we run the risk of accumulating a lot of anger, sadness, and superficiality inside of us...In many families, there is little patience, forgiveness, or gratitude, and because of this young people today don't know how to give thanks, because no one has taught them in a concrete way how to do it. Living in this way, they take everything for granted. We were created, rather, to be good, merciful, patient, and to live a clean and transparent life, in our minds, in our hearts, and in reality. To continue to live in our filth does us harm. We were created for peace and joy, and if we haven't yet found them, we have to ask ourselves why, and begin to search for them inside ourselves.*[27H]

Msgr. Luigi Giussani reminds us of our reward when we and our children live in a virtuous manner: [Christ tells us:] ***"He who follows Me will have eternal life and a hundredfold here below." "He who follows me will have eternal life,*** *may perhaps not interest you," I used to say, but the second phrase cannot help interesting you: **"you will have a hundredfold here below."** According to this, you will live a hundred times better your love for your girl or boyfriend, your father and mother; you will have a hundred times more passion for study, love of work, enjoyment of nature.*[27I] In other words, living the virtues results in a fuller, happier life that positively impacts the lives we come

---

[27G] *Magnificat,* Dec., 2002. [27H] *Ibid.* [27I] *Ibid.*

into contact with. Take for example the influence of Bl. Mother Teresa. In 1992 Princess Diana of Wales traveled to Calcutta, India, just to meet Bl. Mother Teresa. After her visit she confided to her butler/close friend Paul Burrell: *That was when I found my direction in life.* After her visit she transcribed her experience. Burrell explains, her visit was *a spiritual awakening...that became the driving force behind every mission and campaign she worked toward...I read what she had written about the entire experience, and how it had so profoundly changed her outlook on life—and death. On returning from Calcutta, she was driven by a deep feeling to help the sick and dying on a global scale. It was her responsibility, she felt, to use her position as the Princess of Wales to make a difference.* That's precisely what she did until her untimely death.[27J]

But one does not have to be famous to positively change the course of the lives of others. Teach your teens that living the virtues positively impacts all you do and all those you come into contact with. Several years after the death of Princess Diana, Burrell was falsely accused of stealing items from the royal household following her death. It was a nightmare that spanned several years destroying his good reputation. During his trial, the prosecution called one of his fellow workers, a dresser of the Princess. *Out of all the numerous dressers I had worked with, Helen Walsh was probably the most spiritual, a practicing Catholic like Maria* [Burrell's wife]. *Perhaps that was why she walked into the witness box and spoke the truth...*Her evidence helped the defense of Paul rather than the prosecution. It was her evidence and the Queen's intervention that finally had the case dropped with Paul declared innocent. After Walsh's testimony, Paul met her outside the courtroom: *"Thank you, Helen, for being so honest," I told her. "I just told the truth, Paul. That's all I did."*[27K] Telling the truth cleared an innocent man as well as restored his reputation.

On the other hand, not living virtue and our Catholic faith

[27J] Paul Burrell, ***A Royal Duty*** (NY: G. P. Putnam's Sons, 2003) pp. 395-396.
[27K] *Ibid.*, pp. 268-269.

can seriously impact the progress of our civilization. *King Henry VIII's revolt against the Catholic Church and his closing of monasteries may also have...postponed the industrial revolution. Archaeologists have found evidence that the Cistercian monks of Rievaulx Abbey, in North Yorkshire, were developing a prototype blast furnace for the large-scale production of cast iron when they were evicted by the king in 1538.* It was the blast furnace that *ushered in the industrial age..."One of the key things is that the Cistercians had a regular meeting of abbots every year, and they had the means of sharing technological advances across Europe. They effectively had a stranglehold on iron. The breakup of the monasteries broke up this network of technology transfer,"* explained Archaeologist Gerry McDonnell. *"They had the potential to move to blast furnaces that produced nothing but cast iron. They were poised to do it on a large scale, but by breaking up the virtual monopoly, Henry VIII effectively broke up that potential."* [27L]

Explain this to your teens. Suggest to your teens also that they take St. Dominic Savio as their patron. Although his life was brief, only fifteen years, he became a saint not by martyrdom but by living all the virtues heroically. Trained by his parents in the faith at an early age, he was able to serve Holy Mass when he was but five years old. A pupil of St. John Bosco's Oratory School, he wrote to a friend: *Here we make sanctity consist in being joyful all the time and in faithfully performing our duties.* This concisely sums up living a virtuous life! Why not encourage your teens to take St. Dominic's statement as their own motto?

Sometime after his death, St. Dominic Savio appeared to St. John Bosco in a dream. *Savio held out a gorgeous bouquet of roses, violets, sunflowers, gentians, lilies, evergreens, perennials, and sprigs of wheat and he handed it to me..."Give this bouquet to your sons so that, when the time comes, they may offer it to the Lord. See to it that everyone has it, that no one is without it and that no one steals it from*

[27L] Zenit, June 24, 2002.

them. Do this and you can rest assured that they will have enough to make them happy...[T]hese flowers symbolize the virtues which most delight the Lord...The rose is the symbol of charity, the violet of humility, the sunflower of obedience, the gentian of penance and self-denial, and the wheat stalks of frequent Communion. Then, the lily stands for the beautiful virtue of chastity of which it is written [they shall be like God's angels in heaven]. Finally, the evergreens and perennials tell you that these virtues must endure forever. They denote perseverance." St. John Bosco then asked St. Dominic, *Now tell me, you who practiced all these virtues in your lifetime, what comforted you the most at the moment of your death?* Savio responded that **all the virtues were consolations at the moment of death** but *the one thing that consoled me most at the hour of my death was the assistance of the mighty and lovely Mother of the Savior. Tell your sons never to forget to pray to Her as long as they live...*[27M]

As you read this book, the Holy Spirit gave you ideas how to create the same bouquet of virtues in the souls of your children. If your children are older and you feel that you "have missed the boat," don't become discouraged. It's never too late to begin. No situation is hopeless. Take your teens and the various situations to your prayer. Consider specifically how you can begin to educate them in the virtues. Try discussing specific situations with them then pointing out the virtues and vices. Encourage them to read books on the topic such as ***The Devout Life*** by St. Francis de Sales, ***The Way, Furrow*** and ***The Forge*** by St. Josemaría Escrivá, ***The Spiritual Combat*** by Lawrence Scupoli. Show videos/ DVDs mentioned at the end of each chapter then discuss the moral implications. Go to Our Lady for help and guidance. Remember how she arranged the Castellan roses in Blessed Juan Diego's tilma? She will arrange the bouquet of virtues in the souls of your children as well. Then, at the moment of death, the Queen of Heaven will present the bouquet to the Father perfumed by her own personal virtues.

[27M] Rev. Eugene M. Brown, ***Dreams, Visions & Prophecies of Don Bosco*** (New Rochelle, NY: Don Bosco Publications, 1986) pp. 262-263.

Pessimism vs. Reality

"Character is destiny." Ancient Proverb

Everywhere I go I hear people bemoaning the state of the world. On the surface everything does indeed look grim but by cooperating with God's grace, faithfully living lives of virtue, practicing the fullness of the Catholic faith with devotion, you and your family will change our world and culture for the better. Consider these words written by Church historian Daniel-Rops: *Christianity in the fourth century was no longer what it had been in early times, in those heroic days when there had been no middle way between total sacrifice and refusal. But it was sufficient that a few faithful souls should be preserved from staleness to ensure that the salt of the earth retained its savor; and in this triumphant Church there were still innumerable saints. Through them the work of Christian expansion was to be continued, and the ultimate loyalties preserved throughout the worst disasters.*

At this turning-point in history it was not a question of saving a political and social order which was incurably stricken with decadence, but of gathering together the seeds of civilization and of sowing them in new ground, or rather in land that had been renewed by terrible agonies...In order that the world should return to a truer morality, to a more healthy economy, to a less inhuman political system, this society had to die in order to be reborn...Through so much darkness and travail a new civilization was born, the Christian society of the Middle Ages.[27N]

God expects you and your family to give birth to a new Christian civilization. He calls your family to be missionaries to the world. You are now aware of all the tools God has given you to be successful in this endeavor. You simply have to use them! Archbishop John Patrick Foley, president of the Pontifical Council for Social

[27N] H. Daniel-Rops, ***The Church Of Apostles & Martyrs*** (NY: E. P.Dutton & Co., Inc., 1960) pp. 595-596.

Communication, reminds us: *"The greatest barrier to evangelization today is bad example. Our strategy of evangelization must be based upon sanctity, upon our enthusiastic response to Christ's universal call to holiness." Archbishop Foley said that of the 65 million people in the United States who call themselves Catholic, only a third practice their faith. "That is why, if we wish to evangelize the world, each one of us must begin by trying to become a saint."* Redemptorist Fr. Thomas Forest added that we have *to believe in Jesus Christ, to follow Him without timidity or stupidity, and then proclaim Him to those who do not know Him.*[27O]

What Is Joy?

"Joy is the gigantic secret of the common Christian." H. G. Chesterton

Joy is the reward for striving to live all the virtues. It certainly isn't an emotional roller coaster dependent on getting our hearts' desires. Rather, it is a fruit of the Holy Spirit. ***But the fruit of the Spirit is: charity, joy, peace, patience, kindness, goodness, faith, modesty, continency...And they who belong to Christ have crucified their flesh with its passions and desires. If we live by the Spirit, by the Spirit let us also walk. Let us not become desirous of vainglory, provoking one another, envying one another*** (***Galatians*** 5:22-26).

Since this concept is foreign to our culture, St. Alphonsus Rodriguez explains that *true joy and satisfaction is not what one shows in his exterior, talking, laughing, and chatting with this party and that—for that neither fills nor satisfies the soul—but what is within, like fine gold, in the vitals and innermost recesses of the heart.*[27P]

Fr. Francis Fernandez, of the Prelature of Opus Dei, deepens our understanding by explaining: *True joy does not depend on mere physical or material well-being, is not*

[27O] Zenit, Feb. 4, 2003.

[27P] ***Practice of Perfection & Christian Virtues, Vol. 2,*** *Op. Cit.*, p. 128.

diminished by the presence of difficulties, by the absence of health...Deep joy originates in Christ, in the love that God has had for us and in our correspondence with this love.

The Lord's promise is fulfilled—today: ***I will give you a joy which no one will take from you*** (**John** 16:22). *Nobody can. Nor can pain take it away, nor calumny, nor abandonment...nor even weaknesses and falls, if we turn promptly to the Lord. This is the sole condition of our remaining in it: not to separate ourselves from God, not to allow things to divide us from Him; to know at all times that we are His sons and daughters.*[28]

In the love of God, who is our Father and the Father of all men, and in the consequent forgetfulness of ourselves, lies the origin of that profound joy which is the Christian's. And this is usual for those who follow Christ. A pessimistic sadness must always be something foreign to the Christian. It is something, should it ever occur, that will require urgent remedy.

Remoteness from God, waywardness, is the only thing that can disturb us and take away this wonderful gift. Let us struggle, therefore, to seek the Lord in our work and in all our undertakings; let us chastise our caprices and our egotism whenever the occasion arises, each day if necessary. This effort keeps us alert and attentive to the things of God, and on the lookout for everything that can make life more pleasant for others. This interior struggle gives the soul a special youthfulness of spirit. There is no greater youthfulness than the youthfulness of one who knows he is a son [or daughter] of God and acts accordingly.[29]

Dom Hubert Van Zeller notes: *Man is not born to the appreciation of the highest happiness—any more than he is born to the highest wisdom or skill or holiness—he has to direct himself towards it. Sometimes drag himself towards it. As with knowledge, ability, and sanctity, the understanding of what happiness is all about is arrived at*

---

[28] ***In Conversation With God #2***, *Op. Cit.*, p. 300.
[29] *Ibid.*, pp. 301-302.

only as the result of search...the point which needs emphasis here is that we become proficient precisely by working at it. The pleasure is a by-product, just as happiness is a by-produce of sanctity. A necessary by-product...Joy has to be raked out of the embers of suffering...the flower has to be plucked from among the weeds which threaten it. But we rake the embers not for the sake of uncovering the joy, we part the weeds not for the sake of finding flowers. We do these things because they are our job. Within the ambit of our job are found the highest and the safest joys—and by "job" I mean not only our work but our vocation (editorial emphasis).[29A]

Mother Marie Des Douleurs, the foundress of the Benedictine Sisters of Jesus Crucified, concurs. She emphasizes that it is our duty to be joyful: *We say "duty," because supernatural joy is in no way that kind of dissipation, relaxation, and license by which too many people try to force their human dignity. Joy is a duty the importance of which escapes us because we imagine that joy should invade us by itself, without our doing anything to acquire it. This is a great mistake: joy is absolutely necessary for us and it has to be pursued and conquered by a struggle against our evil tendencies which continually plunge us into gloom.*[29B]

Scripture admonishes us to ***serve the Lord with gladness***.[30] Joy, we learned, is the indicator that we are growing in holiness as well as being passionately in love with God. This love is not emotional but a practical, down to earth type of love lived through the practice of our faith and the practice of virtues. If you and your children possess such a love it cannot be taken from you by suffering, contradiction, or unrelenting pain. Jesus reassures us: ***so you have sorrow now, but I will see you again and your hearts will rejoice, and no one will take your joy from you*** (***John*** 16:22).

If you want your teens and young adults to be truly happy

[29A] ***We Die Standing Up,*** *Op. Cit.*, pp. 126-127.

[29B] *Magnificat,* April, 2002.

[30] ***Ps***. 99:2.

and cheerful, teach them the importance of living the eight beatitudes. Why? The ***Catechism of the Catholic Church*** states:

> **#1718** ***The Beatitudes respond to the natural desire for happiness. This desire is of divine origin: God has placed it in the human heart in order to draw man to the One who alone can fulfill it.***

The word "beatitude" means blessed. But another translation is happy. Let's use the word happy for this listing of beatitudes but before we study these let us consider a small book entitled **The Beatitudes** by Fr. F. X. Lasance written in 1940. It is a spiritual treasure. He writes: *Every human being is continually panting for happiness, the good and the wicked are alike desirous of gaining it, but they seek for it by different means. Christ, therefore, commences His Sermon on the Mount with the Beatitudes, as if He were to say, you all desire to be happy; listen then, and I will point out the ways that lead to felicity...Christ honored eight virtues which are contemptible in the eyes of the world, with the titles of beatitudes....They are poverty of spirit, meekness, sorrow for sins, hunger and thirst after justice, mercy, purity of heart, the making of peace both with God and man, and the suffering of persecutions for Christ's sake. You must ascend these steps, if you wish to enter into the joys of your Lord.*[30A]

1. Happy are the poor in spirit, for theirs is the kingdom of God.
2. Happy are those who mourn, for they shall be comforted.
3. Happy are the meek, for they shall inherit the earth.
4. Happy are those who hunger and thirst for justice for they shall be satisfied.
5. Happy are the merciful, for they shall obtain mercy.
6. Happy are the pure in heart, for they shall see God.
7. Happy are the peacemakers, for they shall be called children of God.

[30A] Rev. F. X. Lasance, ***The Beatitudes*** (NY: Benziger Brothers, Inc., 1940) pp. 7-8.

8. Happy are those who are persecuted for righteousness' sake, for theirs is the kingdom of heaven. Happy are you when men revile you and persecute you and utter all kinds of evil against you falsely on my account. Rejoice and be glad, for your reward is great in heaven.[31]

Christ sternly warns those who do not practice virtues:

> ***But woe to you rich! For you are now having your comfort.***
> ***Woe to you who are filled! For you shall hunger.***
> ***Woe to you who laugh now! For you shall mourn and weep.***
> ***Woe to you when all men speak well of you! In the selfsame manner their fathers used to treat the prophets*** [false prophets] (***LK*** 6:24-26).

St. Thomas Aquinas also warned: *A life devoted to pleasure is a false happiness which hinders the true happiness of the life to come; but the happiness of a life active in doing good prepares for true happiness, and the happiness of a contemplative life is already true happiness beginning. The contemplative life does not so much deserve blessing as constitute it.*

Joy Spreads The Faith

"If you are what you should be, you will set the whole world ablaze!" St. Catherine of Siena

It was the great, visible joy of the first Christians that was the force that spread Christianity throughout the known world. H. Daniel-Rops writes: *Though this Christian endeavor possessed outstanding leaders, in the persons of Apostles and disciples, we should not forget that the immense labor of thousands of anonymous believers must have been of at least equal importance in ensuring its success. These unknown folk, by their chance journeyings and meetings, must have done a very great deal indeed to prepare the way for the Lord and to begin the work of winning souls for Christ...[T]his...type of evangelization...was spontaneous,*

[31] ***Matt.*** 5:3-10

and largely unconscious in character. Yet its influence must have been just as decisive...Thus, in the space of about a century, the Gospel had breached all the vital spiritual nerve-centers of the Empire.[35] But that wasn't all. *Christianity was to possess a revolutionary personnel...men who were determined to ensure the triumph of their cause, and who made this their sole aim in life.*[36]

This must likewise be our sole aim in life. *To act effectively in a society, man is bound to accept a certain detachment and separation from that society, as Christ had taught His followers. He had taught them something else besides: the morality of heroism, which asked man to sacrifice himself for the cause in advance, counting his own life as nothing.*[37]

The ripples of goodness must flow from you to influence everyone you meet and that includes your children and teens. In a letter, St. Josemaría insisted everyone who comes close to us should feel the urge to know Christ better and want to love God more.[38]

If this is true, friendships with the most diverse types of people are possible. People will enjoy being with you. Your conversation will be uplifting, showing them possibilities they never thought possible. Attracted by your effort to strive for perfection, they will be motivated to imitate you. This can only happen if your love of God is founded on struggling to grow in virtues. *[S]t. Paul's writing proves in most striking fashion that a spiritual doctrine can be fully efficacious in human society only when it rigidly obeys its own principles,* observes Daniel-Rops.[39]

John Paul II reiterates over and over this same concept: *The Christian cannot limit himself to analyzing historical processes as they happen, maintaining a passive attitude, as if they were beyond his capacity to intervene, as if we were led by blind and impersonal forces. The believer is convinced*

[35] ***The Church of Apostles And Martyrs,*** *Op. Cit.,* pp. 106, 109.
[36] *Ibid.,* p. 139. [37] *Ibid.,* p. 139.
[38] St. Josemaría, *Letter,* 15 October 1948, 31.
[39] ***The Church of Apostles And Martyrs,*** *Op. Cit.,* p. 85.

that every human event is under God's provident hand, who asks each one to collaborate with Him in the orientation of history toward an end worthy of man. Next the Holy Father asks us to consider the following questions: *"How do I live the Christian faith?" "Is it just a collection of beliefs and devotions enclosed in the private sphere, or is it also a force which calls for translation into options that affect my relations with others?"*

It is part of Christian realism to understand that great social changes are the result of small and courageous daily options. You often ask yourselves: ***When will our world be configured to the Gospel message? The answer is simple: When you, in the first place, act and think permanently like Christ, at least part of that world will be given to Him in you.*** *To promote a global culture of those moral absolutes that are a person's rights,* ***it is necessary that each Christian begin with himself, making the effort to reflect the image of Christ in each one of his thoughts and deeds. The world is changed with holiness.***[40]

Fr. Joseph Massmann insists: *Joy is indispensable for physical and spiritual development. Joy is for man what the sun is for plants...Joy improves the breathing, quickens the pulse, aids digestion, stimulates the appetite and strengthens the muscles. Provide...man with joy in life and he enjoys his work...He does great things, overcomes himself and all life's difficulties. Joy charms away adversity.*[41]

In this joy the mind is transformed and the face of the world is renewed. In this joy is to be found the strength to bear all life's little crosses and pinpricks, the strength to conquer one's self and one's selfishness, one's rash judgments, one's preconceived opinions, one's over-readiness to defend one's self. It supplies the strength to bear despondency, depression, moodiness, overstrain, touchiness, taciturnity, fear for one's health, fear lest one should lose the good opinion of others or

[40] Zenit April 9, 2001.
[41] ***Nervousness, Temperament and the Soul,*** *Op. Cit.*, p. 160.

not be appreciated. In the joy of being conscious of God's will, and of being of no account, the true greatness of man before God, the ever-cheerful mind of the true child of God comes to maturity. Therein life is completely renewed; body and soul regain their health and [in this awareness] true happiness exists.[42]

St. Dominic Savio, whom we mentioned earlier, had a most difficult young life filled with suffering, poverty and hard work. Yet it never affected his cheerful disposition. This teen had learned the secret of joy and happiness at a young age.[43]

Fr. Brian Kolodiejchuk, the postulator of the cause for Mother's Teresa's canonization writes of her: *She simply radiated joy to those around her. Her joy was not a matter of temperament and natural inclination but the result of God's grace and her surrender. This required a conscious and resolute effort. When it was hardest, her smile was brightest. Mother Teresa was determined to become "an apostle of joy" and spread the fragrance of Christ's joy wherever she went. Her love for God was such that she desired not just to accept the cross, but to do so with joy...She decided to smile at Jesus every time something was taken from her. "I give Him a big smile in return. Thank God that He still stoops down to take from me."...She radiated the joy of loving Jesus even in the midst of her severest trials. After a brief encounter with Mother Teresa, those who were discouraged or in despair would go away full of consolation and hope...*[43A]

Her philosophy of joy is seen in her writings: *Joy must be one of the pivots of our life. It is the token of a generous personality. Sometimes it is also a mantle that clothes a life of sacrifice and self-giving. A person who has this gift often reaches high summits. He or she is like a sun in a community. Let those who suffer find in us comforting angels.*

Why has the work in the slums been blessed by God?

---

[42] *Ibid.*, p. 170.

[43] ***Lives of the Saints Illustrated Part I***, *Op. Cit.*, p. 100.

[43A] Zenit, Dec. 20, 2002.

Certainly not because of given personal qualities, but because of the joy that the sisters spread as they pass by. The people of the world lack our joy. Those who live in the slums have still less of it. Our joy is the best means to preach Christianity to the heathen.[43B]

Bl. John XXIII wrote in his ***Journal of a Soul*** the secret of joy: *Among the flowers of the altar, that is, among the good results of a sincere devotion to the Blessed Sacrament, spiritual joy has the first place; this joy is a most important element of the spiritual life, the atmosphere of heroic virtues; it is courage, instinct, genius and indescribable grace. Joy is to be thought of as the true source of that liberty of mind which alone is able to unite the apparently incompatible qualities of the spiritual life, giving a freer rein to natural expressions of love while remaining inseparably attached to mortification. In our joy we must be careful to keep our spirit mortified, and practice mortification in order to increase our joy.*

I must therefore remain always and invariably happy while never for one moment desisting from self-denial. It is self-love which stunts the growth of the spirit and saddens us; self-denial restores life, serenity and peace.[44]

True joy for you, your spouse, and children comes only from struggling to grow holy...to become a saint. If you have taken the preceding books and chapters to heart you realize sanctity takes effort. *...[T]he spiritual life has a kind of normal state...struggle, fatigue, and rest...Struggle requires patience. Fatigue must be proof against human respect. Rest must lean upon mortification, for nowhere else can she safely sleep...[T]he spiritual life...is a struggle, strife, combat, battle, warfare, whichever word you may choose...If my life is not sensibly a fight, can it be a spiritual life at all? Or rather am I not in one of the common delusions of easy devotion and unmortified effeminacy. If I am not fighting, I am conquered; and surely I can hardly be fighting and not know*

[43B] ***Heart of Joy,*** *Op. Cit.*, p. 127.

[44] ***Saints & Heroes Speak, Vol. Four***, *Op. Cit.*, pp. 69-70.

it...Yet in these times it seems as if we were all to be invalids of holiness writes Rev. Frederick W. Faber, D.D.[45]

Fr. Faber continues, *Help people to be saints. Not all who ask for help really wish it, when it comes to be painful. But some do. Raise ten souls to detachment from creatures, and to close union with God, and what will happen to this ...city? Who can tell?*[46]

Daniel-Rops insists:*...[T]he greatest mystics are always people possessed of plenty of common sense, their feet on the ground, leading effective, active lives, and quite the opposite of ineffectual daydreamers...*[some such mystics were] *St. Augustine, St. Francis of Assisi, St. Joan of Arc and St. Teresa of Avila.*[47]

Does all of this sound too idealistic considering the times we live in? Around 150 A.D. St. Polycarp cried out to God, *What a dreadful age you have made me live in!*[48] Couldn't we rightly echo his words today? Every age is going to have its crushing evil but also it's glorious saints. You and your children are called to be the glorious saints of this millennium. Before his death, Fr. John Hardon, S.J., warned: *Ordinary Catholics will not survive...The Catholic Church will be preserved only where there are Catholics who are living martyrs, do you hear me?* But his words are not simply for you but also for your children. Each year the Holy Father meets with the children from Catholic Action in Rome. This year he asked them: *Certainly it is obvious that you have grown. At your age, one year more is a lot, and the changes are very noticeable. But, can you say that you have grown as Christians?*[49] As you watch your children grow out of their clothes and physically mature, can you see them also growing as rapidly in their faith and in virtue? Their rate of **spiritual growth depends on your commitment, perseverance, and their cooperation with God's graces**.

---

[45] ***Growth In Holiness***, *Op. Cit.*, pp. 109-110. [46] *Ibid.,* p. 111.
[47] ***The Church of Apostles And Martyrs,*** *Op. Cit.* This quote is a rework of a quote of Bergson., p. 79. [48] *Ibid.,* p. 303.
[49] Zenit, Dec. 21, 2000.

Christ tells us: ***The light has come into the world, yet men have loved the darkness rather than the light, for their works were evil. For everyone who does evil hates the light, and does not come to the light, that his deeds may not be exposed. But he who does the truth comes to the light that his deeds may be made manifest, for they have been performed in God*** (***John*** 3:19-21).

John Paul II, on his visit to St. Louis in 1999, commented on this passage to teens and young adults: *Each of you has a special mission in life, and you are each called to be a disciple of Christ... [A]ll of you must be the light of the world. Christ and the Church need your special talents. Use well the gifts the Lord has given you!...This does not mean that you can put off until later your meeting with Christ and your sharing in the Church's mission...[T]he time for action is now! He does not set you aside for a later time when you will be older and your training will be complete. Your training will never be finished. Christians are always in training. You are ready for what Christ wants of you now. He wants you—all of you—to be the light to the world...It is time to let your light shine...*

I urge you to let His word enter your hearts and then from the bottom of your hearts to tell Him: **"Here I am Lord, Here I am. I come to do Your will"** (***Hebrews*** 10:7)...

Jesus is calling you the light of the world. He is asking you to let your light shine before others. I know that in your hearts you want to say: **"Here I am, Lord. Here I am. I come to do your will."** *But only if you are one with Jesus can you share His light and be a light to the world.*

Sadly, too many people today are living apart from the light—in a world of illusions, a world of fleeting shadows and promises unfulfilled. If you look to Jesus, if you live the truth that is Jesus, you will have in you the light, the light that reveals the truths and values on which to build your own happiness, while building a world of justice, peace and solidarity...Because Jesus is the light, we too become light when we proclaim Him. This is the heart of the Christian mission, to which each of you has been called through baptism and confirmation. You are called to make the light of Christ shine brightly in the world...In ...a thousand different ways, you must reflect the light of Christ through your lives of prayer and of joyful service of others...Remember, Christ is calling you, the church needs you, the pope believes in you, and he expects great things of you!"

If we don't want to let God, the Church, and the Holy Father down, we need to develop a burning love to bring other souls to Christ. As John Paul II reminds us over and over, *the disciple of Christ must not only keep the faith and live on it, but also profess it, confidently bear witness to it, and spread it.* In his Apostolic Letter, ***Novo Millennio Ineunte***, he urges us to cast our nets into the deep with faith and hope.

The Holy Father emphasized in St. Louis: *Today, American Catholics are seriously challenged to know and cherish this immense heritage of holiness and service. Out of that heritage you must draw inspiration and strength for the new evangelization so urgently needed at the approach of the Third Christian Millennium. In the holiness and service of St. Louis' own St. Philippine Duschesne, and of countless faithful priests, religious and laity since the Church's earliest days in this area, Catholic life has appeared in all its rich and varied splendor.* ***Nothing less is asked of you today.***

The Holy Father continued: *The Spirit will truly bring about a new springtime of faith* ***if*** *Christian hearts are filled with new attitudes of humility, generosity and openness to His purifying grace. In parishes and communities across this land, holiness and Christian service will flourish if "you come to know and believe in the love God has for you."*

The Holy Father speaks a great deal about the "new springtime" but it is conditional. The Holy Father ended his talk, saying Mary, *Mother of Mercy, teach the people of St. Louis and of the United States to say yes to your Son, our Lord Jesus Christ!* Will you and your children say yes?

Final Thoughts...

"All the words which the Lord has spoken we will do." *Ex.* 24:3

Our duty as parents is to correct the disordered inclinations of our children before they take root. Once rooted in the soul they become habits of vice, thereby destroying your children's potential for happiness on earth as well as in heaven. The same goes for ourselves. St. John Chrysostom, a Father of the Church, exhorted the early Christians: *I urge you to correct vices energetically and to do battle with the passions affecting us at each age. If, in each period of life we sail outside the path of virtue and undergo constant shipwreck, we will reach port without spiritual cargo and suffer the ultimate torments* (editorial emphasis).[49A]

The Old Testament warns us as well: ***Let a man pamper his children...and he shall find him a spoilt son headstrong and stubborn as a horse unbroken*** (*Sir*. 30:8).

Besides observing the actions of your children, you can tell if they are on the right path by looking into the faces of your children, particularly into their eyes since the eyes are the windows to the soul. Remember the book/movie *The Portrait* of *Dorian Grey* in which a wealthy, handsome gentleman had a portrait done of himself? As his life degenerated, his immorality became visible on his portrait. To hide his sinfulness, he simply covered his portrait. Even though covered and hidden, the portrait grew more and more grotesque, a terrifying sign of the state of his soul. The story rather accurately portrays how sin destroys the beauty of the soul as well as the beauty of the body. Even scripture affirms this. We read in the ***Book of Sirach: A man's heart changes his countenance, either for good or for evil.***

[49A] ***In Matthaeum homiliae***, 81, 5.

The mark of a happy heart is a cheerful face (113: 25-26).

Once the virtues are in the process of being cultivated the effects are far reaching. They refine the soul and clothe it in riches. You and your children will search for ways to bring joy to others. You will contemplate what you can do to make the lives of others more agreeable and fun. You will find yourself thinking, *What can I do to raise that child, relative or friend's spirits? Should I call, send a card, token of affection, possibly visit?* The words of Christ in the Gospel will take on even deeper meaning: ***even as you wish men to do to you, so also do you to them*** (***Lk***. 6:31). Outwardly you and your children will develop an affectionate, friendly, warm manner. You will smile and greet everyone. You will be courteous, thoughtful and helpful. *How can I help you? What can I do for you? Do you need help?* You will display clear-headedness in all situations. But most importantly you will reflect joy in your face, in your actions, in the way you handle the day to day details of living. People know that they can trust you; they can depend on you; they can ask you for help. The confidences they share are locked in your heart, not to be gossiped about with others. At both the human and the supernatural levels, you will find fulfillment through your total self-giving to others. This in turn makes virtue attractive to others.

Fr. Francis Fernandez points out: *When one is happy, one is a stimulus and an encouragement for others; sadness, on the other hand, obscures and causes damage...We do great good around us with our job, for this brings others to God. Joy is frequently the best example of charity for those around us...Many people will find God behind our optimism, in the customary smile, in a cordial attitude. This example of charity to others—of forcing ourselves to flee from gloomy moods and sadness at all times and to remove their cause—is particularly communicated to those closest to us. To be more precise, God wants the home where we live to be a "bright and cheerful home," never a dark unhappy place, full of tension due to egocentricity and lack of mutual comprehension.*

A Christian household must be happy, because supernatural life leads us to practicing those virtues (generosity, cordiality, a spirit of service...) to which joy is so intimately united. A Christian home makes Christ known in an attractive way among families and throughout society.

We must also try to take this serene, kindly joy to our workplace, out into the street, and into all our social relations. This world is apprehensive and anxious. It is in need, above all, of the peace and joy the Lord has given us. So many people have found the road to God in the cordial, smiling conduct of a good Christian. Joy is an enormous help in the apostolate...St. Thomas Aquinas says expressly that "everyone who wants to make progress in the spiritual life needs to have joy." Sadness debilitates us. It is like the heavy clay accumulating on the boots of a walker which, as well as befouling them, makes each step more difficult for him.

This interior joy is also the state of mind necessary for perfectly complying with our obligations. And "the greater these are the greater must be our joy" The greater our responsibility (parents, teachers, priests, superiors...), the greater also our obligation to have this peace and joy to give to others, and the greater the urgency of recovering it when its habitual possession has been interrupted or disturbed.[49B]

As you complete this book, please remember that teaching children and teens virtues is just one aspect of raising happy children. You must also continually enrich your marriage as well as teach your children to live daily the Catholic faith. If you have not read ***Raise Happy Children Through A Happier Marriage!*** nor ***Raise Happy Children...Raise Them Saints!*** you have learned only one phase of raising happy children. I encourage you to read the first two books of the ***Raise Happy Children Series*** so that you can give your children the complete "happiness program."

[49B] ***In Conversation With God #2***, *Op. Cit.*, pp. 303-304.

Remember, St. Gregory the Great stressed that *one does not come from virtues to faith, but from faith to virtues.*

John Paul II, in his address to participants of the 4th World Meeting of Families in Manila in 2003, stressed the importance of the family: *Dear Christian families, proclaim joyfully to the whole world the wonderful treasure which you, as domestic churches, possess! Christian couples, in your communion of life and love, in your mutual self-giving and in your generous openness to children, become, in Christ, the light of the world. The Lord asks you daily to be like a lamp which does not remain hidden, but is put* ***on a stand, and...gives light to all in the house*** (***Matt***. 5:15).

Above all, be "good news" for the third millennium by remaining faithful to your vocation. Whether you are married recently or many years ago, the Sacrament of Matrimony continues to be your own special way of being disciples of Jesus, contributing to the spread of the Kingdom of God and growing in the holiness to which all Christians are called...

Accept fully and without reserve the love which, in the Sacrament of Matrimony, God first gave to you, and through which He enables you to love others in turn (cf. ***1 John*** 4:19). *Stand firm in the one conviction which can give meaning, strength, and joy to your life: Christ's love will never abandon you, His covenant of peace with you will never fail* (cf. ***Is.*** 54:10). *God's gifts and call are irrevocable* (cf. ***Rom***. 11:29). *He has written your name on the palm of His hand* (cf. ***Is*** 49:16).

The grace which you received in marriage remains with you through the years. Its source is in the pierced heart of the Redeemer, who sacrificed Himself on the altar of the Cross...

This grace remains ever close to that source: it is the grace of a self-sacrificing love, a love which both gives and forgives. It is the grace of a selfless love which forgets the hurt it has suffered, a love faithful unto death, a love bursting with new life. It is the grace of a generous love, which believes all things, bears all things, hopes all things, endures all things, a love which has no end, a love which is greater than all else (cf. ***1 Cor***. 13:7-8).

Such a love is not always easy. Daily life is full of pitfalls, tensions, suffering, and even fatigue. But on this journey you are not alone. Jesus is always present at your side, just as He was for the newlyweds at Cana in Galilee during a moment of difficulty. The Second Vatican Council reminds us that the Savior remains close to Christian couples and offers them help, so that, just as He loved the Church and gave Himself up for her, they too might always love each other faithfully and with constant mutual concern (cf. ***Gaudium et Spes***, 48).

Christian couples, be "good news for the third millennium" by bearing convincing and consistent witness to the truth about the family.

The family founded on marriage is a patrimony of humanity, a great good of priceless value, necessary for the life, development and the future of peoples. According to the plan of creation established in the beginning (cf. **Matt.** 19:4-8), *the family is the setting in which the human person, made in the image and likeness of God* (cf. **Gen**. 1:26), *is conceived and born, grows and matures. The family, as the primary school in which the human person is formed* (cf. ***Familiaris Consortio***, 19-27), *is indispensable for a true "human ecology"* (***Centesimus Annus***, 39)...

I urge you, dear Christian families, to show by your daily lives that despite numerous difficulties and obstacles marriage is able to be fully lived out as a meaningful experience and as "good news" for the men and women of today. Be leaders in the Church and in the world: this is a responsibility flowing from your celebration of the Sacrament of Matrimony, from your being a domestic church, and from the marital mission which is yours as the primary cells of society (cf. ***Apostolicam Actuositatem***, 11).

Finally, dear Christian couples, if you wish to be "good news for the third millennium", do not forget that family prayer is a sure way to remain united in a way of life in harmony with God's will...By reciting the rosary, families "place Jesus at the center, they share His joys and sorrows, they place their needs and their plans in His hands, they draw from Him the hope and the strength to go on" (***Rosarium Virginis Mariae***, 42).

I entrust all of you to Mary, Queen of the Family; may she accompany and sustain your life as families...I leave you with a final charge: with God's help, make the Gospel the guiding principle of your families, and make your families a page of the Gospel written for our time! [49D]

Pope John Paul II has led us into the new millennium filled with hope because the only hope for the world rests in the fullness of the Catholic faith lived heroically by its members. Why is this so? Daniel-Rops observed that: *civilizations always die of a drying up of their religious sap, of an antagonism which grows up between the fundamental aspirations of the human soul and the frameworks in which societies seek to confine those aspirations.*[50] You and your family have the spiritual power fueled by God's grace to not only save the world but to present it to God the Father through the merits of His Son Jesus Christ.

As you come to the conclusion of this book, I hope that you are firmly convinced that holiness, the same holiness practiced by the saints, is possible for you and your children. Pope John Paul II insists that great sanctity is not only possible for everyone but God *expects* it from everyone. To prove his point, he has canonized over 447 people, while he has beatified thousands of others. *Since his days as a young priest in Cracow, Karol Wojtyla has been convinced that God is wonderfully profligate in making saints. The new*

[49D] Zenit, Jan. 26, 2003.

[50] ***The Church of Apostles And Martyrs***, *Op. Cit.*, p. 141.

procedures he has put into place, and the range of his beatifications and canonizations, testify to the pope's conviction that saints are, in fact, all around us...John Paul has illustrated this idea by celebrating sanctity in what may seem unlikely places and guises: writes George Weigel. *[A]mong the bright young people of Milan's Roaring Twenties (Blessed Pier Giorgio Frassati); in a South Pacific village catechist (Blessed Peter To Rot); in a feisty Scottish-Australian nun given to challenging her male superiors (Blessed Mary MacKillip); in the mansions of the Philadelphia Main Line (Saint Katherine Drexel); in an anti-czarist rebel and avant-garde Polish painter who spent his last decades tending the homeless (Saint Albert Chmielowski); or in a young Italian pediatrician who gave her life in 1962 to save her child during a dangerous pregnancy (Blessed Gianna Beretet Molla).*

Saints, a contemporary theologian said, are God's "prime numbers," John Paul II insists that there are more of those prime numbers than we may think.[51]

During times of difficulty, go to Our Lady to sustain you under her title "Cause of our joy." St. Bernard assures us that *[w]hen Mary supports you, you will not fail. With her as your protector, you will have nothing to fear. With her as your guide you will not grow weary. When you win her favor, you will reach the port of heaven.* St. Louis de Montfort, a devout son of Our Lady, writes: *Saint Bonaventure seems to say the same thing in even more explicit terms, "The Blessed Virgin," he says, "not only preserves the fullness enjoyed by the saints, but she maintains the saints in their fullness so that it does not diminish. She prevents their virtues from fading away, their merits from being wasted and their graces from being lost. She prevents the devils from doing them harm and she so influences them that her divine Son has no need to punish them when they sin..." She obtains fidelity to God and final perseverance to those who commit themselves to her...It was to Mary that the saints who attained salvation*

---

[51] George Weigel, "A Century of Saints," *The Wall Street Journal*, Oct. 4, 2000.

most firmly anchored themselves as did others who wanted to ensure their perseverance in holiness.[52]

Want to raise happy children? Continually enrich your marriage, raise your children saints, teach them virtues and don't forget about joy! Writing these books has given me the opportunity to meet and chat with many of you either at conferences or over the phone. From this contact I know that you have the ability to raise happy children and to change the world for the better. The times we are living in are immensely exciting. We are called to participate in the greatest spiritual battle in the history of the Church! We cannot be content to sit on the sidelines and watch the various players cheering for the forces of good and booing the forces of evil. We are called to suit up spiritually and physically to participate in this battle for souls beginning with the souls of our children. We can't warm the bench. If we do we will bear the heat of Purgatory or Hell later!

We have been happy together in the light we have shared. We have really enjoyed being together. We have really rejoiced. But as we leave one another, let us not leave Him (St. Augustine). *I pray to God to bring us all together again in heaven, under the feet of the saints!* (Ven. John Henry Newman)

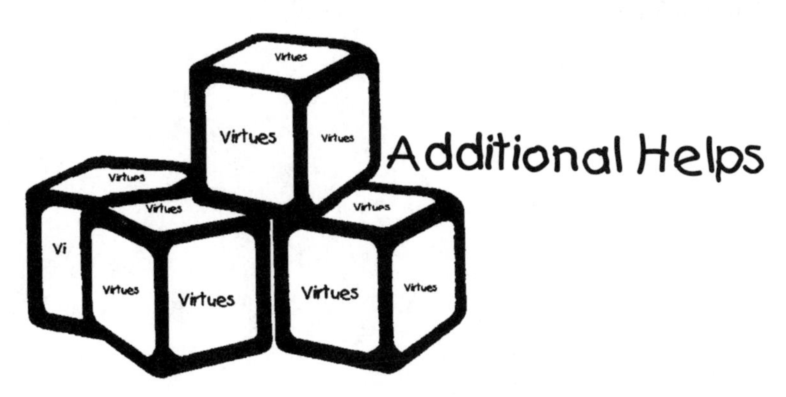

✓ Have your preteen and teen daughters read Jan Karon's ***Mitford Series.*** Discuss the characters with them.

---

[52] St. Louis de Montfort, ***God Alone, The Collected Writings of St. Louis de Montfort*** (NY: Montfort Publications, 1995).

- ✓ View the movie *Portrait of Dorian Grey* then discuss it.
- ✓ View the DVD ***Chronicles of Narnia*** by C. S. Lewis or read the books. Discuss it with your preteens and teens.
- ✓ Read the book ***The Beatitudes*** by Rev. F. X. Lasance (check used bookstores since this is out-of-print) or get the audiotapes from R. B. Media.
- ✓ As a family discuss the importance of cheerfulness. Discuss with your children and teens how they can practice the virtue better.
- ✓ What are your specific resolutions from reading this book? How are you going to implement them? When are you going to implement them? Set up a schedule and a timetable to implement them.

Scripture Verses to Read

Psalm #16; 68:32
Tobias 5:11
Proverbs 25:20
Ecclesiasticus 25:17; 30:22-27; 38:19
1 Corinthians 3:10-15; 9:22-23; 10:6-11; 10: 31-33; 15:58
2 Corinthians 1:3-7; 2:7; 9:7
1 Timothy 6:17-19
2 Timothy 3:1-9

Bibliography

ABC News.com, "Winning Values," Nov. 7, 2003.

Allers, M.D., Ph.D., Rudolf. ***Forming Character in Adolescents***, Fort Collins, CO, 1940.

Alvarez, Fr. Jay. Day of Recollection, 2000.

American Free Press, "News You May Have Missed," Feb. 9, 2004.

"Pro-Christian Activist Blasts Federal Tyranny," July 7, 2003.

"Virginity Scores," Oct. 21, 2002.

Anderson, Joan Wester. ***Forever Young***, Texas, 2000.

Andras, Mary R. "Fashions and their Effect on Society," *Catholic Position Papers,* No. 305, March 2001.

Apostolate of the Little Flower, Jan.-Feb. 1987.

Aquinas, St. Thomas. ***Summa Theologica.***

Araujo, Dr. Ana Maria. "The Awakening of a Sense of Intimacy In the Adolescent," Instituto de Ciencias de la Educación, Universidad de Navarre.

"The Denial of Happiness," audiotape.

Art & Entertainment Program, "Biography of the Millennium".

Associated Press, MSNBC, "High schooler declines tainted record."

Augustine, St. ***Daily Readings with St. Augustine***, Springfield, IL, 1986.

Baurac, Deborah Rissing. "Mothers' smoking tied to behavioral problems in children, doctor says," *Chicago Tribune*, no date.

Beamer, Lisa. ***Let's Roll!*** Wheaton, IL, 2002.

Berg, A. Scott. ***Kate Remembered***, New York, 2003.

Bernal, Salvador. ***A Profile Of Msgr. Escriva, Founder Of Opus Dei***, New York, 1976.

Bernard, St. ***Sermones in Canticas Canticorum,*** 49, 5 (PL 183, 1018).

Bible: Douay Rheims & The Jerusalem Bible.

Billhartz, Cynthia. "Taste Buds in Training," St. Louis Post-Dispatch, Aug. 12, 2001.

Bonaventure, St. ***Meditations on the Life of Christ***, St. Louis, 1934.

Bossis, Gabrielle. ***He & i***, Sherbrooke, Quebec, 1985.

Bowen, Fred, "For the Record...No Defense," washingtonpost.com, Nov. 7,2003.

Branch, Shelly. "Is Food the Next Tobacco?" *The Wall Street Journal,* no date.

Brochure from the Edison Ford Estates.

Brown, Rev. Eugene M. ***Dreams, Visions & Prophecies of Don Bosco,*** New Rochelle, NY, 1986.

Buckman, Rebecca. "A Cottage Industry In Utah Cleans Up Hollywood's Act," The Wall Street Journal, Sept. 19, 2002, p. 1.

Burke, Cormac. ***Man and Values.***

Bukowski, Elizabeth. *The Wall Street Journal,* "Her Bestsellers Are Rated G For Godliness," May 1, 2001.

"Call To Holiness News," Vol. 5, No. 1.

Castillo, Prof. Gerardo. "The Generation Gap, and Trust Within the Family," Instituto de Ciencias de la Educación, Universidad de Navarre, 1988.

"The Influence of Ideologies in the Adolescent," Instituto de Ciencias de la Educación, Universidad de Navarre, 1992.

Catalyst, "Media Ignore Survey On Religion And Teen Sex," Nov. 2001.

Catechism of the Catholic Church, 2nd edition. Vatican, 1997.

Catholic Times, "Fifth-grader gives up TV for Lent, for seventh year," March 11, 2001, p. 16.

"Be chaste, use summer vacation to boost prayer life, pope tells youth." July 13, 2003.

Chandler, Phyllis and Burney, Joan. ***Sharing the Faith with Your Children—From Birth to Age Six,*** Missouri, 1984.

Châu, André Nguyên Vãn. ***The Miracle of Hope***, Boston, 2003.

"GLSEN web site lies about number of homosexual clubs," Jan-April, 2004, p. 1.

Christian Anthropology, Class 6.

Chrysostom, St. John. ***In Matthaeum homiliae*** 7, 7.

Cirrincione, Msgr. Joseph A. ***Ven Jacinta Marto of Fatima***, Rockford,IL,1992.

Clark, Mary Higgins. ***Mount Vernon Love Story,*** New York, 1968.

Cloud, Dr. Henry and Townsend, Dr. John. ***Boundaries***, Michigan, 1992.

Ciszek, S.J., Walter J. with Daniel L. Flaherty, S.J., ***With God In Russia,*** Garden City, 1966.

Colina, Jesús. ***Christ Is My Life,*** Manchester, New Hampshire, 2003.

Colver, Anne. ***Theodosia***, New York, 1962.

Conde, Bertha. ***The Business of Being A Friend***, New York, 1916.

Congregation for Catholic Education. *Educational Guidelines for Human Love,* 1983.

Cowin, Dana. "From the editor", *Food & Wine*, Oct. 2002.

Cowper, W. ***The Winter Walk at Noon,*** Bk. VI, line 96.

Curry, Dayna and Mercer, Heather. ***Prisoners Of Hope*** New York, 2002.

Daniel-Rops, H. ***Cathedral And Crusade***, New York, 1961.
The Church In The Dark Ages, New York, 1960.
The Church Of Apostles & Martyrs, New York, 1960.

de Foucauld, Charles. ***Meditations of a Hermit,*** London, 1974.

de Granada, Ven. Luis. ***Suma de la vida cristiana.***

de Liguori, St. Alphonsus. ***The Incarnation, Birth And Infancy of Jesus Christ***, St. Louis, 1927.

de Montfort, St. Louis. ***God Alone, The Collected Writings of St. Louis de Montfort***, New York, 1995.

de Prada, A. Vazquez. ***Estudio sobre la amistad,*** Madrid, 1975.

de Sales, St. Francis. ***Parochial and Plain Sermons,*** San Francisco, 1997.

DEY/ Almost EVERYTHING. Handout.

Dickens, Gerald Charles. Great-great grandson of Charles Dickens, in his performance in *Mr. Dickens is Coming*, Springfield,IL.

Dietrich, Matthew. "Unplugged," *The State Journal-Register*, April 22, 2001, Springfield, IL.

Dietzen, Fr. John. "Body disfigurement by tattoo or piercing practices," *Catholic Times*, Springfield, IL, June 3, 2001, p. 7.

Doherty, Eddie. ***Bl. Martin de Porres***, St. Paul, 1953.

Diocese of Peoria. ***We Are Family,*** Office of Family Life, 1992.

Drake, Tim. "Reaching Out from Behind Bars," *CMN Trade Journ*al, Vol. 7, Issue 1.

Duff, Christina. "It's My Party, I'll Cry If I Want to, Cry if I Want to, Cry if I..." *The Wall Street Journal,* no date.

Echikson, William. "Wish Upon A Star," *The Wall Street Journal*, Feb. 28, 2003.

Eckert, Allan W. ***A Sorrow In Our Heart, The Life of Tecumseh***, New York, 1993.
Gateway to Empire, New York, 1983.
Twilight of Empire, Boston, 1988.

Eckert, Kristy. "Haas is ready for some privacy," *Springfield State-Journal Register,* Springfield, IL.

Ehrenhalt, Alan. "The Empty Square," *Preservation,* March/April 2000.

Eig, Jonathan. "What's Next? Blankie? The Beloved Sippy Cup Comes Under Attack," *The Wall Street Journal*, Feb. 13, 2002.

Eymard, St. Peter Julian. ***In the Light of the Monstrance,*** Vol. 9, Cleveland, OH, 1947.

Escrivá, St. Josemaría. ***Conversations With Msgr. Escriva De Balaguer*** Dublin, 1969.
Christ Is Passing By, New York, 1982.
Friends of God, New York, 1981.
Furrow, New York, 1987.
The Forge, New York, 1988.
The Way, Chicago, 1954.
The Way of the Cross, New York, 1983.
Letter, 15 October 1948, 31.

Faber, D.D., Rev. Frederick W. ***Growth In Holiness***, Baltimore, 1854.
Fernandez, Francis. ***In Conversation With God #2***, New York, 1989.
Ferrer, St. Vincent. ***Treatise on the Spiritual Life***, Westminster, MD, 1944.
FMA, "Patience and the spirit of God."
Fosdick, Harry Emerson. ***Twelve Tests of Character***, New York, 1923.
Fox, Fr. Robert J. ***Saints & Heroes Speak Vol. 1***, Alexandria, ND, 1996.
Saints & Heroes Speak Vol. Three, Alexandria, ND, 1996.
Saints & Heroes Speak Vol. Four, Alexandria, ND, 1996.
Franklin, Benjamin. ***The Autobiography of Benjamin Franklin***, New York, 1962.
Gerrard, Rev. Thomas J. ***Marriage and Parenthood***, New York, 1911.
Gormley, Beatrice. ***Amelia Earhart***, New York, 2002.
Gottlieg, M.D., Scott. "Fads and Big Fat," *The Wall Street Journal*, Aug. 2, 2002
Gresh, Dannah. www.ridingthewaves.com/article17.htm
Gurdon, Meghan Cox. "A Lot of Groping, Yes, but Not Much Happiness, *The Wall Street Journal*, Oct. 25, 2001.
Hallmark Editions, ***The Treasure of Friendship,*** Kansas City, MO, 1998.
Hardon, S.J., Rev. John. "The Front-Line Defense of Chastity," Bardstown, Eternal Life Publications, Vol. 3, No. 1.
Harman, Rev. Peter. "Taking personal responsibility for morality and media," *Catholic Times,* June 3, 2001, p. 6.
Harvard Women's Health Watch, Volume VII, No. 4, Dec. 1999.
Henderson, Peter. "Cirque Du Soleil Bares All in New Vegas Erotic Show," Reuters, Sept. 29, 2003.
Herbst, S.D.S., Rev. Winfrid. ***Follow The Saints***, New York, 1933.
Hines, Mark. "You Said It," *Reader's Digest,* Feb. 2003.
Hoever, S.O. Cist., Ph.D., Hugo. ***Lives of the Saints Illustrated Part I,*** New Jersey, 1999.
Holböck, Ferdinand. ***Married Saints and Blesseds Through the Centuries***, San Francisco, 2001.
Homan, Helen Walker. ***Francis and Clare, Saints of Assisi,*** New York, 1956.
Hoz, V. García. "Contestación a una pregunta en una entrevista" in *Palabra* (Madrid), March 1972.
Hutchcraft, Ron. ***5 Needs Your Child Must have Met At Home***, Grand Rapids, 1994.
Isaacs, Dr. David. ***Character Building***, Dublin, 1981.
"Teaching Younger Children Virtue," University of Navarre Course Washington, DC, 1986.
"The Education of Friendship," Instituto de Ciencias de la Educación, Universidad de Navarre, 1981.
"The Education of Intimacy," Instituto de Ciencias de la Educación, Universidad de Navarra, 1989.
"The Education of Optimism," Instituto de Ciencias de la Educación, Universidad de Navarre, 1986.
"The Education of Prudence," Insituto de Ciencias de la Educación, Universidad de Navarre, 1984.
Kalvelage, F.I., Bro. Francis Mary. "Fatima Seers, Models for All to Imitate." "Portugal: The Land of Holy Mary."
Kersten Katherine. Commentary, "Cosmopolitan's Philosophy of Unfettered Freedom," *Star Tribune*, June 11, 1997.
Kindred, David. "A record given back sets QB in Illinois apart," *The Sporting News,* Nov. 16, 2003.
King, Henry V. "Work To Develop Virtues In Children, Says Bishop Daily." *The Wanderer*, Jan. 12, 1995.
Kowalska, St. Maria Faustina. ***Diary, Divine Mercy in My Soul***, MA, 1987.
Lague, David. "The Catholic Voice Leading Hong Kong's Opposition," *The Wall Street Journal*, no date.

Lang, Annie. "Teenage Girls And Fashion."
Lappin, Peter. ***Challenge and Change***, Bloomingdale, OH, 1999.
Lasance, Rev. F. X., ***The Beatitudes,*** New York, 1940.
Lee, Thomas & Townsel, Lisa Jones, "Shoppers make a run for the Mills," St. Louis Post-Dispatch, Nov. 14, 2003, Section C, p. C1, C19.
Leen, C.S.S.P., Edward. ***Why The Cross***, New Jersey, 1938.
Leo XIII, Enc. Letter ***Sapientia christianae,*** Janurary 10, 1890.
Lewis, C. S. ***Mere Christianity,*** New York, 1952.
Lindbergh, Charles A. ***The Spirit of St. Louis***, New York, 1953.
Lowman, Rob. "Oh the 'Zumanity!', *Los Angles Daily News*, Nov. 2, 2003.
John Paul II. ***Apost. Exhort. Catechesi Tradendae***, October 16, 1979.
Letter ***Parati semper***, March 31, 1985.
Message for Lent 2003.
The Pope's Challenge, New York, 1979.
World Youth Day Rome Aug. 19, 2000.
Audience, March 4, 2001.
Audience, April 1, 2001.
Magnificat May 2001. Sept. 2002.
Oct. 2002. Dec. 2002.
Nov. 2002. Jan. 2003.
June 2001. April 2003.
July 2001. Sept. 2003.
Dec. 2001. Nov. 2003.
April 2002. Jan. 2003.
July 2002. Feb. 2004.
April 2004.
Malaise, S.J., Joseph. ***Know Yourself***, San Francisco, 1939.
Maritain, Raissa. ***Raissa's Journal***, New York, 1974.
Mark the Ascetic, ***Philokalia*** compiled by St. Nikodimos and St. Makarios.
Matthew, Margaret, and Bunson, Stephen. ***John Paul II's Book Of Saints***, Huntington, IN, 1999.
McAstocker, S. J., David P. ***The Little Virtues***, Milwaukee, 1940.
McCullough, David. ***John Adams***, New York, 2001.
McDonald, Hugh. "We Are What We Watch and Read," Zenit, July 21, 2001.
McMahon, Darrin M. "Disgruntled in the Midst of Plenty," *The Wall Street Journal,* Dec. 4, 2003.
McNulty, Patricia. ***Selected Writings on the Spiritual Life***, London, 1959.
MEF, "Small Goals Lead To Virtue," Spring, 2003.
Merrick, Amy. "The Pared-Down Prom Dress," *The Wall Street Journal*, May 11, 2001.
Messenger, Ph.D., Rev. E. C. ***Two In One Flesh, Vol. 2, The Mystery Of Sex And Marriage***, Westminster, Maryland, 1948.
Meyer, O.F. M., James. ***A Primer of Perfection for Everybody,*** Chicago, 1946.
Meyer, Michelle. "Schools update dress codes as near-naked fashions hit the halls," *St. Louis Post Dispatch*, Dec.12,2001.
Mies, Rich, Editor-In-Chief. "A Touchdown for Integrity, www.totk.com/articleprint.asp?articleid=49817
Morris,O.P., Michael. "Saint Benedict," Magnificat, July 2002, Vol. 4, No. 5.
"St. John of Capistrano," *Magnificat,* Oct. 2003.
Mother Cabrini Messenger, *Vol. 64, No. 2, 2002.*
Murray, Shailagh. "Seminary Article Sparks Alabama Tax-Code Revolt," *The Wall Street Journal*, Feb. 12, 2003.
Newman, St. John Henry. ***Meditations and Devotions.***
Newton, James. ***Uncommon Friends,*** New York, 1987.
Noonan, Peggy. ***When Character Was King***, New York, 2001.

On This Rock, September, 1999.

Otero, Prof. Oliveros F. "Authority in the Education of Children," Instituto de Ciencias de la Educación, Universidad de Navarre, 1982.

Ouzounian, Richard. "Oh, the Zumanity Cirque du Soleil reinvents eroticism," *Toronto Star,* April 5, 2003, p. H01 Arts Section.

"Hypersexual circus for grown-ups," *Toronto Star* (Canada), Sept. 22, 2003, p. B04.

Persica, Michael. "The Man of the Beatitudes," *The Mir Response*, April/May 1995.

Peterson, Karen S. "Changing the shape of the American family," *USA Today,* April 18, 2000, Section D.

Peyret, Rev. Raymond. "Our First Vocation is Love," *Resurrection Magazine,* Year 2, Dec. 2001.

Piat, O.F.M., Fr. Stéphane-Joseph. ***The Story Of A Family***, Rockford, 1994.

Pieper, J. ***Prudence and Temperance***, Madrid, 1969.

Pope, Tara Parker-. "How to Give Your Child A Longer Life," *The Wall Street Journal,* Dec. 9, 2003.

Richmond, Derek. "High School QB Does The Right Thing," *The Hoya, Georgetown University's Newspaper of Record,* Nov, 11, 2003.

Rogers, Dale Evans. ***No Two Ways About It!*** New Jersey, 1963.

Rodriguez, S.J., St. Alphonsus. ***Practice of Perfection And Christian Virtues, Vol. 2***, Chicago, 1929.

Vol. 3, Chicago, 1929.

Russell, Claire. ***Glimpses of the Church Fathers***, New York, 1994.

Ryan, O.P., Bishop Finbar. ***Our Lady of Fatima***.

Sacred Congregation for the Clergy, ***General Catechetical Directory***, April 11, 1971.

Sartwell, Crispin. "Distant Star."

Sattler, C.SS.R, Ph.D., Henry V. ***Parents, Children and the Facts of Life***, New Jersey, 1952.

Schurter, Ted. "Kid's integrity shines after unwise, but heartfelt decision by coach," *Springfield State Journal-Register,* Springfield, IL, *USA Today.*

Scupoli, Fr. Lawrence. ***The Spiritual Combat***, Westminster, Maryland, 1947.

Shamblin, Gwen. ***The Weigh Down Diet***, New York, 1997.

Shellenbarger, Sue. "Work & Family," "Making Time to Veg: Parents Find Their Kids Need Life Balance as Well," *The Wall Street Journal,* Sept. 26, 2002.

Sheen, Archbishop Fulton J. ***Children and Parents***, New York, 1970.

Shepherd, Dr. Jerry. ***Teen Life and Christ***, Sydney, Australia, 2001.

State Journal Register, "Mom admits falsifying claims son is genius," Mar. 3, 2002, Springfield, IL.

"High school girls pummel flasher," Nov. 1, 2003.

Stenson, James. "Peer Pressure." Audiotape.

"How To Be A Successful Father." Audiotape.

Lifeline—The Religious Upbringing of Your Children, New York, 1996.

St. Louis Review, January 30, 2004.

Stopp, Elizabeth. ***St. Francis de Sales***, New York, 1960.

Teresa, Bl. Mother. ***Heart of Joy, The Transforming Power of Self-Giving***, Ann Arbor, 1987.

Thérèse, St. ***Story of a Soul.***

The Eagle, "A lesson in integrity by a young player," Nov. 9, 2003.

The Sacred Congregation for Bishops. Directory ***Ecclesiae imago***, February 22, 1973.

The Wall Street Journal, "A Kid Recession?", July 13, 2001.

"Toddlers Who Watch TV Risk Attention Problems, Study Finds," April 5, 2004.

Tobin, Greg. ***The Wisdom of St. Patrick***, New York, 1999.

Trebay, Guy. "After Nice, A return to Vice," *The New York Times,* June 8, 2003.

Valenta, Fr. Stephen. Hearts to heart Ministries, Dec. 2003.
Vãn Châu, André Nguyên. ***The Miracle of Hope, Political Prisoner, Prophet of Peace,*** Boston, 2003.
Varadarajan, Tunku. "Foghorn Phil Joins the Battle With Bawling Bill," *The Wall Street Journal*, July 18, 2002.
Van Zeller, Dom Hubert. ***We Die Standing Up***, New York, 1949.
Vatican Council II, Past. Const. ***Gaudium et spes.***
von Trapp, Maria. ***Maria, My Own* Story,** Carol Stream, IL, 1972.
The Story Of The Trapp Family Singers, New York, 1971.
Walsh, James E., Titular Bishop of Sato. ***Tales of Xavier,*** New York, 1946.
Webster's New Collegiate Dictionary
Weigel, George. "A Century of Saints," *The Wall Street Journal*, Oct. 4, 2000.
WGN TV April 15, 2002; Dec. 3, 2003; Dec. 4, 2003
White, Erin. "Now There's Something New for Back-to-School: Racy Underwear," *The Wall Street Journal*, Aug. 3, 2000.
Zark, Jenna . "Date Rape, What You Need To Know," *Scholastic Choices Magazine*, Feb. 1990.

Zenit, Aug. 16, 2000.
Zenit, Aug. 23, 2000.
Zenit, Feb. 21, 2000.
Zenit, Dec. 21, 2000.
Zenit, Feb. 2, 2001.
Zenit, Feb. 21, 2001.
Zenit, Feb. 22, 2001.
Zenit, Feb. 27, 2001.
Zenit, Mar. 5, 2001.
Zenit, Mar. 7, 2001.
Zenit, Mar. 8, 2001.
Zenit, Mar. 14, 2001.
Zenit, Mar. 16, 2001.
Zenit, Mar. 26, 2001.
Zenit, Mar. 30, 2001.
Zenit, April 2, 2001.
Zenit, April 5, 2001.
Zenit, April 8, 2001.
Zenit, April 9, 2001.
Zenit, April 12, 2001.
Zenit, July 14, 2001.
Zenit, Nov. 15, 2001.
Zenit, Nov. 18, 2001
Zenit, Nov. 27, 2001.
Zenit, Dec. 9, 2001.
Zenit, Dec. 22, 2001.
Zenit, Jan. 31, 2002.
Zenit, Mar. 23, 2002.
Zenit, April 27, 2002.
Zenit, May 5, 2002.
Zenit, May 6, 2002.
Zenit, May 9, 2002.
Zenit, May 26, 2002.
Zenit, June 28, 2002.
Zenit, July 8, 2002.
Zenit, July 14, 2002.
Zenit, Aug. 18, 2002.
Zenit, Aug. 19, 2002.
Zenit, July 20, 2002.
Zenit, July 23, 2002.
Zenit, July 28, 2002.
Zenit, July 29, 2002.
Zenit, Aug. 30, 2002.
Zenit, Sept. 2, 2002.
Zenit, Sept. 12, 2002.
Zenit, Sept. 29, 2002.
Zenit, Oct. 8, 2002.
Zenit, Oct. 18, 2002.
Zenit Oct. 24, 2002.
Zenit, Nov. 30, 2002.
Zenit, Dec. 11, 2002.
Zenit, Dec. 14, 2002.
Zenit, Dec. 20, 2002.
Zenit, Jan. 16, 2003.
Zenit, Jan. 28, 2003.
Zenit, Jan. 31, 2003.
Zenit, Feb. 4, 2003.
Zenit, Mar. 9, 2003
Zenit, Mar. 19, 2003.
Zenit, Mar. 28, 2003.
Zenit, April 1, 2003.
Zenit, May 9, 2003.
Zenit, May 16, 2003.
Zenit, May 21, 2003.
Zenit, May 23, 2003.
Zenit, May 24, 2003.
Zenit, Oct. 13, 2003.
Zenit, May 25, 2003.
Zenit, June 21,2003.
Zenit, July 6, 2003.
Zenit, July 16, 2003.
Zenit, July 23, 2003.
Zenit, July 25, 2003.
Zenit, Aug. 20, 2003.
Zenit, Aug. 21, 2003.
Zenit, Aug. 25, 2003.
Zenit, Aug. 26, 2003.
Zenit, Aug. 29, 2003.
Zenit, Sept. 1, 2003.
Zenit, Sept. 2, 2003.
Zenit, Sept. 7, 2003.
Zenit, Sept. 15, 2003.
Zenit, Sept. 21, 2003.
Zenit, Oct. 4, 2003.
Zenit, Oct. 9, 2003.
Zenit, Oct. 17, 2003.
Zenit, Oct. 20, 2003.
Zenit, Oct. 29, 2003.
Zenit, Nov. 6, 2003.
Zenit, Nov. 8, 2003.
Zenit, Nov. 11, 2003.
Zenit, Nov. 18, 2003.
Zenit, Nov. 21, 2003.
Zenit, Nov. 23, 2003.
Zenit, Dec. 12, 2003.
Zenit, Dec. 14, 2003.
Zenit, Dec. 17, 2003.
Zenit, Dec. 22, 2003.
Zenit, Jan. 24, 2004.
Zenit, Jan. 25, 2004.
Zenit, Jan. 26, 2004.
Zenit, Jan. 28, 2004.
Zenit, Feb. 7, 2004.
Zenit, Feb. 20, 2004.
Zenit, Mar. 1, 2004.
Zenit, Mar. 5, 2004.
Zenit, Mar. 9, 2004.
Zenit, Mar. 16, 2004.

Index

A

B

C

E

F

G

H

I

J

K

L

M

N

T

ORDER FORM

Thank you for your wonderful, useful book! **Illinois**

This is one of the best books I've ever read! **Kansas**

Your book on marriage is a treasure. It has changed my marriage and family life. God sent your book to me to get me on the road to raise a holy family. Your books are so powerful. Please keep writing! **California**

I couldn't put your book down. **Indiana**

Thank you for such helpful books! **Iowa**

Your books have had a profound effect on my life and the life of my family. **Ohio**

Your books have been two of the best books I've read. Thanks...for writing such wonderful books. **Pennsylvania**

To order books:

Quantity	Title	Unit Price	Amount
____	You Can Become A Saint!	$14.95	________
____	You Can Become A Saint! Workbook	$18.95	________
____	Looking for Peace? Try Confession!	$11.95	________
____	Raise Happy Children Through A Happier Marriage? (Book 1)	$14.95	________
____	Raise Happy Children... Raise Them Saints! (Book 2)	$16.95	________
____	Raise Happy Children... Teach Them Virtues! (Book 3)	$16.95	________
____	Raise Happy Children... Teach Them Joy! (Book 4)	$16.95	________
____	Why Suffer? booklet *	$2.50	________

R.B. Media, Inc., 154 Doral, Springfield, IL 62704

Name: ______________________________ **SUBTOTAL:** ________

Address: ____________________________ **Tax**** ________

City: _______________________________ **Shipping***** ________

State: ______________ Zip: ____________ **TOTAL:** ________

***Illinois residents add 7.25% tax.

****Shipping is $4.50 for one book. Please add $1 for each additional book.

*Shipping is .50 for each "Why Suffer?" booklet.